THE ULTIMATE KEY TO
EATING FOR GOOD HEALTH!

Whether you're restricting salt, lowering fat intake, boosting fiber, or counting calories, here is the best and most comprehensive dietary reference, specially tailored to your needs.

It's easy to be informed. And it's all here, alphabetized for quick reference. You can be in control of what you eat when everything you need to know is at your fingertips. Now you can make the healthful choices that are right for you!

THE COMPLETE BOOK OF FOOD COUNTS

IF YOU CARE ABOUT YOUR HEALTH
TAKE IT WITH YOU WHEREVER YOU GO!

Revised Edition

THE
COMPLETE
BOOK
OF
FOOD COUNTS

Corinne T. Netzer

A DELL BOOK

Published by
Dell Publishing
a division of
Bantam Doubleday Dell Publishing Group, Inc.
666 Fifth Avenue
New York, New York 10103

ISBN: 0-440-20854-8

Printed in the United States of America
Published simultaneously in Canada

March 1991

10 9 8 7 6 5 4

RAD

Introduction

The second edition of *The Complete Book of Food Counts* is the largest compilation of essential food data in this format. It contains data (calories, protein, carbohydrates, fat, cholesterol, sodium, and fiber) for basic generic foods, brand-name foods, and restaurant chains. Whether you are interested in dieting or in nutrition—or in both—you will find this book unique and invaluable as a reference. Should you need even more data, you may wish to consult *Corinne T. Netzer's Encyclopedia of Food Values.*

Since this book is alphabetized, you should have no difficulty finding whatever you wish to look up. There are, however, times when you may have to look in more than one place. If you are searching for a particular food and cannot find it immediately, look for it under a category, such as cakes, puddings, cookies, soups. Wherever sensible, I have cross-referenced listings, but limited space has made it impossible to do that for every item.

Compare only foods listed in similar measures. This rule particularly applies to the confusion between measures by capacity and measures by weight. Eight ounces is not necessarily equivalent to eight fluid ounces or one cup. Eight ounces is a measure of how much something weighs; one cup is a measure of how much space it occupies. For instance, a cup of lightweight food, such as puffed rice or popcorn, weighs about one ounce, so eight ounces of that product would fill many cups. Naturally you can convert a similar unit of measure into a smaller or larger amount. The following table may be useful in making such conversions:

Equivalents by Capacity
(all measures level)

1 quart	=	4 cups
1 cup	=	8 fluid ounces
	=	1/2 pint
	=	16 tablespoons
2 tablespoons	=	1 fluid ounce
1 tablespoon	=	3 teaspoons

Equivalents by Weight

1 pound	=	16 ounces
3.57 ounces	=	100 grams
1 ounce	=	28.35 grams

All the material contained in *The Complete Book of Food Counts* is based on information from the United States government, from producers and processors of brand-name foods, and from food chains. The data contained herein are the most complete and accurate information available as this book goes to press. Please bear in mind that seasonal and regional differences can affect the nutritional value of foods. Also, the food industry often changes recipes and sizes and may discontinue a product or add new ones. In the future I will revise and update this book to keep you completely informed.

Good luck and good dieting.

CORINNE T. NETZER

Abbreviations and Symbols

c . . . . crude fiber*
cal. calories
carbo. . . . . carbohydrates
chol. . . . . cholesterol
cont. . . . . container
d . . . . dietary fiber
diam. . . . . diameter
fl. . . . . fluid
gms . . . . grams
" . . . . inch
< . . . . less than
(0) . . . . may contain trace amounts
m.q. . . . . measurable quantity**
mgs. . . . . milligrams
lb. . . . . pound
n.a. . . . . not available
oz. . . . . ounces
pkg. package
pkt. . . . . packet
prot. protein
sod. sodium
tbsp. . . . . tablespoon
tsp. . . . . teaspoon
tr. . . . . trace
w/ . . . . with
w/out . . . . without

---

* Obtained through crude method of analysis; actual content may be higher.
** Believed to contain measurable quantities, but data are unavailable at this time. (Note: A "measurable quantity" may range from a trace to significant amounts.)

A

Food and Measure	cal.	prot. (gms)	carbo. (gms)	fat (gms)	chol. (mgs)	sod. (mgs)	fiber (gms)
Abalone, meat only:							
raw, 1 oz.	30	4.8	1.7	.2	24	85	0
fried[1], 4 oz.	214	22.3	12.5	7.7	107	670	.1 c
Acapulco dip:							
(Ortega), 1 oz.	8	0	2.0	0	0	0	n.a.
Acerola, fresh:							
trimmed, 1/2 cup . . .	16	.2	3.8	.1	0	4	.2 c
1 medium	2	<.1	.4	<.1	0	tr.	<.1 c
juice, 6 fl. oz.	36	.7	8.7	.5	0	6	.5 c
Acorn squash:							
raw, 1.3-lb. squash	172	3.5	44.9	.4	0	14	6.0 c
baked, cubed, 1/2 cup	57	1.1	14.9	.1	0	4	2.0 c
boiled, mashed,							
1/2 cup	41	.8	10.7	.1	0	3	1.4 c
Adzuki beans:							
boiled, 1/2 cup	147	8.7	28.5	.1	0	9	2.3 c
canned, sweetened,							
1/2 cup	351	5.6	81.4	<.1	0	323	2.3 c
Agar, see "Seaweed"							
Albacore, see "Tuna, canned"							
Alfalfa seeds, sprouted:							
raw, 1/2 cup	5	.7	.6	.1	0	1	.4 d
raw, 1 tbsp.	1	.1	.1	<.1	0	tr.	.1 d
Alfredo sauce:							
refrigerated *(Contadina Fresh),* 6 oz.	540	9.0	10.0	53.0	85	620	n.a.

[1] *Dipped in flour and salted before frying.*

Food and Measure	cal.	prot. (gms)	carbo. (gms)	fat (gms)	chol. (mgs)	sod. (mgs)	fiber (gms)
Alfredo sauce *(cont.)*							
mix *(Lawry's Pasta Alfredo)*, 1 pkg. . . .	226	8.0	19.2	13.3	n.a.	3222	.6 c
Algae, see "Seaweed"							
Allspice, ground:							
1 tsp.	5	.1	1.4	.2	0	1	.4 c
Almond, shelled:							
(Beer Nuts), 1 oz. . .	180	5.0	7.0	14.4	0	51	m.q.
(Dole), 1 oz.	170	6.0	12.0	14.0	0	4	m.q.
dried:							
1 oz.	167	5.7	5.8	14.8	0	3	8.6 d
sliced, 1 cup	554	18.8	19.2	49.1	0	10	4.4 d
slivered, 1 cup . .	795	26.9	27.5	70.5	0	15	6.4 d
blanched, 1 oz. . .	166	5.8	5.3	14.9	0	3	.7 c
(Planters), 1 oz. . .	170	6.0	6.0	15.0	0	0	m.q.
dry-roasted:							
1 oz.	167	4.6	6.9	14.7	0	3	1.4 c
salted, 1 oz.	167	4.6	6.9	14.7	0	221	1.4 c
(Planters), 1 oz. . .	170	6.0	6.0	15.0	0	200	m.q.
oil-roasted:							
1 oz.	176	5.8	4.5	16.4	0	3	3.2 d
salted, 1 oz.	176	5.8	4.5	16.4	0	221	3.2 d
blanched, 1 oz. . .	174	5.4	5.1	16.1	0	3	3.2 d
toasted, 1 oz.	167	5.8	6.5	14.4	0	3	1.4 c
Almond butter:							
1 tbsp.	101	2.4	3.4	9.5	0	2	.2 c
raw *(Hain Natural)*, 2 tbsp.	190	8.0	3.0	18.0	0	5	m.q.
blanched, toasted *(Hain)*, 2 tbsp. . . .	210	8.0	3.0	19.0	0	5	m.q.
salted, 1 tbsp.	101	2.4	3.4	9.5	0	72	.2 c
honey cinnamon, 1 tbsp.	96	2.5	4.3	8.4	0	2	.2 c
Almond meal, partially defatted:							
1 oz.	116	11.2	8.2	5.2	0	2	.7 c
salted, 1 oz.	116	11.2	8.2	5.2	0	211	.7 c

Food and Measure	cal.	prot. (gms)	carbo. (gms)	fat (gms)	chol. (mgs)	sod. (mgs)	fiber (gms)
Almond paste:							
1 oz.	127	3.4	12.4	7.2	0	3	1.7 c
Amaranth, 1/2 cup:							
raw, trimmed	4	.3	.6	<.1	0	3	.1 c
boiled, drained	14	1.4	2.7	.1	0	14	.9 c
Amaranth,							
whole-grain:							
1 oz.	106	4.1	18.8	1.8	0	6	4.3 d
Anchovy, meat only:							
fresh, European, raw,							
1 oz.	37	5.8	0	1.4	m.q.	29	0
canned in olive oil:							
drained, 1 oz.	60	8.2	0	2.8	m.q.	1040	0
5 medium, .7 oz.	42	5.8	0	1.9	m.q.	734	0
Anise seed:							
1 tsp.	7	.4	1.1	.3	0	tr.	.3 c
Apple:							
raw, w/peel:							
23/4"-diam. apple	81	.3	21.1	.5	0	1	3.0 d
sliced, 1/2 cup . . .	32	.1	8.4	.2	0	tr.	1.2 d
raw, peeled:							
23/4"-diam. apple	72	.2	19.0	.4	0	tr.	2.4 d
sliced, 1/2 cup . . .	31	.1	8.2	.2	0	tr.	1.0 d
cooked, sliced,							
peeled:							
boiled, 1/2 cup . . .	46	.2	11.7	.3	0	1	1.6 d
microwaved, 1/2 cup	48	.2	12.3	.4	0	1	2.0 d
canned:							
baked style *(White*							
House), 3.5 oz.	118	0	29.0	0	0	11	m.q.
rings, spiced *(White*							
House), 3.5 oz.	180	0	44.0	0	0	25	m.q.
sliced *(White*							
House), 4 oz. . .	54	0	14.0	0	0	10	m.q.
dried, 2 oz.:							
chunks *(Sun-Maid/*							
Sunsweet) . . .	150	1.0	42.0	0	0	<40	m.q.
sliced *(Del Monte)*	140	0	37.0	0	0	<50	m.q.

Food and Measure	cal.	prot. (gms)	carbo. (gms)	fat (gms)	chol. (mgs)	sod. (mgs)	fiber (gms)
Apple, escalloped,							
frozen:							
(Stouffer's), 4 oz. . .	130	0	27.0	2.0	n.a.	15	m.q.
Apple, glazed:							
frozen, in raspberry							
sauce *(The Budget*							
Gourmet), 5 oz. . . .	110	0	22.0	3.0	10	210	m.q.
Apple butter:							
all varieties *(Smuck-*							
er's), 1 tsp.	12	0	3.0	0	0	0	m.q.
(Bama), 2 tbsp. . . .	25	0	6.0	0	0	5	m.q.
(White House), 1 oz.	50	0	12.0	0	0	5	m.q.
Apple cider, 6 fl. oz.:							
(Indian Summer) . . .	80	<1.0	20.0	<1.0	0	10	m.q.
(Tree Top)	90	0	22.0	0	0	10	m.q.
sparkling *(Lucky Leaf)*	80	0	18.0	0	0	45	m.q.
Apple cobbler, see							
"Cobbler"							
Apple crisp, frozen:							
(Pepperidge Farm							
Berkshire), 1 cup	250	2.0	43.0	8.0	40	130	1.0 d
Apple danish, see							
"Danish"							
Apple drink:							
(Hi-C Candy Apple							
Cooler), 6 fl. oz. . . .	94	<.1	23.1	<.1	0	17	(0)
Apple dumpling:							
frozen *(Pepperidge*							
Farm), 3 oz.	260	2.0	33.0	13.0	n.a.	230	m.q.
Apple fritter:							
frozen *(Mrs. Paul's)*,							
2 pieces	270	3.0	36.0	13.0	n.a.	610	n.a.
Apple fruit roll, see							
"Fruit snack"							
Apple fruit square:							
frozen *(Pepperidge*							
Farm), 1 piece . .	220	2.0	27.0	12.0	n.a.	170	n.a.

Food and Measure	cal.	prot. (gms)	carbo. (gms)	fat (gms)	chol. (mgs)	sod. (mgs)	fiber (gms)
Apple juice 6 fl. oz., except as noted:							
(Campbell's Juice Bowl)	110	0	25.0	0	0	50	m.q.
(Indian Summer) . . .	90	<1.0	21.0	<1.0	0	10	m.q.
(Kraft Pure 100%) . .	80	0	20.0	0	0	5	m.q.
(Minute Maid), 8.45 fl. oz.	128	.2	31.9	.3	0	32	m.q.
(Minute Maid Juices to Go), 9.6 fl. oz. . . .	145	.2	35.3	.3	0	37	m.q.
(Minute Maid On The Go), 10 fl. oz. . . .	152	.2	37.8	.4	0	38	m.q.
(Mott's)	88	0	22.0	0	0	13	m.q.
(Mott's Natural Style)	76	0	19.0	0	0	28	m.q.
(Red Cheek Natural)	97	.2	24.0	0	0	16	m.q.
(Red Cheek 100% Pure)	97	.2	24.0	0	0	7	m.q.
(TreeSweet)	90	0	22.0	0	0	15	m.q.
(Tree Top)	90	0	22.0	0	0	10	.2 c
(Veryfine 100%), 8 fl. oz.	107	<1.0	27.0	0	0	<10	m.q.
blend *(Libby's Juicy Juice)*	90	0	21.0	0	0	5	m.q.
sparkling *(Welch's)*	100	0	24.0	0	0	5	0
chilled or frozen[1]:							
(Minute Maid) . . .	91	.1	22.7	.2	0	23	m.q.
(Sunkist), 8 fl. oz.	79	.2	19.4	.2	0	12	m.q.
(Tree Top)	90	0	22.0	0	0	10	m.q.
cocktail *(Welch's Orchard),* 10 fl. oz.	170	0	42.0	0	0	95	0
Apple pie, see "Pie"							
Apple pie spice:							
(Tone's), 1 tsp. . . .	9	.2	2.4	.2	0	1	.7 d
Apple punch, 6 fl. oz.:							
(Red Cheek)	113	.3	28.0	0	0	7	(0)
Apple sticks, frozen:							
(Farm Rich), 4 oz. . .	260	2.0	44.0	8.0	0	565	m.q.

[1] *Diluted according to package directions.*

Food and Measure	cal.	prot. (gms)	carbo. (gms)	fat (gms)	chol. (mgs)	sod. (mgs)	fiber (gms)
Apple-cherry cider, 6 fl. oz.:							
(Indian Summer) . . .	100	<1.0	25.0	<1.0	0	10	m.q.
Apple-cherry juice, 6 fl. oz.:							
(Musselman's Break- fast Cocktail) . . .	100	1.0	26.0	0	0	5	m.q.
(Red Cheek)	113	.2	28.0	0	0	11	m.q.
Apple-cranberry ci- der, 6 fl. oz.:							
(Indian Summer) . . .	100	<1.0	24.0	<1.0	0	10	m.q.
Apple-cranberry drink:							
(Mott's), 10 oz.	176	0	44.0	0	0	3	(0)
Apple-cranberry juice:							
(Lucky Leaf), 6 fl. oz.	130	0	32.0	0	0	10	m.q.
(Mott's), 9.5-oz. can	147	0	38.0	0	0	27	m.q.
(Mott's), 6 fl. oz. . . .	83	0	24.0	0	0	17	m.q.
(Tree Top), 6 fl. oz.	100	0	25.0	0	0	10	m.q.
cocktail (Veryfine), 8 fl. oz.	130	<1.0	33.0	0	0	<10	m.q.
Apple-grape juice, 6 fl. oz.:							
(Libby's Juicy Juice)	90	0	22.0	0	0	10	m.q.
(Mott's)	86	0	23.0	0	0	17	m.q.
(Red Cheek)	109	.3	27.0	0	0	9	m.q.
(Tree Top)	100	0	25.0	0	0	10	m.q.
cocktail: (Welch's Orchard)	110	0	27.0	0	0	20	0
white grape, frozen[1] (Welch's No Sugar)	40	0	10.0	0	0	5	0
frozen[1] (Welch's Orchard)	110	0	27.0	0	0	10	0

[1] Diluted according to package directions.

Food and Measure	cal.	prot. (gms)	carbo. (gms)	fat (gms)	chol. (mgs)	sod. (mgs)	fiber (gms)
Apple-grape-cherry juice cocktail:							
(Welch's Orchard), 6 fl. oz.	110	0	27.0	0	0	20	0
(Welch's Orchard Cocktails-In-A-Box), 8.45 fl. oz.	150	0	38.0	0	0	20	0
frozen[1] *(Welch's* Orchard), 6 fl. oz.	90	0	22.0	0	0	10	0
Apple-grape-raspberry juice cocktail:							
(Welch's Orchard), 6 fl. oz.	100	0	26.0	0	0	20	0
(Welch's Orchard Cocktails-In-A-Box), 8.45 fl. oz.	140	0	35.0	0	0	20	0
frozen[1] *(Welch's* Orchard), 6 fl. oz.	90	0	22.0	0	0	10	0
Apple-orange-pineapple juice cocktail:							
(Welch's Orchard Tropicals Cocktails-In-A-Box), 8.45 fl. oz.	140	0	35.0	0	0	20	0
bottled or frozen[1] *(Welch's* Orchard Tropicals), 6 fl. oz.	100	0	25.0	0	0	20	0
Apple-pear juice:							
(Tree Top), 6 fl. oz.	90	0	22.0	0	0	10	m.q.
Apple-raspberry drink:							
(Mott's), 10 oz.	158	0	40.0	0	0	17	(0)
Apple-raspberry juice:							
(Mott's), 9.5-oz. can	134	0	35.0	0	0	76	m.q.

[1] *Diluted according to package directions.*

Food and Measure	cal.	prot. (gms)	carbo. (gms)	fat (gms)	chol. (mgs)	sod. (mgs)	fiber (gms)
Apple-raspberry juice *(cont.)*							
(Mott's), 6 fl. oz.	83	0	22.0	0	0	48	m.q.
(Red Cheek), 6 fl. oz.	113	.3	28.0	0	0	8	m.q.
(Tree Top), 6 fl. oz.	80	0	21.0	0	0	10	m.q.
cocktail *(Veryfine)*, 8 fl. oz.	110	<1.0	27.0	0	0	<15	(0)
Applesauce, 1/2 cup, except as noted:							
unsweetened	53	.2	13.8	.1	0	2	1.8 d
sweetened	97	.2	25.5	.2	0	32	1.5 d
(Del Monte)	90	0	24.0	0	0	<5	m.q.
(Del Monte Lite) . . .	50	0	13.0	0	0	<10	m.q.
(Hunt's Snack Pack), 4.25 oz.	80	0	19.0	0	0	n.a.	m.q.
(Mott's), 6 oz.	150	0	36.0	0	0	<1	m.q.
(Mott's Chunky), 6 oz.	86	0	21.0	0	0	11	m.q.
(Mott's Natural), 6 oz.	80	0	20.0	0	0	3	m.q.
(Mott's Natural Single Serve), 4 oz. . . .	53	0	13.0	0	0	2	m.q.
(Mott's Single Serve), 4 oz.	100	0	24.0	0	0	<1	m.q.
(S&W)	90	0	24.0	0	0	10	m.q.
(S&W Unsweetened)	55	0	14.0	0	0	5	m.q.
(Stokely)	90	0	23.0	0	0	30	m.q.
(Stokely Un-sweetened)	45	0	12.0	0	0	5	m.q.
(Tree Top Original)	80	0	21.0	0	0	0	m.q.
cinnamon *(Mott's)*, 6 oz.	152	0	36.0	0	0	<1	m.q.
cinnamon *(Mott's Single Serve)*, 4 oz.	101	0	24.0	0	0	<1	m.q.
Applesauce blends, 4 oz.:							
w/cranberry *(Lucky Leaf)*	80	0	19.0	0	0	15	m.q.
w/peach *(Musselman's* Fruit N'Sauce)	90	0	22.0	0	0	<20	m.q.

Food and Measure	cal.	prot. (gms)	carbo. (gms)	fat (gms)	chol. (mgs)	sod. (mgs)	fiber (gms)
w/pineapple (Mus-selman's Fruit N'Sauce)	110	0	26.0	0	0	<20	m.q.
w/strawberry (Mus-selman's Fruit N'Sauce)	100	0	24.0	0	0	<20	m.q.
Apricot:							
fresh:							
3 medium, 12 per lb.	51	1.5	11.8	.4	0	1	1.4 d
pitted, halves, 1/2 cup	37	1.1	8.6	.3	0	1	1.0 d
canned, 1/2 cup:							
whole, peeled (Del Monte)	100	0	27.0	0	0	<10	m.q.
halves, unpeeled (Del Monte) . . .	100	0	26.0	0	0	<10	m.q.
in juice, halves . .	60	.8	15.3	<.1	0	5	.6 d
in heavy syrup, halves	107	.7	27.7	.1	0	5	.5 c
in heavy syrup, halves (S&W) . .	110	0	28.0	0	0	15	m.q.
in heavy syrup, whole	107	.7	27.7	.1	0	14	.5 c
in heavy syrup, whole (S&W) . .	100	0	26.0	0	0	15	m.q.
dried (Del Monte), 2 oz.	140	2.0	35.0	0	0	<10	m.q.
frozen, sweetened, 1/2 cup	119	.9	30.4	.1	0	5	.7 c
Apricot fruit snack, see "Fruit snack"							
Apricot nectar:							
(Del Monte), 6 fl. oz.	100	1.0	26.0	0	0	<10	m.q.
(Libby's), 6 fl. oz. . .	110	0	26.0	0	0	0	m.q.
(S&W), 6 fl. oz. . . .	100	0	26.0	0	0	10	m.q.
Arby's, 1 serving:							
sandwiches:							
beef 'n cheddar . .	455	25.7	27.7	26.8	63	955	m.q.

Food and Measure	cal.	prot. (gms)	carbo. (gms)	fat (gms)	chol. (mgs)	sod. (mgs)	fiber (gms)
Arby's, sandwiches (cont.)							
chicken breast ..	493	23.0	47.9	25.0	91	1019	m.q.
ham 'n cheese ..	292	22.9	19.2	13.7	45	1350	m.q.
roast beef, regular	353	22.2	31.6	14.8	39	588	m.q.
roast beef, super	501	25.1	50.4	22.1	40	798	m.q.
roast chicken club	610	31.0	40.0	33.0	80	1500	m.q.
turkey deluxe ...	375	23.8	32.5	16.6	39	1047	m.q.
potato cakes, 3 oz.	204	1.8	19.8	12.0	0	397	m.q.
french fries, 2.5 oz.	246	2.1	29.8	13.2	0	114	m.q.
shake, Jamocha ...	368	9.3	59.1	10.5	35	262	(0)
Arrowhead:							
raw, 2⅝"-diam. corm.	12	.6	2.4	<.1	0	3	.1 c
boiled, 1"-diam. corm.	9	.5	1.9	<.1	0	2	.2 c
Arrowroot flour:							
1 cup	457	.4	112.8	.1	0	2	4.4 d
Arthur Treacher's, 1 serving:							
chicken, 2 patties ..	369	27.1	16.5	21.6	65	495	m.q.
chicken sandwich ..	413	16.2	44.0	19.2	32	708	m.q.
chips, 4 oz.	276	4.0	34.9	13.2	<85	39	m.q.
cod tail shape, bake 'n broil	245	19.6	9.7	14.2	m.q.	144	m.q.
coleslaw	123	1.0	11.1	8.2	7	266	m.q.
fish, 2 pieces ...	355	19.2	25.4	19.8	56	450	m.q.
fish sandwich	440	16.4	39.4	24.0	42	836	m.q.
Krunch Pup	203	5.4	12.0	14.8	25	446	m.q.
Lemon Luvs	276	2.6	35.1	13.9	<1	314	m.q.
shrimp, 7 pieces ...	381	13.1	27.2	24.4	93	538	m.q.
Artichoke, globe: fresh, boiled:							
1 medium, 10.6 oz.	60	4.2	13.4	.2	0	114	1.5 c
hearts, ½ cup ..	42	2.9	9.4	.1	0	80	1.1 c
canned, marinated (*S&W*), 3.5 oz. ..	225	2.0	6.0	26.0	0	15	m.q.
frozen, hearts, 3 oz.:							
(*Birds Eye* Deluxe)	30	2.0	7.0	0	0	40	m.q.
(*Seabrook*)	25	3.0	4.0	0	0	6	1.0 c

Food and Measure	cal.	prot. (gms)	carbo. (gms)	fat (gms)	chol. (mgs)	sod. (mgs)	fiber (gms)
Artichoke, Jerusa-lem, see "Jerusa-lem artichoke"							
Asparagus:							
fresh:							
raw, 4 spears, 3.8 oz.	13	1.8	2.1	.1	0	1	.6 d
boiled, 4 spears, 1/2" diam. base	15	1.6	2.6	.2	0	3	.5 c
boiled, drained, cuts, 1/2 cup . .	22	2.3	4.0	.3	0	4	.8 c
canned, 1/2 cup:							
all varieties (Del Monte)	20	2.0	3.0	0	0	355	m.q.
cuts and spears (Green Giant) . .	20	2.0	3.0	0	0	420	1.2 d
spears (S&W Fancy)	18	2.0	3.0	0	0	320	m.q.
spears, colossal (S&W Fancy) . .	20	2.0	4.0	0	0	320	m.q.
(Stokely)	20	2.0	3.0	0	0	380	m.q.
(Stokely No Salt or Sugar)	20	2.0	3.0	0	0	5	m.q.
frozen, 3.3 oz., except as noted:							
cuts and spears, 10-oz. pkg. . . .	69	9.2	11.7	.7	0	24	2.5 c
boiled, 4 spears, ap-prox. 2.1 oz. . .	17	1.8	2.9	.3	0	2	.5 c
spears (Birds Eye)	25	3.0	4.0	0	0	0	m.q.
spears (Frosty Acres)	25	3.0	4.0	0	0	4	1.0 c
cuts (Birds Eye) . .	25	3.0	4.0	0	0	5	m.q.
cuts and spears (Frosty Acres) . .	25	3.0	4.0	0	0	6	m.q.
Asparagus bean, see "Yardlong bean"							

Food and Measure	cal.	prot. (gms)	carbo. (gms)	fat (gms)	chol. (mgs)	sod. (mgs)	fiber (gms)
Asparagus pilaf:							
frozen *(Green Giant Microwave Garden Gourmet)*, 1 pkg.	190	5.0	37.0	4.0	10	610	3.0 d
Au jus gravy:							
canned *(Franco-American)*, 2 oz.	10	0	2.0	0	0	330	n.a.
mix[1] *(French's)*, ¼ cup	10	0	2.0	0	0	260	n.a.
Avocado:							
California:							
trimmed, 1 oz. . . .	50	.6	2.0	4.9	0	3	.8 d
pureed, ½ cup . .	204	2.4	8.0	19.9	0	14	3.1 d
1 medium, 8 oz. . .	306	3.6	12.0	30.0	0	21	4.7 d
Florida:							
trimmed, 1 oz. . . .	32	.5	2.5	2.5	0	1	.6 c
pureed, ½ cup . .	129	1.8	10.3	10.2	0	6	2.4 c
1 medium, 1 lb. . .	339	4.8	27.1	27.0	0	14	6.4 c
Avocado dip:							
(Kraft), 2 tbsp.	50	1.0	3.0	4.0	0	210	n.a.
Avocado oil, see "Oil"							

---

[1] *Prepared according to package directions.*

B

Food and Measure	cal.	prot. (gms)	carbo. (gms)	fat (gms)	chol. (mgs)	sod. (mgs)	fiber (gms)
Bacon, cooked:							
4.5 oz. (1 lb. raw) . .	732	38.7	.8	62.5	107	2026	0
(Black Label), 2 slices	60	4.0	0	5.0	m.q.	298	0
(JM), 2 slices	100	4.0	1.0	9.0	12	370	0
(JM Lower Sodium),							
2 slices	100	4.0	1.0	9.0	m.q.	260	0
(Kahn's American							
Beauty), 2 slices	100	5.0	n.a.	9.0	m.q.	m.q.	0
(Oscar Mayer), 1 slice	35	1.7	.1	3.1	5	118	0
(Oscar Mayer Center							
Cut), 1 slice	24	1.5	.1	2.0	5	96	0
(Oscar Mayer Lower							
Salt), 1 slice	33	2.0	.1	2.7	5	85	0
(Range Brand Sliced),							
2 slices	110	6.0	0	9.0	m.q.	392	0
(Red Label), 3 slices	110	6.0	0	10.0	m.q.	m.q.	0
beef *(JM),* 2 slices	100	7.0	1.0	7.0	20	320	0
thick sliced *(Oscar*							
Mayer), 1 slice . .	64	3.0	.2	5.7	10	208	0
Bacon, Canadian:							
unheated, 1 oz. . . .	45	5.9	.5	2.0	14	399	0
unheated *(Jones Dairy*							
Farm), 1 slice . . .	25	3.2	tr.	1.0	7	144	0
(Hormel Sliced), 1 oz.	45	6.0	0	2.0	m.q.	315	0
(Light & Lean),							
2 slices	35	6.0	0	1.0	m.q.	m.q.	0
(Oscar Mayer), 1-oz.							
slice	35	5.6	.1	1.4	12	389	0

Food and Measure	cal.	prot. (gms)	carbo. (gms)	fat (gms)	chol. (mgs)	sod. (mgs)	fiber (gms)
"Bacon," substitute:							
beef, heated:							
(Oscar Mayer Lean							
'N Tasty), 1 strip	46	2.9	.2	3.8	13	190	0
(Sizzlean), 2 strips	70	6.0	0	5.0	m.q.	480	0
pork, heated:							
(Oscar Mayer Lean							
'N Tasty), 1 strip	54	3.0	.1	4.7	14	215	0
(Sizzlean), 2 strips	90	6.0	0	8.0	m.q.	530	0
brown sugar cured							
(Sizzlean), 2 strips	110	6.0	2.0	9.0	m.q.	490	0
"Bacon," vegetarian:							
frozen *(Morningstar*							
Farms Breakfast							
Strips), 3 strips . .	80	3.0	4.0	6.0	0	350	m.q.
frozen *(Worthington*							
Stripples), 4 strips	120	4.0	6.0	9.0	0	460	m.q.
Bacon bits:							
(Hormel), 1 tbsp. . .	30	3.0	0	2.0	m.q.	313	0
(Oscar Mayer), 1/4 oz.	21	2.6	.2	1.0	6	181	0
imitation:							
(Bac*Os), 2 tsp. . .	25	2.0	2.0	1.0	0	90	n.a.
(Tone's), 1 tsp. . .	7	.8	.4	.3	0	59	n.a.
Bacon horseradish							
dip:							
(Kraft), 2 tbsp.	60	1.0	3.0	5.0	0	200	n.a.
(Kraft Premium),							
2 tbsp.	50	1.0	2.0	4.0	10	250	n.a.
Bacon onion dip:							
(Kraft Premium),							
2 tbsp.	50	1.0	1.0	5.0	10	250	n.a.
Bagel, frozen,							
1 piece:							
plain:							
(Lenders'), 2 oz.	150	6.0	30.0	1.0	0	320	m.q.
(Lender's Bagel-							
ettes), .9 oz. . .	70	3.0	13.0	<1.0	0	170	m.q.

Food and Measure	cal.	prot. (gms)	carbo. (gms)	fat (gms)	chol. (mgs)	sod. (mgs)	fiber (gms)
(Lender's Big'n Crusty), 31/8 oz.	240	9.0	47.0	1.0	0	450	m.q.
(Sara Lee), 3.1 oz.	230	9.0	46.0	1.0	n.a.	540	m.q.
blueberry *(Lender's)*, 21/2 oz.	190	7.0	38.0	1.0	0	250	m.q.
cinnamon and raisin:							
(Lender's Big'n Crusty), 31/8 oz.	250	8.0	49.0	2.0	0	370	m.q.
(Sara Lee), 3.1 oz.	240	8.0	48.0	2.0	n.a.	280	m.q.
egg:							
(Lender's), 2 oz.	150	7.0	29.0	1.0	5	360	m.q.
(Lender's Big'n Crusty), 31/8 oz.	250	9.0	47.0	2.0	15	380	m.q.
(Sara Lee), 3.1 oz.	250	9.0	48.0	2.0	m.q.	410	m.q.
garlic:							
(Lender's), 2 oz.	160	6.0	32.0	1.0	0	340	m.q.
(Lender's Big'n Crusty), 31/8 oz.	250	9.0	50.0	1.0	0	530	m.q.
oat bran *(Lender's)*, 21/2 oz.	170	7.0	36.0	2.0	0	290	3.0 d
onion:							
(Lender's), 2 oz.	160	7.0	31.0	1.0	0	290	m.q.
(Lender's Bagel-ettes), .9 oz. . . .	70	3.0	14.0	<1.0	0	135	<.1 d
(Lender's Big'n Crusty), 31/8 oz.	230	9.0	46.0	1.0	0	480	m.q.
(Sara Lee), 3.1 oz.	230	9.0	45.0	1.0	n.a.	630	m.q.
poppy seed:							
(Lender's), 2 oz.	160	7.0	29.0	1.0	0	370	m.q.
(Sara Lee), 3.1 oz.	230	9.0	46.0	1.0	n.a.	580	m.q.
pumpernickel *(Lend-er's)*, 2 oz.	160	6.0	31.0	1.0	0	330	m.q.
raisin *(Lender's* Bagelettes), .9 oz.	70	2.0	14.0	<1.0	0	110	m.q.
raisin'n honey *(Lend-er's)*, 21/2 oz. . . .	200	8.0	40.0	1.0	0	310	m.q.
rye *(Lender's)*, 2 oz.	150	6.0	30.0	1.0	0	310	m.q.

Food and Measure	cal.	prot. (gms)	carbo. (gms)	fat (gms)	chol. (mgs)	sod. (mgs)	fiber (gms)
Bagel, frozen *(cont.)*							
sesame seed:							
(Lender's), 2 oz.	160	7.0	31.0	1.0	0	320	m.q.
(Sara Lee), 3.1 oz.	260	8.0	50.0	3.0	n.a.	570	m.q.
soft *(Lender's)*,							
2¹/₂ oz.	210	7.0	36.0	3.0	12	350	m.q.
wheat'n raisin *(Lender's)*, 2¹/₂ oz. . . .	190	6.0	39.0	1.0	0	310	m.q.
Baked beans,							
canned, ¹/₂ cup,							
except as noted:							
(Allens)	170	6.0	21.0	6.0	n.a.	330	m.q.
(Campbell's Home							
Style), 8 oz.	230	11.0	48.0	4.0	n.a.	900	m.q.
(Grandma Brown's),							
1 cup	301	14.6	53.9	3.0	<1	655	15.5 d
(Grandma Brown's							
Saucepan), 1 cup	307	13.7	52.3	4.8	<1	592	14.8 d
(S&W Brick Oven) . .	160	7.0	28.0	2.0	n.a.	560	m.q.
pea, small *(B&M)*,							
8 oz.	330	16.0	49.0	8.0	n.a.	770	12.0 d
plain or vegetarian:							
4 oz.	105	5.4	23.3	.5	0	450	8.7 d
(Allens)	110	6.0	19.0	1.0	0	380	m.q.
(B&W), 8 oz. . . .	280	15.0	50.0	2.0	0	750	12.0 d
(Van Camp's Vege-							
tarian Style),							
1 cup	206	10.9	39.2	.6	n.a.	987	2.4 c
barbecue:							
(B&M), 8 oz. . . .	310	15.0	48.0	6.0	n.a.	1000	11.0 d
(Campbell's),							
7⁷/₈ oz.	210	10.0	43.0	4.0	n.a.	900	m.q.
w/beef	161	8.5	22.5	4.6	29	632	1.4 c
brown sugar *(Van							
Camp's)*, 1 cup . .	284	11.6	47.8	5.1	n.a.	892	3.2 c
w/franks *(Van Camp's*							
Beanee Weenee),							
1 cup	326	15.2	31.7	15.4	m.q.	990	2.7 c

Food and Measure	cal.	prot. (gms)	carbo. (gms)	fat (gms)	chol. (mgs)	sod. (mgs)	fiber (gms)
honey (B&W), 8 oz.	280	15.0	50.0	2.0	n.a.	940	11.0 d
molasses, brown sugar sauce (Campbell's Old Fashioned), 8 oz.	230	11.0	49.0	3.0	n.a.	730	m.q.
w/pork:							
(Allens Extra Fancy)	125	5.0	24.0	1.0	m.q.	540	m.q.
(Allens Extra Standard)	90	5.0	15.0	1.0	m.q.	350	m.q.
(Allens Fancy)	110	6.0	18.0	1.0	m.q.	430	m.q.
(Hormel Micro-Cup), 7.5 oz.	254	11.0	41.0	5.0	30	650	m.q.
(Hunt's), 4 oz.	140	6.0	26.0	1.0	m.q.	400	m.q.
(S&W)	130	5.0	22.0	2.0	m.q.	135	m.q.
(Van Camp's), 1 cup	216	10.9	38.8	1.9	m.q.	1011	2.4 c
in tomato sauce (B&W), 8 oz.	230	12.0	48.0	3.0	m.q.	1010	10.0 d
in tomato sauce (Campbell's), 8 oz.	190	9.0	43.0	3.0	m.q.	730	m.q.
in tomato sauce (Green Giant/ Joan of Arc)	90	5.0	21.0	1.0	m.q.	420	5.2 d
ranchero (Campbell's), 7¾ oz.	180	9.0	36.0	4.0	n.a.	860	m.q.
western style (Van Camp's), 1 cup	207	11.1	32.0	3.8	n.a.	1006	2.4 c
Baking powder:							
(Davis), 1 tsp.	8	0	2.0	0	0	330	0
Baking soda:							
(Tone's), 1 tsp.	0	0	0	0	0	821	0
Balsam-pear, fresh:							
leafy-tips, 1/2 cup:							
raw	7	1.3	.8	.2	0	3	.6 c
boiled, drained	10	1.0	2.0	.1	0	4	.5 c
pods, 1/2 cup:							
raw, 1/2" pieces	8	.5	1.7	.1	0	3	.7 c

Food and Measure	cal.	prot. (gms)	carbo. (gms)	fat (gms)	chol. (mgs)	sod. (mgs)	fiber (gms)
Balsam-pear, pods *(cont.)*							
boiled, drained,							
1/2" pieces . . .	12	.5	2.7	.1	0	4	.7 c
Bamboo shoots:							
fresh, 1/2 cup:							
raw, slices	21	2.0	4.0	.2	0	3	2.0 d
boiled, drained,							
1/2" slices	8	.9	1.2	.1	0	3	.4 c
canned:							
drained, 1/2 cup . .	13	1.1	2.1	.3	0	5	.4 c
(La Choy), 1.5 oz.	8	.7	1.4	.2	0	3	m.q.
Banana:							
fresh:							
whole, 1 lb.	271	3.1	69.1	1.4	0	3	4.7 d
1 medium, 8 3/4"							
long	105	1.2	26.7	.6	0	1	1.8 d
mashed, 1/2 cup . .	104	1.2	26.4	.5	0	1	1.8 d
dehydrated, 1/4 cup	87	1.0	22.1	.5	0	1	.5 c
Banana, baking, see "Plantain"							
Banana, red, fresh:							
1 medium, 7 1/4" long	118	1.6	30.7	.3	0	1	m.q.
Banana chips:							
freeze-dried *(Mountain House)*, 1/2 cup . .	248	2.0	15.0	8.0	0	n.a.	m.q.
Banana nectar:							
(Libby's), 6 fl. oz. . .	110	0	26.0	0	0	15	m.q.
Banana squash:							
baked *(Frieda* of California), 1 oz. . . .	18	.5	4.4	.1	0	3	m.q.
Barbecue loaf:							
(Oscar Mayer), 1-oz. slice	48	4.5	1.9	2.5	13	346	0
Barbecue sauce, 1 tbsp. except as noted:							
(Enrico's Original) . .	18	1.0	3.0	1.0	0	4	n.a.

Food and Measure	cal.	prot. (gms)	carbo. (gms)	fat (gms)	chol. (mgs)	sod. (mgs)	fiber (gms)
(Heinz Thick and							
Rich)	20	0	5.0	0	0	230	n.a.
(Hunt Original)	20	0	5.0	0	0	190	n.a.
(Kraft), 2 tbsp.	40	0	9.0	1.0	0	490	n.a.
(Kraft Thick'n Spicy							
Original), 2 tbsp.	50	0	11.0	1.0	0	490	n.a.
(Maull's Genuine) . .	20	<1.0	4.8	<1.0	<1	160	<1.0 d
(Ott's), 1 tbsp.	14	.2	3.2	.1	<1	147	.1 d
Cajun *(Golden Dipt)*,							
2 tbsp.	90	0	5.0	8.0	0	360	n.a.
chunky *(Kraft* Thick'n							
Spicy), 2 tbsp. . . .	60	0	12.0	1.0	0	450	n.a.
Dijon and honey							
(Lawry's), 1/4 cup	203	4.7	27.0	1.2	n.a.	1768	.4 c
garlic *(Kraft)*, 2 tbsp.	40	0	9.0	0	0	530	n.a.
hickory smoke:							
(Heinz Thick and							
Rich)	20	0	5.0	0	0	220	n.a.
(Kraft), 2 tbsp. . .	40	0	9.0	1.0	0	490	n.a.
(Kraft Thick'n							
Spicy), 2 tbsp.	50	0	11.0	1.0	0	510	n.a.
onion bits *(Kraft)*,							
2 tbsp.	50	0	10.0	1.0	0	420	n.a.
honey *(Hain)* . . .	14	0	1.0	1.0	0	120	n.a.
w/honey *(Kraft*							
Thick'n Spicy),							
2 tbsp.	60	0	13.0	1.0	0	350	n.a.
hot:							
(Heinz Thick and							
Rich)	20	0	5.0	0	0	220	n.a.
(Kraft), 2 tbsp. . .	40	0	8.0	1.0	0	510	n.a.
hickory smoke							
(Kraft), 2 tbsp.	40	0	8.0	1.0	0	500	n.a.
Italian seasonings							
(Kraft), 2 tbsp.	50	0	10.0	1.0	0	280	n.a.
Kansas City style:							
(Kraft), 2 tbsp. . .	50	0	11.0	1.0	0	290	n.a.

Food and Measure	cal.	prot. (gms)	carbo. (gms)	fat (gms)	chol. (mgs)	sod. (mgs)	fiber (gms)
Barbecue sauce, Kansas City style *(cont.)*							
(Kraft Thick'n							
Spicy), 2 tbsp.	60	0	13.0	1.0	0	300	n.a.
mesquite:							
(Enrico's)	18	1.0	3.0	1.0	0	4	n.a.
smoke *(Kraft),*							
2 tbsp.	40	0	10.0	1.0	0	420	n.a.
mushroom *(Heinz*							
Thick and Rich) . .	20	0	5.0	0	0	220	n.a.
onion:							
(Heinz Thick and							
Rich)	20	0	5.0	0	0	200	n.a.
(Maull's)	20	<1.0	4.0	<1.0	<1	135	<1.0 d
bits *(Kraft),* 2 tbsp.	50	0	11.0	1.0	0	420	n.a.
w/orange juice							
(Lawry's California							
Grill), 1/4 cup . . .	34	3.8	3.4	.7	n.a.	3846	.1 c
Oriental *(La Choy)* . .	16	.7	3.8	<.1	0	304	<.1 d
sloppy Joe w/beef							
(Libby's), 1/3 cup	110	5.0	7.0	7.0	m.q.	190	n.a.
sweet:							
(Maull's Sweet &							
Mild)	27	<1.0	5.0	<1.0	<1	125	<1.0 d
(Maull's Sweet &							
Smokey)	25	<1.0	6.0	<1.0	<1	140	<1.0 d
Barley:							
uncooked, 1 cup . .	651	23.0	135.2	4.2	0	22	31.8 d
pearled:							
uncooked, 1 cup	704	19.8	155.5	2.3	0	18	31.2 d
cooked, 1 cup . . .	193	3.6	44.3	.7	0	5	.4 c
medium or quick							
(Quaker Scotch),							
1.7 oz., 1/4 cup	172	5.0	36.3	.5	0	5	.4 c
Basella, see ''Vine-							
spinach''							
Basil, dried:							
ground, 1 tbsp. . . .	11	.7	2.7	.2	0	2	.8 c
ground, 1 tsp.	4	.2	.9	.1	0	tr.	.3 c

Food and Measure	cal.	prot. (gms)	carbo. (gms)	fat (gms)	chol. (mgs)	sod. (mgs)	fiber (gms)
Bass, meat only:							
freshwater, raw:							
1 lb.	516	85.5	0	16.7	308	317	0
1 oz.	32	5.3	0	1.0	19	20	0
sea, see "Sea bass"							
striped, raw:							
1 lb.	439	80.4	0	10.6	363	313	0
1 oz.	27	5.0	0	.7	20	23	0
Batter mix (see also specific listings), 1 oz.:							
(Golden Dipt)	100	3.0	21.0	0	0	740	m.q.
(Golden Dipt Corny Dog)	100	3.0	22.0	0	0	490	m.q.
Bay leaf, dried:							
(Spice Islands), 1 tsp.	5	.1	.3	.1	0	<1	.3 c
crumbled, 1 tsp. . . .	2	<.1	.2	<.1	0	tr.	.2 c
Bean mix, 1/2 cup[1]:							
Cajun (Lipton)	160	5.0	28.0	3.0	m.q.	440	m.q.
chicken (Lipton) . . .	150	6.0	26.0	4.0	m.q.	500	m.q.
Bean salad, canned, 1/2 cup, except as noted:							
four bean (Joan of Arc/Read)	100	3.0	23.0	1.0	0	660	3.3 d
green bean, German-style (Joan of Arc/Read), 1 cup . . .	180	3.0	27.0	7.0	n.a.	920	3.6 d
three bean:							
(Green Giant) . . .	70	2.0	15.0	0	0	410	1.5 d
(Joan of Arc/Read)	90	2.0	22.0	0	0	710	3.0 d
Bean sprouts:							
fresh, see specific bean listings							
canned (La Choy), 2 oz.	6	.7	1.4	.1	0	17	.7 d

[1] Prepared according to package directions with 1 tbsp. butter.

Food and Measure	cal.	prot. (gms)	carbo. (gms)	fat (gms)	chol. (mgs)	sod. (mgs)	fiber (gms)
Beans, see specific bean listings							
Beans and frank-furter dinner, frozen:							
(Banquet), 10 oz. . .	520	17.0	57.0	25.0	35	1230	m.q.
(Morton), 10 oz. . . .	350	11.0	46.0	13.0	30	1490	m.q.
(Swanson), 10 1/2 oz.	440	11.0	55.0	20.0	m.q.	900	m.q.
Beans, refried, see "Refried beans"							
Beans, snap, see "Green bean"							
Bearnaise sauce mix:							
dry, .9-oz. pkt.	90	3.5	14.8	2.2	tr.	841	.1 c
Beechnuts, dried:							
shelled, 1 oz.	164	1.8	9.5	14.2	0	m.q.	1.1 c
Beef, choice, meat only[1], 4 oz., except as noted:							
brisket, whole, braised:							
lean w/fat	437	26.6	0	35.8	107	69	0
lean only	274	33.7	0	14.5	105	79	0
chuck, arm pot roast, braised:							
lean w/fat	395	30.6	0	29.2	112	67	0
lean only	255	37.4	0	10.5	115	75	0
chuck, blade roast, braised:							
lean w/fat	412	29.7	0	31.5	117	73	0
lean only	298	35.2	0	16.3	120	81	0
flank steak[2], braised, lean only	298	30.6	0	18.6	82	79	0
ground, raw, 1 oz.:							
extra lean	66	5.3	0	4.8	19	19	0
lean	75	5.0	0	5.9	21	20	0

[1] *Trimmed to 1/4" fat, except as noted.*
[2] *Trimmed to 0" fat.*

Food and Measure	cal.	prot. (gms)	carbo. (gms)	fat (gms)	chol. (mgs)	sod. (mgs)	fiber (gms)
regular	88	4.7	0	7.5	24	19	0
ground, broiled, medium:							
extra lean, 11.9 oz.							
(1 lb. raw)	859	85.3	0	54.9	281	234	0
extra lean	290	28.8	0	18.5	95	79	0
lean, 11.4 oz. (1 lb. raw)	876	79.6	0	59.4	280	248	0
lean	308	28.0	0	20.9	99	87	0
regular, 10.7 oz. (1 lb. raw)	880	73.2	0	62.9	273	251	0
regular	328	27.3	0	23.5	102	94	0
porterhouse steak, broiled:							
lean w/fat	346	28.2	0	25.1	94	69	0
lean only	247	31.9	0	12.2	91	75	0
rib, whole (ribs 6–12), roasted:							
lean w/fat	426	25.1	0	35.4	96	71	0
lean only	276	30.9	0	15.9	91	82	0
rib, large end (ribs 6–9), roasted:							
lean w/fat	434	25.3	0	36.2	96	71	0
lean only	284	31.2	0	16.7	92	83	0
rib, small end (ribs 10–12), broiled:							
lean w/fat	376	26.7	0	31.3	95	70	0
lean only	263	30.4	0	14.8	90	81	0
round, bottom, braised:							
lean w/fat	257	35.1	0	12.0	109	58	0
lean only	249	35.8	0	10.7	109	58	0
round, eye of, roasted:							
lean w/fat	273	30.2	0	16.0	82	67	0
lean only	198	32.9	0	6.5	78	70	0
round, full cut, broiled:							
lean w/fat	272	31.0	0	15.4	91	69	0
lean only	217	33.1	0	8.3	88	73	0

Food and Measure	cal.	prot. (gms)	carbo. (gms)	fat (gms)	chol. (mgs)	sod. (mgs)	fiber (gms)
Beef (cont.)							
round, tip, roasted:							
lean w/fat	280	30.1	0	16.9	94	70	0
lean only	213	32.6	0	8.3	92	74	0
round, top, broiled:							
lean w/fat	254	34.2	0	12.0	96	68	0
lean only	214	35.9	0	6.7	95	69	0
round, top, fried:							
lean w/fat	314	36.7	0	17.4	110	77	0
lean only	257	39.8	0	9.7	110	81	0
shank, crosscuts, simmered:							
lean w/fat	298	34.8	0	16.6	91	69	0
lean only	228	38.2	0	7.2	88	73	0
shortribs, braised:							
lean w/fat	534	24.5	0	47.6	107	57	0
lean only	335	34.9	0	20.6	105	66	0
sirloin, top, broiled:							
lean w/fat	305	31.3	0	19.0	102	70	0
lean only	229	34.4	0	9.1	101	75	0
sirloin, top, fried:							
lean w/fat	370	31.9	0	25.9	111	79	0
lean only	270	36.8	0	12.4	112	87	0
T-bone steak, broiled:							
lean w/fat	338	28.3	0	24.0	94	69	0
lean only	243	31.9	0	11.8	91	75	0
tenderloin, broiled:							
lean w/fat	345	28.4	0	24.8	98	67	0
lean only	252	32.0	0	12.7	95	71	0
top loin, broiled:							
lean w/fat	338	28.8	0	23.8	90	71	0
lean only	243	32.5	0	11.5	86	77	0
Beef, corned, 1 oz., except as noted:							
(Eckrich Slender Sliced)	40	6.0	1.0	1.0	m.q.	270	0
(Healthy Deli)	35	5.7	.7	1.0	11	210	0

Food and Measure	cal.	prot. (gms)	carbo. (gms)	fat (gms)	chol. (mgs)	sod. (mgs)	fiber (gms)
(Healthy Deli St. Paddy's)	24	3.9	1.1	.4	7	290	0
(Hillshire Farm) . . .	31	6.0	<1.0	.4	m.q.	230	0
(Oscar Mayer), .6-oz. slice	16	3.3	.1	.3	5	208	0
brisket, cured, cooked, 4 oz.	285	20.6	.5	21.5	111	1286	0
canned *(Libby's* 12 oz.), 2.4 oz.	160	17.0	2.0	9.0	m.q.	750	0
Beef, corned, hash, canned:							
(Dinty Moore), 2 oz.	130	15.0	0	8.0	m.q.	m.q.	m.q.
(Libby's 15 oz.), 7½ oz.	400	18.0	20.0	27.0	m.q.	1260	m.q.
(Mary Kitchen 25 oz.), 8⅓-oz.	400	22.0	19.0	27.0	m.q.	1429	m.q.
(Mary Kitchen 15 oz.), 7½-oz.	360	20.0	19.0	24.0	m.q.	1386	m.q.
Beef, corned, spread, canned:							
(Hormel), ½ oz. . . .	35	2.0	0	3.0	m.q.	m.q.	(0)
(Underwood), 2¼ oz.	120	6.0	n.a.	10.0	m.q.	605	(0)
Beef, dried:							
cured, 1 oz.	47	8.3	.4	1.1	m.q.	984	0
Beef, roast, see "Beef" and "Beef luncheon meat"							
Beef, roast, hash:							
canned *(Mary Kitchen)*, 7½ oz.	350	20.0	18.0	22.0	m.q.	1142	m.q.
frozen *(Stouffer's)*, 10 oz.	380	30.0	16.0	22.0	m.q.	1340	m.q.
Beef, roast, spread, canned:							
(Hormel), ½ oz. . . .	31	2.0	0	2.0	m.q.	m.q.	m.q.
(Underwood), 2.4 oz.	140	11.0	n.a.	10.0	m.q.	515	m.q.

Food and Measure	cal.	prot. (gms)	carbo. (gms)	fat (gms)	chol. (mgs)	sod. (mgs)	fiber (gms)
"Beef," vegetarian,							
canned:							
slices *(Worthington Savory Slices),* 2 slices	100	8.0	4.0	6.0	0	340	m.q.
steak *(Worthington Prime Stakes),* 3.25-oz. piece	160	10.0	7.0	10.0	0	410	m.q.
steak *(Worthington Vegetable Steaks),* 2 1/2 pieces	110	17.0	5.0	2.0	0	400	m.q.
stew *(Worthington Country Stew),* 9 1/2 oz.	220	10.0	23.0	10.0	0	760	m.q.
frozen:							
(Worthington Stakelets), 2.5 oz.	150	13.0	7.0	8.0	0	460	m.q.
corned, slices *(Worthington),* 4 slices	120	9.0	8.0	6.0	0	740	m.q.
corned, roll *(Worthington),* 2 1/2 oz.	150	12.0	9.0	7.0	0	660	m.q.
pie *(Worthington)* 8-oz. pie	360	9.0	44.0	16.0	0	1940	m.q.
roll *(Worthington),* 4 slices, 2.5 oz.	130	12.0	7.0	6.0	0	750	m.q.
roll, smoked *(Worthington),* 3 slices	120	10.0	7.0	6.0	0	790	m.q.
Beef casserole, see "Beef entree, frozen"							
Beef dinner,							
frozen:							
(Banquet Extra Helping), 16 oz.	870	34.0	50.0	61.0	120	810	m.q.
(Swanson), 11 1/4 oz.	340	27.0	41.0	8.0	m.q.	800	m.q.
in barbecue sauce *(Swanson),* 11 oz.	460	29.0	51.0	15.0	m.q.	850	m.q.

Food and Measure	cal.	prot. (gms)	carbo. (gms)	fat (gms)	chol. (mgs)	sod. (mgs)	fiber (gms)
chopped:							
(Banquet), 11 oz.	420	21.0	14.0	32.0	80	600	m.q.
steak (Swanson Hungry Man),							
16¾ oz.	640	35.0	41.0	37.0	m.q.	1600	m.q.
enchilada, see "Enchilada dinner"							
meat loaf, see "Meat loaf dinner"							
Mexicana (The Budget Gourmet), 12.8 oz.	560	33.0	56.0	23.0	50	1290	m.q.
patty, charbroiled (Freezer Queen),							
10 oz.	300	17.0	20.0	17.0	m.q.	1260	m.q.
patty, cheese, sandwich (Kid Cuisine),							
6.25 oz.	400	12.0	47.0	19.0	40	550	m.q.
pepper steak:							
(Armour Classics Lite), 11.25 oz.	220	17.0	29.0	4.0	35	970	m.q.
(Healthy Choice),							
11 oz.	290	24.0	35.0	6.0	65	530	m.q.
(Le Menu), 11½ oz.	370	25.0	38.0	13.0	m.q.	1030	m.q.
pot roast, Yankee:							
(Armour Classics),							
10 oz.	310	25.0	26.0	12.0	85	670	m.q.
(The Budget Gourmet), 11 oz.	380	27.0	22.0	21.0	70	690	m.q.
(Healthy Choice),							
11 oz.	260	19.0	36.0	4.0	45	310	m.q.
(Le Menu), 11 oz.	370	27.0	31.0	15.0	m.q.	780	m.q.
Salisbury steak:							
(Armour Classics),							
11.25 oz.	350	22.0	26.0	17.0	55	1430	m.q.
(Armour Classics Lite), 11.5 oz. . .	300	21.0	29.0	2.0	35	1020	m.q.
(Banquet), 11 oz.	500	23.0	26.0	34.0	80	600	m.q.

Food and Measure	cal.	prot. (gms)	carbo. (gms)	fat (gms)	chol. (mgs)	sod. (mgs)	fiber (gms)
Beef dinner, Salisbury steak *(cont.)*							
(Banquet Extra Helping), 18 oz.	910	50.0	49.0	60.0	175	740	m.q.
(Freezer Queen), 10 oz.	380	18.0	28.0	22.0	m.q.	1260	m.q.
(Healthy Choice), 11.5 oz.	300	19.0	41.0	7.0	50	480	m.q.
(Le Menu Light Style)*, 10½ oz.	220	18.0	21.0	7.0	m.q.	830	m.q.
(Morton), 10 oz. . .	300	12.0	23.0	17.0	40	1420	m.q.
(Swanson), 10¾ oz.	410	19.0	43.0	18.0	m.q.	880	m.q.
(Swanson Hungry Man), 18¼ oz.	680	41.0	37.0	41.0	m.q.	1730	m.q.
w/gravy and mush-rooms *(Stouffer's Dinner Supreme)*, 11⅝ oz.	400	25.0	24.0	23.0	m.q.	1230	m.q.
w/mushroom gravy *(Banquet Extra Helping)*, 18 oz.	890	51.0	48.0	58.0	169	685	m.q.
parmigiana *(Armour Classics)*, 11.5 oz.	410	22.0	32.0	21.0	60	1120	m.q.
sirloin *(The Budget Gourmet)*, 11.5 oz.	410	26.0	28.0	22.0	105	890	m.q.
short ribs *(Armour Classics)*, 9.75 oz.	380	24.0	34.0	16.0	90	790	m.q.
sirloin:							
chopped *(Le Menu)*, 12¼ oz.	440	25.0	29.0	25.0	m.q.	1030	m.q.
chopped *(Swanson)*, 11 oz.	370	21.0	29.0	19.0	m.q.	850	m.q.
roast *(Armour Classics)*, 10.45 oz.	190	19.0	21.0	4.0	55	970	m.q.
tips *(Armour Classics)*, 10.25 oz.	230	22.0	20.0	7.0	70	820	m.q.

Food and Measure	cal.	prot. (gms)	carbo. (gms)	fat (gms)	chol. (mgs)	sod. (mgs)	fiber (gms)
tips (Healthy Choice), 11.75 oz.	290	25.0	33.0	6.0	70	350	m.q.
tips (Le Menu), 11½ oz.	400	29.0	29.0	19.0	m.q.	780	m.q.
tips, in Burgundy sauce (The Budget Gourmet), 11 oz.	310	24.0	28.0	11.0	65	720	m.q.
sliced:							
(Morton), 10 oz. . .	220	24.0	20.0	5.0	65	950	m.q.
(Swanson Hungry Man), 15¼ oz.	450	37.0	49.0	12.0	m.q.	1060	m.q.
gravy and (Freezer Queen), 10 oz.	210	18.0	18.0	7.0	m.q.	1010	m.q.
steak Diane (Armour Classics Lite), 10 oz.	290	27.0	25.0	9.0	80	440	m.q.
Stroganoff:							
(Armour Classics Lite), 11.25 oz.	250	18.0	33.0	6.0	55	510	m.q.
(Le Menu), 10 oz.	450	25.0	30.0	25.0	m.q.	1000	m.q.
Swiss steak:							
(The Budget Gourmet), 11.2 oz. . .	450	23.0	40.0	22.0	70	1110	m.q.
(Swanson), 10 oz.	340	23.0	38.0	11.0	m.q.	740	m.q.
tamale, see "Tamale dinner"							
Beef entree, canned:							
chow mein (La Choy Bi-Pack), ¾ cup	70	7.0	8.0	1.0	20	840	1.0 d
pepper Oriental (La Choy Bi-Pack), ¾ cup	80	7.0	10.0	2.0	18	950	1.0 d
stew:							
(Dinty Moore 40 oz.) 8 oz.	210	13.0	16.0	11.0	m.q.	971	m.q.
(Dinty Moore 24 oz.), 8 oz.	220	12.0	15.0	12.0	m.q.	980	m.q.

Food and Measure	cal.	prot. (gms)	carbo. (gms)	fat (gms)	chol. (mgs)	sod. (mgs)	fiber (gms)
Beef entree, canned stew *(cont.)*							
(Hormel/Dinty Moore Micro-Cup), 7.5 oz. . .	190	10.0	17.0	9.0	50	860	m.q.
(Libby's 24 oz.), 8 oz.	170	12.0	19.0	6.0	m.q.	930	m.q.
(Libby's 15 oz.), 7.5 oz.	160	12.0	18.0	5.0	m.q.	870	m.q.
(Wolf Brand), 7.5 oz.	179	9.6	18.3	7.5	m.q.	1043	.6 c
Beef entree, freeze-dried, 1 cup:							
and rice w/onions *(Mountain House)*	330	11.0	42.0	12.0	m.q.	265	m.q.
stew *(Mountain House)*	260	16.0	26.0	9.0	m.q.	75	m.q.
Stroganoff *(Mountain House)*	270	10.0	26.0	13.0	m.q.	118	m.q.
Beef entree, frozen:							
(Banquet Platter), 10 oz.	460	22.0	20.0	34.0	75	630	m.q.
and broccoli w/rice *(La Choy Fresh & Lite)*, 11 oz.	260	17.0	42.0	5.0	51	1299	5.2 d
Burgundy *(Le Menu)*, 7½ oz.	330	25.0	5.0	23.0	m.q.	660	n.a.
casserole *(Pillsbury Microwave Classic)*, 1 pkg.	430	16.0	34.0	25.0	m.q.	1100	m.q.
champignon *(Tyson Gourmet Selection)*, 10.5 oz.	370	27.0	31.0	15.0	m.q.	830	m.q.
cheeseburger *(MicroMagic)*, 4.75 oz.	450	17.0	29.0	25.0	80	790	m.q.
chop suey, w/rice *(Stouffer's)*, 12 oz.	300	16.0	38.0	9.0	m.q.	1170	m.q.
creamed, chipped:							
(Banquet Cookin' Bags), 4 oz.	100	7.0	9.0	4.0	m.q.	m.q.	n.a.

Food and Measure	cal.	prot. (gms)	carbo. (gms)	fat (gms)	chol. (mgs)	sod. (mgs)	fiber (gms)
(Freezer Queen Cook-In-Pouch), 5 oz.	80	5.0	11.0	2.0	m.q.	500	n.a.
(Myers), 3.5 oz. . . .	136	9.0	7.0	8.0	m.q.	863	n.a.
(Stouffer's), 5 1/2 oz.	230	12.0	9.0	16.0	m.q.	850	n.a.
Dijon, w/pasta and vegetables *(Right Course)*, 9 1/2 oz.	290	20.0	31.0	9.0	40	580	m.q.
enchilada, see "Enchilada entree"							
fiesta, w/corn pasta *(Right Course)*, 8 7/8 oz.	270	18.0	33.0	7.0	30	590	m.q.
hamburger *(MicroMagic)*, 4 oz.	350	13.0	26.0	18.0	55	500	m.q.
London broil *(Weight Watchers)*, 7.37 oz.	140	18.0	9.0	3.0	40	510	m.q.
meat loaf, see "Meat loaf entree"							
Oriental:							
(The Budget Gourmet Slim Selects), 10 oz.	290	17.0	36.0	9.0	25	690	m.q.
w/vegetables and rice *(Lean Cuisine)*, 8 5/8 oz. . .	250	18.0	28.0	7.0	45	900	m.q.
patty, charbroiled, mushroom gravy and:							
(Banquet Cookin' Bags), 5 oz. . . .	210	9.0	8.0	15.0	m.q.	m.q.	n.a.
(Banquet Family Entrees), 8 oz. . . .	290	13.0	13.0	21.0	m.q.	m.q.	n.a.
(Freezer Queen Cook-In-Pouch), 5 oz.	90	10.0	7.0	3.0	m.q.	900	n.a.
(Freezer Queen Family Suppers), 7 oz.	180	12.0	9.0	11.0	m.q.	1050	n.a.

Food and Measure	cal.	prot. (gms)	carbo. (gms)	fat (gms)	chol. (mgs)	sod. (mgs)	fiber (gms)
Beef entree, frozen *(cont.)*							
patty, onion gravy and:							
(Banquet Family Entrees), 8 oz. . . .	300	12.0	14.0	21.0	m.q.	m.q.	n.a.
(Freezer Queen Family Suppers), 7 oz.	200	13.0	10.0	12.0	m.q.	960	n.a.
and peppers in sauce, w/rice *(Freezer Queen Single Serve)*, 9 oz. . . .	260	21.0	38.0	3.0	m.q.	810	m.q.
pepper Oriental *(Chun King)*, 13 oz.	310	17.0	53.0	3.0	m.q.	1300	m.q.
pepper steak:							
(Dining Lite), 9 oz.	260	18.0	33.0	6.0	40	1050	m.q.
(Healthy Choice), 9.5 oz.	250	18.0	36.0	4.0	40	340	m.q.
(Tyson Gourmet Selection), 11.25 oz.	330	20.0	38.0	11.0	m.q.	1130	m.q.
green, w/rice *(Stouffer's)*, 10 1/2 oz.	330	21.0	36.0	11.0	m.q.	1440	m.q.
w/rice *(The Budget Gourmet)*, 10 oz.	300	15.0	39.0	9.0	25	800	m.q.
w/rice, vegetables *(La Choy Fresh & Lite)*, 10 oz. . . .	280	21.0	33.0	8.0	36	1082	2.0 d
pie:							
(Banquet), 7 oz. . .	510	12.0	39.0	33.0	25	870	m.q.
(Morton), 7 oz. . .	430	11.0	27.0	31.0	30	740	m.q.
(Myers), 3.5 oz. . . .	123	7.0	10.0	6.0	m.q.	343	m.q.
(Stouffer's), 10 oz.	500	20.0	33.0	32.0	m.q.	1300	m.q.
(Swanson Pot Pie), 7 oz.	380	11.0	37.0	20.0	m.q.	700	m.q.
(Swanson Hungry Man Pot Pie), 16 oz.	700	27.0	66.0	36.0	m.q.	1530	m.q.

Food and Measure	cal.	prot. (gms)	carbo. (gms)	fat (gms)	chol. (mgs)	sod. (mgs)	fiber (gms)
microwave *(Banquet Supreme)*, 7 oz.	440	14.0	30.0	29.0	35	730	m.q.
pot roast *(Right Course)*, 9 1/4 oz.	220	17.0	22.0	7.0	35	550	m.q.
ragout, w/rice pilaf *(Right Course)*, 10 oz.	300	19.0	38.0	8.0	50	550	m.q.
Salisbury steak:							
(Dining Lite), 9 oz.	200	18.0	14.0	8.0	55	1000	m.q.
(Swanson Home-style), 10 oz. . .	480	22.0	22.0	34.0	m.q.	1170	m.q.
charbroiled, w/veg-etables *(Freezer Queen* Single Serve), 9 oz. . .	330	22.0	14.0	22.0	m.q.	990	m.q.
gravy and: *(Banquet Cookin' Bags)*, 5 oz.	190	9.0	8.0	14.0	m.q.	m.q.	n.a.
gravy and *(Banquet Family Entrees)*, 8 oz.	300	13.0	12.0	22.0	m.q.	m.q.	n.a.
gravy and *(Freezer Queen Cook-In-Pouch)*, 5 oz. . .	160	9.0	7.0	11.0	m.q.	850	n.a.
gravy and *(Freezer Queen Family Suppers)*, 7 oz.	200	13.0	9.0	13.0	m.q.	1110	n.a.
in gravy *(Stouffer's)*, 9 7/8 oz.	250	21.0	9.0	14.0	m.q.	1070	n.a.
w/Italian style sauce and vege-tables *(Lean Cui-sine)*, 9 1/2 oz. . .	280	25.0	12.0	15.0	100	840	m.q.
Romana *(Weight Watchers)*, 8.75 oz.	310	23.0	26.0	13.0	80	910	m.q.
sirloin *(The Budget Gourmet* Slim Selects), 9 oz.	280	21.0	31.0	8.0	75	870	m.q.

Food and Measure	cal.	prot. (gms)	carbo. (gms)	fat (gms)	chol. (mgs)	sod. (mgs)	fiber (gms)
Beef entree, frozen, Salisbury steak *(cont.)*							
supreme *(Tyson Gourmet Selection)*, 10 oz.	430	16.0	34.0	26.0	m.q.	810	m.q.
short ribs:							
(Tyson Gourmet Selection), 11 oz.	470	25.0	38.0	24.0	m.q.	950	m.q.
in gravy *(Stouffer's)*, 9 oz.	350	30.0	12.0	20.0	m.q.	900	m.q.
sirloin:							
in herb sauce *(The Budget Gourmet Slim Selects)*, 10 oz.	290	19.0	27.0	12.0	25	770	m.q.
roast *(The Budget Gourmet)*, 9.5 oz.	330	13.0	36.0	14.0	85	700	m.q.
tips in Burgundy sauce *(Swanson Homestyle)*, 7 oz.	270	17.0	27.0	10.0	m.q.	570	m.q.
tips w/country style vegetables *(The Budget Gourmet)*, 10 oz.	310	16.0	21.0	18.0	40	570	m.q.
sliced:							
barbecue sauce and *(Banquet Cookin' Bags)*, 4 oz. . . .	100	9.0	11.0	2.0	m.q.	m.q.	n.a.
sliced, gravy and:							
(Banquet Cookin' Bags), 4 oz. . . .	100	8.0	5.0	5.0	m.q.	m.q.	n.a
(Banquet Family Entrees), 8 oz. . . .	160	20.0	8.0	5.0	m.q.	m.q.	n.a.
(Freezer Queen Cook-In-Pouch), 4 oz.	60	9.0	4.0	1.0	m.q.	500	n.a.
(Freezer Queen Deluxe Family Suppers), 7 oz.	130	15.0	10.0	3.0	m.q.	870	n.a.

Food and Measure	cal.	prot. (gms)	carbo. (gms)	fat (gms)	chol. (mgs)	sod. (mgs)	fiber (gms)
steak:							
breaded (Hormel), 4 oz.	370	14.0	13.0	30.0	m.q.	m.q.	m.q.
ranchero (Lean Cuisine), 9¼ oz. . . ,	270	16.0	30.0	9.0	40	950	m.q.
stew:							
(Banquet Family Entrees), 7 oz. . . .	140	6.0	18.0	5.0	m.q.	m.q.	m.q.
(Freezer Queen Family Suppers), 7 oz.	150	9.0	15.0	6.0	m.q.	820	m.q.
Stroganoff:							
(The Budget Gourmet Slim Selects), 8.75 oz.	280	18.0	29.0	10.0	60	560	m.q.
(Myers), 3.5 oz. . .	112	8.0	7.0	6.0	m.q.	346	n.a.
(Weight Watchers), 9 oz.	320	24.0	27.0	13.0	70	900	m.q.
w/parsley noodles (Stouffer's), 9¾ oz.	390	24.0	28.0	20.0	m.q.	1090	m.q.
sauce w/, and noodles (Banquet Family Entrees), 7 oz.	190	17.0	18.0	6.0	m.q.	m.q.	m.q.
Szechuan:							
(Chun King), 13 oz.	340	20.0	57.0	3.0	m.q.	1810	m.q.
w/noodles and vegetables (Lean Cuisine), 9¼ oz. . . .	260	20.0	22.0	10.0	100	680	m.q.
teriyaki:							
(Chun King), 13 oz.	380	22.0	68.0	2.0	m.q.	2200	m.q.
(Dining Lite), 9 oz.	270	20.0	36.0	5.0	45	850	m.q.
w/rice and vegetables (La Choy Fresh & Lite), 10 oz.	240	17.0	39.9	5.0	57	1198	2.0 d

Food and Measure	cal.	prot. (gms)	carbo. (gms)	fat (gms)	chol. (mgs)	sod. (mgs)	fiber (gms)
Beef entree, frozen, teriyaki *(cont.)*							
in sauce, w/rice and vegetables *(Stouffer's)*, 9³/4 oz.	290	22.0	33.0	8.0	m.q.	1450	m.q.
tortellini, see "Tortellini entree"							
Beef entree, packaged:							
pepper steak, Oriental *(Hormel Top Shelf)*, 1 serving	290	25.0	25.0	10.0	45	1700	m.q.
ribs, boneless *(Hormel Top Shelf)*, 1 serving	440	28.0	29.0	24.0	90	550	m.q.
roast, tender *(Hormel Top Shelf)*, 1 serving	240	27.0	18.0	7.0	65	980	m.q.
Salisbury steak, w/potatoes *(Hormel Top Shelf)*, 10 oz. . . .	254	29.0	22.0	6.0	88	1211	m.q.
Stroganoff *(Hormel Top Shelf)*, 1 serving	320	29.0	24.0	12.0	48	1250	m.q.
sukiyaki *(Hormel Top Shelf)*, 1 serving	330	24.0	36.0	10.0	45	1700	m.q.
Beef entree mix:							
Oriental *(Hunt's Minute Gourmet)*, 7.6 oz.[1]	271]	26.1	14.0	12.0	m.q.	1122	m.q.
stew, hearty *(Lipton Microeasy)*, 1/4 pkg.[2]	370	31.0	14.0	20.0	m.q.	800	m.q.
Beef gravy, canned:							
1/4 cup	31	2.2	2.8	1.4	2	326	0
(Franco-American), 2 oz.	25	1.0	3.0	1.0	m.q.	290	n.a.

[1] *Prepared according to package directions.*

[2] *Prepared according to package directions with 1¹/2 lbs. beef stew meat.*

Food and Measure	cal.	prot. (gms)	carbo. (gms)	fat (gms)	chol. (mgs)	sod. (mgs)	fiber (gms)
w/chunky beef (Hormel Great Beginnings), 5 oz.	136	12.0	7.0	7.0	m.q.	904	n.a.
Beef jerky (see also "Sausage sticks"):							
(Frito-Lay's), .21 oz.	25	3.0	1.0	1.0	10	200	0
(Frito-Lay's Tender), .7 oz.	120	5.0	2.0	10.0	25	370	0
(Hickory Farms), 1 oz.	100	16.0	4.0	3.0	73	1360	0
(Hormel Lumberjack), 1 oz.	101	5.0	0	9.0	m.q.	304	0
(Pemmican Arrowhead), 1 piece . . .	70	8.0	2.0	3.0	m.q.	580	0
(Pemmican Steakers), 1 pouch	80	14.0	4.0	1.0	m.q.	470	0
(Pemmican Steakers), 1 strip	40	5.0	2.0	1.0	m.q.	160	0
(Pemmican Tender Brave/Chief/Trail/ Tribe Packs), 1 oz.	80	14.0	2.0	2.0	m.q.	830	0
(Pemmican Tender Tomahawk), 1 piece	20	3.0	1.0	1.0	m.q.	210	0
(Slim Jim), 1 piece	20	2.0	1.0	1.0	m.q.	120	0
(Slim Jim Big Jerk), 1 piece	25	3.0	1.0	1.0	m.q.	220	0
(Slim Jim Giant Jerk), 1 piece	60	7.0	2.0	2.0	m.q.	510	0
natural, peppered, jalapeño or Tabasco:							
(Pemmican), 1.1 oz.	90	13.0	4.0	2.0	m.q.	960	0
(Pemmican), 15/16-oz. slab . .	110	16.0	5.0	3.0	m.q.	1150	0
(Pemmican), 1/4-oz. steak	25	3.0	1.0	1.0	m.q.	220	0
natural style (Pemmican), 1 oz.	80	12.0	4.0	2.0	m.q.	880	0

Food and Measure	cal.	prot. (gms)	carbo. (gms)	fat (gms)	chol. (mgs)	sod. (mgs)	fiber (gms)
Beef jerky *(cont.)*							
regular or *Tabasco*							
(*Slim Jim Super*							
Jerk), 1 piece . . .	30	4.0	1.0	1.0	m.q.	250	0
teriyaki, natural style:							
(Pemmican), 1 oz.	80	12.0	4.0	2.0	m.q.	800	0
(Pemmican),							
15/16-oz. slab . .	100	15.0	5.0	2.0	m.q.	1030	0
(Pemmican), 1/4-oz.							
steak	20	3.0	1.0	1.0	m.q.	200	0
Beef luncheon meat,							
1 oz., except as							
noted:							
(Eckrich Slender							
Sliced)	35	6.0	1.0	1.0	m.q.	270	0
corned, see "Beef,							
corned"							
loaf, jellied *(Hormel*							
Perma-Fresh),							
2 slices	90	14.0	0	4.0	m.q.	900	0
roast:							
(Healthy Deli) . . .	30	6.4	.2	.4	13	130	0
Italian *(Healthy Deli)*	31	6.2	.1	.6	16	140	0
oven-roasted, cured							
(Hillshire Farm							
Deli Select) . . .	31	6.0	<1.0	.5	m.q.	270	0
top round *(Boar's*							
Head)	40	7.0	<1.0	1.0	20	30	0
top round *(Boar's*							
Head Deluxe) . .	45	7.0	<1.0	2.0	20	40	0
sandwich steak							
(Steak-Umm), 2 oz.	180	9.0	0	16.0	m.q.	50	0
smoked:							
(Hillshire Farm Deli							
Select)	31	6.0	<1.0	.5	m.q.	270	0
(Oscar Mayer),							
.5-oz. slice . . .	14	2.6	.3	.3	7	179	0
cured *(Hormel)* . .	50	5.0	0	2.0	m.q.	315	0

Food and Measure	cal.	prot. (gms)	carbo. (gms)	fat (gms)	chol. (mgs)	sod. (mgs)	fiber (gms)
cured, dried (Hormel)	45	8.0	0	1.0	m.q.	822	0
Beef marinade seasoning mix:							
(Lawry's), 1 pkg. . . .	49	1.2	10.7	.2	0	7284	<.1 c
Beef pie, see "Beef entree, frozen"							
Beef pocket sandwich, and broccoli, frozen							
(Lean Pockets), 1 pkg.	250	11.0	30.0	8.0	m.q.	760	m.q.
Beef roll or stick, see "Beef jerky" and "Sausage sticks"							
Beef stew, see "Beef entree"							
Beef stew seasoning mix:							
(French's), 1/6 pkg.	25	0	5.0	0	0	770	n.a.
(Lawry's), 1 pkg. . . .	131	5.4	25.7	.7	0	3181	1.2 c
(McCormick/Schilling), 1 pkg.	130	5.0	25.0	1.0	n.a.	1251	n.a.
Beefalo, meat only:							
roasted, 4 oz.	213	34.8	0	7.2	66	93	0
Beer, ale, and malt liquor 12 fl. oz.:							
(Anheuser Marzen)	168	2.3	15.2	0	0	12	0
(Beck's)	148	1.7	10.0	0	0	14	0
(Bud Light)	110	1.1	6.9	0	0	12	0
(Budweiser)	144	1.2	11.3	0	0	12	0
(Busch)	144	1.2	11.9	0	0	12	0
(Carlsberg)	149	1.2	11.9	0	0	12	0
(Carlsberg Light) . . .	110	1.1	6.5	0	0	12	0
(Coqui Malt Liquor)	208	1.7	9.8	0	0	13	0
(Dribeck's)	94	1.0	7.0	0	0	14	0
(Elephant Malt Liquor)	208	1.6	16.9	0	0	12	0

Food and Measure	cal.	prot. (gms)	carbo. (gms)	fat (gms)	chol. (mgs)	sod. (mgs)	fiber (gms)
Beer, ale, and malt liquor *(cont.)*							
(King Cobra Malt Liquor)	182	1.4	15.2	0	0	12	0
(Knickerbocker) . . .	140	.9	12.3	0	0	9	0
(LA)	114	.8	16.4	0	0	12	0
(Lite)	96	.8	2.8	0	0	6	0
(Lite Genuine Draft)	98	.8	3.5	0	0	6	0
(Lowenbrau Dark Special)	158	1.4	14.3	0	0	7	0
(Lowenbrau Special)	158	1.4	14.3	0	0	7	0
(McSorley's Ale) . . .	166	1.7	14.7	0	0	6	0
(Michelob)	156	1.5	13.6	0	0	12	0
(Michelob Classic Dark)	158	1.5	14.4	0	0	12	0
(Michelob Dry)	133	1.3	7.8	0	0	12	0
(Michelob Light) . . .	134	1.2	11.9	0	0	12	0
(Miller Genuine Draft)	147	1.0	13.1	0	0	7	0
(Miller High Life) . . .	147	1.0	13.1	0	0	7	0
(Miller Magnum) . . .	162	1.3	10.2	0	0	8	0
(Prior Double Dark)	171	1.4	15.4	0	0	10	0
(Rheingold)	148	1.0	12.9	0	0	9	0
(Rheingold Light) . .	96	.7	2.8	0	0	7	0
(Rolling Rock Light)	104	.4	8.0	0	0	<1	0
(Rolling Rock Premium)	145	.4	10.0	0	0	<1	0
(Schmidt Light) . . .	96	.7	2.8	0	0	7	0
(Schmidt's)	148	1.0	12.9	0	0	9	0
(Schmidt's Classic)	144	1.0	12.8	0	0	10	0
(Sharp's)	86	1.0	9.5	0	0	5	0
(Tiger Head Ale) . . .	166	1.7	14.7	0	0	6	0
Beer batter mix:							
(Golden Dipt), 1 oz.	100	2.0	22.0	0	0	650	n.a.
Beerwurst, see "Salami, beer"							
Beet:							
fresh, raw:							
trimmed, sliced, ½ cup	30	1.0	6.8	.1	0	49	.7 d

Food and Measure	cal.	prot. (gms)	carbo. (gms)	fat (gms)	chol. (mgs)	sod. (mgs)	fiber (gms)
2 medium, 2″ diam., approx. 8.6 oz.	71	2.4	16.3	.2	0	118	1.6 d
fresh, boiled, drained:							
sliced, 1/2 cup . . .	26	.9	5.7	<.1	0	42	.7 c
2 medium, 2″ diam., approx. 3.5 oz.	31	1.1	6.7	.1	0	49	.9 c
canned, 1/2 cup:							
w/liquid	36	1.0	8.3	.1	0	324	1.4 d
drained, sliced . .	27	.8	6.1	.1	0	m.q.	1.4 d
(Stokely No Salt or Sugar Added) . .	40	1.0	8.0	0	0	40	m.q.
whole, small (S&W)	40	1.0	9.0	0	0	270	m.q.
whole, tiny or sliced (Del Monte) . . .	35	1.0	8.0	0	0	290	m.q.
whole, sliced or cut (Stokely)	40	1.0	8.0	0	0	300	m.q.
sliced (Del Monte No Salt)	35	1.0	8.0	0	0	100	m.q.
sliced, small, tender (S&W Premium)	40	1.0	9.0	0	0	270	m.q.
diced or julienne (S&W)	40	1.0	9.0	0	0	270	m.q.
diced (Stokely) . .	35	1.0	7.0	0	0	300	m.q.
Harvard (Stokely)	70	1.0	18.0	0	0	135	m.q.
pickled (Stokely)	100	1.0	25.0	0	0	400	m.q.
pickled (Stokely, Jars)	90	1.0	22.0	0	0	280	m.q.
pickled, whole, extra small (S&W) . .	70	1.0	16.0	0	0	215	m.q.
pickled, crinkle sliced (Del Monte)	80	1.0	19.0	0	0	375	m.q.
pickled, w/red wine vinegar (S&W Regular or Party)	70	1.0	16.0	0	0	215	m.q.
Beet greens, 1/2 cup:							
raw, 1″ pieces	4	.4	.8	<.1	0	38	.3 c
boiled, drained, 1″ pieces	20	1.9	3.9	.1	0	173	.8 c

Food and Measure	cal.	prot. (gms)	carbo. (gms)	fat (gms)	chol. (mgs)	sod. (mgs)	fiber (gms)
Berliner:							
pork and beef, 1 oz.	65	4.3	.7	4.9	13	368	0
Berry drink:							
(Hawaiian Punch Very Berry), 6 fl. oz. . . .	90	0	22.0	0	0	30	(0)
wild *(Hi-C)*, 8.45 fl.-oz. pkg.	129	.1	31.7	.1	0	24	(0)
wild *(Hi-C)*, 6 fl. oz.	92	.1	22.5	.1	0	17	(0)
Berry juice:							
(Libby's Juicy Juice), 6 fl. oz.	90	0	22.0	0	0	10	m.q.
Biscuit, 1 piece, except as noted:							
(Wonder)	80	2.0	14.0	1.0	n.a.	140	.6 d
country *(Awrey's 3")*, 2 oz.	160	4.0	23.0	5.0	0	530	1.0 d
round or square *(Awrey's 2")*, 1 oz.	80	2.0	12.0	3.0	0	260	0
sliced or unsliced *(Awrey's)*, 2 oz. . .	160	4.0	23.0	5.0	0	520	1.0 d
square *(Awrey's 3")*, 2 oz.	160	4.0	23.0	5.0	0	520	1.0 d
frozen *(Bridgford)*, 2 oz.	180	4.0	28.0	6.0	1	632	m.q.
mix[1] *(Martha White BixMix)*	100	2.0	15.0	3.0	1	240	m.q.
refrigerated:							
(Ballard Ovenready)	50	1.0	10.0	1.0	0	180	m.q.
(Big Country Butter Tastin')	100	2.0	14.0	4.0	0	320	m.q.
(1869 Brand Butter Tastin)	100	2.0	12.0	5.0	0	300	m.q.
(Pillsbury Big Premium Heat 'n Eat), 2 pieces . .	280	5.0	32.0	15.0	0	610	m.q.
(Pillsbury Country)	50	1.0	10.0	1.0	0	180	m.q.

[1] *Prepared according to package directions.*

Food and Measure	cal.	prot. (gms)	carbo. (gms)	fat (gms)	chol. (mgs)	sod. (mgs)	fiber (gms)
(Roman Meal), 1.2 oz.	89	2.0	16.5	1.6	n.a.	255	m.q.
baking powder *(1869 Brand)* . .	100	2.0	12.0	5.0	0	300	m.q.
butter *(Pillsbury)* . .	50	1.0	10.0	1.0	0	180	m.q.
buttermilk:							
(Ballard Ovenready) . .	50	1.0	10.0	1.0	n.a.	180	m.q.
(Big Country) . .	100	2.0	14.0	4.0	0	320	m.q c
(1869 Brand) . .	100	2.0	12.0	5.0	0	300	m.q c
(Hungry Jack Extra Rich) . . .	50	1.0	9.0	1.0	0	170	m.q.
(Pillsbury)	50	1.0	10.0	1.0	0	180	m.q.
(Pillsbury Heat 'n Eat), 2 pieces	170	4.0	27.0	5.0	0	530	m.q.
(Pillsbury Tender Layer)	60	1.0	9.0	2.0	0	170	m.q.
flaky *(Hungry Jack)*	80	2.0	12.0	4.0	0	300	m.q.
fluffy *(Hungry Jack)*	90	2.0	12.0	4.0	5	280	m.q.
flaky:							
(Hungry Jack) . .	80	2.0	12.0	4.0	0	300	m.q.
(Hungry Jack Butter Tastin')* . .	90	2.0	11.0	4.0	5	280	m.q.
honey *(Hungry Jack)*	90	2.0	13.0	4.0	0	290	m.q.
fluffy *(Pillsbury* Good 'N Buttery) . . .	90	1.0	11.0	5.0	0	270	m.q.
Southern style *(Big Country)*	100	2.0	14.0	4.0	0	320	m.q.
Black beans:							
boiled, 1/2 cup	113	7.6	20.4	.5	0	1	3.6 d
turtle soup:							
raw, 1/2 cup	312	19.6	58.2	.8	0	8	4.9 c
boiled, 1/2 cup . . .	120	7.5	22.4	.3	0	3	1.9 c
canned *(Progresso)*, 8 oz.	205	14.0	37.0	1.0	0	m.q.	m.q.

Food and Measure	cal.	prot. (gms)	carbo. (gms)	fat (gms)	chol. (mgs)	sod. (mgs)	fiber (gms)
Blackberry, 1/2 cup:							
fresh, trimmed	37	.5	9.2	.3	0	tr.	3.3 d
canned:							
in water *(Allens)*	25	1.0	4.0	<1.0	0	15	m.q.
in heavy syrup . .	118	1.7	29.6	.2	0	3	3.3 c
frozen, unsweetened	49	.9	11.8	.3	0	1	2.0 c
Blackeye pea, see "Cowpea"							
Blood sausage:							
1 oz.	107	4.1	.4	9.8	34	m.q.	0
Bloody Mary mix:							
bottled *(Holland House* Smooth N' Spicy), 1 fl. oz. . .	3	0	<1.0	0	0	329	(0)
Blue cheese dip, see "Cheese dip"							
Blueberry, 1/2 cup, except as noted:							
fresh	41	.5	10.2	.3	0	5	1.7 d
canned:							
in water *(Musselman's),* 4 oz.	40	0	9.0	0	0	0	m.q.
in heavy syrup . .	112	.8	28.2	.4	0	4	1.2 c
in heavy syrup *(S&W)*	111	0	30.0	0	0	<10	m.q.
frozen:							
unsweetened . . .	39	.3	9.4	.5	0	1	2.5 d
sweetened	94	.5	25.2	.2	0	2	1.0 c
Blueberry cobbler, see "Cobbler"							
Blueberry-cranberry drink:							
(Ocean Spray Cran-Blueberry), 6 fl. oz.	120	0	30.0	0	0	10	(0)
Blueberry fruit square:							
frozen *(Pepperidge Farm),* 1 piece . .	220	2.0	28.0	11.0	n.a.	190	m.q.

Food and Measure	cal.	prot. (gms)	carbo. (gms)	fat (gms)	chol. (mgs)	sod. (mgs)	fiber (gms)
Blueberry pie, see "Pie"							
Bluefish, meat only:							
raw, 1 lb.	562	90.9	0	19.2	266	272	0
raw, 1 oz.	35	5.7	0	1.2	17	17	0
Boar, wild, meat only:							
roasted, 4 oz.	181	32.1	0	5.0	m.q.	m.q.	0
Bockwurst, raw:							
1 oz.	87	3.8	.1	7.8	m.q.	m.q.	0
Bok-choy, see "Cabbage, Chinese"							
Bologna, 1 oz., except as noted:							
(*Boar's Head*)	80	4.0	<1.0	7.0	15	250	0
(*Boar's Head* Lower Salt)	80	4.0	<1.0	m.q.	20	210	0
(*Eckrich/Eckrich Smorgas Pac*/Sandwich)	100	3.0	1.0	9.0	m.q.	240	0
(*Eckrich German Brand*)	80	4.0	1.0	7.0	m.q.	300	0
(*Eckrich Lean Supreme*)	70	4.0	1.0	6.0	m.q.	240	0
(*Eckrich Thick Sliced, 12 oz.*), 1.7-oz. slice	160	5.0	2.0	15.0	m.q.	420	0
(*Eckrich Thick Sliced, 1 lb.*), 1.8-oz. slice	170	5.0	2.0	15.0	m.q.	430	0
(*Hillshire Farm* Large)	90	3.0	<1.0	8.0	m.q.	m.q.	0
(*Hillshire Farm* Ring)	89	3.0	<1.0	8.0	m.q.	m.q.	0
(*Hormel* Coarse Ground, 1 lb.), 2 oz.	160	8.0	1.0	14.0	m.q.	578	0
(*Hormel* Fine Ground, 1 lb.), 2 oz.	170	7.0	1.0	16.0	m.q.	596	0
(*Hormel* Perma-Fresh), 2 slices	180	7.0	0	16.0	m.q.	599	0
(*JM*)	90	3.0	1.0	8.0	m.q.	350	0
(*JM* German Brand)	70	4.0	1.0	6.0	m.q.	270	0

Food and Measure	cal.	prot. (gms)	carbo. (gms)	fat (gms)	chol. (mgs)	sod. (mgs)	fiber (gms)
Bologna, 1 oz., except as noted *(cont.)*							
(Kahn's Deluxe Club/ Giant Deluxe), 1 slice	90	3.0	1.0	8.0	m.q.	290	0
(Kahn's Deluxe Club Family Pack), 1 slice	70	2.0	1.0	6.0	m.q.	220	0
(Kahn's Giant Thick Deluxe), 1 slice . .	110	4.0	1.0	10.0	m.q.	330	0
(Kahn's Thick Deluxe), 1 slice	140	5.0	1.0	13.0	m.q.	450	0
(Kahn's Thin Sliced Deluxe), 1 slice . .	60	2.0	1.0	5.0	m.q.	190	0
(Light & Lean), 2 slices	140	6.0	2.0	12.0	m.q.	m.q.	0
(Light & Lean Thin Sliced), 2 slices . .	70	3.0	1.0	6.0	m.q.	m.q.	0
(OHSE)	75	3.0	3.0	6.0	m.q.	280	0
(OHSE 15% Chicken)	90	3.0	1.0	8.0	m.q.	320	0
(Oscar Mayer), .53-oz. slice	48	1.7	.3	4.5	10	162	0
(Oscar Mayer)	90	3.1	.6	8.3	19	303	0
(Oscar Mayer), 1.6-oz. slice	144	5.0	.9	13.4	31	487	0
w/cheese *(Eckrich)*	90	3.0	1.0	9.0	m.q.	250	0
w/cheese *(Oscar Mayer),* .8-oz. slice	74	2.7	.6	6.7	16	235	0
beef:							
(Boar's Head) . . .	74	4.0	<1.0	7.0	17	270	0
(Eckrich)	90	3.0	1.0	8.0	m.q.	230	0
(Eckrich Thick Sliced), 1.5-oz. slice	130	4.0	2.0	12.0	m.q.	340	0
(Hebrew National Original Deli Style)	90	3.0	<1.0	3.0	15	330	0
(Hormel Coarse Ground, 1 lb.), 2 oz.	160	8.0	1.0	14.0	m.q.	576	0

Food and Measure	cal.	prot. (gms)	carbo. (gms)	fat (gms)	chol. (mgs)	sod. (mgs)	fiber (gms)
(Hormel Perma-Fresh), 2 slices	170	6.0	1.0	16.0	m.q.	592	0
(JM)	90	3.0	1.0	8.0	m.q.	350	0
(Kahn's/Kahn's Giant), 1 slice . . .	90	3.0	1.0	8.0	m.q.	300	0
(Kahn's Family Pack), 1 slice . .	70	2.0	1.0	6.0	m.q.	230	0
(OHSE)	85	3.0	1.0	8.0	m.q.	310	0
(Oscar Mayer), .53-oz. slice . . .	48	1.6	.3	4.5	10	167	0
(Oscar Mayer) . . .	90	3.0	.6	8.4	18	311	0
(Oscar Mayer), 1.6-oz. slice . . .	145	4.9	1.0	13.5	29	500	0
garlic flavor (Oscar Mayer)	89	3.1	.6	8.3	19	298	0
Lebanon (Oscar Mayer), .8-oz. slice	49	4.7	.4	3.2	16	298	0
beef and cheddar (Kahn's), 1 slice . .	90	4.0	1.0	8.0	m.q.	320	0
beef and pork (Healthy Deli) . . .	41	4.4	1.1	2.0	9	200	0
garlic:							
(Eckrich)	90	3.0	1.0	9.0	m.q.	230	0
(JM)	90	3.0	1.0	8.0	m.q.	350	0
(Kahn's), 1 slice . .	90	3.0	1.0	8.0	m.q.	290	0
turkey, see "Turkey bologna"							
"Bologna," vegetarian, frozen:							
(Worthington Bolono), 2 slices, 1.3 oz. . .	60	7.0	2.0	2.0	0	390	m.q.
Bolognese sauce: refrigerated (Contadina Fresh), 7.5 oz.	230	22.0	12.0	11.0	50	600	m.q.
Bonito, meat only: raw, 1 lb.	585	117.0	1.8	9.1	m.q.	200	0

Food and Measure	cal.	prot. (gms)	carbo. (gms)	fat (gms)	chol. (mgs)	sod. (mgs)	fiber (gms)
Bonito *(cont.)*							
raw, 1 oz.	37	7.3	.1	.6	m.q.	12	0
Borage:							
raw, 1″ pieces, 1/2 cup	9	.8	1.4	.3	0	35	.4 c
boiled, drained, 4 oz.	28	2.4	4.0	.9	0	98	1.2 c
Bouillon (see also "Soup"):							
beef, 1 cube:							
(Steero)	6	<1.0	1.0	<1.0	n.a.	930	(0)
(Wyler's)	6	<1.0	1.0	<1.0	n.a.	930	(0)
beef, instant, 1 tsp.:							
(Steero)	6	<1.0	1.0	<1.0	n.a.	930	(0)
(Wyler's)	6	<1.0	1.0	<1.0	n.a.	930	(0)
chicken, 1 cube:							
(Steero)	8	<1.0	1.0	<1.0	n.a.	990	(0)
(Wyler's)	8	<1.0	1.0	<1.0	n.a.	900	(0)
chicken, instant, 1 tsp.:							
(Steero)	8	<1.0	1.0	<1.0	n.a.	990	(0)
(Wyler's)	8	<1.0	1.0	<1.0	n.a.	900	(0)
onion, instant *(Wyler's)*, 1 tsp. . .	10	<1.0	1.0	<1.0	0	670	(0)
vegetable, instant *(Wyler's)*, 1 tsp. . .	6	<1.0	1.0	<1.0	0	910	(0)
Boysenberry:							
fresh, see "Black-berry"							
canned, in heavy syrup, 1/2 cup . . .	113	1.3	28.6	.2	0	4	2.4 c
frozen, unsweetened, 10-oz. pkg.	141	3.1	34.6	.8	0	4	7.7 c
Boysenberry juice:							
(Smucker's Naturally 100%), 8 fl. oz. . .	120	0	30.0	0	0	10	m.q.
Brains, 4 oz.:							
beef, fried	222	14.3	0	18.0	2262	179	0
lamb, fried	310	19.2	0	25.2	2840	178	0
pork, braised	156	13.8	0	10.8	2894	103	0

Food and Measure	cal.	prot. (gms)	carbo. (gms)	fat (gms)	chol. (mgs)	sod. (mgs)	fiber (gms)
veal, fried	242	16.4	0	19.0	2404	200	0
Bran (see also "Cereal" and specific listings):							
unprocessed (Quaker), 2 tbsp., 1/4 oz. . .	8	1.0	3.8	.2	0	0	3.3 d
Bratwurst:							
(Eckrich), 1 link . . .	310	11.0	1.0	30.0	m.q.	820	0
(Hickory Farms Brotwurst), 1 oz.	90	4.0	1.0	8.0	8	277	0
(Hillshire Farm Fully Cooked), 2 oz. . .	170	7.0	1.0	16.0	m.q.	380	0
(Kahn's), 1 link . . .	190	7.0	2.0	17.0	m.q.	490	0
cheddar (Hickory Farms Cheddy Brots), 1 oz.	98	4.0	1.0	9.0	7	259	0
fresh (Hillshire Farm), 2 oz.	190	7.0	1.0	17.0	m.q.	410	0
hot (Hickory Farms Hot Brots), 1 oz.	96	4.0	1.0	9.0	8	269	0
pork, cooked, 1 oz.	85	4.0	.6	7.3	17	158	0
smoked:							
(Hillshire Farm), 2 oz.	190	8.0	1.0	17.0	m.q.	540	0
(Oscar Mayer International Sausages), 2.7-oz. link	237	10.0	1.1	21.4	40	773	0
spicy (Hillshire Farm), 2 oz.	180	8.0	1.0	17.0	m.q.	m.q.	0
Braunschweiger, 1 oz., except as noted:							
(Hormel)	80	4.0	0	7.0	m.q.	322	0
(JM)	80	3.0	2.0	6.0	m.q.	260	0
(Oscar Mayer German Brand)	94	3.9	.5	8.5	46	345	0
(Oscar Mayer Slices)	96	3.9	.6	8.7	50	327	0

Food and Measure	cal.	prot. (gms)	carbo. (gms)	fat (gms)	chol. (mgs)	sod. (mgs)	fiber (gms)
Braunschweiger *(cont.)*							
(Oscar Mayer Slices),							
.9-oz. slice	89	3.6	.5	8.0	47	303	0
(Oscar Mayer Tube)	96	3.8	.9	8.6	43	321	0
Brazil nuts, shelled:							
1 oz., 6 large or 8 me-							
dium kernels . . .	186	4.1	3.6	18.8	0	tr.	.7 c
Bread, 1 slice, except							
as noted:							
apple walnut *(Arnold)*	64	2.1	12.6	1.3	1	103	1.3 d
(Arnold/Brownberry							
Bran'nola)	85	3.9	17.5	1.4	tr.	137	2.9 d
barbecue *(Colombo*							
Brand BBQ), 2 oz.	139	7.9	23.5	1.6	n.a.	318	m.q.
bran:							
honey *(Roman*							
Light)	40	2.3	9.9	.2	0	108	2.8 d
and oat *(Oatmeal*							
Goodness Light)	40	2.0	6.0	<1.0	0	90	m.q.
whole *(Brownberry*							
Natural)	58	2.3	11.7	1.4	0	167	2.1 d
cinnamon:							
oatmeal *(Oatmeal*							
Goodness) . . .	90	4.0	15.0	2.0	0	140	1.0 d
raisin *(Arnold)* . . .	67	2.1	12.9	1.4	2	86	.8 d
swirl *(Pepperidge*							
Farm)	90	2.0	15.0	3.0	0	110	2.0 d
corn and molasses							
(Pepperidge Farm)	70	2.0	14.0	1.0	0	135	0
date walnut swirl							
(Pepperidge Farm)	90	2.0	14.0	3.0	0	110	2.0 d
French:							
(DiCarlo Parisian)	70	3.0	13.0	1.0	n.a.	180	.7 d
extra sour, sliced							
(Colombo Brand),							
2 oz.	153	7.6	27.2	1.6	0	310	m.q.

Food and Measure	cal.	prot. (gms)	carbo. (gms)	fat (gms)	chol. (mgs)	sod. (mgs)	fiber (gms)
style (Pepperidge Farm 14 oz.), 2 oz.	150	5.0	28.0	2.0	0	320	.5 d
sweet (Colombo Brand Stick), 2 oz.	154	7.2	27.1	1.9	n.a.	331	m.q.
twin (Pepperidge Farm), 1 oz. . . .	80	3.0	15.0	1.0	0	160	0
garlic (Colombo Brand), 2 oz. . . .	185	6.2	17.3	10.1	n.a.	331	m.q.
grain, nutty (Arnold/ Brownberry Bran'nola)	85	3.9	17.4	1.6	tr.	144	3.0 d
granola, oat and honey (Pepperidge Farm)	60	2.0	12.0	2.0	0	105	2.0 d
(Hollywood Dark) . .	70	3.0	13.0	1.0	n.a.	160	.8 d
(Hollywood Light) . .	70	3.0	13.0	1.0	n.a.	150	.7 d
honey bran (Pepper- idge Farm)	90	3.0	18.0	1.0	0	160	1.0 d
Italian:							
(Arnold Francisco)	72	2.9	14.1	1.1	0	190	.8 d
(Brownberry Light)	44	2.3	9.9	.5	tr.	89	2.0 d
(Pepperidge Farm Sliced)	70	2.0	12.0	1.0	0	125	m.q.
(Wonder Family) . .	70	2.0	13.0	1.0	n.a.	160	.7 d
light (Arnold Bakery)	45	2.4	9.9	.5	tr.	90	2.0 d
thick sliced (Arnold Francisco)	66	2.3	13.7	.8	0	111	.9 d
(Monk's Hi-Fibre) . .	70	3.0	13.0	1.0	0	80	1.4 d
multi grain (Pepper- idge Farm Very Thin)	40	1.0	8.0	1.0	0	90	1.0 d
oat (Arnold/ Brownberry Bran'nola Country)	90	3.7	17.8	2.0	tr.	166	2.8 d
oat, crunchy (Pepper- idge Farm), 2 slices	190	8.0	34.0	4.0	0	290	3.0 d

Food and Measure	cal.	prot. (gms)	carbo. (gms)	fat (gms)	chol. (mgs)	sod. (mgs)	fiber (gms)
Bread (cont.)							
oat bran (Awrey's) . .	50	2.0	10.0	0	0	130	1.0 d
oatmeal:							
(Pepperidge Farm							
1 lb.)	70	2.0	12.0	1.0	0	160	1.0 d
(Pepperidge Farm							
1½ lb.)	90	3.0	17.0	1.0	0	200	1.0 d
(Pepperidge Farm							
Very Thin)	40	1.0	8.0	1.0	0	80	0
and bran (Oatmeal							
Goodness) . . .	90	4.0	15.0	2.0	0	140	1.0 d
light (Arnold Bakery)	44	2.3	9.6	.6	tr.	98	1.9 d
w/raisins (Pepper-							
idge Farm) . . .	70	2.0	14.0	1.0	0	120	1.0 d
sunflower seed							
(Oatmeal Good-							
ness)	90	4.0	15.0	2.0	0	140	1.0 d
orange raisin							
(Brownberry) . . .	67	2.3	13.0	1.2	tr.	83	.8 d
pita:							
oat bran (Sahara),							
½ piece	66	2.4	15.3	.3	0	163	1.8 d
wheat, whole (Sa-							
hara), 1 piece . .	150	6.0	28.0	2.0	0	320	.7 c
white (Sahara),							
½ piece	79	2.9	15.6	.5	0	147	m.q.
pumpernickel:							
(Arnold)	70	2.7	14.7	.9	0	198	1.3 d
dark (Pepperidge							
Farm)	80	3.0	15.0	1.0	0	230	2.0 d
small (Pepperidge							
Farm Party),							
4 slices	60	2.0	12.0	1.0	0	160	1.0 d
raisin bran							
(Brownberry) . . .	61	2.2	12.4	1.3	0	108	1.8 d
raisin cinnamon:							
(Brownberry) . . .	66	2.1	12.8	1.3	tr.	107	.9 d
(Monk's)	70	3.0	10.0	2.0	0	85	m.q.

Food and Measure	cal.	prot. (gms)	carbo. (gms)	fat (gms)	chol. (mgs)	sod. (mgs)	fiber (gms)
swirl *(Pepperidge Farm)*	90	2.0	16.0	2.0	0	100	1.0 d
raisin walnut *(Brownberry)* . . .	68	2.2	11.4	2.7	tr.	96	2.3 d
rice bran *(Monk's)* . .	70	3.0	14.0	1.0	0	80	1.6 d
round top *(Roman Meal)*	67	2.9	13.2	.8	0	140	1.2 d
rye:							
(Beefsteak Hearty or Mild)*	70	3.0	13.0	1.0	0	180	.7 d
(Beefsteak Soft)*	70	3.0	13.0	1.0	0	170	.9 d
(Braun's Old Alle- gheny)	70	3.0	13.0	1.0	0	160	.7 d
(Wonder)	70	2.0	13.0	1.0	n.a.	150	.7 d
caraway *(Brownberry* Natu- ral)	73	2.8	15.4	.8	0	185	1.2 d
Dijon *(Pepperidge Farm)*	50	2.0	9.0	1.0	0	175	1.0 d
Dijon, thick sliced *(Pepperidge Farm)*	70	3.0	15.0	1.0	0	260	2.0 d
dill *(Arnold)*	71	2.8	14.4	1.0	0	187	1.3 d
Jewish, seeded *(Levy's)*	76	2.8	15.9	.9	0	181	1.4 d
Jewish, seedless *(Levy's)*	75	2.8	16.0	.8	0	178	1.3 d
onion *(Beefsteak)*	70	3.0	12.0	1.0	0	170	1.0 d
seeded *(Pepperidge Farm* Family) . .	80	3.0	16.0	1.0	0	220	2.0 d
seedless *(Brownberry* Natu- ral Thin)	45	1.7	9.8	.6	0	118	.8 d
seedless *(Pepper- idge Farm* Family)	80	3.0	16.0	1.0	0	210	2.0 d
small *(Pepperidge Farm* Party), 4 slices	60	2.0	12.0	1.0	0	250	1.0 d

Food and Measure	cal.	prot. (gms)	carbo. (gms)	fat (gms)	chol. (mgs)	sod. (mgs)	fiber (gms)
Bread, rye *(cont.)*							
soft *(Pepperidge Farm)*	70	2.0	12.0	1.0	0	120	m.q.
wheatberry *(Beefsteak)*	70	3.0	13.0	1.0	0	160	1.0 d
sandwich *(Roman Meal)*	55	2.4	10.7	.7	0	114	1.0 d
seven grain:							
(Pepperidge Farm), 2 slices	180	5.0	36.0	2.0	0	340	2.0 d
(Roman Light) . . .	40	2.2	9.9	.4	0	108	2.9 d
sourdough *(DiCarlo)*	70	3.0	12.0	1.0	0	140	.7 d
sourdough, French *(Boudin)*	130	5.0	27.0	1.0	0	297	m.q.
sunflower and bran *(Monk's)*	70	3.0	12.0	1.0	0	80	1.6 d
Vienna, thick sliced *(Pepperidge Farm)*	70	2.0	13.0	1.0	0	125	0
wheat:							
(Arnold Brick Oven)	57	2.4	10.6	1.5	tr.	104	1.7 d
(Beefsteak Hearty)	70	3.0	11.0	1.0	0	160	1.4 d
(Beefsteak Soft)	70	3.0	12.0	1.0	0	160	1.6 d
(Brownberry Hearth)	70	3.1	13.6	1.4	0	150	2.0 d
(Brownberry Natural)	80	3.0	17.0	1.3	0	183	2.3 d
(Country Grain) . .	70	3.0	12.0	1.0	n.a.	160	1.3 d
(Fresh & Natural)	70	3.0	13.0	1.0	0	140	1.8 d
(Home Pride Butter Top)	70	3.0	13.0	1.0	n.a.	140	.8 d
(Home Pride 7 Grain)	70	3.0	12.0	1.0	n.a.	140	.8 d
(Home Pride Stoneground)	70	3.0	12.0	1.0	0	140	1.9 d
(Pepperidge Farm 1.5 lb.)	90	3.0	18.0	2.0	0	190	2.0 d
(Pepperidge Farm Family, 2 lb.) . .	70	2.0	13.0	1.0	0	130	2.0 d

Food and Measure	cal.	prot. (gms)	carbo. (gms)	fat (gms)	chol. (mgs)	sod. (mgs)	fiber (gms)
(Pepperidge Farm Very Thin)	35	2.0	7.0	0	0	75	0
(Roman Light) . . .	40	2.2	9.8	.3	0	108	2.7 d
apple honey *(Brownberry)* . .	69	2.3	11.4	1.9	0	148	1.5 d
cracked *(Pepperidge Farm)* . . .	70	2.0	13.0	1.0	0	140	1.0 d
cracked *(Wonder)*	70	3.0	13.0	1.0	n.a.	180	.8 d
dark *(Arnold Bran'nola)*	83	4.1	17.6	1.0	tr.	166	2.8 d
germ *(Pepperidge Farm)*	60	3.0	12.0	0	0	140	1.0 d
hearty *(Arnold/ Brownberry Bran'nola)*	88	3.8	17.1	1.9	tr.	197	2.7 d
honey wheatberry *(Arnold)*	77	3.1	16.5	1.2	tr.	143	2.4 d
honey wheatberry *(Pepperidge Farm)*	70	2.0	14.0	1.0	0	140	1.0 d
honey wheatberry *(Roman Light)*	39	2.3	10.0	.2	0	108	2.9 d
light golden *(Arnold Bakery)*	44	2.3	9.5	.5	tr.	86	2.0 d
multi grain *(Beef-steak)*	70	3.0	11.0	1.0	0	130	1.6 d
oatmeal *(Oatmeal Goodness)* . . .	90	4.0	15.0	2.0	0	140	1.0 d
oatmeal *(Oatmeal Goodness Light)*	40	2.0	6.0	<1.0	0	90	m.q.
sesame *(Pepperidge Farm)*, 2 slices	190	7.0	36.0	3.0	0	340	3.0 d
soft *(Brownberry)*	74	2.8	13.1	1.8	tr.	127	1.0 d
sprouted *(Pepperidge Farm)* . . .	70	3.0	11.0	2.0	0	100	2.0 d
wheat, whole: *(Arnold* Stone-ground 100%)	48	2.4	9.9	.7	tr.	97	1.6 d

Food and Measure	cal.	prot. (gms)	carbo. (gms)	fat (gms)	chol. (mgs)	sod. (mgs)	fiber (gms)
Bread, wheat, whole *(cont.)*							
(Monk's 100%							
Stone Ground)*	70	3.0	13.0	1.0	0	110	m.q.
(Pepperidge Farm							
Thin Sliced, 8 oz.)*	60	2.0	11.0	1.0	0	100	2.0 d
(Pepperidge Farm							
Thin Sliced,*							
16 oz.)*	60	2.0	12.0	1.0	0	110	2.0 d
(Wonder 100%) . .	70	3.0	12.0	1.0	n.a.	160	1.8 d
(Wonder Soft 100%)	70	4.0	10.0	1.0	0	140	1.8 d
(Wonder High Fiber)	40	2.0	6.0	0	0	80	2.9 d
(Wonder Light) . .	40	3.0	7.0	0	0	120	2.0 d
(Wonder Family) . .	70	3.0	13.0	1.0	n.a.	140	.8 d
white:							
(Arnold Brick Oven)	61	2.2	11.3	1.2	tr.	134	.8 d
(Arnold Country							
White)*	98	3.4	18.6	1.8	tr.	204	1.0 d
(Arnold/Brownberry							
Light Premium)*	42	2.3	9.6	.5	tr.	89	2.2 d
(Beefsteak Robust)	70	3.0	13.0	1.0	n.a.	140	.7 d
(Brownberry Natu-							
ral)*	59	2.2	11.1	1.1	tr.	136	.6 d
(Home Pride Butter							
Top)*	70	3.0	13.0	1.0	n.a.	140	.7 d
(Monk's)	60	3.0	10.0	1.0	0	95	m.q.
(Pepperidge Farm							
Country), 2 slices*	190	7.0	38.0	2.0	0	340	2.0 d
(Pepperidge Farm							
Large Family*							
2 lb.)*	70	2.0	13.0	1.0	0	150	0
(Pepperidge Farm							
Thin Sliced 8 oz.)*	70	2.0	13.0	1.0	0	120	0
(Pepperidge Farm							
Thin Sliced*							
16 oz.)*	80	2.0	14.0	2.0	0	130	0
(Pepperidge Farm							
Very Thin)*	40	1.0	8.0	0	0	80	0
(Roman Light) . . .	40	2.1	10.2	.2	0	109	2.7 d

Food and Measure	cal.	prot. (gms)	carbo. (gms)	fat (gms)	chol. (mgs)	sod. (mgs)	fiber (gms)
(Wonder)	70	3.0	13.0	1.0	n.a.	140	.7 d
(Wonder High Fiber)	40	2.0	6.0	0	0	80	2.9 d
(Wonder Light) . .	40	3.0	7.0	0	0	110	2.0 d
(Wonder Thin) . . .	50	2.0	10.0	1.0	0	120	.5 d
w/buttermilk *(Wonder)*	70	2.0	13.0	1.0	n.a.	160	.7 d
extra fiber *(Arnold Brick Oven)* . . .	55	2.2	12.1	.8	tr.	93	2.1 d
sandwich *(Pepperidge Farm)*, 2 slices	130	4.0	24.0	2.0	0	260	0
toasting *(Pepperidge Farm)* . . .	90	3.0	17.0	1.0	0	200	1.0 d
(Wonder)	70	3.0	13.0	1.0	0	180	.7 d
Bread, brown and serve:							
(du Jour Austrian/ French), 1 slice . .	70	3.0	13.0	1.0	0	140	.6 d
Italian *(Pepperidge Farm)*, 1 oz.	80	2.0	14.0	1.0	0	150	0
Bread, brown, canned:							
(S&W New England), 2 slices	76	2.0	17.0	0	0	172	m.q.
plain or w/raisins *(B&M)*, 1/2″ slice	80	2.0	18.0	m.q.	n.a.	220	m.q.
Bread, refrigerated, see "Bread dough"							
Bread, sweet, mix[1], 1/12 loaf, except as noted:							
banana *(Pillsbury)* . .	170	3.0	27.0	6.0	m.q.	200	m.q.
blueberry nut *(Pillsbury)*	150	2.0	26.0	4.0	m.q.	150	m.q.
cherry nut *(Pillsbury)*	180	3.0	29.0	5.0	m.q.	150	m.q.

[1] *Prepared according to package directions, except as noted.*

Food and Measure	cal.	prot. (gms)	carbo. (gms)	fat (gms)	chol. (mgs)	sod. (mgs)	fiber (gms)
Bread, sweet, mix *(cont.)*							
cornbread:							
(Aunt Jemima							
Easy), 1 serving	196	3.5	32.7	6.3	13	679	1.4 d
(Dromedary), 3 tbsp.							
dry	100	2.0	19.0	2.0	n.a.	280	m.q.
(Dromedary), 2″ sq.	130	3.0	20.0	3.0	n.a.	480	m.q.
(Martha White Cotton Pickin'),							
1/4 pan	170	3.0	31.0	3.0	2	540	m.q.
(Pillsbury/Ballard),							
1/8 recipe	140	3.0	25.0	3.0	m.q.	570	m.q.
yellow *(Martha White* Light							
Crust), 2 oz. . .	140	4.0	21.0	4.0	26	400	m.q.
cranberry *(Pillsbury)*	160	2.0	30.0	4.0	m.q.	160	m.q.
date *(Pillsbury)* . . .	160	2.0	32.0	3.0	m.q.	150	m.q.
date nut *(Dromedary)*	183	2.0	26.0	8.0	n.a.	248	m.q.
gingerbread *(Pillsbury),*							
3″ sq.	190	2.0	36.0	4.0	n.a.	310	m.q.
nut *(Pillsbury)*	170	3.0	28.0	6.0	m.q.	190	m.q.
Bread crumbs, 1 oz.:							
plain *(Devonsheer)*	108	3.9	21.6	1.4	0	272	.9 d
Italian style *(Devonsheer)*	104	3.6	21.1	1.3	0	408	.9 d
Bread dough:							
frozen:							
honey walnut							
(Bridgford), 1 oz.	76	3.0	13.8	.9	0	152	m.q.
white:							
(Bridgford), 1 oz.	76	2.5	13.8	1.2	0	156	m.q.
(Rich's), 2 slices	120	4.0	23.0	1.0	0	300	m.q.
refrigerated, 1″ slice, except as noted:							
(Roman Meal), 1 oz.	85	2.3	12.7	2.8	0	199	m.q.
cornbread twists							
(Pillsbury), 1 twist	70	2.0	8.0	4.0	5	140	m.q.

Food and Measure	cal.	prot. (gms)	carbo. (gms)	fat (gms)	chol. (mgs)	sod. (mgs)	fiber (gms)
French, crusty (Pills-bury)	60	2.0	11.0	<1.0	0	120	m.q.
wheat (Pipin' Hot)	80	3.0	12.0	2.0	0	170	m.q.
white (Pipin' Hot)	80	3.0	13.0	2.0	0	170	m.q.
Breadfruit:							
1/2 cup	114	1.2	29.8	.3	0	2	1.6 c
1/4 small, 3.4 oz. . . .	99	1.0	26.0	.2	0	2	1.4 c
Breadfruit seeds, 1 oz.:							
raw[1], shelled	54	2.1	8.3	1.6	0	n.a.	.5 c
boiled[2], shelled . . .	48	1.5	9.1	.7	0	n.a.	.5 c
roasted[1], shelled . .	59	1.8	11.4	.8	0	n.a.	.6 c
Breadsticks, 1 piece:							
plain (Stella D'Oro)	41	1.0	6.5	1.2	n.a.	m.q.	m.q.
onion (Stella D'Oro)	40	1.2	6.1	1.3	n.a.	m.q.	m.q.
pizza (Stella D'Oro)	43	1.3	6.9	1.2	n.a.	m.q.	m.q.
sesame (Stella D'Oro)	51	1.4	6.3	2.2	n.a.	m.q.	m.q.
wheat (Stella D'Oro)	42	1.3	6.1	1.4	n.a.	m.q.	m.q.
refrigerated:							
soft (Pillsbury) . . .	100	3.0	17.0	2.0	0	230	m.q.
soft (Roman Meal)	117	3.1	17.4	3.9	0	274	.8 d
Breakfast, frozen, see specific list-ings							
Breakfast strips, see "Bacon, substi-tute"							
Broad bean:							
raw, 1/2 cup	40	3.1	6.4	.4	0	28	1.2 c
boiled, drained, 4 oz.	64	5.4	11.5	.6	0	47	2.2 c
Broad bean, mature, dry, 1/2 cup:							
boiled	93	6.5	16.7	.3	0	4	4.3 d
canned, w/liquid . . .	91	7.0	15.9	.3	0	580	.5 c

[1] South American cultivar.

[2] Pacific area cultivar.

Food and Measure	cal.	prot. (gms)	carbo. (gms)	fat (gms)	chol. (mgs)	sod. (mgs)	fiber (gms)
Broccoli:							
fresh:							
raw, chopped,							
1/2 cup	12	1.3	2.3	.2	0	12	1.2 d
raw, 1 spear, 8.7 oz.	42	4.5	7.9	.5	0	40	4.2 d
boiled, drained:							
chopped, 1/2 cup	22	2.3	3.9	.2	0	20	2.0 d
1 spear, 6.3 oz. . .	51	5.4	9.1	.6	0	46	4.7 d
frozen, 3.3 oz., except as noted:							
spears, 10-oz. pkg.	84	8.7	15.2	1.0	0	49	6.0 d
spears (Birds Eye)	25	3.0	5.0	0	0	20	3.0 d
spears (Green Giant Harvest Fresh), 1/2 cup	20	2.0	4.0	0	0	190	2.4 d
spears (Seabrook)	25	3.0	5.0	0	0	20	1.0 c
spears, baby (Birds Eye Deluxe) . . .	30	3.0	5.0	0	0	15	3.0 d
spears, baby (Seabrook)	30	3.0	5.0	0	0	14	1.0 c
spears, whole (Birds Eye Farm Fresh), 4 oz.	30	4.0	6.0	0	0	25	3.0 d
florets (Birds Eye Deluxe)	25	3.0	5.0	0	0	20	3.0 d
florets (Frosty Acres)	30	3.0	5.0	0	0	14	1.0 c
cuts (Birds Eye) . .	25	3.0	5.0	0	0	25	3.0 d
cuts (Birds Eye Portion Pack), 3 oz.	20	3.0	4.0	0	0	20	2.0 d
cuts (Green Giant Polybag), 1/2 cup	12	1.0	3.0	0	0	15	2.0 d
cuts (Green Giant Harvest Fresh), 1/2 cup	16	2.0	3.0	0	0	150	2.0 d
cuts (Seabrook) . .	25	3.0	5.0	0	0	50	1.0 c
cuts (Stokely Singles), 3 oz. . . .	25	3.0	5.0	1.0	0	15	m.q.

Food and Measure	cal.	prot. (gms)	carbo. (gms)	fat (gms)	chol. (mgs)	sod. (mgs)	fiber (gms)
chopped, 10-oz. pkg.	75	8.0	13.6	.8	0	68	4.8 d
chopped (Birds Eye)	25	3.0	5.0	0	0	15	3.0 d
chopped (Seabrook)	25	3.0	5.0	0	0	18	1.0 c
frozen, in butter sauce:							
(Green Giant One Serving), 4.5 oz.	45	3.0	7.0	2.0	5	420	2.7 d
spears (Birds Eye Combinations), 3.3 oz. . .	45	2.0	5.0	2.0	5	320	2.0 d
spears (Green Giant), 1/2 cup . . .	40	2.0	6.0	2.0	5	350	2.0 d
frozen, in cheese sauce:							
(Birds Eye Combinations), 5 oz. . . .	130	6.0	12.0	7.0	10	560	2.0 d
(Freezer Queen Family Side Dish), 4.5 oz.	48	2.0	8.0	1.0	n.a.	280	m.q.
cuts (Green Giant One Serving), 5 oz.	70	4.0	11.0	3.0	2	660	2.8 d
(Stokely Singles), 4 oz.	80	5.0	7.0	4.0	15	200	m.q.
flavored (Green Giant), 1/2 cup . . .	60	3.0	9.0	2.0	2	530	2.2 d
Broccoli combinations, frozen:							
and carrots:							
baby, and water chestnuts (Birds Eye Farm Fresh), 4 oz.	45	2.0	10.0	0	0	35	3.0 d
baby, and chestnuts (Stokely Singles), 3 oz.	30	2.0	6.0	1.0	0	22	m.q.
fanfare (Green Giant Valley Combinations), 1/2 cup	20	1.0	6.0	0	0	30	2.1 d

Food and Measure	cal.	prot. (gms)	carbo. (gms)	fat (gms)	chol. (mgs)	sod. (mgs)	fiber (gms)
Broccoli combinations (cont.)							
and cauliflower:							
(Frosty Acres Swiss Mix), 3 oz. . . .	25	2.0	5.0	0	0	36	1.0 c
(Stokely Singles), 3 oz.	20	2.0	4.0	1.0	0	15	m.q.
medley (Green Giant Valley Combinations), 1/2 cup	30	2.0	10.0	1.0	0	80	3.0 d
supreme (Green Giant Valley Combinations), 1/2 cup	20	1.0	5.0	0	0	30	2.1 d
cauliflower and carrots:							
(Birds Eye Farm Fresh), 4 oz. . .	35	2.0	7.0	0	0	40	3.0 d
w/out sauce (Green Giant One Serving), 4 oz.	25	2.0	7.0	0	0	45	3.0 d
baby (Stokely Singles), 3 oz. . . .	25	2.0	5.0	1.0	0	25	m.q.
in butter sauce (Birds Eye Combinations), 3.3 oz.	45	2.0	6.0	2.0	5	290	2.0 d
in butter sauce (Green Giant), 1/2 cup	30	1.0	6.0	1.0	5	240	2.6 d
in cheese sauce (Birds Eye Combinations), 4.5 oz.	110	5.0	11.0	5.0	5	410	2.0 d
in cheese sauce (Birds Eye For One), 5 oz. . . .	110	6.0	11.0	5.0	5	410	2.0 d
in cheese sauce (Green Giant One Serving), 5 oz.	70	3.0	12.0	3.0	5	610	2.8 d
in cheese flavored sauce (Green Giant), 1/2 cup . . .	60	3.0	9.0	2.0	2	490	2.3 d

Food and Measure	cal.	prot. (gms)	carbo. (gms)	fat (gms)	chol. (mgs)	sod. (mgs)	fiber (gms)
in cheese sauce, baby *(Stokely Singles)*, 4 oz. . . .	70	4.0	8.0	3.0	15	180	m.q.
cauliflower and red peppers *(Birds Eye Farm Fresh)*, 4 oz.	30	3.0	5.0	0	0	25	3.0 d
corn and red peppers *(Birds Eye Farm Fresh)*, 4 oz.	60	3.0	14.0	1.0	0	15	3.0 d
fanfare *(Green Giant Valley Combinations)*, 1/2 cup . . .	70	3.0	13.0	2.0	n.a.	330	2.9 d
green beans, pearl onions and red pepper *(Birds Eye Farm Fresh)*, 4 oz.	35	2.0	7.0	0	0	15	3.0 d
red peppers, bamboo shoots and straw mushrooms *(Birds Eye Farm Fresh)*, 4 oz.	30	3.0	5.0	0	0	20	3.0 d
rotini, in cheese sauce *(Green Giant One Serving)*, 5.5 oz.	120	4.0	20.0	3.0	2	550	m.q.
Broth, see "Soup"							
Brown gravy:							
canned or in jars:							
(Heinz), 2 oz.	20	1.0	1.0	2.0	n.a.	130	n.a.
(McCormick/Schilling), 1/3 cup . .	30	.7	4.7	1.0	n.a.	417	n.a.
w/onions *(Franco-American)*, 2 oz.	25	0	4.0	1.0	n.a.	340	n.a.
mix[1]:							
(Lawry's), 1 cup . .	94	3.8	16.5	1.4	n.a.	1500	.1 c
(McCormick/Schilling), 1/4 cup . .	23	.5	3.5	.8	n.a.	313	n.a.

[1] *Prepared according to package directions.*

63

Food and Measure	cal.	prot. (gms)	carbo. (gms)	fat (gms)	chol. (mgs)	sod. (mgs)	fiber (gms)
Brown gravy, mix *(cont.)*							
(McCormick/Schilling Lite), 1/4 cup	10	<1.0	2.0	1.0	n.a.	450	n.a.
(Pillsbury), 1/4 cup	15	<1.0	3.0	0	0	300	n.a.
Brownie (see also "Cookie"), 1 piece, except as noted:							
Dutch chocolate *(Awrey's* Cake), 1/16 cake	340	3.0	40.0	20.0	35	260	1.0 d
fudge:							
(Little Debbie), 2 oz.	240	3.0	39.0	8.0	<1	140	m.q.
(Little Debbie), 3 oz.	350	4.0	57.0	12.0	<1	180	m.q.
nut *(Awrey's* Sheet Cake), 1.25 oz.	150	2.0	16.0	9.0	25	115	1.0 d
nut, iced *(Awrey's* Sheet Cake), 2.5 oz.	300	3.0	36.0	17.0	40	210	1.0 d
walnut *(Tastykake),* 3 oz.	373	4.3	67.6	9.5	n.a.	229	m.q.
frozen:							
chocolate *(Weight Watchers),* 1.25 oz.	100	3.0	16.0	3.0	5	150	m.q.
chocolate chip, double *(Nestlé* Toll House Ready To Bake), 1.4 oz.	150	2.0	19.0	7.0	n.a.	60	m.q.
hot fudge:							
(Pepperidge Farm Newport) . . .	400	4.0	50.0	20.0	80	160	m.q.
chocolate chunk *(Pepperidge Farm* Monterey)	480	5.0	56.0	26.0	65	200	m.q.
refrigerated, fudge, w/ chocolate-flavored chips *(Pillsbury* Ready to Microwave)	180	2.0	25.0	9.0	0	110	m.q.

Food and Measure	cal.	prot. (gms)	carbo. (gms)	fat (gms)	chol. (mgs)	sod. (mgs)	fiber (gms)
Brownie mix[1]:							
caramel fudge chunk (Pillsbury), 2" square	170	2.0	25.0	7.0	m.q.	105	m.q.
chocolate:							
German (Betty Crocker)	160	1.0	24.0	7.0	10	110	m.q.
milk (Duncan Hines)	160	1.0	22.0	7.0	m.q.	95	m.q.
frosted:							
(Betty Crocker) . .	160	1.0	26.0	6.0	10	120	m.q.
(Betty Crocker MicroRave) . . .	180	2.0	27.0	7.0	0	120	m.q.
fudge:							
(Betty Crocker Family Size)	140	1.0	22.0	5.0	10	100	m.q.
(Betty Crocker MicroRave) . . .	150	2.0	22.0	6.0	0	110	m.q.
(Duncan Hines) . .	160	2.0	22.0	7.0	m.q.	105	m.q.
(Pillsbury Microwave)	190	2.0	25.0	9.0	m.q.	105	m.q.
chewy (Duncan Hines)	130	1.0	18.0	5.0	m.q.	90	m.q.
deluxe (Pillsbury), 2" square	150	2.0	21.0	6.0	m.q.	100	m.q.
deluxe (Pillsbury Family Size), 2" square	150	1.0	20.0	7.0	m.q.	95	m.q.
deluxe, w/walnuts (Pillsbury), 2" square	150	2.0	19.0	8.0	m.q.	90	m.q.
double (Pillsbury), 2" square	160	2.0	24.0	6.0	m.q.	105	m.q.
peanut butter (Duncan Hines)	150	3.0	16.0	8.0	m.q.	105	m.q.
supreme (Betty Crocker)	120	1.0	21.0	3.0	10	85	m.q.

[1] Prepared according to basic package directions.

Food and Measure	cal.	prot. (gms)	carbo. (gms)	fat (gms)	chol. (mgs)	sod. (mgs)	fiber (gms)
Brownie mix, fudge *(cont.)*							
triple, chunky *(Pillsbury)*, 2″ square	170	2.0	25.0	7.0	m.q.	105	m.q.
rocky road, fudge *(Pillsbury)*, 2″ square	170	2.0	24.0	8.0	m.q.	95	m.q.
walnut:							
(Betty Crocker) . .	140	1.0	18.0	7.0	10	80	m.q.
(Betty Crocker MicroRave) . . .	160	2.0	21.0	7.0	0	95	m.q.
white, Vienna *(Duncan Hines)*	240	3.0	29.0	12.0	m.q.	135	m.q.
Browning sauce:							
(Gravymaster), 1 tsp.	12	.5	2.4	tr.	0	<1	tr.c
Brussels sprouts:							
fresh:							
raw, 1/2 cup	19	1.5	3.9	.1	0	11	.7 c
boiled, drained, 1 sprout, .7 oz.	8	.5	1.8	.1	0	4	.9 d
boiled, drained, 1/2 cup	30	2.0	6.8	.4	0	17	3.4 d
frozen, 3.3 oz., except as noted:							
boiled, drained, 1/2 cup	33	2.8	6.5	.3	0	18	1.4 d
(Birds Eye)	35	3.0	7.0	0	0	15	3.0 d
(Green Giant Polybag), 1/2 cup	25	2.0	6.0	0	0	10	1.6 d
(Seabrook)	35	3.0	7.0	0	0	12	1.0 c
(Stokely Singles), 3 oz.	35	4.0	7.0	0	0	10	m.q.
baby *(Seabrook)*	40	4.0	7.0	0	0	5	1.0 c
frozen, in butter sauce:							
(Green Giant), 1/2 cup	40	3.0	8.0	1.0	5	280	4.1 d
(Stokely Singles), 4 oz.	50	4.0	10.0	1.0	5	325	m.q.

Food and Measure	cal.	prot. (gms)	carbo. (gms)	fat (gms)	chol. (mgs)	sod. (mgs)	fiber (gms)
frozen, w/cheese sauce, baby *(Birds Eye* Combinations), 4.5 oz.	130	6.0	12.0	7.0	5	500	2.0 d
frozen, w/cauliflower, carrots *(Birds Eye* Farm Fresh), 4 oz.	40	3.0	8.0	0	0	30	4.0 d
Buckwheat, whole-grain:							
1 oz.	97	3.8	20.3	1.0	0	<1	m.q.
1 cup	584	22.5	121.6	5.8	0	1	m.q.
Buckwheat flour:							
1 oz.	95	3.6	20.0	.9	0	n.a.	m.q.
1 cup	402	15.1	84.7	3.7	0	n.a.	m.q.
Buckwheat groats, roasted:							
dry, 1 oz.	98	3.3	21.2	.8	0	3	.5 c
cooked, 1 cup	182	6.7	39.5	1.2	0	8	1.0 c
Bulgur (see also "Tabbouleh mix"):							
dry, 1 oz.	97	3.5	21.5	.4	0	5	5.2 d
dry, 1 cup	479	17.2	106.2	1.9	0	23	25.6 d
cooked, 1 cup	152	5.6	33.8	.4	0	9	.6 c
Buns, see "Rolls"							
Burbot, meat only:							
raw, 1 lb.	407	87.6	0	3.7	270	438	0
raw, 1 oz.	26	5.5	0	.2	17	27	0
Burdock root:							
raw, pieces, 1/2 cup	43	.9	10.3	.1	0	3	1.2 c
raw, 1 medium, 7.3 oz.	112	1.3	13.6	.1	0	4	1.5 c
boiled, drained, 1" pieces, 1/2 cup . .	55	1.3	13.2	.1	0	3	1.2 c
Burger King, 1 serving:							
breakfast bagel sandwich:							
regular	387	17.0	46.0	14.0	268	780	m.q.

Food and Measure	cal.	prot. (gms)	carbo. (gms)	fat (gms)	chol. (mgs)	sod. (mgs)	fiber (gms)
Burger King, breakfast bagel sandwich *(cont.)*							
w/bacon	438	20.0	46.0	19.0	273	905	m.q.
w/ham	418	23.0	46.0	15.0	287	1130	m.q.
w/sausage	731	26.0	46.0	36.0	318	1185	m.q.
breakfast *Croissan'wich:*							
regular	304	11.0	20.0	19.0	243	637	m.q.
w/bacon	354	14.0	20.0	24.0	249	762	m.q.
w/ham	335	17.0	20.0	20.0	262	987	m.q.
w/sausage	538	20.0	20.0	41.0	293	1042	m.q.
French toast sticks	449	49.0	49.0	29.0	74	498	m.q.
Great Danish	500	5.0	40.0	36.0	6	288	m.q.
scrambled egg platter:							
regular	468	15.0	33.0	30.0	370	808	m.q.
w/bacon	536	19.0	33.0	36.0	378	974	m.q.
w/sausage	702	24.0	33.0	52.0	420	1213	m.q.
chicken tenders, 6 pieces	236	16.0	14.0	13.0	46	541	m.q.
fish tenders, 6 pieces	267	12.0	18.0	16.0	28	870	m.q.
sandwiches:							
bacon double cheeseburger . .	510	33.0	27.0	31.0	104	728	m.q.
bacon double cheeseburger deluxe	592	33.0	28.0	39.0	111	804	m.q.
bacon double cheeseburger, barbeque	536	32.0	31.0	31.0	105	795	m.q.
BK Broiler chicken	379	24.0	31.0	18.0	53	764	m.q.
cheeseburger . . .	317	17.0	30.0	15.0	48	651	m.q.
chicken Speciality Sandwich	688	26.0	56.0	40.0	82	1423	m.q.
double cheeseburger	483	30.0	29.0	27.0	100	851	m.q.
ham and cheese Speciality Sandwich	471	24.0	44.0	23.0	70	1534	m.q.
hamburger	275	15.0	29.0	12.0	37	509	m.q.

Food and Measure	cal.	prot. (gms)	carbo. (gms)	fat (gms)	chol. (mgs)	sod. (mgs)	fiber (gms)
mushroom Swiss double cheeseburger, 6.2 oz.	473	31.0	27.0	27.0	95	746	m.q.
Whaler fish sandwich	488	19.0	45.0	27.0	77	592	m.q.
Whopper	628	27.0	46.0	36.0	90	880	m.q.
Whopper, w/cheese	711	32.0	47.0	43.0	113	1164	m.q.
Whopper Jr.	322	15.0	30.0	17.0	41	486	m.q.
Whopper Jr., w/ cheese	364	17.0	31.0	20.0	52	628	m.q.
salad:							
chef salad	180	17.0	7.0	9.0	120	570	m.q.
chicken salad . . .	140	20.0	8.0	4.0	50	440	m.q.
garden salad . . .	90	6.0	7.0	5.0	15	125	m.q.
side salad	20	1.0	4.0	0	0	20	m.q.
dressings and sauces, 1 full pkt., except as noted:							
bleu cheese dressing	300	2.0	3.0	31.0	40	600	n.a.
French dressing . .	280	0	17.0	23.0	0	690	n.a.
house dressing . .	260	2.0	5.0	26.0	20	530	n.a.
Italian dressing, reduced calorie . .	30	0	4.0	2.0	0	870	n.a.
ranch dipping sauce, 1 oz. . .	171	0	2.0	18.0	0	208	n.a.
tartar dipping sauce, 1 oz.	174	0	3.0	18.0	16	303	n.a.
Thousand Island dressing	240	1.0	7.0	23.0	35	470	n.a.
sweet & sour sauce, 1 oz.	45	0	11.0	0	0	52	n.a.
side dishes:							
french fries, regular	227	3.0	24.0	13.0	0	160	m.q.
onion rings	274	4.0	28.0	16.0	0	665	m.q.
tater tenders . . .	213	2.0	25.0	12.0	n.a.	318	m.q.
apple pie	305	3.0	44.0	12.0	4	412	m.q.

Food and Measure	cal.	prot. (gms)	carbo. (gms)	fat (gms)	chol. (mgs)	sod. (mgs)	fiber (gms)
"Burger," vegetarian:							
canned (Worthington Vegetarian Burger), 1/2 cup	150	19.0	9.0	4.0	0	780	m.q.
frozen (Morningstar Farms FriPats/Grillers), 2.25-oz. patty	180	13.0	5.0	12.0	0	350	m.q.
mix[1]:							
(Love Natural Foods Loveburger), 2 oz. mix, 4-oz. burger	245	17.0	20.0	11.0	0	224	8.0 d
(Nature's Burger), 3-oz. burger[2] . .	152	7.0	21.0	4.0	0	228	m.q.
(Worthington Granburger), 6 tbsp. mix . . .	110	19.0	7.0	1.0	0	700	m.q.
barbecue (Nature's Burger), 3-oz. burger[2]	117	4.0	24.0	.8	0	423	m.q.
pizza (Nature's Burger), 3-oz. burger[2]	121	5.0	24.0	1.0	0	406	m.q.
w/tofu (Fantastic Foods), 3.4-oz. burger[2]	133	11.0	14.0	5.0	n.a.	320	m..q.
Burrito, frozen (see also "Burrito entree"):							
(Hormel Burrito Grande), 51/2 oz.	380	14.0	45.0	16.0	m.q.	877	m.q.
beef (Hormel), 1 piece	205	9.0	31.0	8.0	m.q.	780	m.q.
beef and bean:							
(Patio), 5-oz. pkg.	370	11.0	43.0	16.0	m.q.	830	m.q.
(Patio Britos), 3.63 oz.	250	6.0	33.0	10.0	15	340	m.q.

[1] Prepared according to package directions, except as noted.
[2] Does not include fat from butter or oil used in cooking.

Food and Measure	cal.	prot. (gms)	carbo. (gms)	fat (gms)	chol. (mgs)	sod. (mgs)	fiber (gms)
green chili (Patio), 5-oz. pkg.	330	12.0	43.0	12.0	m.q.	770	m.q.
red chili (Patio), 5-oz. pkg.	340	11.0	44.0	13.0	m.q.	810	m.q.
beef nacho (Patio Britos), 3.63 oz. . .	270	9.0	30.0	13.0	25	420	m.q.
cheese:							
(Hormel), 1 piece	210	9.0	32.0	5.0	m.q.	792	m.q.
nacho (Patio Britos), 3.63 oz.	250	7.0	32.0	10.0	20	330	m.q.
chicken:							
and rice (Hormel), 1 piece	200	9.0	32.0	4.0	m.q.	594	m.q.
spicy (Patio Britos), 3.63 oz.	250	6.0	33.0	10.0	25	330	m.q.
chili:							
green (Patio Britos), 3.63 oz.	250	6.0	33.0	10.0	15	420	m.q.
hot (Hormel), 1 piece	240	9.0	33.0	8.0	m.q.	619	m.q.
red (Patio Britos), 3.63 oz.	240	6.0	31.0	10.0	15	370	m.q.
red hot (Patio), 5-oz. pkg.	360	12.0	43.0	15.0	m.q.	800	m.q.
Burrito dinner, fro-zen:							
(Patio), 12 oz.	517	18.0	74.0	16.0	m.q.	1643	m.q.
beef and bean (Old El Paso Festive Din-ners), 11 oz. . . .	470	23.0	72.0	9.0	m.q.	1180	m.q.
Burrito dinner mix: (Tio Sancho Dinner Kit):							
seasoning, 3.25 oz.	265	12.3	49.3	2.1	n.a.	5031	5.5 c
1 tortilla	125	3.3	24.0	1.9	n.a.	569	.1 c
Burrito entree, fro-zen:							
bean and cheese (Old El Paso), 1 pkg. . .	340	19.0	43.0	13.0	m.q.	770	m.q.

Food and Measure	cal.	prot. (gms)	carbo. (gms)	fat (gms)	chol. (mgs)	sod. (mgs)	fiber (gms)
Burrito entree *(cont.)*							
beef and bean:							
hot *(Old El Paso)*,							
1 pkg.	340	11.0	41.0	14.0	m.q.	950	m.q.
medium *(Old El*							
Paso), 1 pkg. . . .	330	11.0	41.0	14.0	m.q.	730	m.q.
mild *(Old El Paso)*,							
1 pkg.	330	12.0	40.0	13.0	m.q.	660	m.q.
beefsteak *(Weight*							
Watchers), 7.62 oz.	310	16.0	36.0	12.0	70	790	m.q.
chicken *(Weight*							
Watchers), 7.62 oz.	310	15.0	34.0	13.0	60	790	m.q.
Burrito filling mix:							
beans *(Del Monte)*,							
1/2 cup	110	6.0	20.0	1.0	n.a.	900	n.a.
Burrito seasoning							
mix:							
(Lawry's), 1 pkg. . . .	132	6.0	23.3	1.7	0	2516	.9 c
Butter:							
regular, unsalted:							
1 stick or 4 oz. . .	813	1.0	0	92.0	248	12	0
1 tbsp.	100	.1	0	11.4	31	1	0
1 tsp.	34	<.1	0	3.8	10	<1	0
regular, salted:							
1 stick or 4 oz. . .	813	1.0	0	92.0	248	937	0
1 tbsp.	100	.1	0	11.4	31	115	0
1 tsp.	34	<.1	0	3.8	10	39	0
1 pat (90 per lb.)	36	<.1	0	4.1	11	41	0
whipped, unsalted:							
1/2 cup or 1 stick	542	.6	<.1	61.3	165	8	0
1 tbsp.	67	.1	tr.	7.6	20	1	0
1 tsp.	23	tr.	tr.	2.6	7	<1	0
1 pat (120 per lb.)	27	<.1	tr.	3.1	8	1	0
whipped, salted:							
1/2 cup or 1 stick	542	.6	<.1	61.3	165	625	0
1 tbsp.	67	.1	tr.	7.6	20	78	0
1 tsp.	23	tr.	tr.	2.6	7	26	0
1 pat (120 per lb.)	27	<.1	tr.	3.1	8	31	0

Food and Measure	cal.	prot. (gms)	carbo. (gms)	fat (gms)	chol. (mgs)	sod. (mgs)	fiber (gms)
Butter oil:							
1 tbsp.	112	<.1	0	12.7	33	n.a.	0
Butterbur:							
fresh:							
raw, 1/2 cup	7	.2	1.7	<.1	0	4	.6 c
raw, 1 stalk, .2 oz.	1	<.1	.2	tr.	0	tr.	.1 c
boiled, drained,							
4 oz.	9	.3	2.4	<.1	0	5	.9 c
canned:							
chopped, 1/2 cup	2	.1	.2	.1	0	3	.6 c
3 stalks, 1.6 oz. . .	1	<.1	.2	<.1	0	2	.4 c
Butterfish, meat only:							
raw, 1 lb.	663	78.4	0	36.4	295	401	0
raw, 1 oz.	41	4.9	0	2.3	18	25	0
Buttermilk, see "Milk" and "Milk, dry"							
Butternuts, dried:							
in shell, 1 lb.	750	30.5	14.8	69.8	0	1	2.3 c
shelled, 1 oz.	174	7.1	3.4	16.2	0	tr.	.5 c
Butternut squash:							
fresh, 1/2 cup:							
raw, cubed	32	.7	8.1	.1	0	3	1.0 c
baked, cubed . . .	41	.9	10.7	.1	0	4	1.3 c
frozen:							
12-oz. pkg.	192	6.0	49.0	.3	0	8	4.2 c
boiled, drained,							
4 oz.	44	1.4	11.4	.1	0	2	1.0 c
mashed, 1/2 cup . .	47	1.5	12.1	.1	0	2	1.0 c
Butterscotch, see "Candy"							
Butterscotch baking:							
chips *(Nestlé* Toll House Morsels),							
1 oz.	150	1.0	19.0	8.0	n.a.	25	(0)

Food and Measure	cal.	prot. (gms)	carbo. (gms)	fat (gms)	chol. (mgs)	sod. (mgs)	fiber (gms)
Butterscotch topping:							
(Kraft), 1 tbsp.	60	0	13.0	1.0	0	70	(0)
caramel flavor *(Smucker's* Special Recipe), 2 tbsp. . . .	160	1.0	33.0	3.0	n.a.	40	(0)
flavor *(Smucker's)*, 2 tbsp.	140	0	33.0	0	0	75	(0)

C

Food and Measure	cal.	prot. (gms)	carbo. (gms)	fat (gms)	chol. (mgs)	sod. (mgs)	fiber (gms)
Cabbage:							
raw:							
5¾"-diam. head,							
2.5 lb.	215	11.0	48.8	1.6	0	164	10.0 d
shredded, ½ cup	8	.4	1.9	.1	0	6	.4 d
boiled, drained:							
1 head, 2.8 lb. . .	270	12.1	60.2	3.1	0	239	7.6 c
shredded, ½ cup	16	.7	3.6	.2	0	14	.5 c
Cabbage, Chinese,							
½ cup, except as							
noted:							
bok-choy:							
raw, whole, 1 lb.	52	6.0	8.7	.8	0	257	4.0 d
raw, shredded . . .	5	.5	.8	.1	0	23	.4 d
boiled, drained,							
shredded	10	1.3	1.5	.1	0	29	1.4 d
pe-tsai:							
raw, whole, 1 lb.	68	5.1	13.6	.8	0	38	4.2 d
raw, shredded . . .	6	.5	1.2	.1	0	3	.4 d
boiled, drained,							
shredded	8	.9	1.4	.1	0	6	1.0 d
Cabbage, red:							
raw, whole, 1 lb. . . .	100	5.0	22.2	.9	0	38	7.2 d
raw, shredded, ½ cup	10	.5	2.1	.1	0	4	.7 d
boiled, drained, shred-							
ded, ½ cup	16	.8	3.5	.2	0	6	1.8 d
Cabbage, savoy:							
raw, whole, 1 lb. . . .	100	7.3	22.1	.4	0	102	2.9 c
raw, shredded, ½ cup	10	.7	2.1	<.1	0	10	.3 c

Food and Measure	cal.	prot. (gms)	carbo. (gms)	fat (gms)	chol. (mgs)	sod. (mgs)	fiber (gms)
Cabbage, savoy *(cont.)*							
boiled, drained, shredded, 1/2 cup	18	1.3	4.0	.1	0	17	.5 c
Cabbage, stuffed, frozen:							
w/meat, in tomato sauce *(Lean Cuisine)*, 10¾ oz. . . .	220	14.0	19.0	10.0	55	930	m.q.
Cabbage, swamp, see "Swamp cabbage"							
Cajun sauce, see "Creole sauce"							
Cajun seasoning:							
(Tone's), 1 tsp. . . .	9	.4	2.1	.2	0	215	.5 d
Cake, 1/12 cake, except as noted:							
apple streusel *(Awrey's)*, 2″ × 2″ piece	160	2.0	18.0	9.0	15	120	0
banana, iced *(Awrey's)*, 2″ × 2″ piece	140	1.0	17.0	8.0	20	120	0
black forest torte *(Awrey's)*, 1/14 cake	350	3.0	38.0	21.0	50	330	1.0 d
carrot, iced; supreme *(Awrey's)*, 2″ × 2″ piece	210	3.0	23.0	12.0	25	170	0
3-layer *(Awrey's)*	390	5.0	44.0	23.0	45	310	1.0 d
chocolate:							
double, iced *(Awrey's)*, 2″ × 2″ piece	130	2.0	21.0	6.0	15	150	1.0 d
double, 2-layer *(Awrey's)*	250	3.0	38.0	11.0	35	260	1.0 d
double, 3-layer *(Awrey's)*	310	3.0	48.0	14.0	35	290	2.0 d

Food and Measure	cal.	prot. (gms)	carbo. (gms)	fat (gms)	chol. (mgs)	sod. (mgs)	fiber (gms)
double torte (Awrey's), 1/14 cake	340	3.0	51.0	15.0	35	300	2.0 d
German, iced (Awrey's) 2″ × 2″ piece	160	2.0	19.0	9.0	20	150	0
German, 3-layer (Awrey's)	350	3.0	46.0	18.0	40	300	1.0 d
milk, yellow, 2-layer (Awrey's)	290	3.0	33.0	17.0	50	320	0
white iced, 2-layer (Awrey's)	270	3.0	34.0	15.0	40	290	1.0 d
coconut:							
butter cream (Awrey's), 2″ × 2″ piece	160	1.0	19.0	9.0	25	180	0
yellow, 3-layer (Awrey's)	350	3.0	40.0	21.0	50	340	0
coffee:							
caramel nut (Awrey's)	140	2.0	15.0	8.0	5	150	0
long John (Awrey's)	160	2.0	19.0	8.0	10	130	0
devil's food, iced (Awrey's), 2″ × 2″ piece	150	1.0	17.0	8.0	25	160	1.0 d
lemon:							
3-layer (Awrey's)	320	2.0	38.0	19.0	45	310	0
yellow, 2-layer (Awrey's)	290	2.0	33.0	17.0	45	310	0
Neapolitan torte (Awrey's), 1/14 cake	380	3.0	43.0	22.0	55	370	0
orange, iced:							
frosty (Awrey's), 2″ × 2″ piece	150	1.0	19.0	8.0	20	170	0
3-layer (Awrey's)	320	2.0	40.0	17.0	35	320	0
peanut butter, torte (Awrey's), 1/14 cake	380	7.0	44.0	22.0	40	340	1.0 d

Food and Measure	cal.	prot. (gms)	carbo. (gms)	fat (gms)	chol. (mgs)	sod. (mgs)	fiber (gms)
Cake *(cont.)*							
pineapple crunch *(Entenmann's)*, 1 oz.	70	1.0	16.0	0	0	85	m.q.
pistachio, torte *(Awrey's)*, 1/14 cake	370	3.0	41.0	22.0	35	370	1.0 d
pound:							
(Drake's), 1/10 cake	110	2.0	16.0	5.0	25	70	m.q.
golden *(Awrey's)*, 1/14 loaf	130	2.0	19.0	5.0	20	150	0
raisin spice, iced *(Awrey's)*, 2" × 2" piece	160	1.0	21.0	8.0	20	120	0
raspberry nut *(Awrey's)*, 1/16 cake	310	3.0	39.0	16.0	30	220	0
sponge *(Awrey's)*, 2" × 2" piece . . .	80	1.0	11.0	3.0	15	125	0
strawberry supreme, torte *(Awrey's)*, 1/14 cake	270	3.0	38.0	12.0	45	310	1.0 d
walnut, torte *(Awrey's)*, 1/14 cake	320	2.0	38.0	19.0	30	290	0
yellow, iced *(Awrey's)*, 2" × 2" piece . . .	150	1.0	18.0	9.0	25	180	0
Cake, frozen, (see also "Cake, snack, frozen"):							
banana, iced *(Sara Lee)*, 1/8 cake . . .	170	1.0	28.0	6.0	n.a.	160	m.q.
black forest:							
(Weight Watchers), 3 oz.	180	4.0	32.0	5.0	5	280	m.q.
(Sara Lee), 1/8 cake	190	2.0	28.0	8.0	n.a.	100	m.q.
Boston cream:							
(Pepperidge Farm Supreme), 1/4 cake	290	3.0	39.0	14.0	50	190	m.q.
(Weight Watchers), 3 oz.	190	4.0	35.0	4.0	5	280	m.q.

Food and Measure	cal.	prot. (gms)	carbo. (gms)	fat (gms)	chol. (mgs)	sod. (mgs)	fiber (gms)
carrot:							
(Weight Watchers), 3 oz.	170	4.0	27.0	5.0	5	310	m.q.
cream cheese iced (Pepperidge Farm Old Fashioned), 1/8 cake	150	1.0	19.0	9.0	15	160	m.q.
iced (Sara Lee), 1/8 cake	260	3.0	31.0	13.0	n.a.	240	m.q.
cheesecake:							
(Weight Watchers), 3.9 oz.	220	10.0	30.0	7.0	25	280	m.q.
French (Sara Lee Light Classics), 1/10 cake	200	3.0	19.0	13.0	n.a.	100	m.q.
strawberry (Weight Watchers), 3.9 oz.	180	7.0	28.0	5.0	20	230	m.q.
strawberry, French (Sara Lee), 1/8 cake	240	3.0	28.0	13.0	20	125	m.q.
cheesecake, nondairy, all varieties (Tofutti Better than Cheesecake), 2 oz.	160	2.0	16.0	10.0	0	110	m.q.
chocolate:							
(Pepperidge Farm Supreme), 1/4 cake	300	3.0	37.0	16.0	25	140	m.q.
(Weight Watchers), 2.5 oz.	190	5.0	31.0	5.0	5	250	m.q.
fudge layer (Pepperidge Farm), 1/10 cake	180	1.0	23.0	10.0	20	140	m.q.
fudge stripe (Pepperidge Farm), 1/10 cake	170	2.0	20.0	9.0	20	140	m.q.
German (Weight Watchers), 2.5 oz.	200	4.0	31.0	7.0	5	350	m.q.

Food and Measure	cal.	prot. (gms)	carbo. (gms)	fat (gms)	chol. (mgs)	sod. (mgs)	fiber (gms)
Cake, frozen, chocolate *(cont.)*							
German, layer *(Pepperidge Farm),*							
1/10 cake	180	1.0	22.0	10.0	20	170	m.q.
mousse *(Sara Lee Light Classics),*							
1/10 cake	200	2.0	18.0	14.0	n.a.	80	n.a.
coconut layer *(Pepperidge Farm),*							
1/10 cake	180	1.0	24.0	8.0	20	120	m.q.
coffee, all butter, 1/8 cake:							
cheese *(Sara Lee)*	210	4.0	23.0	12.0	m.q.	210	m.q.
pecan *(Sara Lee)*	160	3.0	19.0	8.0	m.q.	180	m.q.
streusel *(Sara Lee)*	160	3.0	20.0	7.0	m.q.	160	m.q.
devil's food layer *(Pepperidge Farm),*							
1/10 cake	180	1.0	24.0	9.0	20	135	m.q.
golden layer *(Pepperidge Farm),*							
1/10 cake	180	1.0	24.0	9.0	20	110	m.q.
lemon coconut *(Pepperidge Farm Supreme),* 1/4 cake	280	3.0	38.0	13.0	30	220	m.q.
lemon cream *(Pepperidge Farm Supreme),* 1/12 cake	170	2.0	21.0	9.0	20	120	m.q.
peach Melba *(Pepperidge Farm Supreme),* 1/4 cake	270	2.0	50.0	7.0	35	135	m.q.
pineapple cream *(Pepperidge Farm Supreme),* 1/12 cake	190	2.0	28.0	7.0	20	130	m.q.
pound:							
(Pepperidge Farm Old Fashioned Cholesterol Free),							
1/10 cake	110	1.0	13.0	6.0	0	85	m.q.

Food and Measure	cal.	prot. (gms)	carbo. (gms)	fat (gms)	chol. (mgs)	sod. (mgs)	fiber (gms)
all butter (Sara Lee Original), 1/10 cake	130	2.0	14.0	7.0	m.q.	85	m.q.
butter (Pepperidge Farm Old Fashioned), 1/10 cake	130	1.0	16.0	7.0	60	150	m.q.
strawberry:							
cream (Pepperidge Farm Supreme), 1/12 cake	190	1.0	30.0	7.0	20	120	m.q.
shortcake (Sara Lee), 1/8 cake . .	190	2.0	26.0	8.0	n.a.	90	m.q.
stripe, layer (Pepperidge Farm), 1/12 cake	160	1.0	21.0	8.0	20	120	m.q.
vanilla layer (Pepperidge Farm), 1/10 cake	190	1.0	25.0	8.0	20	120	m.q.
Cake, snack, 1 piece, except as noted:							
apple:							
bar, baked (Sunbelt)	130	1.0	28.0	2.0	<1	130	m.q.
delight (Little Debbie)	140	2.0	24.0	4.0	<1	95	m.q.
spice (Little Debbie)	270	2.0	41.0	11.0	<1	180	m.q.
banana:							
(Hostess Suzy Q's)	240	2.0	40.0	8.0	15	230	m.q.
(Tastykake Banana Treat)	138	1.2	26.9	2.9	n.a.	112	m.q.
twins (Little Debbie)	250	2.0	40.0	9.0	<1	190	m.q.
brownie, see "Brownie"							
butterscotch (Tastykake Krimpets)	118	1.4	23.5	2.1	n.a.	96	m.q.
caramel peanut filled, (Little Debbie Peanut Cluster)	230	3.0	28.0	12.0	<1	120	m.q.

Food and Measure	cal.	prot. (gms)	carbo. (gms)	fat (gms)	chol. (mgs)	sod. (mgs)	fiber (gms)
Cake, snack *(cont.)*							
cherry cordial *(Little Debbie)*	170	1.0	23.0	8.0	n.a.	80	m.q.
chocolate:							
(Hostess Choco Bliss)	200	2.0	34.0	7.0	5	130	m.q.
(Hostess Choco-Diles)	240	2.0	35.0	11.0	7	180	m.q.
(Hostess Ding Dongs/King Dons)	170	1.0	21.0	9.0	6	130	m.q.
(Hostess Ho Hos)	120	1.0	17.0	6.0	8	70	m.q.
(Hostess Suzy Q's)	250	2.0	45.0	8.0	16	260	m.q.
(Little Debbie) . . .	320	2.0	45.0	14.0	<1	135	m.q.
(Little Debbie ChocoCake) . .	270	2.0	37.0	13.0	<1	220	m.q.
(Little Debbie ChocoJel)	150	1.0	21.0	7.0	<1	80	m.q.
(Tastykake Creamie)	174	1.9	26.6	6.7	n.a.	135	m.q.
(Tastykake Juniors)	364	4.3	69.6	7.7	n.a.	298	m.q.
(Tastykake Kandy Kakes)	99	1.0	14.0	4.3	n.a.	46	m.q.
(Tastykake Tempty)	94	1.0	17.8	2.1	n.a.	90	m.q.
cream filled *(Drake's Devil Dog)*	160	2.0	24.0	6.0	0	135	m.q.
cream filled *(Drake's Ring Ding)*	180	2.0	23.0	10.0	0	115	m.q.
fudge crispy *(Little Debbie)*	260	2.0	48.0	7.0	<1	90	m.q.
fudge round *(Little Debbie)*	150	1.0	23.0	6.0	<1	70	m.q.
mint, cream filled *(Drake's Ring Ding)*	190	2.0	22.0	11.0	0	115	m.q.

Food and Measure	cal.	prot. (gms)	carbo. (gms)	fat (gms)	chol. (mgs)	sod. (mgs)	fiber (gms)
roll, cream filled (Drake's Yodel)	150	2.0	16.0	9.0	5	65	m.q.
roll, cream filled, Swiss (Drake's)	170	2.0	22.0	8.0	15	140	m.q.
slices (Little Debbie)	320	3.0	56.0	9.0	<1	280	m.q.
twins (Little Debbie)	240	2.0	41.0	7.0	<1	200	m.q.
chocolate chip (Little Debbie)	320	2.0	40.0	16.0	<1	180	m.q.
coconut: (Tastykake Juniors)	317	4.0	66.1	4.0	n.a.	305	m.q.
covered (Hostess Sno Balls)	140	1.0	14.0	2.0	2	90	m.q.
crunch (Little Debbie)	320	2.0	35.0	19.0	<2	80	m.q.
coffee: (Drake's Jr.)	140	2.0	18.0	6.0	10	90	m.q.
(Drake's Small) . . .	220	3.0	33.0	9.0	15	160	m.q.
(Little Debbie) . . .	250	3.0	39.0	9.0	<1	210	m.q.
(Tastykake Koffee Kake Juniors) . .	317	3.7	47.9	12.3	n.a.	263	m.q.
cinnamon crumb (Drake's)	150	2.0	22.0	6.0	10	110	m.q.
cream filled (Tastykake Koffee Kake)	143	1.5	21.7	5.6	n.a.	106	m.q.
cupcake: butter cream, cream filled (Tastykake)	125	1.4	22.3	3.4	n.a.	141	m.q.
chocolate (Hostess)	170	2.0	32.0	8.0	3	250	m.q.
chocolate (Tastykake)	113	1.5	20.7	2.7	n.a.	144	m.q.
chocolate, cream filled (Drake's Ring Ding) . . .	100	1.0	16.0	4.0	0	110	m.q.
chocolate, cream filled (Tastykake)	130	3.8	22.8	3.6	n.a.	137	m.q.
creme (Tastykake Kreme Kup) . . .	104	1.8	17.3	3.3	n.a.	138	m.q.

Food and Measure	cal.	prot. (gms)	carbo. (gms)	fat (gms)	chol. (mgs)	sod. (mgs)	fiber (gms)
Cake, snack, cupcake (cont.)							
golden, cream filled (Drake's Sunny Doodle)	100	1.0	16.0	3.0	10	100	m.q.
orange (Hostess)	150	2.0	28.0	5.0	10	140	m.q.
crumb cake (Hostess)	160	1.0	25.0	4.0	9	100	m.q.
dessert cup (Little Debbie)	80	1.0	4.0	1.0	<1	170	m.q.
devil's food:							
(Little Debbie Devil Cremes)	300	3.0	43.0	13.0	<1	330	m.q.
(Little Debbie Devil Squares)	270	2.0	41.0	11.0	<1	150	m.q.
donut, see "Donut"							
(Drake's Funny Bone)	150	3.0	18.0	8.0	0	110	m.q.
(Drake's Zoinks) . . .	130	1.0	20.0	5.0	10	130	m.q.
fancy (Little Debbie)	340	2.0	46.0	16.0	<1	150	m.q.
fig (Little Debbie Figaroos)	160	1.0	31.0	4.0	<1	105	m.q.
fruit (Hostess Fruit Loaf)	400	4.0	77.0	9.0	7	520	m.q.
golden cremes (Little Debbie)	270	3.0	41.0	11.0	<1	270	m.q.
honey:							
glazed (Hostess)	370	5.0	41.0	21.0	19	250	m.q.
iced (Hostess) . .	410	6.0	55.0	21.0	16	210	m.q.
(Hostess Lil' Angels)	90	1.0	18.0	1.0	1	120	m.q.
(Hostess O's) . . .	220	3.0	33.0	8.0	14	250	m.q.
(Hostess Tiger Tail)	140	2.0	30.0	2.0	8	160	m.q.
(Hostess Twinkies)	140	1.0	30.0	2.0	10	180	m.q.
jelly (Tastykake Krimpets)	96	1.1	21.3	.8	n.a.	88	m.q.
jelly roll (Little Debbie)	250	1.0	43.0	9.0	<1	160	m.q.
lemon stix (Little Debbie)	220	2.0	29.0	10.0	<1	55	m.q.

Food and Measure	cal.	prot. (gms)	carbo. (gms)	fat (gms)	chol. (mgs)	sod. (mgs)	fiber (gms)
(Little Debbie Caravella)	200	2.0	26.0	9.0	<1	95	m.q.
(Little Debbie Doodle Dandies) . .	320	2.0	44.0	16.0	<1	140	m.q.
marshmallow supreme *(Little Debbie)*	150	1.0	24.0	5.0	<1	60	m.q.
mint wafer, chocolate coated *(Little Debbie Mint Sprints)*	200	2.0	24.0	10.0	<1	90	m.q.
peanut butter: *(Tastykake* Kandy Kakes)	103	2.0	11.7	5.3	n.a.	41	m.q.
bar *(Little Debbie)*	370	8.0	41.0	18.0	<1	270	m.q.
wafer, chocolate coated *(Little Debbie Nutty Bar)*	390	5.0	41.0	23.0	<1	150	m.q.
and jelly sandwich *(Little Debbie)* . .	150	2.0	20.0	6.0	<1	105	m.q.
pecan twins *(Little Debbie)*	220	3.0	34.0	10.0	<1	170	m.q.
pie, see "Pie, snack"							
pudding cakes *(Hostess)*	170	2.0	32.0	4.0	8	200	m.q.
Swiss roll *(Little Debbie)*	270	2.0	38.0	12.0	<1	130	m.q.
vanilla: *(Little Debbie)* . . .	330	2.0	46.0	16.0	<1	135	m.q.
(Tastykake Creamie)	182	1.9	26.9	7.5	n.a.	136	m.q.
cream filled *(Tastykake Krimpets)*	139	1.4	25.4	3.6	n.a.	92	m.q.
wafer, peanut butter filled *(Little Debbie* Naturals)	170	5.0	19.0	10.0	<1	90	m.q.

Food and Measure	cal.	prot. (gms)	carbo. (gms)	fat (gms)	chol. (mgs)	sod. (mgs)	fiber (gms)
Cake, snack, frozen, 1 piece:							
apple'n spice bake *(Pepperidge Farm Dessert Lights)* . .	170	2.0	37.0	2.0	10	105	m.q.
Boston cream *(Pepperidge Farm Hyannis)*	230	4.0	34.0	10.0	70	125	2.0 d
carrot:							
(Pepperidge Farm Classic)	260	2.0	32.0	16.0	50	280	m.q.
(Sara Lee)	170	4.0	26.0	6.0	10	135	m.q.
cheesecake:							
(Sara Lee Classic)	200	4.0	16.0	14.0	n.a.	150	m.q.
strawberry *(Pepperidge Farm Manhattan)*	300	6.0	49.0	9.0	150	250	m.q.
cherries supreme *(Pepperidge Farm Dessert Lights)* . .	170	0	38.0	2.0	80	35	m.q.
chocolate:							
double *(Pepperidge Farm Classic)* . .	250	2.0	31.0	13.0	35	180	m.q.
fudge *(Pepperidge Farm Classic)* . .	260	2.0	34.0	14.0	40	160	m.q.
German *(Pepperidge Farm Classic)*	250	2.0	29.0	13.0	45	230	m.q.
chocolate mousse:							
(Pepperidge Farm Dessert Lights)	190	3.0	25.0	9.0	5	260	m.q.
(Pepperidge Farm San Francisco)	490	4.0	41.0	34.0	150	75	m.q.
(Sara Lee)	180	5.0	20.0	9.0	15	125	m.q.
coconut *(Pepperidge Farm Classic)* . . .	230	2.0	31.0	11.0	20	160	m.q.

Food and Measure	cal.	prot. (gms)	carbo. (gms)	fat (gms)	chol. (mgs)	sod. (mgs)	fiber (gms)
coffee:							
apple cinnamon *(Sara Lee* Individual Wrapped) . .	290	4.0	40.0	13.0	n.a.	270	m.q.
apple crumb *(Pepperidge Farm* Amherst)	220	2.0	30.0	11.0	20	150	1.0 d
butter streusel *(Sara Lee* Individual Wrapped)	230	4.0	27.0	12.0	n.a.	270	m.q.
pecan *(Sara Lee* Individual Wrapped)	280	5.0	30.0	16.0	n.a.	270	m.q.
donut, see "Donut"							
lemon coconut *(Pepperidge Farm* Classic)	220	2.0	30.0	10.0	40	180	m.q.
lemon supreme *(Pepperidge Farm* Dessert Lights)	170	4.0	26.0	5.0	50	100	m.q.
peach Melba shortcake *(Pepperidge Farm* Charleston)	220	2.0	41.0	5.0	135	170	m.q.
peach parfait *(Pepperidge Farm* Dessert Lights)	150	3.0	24.0	5.0	10	70	m.q.
pound, all butter *(Sara Lee)*	200	2.0	23.0	11.0	m.q.	190	m.q.
raspberry-vanilla swirl *(Pepperidge Farm* Dessert Lights) . .	160	4.0	25.0	5.0	15	140	m.q.
strawberry shortcake *(Pepperidge Farm* Dessert Lights) . .	170	2.0	30.0	5.0	70	50	1.0 d
vanilla fudge swirl *(Pepperidge Farm* Classic)	250	2.0	33.0	11.0	35	160	m.q.
Cake frosting, see "Frosting"							

Food and Measure	cal.	prot. (gms)	carbo. (gms)	fat (gms)	chol. (mgs)	sod. (mgs)	fiber (gms)
Cake mix[1], 1/12 cake or pkg., except as noted:							
angel food:							
(Betty Crocker Traditional) . . .	130	3.0	30.0	0	0	170	m.q.
(Duncan Hines) . .	140	3.0	30.0	0	0	130	m.q.
chocolate, confetti, lemon custard or white (Betty Crocker)	150	3.0	34.0	0	0	300	m.q.
strawberry (Betty Crocker)	150	3.0	35.0	0	0	260	m.q.
apple cinnamon (Betty Crocker Supermoist)	250	3.0	36.0	10.0	55	280	m.q.
apple streusel (Betty Crocker MicroRave), 1/6 cake	240	2.0	33.0	11.0	45	190	m.q.
banana (Pillsbury Plus)	250	3.0	36.0	11.0	m.q.	290	m.q.
black forest:							
cherry (Pillsbury Bundt), 1/16 cake	240	3.0	38.0	8.0	m.q.	310	m.q.
mousse (Duncan Hines Tiarra) . .	260	3.0	33.0	13.0	m.q.	270	m.q.
Boston cream:							
(Betty Crocker Classics), 1/8 cake . .	270	4.0	50.0	6.0	m.q.	390	m.q.
(Pillsbury Bundt), 1/16 cake	270	3.0	43.0	10.0	m.q.	310	m.q.
butter pecan (Betty Crocker Supermoist)	250	3.0	35.0	11.0	55	320	m.q.
butter recipe:							
(Pillsbury Plus) . .	260	3.0	34.0	12.0		370	m.q.
golden (Duncan Hines)	270	3.0	36.0	13.0	m.q.	270	m.q.

[1] Prepared according to basic package directions.

Food and Measure	cal.	prot. (gms)	carbo. (gms)	fat (gms)	chol. (mgs)	sod. (mgs)	fiber (gms)
carrot:							
(Betty Crocker Supermoist) . . .	250	3.0	35.0	11.0	55	310	m.q.
(Dromedary)	232	3.0	23.0	15.0	m.q.	292	m.q.
'n spice (Pillsbury Plus)	260	3.0	36.0	11.0	m.q.	330	m.q.
cheesecake, 1/8 cake:							
(Jell-O No Bake)	280	5.0	36.0	13.0	30	350	m.q.
(Jell-O No Bake New York Style)	280	6.0	38.0	12.0	30	420	m.q.
lemon (Jell-O No Bake)	270	5.0	36.0	13.0	25	400	m.q.
lite (Royal No-Bake)	210	5.0	23.0	10.0	m.q.	380	m.q.
real (Royal No-Bake)	280	5.0	31.0	9.0	m.q.	370	m.q.
cherry chip (Betty Crocker Supermoist)	190	3.0	37.0	3.0	0	270	m.q.
cherries and cream (Duncan Hines Tiarra)	250	4.0	34.0	11.0	m.q.	265	m.q.
chocolate:							
(Pillsbury Microwave), 1/8 cake	210	2.0	23.0	13.0	m.q.	260	m.q.
butter (Betty Crocker Supermoist) . . .	270	3.0	35.0	13.0	75	450	m.q.
dark (Pillsbury Plus)	250	3.0	32.0	12.0	m.q.	380	m.q.
double supreme (Pillsbury Microwave), 1/8 cake	330	3.0	39.0	19.0	m.q.	340	m.q.
fudge (Betty Crocker Supermoist) . . .	260	4.0	34.0	12.0	55	470	m.q.
fudge (Duncan Hines Butter Recipe)	270	4.0	34.0	13.0	m.q.	350	m.q.

Food and Measure	cal.	prot. (gms)	carbo. (gms)	fat (gms)	chol. (mgs)	sod. (mgs)	fiber (gms)
Cake mix, chocolate *(cont.)*							
fudge *(Pillsbury Bundt Tunnel of Fudge)*, 1/16 cake	260	3.0	37.0	12.0	m.q.	310	m.q.
fudge *(Pillsbury Bundt Tunnel of Fudge* Microwave), 1/8 cake	290	3.0	36.0	17.0	m.q.	320	m.q.
fudge, dark Dutch *(Duncan Hines)*	280	4.0	33.0	15.0	m.q.	375	m.q.
fudge, marble *(Duncan Hines)*	260	3.0	36.0	11.0	m.q.	285	m.q.
fudge, marble *(Pillsbury Plus)*	270	4.0	36.0	12.0	m.q.	300	m.q.
fudge, w/vanilla frosting *(Betty Crocker MicroRave)*, 1/6 cake	310	3.0	40.0	15.0	35	300	m.q.
German *(Betty Crocker Supermoist)* . . .	260	3.0	35.0	12.0	55	420	m.q.
German *(Pillsbury Plus)*	250	3.0	36.0	11.0	m.q.	340	m.q.
German, w/coconut pecan frosting *(Betty Crocker MicroRave)*, 1/6 cake	320	3.0	37.0	18.0	35	250	m.q.
milk *(Betty Crocker Supermoist)* . . .	260	4.0	35.0	12.0	55	340	m.q.
mousse *(Duncan Hines Tiarra)* . .	270	3.0	29.0	16.0	m.q.	235	m.q.
mousse, Amaretto *(Duncan Hines Tiarra)*	270	3.0	29.0	16.0	m.q.	230	m.q.

Food and Measure	cal.	prot. (gms)	carbo. (gms)	fat (gms)	chol. (mgs)	sod. (mgs)	fiber (gms)
pudding (Betty Crocker Classics), 1/6 cake	230	3.0	44.0	5.0	m.q.	250	m.q.
Swiss (Duncan Hines)	280	4.0	33.0	15.0	m.q.	375	m.q.
w/chocolate frosting (Pillsbury Micro-wave), 1/8 cake	300	2.0	35.0	17.0	m.q.	310	m.q.
w/vanilla frosting (Pillsbury Micro-wave), 1/8 cake	300	2.0	36.0	17.0	m.q.	300	m.q.
chocolate chip:							
(Betty Crocker Supermoist) . . .	280	3.0	36.0	14.0	55	320	m.q.
(Pillsbury Plus) . .	270	3.0	33.0	14.0	m.q.	290	m.q.
chocolate (Betty Crocker Supermoist) . . .	260	4.0	34.0	12.0	55	400	m.q.
chocolate macaroon (Pillsbury Bundt), 1/16 cake	240	3.0	36.0	10.0	m.q.	300	m.q.
cinnamon:							
(Streusel Swirl), 1/16 cake	260	3.0	38.0	11.0	m.q.	200	m.q.
(Streusel Swirl Mi-crowave), 1/8 cake	240	2.0	33.0	11.0	m.q.	180	m.q.
cinnamon pecan streusel (Betty Crocker MicroRave), 1/6 cake	290	3.0	39.0	13.0	45	210	m.q.
coffee:							
(Aunt Jemima Easy), 1 serving	156	2.1	27.1	4.4	1	279	.7 d
apple cinnamon (Pillsbury), 1/8 cake	240	3.0	40.0	7.0	m.q.	150	m.q.

Food and Measure	cal.	prot. (gms)	carbo. (gms)	fat (gms)	chol. (mgs)	sod. (mgs)	fiber (gms)
Cake mix (cont.)							
devil's food:							
(Betty Crocker Supermoist) . . .	260	4.0	35.0	12.0	55	450	m.q.
(Duncan Hines) . .	280	4.0	33.0	15.0	m.q.	375	m.q.
(Pillsbury Plus) . .	270	4.0	32.0	14.0	m.q.	370	m.q.
w/chocolate frosting (Betty Crocker MicroRave), 1/6 cake	310	2.0	37.0	17.0	35	250	m.q.
gingerbread:							
(Betty Crocker Classic), 1/9 cake . .	220	3.0	35.0	7.0	30	330	m.q.
(Dromedary), 2" sq.	100	1.0	19.0	2.0	n.a.	190	m.q.
golden vanilla:							
(Betty Crocker Supermoist) . . .	280	3.0	36.0	14.0	55	270	m.q.
w/rainbow chip frosting (Betty Crocker MicroRave), 1/6 cake	320	2.0	40.0	17.0	35	230	m.q.
lemon:							
(Betty Crocker Supermoist) . . .	260	3.0	36.0	11.0	55	280	m.q.
(Duncan Hines Supreme)	260	3.0	36.0	11.0	m.q.	285	m.q.
(Pillsbury Bundt Tunnel of Lemon), 1/16 cake	270	2.0	45.0	9.0	m.q.	300	m.q.
(Pillsbury Microwave), 1/8 cake	220	2.0	23.0	13.0	m.q.	180	m.q.
(Pillsbury Plus) . .	250	3.0	34.0	11.0	m.q.	290	m.q.
(Streusel Swirl), 1/16 cake	270	3.0	39.0	11.0	m.q.	340	m.q.
chiffon (Betty Crocker Classic)	200	4.0	36.0	5.0	m.q.	200	m.q.

Food and Measure	cal.	prot. (gms)	carbo. (gms)	fat (gms)	chol. (mgs)	sod. (mgs)	fiber (gms)
double supreme *(Pillsbury Microwave)*, 1/8 cake	300	2.0	40.0	15.0	m.q.	210	m.q.
pudding *(Betty Crocker Classics)*, 1/6 cake	230	2.0	45.0	5.0	m.q.	270	m.q.
w/lemon frosting *(Pillsbury MicroRave)*, 1/6 cake	300	2.0	37.0	16.0	45	250	m.q.
marble *(Betty Crocker Supermoist)*	250	2.0	35.0	11.0	55	290	m.q.
pineapple:							
(Duncan Hines Supreme)	260	3.0	36.0	11.0	m.q.	285	m.q.
cream *(Pillsbury Bundt)*, 1/16 cake	260	2.0	41.0	9.0	m.q.	300	m.q.
upside-down *(Betty Crocker Classic)*, 1/9 cake	250	2.0	39.0	10.0	40	210	m.q.
pound:							
(Dromedary), 1/2″ slice	150	2.0	21.0	6.0	n.a.	160	m.q.
(Martha White), 1/10 cake	120	2.0	19.0	4.0	8	110	m.q.
golden *(Betty Crocker Classic)*	200	2.0	28.0	9.0	35	170	m.q.
rainbow chip *(Betty Crocker Supermoist)*	250	3.0	34.0	11.0	55	320	m.q.
sour cream:							
chocolate *(Betty Crocker Supermoist)* . . .	260	3.0	35.0	12.0	55	430	m.q.
white *(Betty Crocker Supermoist)* . . .	180	3.0	36.0	3.0	0	300	m.q.
spice:							
(Betty Crocker Supermoist) . . .	260	3.0	35.0	11.0	55	320	m.q.

Food and Measure	cal.	prot. (gms)	carbo. (gms)	fat (gms)	chol. (mgs)	sod. (mgs)	fiber (gms)
Cake mix, spice *(cont.)*							
(Duncan Hines) . .	260	3.0	36.0	11.0	m.q.	285	m.q.
strawberry:							
(Duncan Hines Supreme)	260	3.0	36.0	11.0	m.q.	285	m.q.
(Pillsbury Plus) . .	260	3.0	37.0	11.0	m.q.	300	m.q.
vanilla, French							
(Duncan Hines) . .	260	3.0	36.0	11.0	m.q.	285	m.q.
white:							
(Betty Crocker Supermoist) . . .	240	3.0	37.0	· 9.0	0	250	m.q.
(Duncan Hines) . .	250	3.0	36.0	10.0	m.q.	260	m.q.
(Pillsbury Plus) . .	240	3.0	35.0	10.0	n.a.	290	m.q.
yellow:							
(Betty Crocker Supermoist) . . .	260	3.0	36.0	11.0	55	300	m.q.
(Duncan Hines) . .	260	3.0	36.0	11.0	m.q.	285	m.q.
(Pillsbury Microwave), 1/8 cake	220	2.0	23.0	13.0	m.q.	170	m.q.
(Pillsbury Plus) . .	260	3.0	36.0	12.0	m.q.	300	m.q.
butter (Betty Crocker Supermoist) . . .	260	3.0	37.0	11.0	75	350	m.q.
w/chocolate frosting (Betty Crocker MicroRave), 1/6 cake	300	2.0	36.0	16.0	35	210	m.q.
w/chocolate frosting (Pillsbury Microwave), 1/8 cake	300	2.0	36.0	17.0	m.q.	220	m.q.
Calves liver, see "Liver, veal"							
Candy, 1 oz., except as noted:							
almond, candy coated (Brach's Jordan Almonds)	120	2.0	23.0	2.0	n.a.	0	m.q.
(Baby Ruth)	130	2.0	18.0	6.0	n.a.	60	m.q.

Food and Measure	cal.	prot. (gms)	carbo. (gms)	fat (gms)	chol. (mgs)	sod. (mgs)	fiber (gms)
(Boyer Smoothie),							
.5-oz. pkg.	75	2.5	12.5	7.5	n.a.	n.a.	n.a.
(Brach Royals)	100	1.0	20.0	2.0	n.a.	60	n.a.
bridge mix *(Brach's)*	130	1.0	19.0	6.0	n.a.	40	m.q.
(Butterfinger)	130	2.0	19.0	6.0	n.a.	60	m.q.
butterscotch *(Callard & Bowser)*	115	0	.9	.1	n.a.	tr.	(0)
candy cane:							
(Brach's)	110	0	27.0	0	0	10	0
(Spangler), 1 piece	60	<1.0	14.0	<1.0	0	0	0
caramel:							
(Brach's Milk Maid)	110	1.0	22.0	2.0	n.a.	70	(0)
(Kraft), 1 piece . .	35	0	6.0	1.0	0	20	(0)
(Sugar Babies), 5/8-oz. pkg. . . .	180	1.0	40.0	2.0	n.a.	85	(0)
(Sugar Daddy), 3/8-oz. pop . . .	150	1.0	33.0	1.0	n.a.	85	(0)
chocolate *(Brach's* Milk Maid)	110	1.0	20.0	3.0	n.a.	55	(0)
chocolate coated *(Pom Poms)* . .	100	1.0	15.0	3.0	n.a.	70	(0)
chocolate coated *(Rolo)*, 1.93 oz. or 8 pieces	270	3.0	37.0	12.0	15	110	(0)
chocolate coated, w/cookies *(Twix)*, 2-oz. piece . . .	140	2.0	19.0	7.0	n.a.	60	m.q.
w/peanut, chocolate coated *(Oh Henry!)*, 2 oz. . .	280	6.0	32.0	14.0	n.a.	85	m.q.
cherry:							
chocolate cream *(Brach's)*	110	1.0	21.0	2.0	n.a.	20	m.q.
dark/milk chocolate coated *(Brach's)*	110	1.0	22.0	2.0	n.a.	20	m.q.
chocolate:							
(Brach's Jots) . . .	130	1.0	21.0	5.0	n.a.	30	m.q.

Food and Measure	cal.	prot. (gms)	carbo. (gms)	fat (gms)	chol. (mgs)	sod. (mgs)	fiber (gms)
Candy, chocolate (cont.)							
·/almonds (Hershey's Golden Almond), 1.6 oz., 1/2 bar	260	5.0	20.0	17.0	5	35	m.q.
w/almonds (Hershey's Solitaires), 1.6 oz., 1/2 bar	260	6.0	20.0	17.0	5	25	m.q.
candy coated (Holidays)	140	2.0	19.0	6.0	n.a.	40	m.q.
candy coated (M&M's), 1.69 oz.	250	3.0	34.0	12.0	n.a.	70	m.q.
w/caramel (Caramello), 1.6 oz.	220	3.0	28.0	11.0	10	60	m.q.
chips, see "Chocolate, baking"							
cream (Callard & Bowser)	120	<.1	.8	.1	n.a.	0	m.q.
dark, sweet (Hershey's Special Dark), 1.45 oz.	220	3.0	25.0	12.0	0	5	m.q.
Easter eggs, in foil (Brach's)	150	2.0	17.0	8.0	n.a.	25	m.q.
w/peanuts, candy coated (M&M's), 1.74 oz.	250	6.0	29.0	13.0	n.a.	55	m.q.
white, w/almonds (Nestlé Alpine), 1.25 oz.	210	3.0	17.0	14.0	n.a.	35	m.q.
chocolate, milk:							
(Brach's Stars) . .	150	2.0	17.0	8.0	n.a.	30	m.q.
(Hershey's), 1.55 oz.	240	4.0	25.0	14.0	10	40	m.q.
(Hershey's Kisses), 1.46 oz., 9 pieces	220	3.0	23.0	13.0	10	35	m.q.
(Nabisco Stars) . .	160	2.0	19.0	8.0	n.a.	35	m.q.
(Nestlé), 1.45 oz.	220	3.0	25.0	13.0	n.a.	25	m.q.

Food and Measure	cal.	prot. (gms)	carbo. (gms)	fat (gms)	chol. (mgs)	sod. (mgs)	fiber (gms)
w/almonds (Hershey's), 1.45 oz.	230	5.0	20.0	14.0	15	55	m.q.
w/almonds (Nestlé), 1.45 oz.	230	4.0	22.0	14.0	n.a.	25	m.q.
w/crisps (Krackel), 1.55 oz.	230	3.0	27.0	13.0	10	80	m.q.
w/crisps (Nestlé Crunch), 1.4 oz.	210	3.0	26.0	10.0	n.a.	35	m.q.
w/crisps and peanuts (Nestlé 100 Grand), 1.5 oz.	200	2.0	31.0	8.0	n.a.	55	m.q.
w/fruit and nuts (Chunky), 1.4 oz.	210	4.0	22.0	12.0	n.a.	20	m.q.
w/peanuts (Brach's Peanut Cluster)	150	3.0	15.0	9.0	n.a.	25	m.q.
w/peanuts (Mr. Goodbar), 1.75 oz.	290	7.0	23.0	19.0	15	20	m.q.
w/pecan and caramel (Demet's Turtles), 1 piece . .	90	1.0	10.0	5.0	n.a.	15	m.q.
cinnamon:							
(Brach's Disks) . .	110	0	27.0	0	0	15	0
(Brach's Imperials)	110	0	27.0	0	0	5	0
coconut, chocolate coated:							
(Mounds), 1.9 oz.	260	2.0	31.0	14.0	0	85	m.q.
(Sunbelt Macaroo), 2 oz.	288	3.0	33.0	16.0	<1	75	m.q.
dark/milk chocolate (Bounty), 1.05 oz.	150	1.0	18.0	8.0	n.a.	50	m.q.
w/almonds (Almond Joy), 1.76 oz. . .	250	3.0	28.0	14.0	0	70	m.q.
coconut, Neapolitan (Brach's)	120	1.0	24.0	2.0	n.a.	40	m.q.
coffee flavor (Brach's)	120	0	25.0	2.0	n.a.	35	0
corn, candy:							
Indian (Brach's) . .	100	0	26.0	0	0	75	0

Food and Measure	cal.	prot. (gms)	carbo. (gms)	fat (gms)	chol. (mgs)	sod. (mgs)	fiber (gms)
Candy, corn, candy *(cont.)*							
three color *(Brach's)*	100	0	26.0	0	n.a.	95	0
cough drops, 1 piece:							
(Beech-Nut)	10	0	3.0	0	0	0	0
(Halls Cough Tablets)	15	tr.	3.7	tr.	0	tr.	0
cremes, chocolate coated, 1 piece:							
(Spangler Opera Creme Chocolate Drop)	80	<1.0	15.0	2.0	0	40	m.q.
caramel w/nuts *(Spangler* Peanut Cluster)	100	2.0	11.0	6.0	0	30	m.q.
cherry creme w/ nuts *(Spangler* Peanut Cluster)	110	2.0	12.0	5.0	0	20	m.q.
maple creme w/ nuts *(Spangler* Peanut Cluster)	110	2.0	12.0	5.0	0	15	m.q.
mint, dark chocolate coated *(Spangler Bittersweets)* . .	80	<1.0	14.0	2.0	0	25	m.q.
fudge w/nuts *(Spangler* Peanut Cluster)	140	2.0	17.0	6.0	0	25	m.q.
fudge w/nuts *(Spangler* Pecan Cluster)	140	1.0	18.0	7.0	0	40	m.q.
vanilla creme w/ nuts *(Spangler* Peanut Cluster)	110	2.0	13.0	5.0	0	20	m.q.
fruit flavored, all flavors:							
(Brach's Fruit Bunch)	90	0	23.0	0	0	20	0
(Skittles), 2.3 oz.	265	0	60.0	3.0	0	35	0

Food and Measure	cal.	prot. (gms)	carbo. (gms)	fat (gms)	chol. (mgs)	sod. (mgs)	fiber (gms)
chews (Bonkers!), 1 piece	20	0	5.0	0	0	0	0
chews (Starburst), 2.07 oz.	240	0	48.0	5.0	0	30	0
fudge:							
(Kraft Fudgies), 1 piece	35	0	6.0	1.0	0	20	m.q.
chocolate cheese or mint w/walnuts (Woodys)	120	2.0	18.0	4.0	5	25	m.q.
maple walnut (Woodys)	120	1.0	19.0	4.0	5	25	m.q.
granola bar, see "Granola and cereal bars"							
gum, chewing, all flavors, 1 piece, except as noted:							
(Beech-Nut)	10	0	2.0	0	0	0	0
(Big Red/Freedent/ Juicy Fruit) . . .	<10	0	2.3	0	0	0	0
(Care*Free)	8	0	2.0	0	0	0	0
(Chewels)	8	tr.	2.0	tr.	0	tr.	0
(Clorets Stick) . . .	9	tr.	2.3	tr.	0	tr.	0
(Dentyne)	6	tr.	1.5	tr.	0	tr.	0
(Dentyne Sugarless)	5	tr.	1.1	tr.	0	tr.	0
(Doublemint/ Wrigley's Spearmint)	<10	0	2.3	0	0	0	0
(Extra)	8	0	0	0	0	0	0
(Freshen-Up) . . .	13	tr.	3.1	tr.	0	tr.	0
(Sticklets)	7	tr.	1.9	tr.	0	tr.	0
bubble (Bubble Yum)	25	0	7.0	0	0	0	0
bubble (Bubblicious)	25	tr.	6.2	tr.	0	tr.	0
bubble (Care*Free)	10	0	2.0	0	0	0	0
bubble (Hubba Bubba)	23	0	5.8	0	0	0	0

Food and Measure	cal.	prot. (gms)	carbo. (gms)	fat (gms)	chol. (mgs)	sod. (mgs)	fiber (gms)
Candy, gum *(cont.)*							
candy coated (*Beechies*) . . .	6	0	2.0	0	0	0	0
candy coated (*Chiclets*)	6	tr.	1.5	tr.	0	tr.	0
candy coated (*Chiclets* Tiny), 1 pkg.	8	tr.	<.1	tr.	0	tr.	0
candy coated (*Clorets*)	6	tr.	1.5	tr.	0	tr.	0
hard, 1 piece, except as noted:							
all fruit flavors (*Life Savers*)	8	0	2.0	0	0	0	0
butter creme mint (*Life Savers*) . .	8	0	2.0	0	0	5	0
butter rum or butterscotch (*Life Savers*)	8	0	2.0	0	0	10	0
cinnamon (*Life Savers* Cin-O-Mon)	8	0	2.0	0	0	0	0
filled, assorted (*Brach's*)	110	0	27.0	0	0	15	n.a.
mint, except butter creme (*Life Savers*)	8	0	2.0	0	0	0	0
root beer (*Life Savers*)	8	0	2.0	0	0	0	0
(*Heath Bits'O Brickle*), 3 oz.	448	1.0	50.0	28.0	n.a.	472	m.q.
(*Heath Soft'n Crunchy Bar*), 2 pieces, 1 3/16 oz.	190	1.0	19.0	12.0	n.a.	85	n.a.
honey (*Bit-O-Honey*), 1.7 oz.	200	1.0	39.0	4.0	n.a.	125	n.a.
(*Hot Tamales*), 1 piece	9	<.1	2.1	tr.	0	1	0

Food and Measure	cal.	prot. (gms)	carbo. (gms)	fat (gms)	chol. (mgs)	sod. (mgs)	fiber (gms)
jellied and gummed:							
(Brach's Gummi Bears/Worms)	100	2.0	22.0	0	0	15	0
(Brach's Jube or Rainbow Bears)	100	0	24.0	0	0	10	0
beans (Brach's) . .	100	0	26.0	0	0	10	0
beans (Just Born Teenee Beanee Gourmet), 1 piece	4	tr.	1.1	tr.	0	<1	0
cherry, sour (Brach's Jels) . .	100	0	26.0	0	0	10	0
cherry hearts (Brach's Jube)	100	0	26.0	0	0	20	0
cinnamon (Brach's Cinnamon Bears)	80	0	21.0	0	0	10	0
eggs (Just Born Petite), 1 piece . .	4	tr.	1.1	tr.	0	<1	0
eggs (Rodda), 1 piece	7	<.1	1.7	tr.	0	1	0
juicy (Callard & Bowser)	90	0	.8	0	0	tr.	0
(Jujyfruits)	100	<1.0	25.0	<1.0	0	n.a.	0
mint, assorted (Brach's)	100	0	26.0	0	0	0	0
spearmint leaves (Brach's)	100	0	24.0	0	0	10	0
(Jolly Joes), 1 piece	9	<.1	2.1	tr.	0	1	0
lemon drops (Brach's Sparkles) . . .	110	0	28.0	0	0	10	0
licorice:							
(Brach's Red Laces/ Twin Twists)	100	2.0	22.0	0	0	10	0
(Brach's Twists) . .	100	2.0	22.0	1.0	0	50	0
(Pearson's Licorice Nip)	120	1.0	23.0	3.0	0	70	0
candy coated (Good & Fruity)	106	.6	25.7	.1	0	8	0

Food and Measure	cal.	prot. (gms)	carbo. (gms)	fat (gms)	chol. (mgs)	sod. (mgs)	fiber (gms)
Candy, licorice *(cont.)*							
candy coated *(Good & Plenty)*	106	1.0	25.9	<.1	0	52	0
cherry *(Y&S Bites)*	100	1.0	23.0	1.0	0	85	0
cherry *(Y&S Nibs)*	100	1.0	23.0	1.0	0	80	0
strawberry *(Y&S Twizzlers)*	100	1.0	23.0	1.0	0	95	0
lollipop, all flavors:							
(Brach's Pops) . .	110	0	27.0	0	0	10	0
(Life Savers), 1 piece	45	0	11.0	0	0	10	0
(Spangler Dum Dums), 1 piece	25	<1.0	6.0	<1.0	0	0	0
(Spangler Saf-T-Pops), 1 piece	45	<1.0	11.0	<1.0	0	0	0
all flavors, except chocolate *(Tootsie Pop)*	111	.1	26.4	.6	tr.	1	(0)
chocolate *(Tootsie Pop)*	110	.1	26.2	.6	tr.	2	(0)
bubble gum center *(Spangler Blo Bubble)*, 1 piece	57	<1.0	14.0	<1.0	0	5	0
lozenge *(Listerine)*, 1 piece	9	tr.	2.0	tr.	0	tr.	0
malted milk balls, chocolate coated							
(Brach's)	130	1.0	21.0	5.0	m.q.	40	m.q.
(Mars), 1.76-oz. bar	240	4.0	30.0	11.0	n.a.	85	m.q.
marshmallow:							
(Campfire), 2 large or 24 mini pieces	40	0	10.0	0	0	10	0
(Funmallows), 1 piece	30	0	7.0	0	0	15	0
(Kraft Jet-Puffed), 1 piece	25	0	6.0	0	0	10	0
cats *(Just Born)*, 1 piece	28	.2	6.7	<.1	n.a.	2	0

Food and Measure	cal.	prot. (gms)	carbo. (gms)	fat (gms)	chol. (mgs)	sod. (mgs)	fiber (gms)
coconut, toasted *(Just Born)*, 1 piece	30	.3	6.1	.6	n.a.	6	.7 d
cup *(Boyer Mallo Cup)*, .5-oz. pkg.	71	1.0	15.0	5.0	n.a.	n.a.	0
eggs *(Brach's)* . .	100	0	25.0	0	0	5	0
eggs *(Just Born)*, 1 large	111	.7	26.8	.1	n.a.	8	0
eggs *(Just Born)*, 1 small	28	.2	6.7	<.1	n.a.	2	0
miniature *(Kraft)*, 10 pieces	18	0	4.0	0	0	5	0
w/peanuts *(Spangler Circus Peanuts)*	110	<1.0	26.0	<1.0	0	5	0
(Mike & Ikes), 1 piece	9	<.1	2.1	tr.	n.a.	1	0
(Milky Way), 2.15 oz.	280	3.0	42.0	11.0	n.a.	150	m.q.
(Milky Way Dark), 1.76 oz.	220	1.0	36.0	8.0	n.a.	115	m.q.
mint:							
(Brach's Coolers/ Starlight)	110	0	27.0	0	0	15	0
(Brach's Creme de Menthe)	150	2.0	16.0	9.0	n.a.	20	0
(Brach's Jots/ Pearls)	120	0	25.0	2.0	n.a.	10	0
(Brach's Kentucky Mints)	110	0	27.0	0	0	0	0
(Certs Sugar Free), 1 piece	6	tr.	1.6	tr.	0	tr.	0
(Mint Meltaway), .33-oz. piece . .	50	0	5.0	3.0	n.a.	10	0
all flavors *(Breath Savers)*, 1 piece	8	0	2.0	0	0	0	0
assorted *(Brach's Dessert Mints)*	110	0	27.0	0	0	0	0
butter or party *(Kraft)*, 1 piece	8	0	2.0	0	0	0	0

Food and Measure	cal.	prot. (gms)	carbo. (gms)	fat (gms)	chol. (mgs)	sod. (mgs)	fiber (gms)
Candy, mint *(cont.)*							
chocolate coated *(Junior Mints)* . .	120	1.0	24.0	3.0	n.a.	10	n.a.
chocolate coated, regular, creme or thin *(Brach's)* . .	110	0	24.0	2.0	n.a.	10	(0)
clear *(Clorets)*, 1 piece	8	tr.	2.1	tr.	0	tr.	0
mini *(Certs Sugar Free)*, 1 piece . .	1	tr.	.4	tr.	0	tr.	0
parfait *(Brach's)* . .	150	2.0	16.0	9.0	n.a.	35	(0)
patty, chocolate coated *(York Peppermint Patty)*, 1.5 oz.	180	1.0	34.0	4.0	0	20	m.q.
pressed *(Clorets)*, 1 piece	6	tr.	1.6	tr.	0	tr.	0
wafer, chocolate coated *(After Eight)*, 1 piece	35	0	6.0	1.0	n.a.	0	(0)
(Munch), 1.42-oz. bar	220	6.0	19.0	14.0	n.a.	110	(0)
(Necco Sky Bar), 1.5-oz. bar	196	1.9	31.5	7.1	n.a.	57	0
nonpareils:							
(Nestlé Sno-Caps)	140	1.0	21.0	6.0	n.a.	0	m.q.
dark chocolate *(Brach's)*	140	1.0	20.0	6.0	n.a.	20	m.q.
nougat:							
(Brach's)	100	0	24.0	1.0	0	35	m.q.
chocolate coated, all flavors *(Charleston Chew!)*	120	1.0	22.0	3.0	n.a.	40	m.q.
nut *(Brach's Nut Goodies)*	130	2.0	21.0	4.0	n.a.	10	m.q.
orange:							
(Brach's Orangettes)	100	0	24.0	0	0	20	0

Food and Measure	cal.	prot. (gms)	carbo. (gms)	fat (gms)	chol. (mgs)	sod. (mgs)	fiber (gms)
sticks, chocolate coated *(Brach's)*	110	1.0	23.0	2.0	n.a.	25	m.q.
peanut:							
(Brach's Jots) . . .	140	3.0	18.0	6.0	n.a.	25	m.q.
butter toffee *(Flavor House)*	150	4.0	17.0	7.0	n.a.	90	m.q.
chocolate coated *(Goobers)*, 1³/₈ oz.	220	6.0	19.0	13.0	n.a.	15	m.q.
chocolate coated *(Nabisco)*	160	4.0	14.0	9.0	n.a.	15	m.q.
filled *(Brach's)* . . .	110	1.0	25.0	1.0	n.a.	20	m.q.
French burnt *(Brach's)*	130	4.0	18.0	5.0	0	5	m.q.
peanut brittle *(Kraft)*	130	3.0	19.0	5.0	0	140	m.q.
peanut butter:							
(PB Max), 1.48 oz.	240	5.0	20.0	16.0	n.a.	160	m.q.
candy coated *(Reese's Pieces)*, 1.85 oz.	260	8.0	32.0	11.0	5	90	m.q.
cup *(Boyer)*, .5-oz. pkg. . . .	75	2.5	12.0	7.5	n.a.	n.a.	m.q.
cup, chocolate coated *(Reese's)*, 1.8 oz.	280	6.0	26.0	17.0	10	180	m.q.
kisses *(Brach's)* . .	110	1.0	22.0	2.0	n.a.	135	m.q.
peanut caramel cluster *(Brach's)*	150	4.0	15.0	8.0	n.a.	50	m.q.
peanut parfait *(Brach's)*	160	3.0	14.0	10.0	n.a.	60	m.q.
popcorn, caramel coated:							
(Orville Redenbacher), 2.5 cups	240	2.0	29.0	14.0	0	90	m.q.
w/peanuts *(Cracker Jack)*	120	2.0	22.0	3.0	0	85	m.q.

Food and Measure	cal.	prot. (gms)	carbo. (gms)	fat (gms)	chol. (mgs)	sod. (mgs)	fiber (gms)
Candy *(cont.)*							
raisins, chocolate coated:							
(Nabisco)	130	1.0	21.0	5.0	n.a.	15	m.q.
(Raisinets), 1³⁄₈ oz.	180	2.0	28.0	6.0	n.a.	10	m.q.
raspberry filled (Brach's)	110	0	27.0	0	0	15	(0)
rock (Brach's Cut Rock)	110	0	27.0	0	0	10	0
(Rolaids), 1 piece . .	4	tr.	1.1	tr.	0	n.a.	0
(Snickers), 2.07 oz.	280	6.0	35.0	14.0	n.a.	160	m.q.
sour balls (Brach's)	110	0	27.0	0	0	15	0
spice (Brach's Spi-cettes)	100	0	26.0	0	0	15	0
straws, mint filled (Brach's)	110	0	26.0	1.0	0	10	0
taffy:							
all flavors (Brach's Salt Water Taffy)	100	0	24.0	1.0	0	30	0
all flavors, except banana, grape, and passion punch chews (Beich'sLaffyTaffy)	110	0	26.0	1.0	0	55	0
banana flavor chews (Beich's Laffy Taffy) . . .	120	0	26.0	1.0	0	55	0
grape flavor chews (Beich's Laffy Taffy)	110	0	26.0	1.0	0	60	0
passion punch fla-vor chews (Beich'sLaffyTaffy)	120	0	26.0	1.0	0	50	0
(3 Musketeers), 2.13 oz.	260	2.0	46.0	8.0	n.a.	120	m.q.
toffee:							
(Brach's)	110	1.0	23.0	2.0	0	80	0
(Callard & Bowser)	135	<.1	.7	.2	0	tr.	0

Food and Measure	cal.	prot. (gms)	carbo. (gms)	fat (gms)	chol. (mgs)	sod. (mgs)	fiber (gms)
(Kraft), 1 piece ..	30	0	5.0	1.0	0	20	0
(Skor), 1.4 oz.	220	2.0	22.0	14.0	25	125	n.a.
English *(Bits 'O Heath)*, 3 1/2 oz.	520	3.0	62.0	31.0	n.a.	390	m.q.
English *(Heath)*, 2 pieces, 1 3/16 oz.	180	1.0	20.0	11.0	n.a.	130	m.q.
(Tootsie Roll)	112	.3	22.8	2.5	tr.	6	(0)
wafer:							
assorted *(Necco)*, 2.02-oz. roll ...	225	.3	56.5	0	0	5	(0)
chocolate *(Necco)*, 2.02-oz. roll ...	226	.5	56.3	.1	0	5	(0)
bar, chocolate coated *(Kit Kat)*, 1.63 oz.	250	3.0	29.0	13.0	10	60	m.q.
Cane syrup:							
1 tbsp.	52	0	13.4	0	0	<1	0
Cannollini dinner, frozen:							
chicken *(Le Menu Light Style)*, 10 1/4 oz.	270	15.0	38.0	5.0	m.q.	590	m.q.
Cannollini entree, frozen:							
beef and pork, w/ mornay sauce *(Lean Cuisine)*, 9 5/8 oz.	260	17.0	25.0	10.0	45	950	m.q.
cheese:							
(Dining Lite), 9 oz.	310	19.0	38.0	9.0	70	650	m.q.
w/tomato sauce *(Lean Cuisine)*, 9 1/8 oz.	260	21.0	22.0	10.0	35	910	m.q.
Florentine *(Celentano)*, 12 oz.	350	21.0	48.0	8.0	n.a.	620	m.q.
Cantaloupe:							
pulp, cubed, 1/2 cup	29	.7	6.7	.2	0	7	.6 d
1/2 of 5"-diam. melon	94	2.3	22.3	.7	0	23	2.1 d

Food and Measure	cal.	prot. (gms)	carbo. (gms)	fat (gms)	chol. (mgs)	sod. (mgs)	fiber (gms)
Capacollo:							
(Hormel), 1 oz. . . .	80	5.0	0	6.0	m.q.	273	0
Capon, see "Chicken"							
Capon giblets, see "Chicken giblets"							
Carambola:							
1 medium, 4.7 oz. . .	42	.7	9.9	.4	0	2	1.5 d
cubed, 1/2 cup	23	.4	5.4	.2	0	1	.8 d
Caramel, see "Candy"							
Caramel topping:							
(Kraft), 1 tbsp.	60	1.0	13.0	0	0	45	0
flavored *(Smucker's),* 2 tbsp.	140	1.0	33.0	0	0	110	0
hot *(Smucker's),* 2 tbsp.	150	1.0	28.0	4.0	0	75	0
Caraway seed:							
1 tsp.	7	.4	1.1	.3	0	tr.	.3 c
Cardamom, 1 tsp.:							
ground *(Tone's)* . . .	6	.2	1.3	.1	0	<1	.2 d
seed *(Spice Islands)*	6	.2	1.3	.1	0	tr.	.2 c
Cardoon:							
raw, shredded, 1/2 cup	18	.6	4.4	.1	0	151	m.q.
boiled, drained, 4 oz.	25	.9	6.0	.1	0	200	m.q.
Carissa:							
1 medium, .8 oz. . .	12	.1	2.7	.3	0	1	.2 c
sliced, 1/2 cup	46	.4	10.2	1.0	0	2	.7 c
Carl's Jr., 1 serving:							
breakfast:							
bacon, 2 strips . .	50	3.0	0	4.0	8	200	0
English muffin w/ margarine	180	4.0	28.0	6.0	0	275	m.q.
French toast dips, w/out syrup . . .	480	8.0	54.0	25.0	54	576	m.q.
hash brown nuggets	170	2.0	20.0	9.0	10	350	m.q.
hot cakes w/marga- rine, w/out syrup	360	7.0	59.0	12.0	15	1190	m.q.

Food and Measure	cal.	prot. (gms)	carbo. (gms)	fat (gms)	chol. (mgs)	sod. (mgs)	fiber (gms)
sausage, 1 patty	190	7.0	1.0	17.0	25	275	0
scrambled eggs . .	120	9.0	2.0	9.0	245	105	0
Sunrise Sandwich, w/bacon	370	17.0	32.0	19.0	120	750	m.q.
Sunrise Sandwich, w/sausage . . .	500	22.0	31.0	32.0	165	990	m.q.
sandwiches:							
California Roast Beef 'n Swiss . .	360	31.0	43.0	8.0	130	1070	m.q.
Charbroiler BBQ Chicken Sandwich	320	28.0	40.0	5.0	50	955	m.q.
Charbroiler Chicken Club Sandwich	510	26.0	53.0	22.0	85	1165	m.q.
Country Fried Steak	610	25.0	54.0	33.0	45	1290	m.q.
Double Western Bacon Cheeseburger	890	42.0	61.0	53.0	145	1620	m.q.
Famous Star Hamburger	590	24.0	42.0	36.0	45	890	m.q.
fish fillet	550	22.0	58.0	26.0	90	945	m.q.
Happy Star hamburger	220	12.0	26.0	8.0	45	445	m.q.
Old Time Star hamburger	400	24.0	38.0	17.0	80	760	m.q.
Super Star hamburger	770	37.0	44.0	50.0	125	990	m.q.
Western Bacon Cheeseburger . .	630	33.0	49.0	33.0	105	1415	m.q.
potatoes:							
bacon and cheese	650	23.0	63.0	34.0	45	1820	m.q.
broccoli and cheese	470	15.0	61.0	17.0	10	690	m.q.
cheese	350	18.0	72.0	22.0	40	785	m.q.
Fiesta	550	25.0	60.0	23.0	40	1230	m.q.
sour cream and chive	350	8.0	49.0	13.0	10	140	m.q.
salad-to-go:							
chef	180	19.0	11.0	7.0	63	581	m.q.

Food and Measure	cal.	prot. (gms)	carbo. (gms)	fat (gms)	chol. (mgs)	sod. (mgs)	fiber (gms)
Carl's Jr., salad-to-go (cont.)							
chicken	206	23.0	12.0	8.0	83	453	m.q.
garden	46	2.0	4.0	2.0	7	57	m.q.
taco	356	29.0	18.0	19.0	99	690	m.q.
salad dressing, 1 oz.:							
blue cheese	151	1.0	0	15.0	18	255	n.a.
French, reduced							
calorie	38	0	5.0	2.0	0	292	n.a.
house	110	1.0	2.0	11.0	10	170	n.a.
Italian	120	0	1.0	13.0	0	210	n.a.
Thousand Island	110	0	4.0	11.0	5	200	n.a.
side dishes:							
fries, regular	360	8.0	43.0	17.0	15	626	m.q.
onion rings	310	4.0	38.0	15.0	10	260	m.q.
zucchini	300	5.0	33.0	16.0	10	480	m.q.
soup, 6.6 oz.:							
Boston clam chow-							
der	140	6.0	12.0	8.0	22	861	m.q.
broccoli, cream of	140	7.0	14.0	6.0	22	845	m.q.
chicken noodle . .	80	4.0	11.0	1.0	14	605	m.q.
Lumber Jack Mix							
vegetable	70	2.0	10.0	3.0	3	807	m.q.
bakery products:							
blueberry muffin . .	256	4.0	40.0	7.0	34	360	m.q.
bran muffin	220	4.0	34.0	6.0	50	300	m.q.
brownie, fudge . .	597	8.0	88.0	27.0	tr.	295	m.q.
cinnamon roll . . .	459	7.0	70.0	16.0	tr.	226	m.q.
chocolate chip							
cookie	327	3.0	41.0	17.0	3	170	m.q.
danish (varieties)	519	7.0	73.0	21.0	tr.	230	m.q.
shake, regular	353	11.0	61.0	7.0	17	255	(0)
Carob drink mix:							
powder, 3 tsp.	45	.2	11.2	tr.	0	12	.2 c
Carob flour:							
1 cup	185	4.8	91.6	.7	0	36	10.9 d
Carp, meat only:							
raw, 1 lb.	574	80.9	0	25.4	298	223	0
raw, 1 oz.	36	5.1	0	1.6	19	14	0

Food and Measure	cal.	prot. (gms)	carbo. (gms)	fat (gms)	chol. (mgs)	sod. (mgs)	fiber (gms)
baked, broiled, or microwaved, 4 oz. . . .	184	25.9	0	8.1	95	71	0
Carrot:							
fresh:							
raw, whole, 7 1/2" long, 2.8 oz. . .	31	.7	7.3	.1	0	25	2.3 d
raw, shredded, 1/2 cup	24	.6	5.6	.1	0	19	1.8 d
boiled, drained, sliced, 1/2 cup . .	35	.9	8.2	.1	0	52	1.5 d
canned, 1/2 cup:							
all cuts *(Del Monte)*	30	0	7.0	0	0	265	m.q.
all cuts *(Stokely)*	35	1.0	7.0	0	0	300	m.q.
all cuts *(Stokely* No Salt/Sugar) . . .	35	1.0	7.0	0	0	35	m.q.
whole, baby *(Allens)*	30	1.0	6.0	<1.0	0	240	m.q.
whole, tiny *(S&W Fancy)*	30	1.0	7.0	0	0	240	m.q.
sliced, w/liquid . .	28	.8	6.2	.2	0	297	1.4 d
sliced, drained . .	17	.5	4.0	.1	0	176	1.1 d
sliced, diced or julienne *(S&W Fancy)*	30	1.0	7.0	0	0	240	m.q.
sliced, small, medium or large *(Allens)*	30	1.0	7.0	<1.0	0	250	m.q.
diced *(Allens)* . . .	30	1.0	5.0	<1.0	0	190	m.q.
frozen, 3.3 oz., except as noted:							
boiled, drained, sliced, 1/2 cup	26	.9	6.0	.1	0	43	1.3 d
(Birds Eye Deluxe Parisienne), 2.6 oz.	30	1.0	7.0	0	0	35	2.0 d
(Seabrook)	40	1.0	9.0	0	0	44	1.0 c
whole, baby *(Birds Eye* Deluxe) . . .	40	1.0	9.0	0	0	45	2.0 d

Food and Measure	cal.	prot. (gms)	carbo. (gms)	fat (gms)	chol. (mgs)	sod. (mgs)	fiber (gms)
Carrot, frozen, 3.3 oz., except as noted: *(cont.)*							
whole, baby *(Stokely Singles),*							
3 oz.	35	1.0	8.0	0	0	50	m.q.
sliced *(Birds Eye),*							
3.2 oz.	35	1.0	8.0	0	0	40	1.0 d
sliced *(Frosty Acres)*	40	1.0	9.0	0	0	44	1.0 c
Carrot, combina- tions, frozen:							
baby, sweet peas and pearl onions *(Birds Eye Deluxe),* 3.3 oz.	50	2.0	10.0	0	0	60	2.0 d
Carrot chips, 1 oz.:							
(Hain)	150	2.0	16.0	9.0	0	160	m.q.
(Hain No Salt)	150	2.0	16.0	7.0	0	30	m.q.
barbecue *(Hain)* . . .	140	2.0	16.0	8.0	0	160	m.q.
Carrot juice, canned:							
6 fl. oz.	73	1.7	17.1	.3	0	54	1.8 c
(Hain), 6 fl. oz.	80	1.0	17.0	0	0	170	m.q.
Casaba:							
1/10 of 73/4″ × 2″							
melon	43	1.5	10.2	.2	0	20	.8 c
pulp, cubed, 1/2 cup	23	.8	5.3	.1	0	10	.4 c
Cashew, 1 oz., except as noted:							
(Beer Nuts)	170	5.0	8.0	13.0	0	65	m.q.
dry-roasted:							
1 oz. or 18 medium	163	4.4	9.3	13.2	0	4	1.7 d
whole or halves,							
1 cup	787	21.0	44.8	63.5	0	21	7.8 d
unsalted *(Planters)*	160	5.0	9.0	13.0	0	0	m.q.
salted *(Planters)*	160	5.0	9.0	13.0	0	230	m.q.
honey-roasted:							
(Planters)	170	4.0	11.0	12.0	0	170	m.q.
w/peanuts *(Plant- ers)*	170	5.0	9.0	12.0	0	170	m.q.
oil-roasted:							
1 oz. or 18 medium	163	4.6	8.1	13.7	0	5	.4 c

Food and Measure	cal.	prot. (gms)	carbo. (gms)	fat (gms)	chol. (mgs)	sod. (mgs)	fiber (gms)
whole or halves,							
1 cup	748	21.0	37.1	62.7	0	22	1.7 c
unsalted, halves							
(Planters)	170	5.0	8.0	14.0	0	0	m.q.
salted (Planters)	170	5.0	8.0	14.0	0	135	m.q.
Cashew butter:							
1 oz.	167	5.0	7.8	14.0	0	4	.2 c
raw (Hain), 2 tbsp.	190	6.0	8.0	15.0	0	5	m.q.
toasted (Hain), 2 tbsp.	190	6.0	8.0	16.0	0	5	m.q.
Cassava:							
trimmed, 1 oz.	34	.9	7.6	.1	0	2	.7 c
Catfish, channel,							
meat only:							
raw, 1 lb.	527	82.5	0	19.3	263	286	0
raw, 1 oz.	33	5.2	0	1.2	16	18	0
Catfish, frozen:							
(Delta Pride), 4 oz.	132	18.0	4.8	4.9	62	<1	0
breaded (Mrs. Paul's							
Light), 1 piece . . .	250	17.0	24.0	10.0	m.q.	389	m.q.
ocean (Booth), 4 oz.	115	20.0	0	20.0	m.q.	85	0
Catjang:							
boiled, 1/2 cup	100	7.0	17.5	.6	0	16	1.4 c
Catsup, 1 tbsp.:							
(Hain Natural)	16	0	4.0	0	0	155	m.q.
(Heinz)	16	0	4.0	0	0	210	m.q.
(Heinz Lite)	8	0	2.0	0	0	115	m.q.
(Hunt's)	16	0	4.0	0	0	170	m.q.
(Stokely)	20	0	5.0	0	0	190	m.q.
Cauliflower:							
fresh:							
raw, 3 flowerets . .	13	1.1	2.8	.1	0	8	1.3 d
raw, 1" pieces,							
1/2 cup	12	1.0	2.5	.1	0	7	1.2 d
boiled, drained, 1"							
pieces, 1/2 cup	15	1.2	2.9	.1	0	4	1.4 d
frozen:							
boiled, drained, 1"							
pieces, 1/2 cup	17	1.5	3.4	.2	0	16	.7 c

Food and Measure	cal.	prot. (gms)	carbo. (gms)	fat (gms)	chol. (mgs)	sod. (mgs)	fiber (gms)
Cauliflower, frozen *(cont.)*							
(Birds Eye), 3.3 oz.	25	2.0	5.0	0	0	20	2.0 d
(Frosty Acres), 3.3 oz.	25	2.0	5.0	0	0	16	1.0 c
(Stokely Singles), 3 oz.	20	2.0	4.0	0	0	20	m.q.
cuts *(Green Giant)*, 1/2 cup	12	1.0	3.0	0	0	25	1.4 d
frozen, in cheese sauce:							
(Birds Eye Combinations), 5 oz. . . .	130	5.0	12.0	7.0	10	560	2.0 d
(Green Giant), 5.5 oz.	80	3.0	14.0	2.0	n.a.	690	3.0 d
(Stokely Singles), 4 oz.	70	4.0	7.0	3.0	15	170	m.q.
cheddar *(The Budget Gourmet)*, 5 oz.	110	6.0	10.0	5.0	25	300	m.q.
cheese flavor sauce *(Green Giant)*, 1/2 cup	60	2.0	10.0	2.0	n.a.	500	2.4 d
Cauliflower combinations, frozen:							
broccoli and carrots, in cheese sauce *(Freezer Queen)*, 5 oz.	60	2.0	10.0	1.0	n.a.	360	m.q.
baby carrots and snow pea pods *(Birds Eye* Farm Fresh), 4 oz.	40	2.0	8.0	0	0	35	3.0 d
zucchini, carrots, red peppers *(Birds Eye* Farm Fresh), 4 oz.	30	2.0	6.0	0	0	25	2.0 d
Cavatelli, frozen:							
(Celentano), 3.2 oz.	250	10.0	52.0	1.0	n.a.	5	m.q.

Food and Measure	cal.	prot. (gms)	carbo. (gms)	fat (gms)	chol. (mgs)	sod. (mgs)	fiber (gms)
Caviar, granular:							
black or red, 1 oz. . .	71	6.9	1.1	5.0	165	420	0
black or red, 1 tbsp.	40	3.9	.6	2.9	94	240	0
Cayenne, see "Pepper"							
Celeriac, fresh:							
raw, 1/2 cup	31	1.2	7.2	.2	0	78	1.0 c
boiled, drained, 4 oz.	28	1.1	6.7	.2	0	69	.9 c
Celery:							
raw:							
71/2″-stalk, 1.6 oz.	6	.3	1.5	.1	0	35	.6 d
diced, 1/2 cup . . .	10	.5	2.2	.1	0	52	1.0 d
boiled, drained, diced,							
1/2 cup	13	.6	3.0	.1	0	68	.7 c
Celery, dried, 1 tsp.:							
flakes or seed							
(Tone's)	9	.4	.9	.5	0	4	.3 d
seed	8	.4	.8	.5	0	3	.2 c
Celery salt:							
(Tone's), 1 tsp. . . .	6	.3	.6	.4	0	1584	.2 d
Cellophane noodles, see "Noodles, Chinese"							
Celtus, raw:							
trimmed, 1 oz.	6	.2	1.0	.1	0	3	.1 c
Cereal, ready-to-eat, (see also specific grains), 1 oz., except as noted:							
bran:							
(All Bran)	70	4.0	22.0	1.0	0	260	10.0 d
(Bran Buds)	70	3.0	22.0	1.0	0	170	8.0 d
(Bran Chex)	90	2.0	24.0	0	0	200	4.0 d
(Kellogg's 40+ Bran Flakes) . .	90	3.0	23.0	0	0	220	5.0 d
(Kellogg's Heartwise) . . .	90	3.0	23.0	1.0	0	125	6.0 d

Food and Measure	cal.	prot. (gms)	carbo. (gms)	fat (gms)	chol. (mgs)	sod. (mgs)	fiber (gms)
Cereal, ready-to-eat, bran *(cont.)*							
(Nabisco 100% Bran)	70	3.0	22.0	2.0	0	190	10.0 d
(Post Natural Bran Flakes)	90	3.0	23.0	0	0	240	5.0 d
(Quaker Crunchy Bran)	89	2.0	22.6	1.3	0	316	5.2 d
apple spice or cinnamon *(Ralston Bran News)* . . .	100	2.0	23.0	0	0	160	3.0 d
extra fiber *(All Bran)*	50	3.0	22.0	1.0	0	140	14.0 d
w/fruit *(Fruitful Bran)* w/.3 oz. fruit	110	3.0	29.0	0	0	230	5.0 d
w/fruit and nuts *(Mueslix)*, w/.4 oz. fruit and nuts	140	3.0	32.0	2.0	0	140	4.0 d
w/raisins *(Kellogg's Raisin Bran)*, w/.4 oz. raisins	120	3.0	31.0	1.0	0	230	5.0 d
w/raisins *(Post Natural Raisin Bran)*, 1.4 oz.	120	3.0	31.0	1.0	0	200	6.0 d
w/raisins and nuts *(Raisin Nut Bran)*	110	3.0	20.0	3.0	0	140	2.5 d
corn:							
(Corn Chex)	110	2.0	25.0	0	0	310	m.q.
(Corn Pops)	110	1.0	26.0	0	0	90	m.q.
(Honeycomb) . . .	110	2.0	25.0	0	0	170	tr.d
(Kellogg's Corn Flakes)	100	2.0	24.0	0	0	250	1.0 d
(Kellogg's Frosted Flakes)	110	1.0	26.0	0	0	200	m.q.
(Nutri-Grain)	100	2.0	24.0	1.0	0	170	3.0 d
(Post Toasties) . .	110	2.0	24.0	0	0	310	tr.d
(Total Corn Flakes)	110	2.0	24.0	1.0	0	280	m.q.

Food and Measure	cal.	prot. (gms)	carbo. (gms)	fat (gms)	chol. (mgs)	sod. (mgs)	fiber (gms)
w/nuts and honey (Nut & Honey Crunch)	110	2.0	24.0	1.0	0	200	m.q.
granola:							
(C.W. Post Hearty)	130	2.0	21.0	4.0	0	80	tr.d
w/almonds (Sun Country 100% Natural)	130	3.1	18.8	5.3	0	11	1.4 d
banana almond (Sunbelt)	130	3.0	20.0	4.0	<1	25	m.q.
fruit and nut (Sunbelt)	120	3.0	19.0	5.0	<1	20	m.q.
w/raisins (Sun Country)	125	2.7	19.4	4.8	0	10	1.8 d
w/raisins and dates (Sun Country 100% Natural)	123	2.5	19.8	4.5	0	9	1.8 d
mixed grain and natural style:							
(Almond Delight)	110	2.0	23.0	2.0	0	200	1.0 d
(Crispix)	110	2.0	22.0	0	0	220	m.q.
(Crunchy Nut Ohls)	127	1.7	21.5	4.2	0	164	.9 d
(Double Chex) . . .	100	2.0	24.0	0	0	190	1.0 d
(Fiber One)	60	2.0	23.0	1.0	0	140	13.0 d
(Grape Nuts) . . .	110	3.0	23.0	0	0	170	3.0 d
(Grape Nuts Flakes)	100	3.0	23.0	1.0	0	160	3.0 d
(Heartland)	130	3.0	18.0	4.0	0	80	m.q.
(Honey Graham Chex)	110	1.0	25.0	1.0	0	180	m.q.
(Honey Graham Ohls)	122	1.4	22.6	3.2	0	217	.7 d
(Just Right)	100	3.0	23.0	1.0	0	190	2.0 d
(Nutri-Grain Nuggets)	100	3.0	23.0	1.0	0	170	3.0 d
(Product 19)	100	3.0	24.0	0	0	320	1.0 d
(Quaker 100% Natural)	127	3.3	18.0	5.5	0	14	2.0 d
(Special K)	110	6.0	20.0	0	0	230	m.q.

Food and Measure	cal.	prot. (gms)	carbo. (gms)	fat (gms)	chol. (mgs)	sod. (mgs)	fiber (gms)
Cereal, ready-to-eat, mixed grain and natural style *(cont.)*							
(Sunflakes Multi-Grain)	100	2.0	24.0	1.0	0	240	3.0 d
w/almonds *(Honey Bunches of Oats)*	120	2.0	22.0	3.0	0	160	1.0 d
w/almonds and raisins *(Nutri-Grain)*, w/.4 oz. nuts and fruit	140	3.0	31.0	2.0	0	220	3.0 d
apple and cinnamon *(Quaker 100% Natural)*	126	3.0	18.9	4.9	0	13	1.6 d
w/apples and raisins *(Apple Raisin Crisp)*, w/.3 oz. fruit	130	2.0	32.0	0	0	230	3.0 d
cinnamon raisin *(Nature Valley)*	120	2.0	20.0	4.0	0	90	1.0 d
coconut *(Heartland)*	130	3.0	18.0	5.0	0	80	m.q.
dates, raisins, walnuts, oat clusters *(Fruit & Fibre)*, 1.25 oz.	120	3.0	27.0	2.0	0	170	5.0 d
w/fruit and nuts *(Just Right)*, w/.3 oz. fruit and nuts	140	3.0	30.0	1.0	0	190	2.0 d
w/fruit and nuts *(Mueslix Five Grain)*, w/.45 oz. fruit and nuts . .	140	4.0	32.0	1.0	0	55	4.0 d
fruit and nut *(Nature Valley)*	130	2.0	19.0	5.0	0	75	1.0 d
fruit, tropical and oat clusters *(Fruit & Fibre)*, 1.25 oz.	120	3.0	27.0	3.0	0	170	5.0 d
honey roasted *(Honey Bunches of Oats)*	110	2.0	24.0	2.0	0	180	1.0 d

Food and Measure	cal.	prot. (gms)	carbo. (gms)	fat (gms)	chol. (mgs)	sod. (mgs)	fiber (gms)
peaches, raisins, almonds and oat clusters *(Fruit & Fibre)*, 1.25 oz.	120	3.0	26.0	2.0	0	170	5.0 d
raisin *(Heartland)*	130	3.0	18.0	4.0	0	80	m.q.
raisin and date *(Quaker 100% Natural)*	123	3.0	18.4	5.0	0	14	1.8 d
raisin, dates, almond *(Ralston Muesli)*, 1.45 oz.	140	4.0	32.0	2.0	0	95	3.0 d
raisin, peach, pecan *(Ralston Muesli)*, 1.45 oz.	150	4.0	30.0	3.0	0	95	3.0 d
raisin, walnut, cranberries *(Ralston Fruit Muesli)*, 1.45 oz.	150	4.0	30.0	3.0	0	95	3.0 d
w/raisins *(Grape Nuts)*	100	3.0	23.0	0	0	140	2.0 d
w/raisins and almonds *(Nutrific)*, w/.5 oz. fruit and nuts	140	4.0	31.0	2.0	0	240	6.0 d
trail mix *(Heartland)*	120	3.0	19.0	4.0	0	80	m.q.
oat:							
(Alpha-Bits)	110	2.0	24.0	1.0	0	190	tr.d
(Cheerios)	110	4.0	20.0	2.0	0	290	2.0 d
(Cinnamon Life) . .	101	5.0	18.9	1.7	0	182	2.5 d
(Life)	101	5.1	18.7	1.7	0	186	2.5 d
(Oat Chex)	100	3.0	22.0	1.0	0	240	1.0 d
(Quaker Oat Squares)	105	3.7	21.3	1.6	0	159	2.4 d
apple cinnamon *(Cheerios)*	110	2.0	22.0	2.0	0	180	1.5 d
honey nut *(Cheerios)*	110	3.0	23.0	1.0	0	250	1.5 d

Food and Measure	cal.	prot. (gms)	carbo. (gms)	fat (gms)	chol. (mgs)	sod. (mgs)	fiber (gms)
Cereal, ready-to-eat, oat *(cont.)*							
toasted *(Nature Valley)*	130	2.0	20.0	5.0	0	90	1.0 d
oat bran:							
(Common Sense)	100	4.0	22.0	1.0	0	270	3.0 d
(Craklin' Oat Bran)	110	3.0	21.0	3.0	150	140	4.0 d
(Post Oat Flakes)	110	4.0	21.0	1.0	0	130	2.0 d
w/raisins *(Common Sense)*, w/.3 oz. raisins	120	4.0	29.0	0	0	250	3.0 d
w/raisins *(General Mills)*, 1.5 oz. . .	150	4.0	31.0	2.0	0	130	3.0 d
w/raisins *(Raisin Oat Bran Options)*, 1.45 oz.	130	4.0	32.0	1.0	0	150	3.0 d
rice:							
(Kellogg's Frosted Krispies)	110	1.0	26.0	0	0	200	m.q.
(Kellogg's Rice Krispies)	110	2.0	25.0	0	0	290	m.q.
(Rice Chex)	110	1.0	25.0	0	0	280	.5 d
puffed *(Quaker)*, 1/2 oz., approx. 1 cup	54	1.0	12.5	.1	0	1	.2 d
w/marshmallow *(Fruity Marshmallow Krispies)*, w/ .3 oz. marshmallows	140	2.0	32.0	0	0	210	m.q.
wheat:							
(Honey Smacks)	110	2.0	25.0	1.0	0	70	1.0 d
(Nutri-Grain)	100	3.0	24.0	0	0	170	3.0 d
(Total)	100	3.0	22.0	1.0	0	140	3.0 d
(Wheat Chex) . . .	100	3.0	23.0	0	0	230	2.0 d
(Wheaties)	100	3.0	23.0	1.0	0	200	3.0 d
apple cinnamon filled *(Kellogg's Apple Cinnamon Squares)*	90	2.0	23.0	0	0	5	2.0 d

Food and Measure	cal.	prot. (gms)	carbo. (gms)	fat (gms)	chol. (mgs)	sod. (mgs)	fiber (gms)
blueberry filled (Kellogg's Blueberry Squares)	90	2.0	23.0	0	0	5	3.0 d
brown sugar, nut and honey filled (Nut & Honey Crunch Biscuits)	100	3.0	22.0	1.0	0	5	3.0 d
puffed (Quaker), 1/2 oz., approx. 1 cup	50	2.4	10.5	.2	0	1	1.0 d
puffs (Super Golden Crisp)	110	2.0	26.0	0	0	45	tr.d
w/raisins (General Mills Raisin Nut Bran)	110	3.0	20.0	3.0	0	140	2.5 d
raisin filled (Kellogg's Raisin Squares)	90	2.0	23.0	0	0	0	2.0 d
w/raisins (Nutri-Grain), w/.4 oz. raisins	130	3.0	32.0	0	0	170	3.0 d
w/raisins (Total Raisin Bran) 1.5 oz., 1 cup	140	3.0	33.0	1.0	0	190	4.0 d
raspberry filled (Fruit Wheats)	90	2.0	23.0	0	0	15	3.0 d
strawberry filled (Kellogg's Strawberry Squares)	90	2.0	23.0	0	0	5	3.0 d
wheat, shredded:							
(Frosted Mini-Wheats)	100	3.0	24.0	0	0	0	3.0 d
(Nabisco), 1 piece	80	2.0	19.0	<1.0	0	0	3.0 d
(Nutri-Grain)	90	4.0	22.0	0	0	0	4.0 d
(Quaker), 2 pieces	132	3.9	31.6	.6	0	1	3.7 d
(S.W. Graham) . .	100	3.0	23.0	0	0	190	3.0 d
bran (Nabisco Shredded Wheat 'n Bran)	90	3.0	23.0	<1.0	0	0	4.0 d

Food and Measure	cal.	prot. (gms)	carbo. (gms)	fat (gms)	chol. (mgs)	sod. (mgs)	fiber (gms)
Cereal, ready-to-eat, wheat, shredded *(cont.)*							
bite size *(Frosted Mini-Wheats)* . .	100	3.0	24.0	0	0	0	3.0 d
cinnamon *(S.W. Graham)*	100	2.0	24.0	0	0	160	2.0 d
mini *(Nabisco Spoon Size)* . . .	90	3.0	23.0	<1.0	0	0	3.0 d
Cereal, cooking[1] (see also specific grains), 1 pkt., except as noted:							
bran *(H-O Brand Super Bran)*, 1/3 cup dry	110	4.0	18.0	2.0	0	0	8.0 d
farina, see "wheat"							
mixed grain:							
(Roman Meal Original), 1 oz.	80	4.0	15.0	<1.0	0	0	5.0 d
w/oats *(Roman Meal Original)*, 1.2 oz.	120	5.0	20.0	2.0	0	5	5.0 d
oat bran:							
(Quaker/Mother's), 2/3 cup cooked	92	5.7	16.6	2.1	0	1	4.2 d
(Roman Meal), 1 oz.	100	5.0	17.0	3.0	0	0	4.0 d
(Wholesome 'N Hearty), 1 oz. . .	100	4.0	18.0	2.0	0	0	5.0 d
apple cinnamon *(Wholesome 'N Hearty Instant)*	130	3.0	30.0	2.0	0	160	5.0 d
honey *(Wholesome 'N Hearty Instant)*	110	3.0	26.0	2.0	0	160	5.0 d
oatmeal and oats:							
(H-O Brand Quick), 1/2 cup dry . . .	130	5.0	23.0	2.0	0	<5	3.0 d
(H-O Brand Gourmet), 1/3 cup dry	100	5.0	18.0	2.0	0	0	3.0 d

[1] Uncooked, except as noted.

Food and Measure	cal.	prot. (gms)	carbo. (gms)	fat (gms)	chol. (mgs)	sod. (mgs)	fiber (gms)
(H-O Brand Instant)	110	4.0	18.0	2.0	0	230	3.0 d
(H-O Brand Instant Box), 1/2 cup dry	130	5.0	22.0	2.0	0	<5	3.0 d
(Instant Quaker) . .	94	3.8	18.0	2.0	0	270	2.8 d
(Maypo 30 Second), 1 oz.	100	4.0	19.0	1.0	0	0	2.0 d
(Quaker Extra) . .	95	4.4	17.6	2.0	0	219	2.9 d
(Quaker Quick/Old Fashioned), 2/3 cup cooked	99	4.4	18.6	2.0	0	1	2.7 d
(Roman Meal Quick/Old Fashioned), 1 oz. . .	100	5.0	17.0	2.0	0	0	3.0 d
(Total), 1.2 oz. . .	110	4.0	22.0	2.0	0	0	2.5 d
(Total Quick), 1 oz.	90	4.0	18.0	2.0	0	0	2.5 d
apple cinnamon *(H-O Brand* Instant)	130	3.0	26.0	2.0	0	220	3.0 d
apple cinnamon *(Instant Quaker)* . .	118	3.3	26.0	1.5	0	128	3.0 d
apple cinnamon *(Total)*, 1.5 oz. . . .	150	4.0	32.0	2.0	0	105	3.0 d
apple spice *(Quaker Extra)*	133	4.3	26.7	1.9	0	191	3.0 d
cinnamon spice *(Instant Quaker)* . .	164	4.5	34.9	2.1	0	322	3.1 d
w/fiber *(H-O Brand* Instant)	110	5.0	18.0	2.0	0	140	3.0 d
w/fiber *(H-O Brand* Instant Box), 1/3 cup dry . . .	100	5.0	15.0	2.0	0	5	3.0 d
w/fiber, apple and bran *(H-O Brand* Instant)	130	3.0	26.0	2.0	0	140	3.0 d
w/fiber, raisin and bran *(H-O Brand* Instant)	150	4.0	32.0	2.0	0	140	3.0 d

Food and Measure	cal.	prot. (gms)	carbo. (gms)	fat (gms)	chol. (mgs)	sod. (mgs)	fiber (gms)
Cereal, cooking, oatmeal and oats *(cont.)*							
maple flavored (*Maypo* Vermont Style), 1 oz. . . .	105	4.0	20.0	1.0	0	0	2.0 d
maple brown sugar (*H-O Brand* Instant)	160	4.0	32.0	2.0	0	285	3.0 d
maple brown sugar (*Instant Quaker*)	152	4.5	31.6	2.1	0	320	2.8 d
maple brown sugar (*Total*), 1.6 oz.	160	4.0	34.0	2.0	0	150	3.0 d
peaches and cream (*Instant Quaker*)	129	3.4	26.3	2.2	0	179	2.3 d
raisin and cinnamon (*Quaker Extra*)	129	4.1	26.6	1.9	0	119	2.7 d
raisin, date and walnut (*Instant Quaker*)	141	4.0	25.1	3.8	0	216	2.4 d
raisin and spice (*H-O Brand* Instant)	150	4.0	32.0	2.0	0	240	3.0 d
raisin and spice (*Instant Quaker*) . .	149	4.1	31.5	2.0	0	266	2.8 d
strawberries and cream (*Instant Quaker*)	129	3.4	26.6	2.0	0	204	2.2 d
sweet'n mellow (*H-O Brand* Instant)	150	5.0	30.0	2.0	0	270	3.0 d
w/wheat, date, raisin and almond (*Roman Meal* Premium), 1/3 cup dry	140	4.0	23.0	3.0	0	0	3.0 d
w/wheat, honey, coconut and almond (*Roman Meal* Premium), 1/3 cup dry	150	5.0	21.0	6.0	0	5	3.0 d

Food and Measure	cal.	prot. (gms)	carbo. (gms)	fat (gms)	chol. (mgs)	sod. (mgs)	fiber (gms)
rye, cream of (Roman Meal), 1/3 cup dry . . .	110	4.0	22.0	<1.0	0	0	5.0 d
wheat:							
(Cream of Wheat Instant), 1 oz. . . .	100	3.0	22.0	0	0	0	1.0 d
(Cream of Wheat Quick), 1 oz. . .	100	3.0	22.0	0	0	80	1.0 d
(Mix'n Eat Cream of Wheat Instant Original)	100	3.0	21.0	0	0	180	1.0 d
(Wheatena), 1 oz.	100	3.0	21.0	1.0	0	0	4.0 d
apple 'n cinnamon (Mix'n Eat Cream of Wheat Instant)	130	2.0	30.0	0	0	300	1.0 d
brown sugar, maple or cinnamon (Mix'n Eat Cream of Wheat Instant)	130	2.0	30.0	0	0	180	1.0 d
farina (H-O Brand Instant)	110	3.0	22.0	0	0	235	3.0 d
farina, cream (H-O Brand), 3 tbsp.	120	3.0	26.0	0	0	0	3.0 d
whole (Quaker/ Mother's Hot Natural), 2/3 cup cooked	92	2.9	20.9	.6	0	1	2.2 d
wheat and barley (Maltex), 1 oz.	105	3.0	21.0	1.0	0	0	3.0 d
Cereal, freeze-dried:							
granola w/blueberries and milk (Mountain House), 1/2 cup . .	290	8.0	44.0	8.0	m.q.	m.q.	m.q.
Cereal beverage, see "Coffee substitute"							
Chard, Swiss, see "Swiss chard"							

Food and Measure	cal.	prot. (gms)	carbo. (gms)	fat (gms)	chol. (mgs)	sod. (mgs)	fiber (gms)
Chayote:							
raw:							
1 medium, 7.2 oz.	49	1.8	11.0	.6	0	8	1.4 c
1" pieces, 1/2 cup	16	.6	3.6	.2	0	3	.5 c
boiled, drained, 1"							
pieces, 1/2 cup	19	.5	4.1	.4	0	1	.5 c
Cheddarwurst:							
(Hillshire Farm Bun							
Size), 2 oz.	200	8.0	1.0	18.0	m.q.	480	(0)
(Hillshire Farm Links),							
2 oz.	190	8.0	1.0	17.0	m.q.	480	(0)
Cheese, (see also							
"Cheese food,"							
and "Cheese							
spread"), 1 oz.,							
except as noted:							
American, processed:							
(Borden)	110	6.0	1.0	9.0	m.q.	460	0
(Dorman's)	110	6.0	1.0	9.0	m.q.	440	0
(Land O'Lakes) . .	110	6.0	<1.0	9.0	25	405	0
loaf *(Kraft* Deluxe)	110	6.0	1.0	9.0	25	430	0
low sodium							
(Dorman's Loaf)	110	6.0	1.0	9.0	m.q.	140	0
slices *(Kraft* Deluxe)	110	6.0	1.0	9.0	25	460	0
hot pepper							
(Sargento) . . .	110	6.0	.5	9.0	27	410	(0)
sharp, loaf *(Old En-*							
glish)	110	6.0	1.0	9.0	30	400	0
sharp, slices *(Old*							
English)	110	6.0	1.0	9.0	30	440	0
asiago, wheel *(Frigo)*	110	7.0	1.0	9.0	m.q.	400	0
babybel *(Laughing*							
Cow)	91	7.0	tr.	7.0	22	227	0
(Bel Paese Domestic							
Traditional)	101	6.0	.7	8.0	20	145	0
(Bel Paese Imported)	90	5.7	.3	7.4	22	196	0
(Bel Paese Lite) . . .	76	7.0	1.0	5.0	16	155	0
(Bel Paese Medallion)	71	3.4	1.3	5.9	18	193	0

Food and Measure	cal.	prot. (gms)	carbo. (gms)	fat (gms)	chol. (mgs)	sod. (mgs)	fiber (gms)
blue:							
(Dorman's Danablu 50%)	100	6.4	.3	8.2	23	200	0
(Dorman's Danablu 60%)	108	4.8	.3	9.7	31	200	0
(Frigo)	100	6.0	1.0	8.0	m.q.	400	0
(Hickory Farms Domestic)	101	6.1	.7	8.3	21	396	0
(Kraft)	100	6.0	1.0	9.0	30	330	0
(Sargento)	100	6.0	1.0	8.0	21	400	0
blue castello or saga *(Dorman's* 70%)	134	3.7	.1	12.3	29	286	0
bonbel *(Laughing Cow)*	100	6.0	tr.	8.0	24	227	0
bonbino *(Laughing Cow)*	103	7.0	tr.	9.0	27	227	0
brick:							
(Dorman's)	110	7.0	1.0	8.0	m.q.	180	0
(Kraft)	110	7.0	0	9.0	30	180	0
(Land O'Lakes) . .	110	7.0	1.0	8.0	25	160	0
Brie:							
(Dorman's)	81	5.1	.3	6.6	20	229	0
(Sargento)	100	6.0	.1	8.0	28	180	0
Cajun *(Sargento)* . .	110	7.0	.3	9.0	28	165	0
caljack *(Churney)* . .	100	6.0	1.0	8.0	m.q.	m.q.	0
Camembert:							
(Dorman's 45%)	82	6.0	.3	6.3	17	226	0
(Dorman's 50%)	89	5.6	.3	7.3	23	285	0
(Sargento)	90	6.0	.1	7.0	20	240	0
caraway *(Kraft)* . . .	100	7.0	1.0	8.0	30	180	0
cheddar:							
(Dorman's)	110	7.0	1.0	9.0	m.q.	200	0
(Frigo)	110	7.0	1.0	9.0	m.q.	200	0
(Kraft)	110	7.0	1.0	9.0	30	180	0
(Land O'Lakes) . .	110	7.0	<1.0	9.0	30	175	0
(Laughing Cow) . .	110	7.0	tr.	9.0	28	227	0
(Sargento)	110	7.0	.4	9.0	30	176	0

Food and Measure	cal.	prot. (gms)	carbo. (gms)	fat (gms)	chol. (mgs)	sod. (mgs)	fiber (gms)
Cheese, cheddar *(cont.)*							
mild, reduced fat *(Kraft* Light Naturals)	80	8.0	1.0	5.0	20	210	0
reduced fat *(Dorman's* Low Sodium)	80	8.0	1.0	5.0	20	100	0
sharp or extra sharp *(Axelrod)*	110	7.0	1.0	9.0	30	200	0
sharp, reduced fat *(Kraft* Light Naturals)	90	8.0	1.0	5.0	20	200	0
sharp, slicing *(Boar's Head)* . .	110	7.0	1.0	9.0	18	100	0
Vermont *(Churny)*	110	7.0	1.0	9.0	30	180	0
Cheshire	110	6.6	1.4	8.7	29	198	0
colby:							
(Dorman's)	110	7.0	1.0	9.0	m.q.	190	0
(Kraft)	110	7.0	1.0	9.0	30	180	0
(Land O'Lakes) . .	110	7.0	1.0	9.0	25	170	0
(Sargento)	110	7.0	1.0	9.0	27	170	0
reduced fat *(Kraft* Light Naturals)	80	8.0	1.0	5.0	20	160	0
colby jack *(Sargento)*	110	7.0	.5	9.0	27	160	0
cottage cheese, creamed, 4% fat, 1/2 cup, except as noted:							
(Bison)	120	14.0	4.0	5.0	20	420	0
(Breakstones Smooth & Creamy), 4 oz.	110	13.0	4.0	5.0	m.q.	380	0
(Crowley)	120	14.0	4.0	5.0	15	390	0
(Darigold), 4 oz. . .	120	14.0	4.0	4.2	17	510	0
(Friendship California Style)	120	14.0	4.0	5.0	17	380	0
chive *(Bison)* . . .	120	14.0	4.0	5.0	20	420	(0)

Food and Measure	cal.	prot. (gms)	carbo. (gms)	fat (gms)	chol. (mgs)	sod. (mgs)	fiber (gms)
garden salad (Bison)	110	12.0	4.0	4.0	15	420	m.q.
w/peaches (Crowley)	140	10.0	17.0	3.0	10	340	m.q.
w/pineapple (Bison)	140	10.0	18.0	4.0	15	340	m.q.
w/pineapple (Crowley)	140	11.0	15.0	4.0	15	330	m.q.
w/pineapple (Friendship) . . .	140	11.0	15.0	4.0	17	300	m.q.
cottage cheese, dry curd, 1/2 cup:							
(Borden)	80	18.0	3.0	1.0	m.q.	20	0
(Darigold)	80	18.0	3.0	1.0	10	15	0
cottage cheese, low fat, 1/2 cup, except as noted:							
2% (Breakstones Hot Pack), 4 oz.	90	13.0	4.0	2.0	m.q.	470	0
2% (Darigold Trim), 4 oz.	100	14.0	4.0	3.2	17	510	0
1% (Bison)	90	14.0	4.0	2.0	5	350	0
1% (Crowley) . . .	90	14.0	4.0	1.0	5	390	0
1% (Crowley No Salt)	90	14.0	4.0	1.0	5	50	0
1% (Friendship) . .	90	14.0	4.0	1.0	5	350	0
1% (Friendship No Salt)	90	14.0	4.0	1.0	5	31	0
w/pineapple, 1% (Crowley)	110	11.0	15.0	1.0	5	330	m.q.
pot style, 2% (Friendship) . . .	100	14.0	4.0	2.0	9	405	0
cream cheese:							
(Crowley)	110	2.0	1.0	9.0	30	100	0
(Dorman's 65%)	90	3.0	.6	8.4	26	200	0
(Dorman's 70%)	102	2.7	.6	9.9	30	200	0
(Philadelphia Brand)	100	2.0	1.0	10.0	30	85	0
w/chives (Philadelphia Brand) . . .	90	2.0	1.0	9.0	30	125	(0)

Food and Measure	cal.	prot. (gms)	carbo. (gms)	fat (gms)	chol. (mgs)	sod. (mgs)	fiber (gms)
Cheese, cream cheese *(cont.)*							
w/pimento *(Phila-delphia Brand)*	90	2.0	1.0	9.0	30	150	(0)
cream cheese, soft:							
(Friendship)	103	1.5	.8	<10.0	31	70	0
(Philadelphia Brand)	100	2.0	1.0	10.0	30	100	0
w/chives and onion *(Philadelphia Brand)*.	100	2.0	2.0	9.0	30	100	(0)
w/honey *(Philadel-phia Brand)* . . .	100	1.0	5.0	8.0	25	55	(0)
w/olives and pi-mento *(Philadel-phia Brand)* . . .	90	2.0	2.0	8.0	25	160	(0)
w/pineapple *(Phila-delphia Brand)*	90	1.0	4.0	8.0	25	90	(0)
w/smoked salmon *(Philadelphia Brand)*.	90	2.0	1.0	9.0	25	180	0
w/strawberries *(Philadelphia Brand)*.	90	1.0	4.0	8.0	25	60	(0)
cream cheese, whipped:							
(Philadelphia Brand)	100	2.0	1.0	10.0	30	85	0
w/chives *(Philadel-phia Brand)* . . .	90	2.0	1.0	8.0	30	150	(0)
w/onion *(Philadel-phia Brand)* . . .	90	2.0	2.0	8.0	25	170	(0)
w/smoked salmon *(Philadelphia Brand)*.	90	2.0	2.0	8.0	30	170	0
danbo *(Dorman's 20%)*	62	8.9	.3	2.8	9	200	0
danbo *(Dorman's 45%)*	98	7.3	.3	7.5	23	200	0
(Dorman's Crema Da-nia 70%)	134	3.7	.1	12.3	29	286	0

Food and Measure	cal.	prot. (gms)	carbo. (gms)	fat (gms)	chol. (mgs)	sod. (mgs)	fiber (gms)
Edam:							
(Dorman's)	100	7.0	1.0	8.0	m.q.	200	0
(Dorman's 45%)	91	6.7	.3	7.0	21	200	0
(Kaukauna)	100	7.0	<1.0	8.0	25	275	0
(Kraft)	90	8.0	0	7.0	20	310	0
(Land O'Lakes) ..	100	7.0	<1.0	8.0	25	275	0
(Laughing Cow) ..	100	6.0	tr.	8.0	26	227	0
(May-Bud)	100	7.0	0	8.0	m.q.	275	0
(Sargento)	100	7.0	.4	8.0	25	270	0
farmer:							
(Friendship), 4 oz.	160	16.0	4.0	12.0	40	356	0
(Kaukauna)	100	7.0	<1.0	8.0	25	m.q.	0
(May-Bud)	90	6.0	1.0	7.0	20	210	0
(Sargento)	100	7.0	1.0	8.0	26	130	0
feta:							
(Churny Natural)	75	4.7	1.2	6.5	25	316	0
(Dorman's 45%)	91	5.9	.4	7.3	m.q.	m.q.	0
(Sargento)	80	4.0	1.0	6.0	25	320	0
fontina (Sargento) ..	110	7.0	.4	9.0	33	m.q.	0
gjetost (Sargento) ..	130	3.0	12.0	8.0	m.q.	170	0
Gouda:							
(Dorman's)	100	7.0	1.0	8.0	m.q.	210	0
(Kaukauna)	100	7.0	1.0	8.0	30	230	0
(Kraft)	110	7.0	0	9.0	30	200	0
(Land O'Lakes) ..	100	7.0	1.0	8.0	30	230	0
(Laughing Cow) ..	110	7.0	tr.	9.0	28	227	0
(Sargento)	100	7.0	1.0	8.0	32	230	0
w/caraway seed							
(Kaukauna) ...	100	7.0	<1.0	8.0	30	230	(0)
w/hickory smoke							
flavor (Kaukauna)	100	7.0	<1.0	8.0	25	230	0
mini (Laughing							
Cow), 3/4 oz. ..	80	5.3	tr.	6.4	21	170	0
Gruyere	117	8.5	.1	9.2	31	95	0
havarti:							
(Casino)	120	6.0	0	11.0	35	140	0
(Dorman's 45%)	91	6.7	.3	7.0	21	200	0
(Dorman's 60%)	118	5.4	.3	10.6	31	200	0

Food and Measure	cal.	prot. (gms)	carbo. (gms)	fat (gms)	chol. (mgs)	sod. (mgs)	fiber (gms)
Cheese, havarti *(cont.)*							
(Sargento)	120	5.0	.3	11.0	31	200	0
Italian style, grated							
(Sargento)	110	8.0	1.0	8.0	26	105	0
Jarlsberg *(Norseland)*	97	7.0	1.0	7.0	18	135	0
limburger:							
(Mohawk Valley Little Gem)	90	6.0	0	8.0	25	250	0
(Sargento)	90	6.0	.1	8.0	26	230	0
mascarpone *(Galbani Imported)*	128	1.5	1.2	13.1	39	17	0
Monterey Jack:							
(Alpine Lace Monti-Jack-Lo)	80	7.0	1.0	5.0	15	75	0
(Axelrod)	100	6.0	1.0	8.0	30	150	0
(Darigold)	110	7.0	<1.0	8.0	25	150	0
(Kaukauna)	110	7.0	<1.0	9.0	25	150	0
(Kraft)	110	6.0	0	9.0	30	190	0
(Sargento)	110	7.0	.2	9.0	25	150	0
w/jalapeños *(Axelrod)*	100	6.0	1.0	8.0	30	220	(0)
w/jalapeños *(Kraft)*	110	7.0	1.0	9.0	30	190	(0)
w/peppers, mild *(Casino)*	110	7.0	0	9.0	30	180	(0)
reduced fat *(Kraft Light Naturals)*	80	8.0	0	5.0	20	180	0
mozzarella:							
(Dorman's)	90	7.0	1.0	6.0	m.q.	190	0
(Polly-O Lite) . . .	70	7.0	1.0	4.0	15	200	0
fresh *(Polly-O Fior di Latte)*	80	5.0	1.0	6.0	20	20	0
whole milk *(Crowley)*	90	5.0	1.0	7.0	25	240	0
whole milk *(Polly-O)*	90	5.0	1.0	6.0	20	280	0
whole milk *(Sargento)* . . .	90	6.0	1.0	7.0	25	120	0
whole milk *(Frigo)*	90	6.0	1.0	7.0	15	190	0

Food and Measure	cal.	prot. (gms)	carbo. (gms)	fat (gms)	chol. (mgs)	sod. (mgs)	fiber (gms)
part skim (Alpine Lace)	70	7.0	1.0	5.0	15	75	0
part skim (Crowley)	70	8.0	1.0	4.0	15	240	0
part skim (Frigo)	80	7.0	1.0	5.0	10	190	0
part skim (Kraft) . .	80	8.0	0	5.0	15	200	0
part skim (Polly-O)	80	6.0	1.0	5.0	15	280	0
part skim (Sargento)	80	8.0	1.0	5.0	15	150	0
part skim (Dorman's Low Sodium) . .	80	8.0	1.0	5.0	15	90	0
part skim, reduced fat (Frigo)	60	8.0	1.0	3.0	10	150	0
part skim, w/ jalapeño pepper (Kraft)	80	8.0	1.0	5.0	20	230	(0)
reduced fat (Dorman's Low Sodium)	80	9.0	1.0	4.0	17	90	0
Muenster:							
(Alpine Lace) . . .	100	7.0	1.0	8.0	30	85	0
(Dorman's)	110	7.0	0	9.0	m.q.	190	0
(Dorman's 50%)	100	6.4	.3	8.2	24	200	0
(Kaukauna)	110	7.0	<1.0	9.0	25	180	0
(Land O'Lakes) . .	100	7.0	<1.0	9.0	25	180	0
reduced fat (Dorman's Low Sodium)	80	8.0	0	5.0	18	140	0
red rind (Sargento)	100	7.0	.3	9.0	27	180	0
Neufchâtel:							
garlic and herbs (Kaukauna) . . .	80	3.0	1.0	7.0	25	150	(0)
light (Philadelphia Brand)	80	3.0	1.0	7.0	25	115	0
vegetable, garden (Kaukauna) . . .	80	3.0	1.0	7.0	25	200	(0)
Parmesan:							
(Kraft)	110	10.0	1.0	7.0	20	450	0
fresh (Sargento) . .	110	10.0	1.0	7.0	19	450	0
grated, 1 tbsp. . .	23	2.1	.2	1.5	4	93	0

Food and Measure	cal.	prot. (gms)	carbo. (gms)	fat (gms)	chol. (mgs)	sod. (mgs)	fiber (gms)
Cheese, Parmesan *(cont.)*							
grated *(Kraft)* ..	130	12.0	1.0	9.0	30	430	0
grated *(Polly-O)* ..	130	11.0	1.0	9.0	20	530	0
grated *(Sargento)*	130	12.0	2.0	9.0	22	530	0
Reggiano *(Galbani Imported)*	105	10.1	n.a.	7.1	21	188	0
wheel or fresh grated *(Frigo)* ..	110	10.0	1.0	7.0	m.q.	350	0
Parmesan and Romano:							
grated *(Frigo)* ...	130	12.0	1.0	9.0	m.q.	510	0
grated *(Sargento)*	110	10.0	1.0	7.0	24	400	0
pimento, processed *(Kraft* Deluxe) ...	100	6.0	1.0	8.0	25	440	(0)
pizza, shredded:							
(Frigo)	90	6.0	1.0	7.0	20	190	0
low fat *(Frigo)* ...	65	9.0	1.0	3.0	10	150	0
Port du Salut	100	6.7	.2	8.0	35	151	0
pot cheese *(Sargento)*	25	5.0	1.0	.2	m.q.	1	0
primavera *(Bel Paese Lite)*	68	6.0	2.0	4.0	14	165	(0)
provolone:							
(Alpine Lace Provo-Lo)	70	7.0	1.0	5.0	15	85	0
(Dorman's)	90	7.0	1.0	7.0	m.q.	290	0
(Kraft)	100	7.0	1.0	7.0	25	260	0
(Land O'Lakes) ..	100	7.0	1.0	8.0	20	250	0
(Sargento)	100	7.0	1.0	8.0	20	250	0
smoked *(Frigo)* ..	100	7.0	1.0	7.0	m.q.	230	0
queso blanco *(Sargento)*	100	7.0	.3	9.0	27	180	0
queso de papa *(Sargento)*	110	7.0	.4	9.0	30	180	0
ricotta, 2 oz., except as noted:							
(Polly-O Lite) ...	80	7.0	3.0	4.0	15	65	0
(Sargento), 1 oz.	40	3.0	1.0	3.0	13	25	0

Food and Measure	cal.	prot. (gms)	carbo. (gms)	fat (gms)	chol. (mgs)	sod. (mgs)	fiber (gms)
(Sargento Lite),							
1 oz.	23	3.0	1.0	1.0	4	20	0
whole milk, 1/2 cup	216	14.0	3.8	16.1	63	104	0
whole milk *(Crow-*							
ley)	100	6.0	3.0	7.0	25	50	0
whole milk *(Polly-O)*	100	7.0	2.0	7.0	20	45	0
part skim *(Crowley)*	80	7.0	3.0	4.0	15	50	0
part skim *(Polly-O)*	90	7.0	2.0	6.0	20	45	0
lowfat *(Frigo)*, 1 oz.	20	3.0	1.0	1.0	5	20	0
Romano:							
(Kraft Natural) . . .	110	9.0	1.0	8.0	30	340	0
(Sargento)	110	9.0	1.0	8.0	29	340	0
grated *(Kraft)* . . .	130	11.0	1.0	9.0	30	350	0
grated *(Polly-O)* . .	130	11.0	1.0	10.0	30	530	0
Roquefort, sheep's							
milk	105	6.1	.6	8.7	26	513	0
Slim Jack *(Dorman's)*	90	6.0	1.0	7.0	m.q.	90	0
smoked *(Sargento*							
Smokestick)	100	7.0	1.0	7.0	24	390	0
string:							
(Frigo)	80	7.0	1.0	5.0	m.q.	190	0
(Polly-O Stick) . . .	90	7.0	2.0	6.0	15	200	0
(Sargento)	80	8.0	1.0	5.0	15	150	0
low moisture *(Kraft)*	80	8.0	1.0	5.0	20	230	0
Swiss:							
(Alpine Lace							
Swiss-Lo)	100	8.0	1.0	7.0	20	35	0
(Boar's Head Do-							
mestic)	110	7.0	1.0	8.0	25	75	0
(Casino)	110	8.0	1.0	8.0	30	35	0
(Dorman's)	100	8.0	0	8.0	m.q.	80	0
(Dorman's Reduced							
Fat)	90	10.0	0	5.0	17	80	0
(Kraft)	110	8.0	1.0	8.0	25	40	0
(Kraft Light							
Naturals)	90	10.0	1.0	5.0	20	45	0
(Kraft 75% Very							
Low Sodium) . .	110	8.0	1.0	8.0	25	10	0

Food and Measure	cal.	prot. (gms)	carbo. (gms)	fat (gms)	chol. (mgs)	sod. (mgs)	fiber (gms)
Cheese, Swiss *(cont.)*							
(Sargento)	110	8.0	1.0	8.0	26	75	0
aged *(Kraft)*	110	8.0	1.0	8.0	25	45	0
Finland *(Sargento)*	110	8.0	1.0	8.0	26	75	0
processed *(Kraft Deluxe)*	90	7.0	1.0	7.0	25	420	0
smoked *(Dorman's)*	100	7.0	1.0	7.0	m.q.	390	0
taco:							
(Sargento)	110	7.0	.5	9.0	27	160	0
shredded *(Frigo)*	110	7.0	1.0	9.0	m.q.	200	0
shredded *(Kraft)*	110	7.0	1.0	9.0	30	190	0
taleggio *(Tal-Fino Brand Imported)*	89	5.4	.2	7.4	m.q.	176	0
Tilsit *(Sargento)* . . .	100	7.0	1.0	7.0	29	210	0
Tybo:							
(Dorman's 45%)	98	7.3	.3	7.5	23	200	0
red wax *(Sargento)*	100	7.0	.3	7.0	23	200	0
"Cheese," imitation and substitute, 1 oz.:							
American:							
caraway *(Churny Delicia)*	80	6.0	1.0	6.0	3	275	0
flavored, imitation *(Golden Image)*	90	7.0	2.0	6.0	5	360	0
hickory smoke *(Churny Delicia)*	80	6.0	0	6.0	1	470	0
plain or hot pepper *(Churny Delicia)*	80	6.0	1.0	6.0	3	300	0
salami *(Churny Delicia)*	80	6.0	1.0	6.0	3	370	0
cheddar:							
imitation *(Frigo)* . .	90	5.0	1.0	7.0	0	280	0
imitation *(Sargento)*	90	7.0	<1.0	6.0	2	350	0
mild, imitation *(Golden Image)*	110	7.0	0	9.0	5	150	0
shredded *(Fisher Ched-O-Mate)*	90	6.0	1.0	7.0	n.a.	330	0

Food and Measure	cal.	prot. (gms)	carbo. (gms)	fat (gms)	chol. (mgs)	sod. (mgs)	fiber (gms)
cheese food							
(Cheeztwin)	90	5.0	3.0	6.0	n.a.	400	0
colby:							
(Dorman's LoChol)	90	7.0	1.0	6.0	1	140	0
imitation (Golden							
Image)	110	7.0	1.0	9.0	5	170	0
longhorn style							
(Churny Delicia)	80	6.0	1.0	6.0	3	550	0
cream cheese, imita-							
tion, all varieties							
(Tofutti Better than							
Cream Cheese) . .	80	1.0	1.0	8.0	0	200	m.q.
mozzarella:							
imitation (Frigo) . .	90	6.0	1.0	7.0	0	240	0
imitation (Sargento)	80	7.0	<1.0	6.0	2	310	0
muenster (Dorman's							
LoChol)	100	7.0	1.0	7.0	1	140	0
(Nucoa Heart Beat)	50	7.0	2.0	2.0	0	280	0
Swiss (Dorman's							
LoChol)	100	7.0	1.0	7.0	1	140	0
Cheese blintz, frozen,							
1 piece:							
(King Kold)	113	6.0	18.9	1.6	m.q.	272	m.q.
(King Kold No Salt)	96	6.4	18.6	.5	m.q.	78	m.q.
Cheese danish, see							
"Danish"							
Cheese dip, 2 tbsp.:							
blue (Kraft Premium)	45	1.0	2.0	4.0	10	200	0
nacho (Kraft Premium)	50	1.0	2.0	4.0	10	190	0
Cheese enchilada,							
see "Enchilada"							
Cheese food, 1 oz.,							
except as noted:							
American:							
(Borden Singles)	90	5.0	3.0	7.0	m.q.	350	0
(Darigold)	80	5.0	2.0	6.0	16	381	0
(Kraft Singles) . . .	90	6.0	2.0	7.0	25	380	0
grated (Kraft) . . .	130	8.0	9.0	7.0	25	740	0

Food and Measure	cal.	prot. (gms)	carbo. (gms)	fat (gms)	chol. (mgs)	sod. (mgs)	fiber (gms)
Cheese food, American *(cont.)*							
sharp *(Borden Sin-gles)*	90	5.0	2.0	7.0	m.q.	470	0
white *(Kraft* Singles)	90	5.0	2.0	7.0	20	400	0
w/bacon:							
(Cracker Barrel) . .	90	5.0	3.0	7.0	20	280	0
(Kraft)	90	5.0	2.0	7.0	20	420	0
(Kraft Cheez'N Ba-con)	90	6.0	2.0	7.0	25	400	0
cheddar:							
(Land O'Lakes La Chedda)*	90	6.0	2.0	7.0	20	335	0
all varieties *(Kaukauna* Cup)	100	6.0	3.0	7.0	25	250	0
port wine *(Cracker Barrel)*	90	5.0	3.0	7.0	20	260	0
sharp or extra sharp *(Cracker Barrel)*	90	5.0	3.0	7.0	20	270	0
sharp or smokey *(Kaukauna* Lite)	70	5.0	5.0	4.0	15	230	0
sharp, cold pack *(Wispride)*	100	5.0	2.0	7.0	25	210	0
w/garlic *(Kraft)* . . .	90	5.0	2.0	7.0	20	370	(0)
horseradish, cold pack *(Kaukauna* Cup) . .	100	6.0	3.0	7.0	25	250	(0)
w/jalapeños:							
(Kraft)	90	5.0	2.0	7.0	20	390	(0)
(Kraft Singles) . . .	90	5.0	2.0	7.0	25	450	(0)
(Land O'Lakes) . .	90	6.0	2.0	7.0	20	360	(0)
hot *(Velveeta* Mexi-can)*	100	6.0	3.0	7.0	25	430	(0)
mild *(Velveeta* Mexi-can)*	100	6.0	3.0	7.0	25	420	(0)
Monterey Jack *(Kraft* Singles)	90	5.0	2.0	7.0	25	390	0
(Nippy)	90	5.0	2.0	7.0	20	380	0
onion *(Land O'Lakes)*	90	6.0	2.0	7.0	15	330	(0)

Food and Measure	cal.	prot. (gms)	carbo. (gms)	fat (gms)	chol. (mgs)	sod. (mgs)	fiber (gms)
pepperoni *(Land O'Lakes)*	90	6.0	1.0	7.0	20	395	0
pimento *(Kraft Singles)*	90	5.0	2.0	7.0	25	390	(0)
port wine, cold pack:							
(Kaukauna Cup) . .	100	6.0	3.0	7.0	25	250	0
(Wispride)	100	5.0	3.0	7.0	25	210	0
salami *(Land O'Lakes)*	100	5.0	2.0	8.0	20	400	0
sharp *(Kraft* Singles)	100	6.0	1.0	8.0	25	400	0
smoked *(Smokelle)*	90	5.0	2.0	7.0	20	370	0
Swiss:							
(Kraft Singles) . . .	90	6.0	2.0	7.0	25	440	0
country *(Kaukauna Lite)*	70	6.0	5.0	4.0	15	200	0
country, cold pack *(Kaukauna* Cup)	100	6.0	3.0	7.0	25	250	0
(Velveeta)	100	6.0	3.0	7.0	20	410	0
Cheese nuggets, frozen:							
mozzarella *(Banquet Hot Bites),* 2.63 oz.	240	14.0	16.0	13.0	m.q.	530	m.q.
Cheese-nut ball or log, 1 oz.:							
all varieties:							
(Cracker Barrel) . .	90	5.0	4.0	6.0	15	410	m.q.
(Kaukauna)	100	6.0	3.0	7.0	25	250	m.q.
log, cheddar, sharp or port wine *(Sargento)*	100	6.0	3.0	7.0	18	250	m.q.
log, Swiss almond *(Sargento)*	90	6.0	2.0	7.0	21	350	m.q.
Cheese product, 1 oz.:							
American flavor:							
(Alpine Lace) . . .	90	6.0	2.0	7.0	20	200	0
(Borden Light) . . .	70	6.0	1.0	5.0	m.q.	420	0
(Harvest Moon) . .	70	6.0	2.0	4.0	15	420	0
(Light N' Lively Singles)	70	6.0	2.0	4.0	15	410	0

Food and Measure	cal.	prot. (gms)	carbo. (gms)	fat (gms)	chol. (mgs)	sod. (mgs)	fiber (gms)
Cheese product *(cont.)*							
cheddar flavor, sharp							
(Light N' Lively) . .	70	6.0	2.0	4.0	15	380	0
cream cheese, light							
(Philadelphia Brand)	60	3.0	2.0	5.0	15	160	0
Muenster flavor							
(Lite-Line)	50	7.0	1.0	2.0	m.q.	450	0
mozzarella flavor							
(Lite-Line)	50	7.0	1.0	2.0	m.q.	340	0
pizza topping							
(Lunch Wagon)	80	6.0	1.0	6.0	0	350	0
port wine flavor							
(Weight Watchers)	70	4.0	7.0	3.0	10	260	0
sandwich slices							
(Lunch Wagon)	90	5.0	2.0	7.0	5	370	0
Swiss flavor *(Light*							
N' Lively Singles)	70	6.0	2.0	3.0	15	350	0
Cheese sauce (see also "Welsh rarebit"):							
aged *(White House)*, 3.5 oz.	213	4.0	10.0	18.0	n.a.	810	n.a.
cheddar, 4 oz.:							
(Musselman's) . .	220	3.0	12.0	18.0	n.a.	1000	n.a.
aged *(Musselman's)*	240	5.0	11.0	20.0	n.a.	920	n.a.
aged, mild *(Musselman's)*	200	5.0	9.0	18.0	n.a.	790	n.a.
aged, sharp *(Musselman's)*	230	9.0	6.0	17.0	n.a.	850	n.a.
jalapeño *(White House)*, 3.5 oz. . . .	193	3.0	10.0	16.0	n.a.	890	n.a.
nacho:							
(Kaukauna), 1 oz.	80	3.0	4.0	6.0	8	330	n.a.
(Musselman's), 4 oz.	220	4.0	11.0	18.0	n.a.	1010	n.a.
(White House), 3.5 oz.	193	3.0	10.0	16.0	n.a.	890	n.a.

Food and Measure	cal.	prot. (gms)	carbo. (gms)	fat (gms)	chol. (mgs)	sod. (mgs)	fiber (gms)
mix, 1 pkg. dry:							
(McCormick/Schilling)	138	8.0	14.0	6.0	m.q.	1908	n.a.
nacho *(McCormick/Schilling)*	167	9.7	18.2	6.1	m.q.	1635	n.a.
refrigerated, four cheese *(Contadina Fresh)*, 6 oz.	470	12.0	8.0	45.0	147	500	n.a.
Cheese spread (see also "Cheese"), 1 oz., except as noted:							
American, processed:							
(Kraft)	80	4.0	2.0	6.0	15	470	0
w/pimento or sharp *(Sargento* Cracker Snacks)	110	6.0	.5	9.0	27	410	(0)
w/bacon:							
(Kraft)	80	5.0	1.0	7.0	20	560	0
(Squeez-A-Snak)	80	5.0	1.0	7.0	20	500	0
blue *(Roka)*	70	3.0	2.0	6.0	20	270	0
brick *(Sargento* Cracker Snacks)	100	6.0	1.0	9.0	25	430	0
(Cheez Whiz)	80	4.0	2.0	6.0	20	470	0
w/garlic *(Kraft)* . . .	80	5.0	2.0	6.0	20	460	(0)
garlic flavor *(Squeez-A-Snak)*	80	5.0	1.0	7.0	20	430	(0)
hickory smoke flavor *(Squeez-A-Snak)*	80	5.0	1.0	7.0	20	440	0
w/jalapeño pepper:							
(Cheez Whiz) . . .	80	4.0	2.0	6.0	15	440	(0)
(Kraft)	70	2.0	3.0	5.0	15	95	(0)
(Squeez-A-Snak)	80	5.0	1.0	6.0	20	510	(0)
loaf *(Kraft)*	80	5.0	2.0	6.0	20	470	(0)
(Land O'Lakes Golden Velvet)	80	5.0	2.0	6.0	15	380	0
(Laughing Cow Cheezbits), 1/6 oz.	13	.8	.1	1.0	3	55	0

Food and Measure	cal.	prot. (gms)	carbo. (gms)	fat (gms)	chol. (mgs)	sod. (mgs)	fiber (gms)
Cheese spread (cont.)							
limburger (Mohawk Valley)	70	4.0	0	6.0	20	420	0
Mexican:							
hot (Cheez Whiz)	80	4.0	2.0	6.0	20	440	(0)
hot (Velveeta) . . .	80	5.0	3.0	6.0	20	520	(0)
mild (Cheez Whiz)	80	4.0	2.0	6.0	20	430	(0)
mild (Velveeta) . .	80	5.0	3.0	6.0	20	440	(0)
(Micro Melt)	80	4.0	2.0	6.0	15	380	0
olives and pimento (Kraft)	60	2.0	2.0	5.0	15	160	(0)
pimento:							
(Kraft)	70	2.0	3.0	5.0	15	120	(0)
(Velveeta)	80	5.0	3.0	6.0	20	400	(0)
pineapple (Kraft) . .	70	2.0	4.0	5.0	15	75	(0)
sharp:							
(Old English) . . .	80	5.0	1.0	7.0	20	480	0
(Squeez-A-Snak)	80	5.0	1.0	7.0	20	440	0
Swiss (Sargento Cracker Snacks)	100	7.0	1.0	7.0	24	390	0
(Velveeta)	80	5.0	3.0	6.0	20	430	0
(Velveeta Slices) . . .	90	5.0	3.0	6.0	20	400	0
Cheese snack sticks:							
cheddar (Flavor Tree), 1/4 cup	129	2.7	11.9	8.1	n.a.	335	.1 c
Cheese sticks, breaded, frozen, 3 oz.:							
cheddar (Farm Rich)	300	10.0	19.0	21.0	m.q.	740	m.q.
hot pepper (Farm Rich)	260	8.0	20.0	17.0	m.q.	700	m.q.
mozzarella (Farm Rich)	240	10.0	19.0	13.0	m.q.	570	m.q.
provolone (Farm Rich)	270	10.0	22.0	16.0	m.q.	820	m.q.
Cheesecake, see "Cake"							
Cherimoya:							
1 medium, 1.9 lb. . .	515	7.1	131.3	2.2	0	m.q.	12.0 c

Food and Measure	cal.	prot. (gms)	carbo. (gms)	fat (gms)	chol. (mgs)	sod. (mgs)	fiber (gms)
Cherry, 1/2 cup, except as noted:							
fresh, sour, red:							
w/pits, 1 oz.	14	.3	3.5	.1	0	1	.1 c
w/pits	26	.5	6.3	.2	0	2	.1 c
pitted	39	.8	9.4	.2	0	3	.2 c
fresh, sweet:							
w/pits	52	.9	12.0	.7	0	1	1.1 d
10 medium, 2.6 oz.	49	.8	11.3	.7	0	tr.	1.0 d
canned, sour, pitted:							
(White House),							
3.5 oz.	43	0	11.0	0	0	5	m.q.
tart (Musselman's),							
4 oz.	50	1.0	11.0	0	0	0	m.q.
in water (Stokely)	45	1.0	10.0	0	0	15	m.q.
in heavy syrup . .	116	.9	29.8	.1	0	9	.1 c
canned, sweet:							
in heavy syrup . .	107	.8	27.4	.2	0	3	.4 c
dark, w/pits (Del Monte)	90	0	23.0	0	0	<10	m.q.
dark, pitted (Del Monte)	90	0	24.0	0	0	<10	m.q.
light, w/pits (Del Monte)	100	0	26.0	0	0	<10	m.q.
packaged (Mott's Cherry Fruit Pak), 3.75 oz.	72	0	17.0	0	0	8	m.q.
frozen, 4 oz.:							
sour, red, unsweetened . . .	52	1.0	12.5	.5	0	1	.3 c
sweet, sweetened	101	1.3	25.4	.1	0	1	.5 c
sweet, sweetened (Lucky Leaf) . .	130	1.0	31.0	0	0	150	m.q.
Cherry, maraschino:							
in jars, w/liquid, 1 oz.	33	.1	8.3	.1	0	n.a.	.1 c
Cherry cobbler, see "Cobbler"							

Food and Measure	cal.	prot. (gms)	carbo. (gms)	fat (gms)	chol. (mgs)	sod. (mgs)	fiber (gms)
Cherry drink mix[1],							
8 fl. oz.:							
(Kool-Aid							
Presweetened) ..	80	0	20.0	0	0	0	(0)
regular or black *(Kool-*							
Aid)	100	0	25.0	0	0	0	(0)
Cherry fruit concen-							
trate:							
black *(Hain),* 2 tbsp.	67	1.0	17.0	0	0	0	n.a.
Cherry fruit roll, see							
"Fruit snack"							
Cherry fruit square,							
frozen, 1 piece							
(Pepperidge Farm)	230	2.0	28.0	12.0	n.a.	180	m.q.
Cherry juice:							
black *(Smucker's* Nat-							
urally 100%),							
8 fl. oz.	130	0	31.0	0	0	10	m.q.
blend, 6 fl. oz.:							
(Dole Pure & Light							
Mountain Cherry)	87	.2	22.0	.1	0	8	m.q.
(Libby's Juicy Juice)	90	0	22.0	0	0	5	m.q.
cocktail *(Welch's*							
Orchard), 6 fl. oz.	180	0	45.0	0	0	10	0
Cherry juice drink:							
(Hi-C), 8.45-fl.-oz.							
cont.	141	.2	34.8	.1	0	24	(0)
(Hi-C), 6 fl. oz.	100	.1	24.7	.1	0	17	(0)
(Kool-Aid Koolers),							
8.45 fl. oz.	140	0	38.0	0	0	10	(0)
(Tang Fruit Box),							
8.45 fl. oz.	120	0	32.0	0	0	10	(0)
Cherry pie, see "Pie"							
Chervil, dried:							
1 tsp.	1	.1	.3	<.1	0	tr.	.1 c

[1] *Prepared according to package directions.*

Food and Measure	cal.	prot. (gms)	carbo. (gms)	fat (gms)	chol. (mgs)	sod. (mgs)	fiber (gms)
Chestnut, Chinese, shelled, 1 oz.:							
raw	64	1.2	13.9	.3	0	1	.5 c
dried	103	1.9	22.7	.5	0	2	.8 c
boiled or steamed . .	44	.8	9.6	.2	0	1	.3 c
roasted, 1 oz.	68	1.3	14.9	.3	0	1	.5 c
Chestnut, European:							
raw, in shell, 1 lb. . .	714	8.1	152.8	7.6	0	9	33.3 d
raw, shelled, w/peel,							
1 cup or 13 kernels	308	3.5	66.0	3.3	0	4	14.5 d
dried, peeled, 1 oz.	105	1.4	22.3	1.1	0	11	1.4 c
boiled or steamed,							
1 oz.	37	.8	7.9	.4	0	8	.2 c
roasted, peeled:							
1 oz.	70	.9	15.0	.6	0	1	3.3 d
1 cup or 17 kernels	350	4.3	75.7	3.2	0	3	16.7 d
Chestnut, Japanese:							
raw, 1 oz.	44	.6	9.9	.2	0	4	.3 c
dried, 1 oz.	102	1.5	23.1	.4	0	10	.6 c
boiled or steamed,							
1 oz.	16	.2	3.6	.1	0	1	.1 c
roasted, 1 oz.	57	.8	12.8	.2	0	m.q.	.3 c
Chewing gum, see "Candy"							
Chicken, fresh:							
broiler-fryer, fried, flour coated, w/skin:							
4 oz.	305	32.4	3.6	16.9	102	95	<.1 c
light meat, 4 oz. . .	279	34.5	2.1	13.7	99	87	<.1 c
dark meat, 4 oz.	323	30.9	4.6	19.2	104	101	<.1 c
skin only, 1 oz. . .	142	5.4	2.6	12.1	21	15	<.1 c
broiler-fryer, roasted:							
w/skin, 1/2 chicken, 10.5 oz. (15.8 oz. w/bone)	715	81.6	0	40.7	263	244	0
w/skin, 4 oz. . . .	271	31.0	0	15.4	100	93	0
meat only, 4 oz. . .	215	32.8	0	8.4	101	98	0

Food and Measure	cal.	prot. (gms)	carbo. (gms)	fat (gms)	chol. (mgs)	sod. (mgs)	fiber (gms)
Chicken, fresh, broiler-fryer, roasted *(cont.)*							
meat only, chopped or diced, 1 cup	266	40.5	0	10.4	125	120	0
skin only, 1 oz. . .	129	5.8	0	11.5	24	18	0
light meat only, 4 oz.	196	35.1	0	5.1	96	87	0
dark meat only, 4 oz.	232	31.0	0	11.0	105	105	0
breast, w/skin, 1/2 breast, 3.5 oz. (8.5 oz. w/bone)	193	29.2	0	7.6	83	69	0
drumstick, w/skin, 1.8 oz. (2.9 oz. w/bone)	112	14.1	0	5.8	48	47	0
leg, w/skin, 4 oz. (5.7 oz. w/bone)	265	29.6	0	15.4	105	99	0
thigh, w/skin, 2.2 oz. (2.9 oz. w/ bone)	153	15.5	0	9.6	58	52	0
wing, w/skin, 1.2 oz. (2.3 oz. w/ bone)	99	9.1	0	6.6	29	28	0
capon, roasted, w/ skin:							
1/2 capon, 1.4 lbs. (2 lbs. w/bone)	1457	184.5	0	74.2	549	313	0
4 oz.	260	32.8	0	13.2	98	56	0
roaster, roasted, w/ skin:							
1/2 chicken, 1 lb. (1.5 lbs. w/bone)	1071	115.0	0	64.3	365	349	0
4 oz.	253	27.2	0	15.2	86	83	0
stewing, stewed:							
w/skin, 1/2 chicken, 9.2 oz. (13.5 oz. w/bone)	744	70.2	0	49.2	205	190	0
w/skin, 4 oz. . . .	323	30.5	0	21.4	90	83	0
meat only, 4 oz. . .	269	34.5	0	13.5	94	88	0

Food and Measure	cal.	prot. (gms)	carbo. (gms)	fat (gms)	chol. (mgs)	sod. (mgs)	fiber (gms)
meat only, chopped or diced, 1 cup	332	42.6	0	16.6	117	109	0
Chicken, boneless and luncheon meat, 1 oz.:							
breast:							
(*Longacre* Premium)	45	4.0	1.0	3.0	20	280	0
(*Mr. Turkey*)	32	4.8	.6	1.1	9	242	0
hickory smoked (*Louis Rich*) . . .	30	5.0	<1.0	1.0	15	355	0
oven-roasted (*Oscar Mayer*)	29	4.9	.6	.7	15	420	0
oven-roasted (*Louis Rich* Deluxe) . .	30	5.0	<1.0	1.0	15	330	0
smoked (*Hillshire Farm* Deli Select)	31	6.0	<1.0	.2	m.q.	290	0
smoked (*Oscar Mayer*)	26	5.3	.3	.4	15	405	0
roll:							
light meat	45	5.5	.7	2.1	14	166	0
sliced (*Longacre*)	60	4.0	1.0	5.0	25	210	0
white meat, oven-roasted (*Louis Rich*)	40	5.0	<1.0	2.0	15	170	0
Chicken, canned:							
chunk:							
breast (*Hormel*), 6¾ oz.	350	41.0	0	20.0	m.q.	855	0
dark (*Hormel*), 6¾ oz.	327	42.0	0	18.0	m.q.	933	0
style (*Swanson* Mixin' Chicken), 2½ oz.	130	14.0	0	8.0	m.q.	230	0
white and dark (*Hormel*), 6¾ oz. . .	340	39.0	0	20.0	m.q.	857	0
white and dark, un-salted (*Hormel*), 6¾ oz.	330	42.0	0	18.0	m.q.	75	0

Food and Measure	cal.	prot. (gms)	carbo. (gms)	fat (gms)	chol. (mgs)	sod. (mgs)	fiber (gms)
Chicken, canned *(cont.)*							
loaf *(Hormel)*, 2 oz.	130	7.0	0	10.0	m.q.	608	0
white *(Swanson)*, 2¹/₂ oz.	100	15.0	0	4.0	m.q.	240	0
white and dark *(Swanson)*, 2¹/₂ oz. . . .	100	16.0	0	4.0	m.q.	240	0
"Chicken," vegetarian:							
canned:							
(Worthington FriChik), 2 pieces	180	11.0	4.0	13.0	0	610	m.q.
sliced *(Worthington)*, 2 slices	90	4.0	2.0	8.0	0	330	m.q.
frozen:							
(Worthington Chik Stiks), 1 stick . .	110	9.0	4.0	7.0	0	390	m.q.
(Worthington Crispy Chik), 3 oz. . . .	280	10.0	17.0	19.0	0	500	m.q.
nuggets *(Morningstar Farms Country Crisps)*, 3 oz. . .	250	8.0	18.0	16.0	0	480	m.q.
patty *(Morningstar Farms Country Crisps)*, 1 patty	220	8.0	13.0	15.0	0	620	m.q.
pie *(Worthington)*, 8-oz. pie	380	7.0	43.0	20.0	0	1200	m.q.
roll *(Worthington Meatless Chicken)*, 2¹/₂ oz.	150	11.0	4.0	10.0	0	570	m.q.
slices *(Worthington Meatless Chicken)*, 2 slices, 2 oz.	130	9.0	3.0	9.0	0	460	m.q.
Chicken entree, packaged, 1 serving:							

Food and Measure	cal.	prot. (gms)	carbo. (gms)	fat (gms)	chol. (mgs)	sod. (mgs)	fiber (gms)
Chicken dinner,							
frozen:							
à la king:							
(Armour Classics							
Lite), 11.25 oz.	290	19.0	38.0	7.0	55	630	m.q.
(Le Menu), 10¼ oz.	330	22.0	28.0	14.0	m.q.	810	m.q.
in barbecue sauce							
(Swanson),							
11¾ oz.	460	28.0	57.0	13.0	m.q.	940	m.q.
barbecue-style *(Stouf-*							
fer's Dinner Su-							
preme), 10.5 oz.	390	22.0	24.0	23.0	m.q.	1250	m.q.
boneless *(Swanson*							
Hungry Man),							
17¾ oz.	700	48.0	65.0	28.0	m.q.	1530	m.q.
breast:							
baked, w/gravy							
(Stouffer's Dinner							
Supreme), 10 oz.	300	30.0	20.0	11.0	m.q.	830	m.q.
glazed *(Le Menu*							
Light Style)*,							
10 oz.	270	26.0	27.0	6.0	m.q.	770	m.q.
Marsala *(Armour*							
Classics Lite),							
10.5 oz.	250	20.0	27.0	7.0	80	930	m.q.
burgundy *(Armour*							
Classics Lite),							
10 oz.	210	23.0	25.0	2.0	45	780	m.q.
cacciatore:							
(The Budget Gour-							
met), 11 oz. . . .	300	20.0	27.0	13.0	60	810	m.q.
(Le Menu Light							
Style)*, 10 oz. . .	270	21.0	28.0	8.0	m.q.	640	m.q.
casserole, 1 pkg.:							
(Pillsbury Microwave							
Classic)	400	21.0	30.0	22.0	m.q.	890	m.q.

Food and Measure	cal.	prot. (gms)	carbo. (gms)	fat (gms)	chol. (mgs)	sod. (mgs)	fiber (gms)
Chicken dinner, frozen, casserole, 1 pkg. *(cont.)*							
and cheese *(Pillsbury Microwave Classic)*	480	21.0	33.0	29.0	m.q.	940	m.q.
chow mein *(Le Menu Light Style)*, 10 oz.	260	18.0	37.0	4.0	m.q.	830	m.q.
Cordon Bleu *(Le Menu)*, 11 oz. . . .	470	23.0	49.0	20.0	m.q.	870	m.q.
and dumplings *(Banquet)*, 10 oz. . . .	430	17.0	34.0	24.0	45	940	m.q.
fettuccini *(Armour Classics)*, 11 oz.	260	17.0	28.0	9.0	50	660	m.q.
Florentine:							
(Le Menu), 10¾ oz.	340	23.0	38.0	10.0	m.q.	990	m.q.
(Stouffer's Dinner Supreme), 11 oz.	430	33.0	32.0	18.0	m.q.	930	m.q.
fried:							
(Banquet), 10 oz.	400	15.0	45.0	22.0	m.q.	1100	m.q.
(Banquet Extra Helping), 16 oz.	570	20.0	70.0	28.0	m.q.	1470	m.q.
(Kid Cuisine), 7.25 oz.	420	15.0	41.0	22.0	m.q.	1050	m.q.
(Stouffer's Dinner Supreme), 10⅝ oz.	450	25.0	35.0	23.0	m.q.	990	m.q.
barbecue flavored *(Swanson)*, 10 oz.[1]	520	25.0	53.0	21.0	m.q.	1000	m.q.
dark meat *(Swanson)*, 9¾ oz. . .	560	22.0	54.0	28.0	m.q.	1100	m.q.
dark meat *(Swanson Hungry Man)*, 14¼ oz.	860	36.0	77.0	45.0	m.q.	1660	m.q.
platter *(Swanson)*, 7¾ oz.	340	8.0	39.0	16.0	m.q.	850	m.q.

[1] *Edible portion.*

Food and Measure	cal.	prot. (gms)	carbo. (gms)	fat (gms)	chol. (mgs)	sod. (mgs)	fiber (gms)
white meat *(Banquet Extra Helping)*, 16 oz. . . .	570	20.0	70.0	28.0	m.q.	1470	m.q.
white meat *(Swanson)*, 10¼ oz.	560	22.0	61.0	25.0	m.q.	1380	m.q.
white meat *(Swanson Hungry Man)*, 14¼ oz.[1]	870	35.0	80.0	46.0	m.q.	2150	m.q.
glazed *(Armour Classics)*, 10.75 oz. . .	300	15.0	24.0	16.0	60	960	m.q.
herb roasted:							
(Le Menu Light Style)*, 9¼ oz.	220	21.0	21.0	6.0	m.q.	610	m.q.
(Healthy Choice), 11 oz.	260	20.0	38.0	3.0	40	300	m.q.
mesquite:							
(Armour Classics), 9.5 oz.	370	15.0	42.0	16.0	55	660	m.q.
(Healthy Choice), 10.5 oz.	310	21.0	52.0	2.0	45	270	m.q.
Mexicana *(The Budget Gourmet)*, 12.8 oz.	510	23.0	70.0	15.0	40	1210	m.q.
and noodles *(Armour Classics)*, 11 oz.	230	19.0	23.0	7.0	50	660	m.q.
nuggets:							
(Kid Cuisine), 6.25 oz.	400	11.0	46.0	19.0	60	610	m.q.
(Swanson), 8¾ oz.	460	19.0	40.0	25.0	m.q.	710	m.q.
w/barbecue sauce *(Banquet Extra Helping)*, 10 oz.	640	29.0	56.0	36.0	m.q.	1390	m.q.
platter *(Freezer Queen)*, 6 oz. . .	410	14.0	36.0	23.0	m.q.	950	m.q.
w/sweet and sour sauce *(Banquet Extra Helping)*, 10 oz.	650	28.0	64.0	34.0	m.q.	m.q.	m.q.

[1] *Edible portion.*

Food and Measure	cal.	prot. (gms)	carbo. (gms)	fat (gms)	chol. (mgs)	sod. (mgs)	fiber (gms)
Chicken dinner, frozen *(cont.)*							
Oriental:							
(Armour Classics							
Lite), 10 oz. . . .	180	18.0	24.0	1.0	35	660	m.q.
(Healthy Choice),							
11.25 oz.	220	21.0	31.0	2.0	55	460	m.q.
parmigiana, 11.5 oz.:							
(Armour Classics)	370	22.0	27.0	19.0	75	1060	m.q.
(Healthy Choice)	280	23.0	38.0	3.0	60	310	m.q.
(Le Menu)	400	26.0	29.0	20.0	m.q.	900	m.q.
(Stouffer's Dinner							
Supreme)	360	31.0	25.0	15.0	m.q.	1150	m.q.
and pasta divan							
(Healthy Choice),							
11.5 oz.	310	23.0	45.0	4.0	60	510	m.q.
pattie platter *(Freezer*							
Queen), 7.5 oz. . .	360	17.0	33.0	17.0	m.q.	1160	m.q.
roast *(The Budget*							
Gourmet), 11.2 oz.	280	19.0	34.0	7.0	40	1110	m.q.
w/Supreme sauce							
(Stouffer's Dinner							
Supreme), 11³/₈ oz.	360	33.0	29.0	12.0	m.q.	990	m.q.
sweet and sour:							
(Armour Classics							
Lite), 11 oz. . . .	240	18.0	39.0	2.0	35	820	m.q.
(Healthy Choice),							
11.5 oz.	280	22.0	44.0	2.0	50	260	m.q.
(Le Menu), 11¼ oz.	450	20.0	42.0	22.0	m.q.	1170	m.q.
(Swanson), 12 oz.	380	20.0	50.0	11.0	m.q.	520	m.q.
teriyaki *(The Budget*							
Gourmet), 12 oz.	360	20.0	44.0	12.0	55	610	m.q.
w/wine and mush-							
room sauce *(Armour*							
Classics), 10.75 oz.	280	22.0	24.0	11.0	50	900	m.q.
Chicken entree,							
canned:							
à la king *(Swanson),*							
5¼ oz.	180	10.0	9.0	12.0	m.q.	690	m.q.

Food and Measure	cal.	prot. (gms)	carbo. (gms)	fat (gms)	chol. (mgs)	sod. (mgs)	fiber (gms)
chow mein (La Choy Bi-Pack), 3/4 cup	80	7.0	8.0	3.0	18	980	1.0 d
and dumplings:							
(Luck's), 7.25 oz.	240	16.0	18.0	11.0	m.q.	605	m.q.
(Swanson), 7 1/2 oz.	220	11.0	19.0	12.0	m.q.	960	m.q.
Oriental (La Choy Bi-Pack), 3/4 cup . . .	240	9.0	47.0	2.0	m.q.	1400	1.0 d
stew:							
(Swanson), 7 5/8 oz. w/dumplings	170	9.0	16.0	7.0	m.q.	960	m.q.
(Heinz), 7 1/2 oz.	210	9.0	22.0	9.0	m.q.	850	m.q.
Chicken entree, frozen:							
à la gratin (Myers), 3.5 oz.	129	9.0	9.0	7.0	m.q.	276	m.q.
à la king:							
(Banquet Cookin' Bags), 4 oz. . . .	110	8.0	9.0	5.0	m.q.	m.q.	m.q.
(Dining Lite), 9 oz.	240	14.0	30.0	7.0	40	780	m.q.
(Freezer Queen Cook-In-Pouch), 4 oz.	70	9.0	6.0	1.0	m.q.	460	m.q.
(Myers), 3.5 oz. . .	137	9.0	6.0	9.0	m.q.	357	m.q.
(Weight Watchers), 9 oz.	220	24.0	15.0	8.0	55	940	m.q.
w/rice (Freezer Queen Single Serve), 9 oz. . .	270	20.0	37.0	5.0	m.q.	520	m.q.
w/rice (Stouffer's), 9 1/2 oz.	290	19.0	34.0	9.0	m.q.	890	m.q.
almond, w/rice, vegetables (La Choy Fresh & Lite), 9.75 oz.	270	14.0	40.1	8.0	42	1092	3.0 d
à l'orange:							
(Healthy Choice), 9 oz.	260	22.0	39.0	2.0	45	90	m.q.

Food and Measure	cal.	prot. (gms)	carbo. (gms)	fat (gms)	chol. (mgs)	sod. (mgs)	fiber (gms)
Chicken entree, frozen, à l'orange *(cont.)*							
(Tyson Gourmet Selection), 9.5 oz.	300	21.0	36.0	8.0	m.q.	670	m.q.
w/almond rice *(Lean Cuisine)*, 8 oz.	260	24.0	30.0	5.0	55	430	m.q.
au gratin *(The Budget Gourmet)*, 9.1 oz.	260	20.0	21.0	11.0	70	820	m.q.
and beef luau *(Tyson Gourmet Selection)*, 10.5 oz.	330	18.0	42.0	10.0	m.q.	1030	m.q.
breast, boneless:							
barbecue marinated *(Tyson)*, 3.75 oz.	120	22.0	5.0	3.0	m.q.	400	n.a.
butter garlic marinated *(Tyson)*, 3.75 oz.	160	21.0	3.0	7.0	m.q.	320	n.a.
chunks *(Tyson)*, 3 oz.	240	13.0	10.0	17.0	30	430	m.q.
fillets *(Tyson)*, 3 oz.	190	13.0	15.0	9.0	25	400	m.q.
in herb cream sauce *(Lean Cuisine)*, 9 1/2 oz.	260	26.0	17.0	10.0	80	840	m.q.
Italian marinated *(Tyson)*, 3.75 oz.	130	22.0	6.0	2.0	m.q.	320	n.a.
lemon pepper marinated *(Tyson)*, 3.75 oz.	120	22.0	4.0	2.0	m.q.	210	n.a.
Marsala w/vegetables *(Lean Cuisine)*, 8 1/8 oz.	190	25.0	11.0	5.0	80	400	m.q.
Parmesan *(Lean Cuisine)*, 10 oz.	260	27.0	19.0	8.0	80	870	m.q.
teriyaki marinated *(Tyson)*, 3.75 oz.	130	22.0	6.0	2.0	m.q.	290	n.a.
breast tenders:							
(Banquet Hot Bites), 2.25 oz.	150	11.0	12.0	6.0	m.q.	280	m.q.

Food and Measure	cal.	prot. (gms)	carbo. (gms)	fat (gms)	chol. (mgs)	sod. (mgs)	fiber (gms)
microwave (Banquet Hot Bites), 4 oz.	260	19.0	24.0	10.0	m.q.	560	m.q.
Southern fried (Banquet Hot Bites), 2.25 oz.	160	10.0	13.0	7.0	m.q.	340	m.q.
Southern fried (Tyson), 3 oz. . . .	220	14.0	15.0	11.0	25	630	m.q.
and broccoli (Green Giant Entrees), 9.5 oz.	340	23.0	28.0	15.0	m.q.	890	m.q.
cacciatore:							
(Freezer Queen Single Serve), 9 oz.	270	20.0	33.0	6.0	m.q.	710	m.q.
(Lean Cuisine), 10 7/8 oz.	250	21.0	26.0	7.0	45	860	m.q.
(Swanson Homestyle Recipe), 11 oz.	260	15.0	33.0	8.0	m.q.	1030	m.q.
cannelloni, see "Cannelloni entree"							
cashew, w/rice (Stouffer's), 9 1/2 oz. . . .	380	31.0	29.0	16.0	m.q.	1140	m.q.
w/cheddar (Tyson Chick'n Cheddar), 2.6 oz.	220	11.0	11.0	15.0	40	310	m.q.
chow mein:							
(Chun King), 13 oz.	370	25.0	53.0	6.0	m.q.	1560	m.q.
(Dining Lite), 9 oz.	180	10.0	31.0	2.0	30	650	m.q.
(Healthy Choice), 8.5 oz.	220	16.0	31.0	3.0	45	440	m.q.
w/out noodles (Stouffer's), 8 oz.	130	13.0	11.0	4.0	m.q.	1080	m.q.
w/rice (Lean Cuisine), 11 1/4 oz.	250	14.0	36.0	5.0	35	980	m.q.
chunks:							
(Country Pride), 3 oz.	240	10.0	15.0	15.0	m.q.	560	m.q.

Food and Measure	cal.	prot. (gms)	carbo. (gms)	fat (gms)	chol. (mgs)	sod. (mgs)	fiber (gms)
Chicken entree, frozen, chunks *(cont.)*							
(Tyson Chick'n Chunks), 2.6 oz.	220	10.0	11.0	15.0	35	500	m.q.
Southern fried *(Country Pride)*, 3 oz.	280	10.0	14.0	20.0	m.q.	690	m.q.
Southern fried *(Tyson* Chick'n Chunks), 2.6 oz.	220	10.0	11.0	15.0	35	540	m.q.
Cordon Bleu *(Swift International)*, 6 oz.	360	30.0	23.0	17.0	m.q.	1010	m.q.
creamed:							
(Myers), 3.5 oz. . . .	151	12.0	5.0	10.0	m.q.	372	m.q.
(Stouffer's), 6½ oz.	300	19.0	8.0	21.0	m.q.	670	m.q.
croquettes:							
(Myers), 3.5 oz. . . .	168	16.0	10.0	7.0	m.q.	364	m.q.
breaded, gravy and *(Freezer Queen Family Suppers)*, 7 oz.	240	12.0	20.0	12.0	m.q.	1000	m.q.
diced *(Tyson)*, 3 oz.	150	26.0	0	5.0	70	50	0
Dijon *(Tyson Gourmet Selection)*, 8.5 oz.	310	17.0	22.0	17.0	m.q.	840	m.q.
dipsters *(Swanson Plump & Juicy)*, 3 oz.[1]	220	12.0	12.0	14.0	m.q.	390	m.q.
Divan *(Stouffer's)*, 8½ oz.	320	24.0	11.0	20.0	m.q.	780	m.q.
drumlets *(Swanson Plump & Juicy)*, 3 oz.[1]	220	13.0	11.0	14.0	m.q.	370	m.q.
drumsnackers:							
(Banquet Hot Bites), 2.63 oz.	220	10.0	13.0	15.0	m.q.	530	m.q.
(Banquet Platters), 7 oz.	430	20.0	49.0	19.0	m.q.	690	m.q.

[1] *Edible portion.*

Food and Measure	cal.	prot. (gms)	carbo. (gms)	fat (gms)	chol. (mgs)	sod. (mgs)	fiber (gms)
and dumplings (Banquet Family Entrees), 7 oz.	280	12.0	28.0	14.0	m.q.	m.q.	m.q.
and egg noodles w/ broccoli (The Budget Gourmet), 10 oz.	450	23.0	31.0	26.0	130	1110	m.q.
enchilada, see "Enchilada entree"							
escalloped, and noodles (Stouffer's), 10 oz.	420	21.0	27.0	25.0	m.q.	1230	m.q.
fajita, see "Fajita entree"							
w/fettuccine (The Budget Gourmet), 10 oz.	400	23.0	29.0	21.0	100	740	m.q.
fiesta (Healthy Choice), 8.5 oz. . . .	250	21.0	29.0	6.0	45	880	m.q.
Francais (Tyson Gourmet Selection), 9.5 oz.	280	19.0	20.0	14.0	m.q.	1130	m.q.
French recipe (The Budget Gourmet Slim Selects), 10 oz.	260	21.0	21.0	10.0	60	790	m.q.
fried:							
(Banquet/Banquet Hot 'n Spicy), 6.4 oz.	330	18.0	29.0	19.0	m.q.	1210	m.q.
(Swanson Homestyle Recipe), 7 oz.[1]	380	18.0	30.0	21.0	m.q.	1030	m.q.
breast portions (Banquet), 5.75 oz.	220	16.0	13.0	11.0	m.q.	710	m.q.

[1] Edible portion.

Food and Measure	cal.	prot. (gms)	carbo. (gms)	fat (gms)	chol. (mgs)	sod. (mgs)	fiber (gms)
Chicken entree, frozen, fried (cont.)							
breast portions (Swanson Plump & Juicy), 4½ oz.[1]	360	21.0	20.0	22.0	m.q.	770	m.q.
thighs and drum-sticks (Banquet), 6.25 oz.	250	14.0	14.0	14.0	m.q.	790	m.q.
white meat, regular or hot'n spicy (Banquet Platter), 9 oz.	430	38.0	21.0	22.0	105	m.q.	m.q.
glazed:							
(Dining Lite), 9 oz.	220	17.0	30.0	4.0	45	680	m.q.
(Healthy Choice), 8.5 oz.	220	21.0	27.0	3.0	50	390	m.q.
w/vegetable rice (Lean Cuisine), 8½ oz.	270	26.0	23.0	8.0	55	810	m.q.
hot'n spicy (Banquet Snack'n), 3.75 oz.	140	6.0	8.0	9.0	m.q.	480	m.q.
Imperial:							
(Chun King), 13 oz.	300	17.0	54.0	1.0	m.q.	1540	m.q.
(Weight Watchers), 9.25 oz.	220	21.0	26.0	4.0	50	910	m.q.
w/rice (La Choy Fresh & Lite), 11 oz.	260	13.0	45.0	6.0	46	1269	3.1 d
Italiano, w/fettuccini, vegetables (Right Course), 9⅝ oz.	280	24.0	29.0	8.0	45	560	m.q.
Kiev:							
(Le Menu), 8 oz.	530	20.0	24.0	39.0	m.q.	780	m.q.
(Swift International), 6 oz.	420	27.0	22.0	24.0	m.q.	1030	m.q.
(Tyson Gourmet Se-lection), 9.25 oz.	520	16.0	40.0	33.0	m.q.	1200	m.q.

[1] Edible portion.

Food and Measure	cal.	prot. (gms)	carbo. (gms)	fat (gms)	chol. (mgs)	sod. (mgs)	fiber (gms)
Mandarin *(The Budget Gourmet)*, 10 oz.	290	19.0	40.0	6.0	25	690	m.q.
Marsala *(Tyson Gourmet Selection)*, 10.5 oz.	300	19.0	26.0	13.0	m.q.	900	m.q.
mesquite *(Tyson Gourmet Selection)*, 9.5 oz.	320	23.0	35.0	10.0	m.q.	700	m.q.
nibbles:							
(Swanson Home-style Recipe), 4¼ oz.[1]	340	10.0	21.0	24.0	m.q.	480	m.q.
(Swanson Plump & Juicy), 3¼ oz.[1]	300	12.0	18.0	20.0	m.q.	660	m.q.
and noodles:							
(Dining Lite), 9 oz.	240	17.0	28.0	7.0	50	570	m.q.
(Myers), 3.5 oz. . .	136	8.0	9.0	8.0	m.q.	399	m.q.
(Stouffer's), 10 oz.	310	23.0	21.0	15.0	m.q.	1020	m.q.
nuggets:							
(Banquet Hot Bites), 2.63 oz.	210	11.0	11.0	14.0	m.q.	550	m.q.
(Banquet Platters), 6.4 oz.	430	17.0	46.0	21.0	m.q.	630	m.q.
(Country Pride), 3 oz.	250	11.0	14.0	16.0	m.q.	460	m.q.
(Freezer Queen Deluxe Family Suppers), 3 oz.	270	14.0	15.0	17.0	m.q.	770	m.q.
(Weight Watchers), 5.9 oz.	270	15.0	24.0	12.0	50	540	m.q.
w/cheddar *(Banquet Hot Bites)*, 2.63 oz.	250	11.0	11.0	18.0	m.q.	560	m.q.
hot'n spicy *(Banquet Hot Bites)*, 2.63 oz.	250	10.0	10.0	19.0	m.q.	380	m.q.

[1] *Edible portion.*

Food and Measure	cal.	prot. (gms)	carbo. (gms)	fat (gms)	chol. (mgs)	sod. (mgs)	fiber (gms)
Chicken entree, frozen, nuggets *(cont.)*							
microwave *(Tyson)*, 3.5 oz.	220	10.0	11.0	15.0	m.q.	m.q.	m.q.
Southern fried *(Banquet Hot Bites)*, 2.63 oz.	220	10.0	13.0	14.0	m.q.	530	m.q.
Oriental:							
(Lean Cuisine), 9³⁄₈ oz.	230	22.0	23.0	6.0	100	790	m.q.
(Le Menu), 10¹⁄₂ oz.	330	16.0	46.0	9.0	m.q.	820	m.q.
(Tyson Gourmet Selection), 10.25 oz.	270	20.0	32.0	7.0	m.q.	1140	m.q.
spicy *(La Choy Fresh & Lite)*, 9.75 oz.	270	11.0	52.0	4.0	42	560	4.0 d
parmigiana:							
(Celantano), 9 oz.	330	32.0	15.0	20.0	m.q.	560	m.q.
(Tyson Gourmet Selection), 11.25 oz.	380	19.0	37.0	17.0	m.q.	1100	m.q.
patties:							
(Banquet Platters), 7.5 oz.	380	15.0	34.0	21.0	m.q.	760	m.q.
(Country Pride), 3 oz.	250	12.0	14.0	16.0	m.q.	570	m.q.
(Tyson Thick & Crispy), 2.6 oz.	220	11.0	13.0	14.0	40	490	m.q.
(Tyson), 2.6 oz. . .	220	10.0	11.0	15.0	35	640	m.q.
patties, breast:							
(Banquet Hot Bites), 2.63 oz.	210	11.0	13.0	13.0	m.q.	460	m.q.
and bun *(Banquet Hot Bites)*, 4 oz.	310	16.0	31.0	14.0	m.q.	664	m.q.
Southern fried *(Country Pride)*, 3 oz.	240	11.0	13.0	16.0	m.q.	630	m.q.
Southern fried *(Banquet Hot Bites)*, 2.63 oz.	210	11.0	13.0	12.0	m.q.	620	m.q.

Food and Measure	cal.	prot. (gms)	carbo. (gms)	fat (gms)	chol. (mgs)	sod. (mgs)	fiber (gms)
Southern fried *(Tyson)*, 2.6 oz. . .	220	11.0	9.0	15.0	35	460	m.q.
Southern fried, and biscuit, microwave *(Banquet* Hot Bites), 4 oz. . . .	320	12.0	37.0	14.0	m.q.	980	m.q.
Southern fried, w/ rice pilaf *(Weight Watchers)*, 6.5 oz.	340	18.0	31.0	16.0	50	800	m.q.
picatta *(Tyson Gourmet Selection)*, 9 oz.	240	19.0	19.0	10.0	m.q.	680	m.q.
pie:							
(Banquet), 7 oz. . . .	550	15.0	39.0	36.0	35	860	m.q.
(Morton), 7 oz. . .	420	14.0	27.0	28.0	35	740	m.q.
(Myers), 3.5 oz. . . .	129	7.0	10.0	7.0	m.q.	253	m.q.
(Stouffer's), 10 oz.	530	22.0	35.0	33.0	m.q.	1260	m.q.
(Swanson), 7 oz.	370	10.0	35.0	22.0	m.q.	810	m.q.
(Swanson Homestyle Recipe), 8 oz.	380	13.0	40.0	19.0	m.q.	860	m.q.
(Swanson Hungry Man), 16 oz. . .	740	27.0	65.0	41.0	m.q.	1630	m.q.
microwave *(Banquet* Supreme), 7 oz.	430	15.0	30.0	28.0	40	740	m.q.
primavera:							
(Banquet Cookin' Bags), 4 oz.	100	6.0	14.0	2.0	m.q.	m.q.	m.q.
(Banquet Family Entrees), 7 oz. . . .	140	9.0	18.0	3.0	m.q.	m.q.	m.q.
(Celantano), 11.5 oz.	270	25.0	18.0	10.0	m.q.	580	m.q.
sesame *(Right Course)*, 10 oz. . .	320	25.0	34.0	9.0	50	590	m.q.
sticks:							
(Banquet Hot Bites), 2.63 oz.	220	10.0	11.0	15.0	m.q.	350	m.q.

Food and Measure	cal.	prot. (gms)	carbo. (gms)	fat (gms)	chol. (mgs)	sod. (mgs)	fiber (gms)
Chicken entree, frozen, sticks *(cont.)*							
(Country Pride),							
3 oz.	240	10.0	16.0	15.0	m.q.	400	m.q.
sweet and sour:							
(Banquet Cookin'							
Bags), 4 oz. . . .	130	5.0	22.0	2.0	m.q.	m.q.	m.q.
(Tyson Gourmet Se-							
lection), 11 oz.	420	22.0	50.0	15.0	m.q.	850	m.q.
w/rice *(The Budget*							
Gourmet), 10 oz.	350	18.0	53.0	7.0	40	640	m.q.
w/rice *(Freezer*							
Queen Single							
Serve), 9 oz. . .	300	20.0	48.0	4.0	m.q.	700	m.q.
w/rice and vegeta-							
bles *(La Choy*							
Fresh & Lite),							
10 oz.	260	13.0	50.1	3.0	53	601	3.7 d
tenders *(Weight*							
Watchers),							
10.19 oz.	240	16.0	43.0	1.0	40	600	m.q.
tenderloins:							
in barbecue sauce							
(Right Course),							
8¾ oz.	270	20.0	35.0	6.0	40	590	m.q.
in peanut sauce							
(Right Course),							
9¼ oz.	330	27.0	32.0	10.0	50	570	m.q.
tenders, microwave							
(Tyson), 3.5 oz. . .	230	16.0	19.0	11.0	m.q.	m.q.	m.q.
thighs and drumsticks							
(Swanson Plump &							
Juicy), 3¼ oz.[1] . .	280	16.0	11.0	19.0	m.q.	550	m.q.
w/vegetables, vermi-							
celli *(Lean Cuisine),*							
11¾ oz.	270	20.0	29.0	7.0	45	980	m.q.
walnut, crunchy *(Chun*							
King), 13 oz. . . .	310	16.0	49.0	5.0	m.q.	1700	m.q.

[1] *Edible portion.*

Food and Measure	cal.	prot. (gms)	carbo. (gms)	fat (gms)	chol. (mgs)	sod. (mgs)	fiber (gms)
wings, all varieties *(Tyson Flyers)*, 3.5 oz., 6–7 wings	220	23.0	0	14.0	m.q.	400	0
Chicken entree, packaged, 1 serving:							
Acapulco *(Hormel Top Shelf)*	390	28.0	41.0	13.0	55	1320	m.q.
breast of, glazed *(Hormel Top Shelf)* . .	210	22.0	22.0	3.0	75	1150	m.q.
sweet and sour *(Hormel Top Shelf)* . .	270	24.0	41.0	1.0	60	280	m.q.
Chicken entree, refrigerated, 5 oz.:							
bleu cheese, Italian *(Chicken By George)*	190	29.0	1.0	8.0	80	650	n.a.
Cajun *(Chicken By George)*	200	29.0	1.0	9.0	80	450	n.a.
lemon herb *(Chicken By George)*	150	27.0	2.0	4.0	70	480	n.a.
mesquite barbecue *(Chicken By George)*	170	29.0	5.0	4.0	70	680	n.a.
mustard and dill *(Chicken By George)*	180	29.0	1.0	7.0	80	530	n.a.
teriyaki *(Chicken By George)*	180	30.0	6.0	4.0	65	340	n.a.
tomato herb and basil *(Chicken By George)*	190	28.0	4.0	7.0	90	430	n.a.
Chicken entree mix[1]: barbecue: *(Hunt's Minute Gourmet)*, 6.8 oz.	320	34.0	37.0	4.0	m.q.	1160	m.q.

[1] *Prepared according to package directions.*

Food and Measure	cal.	prot. (gms)	carbo. (gms)	fat (gms)	chol. (mgs)	sod. (mgs)	fiber (gms)
Chicken entree mix, barbecue *(cont.)*							
style *(Lipton Microeasy)*, 1/4 pkg.[1]	220	16.0	24.0	6.0	m.q.	1020	m.q.
w/scalloped potatoes *(Chicken Applause! Dinner)*, 1/5 box	380	36.0	44.0	7.0	105	1050	m.q.
cacciatore *(Hunt's Minute Gourmet)*, 8.4 oz.	260	34.0	15.0	6.0	m.q.	840	m.q.
country *(Lipton Microeasy)*, 1/4 pkg.[1]	190	18.0	15.0	6.0	m.q.	880	m.q.
mushroom, w/rice *(Chicken Applause! Dinner)*, 1/5 box	380	35.0	46.0	6.0	100	1130	m.q.
sweet and sour: *(Hunt's Minute Gourmet)*, 7.8 oz.	300	33.0	32.0	4.0	m.q.	390	m.q.
w/rice *(Chicken Applause! Dinner)*, 1/5 box	360	34.0	45.0	m.q.	100	850	m.q.
three cheese, w/rice *(Chicken Applause! Dinner)*, 1/5 box	430	39.0	35.0	15.0	130	1130	m.q.
Chicken fat: 1 oz.	178	1.1	0	19.3	16	9	0
Chicken frankfurter:							
(Longacre), 1 oz.	63	4.0	1.0	5.0	30	230	0
batter-wrapped *(Tyson Corn Dogs)*, 3.5 oz.	280	9.0	28.0	14.0	75	70	m.q.
Chicken giblets, simmered:							
broiler-fryer:							
4 oz.	178	29.3	1.1	5.4	446	66	0
chopped, 1 cup	228	37.5	1.4	6.9	570	85	0

[1] *Prepared with 2 1/2 lbs. chicken.*

Food and Measure	cal.	prot. (gms)	carbo. (gms)	fat (gms)	chol. (mgs)	sod. (mgs)	fiber (gms)
Chicken gravy:							
canned:							
(Franco-American), 2 oz.	50	0	3.0	4.0	n.a.	310	n.a.
(Heinz), 2 oz.	25	1.0	3.0	2.0	1	110	n.a.
w/chunky chicken (Hormel Great Beginnings), 5 oz.	147	14.0	5.0	8.0	m.q.	567	n.a.
giblet (Franco-American), 2 oz.	30	1.0	3.0	2.0	n.a.	300	n.a.
mix[1]:							
(Lawry's), 1 cup	99	2.5	15.5	2.8	n.a.	980	.1 c
(McCormick/Schilling), 1/4 cup	22	.8	3.7	.4	n.a.	300	n.a.
Chicken ham:							
(Pilgrim's Pride), 1-oz. slice	35	4.0	.8	1.8	18	430	0
Chicken liver, see "Liver"							
Chicken luncheon meat, see "Chicken, boneless and luncheon meat"							
Chicken pie, see "Chicken entree, frozen"							
Chicken salad, 1 oz.:							
(Longacre)	64	3.0	3.0	5.0	15	110	n.a.
(Longacre Saladfest)	47	4.0	1.0	3.0	15	150	n.a.
Chicken sandwich, frozen:							
(MicroMagic), 4.5 oz.	390	13.0	42.0	16.0	35	650	m.q.
barbecue (Tyson Microwave), 4 oz.	230	16.0	27.0	6.0	m.q.	510	m.q.
breast (Tyson Microwave), 3.5 oz.	275	14.0	27.0	12.0	m.q.	m.q.	m.q.

[1] Prepared according to package directions.

Food and Measure	cal.	prot. (gms)	carbo. (gms)	fat (gms)	chol. (mgs)	sod. (mgs)	fiber (gms)
Chicken sandwich, frozen *(cont.)*							
mini *(Tyson* Microwave), 3.5 oz. . . .	230	12.0	39.0	5.0	m.q.	m.q.	m.q.
pocket:							
(Lean Pockets Supreme), 1 pkg.	240	16.0	33.0	5.0	m.q.	810	m.q.
'n cheddar *(Hot Pockets),* 5 oz.	310	16.0	38.0	11.0	m.q.	720	m.q.
Oriental *(Lean Pockets),* 1 pkg.	250	14.0	35.0	6.0	m.q.	840	m.q.
Parmesan *(Lean Pockets),* 1 pkg.	270	19.0	35.0	6.0	m.q.	750	m.q.
Chicken sauce mix, 1 pkg.:							
cacciatore *(McCormick/Schilling* Sauce Blends) . .	132	3.6	28.0	4.8	n.a.	1092	m.q.
creole *(McCormick/ Schilling* Sauce Blends)	140	2.0	24.0	4.8	n.a.	1084	m.q.
curry *(McCormick/ Schilling* Sauce Blends)	152	2.4	24.0	5.6	n.a.	1288	m.q.
Dijon *(McCormick/ Schilling* Sauce Blends)	156	3.2	20.0	6.8	n.a.	1414	m.q.
mesquite marinade *(McCormick/Schilling* Sauce Blends)	132	1.6	24.0	3.0	n.a.	2068	m.q.
teriyaki *(McCormick/ Schilling* Sauce Blends)	172	.6.8	28.0	3.6	n.a.	1380	m.q.
Chicken seasoning and coating mix:							
(Golden Dipt), 1 oz.	90	2.0	20.0	0	0	1430	m.q.
(McCormick/Schilling Bag'n Season), 1 pkg. . . . .:. . .	177	3.7	22.6	1.4	0	2564	m.q.

Food and Measure	cal.	prot. (gms)	carbo. (gms)	fat (gms)	chol. (mgs)	sod. (mgs)	fiber (gms)
(Shake'n Bake),							
1/4 pouch	80	2.0	14.0	2.0	0	450	m.q.
barbecue *(Shake'n Bake)*, 1/4 pouch	90	1.0	18.0	2.0	0	840	m.q.
batter, Cajun *(Tone's)*, 1 tsp.	12	.3	2.6	.1	0	75	.1 d
extra crispy *(Shake'n Bake Oven Fry)*, 1/4 pouch	110	3.0	20.0	2.0	0	810	m.q.
homestyle *(Shake'n Bake Oven Fry)*, 1/4 pouch	80	1.0	15.0	2.0	0	970	m.q.
Chicken spread, canned:							
(Hormel), 1/2 oz. . . .	30	2.0	0	2.0	m.q.	m.q.	0
chunky *(Swanson)*, 1 oz.	60	4.0	2.0	4.0	m.q.	140	n.a.
chunky *(Underwood)*, 1/2 can, 2.4 oz. . .	150	10.0	3.0	11.0	m.q.	575	n.a.
Chickpeas, 1/2 cup:							
boiled	134	7.3	22.5	2.1	0	6	2.9 d
canned:							
w/liquid	143	5.9	27.1	1.4	0	359	1.6 c
(Allens)	110	5.0	18.0	<1.0	0	320	m.q.
(Old El Paso) . . .	190	5.0	16.0	12.0	0	250	m.q.
Chicory, witloof:							
5–7"-long head, 2.1 oz.	8	.5	1.7	.1	0	4	m.q.
1/2 cup	7	.5	1.7	.1	0	3	m.q.
Chicory greens:							
trimmed, 1 oz.	7	.5	1.3	.1	0	13	.2 c
chopped, 1/2 cup . .	21	1.5	4.2	.3	0	41	.7 c
Chicory root:							
1 medium, 2.6 oz. . .	44	.8	10.5	.1	0	30	1.2 c
1" pieces, 1/2 cup . .	33	.6	7.9	.1	0	23	.9 c

Food and Measure	cal.	prot. (gms)	carbo. (gms)	fat (gms)	chol. (mgs)	sod. (mgs)	fiber (gms)
Chili, canned, 7.5 oz., except as noted:							
(Heinz Chili Con Carne), 7³/₄ oz. . . .	350	15.0	27.0	21.0	m.q.	1000	m.q.
(Heinz Chili Mac) .	250	10.0	26.0	12.0	m.q.	860	m.q.
w/beans:							
(Dennison's, 15 oz.)	310	16.0	27.0	15.0	m.q.	875	8.0 d
(Dennison's Cook-Off)*	340	17.0	25.0	19.0	m.q.	915	8.0 d
(Hormel, 15 oz.) .	310	17.0	23.0	17.0	m.q.	1127	m.q.
(Hormel Micro-Cup)	250	15.0	23.0	11.0	65	980	m.q.
(Van Camp's), 1 cup	352	14.9	20.9	23.2	m.q.	1215	2.3 c
(Wolf Brand), 1 cup	345	15.0	21.8	22.0	m.q.	1013	2.3 c
chunky *(Dennison's)*	310	16.0	28.0	14.0	m.q.	780	10.0 d
extra spicy *(Wolf)*	324	14.1	20.6	20.6	m.q.	926	2.2 c
hot *(Dennison's,* 15 oz.)	310	16.0	26.0	16.0	m.q.	910	7.0 d
hot *(Gebhardt),* 4 oz.	189	7.1	9.2	14.2	17	497	2.1 d
hot *(Heinz),* 7³/₄ oz.	330	15.0	30.0	16.0	m.q.	1140	m.q.
hot *(Hormel,* 15 oz.)	310	16.0	24.0	16.0	m.q.	1121	m.q.
w/out beans:							
(Dennison's, 15 oz.)	300	17.0	15.0	19.0	m.q.	1380	m.q.
(Hormel, 15 oz.) . .	370	17.0	12.0	28.0	m.q.	1012	m.q.
(Hormel), 10.5-oz. can	540	24.0	19.0	41.0	m.q.	1384	m.q.
(Van Camp's), 1 cup	412	15.4	12.1	33.5	m.q.	1499	1.6 c
(Wolf Brand), 1 cup	387	20.7	16.2	26.6	m.q.	1042	2.0 c
(Wolf Brand Chili-Mac)	317	11.5	22.9	19.9	m.q.	854	1.1 c
extra spicy *(Wolf* Brand)	363	19.4	15.3	24.9	m.q.	962	1.9 c
hot *(Hormel,* 15 oz.)	370	17.0	12.0	28.0	m.q.	985	m.q.
w/chicken, spicy *(Hain)*	130	11.0	19.0	2.0	40	1030	m.q.
vegetarian:							
(Gebhardt), 4 oz.	219	9.6	6.9	17.1	0	555	m.q.

Food and Measure	cal.	prot. (gms)	carbo. (gms)	fat (gms)	chol. (mgs)	sod. (mgs)	fiber (gms)
(Worthington),							
²/₃ cup	190	10.0	15.0	10.0	0	550	m.q.
spicy *(Hain)*	160	7.0	29.0	1.0	0	1060	m.q.
spicy *(Hain* Re-							
duced Sodium)	170	7.0	31.0	1.0	0	200	m.q.
tempeh, spicy *(Hain)*	160	7.0	24.0	4.0	0	1350	m.q.
Chili beans, canned:							
(Hunt's), 4 oz.	102	5.7	18.1	0	0	488	m.q.
(S&W), ¹/₂ cup	130	7.0	23.0	1.0	n.a.	520	m.q.
Caliente style *(Green*							
Giant/Joan of Arc),							
¹/₂ cup	100	7.0	21.0	1.0	n.a.	620	7.3 d
in chili gravy *(Den-*							
nison's), 7.5 oz. . .	180	12.0	30.0	1.0	n.a.	770	12.0 d
hot *(Allens),* ¹/₂ cup	90	5.0	17.0	<1.0	n.a.	420	m.q.
Mexican style:							
(Allens), ¹/₂ cup . .	135	8.0	24.0	<1.0	n.a.	430	m.q.
(Van Camp's), 1 cup	210	11.4	35.8	2.4	n.a.	718	2.6 c
in sauce *(Hormel),*							
5 oz.	130	6.0	19.0	3.0	n.a.	453	m.q.
spiced *(Gebhardt),*							
4 oz.	113	7.5	19.7	1.1	0	590	6.7 d
Chili concentrate:							
(Oscar Mayer), 1 oz.	78	3.9	2.5	5.8	14	426	m.q.
Chili dip:							
(La Victoria), 1 tbsp.	6	<1.0	1.0	<1.0	n.a.	90	n.a.
Chili entree, frozen:							
con carne:							
(Swanson Home-							
style Recipe),							
8¹/₄ oz.	270	20.0	26.0	10.0	m.q.	740	m.q.
w/beans *(Stouf-*							
fer's), 8³/₄ oz. . . .	260	19.0	24.0	10.0	m.q.	1270	m.q.
vegetarian *(Right*							
Course), 9³/₄ oz.	280	9.0	45.0	7.0	0	590	m.q.

Food and Measure	cal.	prot. (gms)	carbo. (gms)	fat (gms)	chol. (mgs)	sod. (mgs)	fiber (gms)
Chili entree, pack- aged:							
con carne suprema *(Hormel Top Shelf)*, 1 serving	320	24.0	30.0	12.0	65	1140	m.q.
Chili and hot dog:							
w/beans and bun *(Campbell's Souper-* *Combo)*, 10.8 oz.	470	21.0	49.0	21.0	m.q.	1520	m.q.
Chili mix:[1]							
dry *(Gebhardt Chili* *Quik)*, 1.5-oz. pkt.	82	2.5	16.8	1.1	0	2784	3.0 d
w/beans, 4 oz.:							
(Good Times Chili Fixin's)	80	3.0	16.0	1.0	0	600	m.q.
Texas style *(Good* *Times* Chili Fix- in's)	90	4.0	19.0	1.0	0	560	m.q.
w/out beans, 4 oz.:							
(Good Times Chili Fixin's)	50	2.0	11.0	0	0	570	m.q.
Texas style *(Good* *Times* Chili Fix- in's)	60	2.0	13.0	1.0	0	770	m.q.
Chili pepper, see "Pepper, chili"							
Chili powder:							
1 tbsp.	24	.9	4.1	1.3	0	76	1.7 c
1 tsp.	8	.3	1.4	.4	0	26	.6 c
(Gebhardt), 1 tsp. . . .	6	0	1.0	0	0	30	m.q.
Chili sauce:							
(Del Monte), 1/4 cup	70	1.0	17.0	0	0	835	m.q.
(Heinz), 1 tbsp. . . .	17	.2	3.8	tr.	0	191	m.q.
(S&W Chili Makin's), 1/2 cup	100	5.0	20.0	1.0	0	782	m.q.
green, mild *(El* *Molino)*, 2 tbsp. . .	10	0	2.0	0	0	210	m.q.

[1] *Prepared according to package directions, except as noted.*

Food and Measure	cal.	prot. (gms)	carbo. (gms)	fat (gms)	chol. (mgs)	sod. (mgs)	fiber (gms)
hot dog:							
(Gebhardt), 2 tbsp.	20	1.0	2.0	1.0	n.a.	150	m.q.
(Wolf), 1.25 oz. . . .	44	1.5	4.4	2.3	n.a.	199	.4 c
Chili seasoning mix:							
(Lawry's Seasoning							
Blends), 1 pkg. . . .	143	4.9	26.6	1.8	0	2291	2.1 c
(McCormick/Schilling),							
1 pkg	18	6.5	3.0	0	0	193	m.q.
(Tio Sancho), 1.23 oz.	109	4.1	60.9	2.2	n.a.	832	4.2 c
Chimichanga dinner,							
frozen, 11 oz.:							
beef (Old El Paso							
Festive Dinners) . .	540	23.0	65.0	21.0	m.q.	1200	m.q.
beef and cheese (Old							
El Paso Festive Din-							
ners)	510	22.0	53.0	23.0	m.q.	1400	m.q.
Chimichanga entree,							
frozen, 1 pkg.:							
bean and cheese (Old							
El Paso)	350	12.0	36.0	17.0	m.q.	700	m.q.
beef (Old El Paso)	380	10.0	35.0	23.0	m.q.	470	m.q.
beef and pork (Old El							
Paso)	340	13.0	35.0	16.0	m.q.	700	m.q.
chicken (Old El Paso)	370	10.0	35.0	21.0	m.q.	460	m.q.
Chitterlings, pork:							
simmered, 4 oz. . . .	344	11.6	0	32.6	162	44	0
Chives:							
fresh, 1 oz.	7	.8	1.1	.2	0	2	.9 d
fresh, chopped,							
1 tbsp.	1	.1	.1	<.1	0	tr.	.1 d
freeze-dried, 1/4 cup	2	.2	.5	<.1	0	24	.1 c
freeze-dried, 1 tbsp.	1	<.1	.1	<.1	0	6	<.1 c
Chocolate, see							
"Candy"							

Food and Measure	cal.	prot. (gms)	carbo. (gms)	fat (gms)	chol. (mgs)	sod. (mgs)	fiber (gms)
Chocolate, baking:							
bars, 1 oz., except as noted:							
semi-sweet *(Baker's)*	140	1.0	17.0	9.0	n.a.	0	m.q.
semi-sweet *(Hershey's* Premium)	140	1.0	16.0	8.0	n.a.	0	m.q.
semi-sweet *(Nestlé)*	160	2.0	16.0	9.0	n.a.	0	m.q.
sweet *(Baker's German's)*	140	1.0	17.0	10.0	n.a.	0	m.q.
unsweetened *(Baker's)*	140	3.0	9.0	15.0	n.a.	0	m.q.
unsweetened *(Hershey's)*	190	4.0	7.0	16.0	0	5	m.q.
unsweetened *(Nestlé)*	180	4.0	9.0	14.0	n.a.	0	m.q.
white *(Nestlé* Premier), 1/2 oz. . .	80	1.0	8.0	5.0	n.a.	15	m.q.
chips, 1/4 cup, except as noted:							
milk *(Baker's),* 1 oz.	140	2.0	18.0	8.0	5	25	m.q.
milk *(Baker's* Big Chip)*	240	3.0	30.0	13.0	10	40	m.q.
milk *(Hershey's),* 1 oz.	150	2.0	27.0	12.0	10	55	m.q.
milk *(Nestlé* Toll House Morsels), 1 oz.	150	1.0	19.0	7.0	n.a.	15	m.q.
mint *(Hershey's)*	230	2.0	28.0	12.0	n.a.	<1	m.q.
mint or semi-sweet *(Nestlé* Toll House Morsels), 1 oz.	150	2.0	18.0	8.0	n.a.	0	m.q.
semi-sweet *(Baker's)*	200	2.0	28.0	11.0	n.a.	0	m.q.
semi-sweet *(Baker's* Big Chip)	220	2.0	31.0	13.0	n.a.	0	m.q.

Food and Measure	cal.	prot. (gms)	carbo. (gms)	fat (gms)	chol. (mgs)	sod. (mgs)	fiber (gms)
semi-sweet, chocolate flavor (Baker's)	200	2.0	30.0	9.0	n.a.	30	m.q.
semi-sweet, regular or mini (Hershey's)	220	2.0	26.0	12.0	0	5	m.q.
vanilla (Hershey's)	240	3.0	25.0	14.0	n.a.	65	m.q.
chunks, 1 oz.:							
milk (Hershey's) . .	160	2.0	16.0	9.0	n.a.	25	m.q.
milk (Nestlé Toll House Treasures)	150	2.0	17.0	9.0	n.a.	20	m.q.
semi-sweet (Hershey's)	140	1.0	15.0	8.0	n.a.	n.a.	m.q.
semi-sweet (Nestlé Toll House Treasures)	150	2.0	18.0	8.0	n.a.	0	m.q.
white (Nestlé Toll House Premier Treasures) . . .	160	2.0	15.0	10.0	n.a.	25	m.q.
pre-melted (Nestlé Choco Bake), 1 oz.	190	4.0	7.0	16.0	n.a.	0	m.q.
shreds (Tone's), 1 tsp.	21	.1	2.2	1.4	0	1	.1 d
Chocolate flavor drink:							
canned:							
all varieties (Sego), 10 fl. oz.	225	11.0	43.0	1.0	n.a.	445	(0)
(Frostee), 1 cup . .	200	2.0	30.0	8.0	n.a.	160	(0)
mix, powder:							
(Hershey's), .8 oz. or 3 tsp.	90	1.0	22.0	4.0	0	40	m.q.
(Nestlé Quik), 3/4 oz., approx. 2 1/2 heaping tsp.	90	1.0	20.0	1.0	0	25	m.q.
(Pillsbury Instant Breakfast), 1 pkt.	130	6.0	26.0	0	0	190	m.q.

Food and Measure	cal.	prot. (gms)	carbo. (gms)	fat (gms)	chol. (mgs)	sod. (mgs)	fiber (gms)
Chocolate milk, 1 cup, except as noted:							
(Hershey's)	210	7.0	28.0	9.0	m.q.	120	m.q.
(Meadow Gold) . . .	210	8.0	25.0	8.0	m.q.	240	m.q.
lowfat:							
2% (Borden Dutch)	180	8.0	25.0	5.0	m.q.	180	m.q.
2% (Hershey's) . .	190	8.0	29.0	5.0	20	130	m.q.
Chocolate mousse mix[1]:							
(Jell-O Rich & Luscious), 1/2 cup . . .	150	5.0	21.0	6.0	10	75	n.a.
fudge (Jell-O Rich & Luscious), 1/2 cup	140	5.0	20.0	6.0	10	75	n.a.
Chocolate syrup, 2 tbsp.:							
(Hershey's)	80	1.0	17.0	1.0	0	20	m.q.
(Nestlé Quik)	100	1.0	22.0	1.0	0	45	m.q.
flavored (Smucker's)	130	1.0	27.0	2.0	0	40	m.q.
Chocolate topping, 2 tbsp., except as noted:							
(Kraft), 1 tbsp.	60	1.0	13.0	0	0	15	m.q.
(Smucker's Magic Shell)	190	1.0	16.0	15.0	n.a.	25	m.q.
dark, flavored (Smucker's Special)	130	1.0	31.0	1.0	n.a.	45	m.q.
fudge:							
(Hershey's)	100	1.0	14.0	4.0	5	30	m.q.
(Smucker's)	130	1.0	31.0	1.0	n.a.	45	m.q.
(Smucker's Magic Shell)	190	1.0	16.0	15.0	n.a.	50	m.q.
fudge, hot:							
(Kraft), 1 tbsp. . .	70	1.0	11.0	3.0	0	50	m.q.
(Smucker's)	110	1.0	18.0	4.0	n.a.	55	m.q.
(Smucker's Special)	150	2.0	23.0	5.0	n.a.	60	m.q.

[1] Prepared according to package directions, with whole milk.

Food and Measure	cal.	prot. (gms)	carbo. (gms)	fat (gms)	chol. (mgs)	sod. (mgs)	fiber (gms)
Swiss milk chocolate *(Smucker's)*	140	3.0	31.0	1.0	n.a.	70	m.q.
milk:							
w/almonds *(Nestlé Candytops),* 1.25 oz.	230	2.0	14.0	18.0	m.q.	15	m.q.
w/crisps *(Nestlé Crunch Candytops),* 1.25 oz.	220	2.0	16.0	17.0	m.q.	40	m.q.
nut *(Smucker's Magic Shell)*	200	2.0	15.0	16.0	n.a.	40	m.q.
white w/almonds *(Nestlé Candytops),* 1.25 oz.	230	3.0	12.0	19.0	n.a.	20	m.q.
Chow mein, see specific entree listings							
Chow mein noodles, see "Noodles, Chinese"							
Chrysanthemum garland:							
raw, 1" pieces, ¹/₂ cup	2	.2	.5	<.1	0	7	.1 c
boiled, drained, 1" pieces, ¹/₂ cup	10	.8	2.2	.1	0	27	.6 c
Chub, see "Cisco, smoked"							
Cinnamon, ground:							
(Tone's), 1 tsp. . . .	6	.1	1.8	.1	0	1	.6 d
Cisco, meat only:							
raw, 1 lb.	446	86.1	0	8.7	m.q.	249	0
raw, 1 oz.	28	5.4	0	.5	m.q.	16	0
smoked, 4 oz.	201	18.6	0	13.5	36	545	0
Citrus fruit juice drink, 6 fl. oz:							
(Hi-C Citrus Cooler)	95	.1	23.3	<.1	0	17	(0)

Food and Measure	cal.	prot. (gms)	carbo. (gms)	fat (gms)	chol. (mgs)	sod. (mgs)	fiber (gms)
Citrus fruit juice drink *(cont.)*							
chilled or frozen[1] *(Five Alive)*	87	.6	21.8	0	0	23	(0)
Citrus punch:							
chilled or frozen[1] *(Minute Maid)*, 6 fl. oz.	93	.1	23.1	<.1	0	18	(0)
Citrus salad:							
(Florigold), 8 oz. . . .	120	2.7	27.2	0	0	3	m.q.
Clam, meat only:							
raw:							
1 oz.	21	3.6	7.3	.3	10	16	0
9 large or 20 small, 6.3 oz.	133	23.0	4.6	1.8	60	100	0
boiled, poached or steamed, 4 oz. . .	168	29.0	5.8	2.2	76	127	0
Clam, canned:							
chopped or minced: *(Gorton's)*, 1/2 can	70	12.0	4.0	1.0	m.q.	640	0
w/liquid *(Doxsee)*, 6.5 oz.	100	14.0	8.0	<1.0	m.q.	1160	0
Clam, frozen:							
battered, fried *(Mrs. Paul's)*, 2 1/2 oz. . .	240	8.0	22.0	13.0	m.q.	380	m.q.
strips, crunchy *(Gorton's* Microwave Specialty), 3.5 oz.	330	10.0	24.0	22.0	30	430	m.q.
Clam chowder, see "Soup"							
Clam dip, 2 tbsp.:							
(Kraft)	50	1.0	3.0	4.0	30	240	n.a.
(Kraft Premium) . .	45	1.0	2.0	4.0	20	210	n.a.
Clam juice:							
(Doxsee), 3 fl. oz. . .	4	<1.0	0	0	n.a.	110	0
Clam sauce:							
canned, 4 oz.:							
red *(Ferrara)*	70	5.0	8.0	2.0	10	320	m.q.

[1] *Diluted according to package directions.*

Food and Measure	cal.	prot. (gms)	carbo. (gms)	fat (gms)	chol. (mgs)	sod. (mgs)	fiber (gms)
white *(Ferrara)* ..	80	5.0	4.0	5.0	10	570	m.q.
refrigerated:							
red *(Contadina Fresh)*, 7.5 oz.	120	7.0	15.0	4.0	35	800	m.q.
white *(Contadina Fresh)*, 6 oz. ...	290	8.0	13.0	23.0	94	800	m.q.
Cloves, ground:							
1 tbsp..........	21	.4	4.0	1.3	0	16	.6 c
1 tsp.	7	.1	1.3	.4	0	5	.2 c
Coating mix, see specific listings							
Cobbler:							
apple, deep dish *(Awrey's)*, 1/8 pie	320	2.0	48.0	14.0	0	300	1.0 d
blueberry, deep dish *(Awrey's)*, 1/8 pie	310	2.0	45.0	14.0	0	360	2.0 d
frozen, 1/6 pkg., except as noted:							
apple *(Pet-Ritz)* ..	290	1.0	50.0	9.0	n.a.	m.q.	m.q.
apple *(Stilwell)*, 4 oz.	200	2.0	4.0	4.0	n.a.	225	m.q.
blackberry *(Pet-Ritz)*	250	2.0	39.0	10.0	n.a.	m.q.	m.q.
blackberry *(Stilwell)*, 4 oz.	280	3.0	50.0	8.0	n.a.	220	m.q.
blueberry *(Pet-Ritz)*	370	3.0	50.0	12.0	n.a.	m.q.	m.q.
cherry *(Pet-Ritz)* ..	280	2.0	46.0	10.0	n.a.	m.q.	m.q.
cherry *(Stilwell)*, 4 oz.	250	3.0	46.0	6.0	n.a.	205	m.q.
peach *(Pet-Ritz)* ..	260	2.0	46.0	10.0	n.a.	m.q.	m.q.
peach *(Stilwell)*, 4 oz.	270	2.0	55.0	5.0	n.a.	200	m.q.
strawberry *(Pet-Ritz)*	290	1.0	50.0	9.0	n.a.	m.q.	m.q.
Cocktail sauce, 1 tbsp., except as noted:							
(Del Monte), 1/4 cup	70	1.0	17.0	0	0	765	n.a.
(Great Impressions)	21	.2	4.7	.1	0	182	n.a.
(Sauceworks)	12	0	3.0	0	0	170	n.a.

Food and Measure	cal.	prot. (gms)	carbo. (gms)	fat (gms)	chol. (mgs)	sod. (mgs)	fiber (gms)
Cocktail sauce *(cont.)*							
(Stokely)	18	0	5.0	0	0	90	n.a.
regular or extra hot							
(Golden Dipt) . . .	20	0	5.0	0	0	210	n.a.
seafood:							
Creole *(Great Impressions)*	21	.2	4.7	.1	0	182	n.a.
dipping *(Great Impressions)*	17	.6	2.2	.7	0	129	n.a.
dipping, Polynesian *(Great Impressions)*	38	<1.0	9.5	<1.0	0	127	n.a.
Cocoa:							
powder, 1 oz., except as noted:							
(Bensdorp)	130	6.0	8.0	7.0	<1.0	5	m.q.
(Hershey's)	120	7.0	13.0	4.0	0	10	m.q.
(Nestlé), 1.5 oz. . . .	180	11.0	21.0	6.0	n.a.	6	m.q.
European *(Hershey's)*	90	7.0	8.0	3.0	0	15	m.q.
mix, dry, 1 pkt., except as noted:							
(Carnation 70-Calorie)	70	3.0	16.0	.3	1	135	.2 c
(Hills Bros), 2 tbsp.	110	3.0	23.0	1.0	n.a.	55	m.q.
(Swiss Miss Lite)	70	1.0	17.0	.8	n.a.	160	m.q.
Amaretto or chocolate creme *(Swiss Miss)*, 1.25 oz.	150	2.0	29.0	3.0	n.a.	220	m.q.
chocolate, double rich *(Swiss Miss)*	110	2.0	19.1	3.0	0	161	m.q.
chocolate, milk *(Swiss Miss)* . .	110	1.0	20.0	3.0	<1	170	m.q.
fudge *(Carnation)*, 1-oz. pkt.	110	1.0	24.0	1.3	1	135	.3 d
w/mini marshmallows *(Swiss Miss)*, 1 oz.	110	1.0	20.0	3.0	0	150	m.q.

Food and Measure	cal.	prot. (gms)	carbo. (gms)	fat (gms)	chol. (mgs)	sod. (mgs)	fiber (gms)
Coconut:							
fresh, shelled:							
1 oz.	100	.9	4.3	9.5	0	6	2.6 d
1 piece, 2″×2″×1/2″, approx. 1.6 oz. . .	159	1.5	6.9	15.1	0	9	4.1 d
shredded or grated, 1 cup not packed	283	2.7	12.2	26.8	0	16	7.2 d
canned (Baker's Angel Flake), 1/3 cup . .	110	1.0	10.0	9.0	0	5	m.q.
dried, toasted, 1 oz.	168	1.5	12.6	13.4	0	11	.7 c
packaged, 1/3 cup:							
(Baker's Angel Flake)	120	1.0	10.0	8.0	0	75	m.q.
(Baker's Premium Shred)	140	1.0	12.0	9.0	0	85	m.q.
toasted (Baker's Angel Flake) . .	200	2.0	17.0	17.0	0	85	m.q.
Coconut cream, canned, sweetened:							
(Coco Lopez), 2 tbsp.	120	0	20.0	5.0	0	10	m.q.
(Holland House), 1 fl. oz.	81	0	18.0	m.q.	0	21	m.q.
Coconut milk[1]:							
1 tbsp.	35	.3	.8	3.6	0	2	m.q.
canned, 1 tbsp. . .	30	.3	.4	3.2	0	2	m.q.
Coconut water[2]:							
1 tbsp.	3	.1	.6	<.1	0	16	tr.c
Cod, meat only:							
fresh, Atlantic:							
raw, 1 lb.	372	80.8	0	3.1	195	246	0
raw, 1 oz.	23	5.0	0	.2	12	15	0
baked, broiled or microwaved, 4 oz.	119	25.9	0	1.0	62	88	0

[1] Liquid expressed from mixture of grated coconut meat and water.

[2] Liquid from coconuts.

Food and Measure	cal.	prot. (gms)	carbo. (gms)	fat (gms)	chol. (mgs)	sod. (mgs)	fiber (gms)
Cod *(cont.)*							
fresh, Pacific:							
raw, 1 lb.	372	81.2	0	2.9	168	322	0
raw, 1 oz.	23	5.1	0	.2	10	20	0
canned, Atlantic, w/							
liquid, 4 oz.	119	25.8	0	1.0	62	247	0
dried, Atlantic, salted,							
1 oz.	81	17.6	0	.7	42	1968	0
Cod, frozen:							
(Booth), 4 oz.	89	20.0	0	1.0	m.q.	350	0
(Gorton's Fishmarket							
Fresh), 5 oz.	110	26.0	0	1.0	m.q.	90	0
(SeaPak), 4 oz. . . .	90	20.0	0	1.0	m.q.	135	0
(Van de Kamp's Natu-							
ral), 4 oz.	90	19.0	1.0	1.0	55	65	0
breaded *(Van de*							
Kamp's Light),							
1 piece	250	16.0	19.0	12.0	40	430	m.q.
breaded *(Mrs. Paul's*							
Light), 1 piece . . .	220	17.0	23.0	7.0	m.q.	412	m.q.
individually wrapped							
(Booth), 4 oz.	90	20.0	0	1.0	m.q.	80	0
minced, nuggets,							
crunchy *(Frionor*							
Bunch O'Crunch),							
8 nuggets, 4 oz. . .	320	14.0	19.0	21.0	m.q.	411	<.1 d
Cod entree, frozen,							
9.5 oz.:							
au gratin *(Booth)* . .	280	27.0	18.0	11.0	m.q.	1160	m.q.
Florentine *(Booth)* . .	244	20.0	29.0	6.0	m.q.	880	m.q.
w/lemon butter sauce							
and rice *(Booth)* . .	567	22.0	27.0	38.0	m.q.	1330	m.q.
w/mushroom sauce							
and rice *(Booth)* . .	280	27.0	19.0	11.0	m.q.	1010	m.q.
Cod liver oil, see							
"Oil"							
Coffee:							
brewed, 6 fl. oz. . . .	4	.1	.8	0	0	4	0

Food and Measure	cal.	prot. (gms)	carbo. (gms)	fat (gms)	chol. (mgs)	sod. (mgs)	fiber (gms)
instant, regular, 1 rounded tsp. powder	4	.2	.7	tr.	0	1	0
freeze-dried, all varieties *(Taster's Choice),* 1 cup prepared	4	<1.0	1.0	<1.0	0	0	0
Coffee, flavored[1]:							
6 fl. oz.:							
cafe Amaretto *(General Foods* International)	50	0	7.0	2.0	0	20	(0)
cafe Francais:							
(General Foods International) . . .	60	0	6.0	3.0	0	25	(0)
(General Foods International Sugar Free)	35	0	3.0	2.0	0	30	(0)
cafe Irish creme *(General Foods* International)	50	0	8.0	2.0	0	15	(0)
cafe Vienna:							
(General Foods International) . . .	60	0	10.0	2.0	0	110	(0)
(General Foods International Sugar Free)	30	0	3.0	2.0	0	80	(0)
(Hills Bros Cafe Coffees)	60	1.0	9.0	2.0	n.a.	35	(0)
chocolate, double Dutch *(General Foods* International)	50	0	8.0	2.0	0	15	(0)
chocolate mint, Dutch *(General Foods* International)	50	0	8.0	2.0	0	80	(0)

[1] *Prepared according to package directions.*

Food and Measure	cal.	prot. (gms)	carbo. (gms)	fat (gms)	chol. (mgs)	sod. (mgs)	fiber (gms)
Coffee, flavored *(cont.)*							
mocha:							
(General Foods International Suisse Mocha)	50	0	7.0	3.0	0	15	(0)
(General Foods International Suisse Mocha Sugar Free)	30	0	3.0	2.0	0	15	(0)
(MJB)	52	.6	9.5	1.3	n.a.	54	(0)
banana nut *(MJB* Sugar Free) . . .	39	.8	4.9	1.8	n.a.	60	(0)
cherry *(MJB)* . . .	53	.5	9.7	1.4	n.a.	17	(0)
fudge *(MJB* Sugar Free)	39	1.2	4.5	1.8	n.a.	88	(0)
mint *(MJB)*	53	.4	9.9	1.3	n.a.	16	(0)
mint *(MJB* Sugar Free)	37	.7	5.6	1.3	n.a.	43	(0)
Swiss *(Hills Bros Cafe Coffees)* . .	60	1.0	8.0	2.0	n.a.	10	(0)
Swiss *(Hills Bros Cafe Coffees Sugar Free)* . . .	40	1.0	5.0	2.0	n.a.	25	(0)
vanilla *(MJB* Sugar Free)	39	.7	5.2	1.7	n.a.	50	(0)
orange:							
cappuccino *(General Foods* International)	60	0	10.0	2.0	0	100	(0)
cappuccino *(General Foods* International Sugar Free)	30	0	3.0	2.0	0	60	(0)
capri *(Hills Bros Cafe Coffees)* . .	60	1.0	9.0	2.0	n.a.	30	(0)
Coffee cake, see "Cake"							

Food and Measure	cal.	prot. (gms)	carbo. (gms)	fat (gms)	chol. (mgs)	sod. (mgs)	fiber (gms)
Coffee liqueur,							
1 fl. oz.:							
53 proof	117	tr.	16.3	.1	0	3	n.a.
w/cream, 34 proof	102	.9	6.5	4.9	n.a.	29	n.a.
Coffee substitute,							
cereal grain bev-							
erage:							
powder, 1 tsp.	9	.1	1.9	.1	0	2	tr.c
(Kaffree Roma),							
8 fl. oz.	6	0	1.0	0	0	n.a.	(0)
all varieties *(Postum*							
Instant), 6 fl. oz. . .	12	0	3.0	0	0	0	(0)
Cold cuts, see spe-							
cific listings							
Collards:							
fresh:							
raw, 1 oz.	9	.4	2.0	.1	0	6	.2 c
raw, chopped,							
1/2 cup	6	.3	1.3	<.1	0	4	.1 c
boiled, drained,							
chopped, 1/2 cup	17	.9	3.9	.1	0	10	.3 c
canned, chopped:							
(Allens), 1/2 cup . .	20	2.0	2.0	<1.0	0	15	m.q.
w/pork *(Luck's),*							
7.5 oz.	90	2.0	7.0	7.0	m.q.	420	m.q.
frozen, chopped:							
boiled, drained,							
1/2 cup	31	2.5	6.1	.4	0	42	.9 c
(Seabrook), 3.3 oz.	25	3.0	4.0	0	0	45	1.0 c
(Southern), 3.5 oz.	30	2.7	4.6	.4	0	60	m.q.
Cookies, 1 piece, ex-							
cept as noted:							
almond:							
(Stella D'Oro Break-							
fast Treats) . . .	101	1.6	15.4	3.6	n.a.	m.q.	m.q.
(Stella D'Oro Chi-							
nese Dessert) . .	169	2.4	19.5	8.9	n.a.	m.q.	m.q.

Food and Measure	cal.	prot. (gms)	carbo. (gms)	fat (gms)	chol. (mgs)	sod. (mgs)	fiber (gms)
Cookies, almond (cont.)							
supreme (Pepperidge Farm Special Collection) ...	70	1.0	7.0	5.0	5	25	m.q.
toast (Stella D'Oro Mandel)	58	1.3	10.2	1.4	n.a.	m.q.	m.q.
animal crackers:							
(Barnum's), 5 pieces	60	1.0	11.0	2.0	<2	70	m.q.
(FFV), 1.25-oz. pkg.	160	2.0	26.0	6.0	0	150	m.q.
(Keebler), 5 pieces	70	1.0	11.0	2.0	0	75	m.q.
anise:							
(Stella D'Oro Anisette Sponge) ..	51	1.1	9.9	.8	n.a.	m.q.	m.q.
(Stella D'Oro Anisette Toast) ...	46	.8	9.3	.6	n.a.	m.q.	m.q.
(Stella D'Oro Anisette Toast Jumbo)	109	2.0	23.0	1.0	n.a.	m.q.	m.q.
apple:							
bar (Apple Newtons)	80	1.0	15.0	2.0	<2	45	m.q.
bar, Dutch (Stella D'Oro)	112	1.4	18.9	3.3	n.a.	m.q.	m.q.
n'raisin (Archway)	120	2.0	20.0	3.0	10	169	1.0 d
apricot-raspberry:							
(Pepperidge Farm Fruit Cookies), 2 pieces	100	1.0	15.0	4.0	10	50	m.q.
(Pepperidge Farm Zurich)	60	1.0	10.0	2.0	0	30	m.q.
arrowroot biscuit (National)	20	0	3.0	1.0	<2	15	m.q.
assorted:							
(Archway Select)	50	1.0	7.0	2.0	5	40	m.q.
(Stella D'Oro Hostess)	42	.5	5.5	2.0	n.a.	m.q.	m.q.
(Stella D'Oro Lady Stella)	42	.6	5.5	2.0	n.a.	m.q.	m.q.

Food and Measure	cal.	prot. (gms)	carbo. (gms)	fat (gms)	chol. (mgs)	sod. (mgs)	fiber (gms)
fig, apple, strawberry *(Newtons)*	120	1.0	23.0	3.0	<2	110	m.q.
brownie (see also "Brownie"):							
chocolate nut *(Pepperidge Farm* Old Fashioned) . . .	140	1.0	15.0	8.0	5	65	m.q.
cream sandwich *(Pepperidge Farm* Capri)	80	0	10.0	5.0	0	45	m.q.
nut *(Pepperidge Farm* Beacon Hill)	120	2.0	14.0	7.0	5	65	m.q.
butter flavor:							
(Pepperidge Farm Chessmen), 2 pieces	90	1.0	12.0	4.0	10	60	m.q.
chocolate coated *(Keebler* Baby Bear), 3 pieces	70	1.0	10.0	2.0	0	55	m.q.
chocolate coated *(Keebler* E.L. Fudge), 2 pieces	80	<1.0	10.0	4.0	<5	40	m.q.
caramel patties *(FFV)*, 2 pieces	150	1.0	20.0	7.0	n.a.	125	m.q.
chocolate:							
(Stella D'Oro Castelets)	64	.8	9.0	2.8	n.a.	m.q.	m.q.
(Stella D'Oro Margherite) . . .	72	.9	10.2	3.1	n.a.	m.q.	m.q.
chocolate fudge:							
(Stella D'Oro Swiss)	68	.8	8.5	3.4	n.a.	m.q.	m.q.
bar *(Tastykake)* . .	240	2.5	40.1	7.8	n.a.	125	m.q.
mint *(Keebler* Grasshopper), 2 pieces	70	<1.0	10.0	3.0	0	35	m.q.
middles *(Nabisco)*	80	1.0	9.0	5.0	<5	35	m.q.
snaps *(Nabisco)*, 4 pieces, 1/2 oz.	70	1.0	11.0	2.0	<2	75	m.q.

Food and Measure	cal.	prot. (gms)	carbo. (gms)	fat (gms)	chol. (mgs)	sod. (mgs)	fiber (gms)
Cookies, chocolate fudge *(cont.)*							
wafer *(Nabisco Famous Wafers)*, 1/2 oz.	70	1.0	11.0	2.0	<2	110	m.q.
chocolate chip or chunk:							
all varieties *(Keebler Soft Batch)* . . .	80	<1.0	10.0	4.0	0	70	m.q.
(Almost Home Real)	60	1.0	7.0	3.0	<2	45	m.q.
(Archway)	50	1.0	7.0	3.0	5	40	m.q.
(Chips Ahoy! Pure)	50	1.0	7.0	2.0	0	40	m.q.
(Drake's), 2 pieces	140	1.0	18.0	6.0	0	110	m.q.
(Duncan Hines), 2 pieces	110	1.0	15.0	5.0	n.a.	90	m.q.
(Grandma's Big Cookies), 2 pieces	370	4.0	50.0	17.0	5	270	m.q.
(Keebler Deluxe)	80	<1.0	10.0	4.0	<5	75	m.q.
(Pepperidge Farm Old Fashioned), 2 pieces	100	1.0	12.0	5.0	5	45	m.q.
(Tastykake Soft'n Chewy), 1.4 oz.	188	2.2	27.0	7.8	n.a.	130	m.q.
bar *(Tastykake)* . .	211	2.1	34.6	7.7	n.a.	87	m.q.
w/candy coated chocolate *(Keebler Rainbow Deluxe)*	80	1.0	11.0	3.0	<5	45	m.q.
chewy *(Chips Ahoy!)*	60	1.0	7.0	3.0	<2	40	m.q.
chocolate *(Drake's)*, 2 pieces	130	2.0	19.0	5.0	0	85	m.q.
chocolate *(Tastykake* Soft'n Chewy), 1.4 oz.	199	2.2	30.8	7.4	n.a.	92	m.q.
chocolate, chunk *(Chips Ahoy!* Selections)	90	1.0	10.0	5.0	10	65	m.q.

Food and Measure	cal.	prot. (gms)	carbo. (gms)	fat (gms)	chol. (mgs)	sod. (mgs)	fiber (gms)
chocolate, w/chocolate (Keebler Magic Middles)	80	1.0	9.0	5.0	<5	25	m.q.
chunk (Pepperidge Farm Nantucket)	120	1.0	15.0	6.0	5	60	1.0 d
chunk, pecan (Chips Ahoy! Selections)	100	1.0	10.0	6.0	10	65	m.q.
chunk, pecan (Pepperidge Farm Chesapeake) ..	120	1.0	14.0	7.0	5	60	1.0 d
chunk, pecan (Pepperidge Farm Special Collection)	70	0	8.0	4.0	10	25	m.q.
chunky (Chips Ahoy! Selections) . . .	90	1.0	11.0	5.0	10	90	m.q.
fudge (Almost Home)	70	1.0	9.0	3.0	<2	50	m.q.
fudge (Grandma's Big Cookies), 2 pieces	350	4.0	54.0	13.0	5	380	m.q.
milk (Duncan Hines), 2 pieces	110	1.0	15.0	5.0	n.a.	95	m.q.
milk, macadamia (Pepperidge Farm Sausalito)	120	1.0	14.0	7.0	5	65	0
milk, macadamia (Pepperidge Farm Special Collection)	70	1.0	8.0	4.0	<5	35	m.q.
snaps (Nabisco), 3 pieces, 1/2 oz.	70	1.0	11.0	2.0	<2	50	m.q.
striped (Chips Ahoy!)	90	1.0	10.0	5.0	0	45	m.q.
chocolate sandwich:							
(Little Debbie) . . .	250	3.0	35.0	12.0	<1	260	m.q.
(Oreo)	50	1.0	8.0	2.0	<2	75	m.q.
(Oreo Big Stuf) . .	250	2.0	33.0	12.0	<5	220	m.q.

Food and Measure	cal.	prot. (gms)	carbo. (gms)	fat (gms)	chol. (mgs)	sod. (mgs)	fiber (gms)
Cookies, chocolate sandwich *(cont.)*							
(Oreo Double Stuf)	70	1.0	9.0	4.0	<2	75	m.q.
fudge covered *(Oreo)*	110	1.0	13.0	6.0	<2	80	m.q.
fudge creme filled *(Keebler* Chocolate Creme Sandwich)	80	1.0	12.0	4.0	0	70	m.q.
fudge, fudge creme filled *(Keebler E.L. Fudge)*	70	<1.0	9.0	3.0	0	50	m.q.
fudge, peanut butter creme filled *(Keebler E.L. Fudge)*	50	1.0	7.0	3.0	0	50	m.q.
chocolate filled sandwich:							
(Pepperidge Farm Brussels), 2 pieces	110	1.0	13.0	5.0	0	65	0
(Pepperidge Farm Lido)	90	1.0	10.0	5.0	<5	30	m.q.
(Pepperidge Farm Milano), 2 pieces	120	1.0	15.0	6.0	5	45	0
fudge creme *(Keebler E.L. Fudge)*	60	<1.0	8.0	3.0	<5	35	m.q.
mint *(Pepperidge Farm* Brussels Mint), 2 pieces	130	1.0	17.0	7.0	0	40	m.q.
mint or orange *(Pepperidge Farm* Milano), 2 pieces	150	1.0	17.0	7.0	5	60	m.q.
chocolate peanut bar *(Ideal)*	90	2.0	11.0	5.0	<2	80	m.q.
coconut:							
(Drake's), 2 pieces	130	2.0	20.0	5.0	0	95	m.q.
chocolate filled *(Pepperidge Farm* Tahiti)	90	0	9.0	6.0	5	25	m.q.

Food and Measure	cal.	prot. (gms)	carbo. (gms)	fat (gms)	chol. (mgs)	sod. (mgs)	fiber (gms)
macaroon (Stella D'Oro)	60	.7	6.6	3.4	n.a.	m.q.	m.q.
coffee, chocolate praline filled (Pepperidge Farm Cappucino)	50	0	6.0	3.0	<5	20	m.q.
creme sandwich, see specific listings							
date pecan (Pepperidge Farm Kitchen Hearth)	50	0	7.0	3.0	5	20	m.q.
devils food (FFV Trolley Cakes), 2 pieces, 2 oz. . . .	120	2.0	25.0	2.0	n.a.	80	m.q.
egg biscuit:							
(Stella D'Oro) . . .	43	1.6	6.7	1.1	n.a.	m.q.	m.q.
(Stella D'Oro Anginetti)	31	.5	4.9	1.0	n.a.	m.q.	m.q.
(Stella D'Oro Jumbo)	47	1.0	9.1	.7	n.a.	m.q.	m.q.
Roman (Stella D'Or	137	2.7	20.4	5.0	n.a.	m.q.	m.q.
sugareo , ella D'Oro) . . .	75	1.6	14.3	1.4	n.a.	m.q.	m.q.
(FFV Kreem Pilot Bread)	60	1.0	9.0	2.0	n.a.	60	m.q.
(FFV Royal Dainty), 2 pieces		1.0	14.0	6.0	n.a.	90	m.q.
(FFV T.C. Rounds), 2 pieces	160	1.0	20.0	8.0	n.a.	65	m.q.
(FFV Tango), 2 pieces	160	1.0	26.0	5.0	n.a.	50	m.q.
fig bar:							
(Fig Newtons) . . .	60	1.0	11.0	1.0	<2	60	m.q.
(Keebler)	60	1.0	11.0	2.0	0	70	m.q.
vanilla (FFV) . . .	70	1.0	12.0	1.0	0	55	m.q.
whole wheat (FFV)	70	1.0	11.0	2.0	0	50	m.q.
fruit filled, all varieties (Baker's Own) . . .	70	<1.0	12.0	2.0	0	80	m.q.

Food and Measure	cal.	prot. (gms)	carbo. (gms)	fat (gms)	chol. (mgs)	sod. (mgs)	fiber (gms)
Cookies (cont.)							
fruit slices (Stella D'Oro)	60	1.1	8.7	2.2	n.a.	m.q.	m.q.
fudge bar, caramel and peanut (Heyday)	110	2.0	12.0	6.0	0	60	m.q.
ginger:							
(Pepperidge Farm Gingerman), 2 pieces	70	1.0	10.0	3.0	5	50	m.q.
(FFV), 1.25-oz. pkg.	150	2.0	26.0	5.0	0	210	m.q.
gingersnaps:							
(Archway, 80/pkg.)	25	1.0	4.0	<1.0	0	20	m.q.
(Archway, 54/pkg.)	35	0	6.0	1.0	0	30	m.q.
(FFV), 5 pieces . .	130	2.0	22.0	4.0	0	140	m.q.
(Nabisco Old Fashioned)	30	<1.0	6.0	1.0	<2	45	m.q.
graham cracker:							
(Keebler), 4 pieces	70	1.0	12.0	2.0	0	85	m.q.
(Nabisco), 2 pieces	60	1.0	11.0	1.0	<2	90	m.q.
(Regal), 2 pieces	140	1.0	19.0	7.0	n.a.	120	m.q.
(Rokeach), 8 pieces	120	2.0	21.0	3.0	n.a.	m.q.	m.q.
cinnamon (Keebler Alpha Grahams), 6 pieces	70	1.0	10.0	2.0	0	55	m.q.
cinnamon (Keebler Crisp), 4 pieces	70	1.0	11.0	2.0	0	85	m.q.
cinnamon (Keebler Thin Bits), 12 pieces	70	1.0	10.0	3.0	0	50	m.q.
cinnamon or honey (Honey Maid), 2 pieces	60	1.0	11.0	1.0	<2	90	m.q.
cinnamon or honey (Nabisco Teddy Grahams), 11 pieces	60	1.0	11.0	2.0	0	90	m.q.

Food and Measure	cal.	prot. (gms)	carbo. (gms)	fat (gms)	chol. (mgs)	sod. (mgs)	fiber (gms)
honey (Keebler Grahams), 4 pieces	70	1.0	12.0	2.0	0	85	m.q.
honeycomb, all varieties, except oat bran (Honey Maid Snacks), 11 pieces	60	1.0	11.0	2.0	0	80	m.q.
honeycomb, honey'n oat bran, (Honey Maid Snacks), 11 pieces	60	1.0	11.0	2.0	0	55	m.q.
wheat (Carr's Home Graham)	74	1.0	10.9	3.3	n.a.	<1	m.q.
graham cracker, chocolate:							
(Keebler Thin Bits), 12 pieces	70	1.0	9.0	3.0	0	75	m.q.
(Nabisco)	60	1.0	7.0	3.0	<2	30	m.q.
(Nabisco Teddy Grahams), 11 pieces	60	1.0	10.0	2.0	0	90	m.q.
fudge covered (Keebler Deluxe), 2 pieces	90	<1.0	11.0	4.0	0	60	m.q.
w/fudge (Nabisco Cookies'N Fudge), 1/2 oz.	70	1.0	10.0	3.0	<2	50	m.q.
hazelnut (Pepperidge Farm Old Fashioned), 2 pieces . .	110	1.0	15.0	6.0	0	75	m.q.
jelly tarts (FFV) . . .	60	<1.0	11.0	2.0	0	55	m.q.
lemon nut crunch (Pepperidge Farm Old Fashioned), 2 pieces	110	1.0	13.0	7.0	<5	50	m.q.

Food and Measure	cal.	prot. (gms)	carbo. (gms)	fat (gms)	chol. (mgs)	sod. (mgs)	fiber (gms)
Cookies *(cont.)*							
marshmallow cake:							
(Mallomars)	60	1.0	9.0	3.0	0	20	m.q.
(Nabisco Puffs) . .	90	1.0	14.0	4.0	0	45	m.q.
(Nabisco Twirls) . .	140	1.0	20.0	6.0	0	70	m.q.
(Pinwheels)	130	1.0	20.0	5.0	0	40	m.q.
mint sandwich:							
(FFV), 2 pieces . .	160	2.0	22.0	7.0	n.a.	50	m.q.
(Mystic Mint) . . .	90	1.0	11.0	5.0	<2	65	m.q.
molasses:							
(Archway)	100	1.0	18.0	2.0	10	155	2.0 d
(Grandma's Old Time Big Cookies), 2 pieces, 2.75 oz.	320	4.0	58.0	9.0	5	520	m.q.
(Nabisco Pantry)	80	1.0	13.0	3.0	0	75	m.q.
crisps *(Pepperidge Farm* Old Fashioned)*, 2 pieces	70	1.0	8.0	3.0	0	50	m.q.
oat bran raisin *(Awrey's)*	100	1.0	14.0	4.0	0	115	1.0 d
oatmeal:							
(Archway)	110	2.0	19.0	3.0	5	90	1.0 d
(Archway Ruth's Golden)	120	2.0	20.0	4.0	5	122	1.2 d
(Baker's Bonus) . .	80	1.0	12.0	3.0	<5	65	m.q.
(Drake's), 2 pieces	120	2.0	19.0	4.0	0	50	m.q.
(FFV), 5 pieces . .	130	2.0	20.0	4.0	0	150	m.q.
(Keebler Old Fashion)	80	1.0	12.0	3.0	0	110	m.q.
(Little Debbie), 2.75 oz.	340	5.0	52.0	12.0	<2	440	m.q.
apple filled *(Archway)*	90	1.0	18.0	1.0	5	115	1.0 d
apple spice *(Grandma's* Big Cookies), 2 pieces, 2.75 oz.	330	5.0	51.0	12.0	10	570	m.q.

Food and Measure	cal.	prot. (gms)	carbo. (gms)	fat (gms)	chol. (mgs)	sod. (mgs)	fiber (gms)
chocolate (Pepper-idge Farm Da-kota)	110	1.0	15.0	6.0	5	70	1.0 d
w/chocolate (Kee-bler Magic Mid-dles)	80	1.0	8.0	5.0	0	30	m.q.
date filled (Archway)	100	1.0	18.0	2.0	5	105	1.0 d
iced (Archway) . .	140	2.0	22.0	5.0	5	107	1.7 d
Irish (Pepperidge Farm Old Fash-ioned), 2 pieces	90	1.0	13.0	5.0	5	80	m.q.
oatmeal raisin:							
(Almost Home) . .	70	1.0	10.0	3.0	<2	40	m.q.
(Archway)	100	2.0	18.0	3.0	5	107	.9 d
(Duncan Hines), 2 pieces	110	1.0	15.0	5.0	n.a.	75	m.q.
(Entenmann's), 2 pieces	80	1.0	17.0	0	0	120	m.q.
(Keebler Soft Batch)	70	1.0	10.0	3.0	0	65	m.q.
(Pepperidge Farm Santa Fe)	100	1.0	16.0	4.0	<5	70	1.0 d
(Pepperidge Farm Old Fashioned), 2 pieces	110	1.0	15.0	5.0	10	115	0
(Tastykake Soft'n Chewy), 1.4 oz.	207	2.4	30.9	8.1	n.a.	150	m.q.
bar (Tastykake) . .	224	3.4	35.6	7.6	n.a.	224	m.q.
bran (Archway) . .	100	2.0	18.0	3.0	5	95	1.0 d
peach-apricot:							
bar, vanilla (FFV)	70	<1.0	14.0	1.0	0	50	m.q.
bar, whole wheat (FFV)	70	<1.0	11.0	2.0	0	50	m.q.
pastry (Stella D'Oro)	93	1.2	13.6	3.8	n.a.	m.q.	m.q.
peanut, chocolate filled (Pepperidge Farm Nassau) . . .	80	1.0	9.0	5.0	<5	45	m.q.

Food and Measure	cal.	prot. (gms)	carbo. (gms)	fat (gms)	chol. (mgs)	sod. (mgs)	fiber (gms)
Cookies *(cont.)*							
peanut butter:							
(Grandma's Big Cookies), 2 pieces	410	7.0	43.0	30.0	10	410	m.q.
chocolate chip *(Keebler Soft Batch)*	80	1.0	9.0	5.0	0	55	m.q.
cream filled *(Pitter Patter)*	90	2.0	12.0	4.0	0	115	m.q.
nut *(Keebler Soft Batch)*	80	1.0	9.0	4.0	0	60	m.q.
sandwich *(FFV)*, 2 pieces	170	2.0	21.0	8.0	n.a.	110	m.q.
sandwich *(Nutter Butter)*	70	1.0	9.0	3.0	<2	50	m.q.
peanut creme patties *(Nutter Butter)*, 2 pieces, 1/2 oz. . .	80	2.0	8.0	4.0	0	45	m.q.
pecan crunch *(Archway)*	60	1.0	8.0	3.0	5	45	m.q.
(Pepperidge Farm Venice), 2 pieces	120	1.0	14.0	6.0	<5	70	m.q.
praline pecan *(FFV)*	40	<1.0	10.0	2.0	<5	40	m.q.
raisin:							
(Stella D'Oro Golden Bars) . .	109	1.6	16.0	4.3	n.a.	m.q.	m.q.
bar, iced *(Keebler)*	80	1.0	11.0	4.0	0	85	m.q.
bran *(Pepperidge Farm* Kitchen Hearth)*	50	0	7.0	3.0	0	25	m.q.
oatmeal *(Archway)*	50	1.0	7.0	2.0	0	20	m.q.
soft *(Grandma's* Big Cookies), 2 pieces	320	3.0	54.0	10.0	10	280	m.q.
raspberry filled:							
(Pepperidge Farm Chantilly)	80	1.0	14.0	2.0	<5	35	m.q.

Food and Measure	cal.	prot. (gms)	carbo. (gms)	fat (gms)	chol. (mgs)	sod. (mgs)	fiber (gms)
(Pepperidge Farm Linzer)	120	2.0	20.0	4.0	<5	55	m.q.
(Raspberry Newtons)	80	1.0	15.0	2.0	<2	60	m.q.
sesame (Stella D'Oro Regina)	48	.9	6.1	2.2	n.a.	m.q.	m.q.
shortbread:							
(Lorna Doone), 3 pieces, 1/2 oz.	70	1.0	9.0	4.0	<5	65	m.q.
(Pepperidge Farm Old Fashioned), 2 pieces	150	1.0	17.0	8.0	<5	85	m.q.
w/chocolate cream center (Keebler Magic Middles)	80	1.0	9.0	5.0	<5	25	m.q.
country (FFV) . . .	70	1.0	9.0	4.0	<5	45	m.q.
fudge striped (Keebler Fudge Stripes)	50	<1.0	7.0	3.0	0	55	m.q.
fudge striped (Nabisco Cookies 'N Fudge)	60	1.0	7.0	3.0	0	50	m.q.
pecan (Nabisco)	80	1.0	8.0	5.0	<2	40	m.q.
pecan (Pecan Sandies)	80	<1.0	9.0	5.0	<5	75	m.q.
pecan (Pepperidge Farm Old Fashioned)	70	1.0	7.0	5.0	0	15	m.q.
(Stella D'Oro Angel Bars)	76	1.0	7.3	4.7	n.a.	m.q.	m.q.
(Stella D'Oro Angel Wings)	74	1.1	7.0	4.7	n.a.	m.q.	m.q.
(Stella D'Oro Angelica Goodies)	106	1.7	15.7	4.0	n.a.	m.q.	m.q.
(Stella D'Oro Como Delight)	145	2.1	17.9	7.2	n.a.	m.q.	m.q.

Food and Measure	cal.	prot. (gms)	carbo. (gms)	fat (gms)	chol. (mgs)	sod. (mgs)	fiber (gms)
Cookies *(cont.)*							
strawberry:							
(Pepperidge Farm Fruit Cookies), 2 pieces	100	1.0	15.0	4.0	10	70	m.q.
bar *(Strawberry Newtons)*	80	1.0	15.0	2.0	<2	60	m.q.
sugar:							
(Almost Home Old Fashioned) . . .	70	1.0	10.0	3.0	<2	80	m.q.
(Pepperidge Farm Old Fashioned), 2 pieces	100	1.0	13.0	5.0	10	55	m.q.
sugar wafer:							
(Biscos), 4 pieces	70	<1.0	10.0	3.0	0	20	m.q.
chocolate *(Tastykake),* 1 pkg.	367	2.6	45.6	19.4	n.a.	98	m.q.
vanilla *(Tastykake),* 1 pkg.	366	2.0	43.9	20.2	n.a.	46	m.q.
(Social Tea)	20	<1.0	4.0	1.0	<2	20	m.q.
vanilla:							
(Pepperidge Farm Bordeaux), 2 pieces	70	1.0	11.0	3.0	0	40	0
(Pepperidge Farm Pirouettes), 2 pieces	70	1.0	8.0	4.0	<5	20	m.q.
(Stella D'Oro Castelets)	72	1.0	10.0	3.1	n.a.	m.q.	m.q.
(Stella D'Oro Margherite) . . .	72	1.0	10.8	2.8	n.a.	m.q.	m.q.
chocolate laced *(Pepperidge Farm Pirouettes),* 2 pieces	70	1.0	8.0	4.0	<5	20	m.q.

Food and Measure	cal.	prot. (gms)	carbo. (gms)	fat (gms)	chol. (mgs)	sod. (mgs)	fiber (gms)
chocolate nut coated *(Pepperidge Farm Geneva)*, 2 pieces	130	1.0	14.0	6.0	0	50	m.q.
creme sandwich:							
(Cameo)	70	1.0	10.0	3.0	0	50	m.q.
(Keebler French Vanilla Creme)	80	<1.0	12.0	4.0	0	80	m.q.
(Nabisco Cookie Break)	50	1.0	7.0	2.0	<2	35	m.q.
(Nabisco Giggles)	60	1.0	8.0	3.0	<2	20	m.q.
wafer:							
(Archway)	30	0	6.0	<1.0	0	30	m.q.
(FFV), 1 oz. . . .	130	1.0	19.0	5.0	<5	100	m.q.
(Nabisco Nilla Wafers), 1/2 oz.	60	1.0	11.0	2.0	5	45	m.q.
golden *(Keebler)*, 4 pieces . . .	80	<1.0	10.0	3.0	0	60	m.q.
wafer (see also specific listings):							
brown edged *(Nabisco)*, 1/2 oz.	70	1.0	10.0	3.0	<2	45	m.q.
creme, fudge covered *(Keebler Fudge Sticks)*, 2 pieces	100	<1.0	13.0	5.0	0	35	m.q.
fudge *(Nabisco Cookies'N Fudge)*	70	1.0	9.0	4.0	0	30	m.q.
waffle cremes *(Biscos)*, 2 pieces, 1/2 oz.	70	<1.0	10.0	4.0	0	20	m.q.

Food and Measure	cal.	prot. (gms)	carbo. (gms)	fat (gms)	chol. (mgs)	sod. (mgs)	fiber (gms)
Cookies, frozen, 1.2 oz., approx. 2 pieces:							
chocolate chip:							
(Nestlé Toll House Ready To Bake)	150	1.0	20.0	7.0	n.a.	115	m.q.
double (Nestlé Toll House Ready To Bake)	150	2.0	19.0	7.0	n.a.	60	m.q.
w/nuts (Nestlé Toll House Ready To Bake)	160	2.0	19.0	8.0	n.a.	90	m.q.
oatmeal raisin (Nestlé Toll House Ready To Bake)	130	2.0	21.0	5.0	n.a.	55	m.q.
Cookies, refrigerated, 1 piece:							
chocolate chip (Pillsbury)	70	1.0	9.0	3.0	5	55	m.q.
chocolate chocolate chip (Pillsbury) . .	70	1.0	9.0	3.0	0	35	m.q.
oatmeal raisin (Pillsbury)	70	1.0	9.0	3.0	5	60	m.q.
peanut butter (Pillsbury)	70	1.0	9.0	3.0	5	75	m.q.
sugar (Pillsbury) . . .	70	1.0	9.0	3.0	5	70	m.q.
Coriander:							
fresh, 1/4 cup	1	.1	.1	<.1	0	1	<.1 c
dried, leaf, 1 tsp. . .	2	.1	.3	<.1	0	1	.1 c
seed, 1 tsp.	5	.2	1.0	.3	0	1	.5 c
Corn, 1/2 cup, except as noted:							
fresh, kernels, boiled, drained	89	2.7	20.6	1.1	0	14	3.0 d
canned:							
(Green Giant Delicorn)	80	2.0	19.0	1.0	0	360	m.q.

Food and Measure	cal.	prot. (gms)	carbo. (gms)	fat (gms)	chol. (mgs)	sod. (mgs)	fiber (gms)
on cob, Oriental *(Green Giant)* . .	20	1.0	4.0	0	0	250	m.q.
vacuum pack *(Del Monte)*	90	3.0	22.0	1.0	0	355	m.q.
canned, kernel:							
drained	66	2.2	15.2	.8	0	m.q.	1.1 d
(Green Giant) . . .	80	2.0	18.0	0	0	280	2.7 d
golden *(Del Monte)*	70	2.0	17.0	1.0	0	355	m.q.
golden *(Del Monte No Salt)*	80	2.0	18.0	1.0	0	<10	m.q.
golden *(Stokely)* . .	90	2.0	20.0	0	0	300	m.q.
golden, vacuum pack *(Green Giant Supersweet)*	70	2.0	12.0	1.0	0	280	2.7 d
golden, vacuum pack *(Stokely)* . . .	90	3.0	22.0	0	0	300	m.q.
w/peppers *(Green Giant Mexicorn)* . .	80	2.0	19.0	1.0	0	330	m.q.
white *(Del Monte)*	70	2.0	16.0	0	0	355	m.q.
white *(Stokely)* . .	90	3.0	21.0	0	0	290	m.q.
white shoepeg, vacuum pack *(Green Giant)*	80	2.0	20.0	0	0	290	m.q.
young tender *(S&W Premium)*	90	2.0	20.0	1.0	0	295	m.q.
vacuum pack *(Green Giant Niblets)*	80	3.0	16.0	1.0	0	280	1.7 d
canned, cream-style:							
(Green Giant) . . .	100	2.0	24.0	1.0	0	390	2.0 d
(S&W Premium Homestyle No Starch)	120	3.0	24.0	1.0	0	285	m.q.
(S&W Premium Homestyle w/ Starch)	105	2.0	25.0	1.0	0	435	m.q.
golden *(Del Monte)*	80	2.0	18.0	1.0	0	355	m.q.
golden *(Stokely)*	100	2.0	23.0	0	0	380	m.q.

Food and Measure	cal.	prot. (gms)	carbo. (gms)	fat (gms)	chol. (mgs)	sod. (mgs)	fiber (gms)
Corn canned, cream-style *(cont.)*							
white *(Del Monte)*	90	2.0	21.0	0	0	355	m.q.
white *(Stokely)* ..	100	2.0	23.0	0	0	380	m.q.
dried *(John Cope's)*, 1 oz. dry	101	3.0	20.5	1.2	0	0	m.q.
freeze-dried *(Mountain House)*, 1/2 cup . .	90	2.0	18.0	1.0	0	<1	m.q.
frozen, on cob, 1 ear, except as noted:							
(Birds Eye)	120	4.0	29.0	1.0	0	0	m.q.
(Birds Eye Big Ears)	160	5.0	37.0	1.0	0	0	m.q.
(Birds Eye Little Ears), 2 ears . .	130	4.0	30.0	1.0	0	0	m.q.
(Green Giant Niblets, 4/pkg.)	120	4.0	26.0	1.0	0	10	2.0 d
(Green Giant Niblets Supersweet) . .	90	3.0	19.0	2.0	0	10	2.0 d
(Green Giant Niblers, 6/pkg.), 2 ears	120	4.0	26.0	1.0	0	10	2.0 d
baby *(Birds Eye Deluxe)*, 2.6 oz.	25	2.0	4.0	0	0	10	2.0 d
miniature *(Ore-Ida Mini-Gold)*, 2 ears	180	5.0	39.0	2.0	0	40	m.q.
frozen, kernel, 3.3 oz., except as noted:							
(Birds Eye Sweet/ Tender Sweet Deluxe)	80	3.0	20.0	1.0	0	0	2.0 d
(Green Giant Harvest Fresh Niblets), 1/2 cup	80	2.0	17.0	1.0	0	140	2.0 d
(Green Giant Niblets), 1/2 cup	70	2.0	14.0	<1.0	0	5	1.3 d
(Green Giant Niblets Supersweet), 1/2 cup	60	2.0	11.0	1.0	0	5	1.7 d

Food and Measure	cal.	prot. (gms)	carbo. (gms)	fat (gms)	chol. (mgs)	sod. (mgs)	fiber (gms)
cut (Birds Eye Portion Pack), 3 oz.	70	3.0	18.0	1.0	0	0	2.0 d
cut (Frosty Acres)	80	3.0	20.0	1.0	0	3	1.0 c
petite (Birds Eye Deluxe), 2.6 oz.	70	2.0	16.0	1.0	0	0	2.0 d
white (Seabrook)	80	3.0	19.0	1.0	0	3	1.0 c
white (Green Giant), 1/2 cup	70	2.0	15.0	1.0	0	5	1.5 d
white shoepeg (Green Giant Harvest Fresh), 1/2 cup	90	2.0	20.0	1.0	0	270	2.4 d
frozen, cream-style (Green Giant), 1/2 cup	110	3.0	25.0	1.0	0	370	m.q.
frozen, nuggets (Stilwell Quickkrisp), 3 oz.	210	3.0	30.0	8.0	1	420	m.q.
frozen, in butter sauce:							
(The Budget Gourmet Side Dish), 5.5 oz.	190	4.0	31.0	6.0	15	310	m.q.
(Green Giant Niblets)	100	2.0	18.0	2.0	n.a.	280	2.0 d
(Green Giant Niblets One Serving), 4.5 oz.	120	3.0	24.0	2.0	5	350	m.q.
(Stokely Singles), 4 oz.	110	3.0	23.0	1.0	5	230	m.q.
on cob (Stokely Singles), 1 ear . . .	70	2.0	16.0	1.0	5	200	m.q.
golden (Green Giant)	100	3.0	19.0	2.0	5	310	2.0 d
tender, sweet (Birds Eye Combinations), 3.3 oz. . .	90	2.0	17.0	2.0	5	250	2.0 d
white (Green Giant)	100	2.0	20.0	2.0	5	280	2.3 d

Food and Measure	cal.	prot. (gms)	carbo. (gms)	fat (gms)	chol. (mgs)	sod. (mgs)	fiber (gms)
Corn *(cont.)*							
frozen, country style							
(The Budget Gour-							
met Side Dish),							
5.75 oz.	140	4.0	19.0	5.0	15	290	m.q.
Corn, combinations,							
frozen:							
and broccoli *(Green*							
Giant Valley Combi-							
nations), 1/2 cup . .	45	2.0	10.0	1.0	0	15	1.9 d
Corn, whole-grain:							
1 oz.	103	2.7	21.1	1.3	0	10	.8 c
1 cup	605	15.6	123.3	7.9	0	58	4.8 c
Corn bran, crude:							
1 oz.	64	2.4	24.3	.3	0	2	24.0 d
1 cup	170	6.4	65.1	.7	0	5	64.3 d
Corn cake:							
(Quaker Grain Cakes),							
.32-oz. piece . . .	35	.7	7.4	.2	0	53	.1 d
Corn chips and simi-							
lar snacks, 1 oz.:							
(Bachman)	160	2.0	15.0	10.0	0	160	m.q.
(Dipsy Doodles Rip-							
pled)	160	2.0	15.0	10.0	0	180	m.q.
(Fritos)	150	1.0	16.0	9.0	0	230	m.q.
(Fritos Crisp'N Thin)	160	1.0	16.0	10.0	0	210	m.q.
(Fritos Dip Size) . . .	150	2.0	17.0	9.0	0	210	m.q.
(Planters)	160	2.0	15.0	10.0	0	160	m.q.
(Snyder's)	160	2.0	14.0	11.0	0	150	m.q.
(Wise Corn Chips/							
Crunchies/*Ridgies)*	160	2.0	15.0	10.0	0	180	m.q.
barbecue flavor:							
(Bachman BBQ)	150	<1.0	17.0	9.0	0	230	m.q.
(Fritos Bar-B-Q) . .	150	2.0	16.0	9.0	0	320	m.q.
cheese:							
(Chee•tos Balls)	160	2.0	15.0	10.0	tr.	360	m.q.
(Chee•tos Puffs)	160	1.0	16.0	10.0	tr.	330	m.q.

Food and Measure	cal.	prot. (gms)	carbo. (gms)	fat (gms)	chol. (mgs)	sod. (mgs)	fiber (gms)
(Cheez Doodles Baked)	150	2.0	17.0	8.0	n.a.	360	m.q.
(Cheez Doodles Fried)	160	2.0	15.0	10.0	n.a.	220	m.q.
(Jax Baked) . . .	140	2.0	17.0	7.0	n.a.	290	m.q.
(Jax Crunchy) . . .	160	2.0	14.0	11.0	n.a.	250	m.q.
(Planters Balls) . .	160	2.0	14.0	11.0	5	270	m.q.
(Planters Curls) . .	160	2.0	14.0	11.0	5	290	m.q.
(Wise Cheez Waffies)	140	3.0	14.0	8.0	n.a.	420	m.q.
crunchy (Chee•tos)	150	2.0	15.0	10.0	tr.	280	m.q.
nacho (Wise Corn Spirals)	160	2.0	16.0	10.0	n.a.	190	m.q.
chili cheese (Fritos)	160	2.0	16.0	10.0	0	310	m.q.
ranch (Fritos Wild'N Mild)	150	2.0	16.0	9.0	0	230	m.q.
tortilla:							
(Bachman)	140	2.0	19.0	6.0	0	140	m.q.
(Doritos)	140	2.0	19.0	6.0	0	230	m.q.
(Doritos Cool Ranch)	140	2.0	18.0	7.0	0	190	m.q.
(Doritos Salsa Rio)	140	1.0	19.0	7.0	0	170	m.q.
(La Famous)	140	2.0	18.0	7.0	0	180	m.q.
(Old El Paso Nachips)	150	2.0	18.0	7.0	0	80	m.q.
(Tostitos)	140	2.0	18.0	8.0	0	170	m.q.
blue (Bearitos) . .	146	2.9	17.4	7.0	0	29	.6 d
crispy (Old El Paso)	150	2.0	17.0	8.0	0	105	2.0 d
nacho (Bachman)	140	2.0	18.0	6.0	n.a.	210	m.q.
nacho (Bravos Strips)	140	2.0	18.0	7.0	0	220	m.q.
nacho (Bravos Rounds)	150	2.0	18.0	8.0	n.a.	180	m.q.
nacho (Doritos) . .	140	2.0	18.0	7.0	0	240	m.q.
nacho (Doritos Light)	120	2.0	21.0	4.0	0	290	m.q.
nacho, jalapeño flavor (Bravos) . .	150	2.0	19.0	7.0	0	170	m.q.

Food and Measure	cal.	prot. (gms)	carbo. (gms)	fat (gms)	chol. (mgs)	sod. (mgs)	fiber (gms)
Corn chips and similar snacks, tortilla *(cont.)*							
nacho *(Tostitos)* . .	150	2.0	17.0	8.0	0	200	m.q.
ranch *(Eagle)* . . .	140	2.0	17.0	8.0	1	190	m.q.
sesame *(Hain)* . .	140	2.0	19.0	7.0	0	190	m.q.
sesame, cheese *(Hain)*	160	2.0	20.0	8.0	<5	270	m.q.
taco flavor *(Doritos)*	140	2.0	18.0	7.0	0	220	m.q.
taco style *(Hain)*	160	2.0	15.0	11.0	<5	320	m.q.
yellow *(Bearitos)*	143	2.1	18.1	6.4	0	58	1.1 d
Corn flake crumbs:							
(Kellogg's), 1 oz. . .	100	2.0	24.0	0	0	290	1.0 d
Corn flour:							
whole-grain, 1 oz. . .	102	2.0	21.8	1.1	0	1	3.8 d
whole-grain, 1 cup . .	422	8.1	89.9	4.5	0	6	15.7 d
masa, 1 oz.	103	2.6	21.6	1.1	0	1	.5 c
masa, 1 cup	416	10.7	87.0	4.3	0	6	1.9 c
(Quaker Masa Harina De Maiz), 1.3 oz.	137	3.5	27.4	1.5	0	2	.7 c
(Quaker Masa Trigo), 1.3 oz.	149	3.5	24.7	4.0	0	794	.1 c
Corn fritter, frozen:							
(Mrs. Paul's), 2 pieces	250	4.0	33.0	12.0	n.a.	630	m.q.
Corn grits:							
dry, enriched:							
(Quaker/Aunt Jemima Regular/ Quick), 3 tbsp.	101	2.4	22.4	.2	0	1	.1 c
cooked, 1 cup . . .	146	3.5	31.4	.5	0	tr.	.2 c
instant, dry, 1 pkt.:							
w/imitation bacon bits *(Quaker)* . .	101	2.7	21.6	.4	0	544	.1 c
w/real cheddar cheese flavor *(Quaker)*	104	2.2	21.6	1.0	n.a.	497	.1 c
w/imitation ham bits *(Quaker)*	99	2.7	21.3	.3	0	665	.1 c
white hominy product *(Quaker)* . .	79	1.9	17.7	.1	0	385	.1 c

Food and Measure	cal.	prot. (gms)	carbo. (gms)	fat (gms)	chol. (mgs)	sod. (mgs)	fiber (gms)
Corn oil, see "Oil"							
Corn souffle, frozen:							
(Stouffer's), 4 oz. . .	160	5.0	18.0	7.0	n.a.	560	m.q.
Corn syrup:							
dark (Karo), 1 tbsp.	60	0	15.0	0	0	40	0
light (Karo), 1 tbsp.	60	0	15.0	0	0	30	0
Cornbread, see "Bread, sweet, mix"							
Cornish game hen:							
frozen (Tyson), 3.5 oz.	240	28.0	0	14.0	75	70	0
Cornmeal (see also "Corn flour" and "Polenta"), 1 oz.:							
self-rising, white:							
(Aunt Jemima) . .	98	2.3	21.1	.5	0	381	.2 c
enriched, bolted, (Aunt Jemima)	99	2.3	20.4	.9	0	382	.3 c
white or yellow, enriched (Quaker/Aunt Jemima)	102	2.4	22.2	.5	0	1	.2 c
Cornmeal mix:							
buttermilk, self-rising, white (Aunt Jemima), 3 tbsp.	101	2.5	20.2	1.1	0	439	.3 c
white, bolted (Aunt Jemima), 1 oz.	99	2.4	20.8	.7	0	337	.2 c
yellow, bolted (Aunt Jemima), 1 oz. . . .	97	2.4	20.9	.4	0	369	.1 c
Cornstarch, 1 tbsp.:							
(Argo/Kingsford) . .	30	0	7.0	0	0	0	tr.d
Cottonseed kernels:							
roasted, 1 tbsp. . . .	51	3.3	2.2	3.6	0	3	.2 c
Cottonseed meal:							
partially defatted, 1 oz.	104	13.9	10.9	1.4	0	10	.7 c
Cough drop, see "Candy"							

Food and Measure	cal.	prot. (gms)	carbo. (gms)	fat (gms)	chol. (mgs)	sod. (mgs)	fiber (gms)
Country coating mix:							
mild *(Shake'n Bake)*,							
1/4 pouch	80	1.0	10.0	4.0	0	500	m.q.
Couscous:							
dry, 1 oz.	107	3.6	22.0	.2	0	3	.2 c
pilaf mix:							
(Casbah), 1 oz. dry,							
1/2 cup cooked	100	4.0	20.0	0	0	m.q.	m.q.
savory *(Quick Pilaf)*,							
1/2 cup[1]	124	4.0	19.0	3.0	m.q.	254	m.q.
Cowpea, 1/2 cup, ex-							
cept as noted:							
fresh:							
raw, trimmed . . .	65	2.1	13.6	.3	0	3	1.3 c
boiled, drained . .	79	2.6	16.7	.3	0	3	1.6 c
fresh, leafy tips:							
raw, chopped . . .	5	.7	.9	<.1	0	1	.2 c
boiled, drained,							
4 oz.	25	5.3	3.2	.1	0	7	3.0 c
fresh, pods, w/seeds:							
raw, trimmed . . .	21	1.6	4.5	.1	0	2	.8 c
boiled, drained . .	16	1.2	3.3	.1	0	1	.8 c
canned:							
(Allens)	100	7.0	18.0	<1.0	0	370	m.q.
w/snaps *(Allens)*	100	5.0	20.0	<1.0	0	370	m.q.
frozen:							
boiled, drained . .	112	7.2	20.2	.6	0	5	1.3 c
(Frosty Acres),							
3.3 oz.	130	9.0	23.0	1.0	0	6	1.0 c
Cowpea, mature,							
1/2 cup, except as							
noted:							
boiled	100	6.7	17.9	.5	0	3	8.3 d
canned:							
w/liquid	92	5.7	16.4	.7	0	359	.8 c
(Allens)	105	5.0	20.0	<1.0	0	300	m.q.
w/pork *(Allens)* . .	105	5.0	18.0	1.0	m.q.	300	m.q.

[1] *Prepared according to package directions, with 2 tbsp. salted butter.*

Food and Measure	cal.	prot. (gms)	carbo. (gms)	fat (gms)	chol. (mgs)	sod. (mgs)	fiber (gms)
w/pork (Luck's), 7.5 oz.	200	11.0	25.0	6.0	m.q.	760	7.0 d
Cowpea, catjang, see "Catjang"							
Crab, meat only:							
Alaska king:							
raw, 1 lb.	379	83.0	0	2.7	189	3792	0
raw, 1 oz.	24	5.2	0	.2	12	237	0
boiled, poached, or steamed, 4 oz.	110	21.9	0	1.7	60	1216	0
blue:							
raw, 1 lb.	395	81.9	.2	4.9	355	1329	0
raw, 1 oz.	25	5.1	<.1	.3	22	83	0
boiled, poached, or steamed, 4 oz.	116	22.9	0	2.0	113	316	0
dungeness, raw, 1 oz.	24	4.9	.2	.3	17	84	0
queen, raw, 1 oz. . .	26	5.2	0	.3	16	153	0
Crab, canned:							
blue, 4 oz.	112	23.3	0	1.4	101	378	0
dungeness (S&W), 3.25 oz.	81	18.0	1.0	2.0	m.q.	920	0
Crab, frozen:							
cakes, deviled:							
(Mrs. Paul's), 3-oz. cake . . .	170	8.0	19.0	7.0	m.q.	300	m.q.
miniature (Mrs. Paul's), 3½ oz.	250	8.0	29.0	12.0	m.q.	480	m.q.
snow (Wakefield), 3 oz.	60	13.0	0	1.0	m.q.	270	0
"Crab," imitation[1]:							
1 oz.	29	3.4	3.0	.4	6	238	0
(Icicle Brand), 3.5 oz.	99	12.0	11.0	.1	10	900	0
Crab and shrimp:							
frozen (Wakefield), 3 oz.	60	13.0	0	1.0	m.q.	210	0

[1] Made from surimi (see "Surimi").

Food and Measure	cal.	prot. (gms)	carbo. (gms)	fat (gms)	chol. (mgs)	sod. (mgs)	fiber (gms)
Crabapple:							
fresh, w/peel:							
1 oz.	22	.1	5.7	.1	0	<1	.2 c
sliced, 1/2 cup . . .	42	.2	11.0	.2	0	1	.3 c
canned, spiced (Mus-							
selman's), 4 oz. . .	110	0	28.0	0	0	m.q.	m.q.
Crackers, 1/2 oz., ex-							
cept as noted:							
bacon flavor:							
(Keebler Toasteds),							
4 pieces	60	1.0	8.0	3.0	0	125	m.q.
thins (Nabisco) . .	70	1.0	9.0	4.0	<2	210	m.q.
w/bacon and cheese							
(Handi-Snacks),							
1 pkg.	130	4.0	8.0	9.0	20	410	m.q.
butter flavor:							
(Escort)	70	1.0	9.0	4.0	0	115	m.q.
(Keebler Club Low							
Salt), 4 pieces	60	1.0	9.0	3.0	0	75	m.q.
(Keebler Toasteds							
Buttercrisp),							
4 pieces	60	1.0	8.0	3.0	0	125	m.q.
(Keebler Town							
House), 4 pieces	70	1.0	8.0	4.0	0	120	m.q.
(Pepperidge Farm							
Distinctive),							
4 pieces	70	1.0	10.0	3.0	<5	115	0
(Ritz/Ritz Bits) . .	70	1.0	9.0	4.0	<2	120	m.q.
(Ritz/Ritz Bits Low							
Salt)	70	1.0	9.0	4.0	0	60	m.q.
dairy (Nabisco							
American Classic)	70	1.0	9.0	3.0	<2	140	m.q.
cheese:							
(Cheese Nips) . . .	70	1.0	9.0	3.0	<2	130	m.q.
(Combos), 1.8 oz.	240	5.0	34.0	10.0	n.a.	580	m.q.
(Hain), 1 oz.	130	3.0	17.0	6.0	n.a.	280	m.q.

Food and Measure	cal.	prot. (gms)	carbo. (gms)	fat (gms)	chol. (mgs)	sod. (mgs)	fiber (gms)
(Pepperidge Farm Snack Sticks), 8 pieces	130	4.0	19.0	5.0	0	400	1.0 d
(Ritz Bits)	70	1.0	9.0	4.0	<2	150	m.q.
(Tid Bits)	70	1.0	8.0	4.0	<2	200	m.q.
cheddar *(Better Cheddars)*	70	2.0	8.0	4.0	<2	130	m.q.
cheddar *(Better Cheddars Low Salt)*	70	2.0	8.0	4.0	<2	65	m.q.
cheddar *(Guppies),* 1/4 oz.	40	1.0	5.0	2.0	m.a.	95	m.q.
cheddar *(Keebler Town House Jrs.),* 8 pieces	80	1.0	8.0	4.0	<5	95	m.q.
cheddar *(Pepperidge Farm Goldfish),* 1 oz. . . .	120	4.0	19.0	4.0	5	230	1.0 d
Parmesan *(Pepperidge Farm Tiny Goldfish),* 1 oz.	120	4.0	19.0	4.0	<5	330	1.0 d
Swiss *(Nabisco Swiss Cheese)*	70	1.0	11.0	3.0	<2	170	m.q.
thins *(Pepperidge Farm Goldfish),* 4 pieces	50	1.0	8.0	2.0	0	160	m.q.
cheese sandwich: cheddar *(Keebler Town House & Cheddar),* 1 piece	70	1.0	6.0	4.0	<5	105	m.q.
and peanut butter *(Keebler),* 2 pieces	70	2.0	9.0	3.0	0	150	m.q.
wheat and American cheese *(Keebler),* 1 piece . .	70	1.0	7.0	4.0	<5	85	m.q.
and cheese *(Handi-Snacks),* 1 pkg. . .	130	4.0	8.0	9.0	15	440	m.q.

Food and Measure	cal.	prot. (gms)	carbo. (gms)	fat (gms)	chol. (mgs)	sod. (mgs)	fiber (gms)
Crackers, *(cont.)*							
(Chicken In A Biskit)	80	1.0	8.0	5.0	<2	130	m.q.
crispbread (see also specific cracker listings):							
(Kavli Norwegian), 1 thick piece . .	35	1.0	7.5	.3	0	31	m.q.
(Kavli Norwegian), 2 thin pieces . .	40	1.0	8.0	.3	0	32	m.q.
(Wasa Breakfast), 1 piece	50	2.0	8.0	1.0	0	65	.7 d
(Wasa Extra Crisp), 1 piece	25	1.0	5.0	0	0	40	m.q.
(Wasa Fiber Plus), 1 piece	35	1.0	5.0	1.0	0	65	2.8 d
dark, regular or w/ caraway *(Finn Crisp),* 2 pieces	38	1.0	9.0	<1.0	0	130	1.6 d
high fiber:							
(Ryvita Crisp Bread), 1 piece	23	.9	4.0	<1.0	0	10	2.0 d
(Ryvita Snackbread), 1 piece	14	.6	3.0	<1.0	0	25	1.0 d
croissant *(Carr's),* 1 piece	25	n.a.	3.0	1.3	n.a.	19	m.q.
(FFV Schooners), 33 pieces	60	1.0	10.0	2.0	0	130	m.q.
graham, see "Cookies"							
grain, mixed *(Harvest Crisps* 5 Grain) . .	60	1.0	10.0	2.0	0	135	m.q.
(Hain Rich), 1 oz. . .	130	3.0	18.0	5.0	0	160	m.q.
(Hickory Farms Old Fashioned), 10 pieces	90	2.0	16.0	3.0	n.a.	170	m.q.
matzo, 1 board:							
(Manischewitz Daily Unsalted)	110	3.0	24.0	.3	0	1	.1 d

Food and Measure	cal.	prot. (gms)	carbo. (gms)	fat (gms)	chol. (mgs)	sod. (mgs)	fiber (gms)
(Manischewitz Passover)	129	3.3	27.0	.4	0	<5	m.q.
American (Manischewitz)	115	2.9	22.0	1.9	0	m.q.	m.q.
egg (Manischewitz Passover)	132	4.0	27.0	2.0	25	<5	m.q.
egg n' onion (Manischewitz)	112	3.1	23.0	1.0	15	180	m.q.
tea, thin (Manischewitz Daily) . .	103	3.0	22.0	.3	0	1	.1 d
thin (Manischewitz)	100	3.0	21.0	.3	0	m.q.	.1 d
whole wheat w/bran (Manischewitz)	110	4.0	21.0	.6	0	1	.6 d
melba toast:							
(Devonsheer), 1 piece	16	1.0	3.0	.4	0	30	.2 d
(Devonsheer Rounds)	53	2.0	11.0	.6	0	111	.8 d
bacon (Old London Rounds)	53	2.1	10.1	1.0	0	126	.9 d
garlic (Devonsheer/ Ol London Rounds)	56	2.1	10.0	1.2	0	132	.6 d
honey bran (Devonsheer), 1 piece	16	1.0	3.0	.4	0	25	.2 d
honey bran (Devonsheer Rounds)	52	2.1	10.2	.9	0	98	.9 d
oat (Harvest Crisps)	60	1.0	10.0	2.0	0	135	m.q.
onion (Devonsheer Rounds)	51	1.9	10.7	.6	0	120	.8 d
onion (Old London Rounds)	52	2.0	10.2	.8	0	121	.7 d
pumpernickel (Old London)	54	1.6	11.0	.6	0	156	.8 d
rye (Devonsheer), 1 piece	16	1.0	3.0	.4	0	30	.2 d
rye (Devonsheer Rounds)	53	1.8	10.7	.6	0	130	.9 d

Food and Measure	cal.	prot. (gms)	carbo. (gms)	fat (gms)	chol. (mgs)	sod. (mgs)	fiber (gms)
Crackers, melba toast *(cont.)*							
rye *(Old London)*	52	1.8	10.9	.7	0	132	.8 d
sesame *(Devonsheer)*, 1 piece	16	1.0	3.0	.5	0	25	.2 d
sesame *(Devonsheer* Rounds)	57	2.3	9.0	1.8	0	131	.9 d
sesame *(Old London)*	55	2.3	8.9	1.8	0	148	.9 d
sesame *(Old London* Rounds) . .	56	2.3	8.9	1.8	0	149	.9 d
vegetable *(Devonsheer)*, 1 piece	16	1.0	3.0	.4	0	25	.2 d
wheat *(Old London)*	51	2.1	10.5	.7	0	121	.9 d
wheat, whole *(Devonsheer)*, 1 piece	16	1.0	3.0	.4	0	30	.2 d
white *(Old London)*	51	2.0	10.4	.6	0	111	.8 d
white *(Old London* Rounds)	48	2.0	9.8	.6	0	111	.8 d
whole grain *(Old London)*	52	2.1	10.1	.9	0	116	.8 d
whole grain *(Old London* Rounds)	54	2.1	9.9	1.2	0	102	.9 d
oat *(Oat Thins)* . . .	70	1.0	10.0	3.0	0	90	m.q.
oat bran *(Oat Bran Krisp)*	60	1.0	9.0	3.0	0	140	3.2 d
onion:							
(Hain), 1 oz.	130	3.0	17.0	6.0	0	160	m.q.
(Keebler Toasteds), 4 pieces	60	1.0	9.0	3.0	0	140	m.q.
peanut butter:							
(Combos), 1.8 oz.	240	6.0	30.0	10.0	n.a.	360	m.q.
(Handi-Snacks), 1 pkg.	190	6.0	11.0	13.0	0	250	m.q.
cheese *(Little Debbie)*, .93 oz. . . .	130	4.0	14.0	6.0	<1	260	m.q.
toasty *(Little Debbie)*, .93 oz. . . .	140	4.0	14.0	7.0	<1	250	m.q.

Food and Measure	cal.	prot. (gms)	carbo. (gms)	fat (gms)	chol. (mgs)	sod. (mgs)	fiber (gms)
sandwich *(Ritz Bits)*	80	2.0	8.0	4.0	0	80	m.q.
toast and *(Keebler)*, 2 pieces	70	2.0	9.0	3.0	0	120	m.q.
(Pepperidge Farm Original Goldfish), 1 oz.	130	3.0	18.0	5.0	0	190	1.0 d
(Pepperidge Farm Snack Sticks), 8 pieces :	130	2.0	20.0	5.0	0	320	m.q.
pizza flavor *(Pepperidge Farm Goldfish)*, 1 oz.	130	4.0	19.0	5.0	<5	220	1.0 d
poppy, toasted *(Nabisco American Classic)*	70	1.0	9.0	3.0	0	140	m.q.
pretzel:							
(Pepperidge Farm Goldfish), 1 oz.	110	3.0	20.0	3.0	0	160	1.0 d
(Pepperidge Farm Snack Sticks), 8 pieces	120	3.0	23.0	3.0	0	430	1.0 d
pumpernickel *(Pepperidge Farm Snack Sticks)*, 8 pieces	140	3.0	20.0	6.0	0	330	1.0 d
rye:							
(Hain), 1 oz.	120	3.0	19.0	4.0	0	200	m.q.
(Keebler Toasteds), 4 pieces	60	1.0	8.0	3.0	0	140	m.q.
(Rykrisp)	40	1.0	11.0	0	0	75	3.6 d
dark *(Ryvita* Crisp Bread), 1 piece	26	.7	6.0	<1.0	0	35	1.3 d
golden *(Wasa* Crispbread), 1 piece	35	1.0	7.0	0	0	55	1.4 d
hearty *(Wasa* Crispbread), 1 piece	45	2.0	9.0	0	0	70	2.6 d
light *(Finn Crisp* Hi-Fiber), 1 piece	35	1.0	8.0	1.0	0	60	m.q.

Food and Measure	cal.	prot. (gms)	carbo. (gms)	fat (gms)	chol. (mgs)	sod. (mgs)	fiber (gms)
Crackers, rye *(cont.)*							
light *(Ryvita* Crisp Bread), 1 piece	26	.7	6.0	<1.0	0	20	1.3 d
light *(Wasa* Crispbread), 1 piece	25	1.0	5.0	0	0	40	1.2 d
original *(Finn Crisp* Hi-Fiber), 1 piece	40	1.0	10.0	0	0	95	m.q.
seasoned *(Rykrisp)*	45	1.0	11.0	1.0	0	105	3.0 d
sesame *(Rykrisp)*	50	1.0	10.0	2.0	0	105	3.0 d
sesame, toasted *(Ryvita* Crisp Bread), 1 piece	31	1.1	5.0	<1.0	0	10	1.4 d
saltine:							
(Premium)	60	1.0	10.0	2.0	<2	180	m.q.
(Premium Bits) . .	70	1.0	9.0	3.0	0	160	m.q.
(Premium Low Salt)	60	1.0	10.0	2.0	<2	115	m.q.
(Premium Unsalted Tops)	60	1.0	10.0	2.0	<2	135	m.q.
(Zesta Low Salt), 5 pieces	60	1.0	10.0	2.0	0	95	m.q.
original or wheat *(Zesta)*, 5 pieces	60	1.0	10.0	2.0	0	190	m.q.
wheat, whole *(Premium Plus)* . . .	60	1.0	10.0	2.0	0	130	m.q.
sandwich, see specific cracker listings							
sesame:							
(FFV Crisp), 1 piece	60	1.0	10.0	2.0	0	120	m.q.
(Hain), 1 oz.	140	3.0	16.0	7.0	n.a.	210	m.q.
(Keebler Toasteds), 4 pieces	60	1.0	8.0	3.0	0	130	m.q.
(Pepperidge Farm Distinctive), 4 pieces	80	2.0	12.0	4.0	0	140	2.0 d
(Pepperidge Farm Snack Sticks), 8 pieces	140	4.0	19.0	5.0	0	280	1.0 d

Food and Measure	cal.	prot. (gms)	carbo. (gms)	fat (gms)	chol. (mgs)	sod. (mgs)	fiber (gms)
bread wafer (Meal Mates)	70	1.0	9.0	3.0	0	160	m.q.
golden (Nabisco American Classic)	70	1.0	9.0	3.0	0	120	m.q.
savory (Wasa Crispbread), 1 piece	30	2.0	4.0	1.0	0	40	2.4 d
wafer (FFV Crisp), 4 pieces	60	2.0	9.0	2.0	0	140	m.q.
sesame and cheese (Twigs Snack Sticks)	70	1.0	8.0	4.0	<2	140	m.q.
sesame wheat (Wasa Crispbread), 1 piece	50	2.0	8.0	2.0	0	65	.6 d
soda or water:							
(Carr's Table Water, Bite Size), 2 pieces	25	1.0	5.0	1.0	n.a.	15	m.q.
(Crown Pilot) . . .	70	1.0	11.0	2.0	<2	70	m.q.
(FFV Ocean Crisps), 1 piece	60	1.0	10.0	2.0	0	120	m.q.
(Pepperidge Farm English Water Biscuit), 4 pieces	70	2.0	13.0	1.0	0	100	0
(Royal Lunch) . . .	60	1.0	10.0	2.0	<5	80	m.q.
(Sailor Boy Pilot), 1 piece	100	2.0	17.0	3.0	0	125	m.q.
soup and oyster:							
(Dandy)	60	1.0	10.0	2.0	<2	220	m.q.
(Oysterettes), 18 pieces, 1 oz.	60	1.0	10.0	1.0	<2	140	m.q.
sour cream and chive (Hain), 1 oz.	130	3.0	15.0	6.0	n.a.	150	m.q.
sourdough (Hain) . .	65	2.0	9.0	3.0	0	100	m.q.
toast (Uneeda Biscuits Unsalted Tops) . .	60	1.0	10.0	2.0	0	100	m.q.
vegetable:							
(Hain), 1 oz.	130	3.0	10.0	5.0	0	180	m.q.
(Vegetable Thins)	70	1.0	8.0	4.0	<2	140	m.q.

Food and Measure	cal.	prot. (gms)	carbo. (gms)	fat (gms)	chol. (mgs)	sod. (mgs)	fiber (gms)
Crackers, *(cont.)*							
(Waverly)	70	1.0	10.0	3.0	0	160	m.q.
wheat:							
(FFV Crispy Wafer),							
6 pieces	70	1.0	9.0	3.0	n.a.	80	m.q.
(FFV Stoned Wheat							
Wafer), 4 pieces	60	1.0	10.0	2.0	0	170	m.q.
(Ryvita Original							
Snackbread),							
1 piece	20	.5	4.0	<1.0	0	20	.2 d
(Sociables)	70	1.0	9.0	3.0	<2	135	m.q.
(Triscuit/Triscuit							
Bits)	60	1.0	10.0	2.0	0	75	m.q.
(Triscuit Low Salt)	60	1.0	10.0	2.0	0	35	m.q.
(Wheat Thins) . . .	70	1.0	9.0	3.0	0	120	m.q.
(Wheat Thins Low							
Salt)	70	1.0	9.0	3.0	0	60	m.q.
(Wheatsworth Stone							
Ground)	70	1.0	9.0	3.0	0	135	m.q.
cracked *(Nabisco*							
American Classic)	70	1.0	8.0	4.0	0	140	m.q.
cracked *(Pepper-*							
idge Farm Distinc-							
tive), 3 pieces	100	2.0	14.0	4.0	0	180	1.0 d
hearty *(Pepperidge*							
Farm Distinctive),							
4 pieces	100	2.0	13.0	5.0	0	140	1.0 d
nutty *(Wheat Thins)*	70	1.0	9.0	4.0	0	170	m.q.
toasted, w/onion							
(Pepperidge							
Farm), 4 pieces	80	2.0	12.0	3.0	0	140	0
whole *(Carr's)*,							
2 pieces	70	1.0	12.0	1.0	n.a.	15	m.q.
whole *(Keebler*							
Wheatables),							
12 pieces	70	1.0	9.0	3.0	0	140	m.q.

Food and Measure	cal.	prot. (gms)	carbo. (gms)	fat (gms)	chol. (mgs)	sod. (mgs)	fiber (gms)
whole grain (Keebler Harvest Wheats), 4 pieces	60	1.0	8.0	3.0	0	95	m.q.
whole grain (Wasa Crispbread), 1 slice	30	2.0	4.0	1.0	0	40	2.4 d
wheat'n bran (Triscuit)	60	1.0	10.0	2.0	0	75	m.q.
zwieback toast (Nabisco)	60	2.0	10.0	1.0	<2	20	m.q.
Cracker crumbs and meal:							
(Golden Dipt), 1 oz.	100	3.0	22.0	0	0	0	m.q.
matzo (Manischewitz Farfel), 1 cup . . .	180	6.8	60.0	.8	0	2	.2 d
matzo meal (Manischewitz Daily), 1 cup	514	13.0	109.0	1.4	0	3	.5 d
Cranberry:							
fresh, raw, 1/2 cup:							
whole	23	.2	6.0	.1	0	1	.6 c
chopped	27	.2	7.0	.1	0	1	.7 c
canned, see "Cranberry sauce"							
Cranberry bean:							
boiled, 1/2 cup	120	8.2	21.5	.4	0	1	3.0 d
canned, w/liquid, 1/2 cup	108	7.2	19.7	.4	0	431	1.2 c
Cranberry fruit concentrate:							
(Hain), 1 oz., 2 tbsp.	45	0	12.0	0	0	9	<1.0 d
Cranberry juice, 6 fl. oz., except as noted:							
(Lucky Leaf)	110	0	26.0	0	0	10	(0)
(Smucker's Naturally 100%), 8 fl. oz. . .	130	0	30.0	0	0	10	(0)
cocktail:							
(Ocean Spray) . .	110	0	26.0	0	0	10	(0)

Food and Measure	cal.	prot. (gms)	carbo. (gms)	fat (gms)	chol. (mgs)	sod. (mgs)	fiber (gms)
Cranberry juice, cocktail *(cont.)*							
(Sunkist)	110	.1	28.2	.1	0	8	(0)
(Veryfine), 8 fl. oz.	160	<1.0	40.0	0	0	<10	(0)
cocktail, frozen[1]:							
(Sunkist)	110	.1	28.2	.1	0	8	(0)
(Welch's)	100	0	26.0	0	0	0	0
Cranberry juice drink:							
blend *(Ocean Spray Cran-Tastic)*, 6 fl. oz.	110	0	27.0	0	0	15	(0)
Cranberry-apple drink:							
(Ocean Spray Cran-Apple), 6 fl. oz. . .	130	0	32.0	0	0	10	(0)
Cranberry-apple juice cocktail:							
frozen[1] *(Welch's)*, 6 fl. oz.	120	0	30.0	0	0	0	0
Cranberry-apricot juice drink:							
(Ocean Spray Cran-icot), 6 fl. oz. . . .	110	0	26.0	0	0	5	(0)
Cranberry-blueberry juice cocktail:							
frozen *(Welch's)*, 6 fl. oz.	110	0	27.0	0	0	0	0
Cranberry-grape drink:							
(Ocean Spray Cran-Grape), 6 fl. oz. . .	130	0	32.0	0	0	5	(0)
Cranberry-grape juice cocktail:							
frozen[1] *(Welch's)*, 6 fl. oz.	110	0	27.0	0	0	0	0

[1] *Diluted according to package directions.*
[1] *Diluted according to package directions.*

Food and Measure	cal.	prot. (gms)	carbo. (gms)	fat (gms)	chol. (mgs)	sod. (mgs)	fiber (gms)
Cranberry-orange relish, canned:							
1/2 cup	246	.4	63.8	.1	0	44	.8 c
Cranberry-raspberry drink, 6 fl. oz.:							
(Ocean Spray Cran-Raspberry)	110	0	27.0	0	0	10	(0)
Cranberry-raspberry juice cocktail:							
frozen[1] *(Welch's),* 6 fl. oz.	110	0	28.0	0	0	0	0
Cranberry sauce, canned:							
whole or jellied:							
1/2 cup	209	.3	53.7	.2	0	40	.4 c
(Ocean Spray), 2 oz.	90	0	22.0	0	0	15	m.q.
(S&W Old Fashioned), 1/2 cup	90	0	22.0	0	0	20	m.q.
Cranberry sauce blends, 2 oz.:							
all varieties, except w/ apple *(Ocean Spray Cran-Fruit)*	100	0	23.0	0	0	10	m.q.
w/apple *(Ocean Spray Cran-Fruit)*	100	0	24.0	0	0	20	m.q.
Crayfish, meat only:							
raw, 1 lb.	405	84.6	0	4.8	628	241	0
raw, 1 oz., 8 medium	25	5.3	0	.3	39	15	0
boiled or steamed, 4 oz.	129	27.1	0	1.5	202	77	0
Cream:							
half and half:							
1 cup	315	7.2	10.4	27.8	89	98	0
1 tbsp.	20	.4	.6	1.7	6	6	0
(Crowley), 1 fl. oz.	35	1.0	1.0	3.0	15	10	0

[1] *Diluted according to package directions.*

Food and Measure	cal.	prot. (gms)	carbo. (gms)	fat (gms)	chol. (mgs)	sod. (mgs)	fiber (gms)
Cream (cont.)							
light, coffee or table:							
1 cup	469	6.5	8.8	46.3	159	95	0
1 tbsp.	29	.4	.6	2.9	10	6	0
medium (25% fat):							
1 cup	583	5.9	8.3	59.8	209	88	0
1 tbsp.	37	.4	.5	3.8	13	6	0
sour, see "Cream, sour"							
whipping[1], light:							
1 cup	699	5.2	7.1	73.9	265	82	0
1 tbsp.	44	.3	.4	4.6	17	5	0
whipping[1], heavy:							
1 cup	821	4.9	6.6	88.1	326	89	0
1 tbsp.	52	.3	.4	5.6	21	6	0
whipped topping:							
frozen (Kraft Real Cream), 1/4 cup	30	0	2.0	2.0	10	5	0
nondairy, see "Cream topping, nondairy"							
pressurized:							
1 tbsp.	8	.1	.4	.7	2	4	0
(Crowley), 1 tbsp.	20	<1.0	<1.0	1.0	5	10	0
Cream, sour:							
1 cup	493	7.3	9.8	48.2	102	123	0
1 tbsp.	26	.4	.5	2.5	5	6	0
(Crowley), 1 oz. . . .	50	1.0	1.0	5.0	20	15	0
(Friendship), 1 oz., 2 tbsp.	55	1.0	1.0	5.0	42	15	0
half and half, 1 oz.	38	.8	1.2	3.4	11	11	0
half and half, 1 tbsp.	20	.4	.6	1.8	6	6	0
light (Crowley), 1 oz.	30	1.0	2.0	2.0	5	25	0
lowfat (Friendship Lite Delite), 1 oz. . . .	35	1.0	2.0	2.0	8	25	0

[1] Unwhipped; volume approximately doubled when whipped.

Food and Measure	cal.	prot. (gms)	carbo. (gms)	fat (gms)	chol. (mgs)	sod. (mgs)	fiber (gms)
Cream, sour, nondairy:							
1 oz.	59	.7	1.9	5.5	0	29	0
dressing *(Crowley)*, 1 oz.	40	1.0	1.0	4.0	0	5	0
Creme de menthe:							
72 proof, 1 fl. oz. . . .	125	0	14.0	.1	0	2	0
Cream puff, frozen:							
Bavarian *(Rich's)*, 1 piece	150	2.0	17.0	8.0	25	70	m.q.
Cream of tartar:							
(Tone's), 1 tsp. . . .	2	0	.6	0	0	n.a.	0
Cream topping, dairy, see "Cream"							
Cream topping, nondairy:							
frozen:							
1 cup	239	.9	17.3	19.0	0	19	0
1 tbsp.	13	.1	.9	1.0	0	1	0
(Birds Eye Cool Whip), 1 tbsp. . .	12	0	1.0	1.0	0	0	0
(Birds Eye Cool Whip Dairy Recipe), 1 tbsp. . . .	14	0	1.0	1.0	0	0	0
(Birds Eye Cool Whip Lite), 1 tbsp.	8	0	1.0	<1.0	0	0	0
(Kraft Whipped Topping), 1/4 cup . .	35	0	2.0	3.0	0	10	0
mix[1]:							
1 cup	151	2.9	13.2	9.9	0	53	0
(D-Zerta), 1 tbsp.	8	0	0	1.0	0	5	0
(Dream Whip), 1 tbsp.	10	0	1.0	0	0	0	0
pressurized *(Rich's Richwhip)*, 1/4 oz.	20	0	1.0	2.0	0	5	0

[1] *Prepared according to package directions.*

Food and Measure	cal.	prot. (gms)	carbo. (gms)	fat (gms)	chol. (mgs)	sod. (mgs)	fiber (gms)
Cream topping, nondairy *(cont.)*							
prewhipped *(Rich's Richwhip)*, 1 tbsp.	12	0	1.0	1.0	0	0	0
unwhipped *(Rich's Richwhip)*, 1/4 oz.	20	0	1.0	2.0	0	10	0
Creamer, nondairy:							
(Crowley), 1/2 oz. . . .	16	<1.0	1.0	1.0	5	5	0
(Rich's Coffee Rich), 1/2 oz.	20	0	2.0	2.0	0	10	0
(Rich's Farm/Poly Rich), 1/2 oz. . . .	20	0	1.0	2.0	0	5	0
liquid *(Coffee-mate)*, 1 tbsp.	16	0	2.0	1.0	0	5	0
powder *(Cremora)*, 1 tsp.	10	0	1.0	<1.0	0	5	0
Creole sauce:							
Cajun *(Enrico's Light)*, 4 oz.	76	2.0	9.0	2.8	0	284	n.a.
Cress, garden, 1/2 cup:							
raw	8	.7	1.4	.2	0	4	.3 c
boiled, drained	16	1.3	2.6	.4	0	5	.6 c
Cress, water, see "Watercress"							
Croaker, meat only:							
raw, Atlantic, 1 lb. . .	474	80.7	0	14.4	277	252	0
raw, Atlantic, 1 oz.	29	5.0	0	.9	17	16	0
Croissant, 1 piece:							
(Pepperidge Farm Sandwich Quartets)	170	4.0	22.0	7.0	n.a.	250	tr.
butter:							
(Awrey's), 2 oz. . .	200	3.0	21.0	11.0	30	190	1.0 d
petite *(Pepperidge Farm)*	120	3.0	13.0	6.0	m.q.	170	m.q.
margarine *(Awrey's)*	250	4.0	26.0	14.0	5	360	1.0 d
wheat *(Awrey's)* . . .	240	4.0	24.0	14.0	5	390	1.0 d
frozen, butter:							
(Sara Lee), 1.5 oz.	170	4.0	19.0	9.0	m.q.	250	m.q.

Food and Measure	cal.	prot. (gms)	carbo. (gms)	fat (gms)	chol. (mgs)	sod. (mgs)	fiber (gms)
petite (Pepperidge Farm)	140	3.0	13.0	7.0	m.q.	160	m.q.
petite (Sara Lee)	120	3.0	13.0	6.0	m.q.	160	m.q.
Croissant sandwich, frozen, 1 piece:							
chicken and broccoli (Sara Lee), 4.5 oz.	340	16.0	32.0	17.0	m.q.	600	m.q.
ham and Swiss cheese (Sara Lee), 4.25 oz.	340	14.0	30.0	18.0	m.q.	860	m.q.
w/soup, see "Soup combinations"							
Crookneck squash, 1/2 cup:							
fresh, sliced:							
raw, ends trimmed	12	.6	2.6	.2	0	1	.7 d
boiled, drained . .	18	.8	3.9	.3	0	1	1.0 d
canned, cut:							
drained, no salt . .	14	.7	3.2	.1	0	5	1.1 d
yellow (Allens) . .	16	1.0	3.0	<1.0	0	230	m.q.
frozen, boiled, drained, sliced . .	24	1.2	5.3	.2	0	6	1.2 d
Croutons, 1/2 oz.:							
Caesar salad (Brownberry) . . .	62	1.8	8.0	2.6	<1	165	.5 d
cheddar (Brownberry)	63	1.8	8.3	2.8	3	155	.3 d
cheddar and Romano (Pepperidge Farm)	60	2.0	10.0	2.0	0	200	m.q.
cheese and garlic (Pepperidge Farm)	70	2.0	9.0	3.0	0	180	m.q.
onion and garlic:							
(Brownberry) . . .	60	1.6	8.8	2.2	1	190	.4 d
(Pepperidge Farm)	70	2.0	9.0	3.0	0	160	m.q.
seasoned:							
(Brownberry) . . .	59	1.6	8.5	2.2	<1	155	.5 d
(Pepperidge Farm)	70	2.0	9.0	3.0	0	180	m.q.
sour cream and chive (Pepperidge Farm)	70	2.0	9.0	3.0	0	170	m.q.

Food and Measure	cal.	prot. (gms)	carbo. (gms)	fat (gms)	chol. (mgs)	sod. (mgs)	fiber (gms)
Croutons, *(cont.)*							
toasted *(Brownberry)*	56	1.7	9.7	1.4	0	145	.4 d
Crowder peas, see "Peas, crowder"							
Cucumber, w/peel:							
1 medium, 8¼" long	39	1.6	8.8	.4	0	6	3.0 d
sliced, ½ cup . . .	7	.3	1.5	.1	0	1	.5 d
Cucumber dip, 2 tbsp.:							
creamy *(Kraft* Premium)	50	1.0	2.0	4.0	10	130	(0)
Cumin seed:							
1 tsp.	8	.4	.9	.5	0	4	.2 c
Cupcake, see "Cake, snack"							
Currant,							
trimmed ½ cup:							
black, European . . .	36	.8	8.6	.2	0	1	3.0 d
red or white	31	.8	7.7	.1	0	1	1.9 c
zante, dried	204	2.9	53.3	.2	0	6	1.1 c
Curry powder:							
1 tbsp.	20	.8	3.7	.9	0	3	1.0 c
1 tsp.	6	.3	1.2	.3	0	1	.3 c
Curry sauce mix:							
1.25-oz. pkt.	151	3.3	17.9	8.2	tr.	1444	.5 c
Cusk, meat only:							
raw, 1 lb.	396	86.2	0	3.1	186	143	0
raw, 1 oz.	25	5.4	0	.2	12	9	0
Custard, see "Pudding mix"							
Custard apple:							
trimmed, 1 oz.	29	.5	7.1	.2	0	1	1.0 c
Cuttlefish, meat only:							
raw, 1 lb.	359	73.7	3.7	3.2	507	1686	0
raw, 1 oz.	22	4.6	.2	.2	32	105	0

D

Food and Measure	cal.	prot. (gms)	carbo. (gms)	fat (gms)	chol. (mgs)	sod. (mgs)	fiber (gms)
Daikon, see "Radish, Oriental"							
Daiquiri mix:							
bottled, 1 fl. oz.:							
(Holland House) . .	36	0	9.0	0	0	111	(0)
raspberry (Holland House)	30	0	7.0	0	0	4	(0)
strawberry (Holland House)	31	0	7.0	0	0	3	(0)
instant (Holland House), .56 oz. dry	65	0	16.0	0	0	21	(0)
Dairy Queen, 1 serving:							
sandwiches:							
chicken breast fillet	608	27.0	46.0	34.0	78	725	m.q.
chicken breast fillet w/cheese	661	30.0	47.0	38.0	87	921	m.q.
DQ Hounder . . .	480	16.0	21.0	36.0	80	1192	m.q.
DQ Hounder w/ cheese	533	19.0	22.0	40.0	89	1210	m.q.
DQ Hounder w/chili	575	22.0	25.0	41.0	89	913	m.q.
fish fillet	430	20.0	45.0	18.0	40	674	m.q.
fish fillet w/cheese	483	23.0	46.0	22.0	49	870	m.q.
hamburger, single	360	21.0	33.0	16.0	45	630	m.q.
hamburger, double	530	36.0	33.0	28.0	85	660	m.q.
hamburger, triple	710	51.0	33.0	45.0	135	690	m.q.
cheeseburger, single	410	24.0	33.0	20.0	50	790	m.q.
cheeseburger, double	650	43.0	34.0	37.0	95	980	m.q.

225

Food and Measure	cal.	prot. (gms)	carbo. (gms)	fat (gms)	chol. (mgs)	sod. (mgs)	fiber (gms)
Dairy Queen, sandwiches (cont.)							
cheeseburger, triple	820	58.0	34.0	50.0	145	1010	m.q.
hot dog	280	11.0	21.0	16.0	45	830	m.q.
hot dog w/cheese	330	15.0	21.0	21.0	55	990	m.q.
hot dog w/chili . .	320	13.0	23.0	20.0	55	985	m.q.
chicken nuggets . . .	276	16.0	13.0	18.0	39	505	m.q.
chicken nuggets							
sauce, BBQ, 1 oz.	41	n.a.	9.0	n.a.	n.a.	130	m.q.
side dishes:							
french fries	200	2.0	25.0	10.0	10	115	m.q.
french fries, large	320	3.0	40.0	16.0	15	185	m.q.
onion rings	280	4.0	31.0	16.0	15	140	m.q.
desserts and shakes:							
Buster Bar	448	10.0	41.0	29.0	10	175	(0)
Chipper Sandwich	318	5.0	56.0	7.0	13	170	m.q.
cone, regular . . .	240	6.0	38.0	7.0	15	80	m.q.
cone, dipped, regu-							
lar	340	6.0	42.0	16.0	20	100	m.q.
Dilly Bar	210	3.0	21.0	13.0	10	50	(0)
DQ Sandwich . . .	140	3.0	24.0	4.0	5	40	m.q.
float	410	5.0	82.0	7.0	20	85	(0)
freeze	500	9.0	89.0	12.0	30	180	(0)
Fudge Nut Bar . .	406	8.0	40.0	25.0	10	167	m.q.
Heath Blizzard, reg-							
ular	800	15.0	25.0	24.0	65	325	(0)
malt, regular	760	14.0	134.0	18.0	50	260	(0)
Mr. Misty, regular	250	0.0	63.0	0.0	0	10	(0)
Mr. Misty Float . .	390	5.0	74.0	7.0	20	95	(0)
Mr. Misty Freeze	500	9.0	91.0	12.0	30	140	(0)
Mr. Misty Kiss . . .	89	0.0	17.0	0.0	0	10	(0)
parfait	430	8.0	76.0	8.0	30	250	(0)
Peanut Buster Par-							
fait	740	16.0	94.0	34.0	30	250	(0)
shake, regular . . .	710	14.0	120.0	19.0	50	260	(0)
sundae, regular . .	310	5.0	56.0	8.0	20	120	(0)
Dandelion greens:							
raw, 1 oz. or 1/2 cup							
chopped	13	.8	2.6	.2	0	22	.5 c

Food and Measure	cal.	prot. (gms)	carbo. (gms)	fat (gms)	chol. (mgs)	sod. (mgs)	fiber (gms)
boiled, drained, chopped, 1/2 cup	17	1.0	3.3	.3	0	23	.7 c
Danish, 1 piece:							
apple (*Awrey's* Round), 2.75 oz.	270	3.0	34.0	14.0	5	310	1.0 d
cheese (*Awrey's* Round), 2.75 oz.	280	3.0	34.0	15.0	10	350	1.0 d
cinnamon raisin (*Awrey's* Sq.), 3 oz.	290	3.0	41.0	12.0	15	280	1.0 d
cinnamon walnut (*Awrey's* Round), 2.75 oz.	300	4.0	31.0	18.0	5	290	1.0 d
pineapple, miniature (*Awrey's*), 1.7 oz.	157	2.0	21.0	8.0	5	180	1.0 d
raspberry (*Awrey's* Sq.), 3 oz.	260	3.0	45.0	8.0	10	210	1.0 d
strawberry (*Awrey's* Round), 2.75 oz.	270	3.0	34.0	14.0	5	320	1.0 d
frozen:							
apple (*Pepperidge Farm*), 2 1/4 oz.	220	2.0	35.0	8.0	n.a.	130	m.q.
apple (*Sara Lee* Individual), 1.3 oz.	120	2.0	15.0	6.0	n.a.	120	m.q.
cheese (*Pepperidge Farm*), 2 1/4 oz.	240	3.0	25.0	14.0	m.q.	230	m.q.
cheese (*Sara Lee* Individual), 1.3 oz.	130	2.0	13.0	8.0	m.q.	130	m.q.
cinnamon raisin (*Pepperidge Farm*), 2 1/4 oz.	250	3.0	35.0	11.0	n.a.	170	m.q.
cinnamon raisin (*Sara Lee* Individual), 1.3 oz. . . .	150	2.0	17.0	8.0	n.a.	140	m.q.
raspberry (*Pepperidge Farm*), 2 1/4 oz.	220	3.0	31.0	9.0	n.a.	140	m.q.

Food and Measure	cal.	prot. (gms)	carbo. (gms)	fat (gms)	chol. (mgs)	sod. (mgs)	fiber (gms)
Danish *(cont.)*							
refrigerated:							
caramel, w/nuts							
(Pillsbury)	160	2.0	19.0	8.0	5	240	m.q.
cinnamon raisin							
(Pillsbury)	140	2.0	20.0	7.0	5	230	m.q.
orange *(Pillsbury)*	140	2.0	19.0	7.0	5	240	m.q.
Dasheen, see "Taro"							
Date, pitted:							
(Bordo), 2 oz.	204	1.2	47.2	1.2	0	5	1.5 c
(Dole), 1/2 cup	280	5.0	62.0	.0	0	0	m.q.
(Dromedary), 1 oz. or							
5 dates	100	1.0	23.0	0	0	0	m.q.
chopped *(Dromedary),*							
1/4 cup	130	1.0	31.0	0	0	0	m.q.
diced *(Bordo),* 2 oz.	203	1.0	47.5	1.1	0	5	1.2 c
domestic, natural and							
dry, 10 dates,							
2.9 oz.	228	1.6	61.0	.4	0	2	4.2 d
Diable sauce:							
(Escoffier), 1 tbsp. . .	20	0	4.0	0	0	160	n.a.
Dill dip:							
creamy *(Nasoya Vegi-*							
Dip), 1 oz.	60	2.0	4.0	4.0	0	100	n.a.
Dill seasoning:							
(McCormick/Schilling							
Parsley Patch It's a							
Dilly), 1 tsp.	11	.4	2.0	.4	0	5	(0)
Dill seed:							
1 tsp.	6	.3	1.2	.3	0	tr.	.4
Dill weed, dried:							
1 tsp.	3	.2	.6	<.1	0	2	.1
Dip, see specific list-							
ings							
Dock:							
boiled, drained, 4 oz.	23	2.1	3.3	.7	0	3	.8 c

Food and Measure	cal.	prot. (gms)	carbo. (gms)	fat (gms)	chol. (mgs)	sod. (mgs)	fiber (gms)
Dolphin fish, meat only:							
raw, 1 lb.	387	83.9	0	3.2	331	397	0
raw, 1 oz.	24	5.2	0	.2	21	25	0
Domino's Pizza, 2 slices:							
cheese	376	21.6	56.3	10.1	19	483	6.4 d
deluxe	498	26.7	59.2	20.4	40	954	7.0 d
double cheese/pepperoni	545	32.1	55.2	25.3	48	1042	8.0 d
ham	417	23.2	58.0	11.0	26	805	2.1 d
pepperoni	460	24.1	55.6	17.5	28	825	4.5 d
sausage/mushroom	430	24.2	55.3	15.8	28	552	7.6 d
veggie	498	31.0	60.0	18.5	36	1035	8.1 d
Donut, 1 piece:							
plain:							
(Hostess)	110	1.0	12.0	7.0	5	135	m.q.
(Tastykake Assorted), 1.7 oz.	172	2.7	20.0	9.1	n.a.	256	m.q.
chocolate coated:							
(Hostess)	130	1.0	15.0	7.0	4	100	m.q.
(Tastykake Choco-Dipped), 1.25 oz.	181	2.6	20.9	9.7	n.a.	162	m.q.
mini *(Hostess* Donettes)	60	1.0	6.0	3.0	4	50	m.q.
cinnamon:							
(Hostess)	110	1.0	15.0	6.0	6	140	m.q.
(Tastykake Assorted), 1.7 oz.	201	2.7	26.8	9.3	n.a.	261	m.q.
coated, mini *(Tastykake),* .5 oz. . . .	81	1.0	8.7	4.7	n.a.	70	m.q.
crunch *(Hostess* Krunch)	110	1.0	16.0	4.0	4	130	m.q.
fudge iced *(Tastykake* Premium), 2.5 oz.	350	3.3	37.0	21.2	n.a.	250	m.q.
glazed *(Hostess* Old Fashioned)	230	2.0	30.0	12.0	11	200	m.q.

Food and Measure	cal.	prot. (gms)	carbo. (gms)	fat (gms)	chol. (mgs)	sod. (mgs)	fiber (gms)
Donut *(cont.)*							
honey wheat:							
(Tastykake Mini), .4 oz.	65	.7	9.0	2.9	n.a.	75	m.q.
(Tastykake Premium), 2.5 oz.	342	2.9	41.8	18.2	n.a.	238	m.q.
(Hostess Old Fashioned)	180	2.0	22.0	10.0	9	220	m.q.
orange glazed *(Tastykake* Premium)	357	2.9	42.5	19.5	n.a.	239	m.q.
powdered sugar:							
(Hostess)	110	1.0	17.0	4.0	5	118	m.q.
(Hostess Donettes)	40	1.0	5.0	1.0	1	40	m.q.
(Tastykake, 12/ pkg.)	123	1.8	16.1	5.8	n.a.	m.q.	m.q.
(Tastykake Assorted)	195	2.8	26.1	8.8	n.a.	263	m.q.
(Tastykake Mini, 6/ pkg.)	58	.7	6.9	3.1	n.a.	67	m.q.
stick *(Little Debbie)*	230	2.0	26.0	13.0	<1	180	m.q.
frozen:							
glazed *(Rich's Ever Fresh)*	141	2.4	17.2	7.0	n.a.	m.q.	m.q.
jelly *(Rich's Ever Fresh)*	213	3.6	26.0	9.5	n.a.	m.q.	m.q.
Drum, freshwater, meat only:							
raw, 1 lb.	541	79.5	0	22.4	290	340	0
raw, 1 oz.	34	5.0	0	1.4	18	21	0
***Druther's*[1],** 1 serving:							
breakfast:							
bacon and egg biscuit	258	11.8	15.2	16.3	253	653	.6 d
bacon and fried egg plate	721	24.9	62.2	41.9	500	1224	1.7 d

[1] *Values for all dishes and dinners are complete as served, including accompanying biscuits, potatoes, coleslaw, hush puppies, etc.*

Food and Measure	cal.	prot. (gms)	carbo. (gms)	fat (gms)	chol. (mgs)	sod. (mgs)	fiber (gms)
bacon and scrambled egg plate	742	25.9	63.9	43.0	501	1243	1.7 d
ham and egg biscuit	217	13.0	15.1	11.2	256	796	.6 d
ham and fried egg plate	681	29.4	62.1	35.3	511	1622	1.7 d
ham and scrambled egg plate	762	27.0	64.1	44.6	515	1408	1.7 d
sausage and egg biscuit	246	11.2	15.3	15.1	257	674	.6 d
sausage and fried egg plate	741	26.0	62.5	43.4	515	1390	1.7 d
sausage and scrambled egg plate	762	27.0	64.1	44.6	515	1408	1.7 d
1 sausage, 1 biscuit	179	5.9	13.1	11.1	17	447	.6 d
biscuits and gravy . .	331	5.6	41.8	14.7	3	1233	1.2 d
cheeseburger:							
regular	380	18.7	35.1	17.8	69	585	.3 d
deluxe quarter . . .	660	32.9	45.5	37.6	127	768	.6 d
double	500	29.3	35.1	26.1	105	618	.3 d
chicken dinner:							
2-piece, breast and wing, 14 oz. . . .	970	53.7	76.0	49.9	159	1899	2.2 d
2-piece, leg and thigh, 13.4 oz.	925	44.0	77.3	49.0	157	1530	2.2 d
3-piece, breast, thigh, and leg, 1.1 lb.	1281	78.0	89.6	66.9	273	2566	2.3 d
3-piece, breast, thigh, and wing, 1.1 lb.	1309	80.2	86.5	70.3	271	2465	2.2 d
chicken snack:							
breast and wing, 14 oz.	970	53.7	76.0	49.9	159	"1899	2.2 d
thigh and leg, 13.4 oz.	925	44.0	77.3	49.0	157	1497	2.2 d
breast and wing, 7.5 oz.	595	48.0	28.0	30.7	154	1607	.6 d
thigh and leg, 7 oz.	549	38.2	29.4	29.8	152	1205	.6 d

Food and Measure	cal.	prot. (gms)	carbo. (gms)	fat (gms)	chol. (mgs)	sod. (mgs)	fiber (gms)
Druther's (cont.)							
Fish and Chips . . .	729	42.3	71.2	29.8	112	1292	3.5 d
fish dinner	770	43.1	78.7	31.3	117	1306	3.9 d
fish sandwich	349	22.1	33.0	14.4	56	821	2.3 d
hamburger	327	15.6	34.9	13.4	55	382	.3 d
Duck, domesticated, roasted:							
meat w/skin, 4 oz.	382	21.5	0	32.1	95	67	0
meat only, 4 oz. . . .	228	26.6	0	12.7	101	74	0
Duck, wild, raw:							
meat w/skin, 1 oz.	60	4.9	0	4.3	23	16	0
breast meat only, 1 oz.	35	5.6	0	1.2	m.q.	16	0
Duck sauce, see "Sweet and sour sauce"							
Dulcita, frozen:							
apple (Hormel), 4 oz.	290	5.0	44.0	10.0	n.a.	350	n.a.
cherry (Hormel), 4 oz.	300	5.0	48.0	9.0	n.a.	345	n.a.
Dutch brand loaf:							
(Eckrich/Eckrich Smorgas Pac), 1-oz. slice	70	3.0	2.0	6.0	m.q.	300	(0)
(Eckrich Lean Supreme), 1-oz. slice	60	4.0	2.0	4.0	m.q.	250	(0)
(Kahn's), 1 slice . . .	80	3.0	1.0	7.0	m.q.	280	(0)

E

Food and Measure	cal.	prot. (gms)	carbo. (gms)	fat (gms)	chol. (mgs)	sod. (mgs)	fiber (gms)
Eclair, chocolate, frozen:							
(Rich's), 1 piece . . .	210	2.0	27.0	10.0	35	110	m.q.
Eel, meat only:							
raw, 1 oz.	52	5.2	0	3.3	36	14	0
baked, broiled or microwaved, 4 oz. . . .	268	26.8	0	17.0	183	74	0
Egg, chicken:							
raw, fresh or frozen:							
whole, 1 large . . .	75	6.3	.6	5.0	213	63	0
white from 1 large egg	17	3.5	.3	0	0	55	0
yolk from 1 large egg[1]	59	2.8	.3	5.1	213	7	0
cooked:							
hard-boiled, 1 large	77	6.3	.6	5.3	213	62	0
hard-boiled, chopped, 1 cup	210	17.1	1.5	14.4	578	169	0
poached, 1 large	74	6.2	.6	5.0	212	140	0
dried, 1 oz.:							
whole	168	13.0	1.4	11.9	544	148	0
whole, stabilized	174	13.7	.7	12.5	572	155	0
white, stabilized, flakes	100	21.8	1.2	<.1	0	328	0
yolk	195	8.7	.1	17.4	830	26	0
"Egg," substitute or imitation:							
(Fleischmann's Egg Beaters), 1/4 cup	25	5.0	1.0	0	0	80	0

[1] *Includes a small portion of white.*

Food and Measure	cal.	prot. (gms)	carbo. (gms)	fat (gms)	chol. (mgs)	sod. (mgs)	fiber (gms)
"Egg," substitute or imitation *(cont.)*							
w/cheez							
(Fleischmann's Egg Beaters), 1/2 cup	130	14.0	3.0	6.0	5	440	0
frozen:							
(Morningstar Farms Scramblers), 1/4 cup	60	6.0	3.0	3.0	0	n.a.	0
(Tofutti Egg Watchers), 2 oz.	50	7.0	2.0	2.0	0	100	n.a.
mix[1] (Tofu Scrambler), 1/2 cup	158	11.0	7.0	12.0	m.q.	335	m.q.
Egg, duck, fresh:							
whole, raw, 1 egg	130	9.0	1.0	9.6	619	102	0
Egg, goose, fresh:							
whole, raw, 1 egg	267	20.0	1.9	19.1	m.q.	n.a.	0
Egg, pickled:							
(Penrose), 1 egg	80	8.0	1.0	5.0	m.q.	230	0
Egg, quail, fresh:							
whole, raw, 1 egg	14	1.2	<.1	1.0	76	n.a.	0
Egg, turkey, fresh:							
whole, raw, 1 egg	135	10.8	.9	9.4	737	n.a.	0
Egg breakfast, freeze-dried, 1/2 pkg.:							
w/bacon (Mountain House)	170	12.0	7.0	10.0	m.q.	165	n.a.
w/butter (Mountain House)	160	11.0	8.0	8.0	m.q.	174	n.a.
precooked, w/bacon (Mountain House)	180	12.0	3.0	12.0	m.q.	m.q.	n.a.
omelet, cheese (Mountain House)	180	13.0	8.0	9.0	m.q.	207	n.a.

---

[1] *Prepared according to package directions, with tofu and 3 tbsp. salted butter.*

Food and Measure	cal.	prot. (gms)	carbo. (gms)	fat (gms)	chol. (mgs)	sod. (mgs)	fiber (gms)
Egg breakfast, frozen:							
omelet, w/cheese sauce and ham *(Swanson Great Starts)*, 7 oz. . . .	380	18.0	12.0	29.0	m.q.	1200	m.q.
omelet, Spanish style *(Swanson Great Starts)*, 7³/4 oz. . . .	240	8.0	15.0	16.0	m.q.	800	m.q.
scrambled:							
w/bacon, home fries *(Swanson Great Starts)*, 5¹/4 oz.	360	10.0	18.0	28.0	m.q.	690	m.q.
w/home fries *(Swanson Great Starts)*, 4³/8 oz.	280	7.0	15.0	21.0	m.q.	500	m.q.
w/sausages, hash browns *(Swanson Great Starts)*, 6¹/4 oz.	430	12.0	18.0	35.0	m.q.	780	m.q.
"Egg" breakfast, vegetarian, frozen:							
Scramblers, hash browns and links *(Morningstar Farms)*, 7 oz.	360	16.0	22.0	23.0	0	660	m.q.
Scramblers, pancakes and links *(Morningstar Farms)*, 6.8 oz. . .	380	18.0	33.0	19.0	0	900	m.q.
Egg breakfast biscuit, frozen:							
Canadian bacon and cheese *(Swanson Great Starts)*, 5¹/4 oz.	420	16.0	37.0	22.0	m.q.	1850	m.q.

Food and Measure	cal.	prot. (gms)	carbo. (gms)	fat (gms)	chol. (mgs)	sod. (mgs)	fiber (gms)
Egg breakfast biscuit, frozen *(cont.)*							
sausage and cheese *(Swanson Great Starts)*, 5 1/2 oz. . .	460	17.0	34.0	29.0	m.q.	1400	m.q.
Egg breakfast muffin, frozen:							
beefsteak and cheese *(Swanson Great Starts)*, 4.9 oz. . .	380	18.0	27.0	22.0	m.q.	770	m.q.
Canadian bacon and cheese *(Swanson Great Starts)*, 4.1 oz.	300	14.0	25.0	16.0	m.q.	780	m.q.
Egg foo yung, mix[1]:							
(La Choy), 8.8 oz. . .	164	8.2	19.2	7.0	n.a.	1250	m.q.
Egg roll, frozen:							
chicken:							
(Chun King), 3.6 oz.	220	5.0	32.0	8.0	m.q.	600	m.q.
(Jeno's Snacks), 3 oz.	190	5.0	21.0	9.0	m.q.	350	m.q.
meat and shrimp:							
(Chun King), 3.6 oz.	220	6.0	31.0	8.0	m.q.	680	m.q.
(Jeno's Snacks), 3 oz.	200	5.0	21.0	11.0	m.q.	420	m.q.
pork *(Chun King* Restaurant Style), 3 oz.	180	6.0	23.0	6.0	m.q.	450	m.q.
shrimp:							
(Chun King), 3.6 oz.	200	4.0	31.0	6.0	m.q.	480	m.q.
and cheese *(Jeno's* Snacks), 3 oz.	190	7.0	22.0	8.0	m.q.	290	m.q.
vegetable, w/soup, see "Soup combinations"							
vegetarian *(Worthington)*, 3 oz.	160	6.0	20.0	6.0	0	530	m.q.
Egg roll wrapper:							
(Nasoya), 1 piece . .	23	1.0	4.5	0	0	19	m.q.

[1] *Prepared according to package directions.*

Food and Measure	cal.	prot. (gms)	carbo. (gms)	fat (gms)	chol. (mgs)	sod. (mgs)	fiber (gms)
Eggnog, nonalcoholic:							
(Crowley), 6 fl. oz. . . .	270	6.0	34.0	13.0	100	200	(0)
(Darigold), 8 fl. oz. . . .	350	6.0	43.0	17.0	m.q.	120	(0)
(Darigold Classic),							
8 fl. oz.	390	10.0	48.0	17.0	m.q.	170	(0)
canned (Borden),							
1/2 cup	160	3.0	16.0	9.0	m.q.	80	0
Eggplant:							
raw, trimmed,							
1" pieces, 1/2 cup	11	.5	2.6	<.1	0	1	.6 d
boiled, drained,							
1" cubes, 1/2 cup	13	.4	3.2	.1	0	2	.5 c
Eggplant entree, fro-							
zen:							
parmigiana:							
(Celentano),							
6.25 oz.	260	9.0	36.0	10.0	m.q.	220	m.q.
(Celentano), 10 oz.	350	18.0	29.0	19.0	m.q.	500	m.q.
(Mrs. Paul's), 4 oz.	240	6.0	18.0	16.0	15	600	m.q.
rollettes (Celentano),							
11 oz.	320	14.0	36.0	14.0	n.a.	210	m.q.
Elderberry:							
1/2 cup	53	.5	13.3	.4	0	n.a.	5.1 c
Enchilada dinner, fro-							
zen:							
beef:							
(Banquet), 12 oz.	500	19.0	72.0	15.0	m.q.	1810	m.q.
(Old El Paso),							
11 oz.	390	24.0	56.0	8.0	m.q.	1200	m.q.
(Patio), 13.25 oz.	520	16.0	59.0	24.0	40	1810	m.q.
(Swanson),							
13 3/4 oz.	480	16.0	54.0	22.0	m.q.	1300	m.q.
(Van de Kamp's),							
1/2 pkg.	200	8.0	27.0	7.0	m.q.	740	m.q.
cheese:							
(Banquet), 12 oz.	550	22.0	71.0	19.0	m.q.	2170	m.q.
(Old El Paso),							
11 oz.	590	24.0	51.0	31.0	m.q.	1200	m.q.

Food and Measure	cal.	prot. (gms)	carbo. (gms)	fat (gms)	chol. (mgs)	sod. (mgs)	fiber (gms)
Enchilada dinner, frozen, cheese *(cont.)*							
(Patio), 12.25 oz.	380	14.0	59.0	10.0	20	2010	m.q.
(Van de Kamp's),							
1/2 pkg.	220	8.0	26.0	9.0	m.q.	620	m.q.
chicken *(Old El Paso)*,							
11 oz.	460	21.0	54.0	18.0	m.q.	770	m.q.
Enchilada dinner mix:							
(Tio Sancho Dinner Kit)*:							
sauce mix, 3 oz.	278	4.5	62.0	1.5	n.a.	4058	1.8 c
1 shell	80	1.3	10.8	3.5	n.a.	2	.6 c
Enchilada entree, frozen:							
beef:							
(Hormel), 1 piece	140	6.0	17.0	5.0	m.q.	573	m.q.
(Old El Paso),							
1 pkg.	210	8.0	16.0	13.0	m.q.	720	m.q.
(Van de Kamp's),							
1 pkg.	270	11.0	30.0	12.0	m.q.	1040	m.q.
chili gravy *(Banquet Family Entrees)*,							
7 oz.	270	10.0	28.0	13.0	m.q.	m.q.	m.q.
Ranchero *(Weight Watchers)*,							
9.12 oz.	300	19.0	25.0	13.0	45	930	m.q.
shredded *(Van de Kamp's)*, 1 pkg.	360	20.0	40.0	14.0	m.q.	1010	m.q.
sirloin Ranchero *(The Budget Gourmet)*, 9 oz.	290	19.0	20.0	15.0	35	770	m.q.
cheese:							
(Hormel), 1 piece	151	6.0	18.0	6.0	m.q.	676	m.q.
(Old El Paso),							
1 pkg.	250	10.0	24.0	12.0	m.q.	830	m.q.
(Stouffer's),							
10 1/8 oz.	590	23.0	34.0	40.0	m.q.	880	m.q.

Food and Measure	cal.	prot. (gms)	carbo. (gms)	fat (gms)	chol. (mgs)	sod. (mgs)	fiber (gms)
(Van de Kamp's),							
1 pkg.	300	11.0	31.0	15.0	m.q.	980	m.q.
Ranchero *(Van de*							
Kamp's), 1/2 pkg.	260	11.0	26.0	12.0	m.q.	630	m.q.
Ranchero *(Weight*							
Watchers),							
8.87 oz.	360	18.0	30.0	18.0	60	900	m.q.
chicken:							
(Old El Paso),							
1 pkg.	220	8.0	20.0	12.0	m.q.	740	m.q.
(Stouffer's), 10 oz.	490	22.0	34.0	29.0	m.q.	910	m.q.
(Van de Kamp's),							
1 pkg.	260	13.0	27.0	11.0	m.q.	1010	m.q.
w/sour cream							
sauce *(Old El*							
Paso), 1 pkg. . . .	280	10.0	18.0	19.0	m.q.	520	m.q.
Suiza:							
(The Budget							
Gourmet), 9 oz.	270	17.0	30.0	9.0	50	1080	m.q.
(Van de Kamp's),							
1 pkg.	230	12.0	23.0	10.0	m.q.	390	m.q.
(Weight Watch-							
ers), 9.37 oz.	330	21.0	26.0	15.0	50	970	m.q.
vegetable, w/tofu							
(Legume), 11 oz.	270	14.0	36.0	8.0	0	390	10.3 d
Enchilada sauce:							
(Rosarita), 3 oz. . . .	19	n.a.	4.0	n.a.	0	429	(0)
green chili *(Old El*							
Paso), 1/4 cup . . .	18	0	4.0	0	0	400	(0)
hot:							
(Del Monte), 1/2 cup	45	1.0	11.0	0	0	1090	(0)
(Old El Paso),							
1/4 cup	30	0	4.0	1.0	0	250	(0)
hot or mild *(Ortega),*							
1 oz.	12	0	3.0	0	0	280	(0)
mild:							
(Del Monte), 1/2 cup	45	1.0	11.0	0	0	1150	(0)

Food and Measure	cal.	prot. (gms)	carbo. (gms)	fat (gms)	chol. (mgs)	sod. (mgs)	fiber (gms)
Enchilada sauce mild *(cont.)*							
(Old El Paso),							
1/4 cup	25	0	4.0	1.0	0	250	(0)
Enchilada seasoning:							
(Lawry's), 1 pkg. . . .	152	5.3	29.9	1.2	n.a.	1723	1.2 c
Endive:							
1 head, 1.3 lb.	86	6.4	17.2	1.0	0	54	m.q.
chopped, 1/2 cup . .	4	.3	.8	.1	0	6	.2 c
Endive, Belgian, see "Chickory, witloof"							
Eppaw:							
1/2 cup	75	2.3	15.8	.9	0	6	m.q.
Escarole, see "Endive"							

F

Food and Measure	cal.	prot. (gms)	carbo. (gms)	fat (gms)	chol. (mgs)	sod. (mgs)	fiber (gms)
Fajita entree:							
frozen, 6.75 oz.:							
beef *(Weight Watchers)*	250	16.0	31.0	7.0	30	730	m.q.
chicken *(Weight Watchers)*	230	17.0	30.0	5.0	30	590	m.q.
refrigerated, chicken *(Chicken By George)*, 5 oz. . .	170	28.0	2.0	6.0	85	370	n.a.
Fajita seasoning:							
(Lawry's), 1 pkg. . . .	63	2.0	14.0	.4	n.a.	2118	.5 c
Falafel mix:							
(Casbah), 1 oz. dry	103	7.0	15.0	2.0	0	m.q.	m.q.
(Near East), 3 patties[1]	270	13.0	22.0	15.0	n.a.	680	m.q.
Farina, whole-grain (see also "Cereal"):							
dry, 1 oz.	105	3.0	22.1	.1	0	1	.8 d
cooked, 1 cup	116	3.4	24.6	.2	0	1	3.3 d
Fat, see specific listings							
"Fat," imitation:							
(Rokeach Neutral Nyafat), 1 tbsp. . . .	99	0	0	11.0	0	0	0
Fava bean, canned:							
(Progresso), 8 oz. . .	180	14.0	31.0	1.0	0	m.q.	m.q.

[1] *Prepared according to package directions.*

241

Food and Measure	cal.	prot. (gms)	carbo. (gms)	fat (gms)	chol. (mgs)	sod. (mgs)	fiber (gms)
Fennel, fresh:							
(Frieda of California),							
1 oz.	4	.3	.7	<.1	0	26	m.q.
Fennel seed:							
1 tsp.	7	.3	1.1	.3	0	2	.3 c
Fenugreek seed:							
1 tsp.	12	.9	2.2	.2	0	2	.4 c
Fettuccini entree, frozen:							
Alfredo:							
(Healthy Choice),							
8 oz.	240	10.0	36.0	7.0	45	370	m.q.
(Stouffer's), 5 oz.	270	8.0	17.0	19.0	n.a.	560	m.q.
w/broccoli *(Dining Lite),* 9 oz.	290	12.0	33.0	12.0	35	1020	m.q.
w/meat sauce *(The Budget Gourmet),* 10 oz.	290	16.0	34.0	10.0	25	980	m.q.
primavera:							
(Green Giant), 1 pkg.	230	13.0	26.0	8.0	25	610	6.0 d
(Green Giant Microwave Garden Gourmet), 1 pkg.	260	17.0	25.0	13.0	n.a.	640	6.0 d
Fettuccini entree mix:							
Alfredo *(Hain* Pasta & Sauce), 1/4 pkg. . .	180	5.0	27.0	4.0	n.a.	420	m.q.
Fig:							
fresh:							
1 large, 2.3 oz. . .	47	.5	12.3	.2	0	1	.8 c
1 medium, 1.8 oz.	37	.4	9.6	.2	0	1	.6 c
canned, 1/2 cup:							
in heavy syrup, whole *(Del Monte)*	100	0	28.0	0	0	<10	m.q.

Food and Measure	cal.	prot. (gms)	carbo. (gms)	fat (gms)	chol. (mgs)	sod. (mgs)	fiber (gms)
in heavy syrup, whole kadota (S&W Fancy) . .	100	0	28.0	0	0	<10	m.q.
in extra heavy syrup, 1/2 cup . .	140	.5	36.4	.1	0	2	.7 c
dried, 10 figs, 6.6 oz.	477	5.7	122.2	2.2	0	20	17.4 d
Filberts:							
dried:							
1 oz.	179	3.7	4.4	17.8	0	1	1.1 c
chopped, 1 cup . .	727	15.0	17.6	72.0	0	3	4.4 c
blanched, 1 oz. . . .	191	3.6	4.5	19.1	0	1	.5 c
dry-roasted:							
1 oz.	188	2.8	5.1	18.8	0	1	1.1 c
salted, 1 oz.	188	2.8	5.1	18.8	0	221	1.1 c
oil-roasted:							
1 oz.	187	4.1	5.4	18.1	0	1	1.8 d
salted, 1 oz.	187	4.1	5.4	18.1	0	223	1.8 d
Finnan haddie, see "Haddock, smoked"							
Fish, see specific listings							
Fish batter mix, see "Fish seasoning and coating mix"							
Fish dinner, frozen (see also specific fish listings):							
(Morton), 9.75 oz. . . .	370	18.0	46.0	13.0	65	910	m.q.
'n' chips (Swanson), 10 oz.	500	19.0	60.0	20.0	m.q.	930	m.q.
nuggets (Kid Cuisine), 7 oz.	320	13.0	33.0	15.0	45	750	m.q.
nuggets (Swanson), 91/2 oz.	410	17.0	43.0	19.0	m.q.	930	m.q.

Food and Measure	cal.	prot. (gms)	carbo. (gms)	fat (gms)	chol. (mgs)	sod. (mgs)	fiber (gms)
Fish entree, frozen (see also specific fish listings):							
(Banquet Platters), 8.75 oz.	450	31.0	33.0	22.0	95	m.q.	m.q.
battered, 2 pieces, except as noted:							
(Gorton's Crispy)	300	12.0	18.0	20.0	35	580	m.q.
(Gorton's Crunchy)	320	12.0	24.0	20.0	35	400	m.q.
(Gorton's Crunchy Microwave) . . .	340	10.0	17.0	26.0	30	400	m.q.
(Gorton's Potato Crisp)	310	14.0	19.0	20.0	30	380	m.q.
(Mrs. Paul's)	430	17.0	27.0	28.0	50	800	m.q.
(Mrs. Paul's Crunchy)	280	12.0	26.0	14.0	22	730	m.q.
(Van de Kamp's), 1 piece	170	9.0	14.0	9.0	25	340	m.q.
minced *(Mrs. Paul's)*	300	11.0	21.0	19.0	33	540	m.q.
tempura *(Gorton's Light Recipe),* 1 piece	200	10.0	8.0	14.0	30	400	m.q.
breaded, 2 pieces, except as noted:							
(Gorton's Light Recipe), 1 piece . .	180	11.0	16.0	8.0	30	380	m.q.
(Mrs. Paul's Crispy Crunchy)	220	13.0	23.0	9.0	22	380	m.q.
(Van de Kamp's)	260	10.0	23.0	15.0	30	430	m.q.
crispy *(Van de Kamp's* Microwave), 1 piece	130	7.0	9.0	7.0	15	250	m.q.
minced *(Mrs. Paul's Crispy Crunchy)*	230	10.0	14.0	15.0	25	300	m.q.
buttered *(Mrs. Paul's),* 2 pieces	160	21.0	1.0	8.0	105	230	m.q.
cakes *(Mrs. Paul's),* 2 pieces	250	11.0	27.0	11.0	m.q.	840	m.q.

Food and Measure	cal.	prot. (gms)	carbo. (gms)	fat (gms)	chol. (mgs)	sod. (mgs)	fiber (gms)
coated, ranch							
(Gorton's Micro-							
wave, Large), 1 fillet	330	12.0	24.0	21.0	m.q.	520	m.q.
Dijon (Mrs. Paul's							
Light), 8¾ oz. . .	200	21.0	17.0	5.0	60	650	m.q.
fillet of:							
almondine							
(Gorton's), 1 pkg.	340	27.0	2.0	25.0	100	450	m.q.
Divan (Lean Cui-							
sine), 12⅜ oz.	260	31.0	17.0	7.0	85	750	m.q.
Florentine (Lean							
Cuisine), 9 oz.	230	26.0	13.0	8.0	100	700	m.q.
in herb butter							
(Gorton's), 1 pkg.	190	26.0	3.0	8.0	90	450	m.q.
jardiniere (Lean Cui-							
sine), 11¼ oz.	290	31.0	18.0	10.0	110	840	m.q.
Florentine (Mrs. Paul's							
Light), 8 oz.	215	25.0	10.0	8.0	93	820	m.q.
'n' fries (Swanson							
Homestyle), 6½ oz.	350	15.0	35.0	17.0	m.q.	690	m.q.
gems, fancy (Wake-							
field), 4 oz.	80	11.0	11.0	1.0	m.q.	m.q.	m.q.
gems, salad (Wake-							
field), 3 oz.	70	10.0	8.0	1.0	m.q.	m.q.	n.a.
mornay (Mrs. Paul's							
Light), 9 oz.	230	24.0	12.0	10.0	80	670	m.q.
sticks, battered,							
4 pieces, except							
as noted:							
(Gorton's Crispy)	260	9.0	16.0	18.0	25	480	m.q.
(Gorton's Crunchy)	220	7.0	15.0	15.0	20	280	m.q.
(Gorton's Crunchy							
Microwave),							
6 pieces	340	11.0	24.0	22.0	35	420	m.q.
(Gorton's Potato							
Crisp)	260	8.0	21.0	16.0	25	390	m.q.
(Mrs. Paul's							
Crunchy)	180	8.0	16.0	10.0	25	560	m.q.

Food and Measure	cal.	prot. (gms)	carbo. (gms)	fat (gms)	chol. (mgs)	sod. (mgs)	fiber (gms)
Fish entree, frozen sticks, battered, 4 pieces *(cont.)*							
(Van de Kamp's)	170	9.0	14.0	9.0	25	340	m.q.
minced *(Mrs. Paul's)*	220	8.0	20.0	13.0	20	630	m.q.
sticks, breaded, 4 pieces, except as noted:							
(Frionor Bunch O' Crunch)	210	9.0	13.0	14.0	m.q.	267	<.1 d
(Mrs. Paul's Crispy Crunchy)	190	9.0	18.0	8.0	25	560	m.q.
(Van de Kamp's)	190	7.0	18.0	10.0	25	280	m.q.
(Van de Kamp's Microwave), 3 pieces	150	8.0	11.0	8.0	20	270	m.q.
minced *(Mrs. Paul's* Crispy Crunchy)	200	10.0	18.0	10.0	m.q.	340	m.q.
whole wheat *(Booth* Microwave), 2 oz.	150	6.0	14.0	8.0	m.q.	210	m.q.
Fish seasoning and coating, mix:							
(Shake'n Bake), ¼ pouch	70	1.0	14.0	1.0	0	410	m.q.
batter:							
Cajun *(Tone's),* 1 tsp.	12	.3	2.6	.1	0	49	.1 d
fish & chips *(Golden Dipt),* 1¼ oz. . .	120	2.0	27.0	0	0	910	m.q.
blackened Redfish *(Golden Dipt),* ¼ tsp.	2	0	0	0	0	140	n.a.
broiled *(Golden Dipt),* ¼ tsp.	2	0	0	0	0	125	n.a.
fish fry, ⅔ oz.:							
(Golden Dipt) . . .	60	2.0	14.0	0	0	430	m.q.
Cajun style *(Golden Dipt)*	60	2.0	14.0	0	0	470	m.q.

Food and Measure	cal.	prot. (gms)	carbo. (gms)	fat (gms)	chol. (mgs)	sod. (mgs)	fiber (gms)
seafood:							
(Golden Dipt),							
2/3 oz.	60	1.0	14.0	0	0	600	m.q.
(Tone's), 1 tsp. . . .	10	.5	.9	.7	0	1	.3 d
all purpose *(Golden*							
Dipt), 1/4 tsp. . . .	2	0	0	0	0	85	n.a.
Chesapeake							
(Tone's), 1 tsp.	8	.4	.9	.3	0	1032	.3 d
lemon pepper							
(Golden Dipt),							
1/4 tsp.	8	1	1	0	0	115	n.a.
shrimp and crab, Ca-							
jun style *(Golden*							
Dipt), 1/4 tsp. . . .	2	0	0	0	0	200	n.a.
Flatfish, meat only:							
raw, 1 lb.	414	85.5	0	5.4	217	367	0
raw, 1 oz.	26	5.3	0	.3	14	23	0
baked, broiled, or mi-							
crowaved, 4 oz. . .	133	27.4	0	1.7	77	119	0
Flounder, fresh, see							
"Flatfish"							
Flounder, frozen:							
(Gorton's Fishmarket							
Fresh), 5 oz.	110	23.0	1.0	1.0	m.q.	170	0
(SeaPak), 4 oz. . . .	90	20.0	0	1.0	m.q.	120	0
(Van de Kamp's Natu-							
ral), 4 oz.	80	18.0	0	1.0	65	70	0
Atlantic *(Booth),* 4 oz.	90	19.0	0	1.0	m.q.	180	0
Flounder entree, fro-							
zen:							
battered *(Mrs. Paul's*							
Crunchy), 2 pieces	260	13.0	20.0	14.0	m.q.	610	m.q.
breaded:							
(Mrs. Paul's Light),							
1 piece, 41/2 oz.	260	14.0	28.0	11.0	m.q.	536	m.q.
(Van de Kamp's							
Light), 1 piece	240	15.0	19.0	12.0	45	460	m.q.

Food and Measure	cal.	prot. (gms)	carbo. (gms)	fat (gms)	chol. (mgs)	sod. (mgs)	fiber (gms)
Flounder entree, frozen, breaded (cont.)							
(Mrs. Paul's Crispy Crunchy), 2 pieces	300	14.0	17.0	19.0	45	520	m.q.
stuffed (Gorton's Microwave Entrees), 1 pkg.	350	25.0	21.0	18.0	120	850	m.q.
Flour, see specific grain listings							
Forestiera sauce:							
refrigerated (Contadina Fresh), 7.5 oz.	270	6.0	15.0	9.0	15	830	n.a.
Frankfurter, 1 link, except as noted:							
(Eckrich 1 lb.)	160	5.0	2.0	14.0	m.q.	420	0
(Eckrich Bunsize/ Jumbo)	190	6.0	2.0	17.0	m.q.	500	0
(Eckrich Jumbo Lean)	140	7.0	2.0	12.0	m.q.	490	0
(Hillshire Farm Bun Size), 2 oz.	180	7.0	2.0	16.0	m.q.	550	0
(Hormel 12 oz.) . . .	110	4.0	1.0	10.0	m.q.	378	0
(Hormel 1 lb.)	140	5.0	1.0	13.0	m.q.	486	0
(JM)	110	4.0	1.0	10.0	16	370	0
(JM, 10/lb.)	140	5.0	1.0	13.0	22	490	0
(JM German Brand)	160	7.0	1.0	14.0	m.q.	620	0
(JM Jumbo), 2 oz. . .	190	6.0	2.0	17.0	27	620	0
(Kahn's)	140	5.0	1.0	13.0	m.q.	500	0
(Kahn's Bun Size) . .	190	6.0	3.0	17.0	m.q.	560	0
(Kahn's Jumbo) . . .	190	6.0	3.0	18.0	m.q.	560	0
(OHSE Wieners), 1 oz.	90	3.0	1.0	8.0	m.q.	300	0
(Oscar Mayer German)	230	9.3	1.5	20.7	30	731	0
(Oscar Mayer Wieners, 8/lb.)	182	6.2	1.4	16.8	35	580	0
(Oscar Mayer Bun Length)	181	6.2	1.7	16.6	27	606	0

Food and Measure	cal.	prot. (gms)	carbo. (gms)	fat (gms)	chol. (mgs)	sod. (mgs)	fiber (gms)
bacon and cheddar *(Oscar Mayer, 10/ lb.)*	143	6.1	1.1	12.7	30	510	0
batter-wrapped, frozen:							
(Hormel Corn Dogs)	220	7.0	21.0	12.0	m.q.	656	0
(Hormel Tater Dogs)	210	6.0	15.0	14.0	m.q.	170	0
beef:							
(Boar's Head), 1 oz.	80	4.0	<1.0	7.0	15	m.q.	0
(Eckrich, 1 lb.) . .	150	5.0	2.0	14.0	m.q.	400	0
(Eckrich Bunsize/ Jumbo)	190	6.0	2.0	17.0	m.q.	520	0
(Hebrew National)	149	5.8	<1.0	14.0	15	497	0
(Hillshire Farm Bun Size), 2 oz. . . .	180	7.0	2.0	16.0	m.q.	560	0
(Hormel 12 oz.) . .	100	4.0	1.0	10.0	m.q.	362	0
(Hormel 1 lb.) . . .	140	5.0	1.0	13.0	m.q.	463	0
(JM)	100	4.0	1.0	9.0	20	350	0
(JM, 10/lb.)	140	5.0	1.0	13.0	26	480	0
(JM Jumbo)	180	6.0	2.0	16.0	33	600	0
(Kahn's)	140	5.0	2.0	13.0	m.q.	500	0
(Kahn's Bun Size)	190	6.0	3.0	17.0	m.q.	560	0
(Kahn's Jumbo) . .	190	6.0	3.0	18.0	m.q.	560	0
(King Kold), 2 oz.	173	9.0	1.0	16.3	m.q.	815	0
(OHSE), 1 oz. . . .	85	3.0	1.0	8.0	m.q.	280	0
(Oscar Mayer, 8/lb.)	181	6.3	1.3	16.8	36	580	0
(Oscar Mayer, 4/lb.)	363	12.6	2.6	33.6	73	1160	0
(Oscar Mayer Bun Length)	186	6.0	1.8	17.1	32	559	0
w/cheddar *(Kahn's)*	180	7.0	2.0	16.0	m.q.	640	0
w/cheddar *(Oscar Mayer,* 10/lb.)	130	5.9	.9	11.3	29	520	0
hot *(Hillshire Farm)*, 2 oz.	190	8.0	1.0	17.0	m.q.	560	0
cheese (cheesefurter or cheese smokie):							
(Eckrich)	180	7.0	2.0	16.0	m.q.	530	0

Food and Measure	cal.	prot. (gms)	carbo. (gms)	fat (gms)	chol. (mgs)	sod. (mgs)	fiber (gms)
Frankfurter, cheese *(cont.)*							
(Hillshire Farm),							
2 oz.	180	7.0	2.0	16.0	m.q.	530	0
(JM)	140	5.0	2.0	13.0	m.q.	540	0
(JM German) . . .	160	8.0	2.0	14.0	37	620	0
(Kahn's)	150	6.0	1.0	13.0	m.q.	490	0
(Oscar Mayer, 10/ lb.)	145	5.5	1.0	13.2	31	486	0
chicken, see "Chicken frankfurter"							
chicken, beef and pork *(OHSE),* 1 oz.	85	3.0	1.0	8.0	m.q.	260	0
chili *(Hormel* Frank'n Stuff)	165	7.0	2.0	15.0	m.q.	517	n.a.
cocktail *(Oscar Mayer)*	28	1.1	.2	2.6	5	92	0
hot *(Hillshire Farm),* 2 oz.	190	8.0	2.0	16.0	m.q.	530	0
Mexacali *(Hormel),* 5 oz.	400	14.0	41.0	21.0	m.q.	952	n.a.
natural casing *(Hillshire Farm),* 2 oz.	180	6.0	2.0	17.0	m.q.	470	0
pork and beef *(Boar's Head),* 1 oz.	80	4.0	<1.0	7.0	15	250	0
smoked:							
(Hormel Range Brand Wranglers)	170	7.0	1.0	16.0	m.q.	600	0
(Kahn's Big Red Smokey)	170	8.0	2.0	14.0	m.q.	550	0
(Kahn's Bun Size Smokey)	180	8.0	2.0	15.0	m.q.	550	0
beef *(Hormel* Wranglers)	170	7.0	2.0	15.0	m.q.	619	0
beef *(Kahn's* Bun Size Beef Smokey)	190	7.0	2.0	17.0	m.q.	530	0
w/cheese *(Hormel* Wranglers) . . .	180	8.0	1.0	16.0	m.q.	546	0

Food and Measure	cal.	prot. (gms)	carbo. (gms)	fat (gms)	chol. (mgs)	sod. (mgs)	fiber (gms)
turkey, see "Turkey frankfurter"							
"Frankfurter," vegetarian:							
canned:							
(Worthington Veja-Links), 2 links . .	140	8.0	4.0	10.0	0	330	m.q.
(Worthington Super-Links), 1 link . .	100	7.0	3.0	7.0	0	440	m.q.
frozen, 1 link:							
(Worthington Leanies)	100	8.0	2.0	6.0	0	440	m.q.
on a stick (Worthington Dixie Dogs)	200	8.0	21.0	10.0	0	640	m.q.
Frankfurter wrap:							
(Weiner Wrap), 1 piece	60	1.0	10.0	2.0	n.a.	430	m.q.
French toast, frozen, 3 oz., except as noted:							
(Aunt Jemima Original)	166	6.7	26.5	4.4	46	554	1.3 d
(Downyflake), 2 slices	270	4.0	30.0	14.0	n.a.	380	m.q.
cinnamon swirl (Aunt Jemima)	171	6.7	27.5	4.3	41	516	1.3 d
raisin (Aunt Jemima)	172	7.3	27.2	4.4	46	492	1.3 d
sticks:							
apple cinnamon (Farm Rich) . . .	310	6.0	39.0	15.0	n.a.	300	m.q.
blueberry (Farm Rich)	310	6.0	37.0	14.0	n.a.	280	m.q.
original (Farm Rich)	300	5.0	37.0	15.0	n.a.	280	m.q
French toast breakfast, frozen, 6 1/2 oz.:							
w/sausages (Swanson Great Starts) . . .	450	15.0	42.0	25.0	m.q.	640	m.q.

Food and Measure	cal.	prot. (gms)	carbo. (gms)	fat (gms)	chol. (mgs)	sod. (mgs)	fiber (gms)
French toast breakfast, frozen *(cont.)*							
cinnamon swirl, w/ sausages *(Swanson Great Starts)* ..	470	16.0	42.0	26.0	m.q.	660	m.q.
vegetarian, cinnamon swirl, w/patty *(Morningstar Farms)*	380	24.0	37.0	15.0	0	1220	4.0 d
Frog's legs, meat only:							
raw, 1 oz.	21	4.6	0	<1.0	m.q.	m.q.	0
Frosting, ready-to-use, 1/12 can, except as noted:							
Amaretto almond *(Betty Crocker Creamy Deluxe)* ..	160	0	2670	6.0	0	50	(0)
butter pecan *(Betty Crocker Creamy Deluxe)*	170	0	26.0	7.0	0	50	(0)
caramel pecan *(Pillsbury Frosting Supreme)*	160	0	21.0	8.0	n.a.	70	(0)
cherry *(Betty Crocker Creamy Deluxe)* . .	160	0	27.0	6.0	0	50	(0)
chocolate:							
(Betty Crocker Creamy Deluxe)	160	<1.0	24.0	7.0	0	60	(0)
(Duncan Hines) . .	160	0	24.0	7.0	n.a.	90	(0)
double Dutch *(Pillsbury Frosting Supreme)*	140	1.0	22.0	6.0	n.a.	45	(0)
mint *(Pillsbury Frosting Supreme)* . .	150	<1.0	24.0	7.0	n.a.	80	(0)
mocha *(Pillsbury Frosting Supreme)*	150	<1.0	24.0	6.0	n.a.	60	(0)
chocolate, milk:							
(Betty Crocker Creamy Deluxe)	160	<1.0	25.0	6.0	0	55	(0)

Food and Measure	cal.	prot. (gms)	carbo. (gms)	fat (gms)	chol. (mgs)	sod. (mgs)	fiber (gms)
(Duncan Hines) . .	160	0	24.0	7.0	n.a.	85	(0)
(Pillsbury Frosting Supreme)	150	0	23.0	6.0	n.a.	60	(0)
chocolate chip:							
(Betty Crocker Creamy Deluxe)	170	<1.0	27.0	7.0	0	30	(0)
(Pillsbury Frosting Supreme)	150	0	27.0	5.0	n.a.	70	(0)
double *(Betty Crocker Creamy Deluxe)*	170	<1.0	24.0	8.0	0	60	(0)
chocolate coconut almond *(Betty Crocker Creamy Deluxe)*	160	1.0	21.0	8.0	0	55	(0)
chocolate fudge:							
(Pillsbury), 1/8 cake	110	0	17.0	5.0	n.a.	65	(0)
(Pillsbury Frosting Supreme)	150	<1.0	24.0	6.0	n.a.	80	(0)
(Pillsbury Funfetti)	140	<1.0	22.0	6.0	n.a.	80	(0)
dark Dutch *(Betty Crocker Creamy Deluxe)*	160	1.0	22.0	7.0	0	70	(0)
dark Dutch *(Duncan Hines)*	160	0	24.0	7.0	n.a.	95	(0)
coconut almond:							
(Pillsbury)	160	1.0	16.0	10.0	n.a.	85	(0)
(Pillsbury Frosting Supreme)	150	1.0	17.0	9.0	n.a.	60	(0)
coconut pecan:							
(Betty Crocker Creamy Deluxe)	160	<1.0	20.0	9.0	0	80	(0)
(Pillsbury)	150	1.0	20.0	7.0	n.a.	105	(0)
(Pillsbury Frosting Supreme)	160	0	17.0	10.0	n.a.	60	(0)
cream cheese:							
(Betty Crocker Creamy Deluxe)	160	0	27.0	6.0	0	75	(0)

Food and Measure	cal.	prot. (gms)	carbo. (gms)	fat (gms)	chol. (mgs)	sod. (mgs)	fiber (gms)
Frosting, ready-to-use, cream cheese *(cont.)*							
(Pillsbury Frosting Supreme)	160	0	26.0	6.0	n.a.	115	(0)
decorator:							
all flavors except chocolate *(Pillsbury)*, 1 tbsp. . . .	70	0	12.0	2.0	n.a.	0	(0)
chocolate *(Pillsbury)*, 1 tbsp. . . .	60	0	11.0	2.0	n.a.	0	(0)
lemon:							
(Betty Crocker Creamy Deluxe)	170	0	28.0	6.0	0	70	(0)
(Pillsbury Frosting Supreme)	160	0	26.0	6.0	n.a.	80	(0)
rainbow chip *(Betty Crocker Creamy Deluxe)*	170	<1.0	27.0	7.0	0	30	(0)
rocky road *(Betty Crocker Creamy Deluxe)*	150	<1.0	20.0	8.0	0	50	(0)
sour cream:							
chocolate *(Betty Crocker Creamy Deluxe)*	160	<1.0	23.0	7.0	0	110	(0)
vanilla *(Pillsbury Frosting Supreme)*	160	0	27.0	6.0	n.a.	80	(0)
white *(Betty Crocker Creamy Deluxe)*	160	0	27.0	6.0	0	50	(0)
strawberry *(Pillsbury Frosting Supreme)*	160	0	26.0	6.0	n.a.	75	(0)
vanilla:							
(Betty Crocker Creamy Deluxe)	160	0	27.0	6.0	0	30	(0)
(Duncan Hines) . .	160	0	24.0	7.0	n.a.	80	(0)
(Pillsbury), 1/8 cake	120	0	19.0	5.0	n.a.	60	(0)
(Pillsbury Frosting Supreme)	160	0	26.0	6.0	n.a.	75	(0)
(Pillsbury Funfetti)	150	0	24.0	6.0	n.a.	70	(0)

Food and Measure	cal.	prot. (gms)	carbo. (gms)	fat (gms)	chol. (mgs)	sod. (mgs)	fiber (gms)
white *(Pillsbury* Fluffy)	60	0	15.0	0	n.a.	65	(0)
Frozen dessert, see specific listings							
Fructose:							
(Featherweight), 1 tsp.	12	0	3.0	0	0	0	0
Fruit, see specific listings							
Fruit, mixed:							
canned (see also "Fruit cocktail" and "Fruit salad"), 1/2 cup, except as noted:							
(Del Monte Fruit Cup), 5 oz. . . .	100	0	27.0	0	0	<10	m.q.
chunky *(Del Monte)*	80	0	23.0	0	0	<10	m.q.
chunky *(Del Monte Lite)*	50	0	14.0	0	0	<10	m.q.
in juice *(S&W)* . . .	90	1.0	21.0	0	0	5	m.q.
dried, 2 oz.:							
(Del Monte)	130	1.0	34.0	0	0	10	m.q.
(Sun-Maid/Sunsweet)	150	1.0	39.0	0	0	<20	m.q.
bits *(Sun-Maid/Sunsweet)*	150	2.0	40.0	<1.0	0	<50	m.q.
frozen, in syrup *(Birds Eye* Quick Thaw), 5 oz. . .	120	1.0	31.0	0	0	5	1.0 d
Fruit bar,							
frozen (see also "Ice bar"), 1 bar:							
berry, wild *(Sunkist* Fruit & Juice Bar)	103	.1	24.6	.5	0	11	n.a.
cherry *(Dole Fresh Lites)*	25	<1.0	6.0	<1.0	0	6	n.a.
coconut *(Sunkist)* . .	137	2.7	12.8	8.4	0	58	1.4 c
grape *(Dole SunTops)*	40	<1.0	9.0	<1.0	0	5	n.a.

Food and Measure	cal.	prot. (gms)	carbo. (gms)	fat (gms)	chol. (mgs)	sod. (mgs)	fiber (gms)
Fruit bar *(cont.)*							
lemon *(Dole Fresh Lites)*	25	<1.0	6.0	<1.0	0	16	n.a.
lemonade or orange *(Dole SunTops)* . .	40	<1.0	9.0	<1.0	0	5	n.a.
lemonade *(Sunkist)*	68	.1	17.6	.1	0	3	n.a.
orange *(Sunkist Juice Bar)*	72	.7	17.6	.1	0	1	n.a.
piña colada *(Dole Fruit'n Juice)* . . .	90	n.a.	16.0	3.0	0	2	n.a.
pineapple *(Dole Fruit'n Juice)*	70	.3	17.0	<.1	0	4	n.a.
pineapple orange *(Dole Fresh Lites)*	25	<1.0	6.0	<1.0	0	7	n.a.
punch *(Dole SunTops)*	40	<1.0	9.0	<1.0	0	5	n.a.
raspberry:							
(Dole Fresh Lites)	25	<1.0	6.0	<1.0	0	6	n.a.
(Dole Fruit'n Juice)	70	.2	16.0	<.1	0	14	n.a.
strawberry *(Dole Fruit'n Juice)* . . .	70	.2	16.0	<.1	0	6	n.a.
and cream:							
blueberry *(Dole Fruit & Cream)*	90	1.0	19.4	1.4	5	20	n.a.
chocolate/banana *(Dole Fruit & Cream)*	175	2.0	22.0	9.0	n.a.	20	n.a.
chocolate/straw-berry *(Dole Fruit & Cream)*	140	2.0	23.0	8.0	n.a.	20	n.a.
orange *(Sunkist)*	84	.9	16.6	1.5	n.a.	15	n.a.
peach *(Dole Fruit & Cream)*	90	1.0	19.4	1.4	5	19	n.a.
raspberry *(Dole Fruit & Cream)*	90	1.0	20.0	1.4	5	23	n.a.
strawberry *(Dole Fruit & Cream)*	90	1.0	19.3	1.4	5	22	n.a.

Food and Measure	cal.	prot. (gms)	carbo. (gms)	fat (gms)	chol. (mgs)	sod. (mgs)	fiber (gms)
and yogurt:							
cherry (*Dole* Fruit & Yogurt)	80	2.0	17.0	<1.0	n.a.	22	n.a.
raspberry (*Dole* Fruit & Yogurt)	70	1.0	17.0	<1.0	n.a.	18	n.a.
strawberry (*Dole* Fruit & Yogurt)	70	1.0	17.0	<1.0	n.a.	16	n.a.
Fruit cocktail, canned, 1/2 cup:							
(*Del Monte*)	80	0	23.0	0	0	<10	m.q.
(*Del Monte Lite*) . . .	50	0	15.0	0	0	<10	m.q.
in water	40	.5	10.4	.1	0	5	.6 c
in juice:							
(*IGA*)	60	0	15.0	0	0	10	m.q.
(*Libby Lite*)	50	0	13.0	0	0	10	m.q.
(*S&W*)	90	1.0	21.0	0	0	5	m.q.
in light syrup	72	.5	18.8	.1	0	7	.6 c
in heavy syrup (*S&W*)	90	0	24.0	0	0	15	m.q.
Fruit drink (see also specific listings), canned, 6 fl. oz.:							
(*Hi-C* Double Fruit Cooler)	93	<.1	22.9	<.1	0	18	(0)
(*Hi-C* Ecto Cooler) . .	95	.1	23.3	<.1	0	17	(0)
(*Hi-C* Hula Cooler) . .	97	.1	23.9	<.1	0	17	(0)
Fruit juice (see also specific listings), 6 fl. oz.:							
tropical (*Libby's Juicy Juice*)	100	1.0	24.0	0	0	5	(0)
cocktail:							
(*Welch's* Orchard Harvest Blend)	110	0	27.0	0	0	20	0
frozen[1] (*Welch's* Orchard Harvest Blend)	110	0	27.0	0	0	10	0

[1] *Diluted according to package directions.*

Food and Measure	cal.	prot. (gms)	carbo. (gms)	fat (gms)	chol. (mgs)	sod. (mgs)	fiber (gms)
Fruit juice drink:							
mixed *(Tang* Fruit Box), 8.45 fl. oz.	140	0	36.0	0	0	10	0
Fruit and nut mix:							
(Planter's Fruit'Nut), 1 oz.	150	5.0	13.0	9.0	0	90	m.q.
Fruit punch:							
canned:							
(Minute Maid), 8.45 fl. oz. . . .	128	.1	32.0	.1	0	24	(0)
(Minute Maid Juices to Go), 9.6 fl. oz.	145	.1	36.8	.1	0	28	(0)
(Minute Maid On The Go), 10 fl. oz.	152	.1	37.9	.1	0	29	(0)
(Veryfine 100% Juice Punch), 8 fl. oz.	122	<1.0	30.0	0	0	<10	(0)
blend *(Libby's Juicy Juice),* 6 fl. oz.	100	1.0	23.0	0	0	10	(0)
Concord *(Minute Maid)*, 8.45 fl. oz.	131	.2	32.7	.1	0	25	(0)
Concord *(Minute Maid* Juices to Go), 9.6 fl. oz.	148	.2	37.1	.1	0	28	(0)
Concord *(Minute Maid On The Go),* 10 fl. oz.	155	.2	38.7	.1	0	29	(0)
tropical *(Minute Maid)*, 8.45 fl. oz.	130	.1	32.0	<.1	0	24	(0)
tropical *(Minute Maid* Juices to Go), 9.6 fl. oz.	147	.1	36.4	<.1	0	28	(0)
chilled or frozen[1] *(Minute Maid)*, 6 fl. oz.	91	.1	22.7	.1	0	17	(0)

---

[1] *Diluted according to package directions.*

Food and Measure	cal.	prot. (gms)	carbo. (gms)	fat (gms)	chol. (mgs)	sod. (mgs)	fiber (gms)
cocktail:							
(Welch's Orchard Harvest Punch), 10 fl. oz.	180	0	45.0	0	0	0	0
island fruit *(Hawaiian Punch)*, 6 fl. oz.	90	0	22.0	0	0	30	(0)
Fruit punch drink, 6 fl. oz., except as noted:							
(Bama), 8.45 fl. oz.	130	0	32.0	0	0	15	(0)
(Hi-C)	96	.1	23.7	<.1	0	17	(0)
(Hi-C Hula Punch) . .	87	.1	21.4	<.1	0	17	(0)
(Mott's), 9.5 fl. oz. . .	161	0	40.0	0	0	4	(0)
(Wylers)	84	0	21.3	.1	0	8	(0)
mountain berry *(Kool-Aid Koolers),* 8.45 fl. oz.	140	0	37.0	0	0	10	(0)
rainbow *(Kool-Aid Koolers),* 8.45 fl. oz.	130	0	36.0	0	0	10	(0)
red:							
(Hawaiian Punch)	90	0	22.0	0	0	20	(0)
(Hawaiian Punch Lite)	60	0	15.0	0	0	30	(0)
tropical:							
(Hawaiian Punch)	90	0	22.0	0	0	30	(0)
(Kool-Aid Koolers), 8.45 fl. oz. . . .	130	0	35.0	0	0	10	(0)
wild fruit *(Hawaiian Punch)*	90	0	23.0	0	0	35	(0)
chilled:							
(Crowley), 1 cup	130	0	32.0	0	0	15	(0)
(Minute Maid Light'N Juicy) . .	14	.1	2.9	.1	0	17	(0)
Fruit roll, see "Fruit snack"							

Food and Measure	cal.	prot. (gms)	carbo. (gms)	fat (gms)	chol. (mgs)	sod. (mgs)	fiber (gms)
Fruit salad, canned, ½ cup:							
(*Del Monte* Fruit for Salad)	90	0	22.0	0	0	<10	m.q.
(*Kraft* Pure)	80	1.0	18.0	0	0	10	m.q.
tropical:							
(*Del Monte*)	90	0	26.0	0	0	<10	m.q.
in heavy syrup . .	110	.5	28.6	.1	0	3	.6 c
Fruit snack (see also specific fruit listings):							
all varieties (*Fruit Corners/Fruit Roll-Ups*), ½ oz.	50	<1.0	12.0	<1.0	0	40	m.q.
all varieties, except yogurt-coated (*Sunkist Fun Fruits*), 1 pouch	100	.1	21.8	1.4	0	10	n.a.
apple roll (*Flavor Tree*), 1 piece . . .	75	.2	18.5	0	0	17	m.q.
apricot roll (*Flavor Tree*), 1 piece . . .	76	.3	17.7	.5	0	17	m.q.
cherry roll (*Flavor Tree*), 1 piece . . .	75	.3	18.3	.1	0	18	m.q.
fruit punch roll (*Flavor Tree*), 1 piece . . .	74	.2	18.2	0	0	12	m.q.
grape roll (*Flavor Tree*), 1 piece . . .	76	.2	18.5	.1	0	13	m.q.
raspberry roll (*Flavor Tree*), 1 piece . . .	75	.2	18.3	.1	0	20	m.q.
strawberry roll (*Flavor Tree*), 1 piece . . .	74	.2	18.0	.1	0	11	m.q.
yogurt coated (*Sunkist Fun Fruits*), 1 pouch	114	.2	20.1	3.6	n.a.	19	n.a.

Food and Measure	cal.	prot. (gms)	carbo. (gms)	fat (gms)	chol. (mgs)	sod. (mgs)	fiber (gms)
Fruit spread (see also "Jam and preserves"):							
all flavors, 1 tsp.:							
(Polaner All Fruit)	14	0	4.0	0	0	0	m.q.
(Smucker's Simply Fruit)	16	0	4.0	0	0	0	m.q.
(Smucker's Low Sugar)	8	0	2.0	0	0	<10	m.q.
Fruit syrup, 2 tbsp.:							
all flavors *(Smucker's)*	100	0	26.0	0	0	0	n.a.
Fudge, see "Candy"							
Fudge topping, see "Chocolate topping"							

G

Food and Measure	cal.	prot. (gms)	carbo. (gms)	fat (gms)	chol. (mgs)	sod. (mgs)	fiber (gms)
Garbanzo, see "Chickpea"							
Garden salad, 1/2 cup:							
(Joan of Arc/Read)	70	2.0	17.0	0	0	500	2.4 d
marinated (S&W) . .	60	2.0	11.0	0	0	670	m.q.
Garlic:							
trimmed, 1 oz.	42	1.8	9.4	.1	0	5	.4 c
1 clove, approx. .1 oz.	4	.2	1.0	<.1	0	1	.1 c
Garlic herb dip:							
(Nasoya Vegi-Dip), 1 oz.	50	2.0	6.0	2.0	0	100	m.q.
Garlic powder, 1 tsp.:							
w/parsley (Lawry's)	12	.5	2.3	.9	0	5	.1 c
Garlic salt, 1 tsp.:							
(Lawry's)	4	.1	.8	<.1	0	968	<.1 c
Garlic seasoning:							
(McCormick/Schilling Season All), 1/4 tsp.	2	<.1	.1	n.a.	n.a.	163	n.a.
(McCormick/Schilling Parsley Patch), 1 tsp.	13	.5	2.0	.5	n.a.	1	m.q.
bread spread (Lawry's), 1/2 tbsp.	47	.2	1.0	4.6	n.a.	15	<.1 c
spread, concentrate (Lawry's), 1 tbsp.	15	0	.2	1.6	0	21	0
Gelatin, unflavored:							
(Knox), 1 pkt.	25	6.0	0	0	0	10	0
Gelatin bar, frozen:							
all flavors (Jell-O Gelatin Pops), 1 bar	35	1.0	8.0	0	0	5	(0)

Food and Measure	cal.	prot. (gms)	carbo. (gms)	fat (gms)	chol. (mgs)	sod. (mgs)	fiber (gms)
Gelatin dessert mix[1],							
1/2 cup:							
all flavors:							
(Jell-O)	80	2.0	19.0	0	0	— [2]	0
except lemon, lime,							
peach, pineapple,							
strawberry (Royal)	80	2.0	19.0	0	0	95	0
lemon, peach or							
strawberry (Royal)	80	2.0	19.0	0	0	100	0
lime or pineapple							
(Royal)	80	2.0	19.0	0	0	90	0
Gelatin drink mix:							
orange flavor, w/Nu-							
trasweet (Knox),							
1 pkt.	39	5.7	4.0	.1	0	17	(0)
German sausage:							
(Hickory Farms), 1 oz.	100	5.0	1.0	8.0	20	385	0
Ginger, trimmed root:							
1 oz.	20	.5	4.3	.2	0	4	.3 c
sliced, 1/4 cup	17	.4	3.6	.2	0	3	.3 c
Ginger, ground:							
1 tsp.	6	.2	1.3	.1	0	1	.1 c
Ginger, pickled:							
Japanese, 1 oz. . . .	10	.1	2.1	<.1	0	105	m.q.
Ginko nut shelled:							
raw, 1 oz.	52	1.2	10.7	.5	0	2	.1 c
canned, drained, 1 oz.	32	.6	6.3	.5	0	87	.5 c
dried, 1 oz.	99	2.9	20.6	.8	0	4	.3 c
Goat, meat only:							
roasted, 4 oz.	162	30.7	0	3.4	85	98	0
Godfather's Pizza:							
original cheese:							
mini, 1/4 pie	190	8.0	31.0	4.0	8	260	m.q.
small, 1/6 pie . . .	240	12.0	32.0	7.0	15	400	m.q.

[1] Prepared according to package directions.
[2] Sodium values vary according to flavor: black raspberry and concord grape, 35 mg.; lemon and wild strawberry, 75 mg.; lime, 55 mg.; orange-pineapple, 65 mg.; cherry, 70 mg.; all other flavors, 50 mg.

Food and Measure	cal.	prot. (gms)	carbo. (gms)	fat (gms)	chol. (mgs)	sod. (mgs)	fiber (gms)
Godfather's Pizza, **original cheese** *(cont.)*							
medium, 1/8 pie . .	270	13.0	36.0	8.0	15	430	m.q.
large, 1/10 pie . . .	297	15.0	39.0	9.0	20	494	m.q.
large, hot slice,							
1/8 pie	370	18.0	48.0	11.0	25	620	m.q.
original combo:							
mini, 1/4 pie	240	10.0	32.0	7.0	10	450	m.q.
small, 1/6 pie . . .	360	18.0	35.0	15.0	30	830	m.q.
medium, 1/8 pie . .	400	20.0	39.0	17.0	35	930	m.q.
large, 1/10 pie . . .	437	22.0	42.0	19.0	36	1019	m.q.
large, hot slice,							
1/8 pie	550	27.0	52.0	24.0	45	1270	m.q.
thin crust cheese:							
small, 1/6 pie . . .	180	9.0	21.0	6.0	10	370	m.q.
medium, 1/8 pie . .	210	10.0	26.0	7.0	14	410	m.q.
large, 1/10 pie . . .	228	11.0	28.0	7.0	16	464	m.q.
thin crust combo:							
small, 1/6 pie . . .	270	13.0	23.0	13.0	25	710	m.q.
medium, 1/8 pie . .	310	15.0	29.0	14.0	25	790	m.q.
large, 1/10 pie . . .	336	17.0	31.0	16.0	27	870	m.q.
stuffed pie, cheese:							
small, 1/6 pie . . .	310	13.0	38.0	11.0	25	560	m.q.
medium, 1/8 pie . .	350	14.0	42.0	13.0	25	610	m.q.
large, 1/10	381	16.0	44.0	16.0	32	677	m.q.
stuffed pie, combo:							
small, 1/6 pie . . .	430	19.0	41.0	20.0	40	1000	m.q.
medium, 1/8 pie . .	480	21.0	45.0	23.0	43	1105	m.q.
large, 1/10 pie . . .	521	23.0	47.0	26.0	48	1204	m.q.
Goose, domesticated, roasted:							
meat w/skin, 4 oz.	346	28.5	0	24.9	103	79	0
meat only, 4 oz. . . .	270	32.9	0	14.4	109	86	0
Goose fat:							
1 oz.	255	0	0	28.3	28	0	0
Goose liver, see "Liver" and "Pate"							

Food and Measure	cal.	prot. (gms)	carbo. (gms)	fat (gms)	chol. (mgs)	sod. (mgs)	fiber (gms)
Gooseberry:							
fresh, 1/2 cup	34	.7	7.6	.4	0	1	1.4 c
canned, in light syrup,							
1/2 cup	93	.8	23.6	.3	0	3	1.5 c
Gourd, 1/2 cup:							
dishcloth, boiled,							
drained, 1"slices	50	.6	12.8	.3	0	18	.4 d
white-flowered, boiled,							
drained, 1"cubes	11	.4	2.7	<.1	0	1	.5 c
Gourmet loaf:							
(Eckrich), 1-oz. slice	30	4.0	1.0	1.0	m.q.	340	(0)
Granola, see "Cereal"							
Granola and cereal bars, 1 piece:							
w/almonds, chewy (Sunbelt)	120	.3.0	18.0	6.0	<1	65	m.q.
caramel nut (Quaker Granola Dipps) ..	148	1.9	20.9	6.4	2	81	.7 d
chocolate chip:							
(Kudos)	180	3.0	21.0	9.0	n.a.	60	m.q.
(Quaker Chewy) ..	128	2.0	19.3	4.7	<1	90	1.4 d
(Quaker Granola Dipps)	139	1.8	18.7	6.3	1	78	1.0 c
chocolate coated (Hershey's) ...	170	2.0	22.0	8.0	n.a.	50	m.q.
chocolate fudge (Quaker Granola Dipps)	160	2.1	20.0	7.9	n.a.	74	m.q.
chocolate, graham and marshmallow (Quaker Chewy) ..	126	1.9	19.7	4.4	<1	108	1.1 d
cocoa creme, chocolate coated (Hershey's)	180	2.0	22.0	9.0	5	50	m.q.
Common Sense, raspberry filled (Kellogg's Smart Start)	170	2.0	28.0	6.0	0	160	1.0 d

Food and Measure	cal.	prot. (gms)	carbo. (gms)	fat (gms)	chol. (mgs)	sod. (mgs)	fiber (gms)
Granola and cereal bars *(cont.)*							
cookies & creme, chocolate coated *(Hershey's)*	170	2.0	22.0	8.0	n.a.	50	m.q.
corn flakes, mixed berry filled *(Kellogg's Smart Start)*	170	2.0	27.0	7.0	0	160	1.0 d
fudge, nutty *(Kudos)*	190	4.0	19.0	11.0	n.a.	60	m.q.
honey and oats *(Quaker Chewy)* . .	125	2.3	19.1	4.4	<1	95	1.3 d
nut and raisin, chunky *(Quaker Chewy)* . .	131	2.5	17.2	5.8	<1	86	1.6 d
Nutri-Grain, blueberry or strawberry *(Kellogg's Smart Start)*	180	2.0	26.0	8.0	0	170	1.0 d
oats and honey, chewy:							
(Sunbelt)	130	2.0	18.0	5.0	<1	35	m.q.
w/fudge *(Sunbelt)*	190	2.0	24.0	10.0	<1	55	m.q.
peanut butter:							
(Quaker Chewy) . .	128	3.1	17.8	4.9	<1	116	1.2 d
(Quaker Granola Dipps)	170	3.6	18.5	9.1	2	74	1.0 d
and chocolate chip *(Quaker Chewy)*	131	3.1	17.0	5.7	<1	112	1.2 d
chocolate chip *(Quaker Granola Dipps)*	174	3.6	17.4	10.0	n.a.	102	m.q.
chocolate coated *(Hershey's)* . . .	180	4.0	19.0	10.0	5	65	m.q.
chocolate coated *(Kudos)*	190	4.0	18.0	12.0	n.a.	70	m.q.
raisin bran *(Kellogg's Smart Start)*	160	2.0	28.0	5.0	0	170	2.0 d
w/raisin, chewy *(Sunbelt)*	150	2.0	24.0	6.0	<1	65	m.q.

Food and Measure	cal.	prot. (gms)	carbo. (gms)	fat (gms)	chol. (mgs)	sod. (mgs)	fiber (gms)
w/raisin, fudge dipped, chewy *(Sunbelt)*	200	4.0	24.0	12.0	<1	60	m.q.
raisin and cinnamon *(Quaker Chewy)* . .	128	2.2	18.6	5.0	<1	92	1.2 d
Rice Krispies w/almonds *(Kellogg's Smart Start)*	130	2.0	18.0	6.0	0	65	1.0 d
Grape:							
fresh, American type (slipskin):							
10 medium	15	.2	4.1	.1	0	tr.	.2 c
peeled and seeded, 1/2 cup	29	.3	7.9	.2	0	1	.4 c
fresh, European type (adherent skin):							
seeded, 1 lb. . . .	287	2.7	72.0	2.3	0	7	2.8 d
seedless, 10 medium	36	.3	8.9	.3	0	1	.4 d
seedless or seeded, 1/2 cup	57	.5	14.2	.5	0	2	.6 d
canned, Thompson seedless, 1/2 cup:							
in water	48	.6	12.6	.1	0	7	.3 c
in heavy syrup . .	94	.6	25.2	.1	0	7	.3 c
Grape drink:							
canned, bottled or chilled:							
(Bama), 8.45 fl. oz.	120	0	29.0	0	0	25	0
(Crowley), 1 cup	130	0	32.0	0	0	15	0
(Minute Maid Light'N Juicy), 6 fl. oz.	13	.2	2.7	<.1	0	18	0
(Veryfine), 8 fl. oz.	130	.1	34.0	0	0	<10	0
mix[1], 8 fl. oz.:							
(Kool-Aid)	100	0	25.0	0	0	0	0

[1] Prepared according to package directions.

Food and Measure	cal.	prot. (gms)	carbo. (gms)	fat (gms)	chol. (mgs)	sod. (mgs)	fiber (gms)
Grape drink mix, 8 fl. oz. *(cont.)*							
(Kool-Aid Presweetened)	80	0	20.0	0	0	25	0
Grape fruit roll, see "Fruit snack"							
Grape juice, 6 fl. oz., except as noted:							
canned:							
(Campbell's Juice Bowl)	110	0	27.0	0	0	50	0
(Kraft Pure 100%)	104	1.0	25.0	0	0	0	0
(Minute Maid), 8.45 fl. oz. . . .	150	.6	37.4	.3	0	30	0
(Veryfine 100%), 8 fl. oz.	153	1.0	37.0	0	0	<20	0
(Welch's USDA) . .	120	0	30.0	0	0	10	0
blend *(Libby's Juicy Juice)*	100	0	25.0	0	0	5	0
Concord *(S&W)* . .	100	1.0	25.0	0	0	9	0
purple *(Welch's)* . .	120	0	30.0	0	0	10	0
red or white *(Welch's)*	120	0	30.0	0	0	15	0
sparkling, red *(Welch's)*	128	0	30.0	0	0	30	0
sparkling, white *(Welch's)*	120	0	30.0	0	0	30	0
chilled or frozen[2] *(Minute Maid)*	100	.4	25.0	.2	0	21	0
frozen[2]:							
(Sunkist)	69	.3	17.1	.1	0	3	0
purple or white *(Welch's)*	100	0	25.0	0	0	0	0
cocktail:							
(Welch's Orchard)	110	0	27.0	0	0	20	0
frozen[1] *(Welch's No Sugar Added)* . .	40	0	10.0	0	0	5	0

[2] *Diluted according to package directions.*

Food and Measure	cal.	prot. (gms)	carbo. (gms)	fat (gms)	chol. (mgs)	sod. (mgs)	fiber (gms)
Grape juice drink:							
canned:							
(Hi-C), 6 fl. oz. . .	96	.1	23.7	.1	0	17	0
(Kool-Aid Koolers),							
8.45 fl. oz.	140	0	35.0	0	0	10	0
(Tang Fruit Box),							
8.45 fl. oz.	130	0	34.0	0	0	10	0
frozen[1] (Sunkist),							
6 fl. oz.	69	.3	17.0	.1	0	3	0
Grape-apple drink:							
(Mott's), 9.5 fl. oz. . . .	158	0	40.0	0	0	<1	0
Grapeade, 6 fl. oz.:							
(Minute Maid)	94	.1	23.4	<.1	0	18	0
Grapefruit:							
fresh, pink or red, California or Arizona:							
1/2 medium, 33/4"							
diam.	46	.6	11.9	.1	0	<1	.3 c
sections w/juice,							
1/2 cup	43	.6	11.1	.1	0	<1	.2 c
fresh, pink or red, Florida:							
1/2 medium, 33/4"							
diam.	37	.7	9.2	.1	0	<1	.3 c
sections w/juice,							
1/2 cup	34	.6	8.6	.1	0	<1	.2 c
fresh, white, California:							
1/2 medium, 33/4"							
diam.	43	1.0	10.7	.1	0	tr.	.2 c
sections w/juice,							
1/2 cup	42	1.0	10.5	.1	0	tr.	.2 c
fresh, white, Florida:							
1/2 medium, 33/4"							
diam.	38	.7	9.7	.1	0	tr.	.2 d
sections w/juice,							
1/2 cup	38	.7	9.4	.1	0	tr.	.2 d

[1] Diluted according to package directions.

Food and Measure	cal.	prot. (gms)	carbo. (gms)	fat (gms)	chol. (mgs)	sod. (mgs)	fiber (gms)
Grapefruit, *(cont.)*							
canned or chilled,							
1/2 cup:							
(Kraft Pure)	50	1.0	12.0	0	0	0	m.q.
(S&W Un-							
sweetened) . . .	40	0	9.0	0	0	<10	m.q.
in water	44	.7	11.2	.1	0	2	.4 c
in juice	46	.9	11.4	.1	0	9	.3 d
in light syrup *(S&W)*	80	<1.0	14.0	0	0	0	m.q.
in light syrup							
(Stokely)	90	1.0	23.0	1.0	0	5	m.q.
Grapefruit juice,							
6 fl. oz., except							
as noted:							
fresh, 4 fl. oz.	48	.6	11.4	.1	0	1	m.q.
canned or chilled:							
(Campbell's Juice							
Bowl)	80	0	17.0	0	0	30	tr.
(Del Monte)	70	1.0	17.0	0	0	<10	tr.
(Kraft Pure 100%)	70	1.0	16.0	0	0	0	tr.
(Minute Maid) . . .	78	1.0	18.4	.3	0	19	tr.
(Minute Maid On							
The Go), 10 fl. oz.	130	1.7	30.7	.4	0	31	tr.
(Mott's), 9.5 fl. oz.	118	1.0	29.0	0	0	5	tr.
(Ocean Spray) . .	70	1.0	16.0	0	0	10	tr.
(S&W)	80	1.0	18.0	0	0	<10	tr.
(Stokely)	76	1.0	18.0	1.0	0	5	tr.
(Sunkist Fresh							
Squeezed),							
8 fl. oz.	96	1.2	22.7	.2	0	3	tr.
(Tree Top)	80	1.0	19.0	0	0	0	tr.
(Veryfine 100%),							
8 fl. oz.	101	1.4	23.0	0	0	<10	tr.
pink *(Ocean Spray)*	60	1.0	15.0	0	0	10	tr.
regular or pink							
(TreeSweet) . . .	72	0	17.0	0	0	15	tr.

Food and Measure	cal.	prot. (gms)	carbo. (gms)	fat (gms)	chol. (mgs)	sod. (mgs)	fiber (gms)
frozen[1]:							
(Minute Maid) . . .	83	1.1	19.7	.3	0	19	tr.
(Sunkist)	56	.8	13.3	.2	0	1	tr.
(TreeSweet)	78	1.0	18.0	0	0	15	tr.
or chilled, pink (Minute Maid)	78	1.0	18.4	.3	0	19	tr.
cocktail, pink:							
(IGA)	80	0	20.0	0	0	15	(0)
(Minute Maid Juices to Go), 9.6 fl. oz.	136	.7	33.5	.1	0	29	(0)
(Ocean Spray) . .	80	0	20.0	0	0	15	(0)
(TreeSweet Lite)	40	1.0	10.0	0	0	15	(0)
(Veryfine), 8 fl. oz.	120	<1.0	29.0	0	0	<15	(0)
chilled or frozen[1]							
(Minute Maid) . .	85	.5	20.9	.1	0	18	(0)
Grapefruit juice drink:							
(Citrus Hill Plus Calcium), 6 fl. oz. . . .	70	<1.0	19.0	<1.0	0	10	(0)
Gravy, see specific listings							
Great northern bean:							
boiled, 1/2 cup	104	7.3	18.6	.4	0	2	4.7 d
canned, 1/2 cup, except as noted:							
(Allens)	105	5.0	17.0	<1.0	0	440	m.q.
(Green Giant/Joan of Arc)	80	6.0	18.0	1.0	0	290	5.0 d
w/pork (Allens) . .	100	5.0	19.0	1.0	m.q.	320	m.q.
w/pork (Luck's), 7.25 oz.	220	12.0	32.0	5.0	m.q.	645	13.0 d
Green bean:							
fresh:							
raw, untrimmed, 1 lb.	123	7.3	28.5	.5	0	23	8.4 d
raw, 1/2 cup	17	1.0	3.9	.1	0	3	1.2 d

[1] Diluted according to package directions.

Food and Measure	cal.	prot. (gms)	carbo. (gms)	fat (gms)	chol. (mgs)	sod. (mgs)	fiber (gms)
Green bean, fresh *(cont.)*							
boiled, drained, ½ cup	22	1.2	4.9	.2	0	2	1.1 d
canned, ½ cup, except as noted:							
(Stokely)	20	1.0	4.0	0	0	360	m.q.
(Stokely No Salt/ Sugar)	20	1.0	4.0	0	0	5	m.q.
whole *(S&W)* . . .	20	1.0	4.0	0	0	385	m.q.
whole, cut or French *(Del Monte)*	20	1.0	4.0	0	0	355	m.q.
stringless *(S&W)*	20	1.0	4.0	0	0	385	m.q.
cut *(Green Giant)*	20	1.0	4.0	0	0	300	1.2 d
cut *(S&W Premium Golden)*	20	1.0	5.0	0	0	385	m.q.
cut *(Del Monte No Salt)*	20	1.0	4.0	0	0	<10	m.q.
cut or French *(Allens)*	20	1.0	4.0	<1.0	0	350	m.q.
dilled *(S&W)*	60	1.0	15.0	0	0	385	m.q.
French *(Green Giant)*	20	1.0	4.0	0	0	330	1.2 d
French or cut *(S&W Premium Blue Lake)*	20	1.0	4.0	0	0	385	m.q.
Italian *(Allens)* . . .	18	1.0	3.0	<1.0	0	260	m.q.
Italian *(Del Monte)*	25	1.0	6.0	0	0	355	m.q.
kitchen sliced *(Green Giant)* . .	20	1.0	4.0	0	0	280	1.2 d
seasoned, French *(Del Monte)* . . .	20	1.0	4.0	0	0	355	m.q.
w/shelled beans and pork *(Luck's)*, 8 oz.	200	9.0	24.0	8.0	m.q.	840	9.0 d
shelly beans *(Allens)*	35	2.0	6.0	<1.0	0	395	m.q.

Food and Measure	cal.	prot. (gms)	carbo. (gms)	fat (gms)	chol. (mgs)	sod. (mgs)	fiber (gms)
freeze-dried (Mountain House), 1/2 cup . .	35	1.0	6.0	0	0	tr.	m.q.
frozen, 3 oz., except as noted:							
(Green Giant), 1/2 cup	14	1.0	4.0	0	0	10	1.5 d
whole (Birds Eye Deluxe)	25	1.0	5.0	0	0	0	2.0 d
whole (Birds Eye Farm Fresh), 4 oz.	30	2.0	7.0	0	0	0	2.0 d
whole (Seabrook)	25	1.0	5.0	0	0	1	1.0 c
whole (Southern), 3.5 oz.	33	1.6	6.8	.1	0	20	m.q.
cut (Birds Eye Portion Pack)	25	1.0	6.0	0	0	0	2.0 d
cut (Frosty Acres)	25	1.0	6.0	0	0	3	1.0 c
cut (Green Giant Harvest Fresh), 1/2 cup	16	1.0	4.0	0	0	150	1.7 d
cut (Seabrook) . .	25	1.0	6.0	0	0	3	1.0 c
cut (Stokely Singles)	30	2.0	6.0	1.0	0	5	m.q.
cut or French (Birds Eye)	25	1.0	6.0	0	0	0	2.0 d
French (Frosty Acres)	25	1.0	6.0	0	0	3	1.0 c
Italian (Birds Eye)	30	2.0	7.0	0	0	0	3.0 d
petite (Birds Eye Deluxe), 2.6 oz.	20	1.0	5.0	0	0	0	2.0 d
in butter sauce (Green Giant One Serving), 5.5 oz.	60	2.0	10.0	2.0	5	360	m.q.
in butter sauce, cut (Green Giant), 1/2 cup	30	1.0	4.0	1.0	5	230	1.5 d

Food and Measure	cal.	prot. (gms)	carbo. (gms)	fat (gms)	chol. (mgs)	sod. (mgs)	fiber (gms)
Green bean combinations, frozen:							
Bavarian style, w/ spaetzle (Birds Eye), 3.3 oz. . . .	100	2.0	11.0	5.0	10	350	2.0 d
French w/toasted almond (Birds Eye Combinations), 3 oz.	50	3.0	8.0	2.0	0	340	2.0 d
and mushroom, creamy (Green Giant Garden Gourmet), 1 pkg.	220	6.0	29.0	11.0	25	860	4.0 d
mushroom casserole (Stouffer's), 4.75 oz.	160	3.0	13.0	11.0	n.a.	680	m.q.
Grenadine:							
(Rose's), 1 fl. oz. . .	65	0	16.0	0	0	27	(0)
Grits, see "Corn grits"							
Ground cherry:							
trimmed, 1/2 cup . . .	37	1.3	7.8	.5	0	m.q.	2.0 c
Grouper, meat only:							
raw, 1 lb.	417	87.9	0	4.6	166	239	0
raw, 1 oz.	26	5.5	0	.3	10	15	0
baked, broiled, or microwaved, 4 oz. . . .	134	28.2	0	1.5	53	60	0
Guacamole, see "Avocado dip"							
Guacamole seasoning:							
(Lawry's), 1 pkg. . . .	60	1.7	12.6	.4	0	1495	.8 c
Guava:							
1 medium, 4 oz. . . .	45	.7	10.7	.5	0	2	5.0 c
1/2 cup	42	.7	9.8	.5	0	2	4.6 c
strawberry, 1/2 cup	85	.7	21.2	.7	0	45	7.8 c
Guava fruit drink:							
(Ocean Spray Mauna La'I), 6 fl. oz. . . .	100	0	25.0	0	0	10	(0)

Food and Measure	cal.	prot. (gms)	carbo. (gms)	fat (gms)	chol. (mgs)	sod. (mgs)	fiber (gms)
Guava juice, 6 fl. oz.:							
bottled or frozen[1]							
(Welch's Orchard							
Tropicals)	100	0	25.0	0	0	20	0
Guava nectar:							
(Libby's), 6 fl. oz. . . .	110	0	26.0	0	0	15	m.q.
Guava sauce:							
cooked, 1/2 cup . . .	43	.4	11.3	.2	0	4	2.4 c
Guava-passion fruit							
drink:							
(Ocean Spray Mauna							
La'I), 6 fl. oz. . . .	100	0	25.0	0	0	10	(0)
Guava-strawberry							
tropical re-							
fresher:							
(Veryfine), 8 fl. oz. . .	120	.3	30.0	0	0	<25	(0)
Guinea hen, raw:							
meat w/skin, 1 oz.	45	6.6	0	1.8	m.q.	m.q.	0
meat only, 1 oz. . . .	31	5.9	0	.7	18	m.q.	0

---

[1] *Diluted according to package directions.*

H

Food and Measure	cal.	prot. (gms)	carbo. (gms)	fat (gms)	chol. (mgs)	sod. (mgs)	fiber (gms)
Haddock, meat only:							
raw, 1 lb.	396	85.8	0	3.3	261	310	0
raw, 1 oz.	25	5.4	0	.2	16	19	0
baked, broiled, or mi-							
crowaved, 4 oz. . .	127	27.5	0	1.1	84	99	0
smoked, 4 oz.	132	28.6	0	1.1	87	865	0
Haddock, frozen:							
(Gorton's Fishmarket							
Fresh), 5 oz.	110	25.0	0	1.0	m.q.	120	0
(SeaPak), 4 oz. . . .	90	18.0	0	1.0	m.q.	120	0
(Van de Kamp's),							
4 oz.	90	19.0	0	1.0	65	70	0
Haddock entree, fro-							
zen:							
battered, 2 pieces:							
(Mrs. Paul's							
Crunchy)	280	11.0	25.0	15.0	m.q.	580	m.q.
(Van de Kamp's)	250	12.0	20.0	13.0	50	520	m.q.
breaded:							
(Mrs. Paul's Crispy							
Crunchy),							
2 pieces	280	16.0	23.0	14.0	40	460	m.q.
(Mrs. Paul's Light),							
4¼ oz.	220	19.0	24.0	5.0	m.q.	456	m.q.
(Van de Kamp's),							
2 pieces	260	10.0	23.0	15.0	30	430	m.q.
(Van de Kamp's							
Light), 1 piece	250	17.0	19.0	12.0	35	380	m.q.

Food and Measure	cal.	prot. (gms)	carbo. (gms)	fat (gms)	chol. (mgs)	sod. (mgs)	fiber (gms)
in lemon butter *(Gorton's Microwave Entrees),* 1 pkg.	360	23.0	19.0	21.0	100	730	m.q.
Hake, see "Whiting"							
Halibut, meat only:							
raw, 1 lb.	497	94.4	0	10.4	146	245	0
raw, 1 oz.	31	5.9	0	.6	9	15	0
baked, broiled, or microwaved, 4 oz. . .	159	30.3	0	3.3	46	78	0
Halibut, frozen:							
battered *(Van de Kamp's),* 2 pieces	180	9.0	14.0	9.0	35	340	m.q.
steak, w/out seasoning *(SeaPak),* 6-oz. pkg.	160	36.0	0	1.0	m.q.	120	0
Halvah, 1 bar:							
(Fantastic Foods) . .	232	8.0	17.0	10.0	0	0	m.q.
Ham, fresh, meat only:							
whole leg, roasted:							
lean w/fat, 4 oz.	333	28.4	0	23.5	105	67	0
lean w/fat, chopped or diced, 1 cup	411	35.0	0	29.0	131	83	0
lean only, 4 oz. . .	249	32.1	0	12.5	107	73	0
lean only, chopped or diced, 1 cup	309	39.7	0	15.4	131	90	0
rump half, roasted:							
lean w/fat, 4 oz.	311	30.2	0	20.2	108	69	0
lean only, 4 oz. . .	251	33.0	0	12.1	109	74	0
shank half, roasted:							
lean w/fat, 4 oz.	344	27.6	0	25.1	104	66	0
lean only, 4 oz. . .	244	32.0	0	11.9	104	73	0
Ham, cured:							
whole leg, lean w/fat:							
unheated, 1 oz. . .	70	5.2	<.1	5.3	16	364	0
roasted, 4 oz. . . .	276	24.5	0	19.0	70	1346	0

Food and Measure	cal.	prot. (gms)	carbo. (gms)	fat (gms)	chol. (mgs)	sod. (mgs)	fiber (gms)
Ham, cured, whole leg, lean w/fat *(cont.)*							
roasted, chopped or							
diced, 1 cup	341	30.2	0	23.5	86	1661	0
whole leg, lean only:							
unheated, 1 oz. . .	42	6.3	<.1	1.6	15	430	0
roasted, 4 oz. . . .	178	28.4	0	6.2	62	1505	0
roasted, chopped or							
diced, 1 cup	219	35.1	0	7.7	78	1858	0
boneless (11% fat):							
unheated, 1 oz. . .	52	5.0	.9	3.0	16	373	0
roasted, 4 oz. . . .	202	25.7	0	10.2	67	1701	0
roasted, chopped or							
diced, 1 cup	249	31.7	0	12.6	83	2100	0
boneless, extra lean							
(5% fat):							
unheated, 1 oz. . .	37	5.5	.3	1.4	13	405	0
roasted, 4 oz. . . .	164	23.7	1.7	6.3	60	1364	0
roasted, chopped or							
diced, 1 cup	203	29.3	2.1	7.7	74	1684	0
Ham, canned, 4 oz.,							
except as noted:							
(Black Label, 5 lb.)	140	20.0	0	7.0	m.q.	1245	0
(Black Label, 3 lb.)	140	20.0	0	7.0	m.q.	1315	0
(Black Label, 1.5 lb.)	150	21.0	0	7.0	m.q.	1324	0
(Hormel Bone In) . .	210	17.0	1.0	15.0	m.q.	m.q.	0
(Hormel Cure 81) . .	160	22.0	0	8.0	m.q.	1322	0
(Hormel Curemaster)	140	22.0	1.0	5.0	m.q.	1361	0
(EXL)	120	22.0	0	4.0	m.q.	1382	0
(EXL Deli Ham, 10 lb.)	130	20.0	0	6.0	m.q.	1368	0
(JM 95% Fat Free),							
2 oz.	60	10.0	1.0	2.0	m.q.	680	0
(Oscar Mayer Jubilee),							
1 oz.	31	5.2	0	1.1	13	285	0
chopped:							
(Hormel 8 lb.), 3 oz.	240	12.0	1.0	21.0	m.q.	1062	0
(Hormel 12 oz.),							
2 oz.	120	10.0	0	9.0	m.q.	703	0

Food and Measure	cal.	prot. (gms)	carbo. (gms)	fat (gms)	chol. (mgs)	sod. (mgs)	fiber (gms)
chunk (Hormel), 6¾ oz.	310	32.0	0	20.0	m.q.	2241	0
hickory smoked (Rath Black Hawk), 2 oz.	60	10.0	1.0	2.0	m.q.	720	0
roll (Hormel)	170	21.0	0	10.0	m.q.	1338	0
spiced (Hormel), 3 oz.	240	13.0	1.0	21.0	m.q.	1093	0
"Ham," vegetarian, frozen:							
roll or slices (Worthington Wham), 3 slices or 2.4 oz.	120	11.0	3.0	7.0	0	940	m.q.
Ham breakfast taco: (Owens Border Breakfasts), 2.17 oz.	90	7.0	13.0	6.0	50	430	m.q.
Ham dinner, frozen: (Morton), 10 oz. . . .	290	15.0	49.0	4.0	45	1400	m.q.
steak: (Armour Classics), 10.75 oz.	270	15.0	36.0	7.0	50	1320	m.q.
(Le Menu), 10 oz.	300	18.0	33.0	10.0	m.q.	1490	m.q.
glazed (Stouffer's Dinner Supreme), 10.5 oz.	380	25.0	35.0	15.0	m.q.	1960	m.q.
Ham entree, frozen: (Banquet Platters), 10 oz.	400	20.0	43.0	17.0	50	1180	m.q.
and asparagus: au gratin (The Budget Gourmet Slim Selects), 9 oz.	280	14.0	33.0	10.0	40	1130	m.q.
bake (Stouffer's), 9.5 oz.	510	18.0	31.0	35.0	m.q.	900	m.q.
scalloped potatoes and (Swanson Homestyle Recipe), 9 oz.	340	19.0	31.0	16.0	m.q.	990	m.q.

Food and Measure	cal.	prot. (gms)	carbo. (gms)	fat (gms)	chol. (mgs)	sod. (mgs)	fiber (gms)
Ham, luncheon meat, 1 oz., except as noted:							
(*Boar's Head* Lower Salt)	28	5.0	<1.0	<1.0	15	250	0
(*Healthy Deli* Deluxe)	31	4.7	1.1	.9	12	245	0
(*Healthy Deli* Lessalt)	32	4.7	1.4	.9	13	190	0
(*Healthy Deli* Light AM)	27	3.9	1.4	.6	11	200	0
(*Healthy Deli* Taverne)	31	5.4	.3	.8	15	210	0
(*JM* Slice'N Eat 93% Fat Free), 2 oz. . . .	70	10.0	1.0	3.0	24	630	0
(*Jones Dairy Farm*), 1 slice	50	8.8	tr.	1.1	21	381	0
(*Jones Dairy Farm* Family Ham)	35	5.8	tr.	1.2	14	298	0
(*Oscar Mayer* Breakfast Ham), 1.5-oz. slice	52	7.4	1.2	1.9	21	583	0
(*Oscar Mayer* Jubilee)	46	5.2	.1	2.7	15	369	0
(*Swift Premium* Hostess)	30	5.0	0	1.0	m.q.	330	0
(*Swift Premium* Sugar Plum)	30	5.0	1.0	1.0	m.q.	280	0
baked:							
(*Oscar Mayer*), 3/4 oz.	21	3.9	.4	.4	10	238	0
Virginia (*Healthy Deli*)	34	4.8	1.6	.9	12	245	0
barbecue (*Light & Lean*), 2 slices . .	50	8.0	0	2.0	m.q.	m.q.	0
Black Forest (*Healthy Deli*)	32	5.9	.4	.6	16	220	0
boiled:							
(*Boar's Head* Deluxe)	28	5.0	1.0	<1.0	15	275	0
(*Oscar Mayer*), 3/4 oz.	23	3.8	.3	.7	12	290	0

Food and Measure	cal.	prot. (gms)	carbo. (gms)	fat (gms)	chol. (mgs)	sod. (mgs)	fiber (gms)
Cajun (Hillshire Farm Deli Select)	31	6.0	<1.0	.9	m.q.	350	(0)
chopped:							
(Eckrich)	45	5.0	<1.0	2.0	m.q.	350	0
(Eckrich Lean Supreme)	35	10.0	<1.0	2.0	m.q.	350	0
(Hormel Perma-Fresh), 2 slices	88	11.0	0	5.0	m.q.	685	0
(JM)	80	4.0	1.0	7.0	m.q.	370	0
(Kahn's), 1 slice . .	50	5.0	1.0	3.0	m.q.	360	0
(Oscar Mayer) . . .	55	4.5	1.0	3.7	17	327	0
cooked:							
(JM)	30	4.0	1.0	1.0	m.q.	360	0
fresh (Healthy Deli)	33	5.9	.2	.8	13	120	0
glazed (Light & Lean), 2 slices	50	9.0	0	2.0	m.q.	m.q.	0
honey:							
(Healthy Deli Honey Valley)	31	4.8	1.2	.8	10	260	0
(Hillshire Farm Deli Select)	31	6.0	<1.0	.9	m.q.	270	0
(Oscar Mayer), 3/4 oz.	26	3.7	.7	1.0	11	276	0
jalapeño (Healthy Deli)	25	3.7	.8	.6	11	260	(0)
loaf (Eckrich)	50	5.0	1.0	4.0	m.q.	290	0
minced	75	4.6	.5	5.9	20	353	0
pepper, cracked (Oscar Mayer), 3/4 oz.	24	3.8	.2	.8	11	296	(0)
smoked:							
(Eckrich Slender Sliced)	40	5.0	1.0	2.0	m.q.	360	0
(Hillshire Farm Deli Select)	31	6.0	<1.0	.9	m.q.	300	0
cooked (Oscar Mayer), 3/4 oz.	23	3.8	.1	.9	12	268	0
golden (JM), 2 oz.	80	8.0	1.0	5.0	m.q.	630	0
Virginia (Healthy Deli Lessalt)	32	4.7	1.4	.9	13	190	0

Food and Measure	cal.	prot. (gms)	carbo. (gms)	fat (gms)	chol. (mgs)	sod. (mgs)	fiber (gms)
Ham patty, 1 piece:							
(Swift Premium Brown 'N Serve)	130	3.0	1.0	13.0	m.q.	260	0
canned *(Hormel)* . .	180	7.0	0	16.0	m.q.	456	0
Ham salad spread:							
(Oscar Mayer), 1 oz.	59	2.5	3.6	3.8	10	268	n.a.
Ham spread, deviled:							
(Hormel), 1 tbsp.	35	2.0	0	3.0	m.q.	108	0
(Underwood), 2¼ oz.	220	9.0	0	20.0	m.q.	640	0
Ham and cheese breakfast sand- wich:							
(Owens Border Break- fasts), 2 oz.	150	7.0	14.0	6.0	m.q.	600	m.q.
Ham and cheese casserole, fro- zen:							
(Pillsbury Microwave Classic), 1 pkg. . .	470	18.0	34.0	29.0	m.q.	1300	m.q.
Ham and cheese loaf:							
(Eckrich), 1-oz. slice	50	4.0	1.0	4.0	m.q.	300	0
(Hormel Perma-Fresh), 2 slices	110	11.0	0	7.0	m.q.	668	0
(Kahn's), 1 slice . . .	70	4.0	1.0	6.0	m.q.	310	0
(Oscar Mayer), 1 oz.	76	4.5	.6	6.2	18	360	0
canned *(Hormel,* 8 lb.), 3 oz.	260	13.0	1.0	22.0	m.q.	1135	0
Ham and cheese patty:							
(Hormel), 1 piece . .	190	7.0	0	18.0	m.q.	468	0
Ham and cheese pocket sand- wich, frozen:							
(Hot Pockets), 5 oz.	360	19.0	36.0	16.0	90	1320	m.q.

Food and Measure	cal.	prot. (gms)	carbo. (gms)	fat (gms)	chol. (mgs)	sod. (mgs)	fiber (gms)
Ham and cheese spread:							
(Oscar Mayer), 1 oz.	67	4.5	.6	5.2	15	323	0
Hamburger entree mix[1], 1 cup, except as noted:							
beef:							
noodle *(Hamburger Helper)*	320	20.0	26.0	15.0	m.q.	1050	m.q.
Romanoff *(Hamburger Helper)*	350	22.0	31.0	16.0	m.q.	1070	m.q.
cheeseburger macaroni *(Hamburger Helper)*	370	21.0	28.0	19.0	m.q.	1030	m.q.
chili:							
w/beans *(Hamburger Helper)*, 1¼ cup	350	24.0	25.0	17.0	m.q.	1740	m.q.
tomato *(Hamburger Helper)*	330	20.0	31.0	14.0	m.q.	1410	m.q.
hamburger:							
hash *(Hamburger Helper)*	320	18.0	27.0	15.0	m.q.	1020	m.q.
stew *(Hamburger Helper)*	300	18.0	25.0	14.0	m.q.	1010	m.q.
Italian:							
cheesy *(Hamburger Helper)*[2]	360	22.0	30.0	17.0	m.q.	1040	m.q.
zesty *(Hamburger Helper)*	340	21.0	35.0	13.0	m.q.	980	m.q.
lasagne *(Hamburger Helper)*	340	21.0	33.0	14.0	m.q.	1050	m.q.
meatloaf *(Hamburger Helper)*	360	27.0	14.0	22.0	m.q.	710	m.q.

[1] *Prepared according to package directions, except as noted.*
[2] *Prepared with 2% lowfat milk.*

Food and Measure	cal.	prot. (gms)	carbo. (gms)	fat (gms)	chol. (mgs)	sod. (mgs)	fiber (gms)
Hamburger entree mix, 1 cup, except as noted *(cont.)*							
pizza:							
(Hamburger Helper Pizzabake),							
4.5 oz.	320	19.0	29.0	14.0	m.q.	840	m.q.
dish *(Hamburger Helper)*	360	21.0	37.0	14.0	m.q.	1010	m.q.
potato:							
au gratin *(Hamburger Helper)*	320	19.0	28.0	15.0	m.q.	910	m.q.
Stroganoff *(Hamburger Helper)*	320	18.0	28.0	15.0	m.q.	950	m.q.
rice Oriental *(Hamburger Helper)* . .	340	19.0	38.0	14.0	m.q.	1120	m.q.
sloppy Joe *(Hamburger Helper Sloppy Joe Bake),*							
5 oz.	340	18.0	33.0	15.0	m.q.	1100	m.q.
spaghetti *(Hamburger Helper)*	340	20.0	32.0	15.0	m.q.	1110	m.q.
Stroganoff, creamy *(Hamburger Helper)*[1]	390	22.0	30.0	20.0	m.q.	870	m.q.
taco *(Hamburger Helper Tacobake),*							
5.75 oz.	320	17.0	31.0	15.0	m.q.	940	m.q.
tamale pie *(Hamburger Helper)* . .	380	19.0	39.0	16.0	m.q.	940	m.q.
Hardee's, 1 serving:							
Big Country Breakfast:							
bacon	660	24.0	51.0	40.0	305	1540	m.q.
country ham	670	29.0	52.0	38.0	345	2870	m.q.
ham	620	28.0	51.0	33.0	325	1780	m.q.
sausage	850	33.0	51.0	57.0	340	1980	m.q.
Biscuit 'N' Gravy . .	440	9.0	45.0	24.0	15	1250	m.q.
breakfast biscuit:							
bacon	360	10.0	34.0	21.0	10	950	m.q.
bacon and egg . .	410	15.0	35.0	24.0	155	990	m.q.

[1] *Prepared with whole milk.*

Food and Measure	cal.	prot. (gms)	carbo. (gms)	fat (gms)	chol. (mgs)	sod. (mgs)	fiber (gms)
bacon, egg and							
cheese	460	17.0	35.0	28.0	165	1220	m.q.
country ham	350	11.0	35.0	18.0	25	1550	m.q.
country ham and							
egg	400	16.0	35.0	22.0	175	1600	m.q.
ham	320	10.0	34.0	16.0	15	1000	m.q.
ham and egg . . .	370	15.0	35.0	19.0	160	1050	m.q.
ham, egg and							
cheese	420	18.0	35.0	23.0	170	1270	m.q.
Canadian Rise 'N'							
Shine	470	22.0	35.0	27.0	180	1550	m.q.
chicken	430	17.0	42.0	22.0	45	1330	m.q.
Cinnamon 'N' Raisin	320	4.0	37.0	17.0	0	510	m.q.
Rise 'N' Shine . . .	320	5.0	34.0	18.0	0	740	m.q.
sausage	440	13.0	34.0	28.0	25	1100	m.q.
sausage and egg	490	18.0	35.0	31.0	170	1150	m.q.
steak	500	15.0	46.0	29.0	30	1320	m.q.
steak and egg . . .	550	20.0	47.0	32.0	175	1370	m.q.
Hash Rounds	230	3.0	24.0	14.0	0	560	m.q.
pancakes, three:							
1 serving	280	8.0	56.0	2.0	15	890	m.q.
w/2 bacon strips	350	13.0	56.0	9.0	25	1110	m.q.
w/1 sausage patty	430	16.0	56.0	16.0	40	1290	m.q.
pancake syrup, 1.5 oz.	120	<1.0	31.0	<1.0	0	25	0
sandwiches, 1 serving:							
Big Deluxe burger	500	27.0	32.0	30.0	70	760	m.q.
Big Roast Beef . .	300	18.0	32.0	11.0	45	880	m.q.
Big Twin	450	23.0	34.0	25.0	55	580	m.q.
cheeseburger . . .	320	16.0	33.0	14.0	30	710	m.q.
cheeseburger, ba-							
con	610	34.0	31.0	39.0	80	1030	m.q.
cheeseburger,							
1/4 lb.	500	29.0	34.0	29.0	70	1060	m.q.
chicken breast							
sandwich, grilled	310	24.0	34.0	9.0	60	890	m.q.
Chicken Fillet . . .	370	19.0	44.0	13.0	55	1060	m.q.
Fisherman's Fillet	500	23.0	49.0	24.0	70	1030	m.q.
hamburger	270	13.0	33.0	10.0	20	490	m.q.

Food and Measure	cal.	prot. (gms)	carbo. (gms)	fat (gms)	chol. (mgs)	sod. (mgs)	fiber (gms)
Hardee's, sandwiches, 1 serving *(cont.)*							
hot dog, all beef	300	11.0	25.0	17.0	25	710	m.q.
Hot Ham 'N'							
Cheese	330	23.0	32.0	12.0	65	1420	m.q.
Mushroom 'N' Swiss							
burger	490	30.0	33.0	27.0	70	940	m.q.
roast beef, regular	260	15.0	31.0	9.0	35	730	m.q.
Turkey Club	390	29.0	32.0	16.0	70	1280	m.q.
side dishes and special items:							
Chicken Stix,							
9 piece	310	28.0	20.0	14.0	55	1020	m.q.
Chicken Stix,							
6 piece	210	19.0	13.0	9.0	35	680	m.q.
Crispy Curls, 3 oz.	300	4.0	36.0	16.0	0	840	m.q.
french fries, large	360	4.0	48.0	17.0	0	135	m.q.
french fries, regular	230	3.0	30.0	11.0	0	85	m.q.
salads:							
chef	240	22.0	5.0	15.0	115	930	m.q.
chicken 'N' pasta	230	27.0	23.0	3.0	55	380	m.q.
garden	210	14.0	3.0	14.0	105	270	m.q.
side	20	2.0	1.0	<1.0	0	15	m.q.
dressings, 2 oz.:							
blue cheese	210	1.0	10.0	18.0	20	790	n.a.
house	290	1.0	6.0	29.0	25	510	n.a.
Thousand Island	250	1.0	9.0	23.0	35	540	n.a.
sauces:							
barbecue dipping,							
1 oz.	30	<1.0	8.0	<1.0	0	300	n.a.
barbecue, 1 pkt.	14	<1.0	4.0	<1.0	0	140	n.a.
Big Twin, .5 oz. . .	50	<1.0	4.0	4.0	5	35	n.a.
honey, .5 oz. . . .	45	<1.0	11.0	<1.0	0	0	0
sweet mustard dipping, 1 oz. . . .	50	<1.0	10.0	<1.0	0	160	n.a.
sweet 'n' sour dipping, 1 oz. . . .	40	<1.0	10.0	<1.0	0	95	n.a.
tartar, .7 oz.	90	<1.0	2.0	9.0	10	160	n.a.

Food and Measure	cal.	prot. (gms)	carbo. (gms)	fat (gms)	chol. (mgs)	sod. (mgs)	fiber (gms)
desserts and shakes:							
apple turnover . .	270	3.0	38.0	12.0	0	250	m.q.
Big Cookie	250	3.0	31.0	13.0	5	240	m.q.
Cool Twist cone, 4.2 oz.:							
chocolate	200	4.0	31.0	6.0	20	65	m.q.
vanilla	190	5.0	28.0	6.0	15	100	m.q.
vanilla/chocolate	190	4.0	29.0	6.0	20	80	m.q.
Cool Twist sundae:							
caramel, 6 oz.	330	6.0	54.0	10.0	20	290	(0)
hot fudge, 5.9 oz.	320	7.0	45.0	12.0	25	270	(0)
strawberry, 5.9 oz.	260	5.0	43.0	8.0	15	115	(0)
shake, 12 oz.:							
chocolate	460	11.0	85.0	8.0	45	340	(0)
strawberry . . .	440	11.0	82.0	8.0	40	300	(0)
vanilla	400	13.0	66.0	9.0	50	320	0
Hazelnut, see "Filberts"							
Head cheese:							
(Oscar Mayer), 1 oz.	55	4.5	0	4.1	26	347	0
Heart, braised or simmered, 4 oz.:							
beef	199	32.6	.5	6.4	219	71	0
chicken, broiler-fryer	210	30.0	.1	9.0	274	54	0
lamb	210	28.3	2.2	9.0	282	71	0
pork	168	26.8	.5	5.7	251	40	0
turkey	201	30.3	2.3	6.9	256	62	0
veal	211	33.0	.1	7.7	200	66	0
Herb garlic sauce:							
w/lemon juice *(Lawry's),* 1/4 cup	36	3.6	3.8	.4	n.a.	3688	<.1 c
Herb seasoning and coating mix, Italian:							
(McCormick/Schilling Bag'n Season), 1 pkg.	94	2.0	21.0	.2	n.a.	1367	m.q.

Food and Measure	cal.	prot. (gms)	carbo. (gms)	fat (gms)	chol. (mgs)	sod. (mgs)	fiber (gms)
Herb seasoning and coating mix, Italian *(cont.)*							
(Shake'n Bake),							
1/4 pkg.	80	2.0	14.0	1.0	0	620	m.q.
Herbs, see specific listings							
Herbs, mixed, 1 tsp.:							
(Lawry's Pinch of Herbs)	9	.3	.9	.5	0	259	.2 c
Herring, fresh:							
Atlantic, meat only:							
raw, 1 lb.	718	81.5	0	41.0	272	407	0
raw, 1 oz.	45	5.1	0	2.6	17	26	0
baked, broiled or microwaved, 4 oz.	230	26.1	0	13.1	87	130	0
kippered, 4 oz. . .	246	27.9	0	14.0	93	1041	0
pickled, 4 oz. . . .	297	16.1	10.9	20.4	15	987	0
lake, see "Cisco"							
Pacific, meat only:							
raw, 1 lb.	885	74.4	0	63.0	348	335	0
raw, 1 oz.	55	4.6	0	3.9	22	21	0
Herring, canned, see "Sardine"							
Herring, lake, see "Cisco"							
Hickory nut, dried:							
shelled, 1 oz.	187	3.6	5.2	18.3	0	tr.	.9 c
Hollandaise sauce:							
(Great Impressions),							
2 tbsp.	192	.5	.3	21.0	48	107	m.q.
mix *(McCormick/ Schilling)*, 1 pkg.	203	3.3	14.3	14.8	n.a.	678	m.q.
Homestyle gravy mix[1]:							
(French's), 1/4 cup	20	1.0	4.0	1.0	n.a.	250	n.a.
(Pillsbury), 1/4 cup	15	<1.0	3.0	0	0	300	n.a.

[1] *Prepared according to package directions, with water.*

Food and Measure	cal.	prot. (gms)	carbo. (gms)	fat (gms)	chol. (mgs)	sod. (mgs)	fiber (gms)
Hominy, canned:							
golden:							
(Allens), 1/2 cup . .	80	2.0	16.0	<1.0	0	370	m.q.
(Van Camp's), 1 cup	128	2.7	27.9	.6	0	701	.8 c
w/peppers *(Van*							
Camp's), 1 cup	129	2.6	28.5	.5	0	685	.7 c
Mexican *(Allens)*,							
1/2 cup	80	2.0	16.0	<1.0	0	330	m.q.
white:							
(Allens), 1/2 cup . .	70	2.0	16.0	<1.0	0	430	m.q.
(Van Camp's), 1 cup	138	3.0	30.0	.7	0	708	.8 c
Hominy grits, see							
"Corn grits"							
Honey, 1 tbsp.:							
(Golden Blossom) . .	60	0	16.0	0	0	n.a.	0
Honey butter:							
(Honey Butter), 1 tbsp.	50	<1.0	11.0	1.0	m.q.	5	0
Honey loaf:							
(Eckrich), 1 oz. . . .	35	4.0	2.0	1.0	m.q.	280	0
(Eckrich Smorgas							
Pac), 1 oz.	35	4.0	2.0	1.0	m.q.	280	0
(Hormel Perma-Fresh),							
2 slices	90	1.0	0	5.0	m.q.	584	0
(Kahn's), 1 slice . . .	40	4.0	1.0	2.0	m.q.	320	0
(Oscar Mayer), 1 oz.	35	5.1	1.0	1.2	14	365	0
Honey roll sausage:							
beef, 1 oz.	52	5.3	.6	3.0	14	375	0
Honeydew:							
1/10 melon, 7" × 2"	46	.6	11.8	.1	0	13	.8 c
pulp, cubed, 1/2 cup	30	.4	7.8	.1	0	9	.5 c
Horseradish:							
fresh, 1/2 cup:							
leafy tips, raw,							
chopped	6	.9	.8	.1	0	1	.2 c
leafy tips, boiled,							
drained, chopped	13	1.1	2.3	.2	0	2	.4 c
pods, raw, sliced	19	1.1	4.3	.1	0	21	.7 c

Food and Measure	cal.	prot. (gms)	carbo. (gms)	fat (gms)	chol. (mgs)	sod. (mgs)	fiber (gms)
Horseradish, fresh, 1/2 cup *(cont.)*							
pods, boiled,							
drained, sliced	21	1.2	4.8	.1	0	25	1.1 c
prepared:							
(Kraft), 1 tbsp. . . .	10	0	1.0	0	0	140	m.q.
cream style *(Kraft)*,							
1 tbsp.	10	0	1.0	0	0	85	m.q.
hot *(Gold's)*, 1 tsp.	4	<1.0	<1.0	<1.0	0	60	m.q.
Horseradish sauce:							
(Great Impressions),							
1 tbsp.	74	0	1.4	7.6	1	199	m.q.
(Sauceworks), 1 tbsp.	50	0	2.0	5.0	5	105	m.q.
Hubbard squash:							
baked, cubed, 1/2 cup	51	2.5	11.0	.6	0	8	1.8 c
boiled, drained,							
mashed, 1/2 cup . .	35	1.8	7.6	.4	0	6	1.2 c
Hummus:							
dip mix *(Fantastic*							
Foods), 1/4 cup . .	111	4.0	9.5	6.5	0	263	m.q.
mix *(Casbah)*, 1 oz.							
dry	110	5.0	10.0	5.0	0	n.a.	m.q.
Hushpuppy:							
frozen *(SeaPak)*, 4 oz.	330	6.0	56.0	9.0	n.a.	690	m.q.
mix, 1 1/4 oz.:							
deluxe *(Golden*							
Dipt)	120	3.0	26.0	0	0	520	m.q.
jalapeño *(Golden*							
Dipt)	120	3.0	27.0	0	0	570	m.q.
w/onion *(Golden*							
Dipt)	120	3.0	27.0	0	0	520	m.q.
Hyacinth bean:							
fresh:							
raw, trimmed,							
1/2 cup	19	.8	3.7	.1	0	1	.5 c
boiled, drained,							
1/2 cup	22	1.3	4.1	.1	0	1	.8 c
dried, boiled, 1/2 cup	114	7.9	20.1	.6	0	7	2.4 c

Food and Measure	cal.	prot. (gms)	carbo. (gms)	fat (gms)	chol. (mgs)	sod. (mgs)	fiber (gms)
Ice (see also "Sherbet" and "Sorbet"):							
cherry, Italian (Good Humor), 6 fl. oz. . .	138	0	34.2	.1	0	0	(0)
daiquiri (Baskin-Robbins), 1 regular scoop	140	0	35.0	0	0	15	(0)
Ice bar (see also "Gelatin bar" and "Fruit bar"), 1 bar:							
all flavors (Good Humor Ice Stripes) . .	35	0	8.6	0	0	0	(0)
cherry (Good Humor Calippo)	138	.1	34.9	.1	0	5	(0)
lemon (Good Humor Calippo)	112	0	27.6	.1	0	0	(0)
orange (Good Humor Calippo)	111	0	27.2	.2	0	0	(0)
Ice cream, 1/2 cup, except as noted:							
butter almond:							
(Breyers)	170	4.0	15.0	10.0	25	125	m.q.
(Sealtest)	160	3.0	16.0	9.0	20	140	m.q.
butter crunch (Sealtest)	150	2.0	18.0	7.0	m.q.	90	(0)
butter pecan:							
(Breyers)	180	3.0	15.0	11.0	25	125	m.q.
(Frusen Glädjé) . .	280	5.0	16.0	21.0	85	160	m.q.

Food and Measure	cal.	prot. (gms)	carbo. (gms)	fat (gms)	chol. (mgs)	sod. (mgs)	fiber (gms)
Ice cream, butter pecan *(cont.)*							
(Häagen-Dazs) . .	290	5.0	29.0	17.0	m.q.	95	m.q.
(Sealtest)	160	3.0	16.0	10.0	15	115	m.q.
cherry vanilla							
(Breyers)	150	3.0	17.0	7.0	20	45	(0)
chocolate:							
(Breyers)	160	3.0	20.0	8.0	20	30	(0)
(Darigold)	140	2.0	17.0	7.0	m.q.	70	(0)
(Frusen Glädjé) . .	240	5.0	17.0	17.0	90	65	(0)
(Häagen-Dazs) . .	270	5.0	24.0	17.0	m.q.	50	(0)
(Sealtest)	140	2.0	18.0	6.0	20	50	(0)
Dutch *(Borden Olde Fashioned Recipe)*	130	2.0	16.0	6.0	m.q.	65	(0)
swirl *(Borden)* . . .	130	2.0	18.0	6.0	m.q.	65	(0)
triple *(Sealtest)* . .	140	2.0	17.0	7.0	m.q.	50	(0)
chocolate chip:							
(Dreyer's)	150	3.0	16.0	9.0	30	40	(0)
(Sealtest)	150	2.0	17.0	8.0	15	50	(0)
mint *(Breyers)* . . .	170	3.0	17.0	10.0	25	45	(0)
vanilla *(Frusen Glädjé)*	280	6.0	22.0	19.0	85	70	(0)
chocolate chocolate chip:							
(Breyers)	180	3.0	21.0	9.0	20	25	(0)
(Frusen Glädjé) . .	270	6.0	21.0	18.0	80	60	(0)
(Häagen-Dazs) . .	290	5.0	28.0	18.0	m.q.	40	(0)
chocolate, Swiss almond *(Frusen Glädjé)*	270	6.0	18.0	19.0	80	60	m.q.
coffee:							
(Breyers)	140	3.0	15.0	8.0	30	50	(0)
(Frusen Glädjé) . .	260	5.0	23.0	17.0	90	65	(0)
(Häagen-Dazs) . .	260	5.0	25.0	15.0	m.q.	55	(0)
(Sealtest)	140	2.0	16.0	7.0	15	50	(0)
cookies N' cream							
(Breyers)	170	3.0	19.0	9.0	20	60	(0)

Food and Measure	cal.	prot. (gms)	carbo. (gms)	fat (gms)	chol. (mgs)	sod. (mgs)	fiber (gms)
fudge, marble (Dreyer's)	150	3.0	18.0	8.0	28	50	0
heavenly hash (Sealtest)	150	2.0	19.0	7.0	15	50	(0)
macadamia nut (Häagen-Dazs) . .	330	5.0	24.0	24.0	m.q.	80	m.q.
maple walnut (Sealtest)	150	3.0	16.0	9.0	20	50	m.q.
mocha chip (Frusen Glädjé)	280	5.0	26.0	18.0	85	55	(0)
peach (Breyers) . . .	140	2.0	19.0	6.0	15	35	(0)
praline and cream (Frusen Glädjé) . .	280	5.0	25.0	18.0	75	115	(0)
rocky road (Dreyer's)	170	3.0	18.0	10.0	30	30	(0)
rum raisin (Häagen-Dazs)	250	4.0	21.0	17.0	m.q.	45	(0)
strawberry:							
(Borden)	130	2.0	18.0	6.0	m.q.	55	(0)
(Breyers)	130	2.0	17.0	6.0	20	40	(0)
(Frusen Glädjé) . .	230	4.0	20.0	15.0	75	60	(0)
(Häagen-Dazs) . .	250	4.0	23.0	15.0	m.q.	40	(0)
(Sealtest)	130	2.0	18.0	5.0	15	40	(0)
vanilla:							
(Borden Olde Fashioned Recipe) . .	130	2.0	15.0	7.0	m.q.	55	0
(Breyers Natural)	150	3.0	15.0	8.0	30	50	0
(Darigold)	130	2.0	15.0	7.0	m.q.	50	0
(Dreyer's)	160	2.0	14.0	10.0	40	30	0
(Eagle Homestyle)	150	3.0	16.0	9.0	m.q.	55	0
(Frusen Glädjé) . .	230	5.0	16.0	17.0	90	70	0
(Häagen-Dazs) . .	260	5.0	23.0	17.0	m.q.	55	0
(Sealtest)	140	2.0	16.0	7.0	20	50	0
French (Sealtest)	140	2.0	16.0	7.0	35	50	0
French, soft-serve	189	3.5	19.1	11.3	77	77	0
nuggets, dark chocolate coated (Carnation Bon Bons), 5 pieces	170	2.0	15.0	11.0	14	50	(0)

Food and Measure	cal.	prot. (gms)	carbo. (gms)	fat (gms)	chol. (mgs)	sod. (mgs)	fiber (gms)
Ice cream, vanilla *(cont.)*							
nuggets, milk chocolate coated *(Carnation Bon Bons),* 5 pieces	165	2.0	14.0	11.0	16	50	(0)
honey *(Häagen-Dazs)*	250	5.0	22.0	16.0	m.q.	55	0
vanilla fudge:							
(Sealtest)	140	3.0	19.0	7.0	15	55	(0)
twirl *(Breyers)* . . .	160	3.0	19.0	8.0	20	55	(0)
vanilla Swiss almond:							
(Frusen Glädjé) . .	270	6.0	18.0	19.0	85	65	m.q.
(Häagen-Dazs) . .	290	5.0	24.0	19.0	m.q.	55	m.q.
vanilla toffee chunk *(Frusen Glädjé)* . .	270	5.0	22.0	17.0	85	160	0
vanilla-chocolate-strawberry:							
(Breyers)	150	3.0	17.0	8.0	25	40	(0)
(Sealtest)	130	2.0	18.0	6.0	20	50	(0)
(Sealtest Cubic Scoops)	140	2.0	18.0	6.0	20	50	(0)
vanilla-orange *(Sealtest Cubic Scoops)*	130	2.0	22.0	4.0	15	40	(0)
vanilla-raspberry:							
(Sealtest Cubic Scoops)	130	2.0	22.0	4.0	15	40	(0)
swirl *(Frusen Glädjé)*	230	4.0	22.0	13.0	75	60	(0)
Ice cream bar, 1 bar:							
(Good Humor Fat Frog)	154	1.8	16.0	9.2	m.q.	36	n.a.
(Good Humor Halo Bar)	230	3.7	22.8	13.7	m.q.	64	n.a.
(Heath)	170	3.0	16.0	13.0	m.q.	155	n.a.
(Klondike)	280	4.0	23.0	19.0	m.q.	65	n.a.
(Klondike Krispy) . .	290	4.0	26.0	19.0	m.q.	70	n.a.
(Klondike Lite)	140	3.0	10.0	10.0	10	45	n.a.
assorted *(Good Humor Whammy)* . .	95	.8	6.6	7.2	m.q.	17	n.a.

Food and Measure	cal.	prot. (gms)	carbo. (gms)	fat (gms)	chol. (mgs)	sod. (mgs)	fiber (gms)
almond, toasted *(Good Humor)* . . .	212	1.8	24.3	11.8	m.q.	34	m.q.
chip candy crunch *(Good Humor)* . . .	255	2.2	21.2	17.9	m.q.	40	n.a.
chocolate:							
(Klondike)	270	4.0	23.0	19.0	m.q.	60	n.a.
dark chocolate coating *(Häagen-Dazs)*	390	5.0	32.0	27.0	m.q.	60	0
fudge cake *(Good Humor)*	214	1.7	18.1	15.0	m.q.	50	n.a.
fudge sundae *(Bakers Fudgetastic)*	220	3.0	23.0	15.0	20	45	n.a.
fudge sundae, crunchy *(Bakers Fudgetastic)* . . .	230	3.0	24.0	14.0	20	40	n.a.
milk, w/almonds, milk chocolate coated *(Nestlé Premium)*	350	6.0	28.0	23.0	5	45	m.q.
milk chocolate coating *(Nestlé Quik)*	210	3.0	19.0	14.0	m.q.	40	n.a.
chocolate eclair *(Good Humor)*	188	2.1	22.6	9.9	m.q.	54	n.a.
fudge *(Good Humor)*	127	3.7	26.5	.6	n.a.	91	n.a.
strawberry finger *(Good Humor)*	49	0	12.2	.1	n.a.	0	n.a.
strawberry short-cake *(Good Humor)*	176	1.7	23.8	8.2	m.q.	88	n.a.
vanilla, chocolate coated:							
(Good Humor) . . .	198	1.9	16.8	13.7	m.q.	44	n.a.
caramel peanut center *(Oh Henry!)*	320	1.0	34.0	20.0	m.q.	75	n.a.
dark *(Häagen-Dazs)*	390	5.0	32.0	27.0	m.q.	65	n.a.

Food and Measure	cal.	prot. (gms)	carbo. (gms)	fat (gms)	chol. (mgs)	sod. (mgs)	fiber (gms)
Ice cream bar, vanilla, chocolate coated *(cont.)*							
milk *(Häagen-Dazs)*	360	4.0	26.0	27.0	m.q.	55	n.a.
milk, and almonds *(Häagen-Dazs)*	370	5.0	27.0	27.0	m.q.	55	m.q.
milk, and crisps *(Nestlé Crunch)*	180	2.0	15.0	13.0	m.q.	m.q.	n.a.
white chocolate *(Nestlé Alpine)*	350	6.0	25.0	25.0	5	50	n.a.
Ice cream cone or cup, 1 piece:							
plain:							
(Little Debbie Ice Cream Cup*)* . . .	15	.4	3.0	.1	<1	15	m.q.
waffle *(Baskin-Robbins)*	140	3.0	28.0	2.0	0	5	m.q.
filled:							
(Good Humor King Cone*)*	290	4.5	40.9	12.0	m.q.	119	m.q.
boysenberry *(Good Humor* King Cone*)*	340	3.9	51.6	13.1	m.q.	151	m.q.
vanilla-chocolate cup *(Good Humor* Combo*)*	201	3.8	25.6	9.2	m.q.	80	m.q.
Ice cream sandwich, 1 piece:							
chocolate chip cookie, chocolate *(Good Humor),* 4 fl. oz. . . .	246	2.9	35.1	10.5	m.q.	181	m.q.
vanilla *(Good Humor),* 3 fl. oz.	191	3.7	31.1	5.7	m.q.	155	m.q.
vanilla *(Klondike),* 5 fl. oz.	230	5.0	33.0	9.0	m.q.	220	m.q.
Ice cream and sorbet, see "Sorbet"							

Food and Measure	cal.	prot. (gms)	carbo. (gms)	fat (gms)	chol. (mgs)	sod. (mgs)	fiber (gms)
"Ice cream," substitute and imitation, 1/2 cup, except as noted:							
all flavors (Lite-Lite Tofutti)	90	2.0	20.0	<1.0	0	80	n.a.
cappuccino (Tofutti Love Drops)	230	3.0	26.0	12.0	0	120	n.a.
cherry, black (Sealtest Free)	90	2.0	23.0	0	0	50	(0)
chocolate:							
(Sealtest Free) . .	100	3.0	23.0	0	0	55	(0)
(Simple Pleasures), 4 oz.	140	9.0	25.0	<1.0	15	n.a.	0
(Tofutti Love Drops)	230	3.0	26.0	13.0	0	100	n.a.
soft-serve (Lite-Lite Tofutti)	90	2.0	20.0	<1.0	0	80	n.a.
supreme (Tofutti)	210	3.0	20.0	13.0	0	130	n.a.
chocolate chip (Low, Lite'n Luscious) . .	100	3.0	19.0	2.0	4	80	n.a.
coffee (Simple Pleasures), 4 oz.	120	8.0	22.0	<1.0	15	n.a.	0
Jamoca Swiss almond (Low, Lite'n Luscious)	90	3.0	19.0	2.0	4	100	n.a.
peach:							
(Sealtest Free) . .	90	2.0	22.0	0	0	40	(0)
(Simple Pleasures), 4 oz.	135	9.0	24.0	<1.0	5	n.a.	0
pineapple coconut (Low, Lite'n Luscious)	90	3.0	19.0	1.0	3	70	n.a.
rum raisin (Simple Pleasures), 4 oz.	130	7.0	25.0	<1.0	10	n.a.	0
strawberry:							
(Low, Lite'n Luscious)	80	3.0	17.0	1.0	3	70	n.a.
(Sealtest Free) . .	90	2.0	21.0	0	0	45	(0)

Food and Measure	cal.	prot. (gms)	carbo. (gms)	fat (gms)	chol. (mgs)	sod. (mgs)	fiber (gms)
"Ice cream," substitute and imitation, strawberry *(cont.)*							
(Simple Pleasures),							
4 oz.	120	8.0	22.0	<1.0	11	55	0
vanilla:							
(Sealtest Free) . .	100	2.0	23.0	0	0	50	n.a.
(Tofutti)	200	2.0	21.0	11.0	0	90	n.a.
(Tofutti Love Drops)	220	3.0	26.0	12.0	0	100	n.a.
chocolate dipped							
(Tofutti O's),							
1 piece	40	1.0	4.0	2.0	0	20	n.a.
vanilla almond bark							
(Tofutti)	230	3.0	23.0	14.0	0	95	n.a.
vanilla-fudge *(Sealtest*							
Free)	100	3.0	24.0	0	0	65	n.a.
vanilla-strawberry							
(Sealtest Free) . .	100	2.0	23.0	0	0	45	n.a.
vanilla-chocolate-							
strawberry *(Sealtest*							
Free)	90	3.0	22.0	0	0	45	n.a.
wildberry *(Tofutti)* . .	210	2.0	22.0	12.0	0	100	n.a.
Ice milk, 1/2 cup:							
caramel nut *(Light N'*							
Lively)	120	3.0	18.0	4.0	10	100	m.q.
chocolate:							
(Borden)	100	3.0	18.0	2.0	n.a.	80	0
(Breyers Light) . .	120	3.0	18.0	4.0	15	55	(0)
(Darigold Lite) . . .	110	3.0	19.0	3.0	n.a.	65	0
fudge *(Breyers*							
Light)	130	4.0	21.0	4.0	10	60	(0)
chocolate chip *(Light*							
N' Lively)	120	3.0	18.0	4.0	10	50	0
coffee *(Light N' Lively)*	100	3.0	17.0	3.0	10	55	0
cookies n' cream							
(Light N' Lively) . .	120	3.0	19.0	3.0	10	80	0
heavenly hash:							
(Breyers Light) . .	150	3.0	21.0	5.0	10	55	(0)
(Light N' Lively) . .	120	3.0	20.0	3.0	10	45	0

Food and Measure	cal.	prot. (gms)	carbo. (gms)	fat (gms)	chol. (mgs)	sod. (mgs)	fiber (gms)
praline almond							
(*Breyers* Light) . .	130	3.0	19.0	5.0	10	70	m.q.
strawberry:							
(*Borden*)	90	2.0	17.0	2.0	n.a.	65	0
(*Breyers* Light) . .	110	3.0	18.0	3.0	15	50	(0)
toffee fudge swirl							
(*Breyers* Light) . .	150	3.0	22.0	5.0	10	90	(0)
vanilla:							
(*Borden*)	90	2.0	17.0	2.0	n.a.	65	0
(*Breyers* Light) . .	120	3.0	18.0	4.0	10	60	0
(*Darigold*)	110	2.0	18.0	3.0	n.a.	66	0
(*Light N' Lively*) . .	100	3.0	17.0	3.0	10	55	0
vanilla chocolate al-mond (*Light N' Lively*)	120	4.0	17.0	4.0	10	55	0
vanilla-chocolate-strawberry (*Breyers* Light)	120	3.0	18.0	4.0	15	55	(0)
vanilla-chocolate-strawberry (*Light N' Lively*)	110	3.0	17.0	3.0	10	45	0
vanilla fudge swirl (*Light N' Lively*) . .	110	3.0	19.0	3.0	10	55	0
vanilla raspberry:							
(*Breyers* Light) . .	130	3.0	23.0	3.0	15	50	(0)
swirl (*Light N' Lively*)	110	3.0	19.0	3.0	10	50	0
icing, cake, see "Frosting"							
Iowa brand loaf:							
(*Hormel* Perma-Fresh), 2 slices	90	10.0	0	6.0	m.q.	607	0
Italian sausage:							
hot (*Hillshire Farm* Links), 2 oz.	180	7.0	1.0	17.0	m.q.	m.q.	0
mild (*Hillshire Farm* Links), 2 oz.	190	7.0	1.0	17.0	m.q.	m.q.	0

Food and Measure	cal.	prot. (gms)	carbo. (gms)	fat (gms)	chol. (mgs)	sod. (mgs)	fiber (gms)
Italian sausage *(cont.)*							
pork, cooked:							
1 oz.	92	5.7	.4	7.3	22	261	0
1 link (4 oz. raw)	268	16.6	1.2	21.3	65	765	0
smoked:							
(Hillshire Farm							
Flavorseal), 2 oz.	200	7.0	1.0	18.0	m.q.	500	0
cooked *(Oscar*							
Mayer), 2.7-oz.							
link	264	10.7	2.0	23.7	39	712	0
Italian seasoning:							
(Tone's), 1 tsp. . . .	3	.1	.7	.1	0	<1	.2 d

J

Food and Measure	cal.	prot. (gms)	carbo. (gms)	fat (gms)	chol. (mgs)	sod. (mgs)	fiber (gms)
Jack-in-the-Box,							
1 serving:							
breakfast:							
Breakfast Jack . .	307	18.0	30.0	13.0	203	871	m.q.
crescent, Canadian	452	19.0	25.0	31.0	226	851	m.q.
crescent, sausage	584	22.0	28.0	43.0	187	1012	m.q.
crescent, supreme	547	20.0	27.0	40.0	178	1053	m.q.
hash browns . . .	116	2.0	11.0	7.0	3	211	m.q.
pancake platter . .	612	15.0	87.0	22.0	99	888	m.q.
scrambled egg plat-							
ter	662	24.0	52.0	40.0	354	1188	m.q.
sandwiches:							
bacon cheeseburger	705	35.0	48.0	39.0	85	1127	m.q.
beef fajita pita . . .	333	24.0	27.0	14.0	45	635	m.q.
cheeseburger . . .	315	15.0	33.0	14.0	41	746	m.q.
cheeseburger,							
double	467	21.0	33.0	27.0	72	842	m.q.
cheeseburger, ulti-							
mate	942	47.0	33.0	69.0	127	1176	m.q.
chicken fajita pita	292	24.0	29.0	8.0	34	703	m.q.
chicken fillet, grilled	408	31.0	33.0	17.0	64	1130	m.q.
chicken supreme	575	27.0	34.0	36.0	62	1525	m.q.
fish supreme . . .	554	20.0	47.0	32.0	66	1047	m.q.
hamburger	267	13.0	28.0	11.0	26	556	m.q.
Jumbo Jack	584	26.0	42.0	34.0	73	733	m.q.
Jumbo Jack, w/							
cheese	677	32.0	46.0	40.0	102	1090	m.q.
Swiss and bacon							
burger	678	31.0	34.0	47.0	92	1458	m.q.
Mexican food:							
guacamole, 1 oz.	55	.9	1.8	5.0	0	130	m.q.
salsa, 1 oz.	8	.2	2.0	<1.0	0	129	m.q.

Food and Measure	cal.	prot. (gms)	carbo. (gms)	fat (gms)	chol. (mgs)	sod. (mgs)	fiber (gms)
Jack-in-the-Box, Mexican food (cont.)							
taco	191	8.0	16.0	11.0	21	406	m.q.
taco, super	288	12.0	21.0	17.0	37	765	m.q.
salad:							
chef	295	32.0	3.0	18.0	107	812	m.q.
Mexican chicken	442	28.0	30.0	23.0	89	1500	m.q.
side	51	7.0	<1.0	3.0	<1	84	m.q.
taco	503	34.0	28.0	31.0	92	1600	m.q.
finger foods:							
chicken strips,							
4 pieces	349	29.0	28.0	14.0	68	748	m.q.
chicken strips,							
6 pieces	523	43.0	42.0	20.0	103	1122	m.q.
egg rolls, 3 pieces	405	15.0	42.0	19.0	30	903	m.q.
egg rolls, 5 pieces	675	26.0	70.0	32.0	50	1505	m.q.
shrimp, 10 pieces	270	10.0	22.0	16.0	84	669	m.q.
shrimp, 15 pieces	404	15.0	34.0	24.0	126	1003	m.q.
taquitos, 5 pieces	363	16.0	40.0	16.0	37	467	m.q.
taquitos, 7 pieces	508	22.0	56.0	22.0	52	654	m.q.
side dishes:							
fries, small	221	2.0	27.0	12.0	8	164	m.q.
fries, regular	353	3.0	43.0	19.0	13	262	m.q.
onion rings	382	5.0	39.0	23.0	27	407	m.q.
sauces:							
BBQ, 1 oz.	44	.5	10.6	<1.0	0	300	n.a.
mayo-mustard,							
.7 oz.	124	.5	2.0	13.0	10	247	n.a.
mayo-onion, .7 oz.	143	.3	1.0	15.0	20	140	n.a.
seafood cocktail,							
1 oz.	32	<1.0	6.8	<1.0	0	206	n.a.
sweet and sour,							
1 oz.	40	<1.0	11.0	<1.0	<1	160	n.a.
dressings, 2.5 oz.:							
bleu cheese	262	<1.0	14.0	22.0	18	918	n.a.
buttermilk	362	<1.0	8.0	36.0	21	694	n.a.
French, reduced							
calorie	176	<1.0	26.0	8.0	0	600	n.a.
Thousand Island	312	<1.0	12.0	30.0	23	700	n.a.

Food and Measure	cal.	prot. (gms)	carbo. (gms)	fat (gms)	chol. (mgs)	sod. (mgs)	fiber (gms)
desserts:							
apple turnover . .	410	4.0	45.0	24.0	15	350	m.q.
cheesecake	309	8.0	29.0	17.5	63	208	n.a.
shakes:							
chocolate	330	11.0	55.0	7.0	25	270	(0)
strawberry	320	10.0	55.0	7.0	25	240	(0)
vanilla	320	10.0	57.0	6.0	25	230	0
Jackfruit:							
trimmed, 1 oz.	27	.4	6.8	.1	0	1	.3 c
Jalapeño dip:							
(Kraft), 2 tbsp.	50	1.0	3.0	4.0	0	160	n.a.
(Kraft Premium),							
2 tbsp.	50	1.0	2.0	4.0	10	160	n.a.
bean *(Wise)*, 2 tbsp.	25	1.0	5.0	0	0	100	n.a.
bean *(Hain)*, 4 tbsp.	70	4.0	10.0	1.0	5	250	n.a.
nacho *(Price's)*, 1 oz.	80	2.6	2.0	7.1	n.a.	m.q.	n.a.
Jalapeño loaf:							
(Kahn's), 1 slice . . .	70	3.0	2.0	6.0	m.q.	340	n.a.
(Oscar Mayer), 1 oz.	72	3.1	2.4	5.5	10	464	n.a.
Jalapeño pepper,							
see "Pepper,							
jalapeño"							
Jam and preserves,							
2 tsp., except as							
noted:							
all flavors:							
(Bama)	30	0	8.0	0	0	5	m.q.
(Kraft), 1 tsp. . . .	17	0	4.0	0	0	0	m.q.
(Polaner)	35	0	9.0	0	0	n.a.	m.q.
(Smucker's), 1 tsp.	18	0	4.0	0	0	0	m.q.
grape, raspberry-apple							
or strawberry							
(Welch's)	35	0	9.0	0	0	5	0
strawberry *(Smucker's*							
Imitation), 1 tsp. . .	2	0	1.0	0	0	2	n.a.
Java plum:							
3 medium, .4 oz. . .	5	.1	1.4	<.1	0	1	<.1 c
seeded, 1/2 cup . . .	41	.5	10.5	.2	0	9	.2 c

Food and Measure	cal.	prot. (gms)	carbo. (gms)	fat (gms)	chol. (mgs)	sod. (mgs)	fiber (gms)
Jelly:							
all flavors:							
(Bama), 2 tsp.	30	0	8.0	0	0	5	0
(Kraft), 1 tsp.	17	0	4.0	0	0	0	0
(Polaner), 2 tsp. . . .	35	0	9.0	0	0	n.a.	0
(Smucker's), 1 tsp. . .	18	0	4.0	0	0	0	0
(Welch's), 2 tsp. . . .	35	0	9.0	0	0	5	0
grape (Smucker's Imitation), 1 tsp.	2	0	1.0	0	0	2	0
green pepper (Great Impressions), 1 tbsp.	50	0	12.6	0	0	<1	0
jalapeño (Great Impressions), 1 tbsp.	58	0	14.6	0	0	51	0
red pepper (Great Impressions), 1 tbsp.	50	0	12.6	0	0	9	0
strawberry (Finast), 2 tsp.	35	0	9.0	0	0	2	0
Jelly and peanut butter:							
(Bama), 2 tbsp. . . .	150	3.0	20.0	7.0	0	75	0
Jerky, see "Beef jerky" and "Sausage stick"							
Jerusalem artichoke:							
untrimmed, 1 lb.	238	6.3	54.6	<.1	0	n.a.	2.5 c
sliced, 1/2 cup	57	1.5	13.1	<.1	0	n.a.	.6 c
Jicama, see "Yam bean tuber"							
Jujube:							
raw, w/seeds, 1 lb. . .	331	5.1	85.3	.8	0	11	5.9 c
raw, seeded, 1 oz. . .	22	.3	5.7	.1	0	1	.4 c
dried, 1 oz.	81	1.0	20.1	.3	0	3	.9 c
Jute, potherb:							
raw, 1/2 cup	5	.7	.8	<.1	0	1	.2 c
boiled, drained, 1/2 cup	16	1.6	3.1	.1	0	5	.8 c

K

Food and Measure	cal.	prot. (gms)	carbo. (gms)	fat (gms)	chol. (mgs)	sod. (mgs)	fiber (gms)
Kale:							
fresh, 1/2 cup:							
raw, chopped . . .	17	1.1	3.4	.2	0	15	.5 c
boiled, drained,							
chopped	21	1.2	3.7	.3	0	15	.5 c
canned, chopped (Allens), 1/2 cup . . .	25	2.0	3.0	<1.0	0	15	m.q.
frozen, chopped:							
(Frosty Acres),							
3.3 oz.	25	3.0	5.0	0	0	15	1.0 c
(Seabrook), 3.3 oz.	25	3.0	5.0	0	0	14	1.0 c
(Southern), 3.5 oz.	30	2.6	4.8	.5	0	30	m.q.
Kale, Scotch:							
raw, chopped, 1/2 cup	14	1.0	2.8	.2	0	24	.4 c
boiled, drained,							
chopped, 1/2 cup	18	1.2	3.7	.3	0	29	.6 c
Kasha, see "Buckwheat groats"							
Kelp, see "Seaweed"							
Kentucky Fried Chicken:							
chicken, original recipe:							
breast, center,							
4.1 oz.	283	27.5	8.8	15.3	93	672	m.q.
breast, side, 3.2 oz.	267	18.8	10.8	16.5	77	735	m.q.
drumstick, 2 oz. . .	146	13.1	4.2	8.5	67	275	m.q.
thigh, 3.7 oz. . . .	294	17.9	11.1	19.7	123	619	m.q.
wing, 1.9 oz. . . .	178	12.2	6.0	11.7	64	372	m.q.

Food and Measure	cal.	prot. (gms)	carbo. (gms)	fat (gms)	chol. (mgs)	sod. (mgs)	fiber (gms)
Kentucky Fried Chicken (cont.)							
chicken, extra crispy:							
breast, center,							
4.2 oz.	353	26.9	14.4	20.9	93	842	m.q.
breast, side, 3.5 oz.	354	17.7	17.3	23.7	66	797	m.q.
drumstick, 2.1 oz.	173	12.7	5.9	10.9	65	346	m.q.
thigh, 4 oz.	371	19.6	13.8	26.3	121	766	m.q.
wing, 2 oz.	218	11.5	7.8	15.6	63	437	m.q.
chicken, Kentucky nuggets, .6 oz.							
piece	46	2.8	2.2	2.9	12	140	m.q.
Chicken Littles sandwich, 1.7 oz. . . .	169	5.7	13.8	10.1	18	331	m.q.
Kentucky nuggets sauces:							
barbeque, 1 oz. . .	35	.3	7.1	.6	<1	450	n.a.
honey, .5 oz. . . .	49	0	12.1	<.1	<1	<15	n.a.
mustard, 1 oz. . . .	36	.9	6.0	.9	<1	346	n.a.
sweet and sour, 1 oz.	58	.1	13.0	.6	<1	148	n.a.
side dishes:							
buttermilk biscuit	232	4.2	27.1	11.9	1	539	m.q.
coleslaw	119	1.5	13.3	6.6	5	197	m.q.
corn-on-the-cob . .	176	5.1	31.9	3.1	<1	<21	m.q.
fries, regular	244	3.2	31.1	11.9	2	139	m.q.
mashed potatoes w/gravy, 3.5 oz.	71	2.4	11.9	1.6	<1	342	m.q.
Ketchup, see "Catsup"							
Kidney bean, canned, 1/2 cup, except as noted:							
red:							
(Hunt's), 4 oz.	120	7.0	21.0	0	0	400	m.q.
(Progresso), 8 oz.	190	12.0	34.0	1.0	0	1080	m.q.
dark *(Allens)* . . .	105	5.0	20.0	<1.0	0	290	m.q.
dark *(S&W Lite 50% Less Salt)*	120	7.0	22.0	1.0	0	355	m.q.

Food and Measure	cal.	prot. (gms)	carbo. (gms)	fat (gms)	chol. (mgs)	sod. (mgs)	fiber (gms)
dark (S&W Premium)	120	6.0	22.0	1.0	0	596	m.q.
dark (Van Camp's), 1 cup	182	11.7	32.6	.5	0	732	2.3 c
dark or light (Joan of Arc/Green Giant)	90	7.0	20.0	0	0	250	5.9 d
light (Allens)	105	5.0	2.0	<1.0	0	290	m.q.
light (Van Camp's), 1 cup	184	11.5	33.4	.5	0	688	2.2 c
New Orleans (Van Camp's), 1 cup	178	12.1	31.0	.6	n.a.	793	2.4 c
white (Progresso Cannellini), 8 oz. . . .	180	12.0	30.0	1.0	0	717	m.q.
baked (B&M), 7/8 cup	290	15.0	42.0	7.0	n.a.	640	11.0 d
Kidney bean, sprouted:							
raw, 1/2 cup	27	3.9	3.8	.5	0	m.q.	m.q.
boiled, drained, 4 oz.	37	5.5	5.4	.7	0	m.q.	m.q.
Kidneys, braised or simmered:							
beef, 4 oz.	163	28.9	1.1	3.9	439	152	0
lamb, 4 oz.	155	26.8	1.1	4.1	641	171	0
pork, 4 oz.	171	28.8	0	5.3	544	91	0
pork, chopped, 1 cup	211	35.6	0	6.6	673	111	0
veal, 4 oz.	185	29.8	0	6.4	897	125	0
Kielbasa(see also "Polish sausage"), 2 oz., except as noted:							
(Hillshire Farm Polska Flavorseal)	190	8.0	2.0	17.0	m.q.	540	0
(Hillshire Farm Polska Flavorseal Lite) . .	160	8.0	2.0	13.0	m.q.	m.q.	0
(Hillshire Farm Polska Links)	190	7.0	2.0	17.0	m.q.	530	0
(Hormel Kolbase), 3 oz.	220	12.0	1.0	19.0	m.q.	904	0

Food and Measure	cal.	prot. (gms)	carbo. (gms)	fat (gms)	chol. (mgs)	sod. (mgs)	fiber (gms)
Kielbasa (cont.)							
(Eckrich Lean Supreme Polska),							
1 oz.	72	4.0	1.0	6.0	m.q.	224	0
(Oscar Mayer International Sausages),							
1 oz.	83	3.5	.5	7.5	14	261	0
beef (Hillshire Farm Polska Flavorseal)	190	7.0	1.0	17.0	m.q.	550	0
mild (Hillshire Farm Polska Flavorseal)	190	7.0	2.0	17.0	m.q.	530	0
skinless (Eckrich Polska), 1 link	180	7.0	2.0	16.0	m.q.	420	0
skinless (Hormel), 1/2 link	180	12.0	1.0	14.0	m.q.	826	0
Kiwifruit:							
1 large, 3.7 oz. . . .	55	.9	13.5	.4	0	4	3.1 d
1 medium, 3.1 oz. . .	46	.8	11.3	.3	0	4	2.6 d
Knockwurst:							
(Hillshire Farm), 2 oz.	180	7.0	1.0	16.0	m.q.	460	0
beef (Hebrew National), 1 link . . .	263	10.2	<1.0	25.0	26	877	0
Kohlrabi:							
raw, sliced, 1/2 cup	19	1.2	4.3	.1	0	14	.8 d
boiled, drained, sliced,							
1/2 cup	24	1.5	5.5	.1	0	17	.9 c
Kumquat:							
1 medium, .7 oz. . .	12	.2	3.1	<.1	0	1	.7 c
seeded, 1 oz.	18	.3	4.7	<.1	0	2	1.0 c

L

Food and Measure	cal.	prot. (gms)	carbo. (gms)	fat (gms)	chol. (mgs)	sod. (mgs)	fiber (gms)
Lamb, choice, meat only, 4 oz., except as noted:							
cubed, leg/shoulder:							
braised or stewed	253	38.2	0	10.0	122	79	0
broiled	211	31.8	0	8.3	102	86	0
foreshank, braised:							
lean w/fat	276	32.2	0	15.3	120	82	0
lean w/fat, diced, 1 cup, 4.9 oz. . . .	340	39.7	0	18.8	148	101	0
lean only	212	35.2	0	6.8	118	84	0
lean only, diced, 1 cup, 4.9 oz. . . .	262	43.4	0	8.4	146	104	0
ground:							
raw, 1 oz.	80	4.7	0	6.7	21	17	0
broiled	321	28.1	0	22.3	110	92	0
broiled, 1 cup . . .	328	28.7	0	23.1	113	94	0
leg, whole, roasted:							
lean w/fat	293	29.0	0	18.7	105	75	0
lean w/fat, 1 slice, 3″ diam. × 1/4″	73	7.2	0	4.7	26	19	0
lean only	217	32.1	0	8.8	101	77	0
lean only, 3″ slice	54	8.0	0	2.2	25	19	0
leg, shank, roasted:							
lean w/fat	255	29.9	0	14.1	102	74	0
lean w/fat, 1 slice, 3″ diam. × 1/4″	64	7.5	0	3.5	26	18	0
lean only	204	31.9	0	7.6	99	75	0
lean only, 3″ slice	51	8.0	0	1.9	25	19	0

Food and Measure	cal.	prot. (gms)	carbo. (gms)	fat (gms)	chol. (mgs)	sod. (mgs)	fiber (gms)
Lamb *(cont.)*							
leg, sirloin, roasted:							
lean w/fat	331	27.9	0	23.4	110	77	0
lean w/fat, 1 slice,							
3″ diam. × 1/4″	83	7.0	0	5.9	27	19	0
lean only	231	32.1	0	10.4	104	81	0
lean only, 3″ slice	58	8.0	0	2.6	26	20	0
loin chop, broiled:							
lean w/fat, 2.25 oz.							
(4.2 oz. raw w/							
bone)	201	16.1	0	14.7	64	49	0
lean w/fat	358	28.5	0	26.2	113	87	0
lean only, 1.6 oz.							
(4.2 oz. raw w/							
bone and fat) . .	100	13.9	0	4.5	44	39	0
lean only	245	34.0	0	11.0	108	95	0
loin, roasted:							
lean w/fat	350	25.6	0	26.8	108	73	0
lean only	229	30.2	0	11.1	99	75	0
rib:							
broiled, lean w/fat	409	25.1	0	33.6	112	86	0
broiled, lean only	266	31.5	0	14.7	103	96	0
roasted, lean w/fat	407	24.0	0	33.8	110	83	0
roasted, lean only	263	29.7	0	15.1	100	92	0
shoulder, whole:							
braised, lean w/fat	390	32.5	0	27.8	132	85	0
braised, lean only	321	37.2	0	18.0	133	90	0
roasted, lean w/fat	313	25.5	0	22.6	104	75	0
roasted, lean only	231	28.3	0	12.2	99	77	0
Lamb, New Zealand,							
frozen, meat only,							
4 oz., except as							
noted:							
foreshank, braised:							
lean w/fat	293	30.6	0	18.0	116	53	0
lean only	211	34.9	0	6.8	115	56	0
leg, whole, roasted:							
lean w/fat	279	28.1	0	17.6	115	49	0

Food and Measure	cal.	prot. (gms)	carbo. (gms)	fat (gms)	chol. (mgs)	sod. (mgs)	fiber (gms)
lean only	205	31.4	0	7.9	113	51	0
loin chop, broiled:							
lean w/fat, 1.5 oz.							
(3 oz. raw w/							
bone)	135	10.0	0	10.2	48	21	0
lean w/fat	357	26.6	0	27.1	127	56	0
lean only, 1.1 oz.							
(3 oz. raw w/							
bone and fat) . .	60	8.8	0	2.5	34	16	0
lean only	226	33.2	0	9.3	129	62	0
rib, roasted:							
lean w/fat	386	21.5	0	32.6	113	49	0
lean only	222	27.7	0	11.5	107	54	0
shoulder, braised:							
lean w/fat	398	32.5	0	28.8	139	59	0
lean only	323	38.6	0	17.6	144	64	0
Lambsquarters:							
raw, trimmed, 1 lb.	195	19.1	33.1	3.6	0	m.q.	9.5 c
boiled, drained,							
chopped, 1/2 cup	29	2.9	4.5	.6	0	m.q.	1.6 c
Lard, pork:							
1 tbsp.	115	0	0	12.8	12	tr.	0
Lasagna dinner, fro-zen:							
(Banquet Extra Help-ing), 16.5 oz. . . .	645	24.0	88.0	23.0	38	1582	m.q.
Lasagna entree, fro-zen:							
(Celentano), 8 oz. . .	370	19.0	32.0	19.0	m.q.	700	m.q.
(Green Giant Entrees), 12 oz.	490	33.0	44.0	20.0	m.q.	1660	m.q.
(Stouffer's), 101/2-oz. pkg.	360	28.0	33.0	13.0	m.q.	1020	m.q.
(Tyson Gourmet Se-lection), 11.5 oz.	380	20.0	47.0	14.0	m.q.	840	m.q.
cheese:							
(Dining Lite), 9 oz.	260	14.0	36.0	6.0	30	800	m.q.

Food and Measure	cal.	prot. (gms)	carbo. (gms)	fat (gms)	chol. (mgs)	sod. (mgs)	fiber (gms)
Lasagna entree, frozen, cheese (cont.)							
three cheese (The Budget Gourmet), 10 oz.	400	22.0	38.0	17.0	65	760	m.q.
fiesta (Stouffer's), 10¼ oz.	430	24.0	35.0	22.0	m.q.	960	m.q.
meat (Buitoni Single Serving), 9 oz. . .	580	23.0	57.0	19.0	110	820	m.q.
w/meat sauce:							
(Banquet Family Entrees), 7 oz. . . .	270	15.0	30.0	10.0	m.q.	m.q.	m.q.
(The Budget Gourmet Slim Selects), 10 oz.	290	18.0	32.0	10.0	25	890	m.q.
(Dining Lite), 9 oz.	240	13.0	36.0	5.0	25	800	m.q.
(Freezer Queen Deluxe Family Suppers), 7 oz.	200	8.0	28.0	6.0	m.q.	730	m.q.
(Healthy Choice), 9 oz.	260	18.0	37.0	5.0	20	420	m.q.
(Swanson Homestyle), 10½ oz.	400	25.0	39.0	16.0	m.q.	870	m.q.
primavera (Celentano), 11 oz.	330	18.0	34.0	14.0	n.a.	470	m.q.
in sauce (Buitoni Family Style), 7.3 oz.	370	13.0	30.0	13.0	55	940	m.q.
sausage, Italian (The Budget Gourmet), 10 oz.	420	20.0	38.0	20.0	80	950	m.q.
seafood (Mrs. Paul's Light), 9½ oz. . .	290	14.0	39.0	8.0	57	750	m.q.
w/tofu (Legume Classic), 8 oz.	210	15.0	20.0	8.0	0	410	8.2 d
tuna, w/spinach noodles and vegetables (Lean Cuisine), 9¾ oz.	270	17.0	29.0	10.0	35	890	m.q.

Food and Measure	cal.	prot. (gms)	carbo. (gms)	fat (gms)	chol. (mgs)	sod. (mgs)	fiber (gms)
vegetable:							
(Stouffer's),							
10½ oz.	420	23.0	29.0	24.0	n.a.	970	m.q.
garden *(Le Menu Light Style),*							
10½ oz.	260	11.0	35.0	8.0	25	500	m.q.
w/tofu *(Legume),*							
12 oz.	240	14.0	26.0	8.0	0	520	5.8 d
zucchini *(Lean Cuisine),* 11 oz.	260	20.0	28.0	7.0	25	950	m.q.
Lasagna entree, packaged:							
Italian *(Hormel Top Shelf),* 1 serving	360	24.0	28.0	17.0	40	1350	m.q.
vegetable *(Hormel Top Shelf),*							
10.6 oz.	275	18.0	34.0	8.0	35	1024	m.q.
Leek:							
fresh:							
raw, 9.9-oz. leek	76	1.9	17.6	.4	0	25	1.5 d
raw, trimmed, chopped, ½ cup	32	.8	7.4	.2	0	10	.6 d
boiled, drained, chopped, ½ cup	16	.4	4.0	.1	0	6	.4 c
freeze-dried, 1 tbsp.	1	<.1	.2	tr.	0	tr.	<.1 c
Lemon:							
w/peel, 2⅛″-diam. lemon, 3.9 oz. . .	22	1.3	11.6	.3	0	3	m.q.
1 wedge, ¼ medium	5	.3	2.9	.1	0	1	m.q.
peeled, 2⅛″-diam. lemon	17	.6	5.4	.2	0	1	.2 c
Lemon butter dill cooking sauce:							
(Golden Dipt), 1 fl. oz.	110	0	5.0	10.0	0	180	m.q.

Food and Measure	cal.	prot. (gms)	carbo. (gms)	fat (gms)	chol. (mgs)	sod. (mgs)	fiber (gms)
Lemon dill seasoning:							
(McCormick/Schilling Bag'n Season), 1 pkg.	161	3.0	15.0	11.0	0	2035	m.q.
Lemon drink:							
(Crowley), 8 fl. oz. . .	130	0	32.0	0	0	15	(0)
Lemon extract:							
(Virginia Dare), 1 tsp.	22	0	0	0	0	0	0
Lemon-herb marinade:							
(Golden Dipt), 1 fl. oz.	130	0	2.0	14.0	0	210	n.a.
Lemon juice:							
fresh, 1 tbsp.	4	.1	1.3	0	0	tr.	(0)
canned *(Minute Maid 100% Pure),* 1 tbsp.	4	.1	1.0	.1	0	2	(0)
reconstituted, 1 fl. oz.:							
(ReaLemon)	6	0	2.0	0	0	10	(0)
refrigerated *(ReaLemon 100%)*	6	0	2.0	0	0	5	(0)
frozen *(Sunkist),* 1 fl. oz.	7	.1	2.0	.1	0	<1	(0)
Lemon peel:							
(Tone's), 1 tsp. . . .	0	tr.	.3	0	0	0	0
Lemon pepper seasoning, 1 tsp.:							
(Lawry's)	6	.2	1.2	.1	0	340	.1 c
(McCormick/Schilling Parsley Patch) . .	13	.4	1.0	.6	0	2	m.q.
(McCormick/Schilling Spice Blends) . . .	7	.2	.8	0	0	618	m.q.
Lemon-lime drink, 8 fl. oz.:							
(Veryfine)	120	.1	30.0	0	0	<10	(0)
mix[1] *(Kool-Aid)* . . .	100	0	25.0	0	0	0	0

[1] *Prepared according to package directions.*

Food and Measure	cal.	prot. (gms)	carbo. (gms)	fat (gms)	chol. (mgs)	sod. (mgs)	fiber (gms)
Lemonade:							
canned or bottled:							
(Hi-C), 8.45 fl. oz.	109	.1	27.2	.1	0	73	(0)
(Shasta), 12 fl. oz.	146	0	39.0	0	0	106	(0)
(Sunkist), 8 fl. oz.	141	0	36.0	0	0	0	(0)
(Veryfine), 8 fl. oz.	120	.2	30.0	0	0	<25	(0)
(Wylers), 6 fl. oz.	64	0	16.5	0	0	33	(0)
chilled (Minute Maid), 6 fl. oz.	81	.2	21.3	0	0	23	(0)
frozen[1]							
(Sunkist), 8 fl. oz.	92	.1	24.2	0	0	1	(0)
(Minute Maid), 6 fl. oz.	77	.2	20.1	0	0	23	(0)
mix[2], 8 fl. oz.:							
(Country Time) . .	80	0	20.0	0	0	20	0
(Kool-Aid)	100	0	25.0	0	0	0	0
(Kool-Aid Presweetened)	80	0	20.0	0	0	0	0
(Wyler's Crystals, 4 servings/pkg.)	92	0	19.6	1.5	0	44	0
punch (Country Time)	80	0	20.0	0	0	15	0
Lentil:							
boiled, 1/2 cup	115	8.9	19.9	.4	0	2	4.0 d
Lentil, sprouted:							
raw, 1/2 cup	40	3.4	8.4	.2	0	4	1.2 c
Lentil pilaf mix:							
(Casbah), 1 oz. dry or 1/2 cup cooked . .	100	5.0	20.0	0	0	m.q.	m.q.
Lentil rice loaf, frozen:							
(Harvest Bake), 4 oz.	190	8.0	18.0	9.0	0	620	m.q.
Lettuce:							
bibb or Boston:							
untrimmed, 1 lb. . .	45	4.3	7.8	.7	0	18	3.4 d
1 head, 5″ diam.	21	2.1	3.8	.4	0	8	1.6 d

[1] Diluted according to package directions.
[2] Prepared according to package directions.

Food and Measure	cal.	prot. (gms)	carbo. (gms)	fat (gms)	chol. (mgs)	sod. (mgs)	fiber (gms)
Lettuce, bibb or Boston *(cont.)*							
2 inner leaves . . .	2	.2	.4	<.1	0	1	.5 d
cos or romaine:							
untrimmed, 1 lb. . .	68	6.9	10.1	.9	0	32	7.2 d
1 inner leaf	2	.2	.2	<.1	0	1	.2 d
shredded, 1/2 cup	4	.5	.7	.1	0	2	.5 d
iceberg:							
untrimmed, 1 lb. . .	55	4.3	9.0	.8	0	39	4.3 d
1 head, 6" diam.	70	5.4	11.3	1.0	0	48	5.4 d
1 leaf, .7 oz.	3	.2	.4	<.1	0	2	.2 d
looseleaf:							
untrimmed, 1 lb. . .	52	3.8	10.2	.9	0	26	2.0 c
shredded, 1/2 cup	5	.4	1.0	.1	0	3	.2 c
Lima bean:							
fresh:							
raw, trimmed,							
1/2 cup	88	5.3	15.7	.7	0	6	2.9 d
boiled, drained,							
1/2 cup	104	5.8	20.1	.3	0	14	3.6 d
canned, 1/2 cup, except as noted:							
(Allens Butterbeans)	110	5.0	18.0	<1.0	0	370	m.q.
(Green Giant/Joan of Arc)	80	6.0	16.0	0	0	420	3.7 d
(S&W)	100	6.0	19.0	1.0	0	440	m.q.
(Stokely)	80	5.0	16.0	0	0	390	m.q.
(Stokely No Salt/Sugar)	80	5.0	16.0	0	0	5	m.q.
(Van Camp's Butterbeans), 1 cup	162	11.0	28.4	.5	0	752	2.8 c
Fordhook *(Stokely)*	80	5.0	14.0	0	0	300	m.q.
green *(Del Monte)*	70	4.0	14.0	0	0	355	m.q.
green, small *(S&W Fancy)*	80	6.0	16.0	0	0	390	m.q.
green, tiny, small or medium *(Allens)*	90	5.0	15.0	<1.0	0	350	m.q.
green and white *(Allens)*	90	5.0	15.0	<1.0	0	370	m.q.

316

Food and Measure	cal.	prot. (gms)	carbo. (gms)	fat (gms)	chol. (mgs)	sod. (mgs)	fiber (gms)
green, small, w/ pork (Luck's), 7.5 oz.	220	10.0	33.0	7.0	m.q.	640	8.0 d
w/ham (Dennison's), 7.5 oz.	250	14.0	33.0	7.0	m.q.	935	9.0 d
w/pork (Luck's), 7.5 oz.	230	12.0	34.0	7.0	m.q.	720	9.0 d
frozen, 3.3 oz., except as noted:							
(Green Giant), 1/2 cup	100	6.0	19.0	0	0	30	5.0 d
(Green Giant Harvest Fresh), 1/2 cup	60	5.0	15.0	0	0	180	5.2 d
baby (Birds Eye)	130	7.0	24.0	0	0	115	m.q.
baby (Seabrook)	130	7.0	24.0	0	0	125	2.0 c
baby, butter (Seabrook)	140	7.0	26.0	1.0	0	213	2.0 c
Fordhook (Birds Eye)	100	6.0	19.0	0	0	100	m.q.
Fordhook (Seabrook)	100	6.0	19.0	0	0	71	2.0 c
speckled (Seabrook)	120	7.0	23.0	0	0	19	2.0 c
tiny (Seabrook) . .	110	6.0	21.0	1.0	0	144	2.0 c
in butter sauce (Green Giant), 1/2 cup	100	6.0	17.0	2.0	5	310	2.0 d
in butter sauce, baby (Stokely Singles), 4 oz. . . .	140	7.0	25.0	2.0	5	450	m.q.
Lima bean, mature, 1/2 cup:							
baby, boiled	115	7.3	21.2	.3	0	2	3.9 d
large, boiled	108	7.3	19.6	.4	0	2	6.8 d
canned, w/liquid . . .	95	5.9	17.9	.2	0	403	1.5 c
Lime:							
2"-diam. lime	20	.5	7.1	.1	0	1	.3 c

Food and Measure	cal.	prot. (gms)	carbo. (gms)	fat (gms)	chol. (mgs)	sod. (mgs)	fiber (gms)
Lime *(cont.)*							
peeled, seeded, 1 oz.	9	.2	3.0	.1	0	1	.1 c
Lime juice:							
fresh, 1 tbsp.	4	.1	1.4	<.1	0	tr.	(0)
reconstituted							
(*ReaLime*), 1 fl. oz.	6	0	2.0	0	0	10	(0)
sweetened (*Rose's*),							
1 fl. oz.	48	0	12.0	0	0	6	(0)
Limeade, frozen[1]							
(*Minute Maid*), 6 fl. oz.	71	0	19.2	0	0	20	(0)
Ling, meat only:							
raw, 1 lb.	394	86.1	0	2.9	m.q.	612	0
raw, 1 oz.	25	5.4	0	.2	m.q.	38	0
Ling cod, meat only:							
raw, 1 lb.	385	80.1	0	4.8	236	266	0
raw, 1 oz.	24	5.0	0	.3	15	17	0
Linguine, see "Pasta"							
Linguine entree:							
frozen:							
w/scallops and clams (*The Budget Gourmet*), 9.5 oz.	280	16.0	28.0	11.0	60	630	m.q.
seafood (*Weight Watchers*), 9 oz.	210	11.0	27.0	7.0	5	750	m.q.
w/shrimp (*The Budget Gourmet*), 10 oz.	330	15.0	33.0	15.0	75	1250	m.q.
w/shrimp (*Healthy Choice*), 9.5 oz.	230	12.0	40.0	2.0	55	390	m.q.
packaged, w/clam sauce (*Hormel Top Shelf*), 1 serving	330	12.0	30.0	18.0	85	1420	m.q.
Liquor[1], 1 fl. oz.:							
80 proof	65	0	tr.	0	0	tr.	0

[1] *Diluted according to package directions.*

[1] *Includes all pure distilled liquors (bourbon, brandy, gin, rum, rye, Scotch, tequila, vodka, whiskey, etc.).*

Food and Measure	cal.	prot. (gms)	carbo. (gms)	fat (gms)	chol. (mgs)	sod. (mgs)	fiber (gms)
86 proof	70	0	tr.	0	0	tr.	0
90 proof	74	0	tr.	0	0	tr.	0
100 proof	83	0	tr.	0	0	tr.	0
Little Caesars, 1 serving:							
Caesars Sandwich:							
ham and cheese	520	28.0	55.0	21.0	45	1045	.5 d
Italian sub	590	29.0	55.0	28.0	60	1230	1.7 d
tuna melt	700	34.0	58.0	37.0	65	825	.6 d
vegetarian	620	30.0	58.0	30.0	55	1000	1.3 d
pizza, w/salad:							
cheese	600	30.0	73.0	21.0	35	1605	3.0 d
combination	640	34.0	76.0	22.0	40	1715	3.6 d
pizza, single slice:							
cheese	170	9.0	20.0	6.0	10	285	.2 d
combination	190	10.0	20.0	7.0	15	340	.8 d
salad, w/low-calorie dressing:							
antipasto, 12 oz.	170	10.0	12.0	9.0	40	1145	m.q.
Greek, 11 oz. . . .	140	8.0	8.0	8.0	25	1075	m.q.
tossed, 11 oz. . . .	8	4.0	11.0	2.0	0	745	m.q.
Liver:							
beef, pan-fried, 4 oz.	246	30.3	8.9	9.1	547	120	0
chicken, simmered:							
4 oz.	178	27.6	1.0	6.2	716	58	0
chopped, 1 cup . .	219	34.1	1.2	7.6	883	71	0
duck, raw, 1 oz. . . .	39	5.3	1.0	1.3	146	m.q.	0
goose, raw, 1 oz. . .	38	4.6	1.8	1.2	m.q.	40	0
lamb, pan-fried, 4 oz.	270	29.0	4.3	14.3	559	141	0
pork, braised, 4 oz.	187	29.5	4.3	5.0	403	56	0
turkey, simmered:							
4 oz.	192	27.2	3.9	6.7	710	73	0
chopped, 1 cup . .	237	33.6	4.8	8.3	876	89	0
veal (calves):							
braised, 4 oz. . . .	187	24.5	3.1	7.8	636	60	0
pan-fried, 4 oz. . .	278	33.8	4.5	12.9	374	150	0
Liver cheese:							
(JM), 1-oz. slice . . .	70	4.0	1.0	6.0	m.q.	m.q.	0

Food and Measure	cal.	prot. (gms)	carbo. (gms)	fat (gms)	chol. (mgs)	sod. (mgs)	fiber (gms)
Liver cheese (cont.)							
(Oscar Mayer),							
1.34 oz. slice . . .	116	5.8	.7	10.0	76	432	0
Liver loaf:							
(Hormel Perma-Fresh),							
2 slices	160	9.0	1.0	13.0	m.q.	704	0
(Kahn's), 1 slice . . .	170	6.0	3.0	15.0	m.q.	370	0
Liver pâté, see							
"Pâté"							
Liver sausage, see							
"Braunschweiger"							
Liverwurst:							
(Hickory Farms), 1 oz.	97	4.0	1.0	9.0	74	249	0
(Jones Dairy Farm),							
1 slice	75	3.5	tr.	6.6	43	186	0
(Jones Dairy Farm							
Chub), 1 oz.	80	4.5	tr.	6.3	43	254	0
Liverwurst spread,							
canned:							
(Hormel), 1/2 oz. . . .	35	2.0	0	3.0	m.q.	m.q.	0
(Underwood), 1/2 can	190	8.0	4.0	16.0	m.q.	470	n.a.
Lobster, northern,							
meat only:							
raw, 1 oz.	26	5.3	.1	.3	27	m.q.	0
boiled or steamed:							
4 oz.	111	23.2	1.5	.7	82	431	0
1 cup, 5.1 oz. . . .	142	29.7	1.9	.9	104	551	0
Lobster, spiny, see							
"Spiny lobster"							
Lobster Newburg,							
frozen:							
(Stouffer's), 61/2 oz.	380	14.0	9.0	32.0	m.q.	870	m.q.
Loganberry:							
fresh, 1 cup	89	1.4	21.5	.9	0	1	4.3 c
frozen, 1/2 cup	40	1.1	9.6	.2	0	1	m.q.
Longan, shelled:							
fresh, seeded, 1 oz.	17	.4	4.3	<.1	0	tr.	.1 c
dried, 1 oz.	81	1.4	21.0	.1	0	14	.6 c

Food and Measure	cal.	prot. (gms)	carbo. (gms)	fat (gms)	chol. (mgs)	sod. (mgs)	fiber (gms)
Loquat:							
1 medium, .6 oz. . .	5	<.1	1.2	<.1	0	tr.	.1 c
peeled, seeded, 1 oz.	13	.1	3.4	.1	0	<1	.1 c
Lotus root:							
raw, trimmed, 1 oz.	16	.7	4.9	<.1	0	11	.2 c
boiled, drained, 4 oz.	75	1.8	18.2	.1	0	51	1.0 c
Lotus seed:							
raw, 1 oz.	25	1.2	4.9	.2	0	tr.	.2 c
dried, 1 oz.	94	4.4	18.3	.6	0	1	.7 c
fried, 1 cup	106	4.9	20.6	.6	0	1	.8 c
Lox, see "Salmon, Chinook"							
Luncheon meat (see also specific listings):							
(Oscar Mayer), 1-oz. slice	98	3.5	.7	9.1	20	333	0
spiced:							
(JM), 1-oz. slice . .	70	4.0	1.0	6.0	m.q.	370	0
(Hormel Perma-Fresh), 2 slices	118	9.0	1.0	9.0	m.q.	702	0
(Kahn's Luncheon Loaf), 1 slice . .	80	3.0	1.0	7.0	m.q.	240	0
(Light & Lean), 2 slices	120	8.0	1.0	9.0	m.q.	m.q.	0
canned:							
(Spam, 12 oz.), 2 oz.	170	8.0	0	15.0	m.q.	862	0
w/cheese chunks *(Spam),* 2 oz. . .	170	8.0	0	16.0	m.q.	811	0
deviled *(Spam),* 1 tbsp.	35	2.0	0	3.0	m.q.	125	0
smoke flavored *(Spam),* 2 oz. . .	170	8.0	0	15.0	m.q.	774	0
spiced *(Hormel),* 3 oz.	280	11.0	2.0	26.0	m.q.	1110	0

Food and Measure	cal.	prot. (gms)	carbo. (gms)	fat (gms)	chol. (mgs)	sod. (mgs)	fiber (gms)
Luncheon "meat," **vegetarian,** canned, 1/2" slice:							
(Worthington Numete)	160	8.0	6.0	11.0	0	570	m.q.
(Worthington Protose)	180	17.0	9.0	8.0	0	470	m.q.
Lupin:							
boiled, 1/2 cup	98	12.9	8.2	2.4	0	3	.6 c
Luxury loaf:							
(Oscar Mayer), 1 oz.	38	5.2	1.4	1.2	13	300	0
Lychee, shelled:							
raw, seeded, 1 oz.	19	.2	4.7	.1	0	<1	.1 c
dried, 1 oz.	79	1.1	20.0	.3	0	1	.4 c

M

Food and Measure	cal.	prot. (gms)	carbo. (gms)	fat (gms)	chol. (mgs)	sod. (mgs)	fiber (gms)
Macadamia nut:							
(Mauna Loa), 1 oz.	210	2.0	4.0	21.0	0	75	m.q.
dried, shelled:							
1 oz.	199	2.4	3.9	20.9	0	1	1.5 c
1 cup	940	11.1	18.4	98.8	0	6	7.1 c
oil-roasted:							
1 oz.	204	2.1	3.7	21.7	0	2	.5 c
Macaroni (see also "Pasta"):							
uncooked							
2 oz.	211	7.3	42.6	.9	0	4	1.4 d
elbow, 1 cup . . .	389	13.4	78.4	1.7	0	8	2.5 d
(Prince), 2 oz. . . .	210	7.0	43.0	1.0	0	5	m.q.
(Ronzoni), 2 oz. . .	210	7.0	41.0	1.0	0	<5	m.q.
cooked:							
4 oz.	160	5.4	32.1	.8	0	1	1.8 d
elbow, 1 cup . . .	197	6.7	39.7	.9	0	1	2.2 d
small shells, 1 cup	162	5.5	32.6	.8	0	1	1.8 d
spirals, 1 cup . . .	189	6.4	38.0	.9	0	1	2.1 d
vegetable (tricolor), 4 oz.	145	5.1	30.2	.1	0	7	m.q.
whole-wheat, 4 oz.	141	6.0	30.1	.6	0	3	1.1 c
Macaroni dinner, frozen:							
and beef (Swanson), 12 oz.	370	11.0	48.0	15.0	m.q.	870	m.q.
and cheese:							
(Banquet), 10 oz.	420	14.0	46.0	20.0	30	450	m.q.
(Swanson), 12¼ oz.	380	12.0	49.0	15.0	m.q.	990	m.q.

Food and Measure	cal.	prot. (gms)	carbo. (gms)	fat (gms)	chol. (mgs)	sod. (mgs)	fiber (gms)
Macaroni dinner, frozen, and cheese *(cont.)*							
w/mini franks *(Kid Cuisine)*, 9 oz.	380	9.0	55.0	14.0	40	1000	m.q.
Macaroni entree, canned, 7.5 oz., except as noted:							
and beef:							
(Chef Boyardee Beefaroni)	220	8.0	29.0	8.0	m.q.	1070	m.q.
and beef, in tomato sauce:							
(Franco-American Hearty Pasta) . .	200	8.0	30.0	5.0	m.q.	790	m.q.
(Heinz), 7¼ oz. . . .	200	8.0	23.0	8.0	m.q.	850	m.q.
and cheese:							
(Franco-American), 7³⁄₈ oz.	170	6.0	24.0	5.0	m.q.	960	m.q.
(Heinz)	190	5.0	26.0	8.0	m.q.	1105	m.q.
(Hormel Micro-Cup)	189	7.0	26.0	6.0	17	874	m.q.
shells and cheddar *(Lipton Hearty Ones)*, 11 oz. . . .	367	15.4	60.0	7.4	14	1406	m.q.
shells, in tomato sauce *(Chef Boyardee)*	150	6.0	31.0	1.0	n.a.	930	m.q.
Macaroni entree, frozen:							
and beef *(Stouffer's)*, 5³⁄₄ oz.	170	11.0	15.0	7.0	m.q.	810	m.q.
and cheese:							
(Banquet Casserole), 8 oz. . . .	350	11.0	36.0	17.0	m.q.	930	m.q.
(Banquet Family Entrees), 8 oz. . . .	290	12.0	32.0	13.0	m.q.	m.q.	m.q.
(The Budget Gourmet Side Dish), 5.3 oz.	210	9.0	23.0	8.0	25	370	m.q.

Food and Measure	cal.	prot. (gms)	carbo. (gms)	fat (gms)	chol. (mgs)	sod. (mgs)	fiber (gms)
(Freezer Queen Family Side Dish), 4 oz.	110	3.0	19.0	2.0	m.q.	420	m.q.
(Green Giant One Serving), 5¾ oz.	230	9.0	28.0	9.0	25	590	m.q.
(Myers), 3.5 oz. . . .	168	7.0	16.0	9.0	m.q.	516	m.q.
(Stouffer's), 6 oz.	250	12.0	22.0	13.0	m.q.	730	m.q.
(Stouffer's), 5 oz.	210	10.0	18.0	11.0	m.q.	610	m.q.
(Swanson Home-style Recipe), 10 oz.	400	15.0	38.0	21.0	m.q.	980	m.q.
pie *(Swanson)*, 7 oz.	220	8.0	27.0	9.0	m.q.	880	m.q.
Macaroni entree mix[1] ¾ cup, except as noted:							
and cheese:							
(Golden Grain), 1 serving	310	8.0	36.0	15.0	m.q.	620	m.q.
(Kraft Dinner)[2] . . .	290	9.0	34.0	13.0	5	530	m.q.
(Kraft Deluxe Dinner)	260	11.0	36.0	8.0	20	590	m.q.
(Kraft Family Size Dinner)	290	9.0	34.0	13.0	5	490	m.q.
cheddar *(Fantastic Foods)*, ½ cup[3]	112	5.0	19.0	2.0	m.q.	205	m.q.
Parmesan and herbs *(Fantastic Foods)*, ½ cup[3]	109	5.0	19.0	2.0	m.q.	264	m.q.
shells *(Velveeta Dinner)*	260	12.0	32.0	10.0	25	720	m.q.
spiral *(Kraft Dinner)*[2]	330	9.0	36.0	17.0	10	560	m.q.
and curry *(Tofu Classics)*, ½ cup[4] . . .	143	8.0	15.0	7.0	m.q.	330	m.q.

[1] *Prepared according to package directions, except as noted.*
[2] *Prepared without added salt.*
[3] *Prepared with whole milk.*
[4] *Prepared with tofu and 2 tbsp. salted butter.*

Food and Measure	cal.	prot. (gms)	carbo. (gms)	fat (gms)	chol. (mgs)	sod. (mgs)	fiber (gms)
Macaroni and cheese, see "Macaroni dinner" and "Macaroni entree"							
Macaroni and cheese loaf, 1 oz.:							
(Eckrich)	75	3.0	3.0	6.0	m.q.	320	m.q.
Mace, ground:							
1 tsp.	8	.1	.9	.6	0	1	.1 c
Mackerel, meat only:							
Atlantic:							
raw, 1 lb.	929	84.4	0	63.0	318	408	0
raw, 1 oz.	58	5.3	0	3.9	20	26	0
baked, broiled or microwaved, 4 oz.	297	27.0	0	20.2	85	94	0
king:							
raw, 1 lb.	475	92.0	0	9.1	242	717	0
raw, 1 oz.	30	5.7	0	.6	15	45	0
Pacific and jack:							
raw, 1 lb.	712	91.0	0	35.8	213	391	0
raw, 1 oz.	45	5.7	0	2.2	13	24	0
Spanish:							
raw, 1 lb.	631	87.5	0	28.6	345	266	0
raw, 1 oz.	39	5.5	0	1.8	22	17	0
baked, broiled, or microwaved, 4 oz.	179	26.8	0	7.2	83	75	0
Mackerel, canned:							
jack, drained, 4 oz.	177	26.3	0	7.1	90	430	0
Mahi mahi, see "Dolphinfish"							
Mai tai mix:							
bottled (Holland House), 1 fl. oz.	32	0	8.0	0	0	60	(0)
instant (Holland House), .56 oz.	64	0	16.0	0	0	4	(0)

Food and Measure	cal.	prot. (gms)	carbo. (gms)	fat (gms)	chol. (mgs)	sod. (mgs)	fiber (gms)
Malted milk powder, 2–3 heaping tsp.:							
natural flavor	86	2.7	15.2	1.8	4	96	.1 c
chocolate flavor . . .	83	1.4	17.8	.9	1	49	.1 c
Mammy apple:							
peeled, seeded, 1 oz.	14	.1	3.5	.1	0	4	.3 c
Mango:							
10.6-oz. mango . . .	135	1.1	35.2	.6	0	4	2.2 d
sliced, 1/2 cup	54	.4	14.0	.2	0	2	.9 d
Mango nectar:							
(Libby's), 6 fl. oz. . .	110	0	26.0	0	0	0	m.q.
Manhattan mix:							
bottled (Holland House), 1 fl. oz. . .	28	0	7.0	0	0	5	0
Manicotti entree, frozen:							
(Buitoni Single Serving), 9 oz.	470	18.0	45.0	14.0	130	830	m.q.
(Celentano), 7 oz. . . .	360	21.0	35.0	16.0	m.q.	580	m.q.
cheese:							
(Le Menu), 81/2 oz.	410	17.0	40.0	20.0	m.q.	1030	m.q.
(Weight Watchers), 91/4 oz.	300	17.0	28.0	13.0	90	660	m.q.
w/meat sauce (The Budget Gourmet), 10 oz.	450	20.0	33.0	26.0	50	920	m.q.
w/spinach, tofu (Legume Florentine), 11 oz.	260	18.0	30.0	7.0	0	650	8.7 d
w/tofu (Legume Classic), 8 oz.	220	17.0	24.0	11.0	0	370	7.0 d
Maple sugar, see "Sugar, maple"							
Maple syrup:							
1 tbsp.	50	0	12.8	0	0	2	0

Food and Measure	cal.	prot. (gms)	carbo. (gms)	fat (gms)	chol. (mgs)	sod. (mgs)	fiber (gms)
Margarine, 1 tbsp., except as noted:							
(Country Morning Stick), 1 tsp.	35	0	0	4.0	5	35	0
(Country Morning Tub), 1 tsp.	30	0	0	3.0	5	25	0
(Diet Mazola)	50	0	0	6.0	0	130	0
(Land O'Lakes), 1 tsp.	35	0	0	4.0	0	35	0
(Mazola)	100	0	0	11.0	0	100	0
(Nucoa)	100	0	0	11.0	0	160	0
(Parkay)	100	0	0	11.0	0	115	0
safflower *(Hain)* . . .	100	0	0	11.0	0	170	0
soft:							
(Chiffon Cup) . . .	90	0	0	10.0	0	105	0
(Chiffon Stick) . . .	100	0	0	11.0	0	110	0
(Diet Parkay) . . .	50	0	0	6.0	0	110	0
(Nucoa)	90	0	0	10.0	0	150	0
(Parkay)	100	0	0	11.0	0	105	0
safflower *(Hain)* . .	100	0	0	11.0	0	170	0
spread:							
(Kraft "Touch of Butter" Bowl) . .	50	0	0	6.0	0	110	0
(Kraft "Touch of Butter" Stick) . .	60	0	0	7.0	0	105	0
(Land O'Lakes Tub), 1 tsp.	25	0	0	3.0	0	25	0
(Parkay 50% Vegetable Oil)	60	0	0	7.0	0	110	0
corn oil *(Mazola Light)*	50	0	0	6.0	0	100	0
corn oil *(Parkay Light),* 1 tbsp. . . .	70	0	0	8.0	0	110	0
squeeze *(Parkay)* . .	100	0	0	11.0	0	100	0
whipped:							
(Chiffon)	70	0	0	8.0	0	80	0
(Miracle Brand Cup)	60	0	0	7.0	0	70	0
(Miracle Brand Stick)	70	0	0	7.0	0	65	0

Food and Measure	cal.	prot. (gms)	carbo. (gms)	fat (gms)	chol. (mgs)	sod. (mgs)	fiber (gms)
(Parkay Cup) . . .	60	0	0	7.0	0	70	0
(Parkay Stick) . . .	60	0	0	7.0	0	65	0
Margarita mix, bottled, 1 fl. oz.:							
(Holland House) . . .	27	0	6.0	0	0	92	n.a.
strawberry *(Holland House)*	31	0	7.0	0	0	3	n.a.
Marinade, see specific listings							
Marjoram, dried:							
1 tsp.	2	.1	.4	<.1	0	tr.	.1 c
Marmalade, orange:							
(Smucker's), 1 tsp.	18	0	4.0	0	0	0	m.q.
Marrow squash:							
raw, trimmed, 1 oz.	4	.2	1.0	<.1	0	n.a.	.1 c
Marshmallow topping:							
(Marshmallow Fluff), 1 heaping tsp. . . .	59	0	15.0	0	0	12	0
creme *(Kraft),* 1 oz.	90	0	23.0	0	0	20	0
Mayonnaise, 1 tbsp.:							
(Bennett's Real) . . .	110	0	1.0	12.0	m.q.	65	0
(Cains)	100	0	0	11.0	10	80	0
(Hain Light Low Sodium)	60	0	2.0	6.0	10	95	0
(Hellmann's/Best Foods)	100	0	0	11.0	5	80	0
(Hellmann's/Best Foods Light)	50	0	1.0	5.0	5	115	0
(Kraft)	100	0	0	12.0	5	70	0
(Kraft Light)	50	0	1.0	5.0	<5	95	0
(Rokeach)	100	0	0	11.0	10	70	0
(Weight Watchers Reduced Calorie) . .	50	0	1.0	5.0	5	100	0
cholesterol free *(Hellmann's)*	50	0	1.0	5.0	0	80	0
cold processed *(Hain)*	110	0	0	12.0	5	70	0
eggless *(Hain* No Salt)	110	0	0	12.0	0	<5	0

Food and Measure	cal.	prot. (gms)	carbo. (gms)	fat (gms)	chol. (mgs)	sod. (mgs)	fiber (gms)
Mayonnaise *(cont.)*							
safflower *(Hain)* . . .	110	0	0	12.0	5	70	0
soy *(Featherweight*							
Soyamaise)	100	0	0	11.0	5	3	0
tofu *(Nasoya*							
Nayonaise)	40	1.0	1.0	4.0	0	50	(0)
McDonald's, 1 serv-							
ing:							
breakfast dishes:							
eggs, scrambled	140	12.4	1.2	9.8	399	290	0
hashbrown potatoes	130	1.4	14.9	7.3	9	330	m.q.
hotcakes w/butter							
and syrup	410	8.2	74.4	9.2	21	640	m.q.
sausage, pork . . .	180	8.4	0	16.3	48	350	0
breakfast biscuit or							
sandwich:							
w/bacon, egg and							
cheese	440	17.5	33.3	26.4	253	1230	m.q.
w/biscuit spread	260	4.6	31.9	12.7	1	730	m.q.
Egg McMuffin . . .	290	18.2	28.1	11.2	226	740	m.q.
w/sausage	440	13.0	31.9	29.0	49	1080	m.q.
w/sausage and egg	520	19.9	32.6	34.5	275	1250	m.q.
Sausage McMuffin	370	16.5	27.3	21.9	64	830	m.q.
Sausage McMuffin							
w/egg	440	22.6	27.9	26.8	263	980	m.q.
danish:							
apple	390	5.8	51.2	17.9	25	370	m.q.
cinnamon raisin . .	440	6.4	57.5	21.0	34	430	m.q.
iced cheese	390	7.4	42.3	21.8	47	420	m.q.
raspberry	410	6.1	61.5	15.9	26	310	m.q.
muffin:							
apple bran	190	5.0	46.0	0	0	230	m.q.
English, w/butter	170	5.4	26.7	4.6	9	270	m.q.
sandwiches and							
chicken:							
Big Mac	560	25.2	42.5	32.4	103	950	m.q.
cheeseburger . . .	310	15.0	31.2	13.8	53	750	m.q.
Chicken McNuggets	290	19.0	16.5	16.3	65	520	m.q.

Food and Measure	cal.	prot. (gms)	carbo. (gms)	fat (gms)	chol. (mgs)	sod. (mgs)	fiber (gms)
Filet-O-Fish	440	13.8	37.9	26.1	50	1030	m.q.
hamburger	260	12.3	30.6	9.5	37	500	m.q.
McChicken	490	19.2	39.8	28.6	43	780	m.q.
McD.L.T.	580	26.3	36.0	36.8	109	990	m.q.
Quarter Pounder	410	23.1	34.0	20.7	86	660	m.q.
Quarter Pounder w/							
cheese	520	28.5	35.1	29.2	118	1150	m.q.
french fries, medium	320	4.4	36.3	17.1	0	150	m.q.
salads:							
chef	230	20.5	7.5	13.3	128	490	m.q.
chunky chicken . .	140	23.1	5.3	3.4	78	230	m.q.
garden	110	7.1	6.2	6.6	83	160	m.q.
side	60	3.7	3.3	3.3	41	85	m.q.
salad dressing,							
1/5 pkg.:							
blue cheese	70	.5	1.2	6.9	6	150	0
peppercorn	80	.2	.1	8.7	7	85	n.a.
Thousand Island	78	.2	2.4	7.5	8	100	n.a.
sauces:							
barbeque	50	.3	12.1	.5	0	340	n.a.
honey	45	0	11.5	0	0	0	n.a.
hot mustard	70	.5	8.2	3.6	5	250	n.a.
sweet and sour . .	60	.2	13.8	.2	0	190	n.a.
pies and cookies:							
apple pie	260	2.2	30.0	14.8	6	240	m.q.
cookies, chocolate							
chip	330	4.2	41.9	15.6	4	280	m.q.
cookies, McDonald-							
land	290	4.2	47.1	9.2	0	300	m.q.
shakes, lowfat:							
chocolate	320	11.6	66.0	1.7	10	240	(0)
strawberry	320	10.7	67.0	1.3	10	170	(0)
vanilla	290	10.8	60.0	1.3	10	170	0
yogurt, frozen, lowfat:							
cone, vanilla	100	4.0	22.0	.8	3	80	m.q.
sundae, hot caramel	270	6.6	59.3	2.8	13	180	(0)
sundae, hot fudge	148	7.3	50.5	3.2	6	170	(0)
sundae, strawberry	210	5.7	49.2	1.1	5	95	(0)

Food and Measure	cal.	prot. (gms)	carbo. (gms)	fat (gms)	chol. (mgs)	sod. (mgs)	fiber (gms)
Meat, see specific listings							
Meat, potted:							
canned *(Hormel* Food Product), 1 tbsp.	30	2.0	0	2.0	m.q.	145	0
"Meat" loaf, vegetarian, mix:							
(Natural Touch), 4 oz.	180	21.0	7.0	7.0	0	25	m.q.
Meat loaf dinner, frozen:							
(Armour Classics), 11¼ oz.	360	20.0	32.0	17.0	65	1170	m.q.
(Banquet), 11 oz. . .	440	26.0	27.0	27.0	85	770	m.q.
(Freezer Queen), 10 oz.	350	19.0	26.0	19.0	m.q.	910	m.q.
(Morton), 10 oz. . . .	310	11.0	26.0	17.0	50	1520	m.q.
(Swanson), 10¾ oz.	430	17.0	41.0	22.0	m.q.	1030	m.q.
(Stouffer's Dinner Supreme), 12⅛ oz.	410	25.0	29.0	22.0	m.q.	1170	m.q.
Meat loaf entree:							
frozen:							
(Banquet Cookin' Bags), 4 oz. . . .	200	10.0	8.0	14.0	m.q.	m.q.	m.q.
tomato sauce and *(Freezer Queen Family Suppers),* 7 oz.	230	12.0	15.0	13.0	m.q.	850	m.q.
mix[1], *(Lipton Microeasy),* ¼ pkg.	390	31.0	15.0	22.0	m.q.	700	m.q.
Meat loaf seasoning:							
(Lawry's Seasoning Blends), 1 pkg. . .	355	15.5	64.5	1.2	n.a.	6547	1.8 c
Meat Marinade mix:							
(French's), ⅛ pkg.	10	0	2.0	0	0	540	n.a.
Meat tenderizer:							
unseasoned *(Tone's),* 1 tsp.	7	0	1.2	.2	0	1760	tr.d

[1] *Prepared according to package directions, with 1½ lbs. ground beef.*

Food and Measure	cal.	prot. (gms)	carbo. (gms)	fat (gms)	chol. (mgs)	sod. (mgs)	fiber (gms)
"Meatball," vegetarian, canned: (Worthington Non-Meat Balls), 3 pieces	100	7.0	4.0	6.0	0	220	m.q.
Meatball dinner, frozen:							
Swedish (Armour Classics), 11 1/4 oz.	330	19.0	23.0	18.0	80	720	m.q.
Meatball entree:							
frozen:							
Italian style (The Budget Gourmet), 10 oz.	310	20.0	29.0	12.0	55	1120	m.q.
stew (Lean Cuisine), 10 oz.	250	21.0	20.0	10.0	85	940	m.q.
Swedish (Swanson Homestyle Recipe), 8 1/2 oz. . .	350	17.0	22.0	22.0	m.q.	780	m.q.
Swedish, w/parsley noodles (Stouffer's), 11 oz. . .	480	24.0	37.0	26.0	m.q.	1510	m.q.
Swedish, w/pasta and vegetables (Le Menu Light Style), 8 1/2 oz.	260	18.0	30.0	8.0	40	700	m.q.
Swedish, w/noodles (The Budget Gourmet), 10 oz.	600	23.0	40.0	39.0	140	1085	m.q.
Swedish, sauce and (Dining Lite), 9 oz.	280	14.0	34.0	10.0	55	660	m.q.
mix[1], Italian (Hunt's Minute Gourmet), 7.6 oz.	331	21.0	20.0	18.0	m.q.	942	m.q.

---

[1] Prepared according to package directions.

Food and Measure	cal.	prot. (gms)	carbo. (gms)	fat (gms)	chol. (mgs)	sod. (mgs)	fiber (gms)
Meatball stew, canned:							
(Chef Boyardee), 8 oz.	350	9.0	24.0	24.0	m.q.	1315	m.q.
(Dinty Moore), 8 oz.	240	13.0	15.0	15.0	m.q.	m.q.	m.q.
Melon balls, cantaloupe and honeydew:							
frozen, 1/2 cup	28	.7	6.9	.2	0	27	m.q.
Mesquite sauce:							
w/lime juice *(Lawry's),* 1/4 cup	24	3.0	3.0	.4	0	4142	.1 c
Mesquite seasoning:							
(Tone's), 1 tsp. . . .	13	.1	3.2	<.1	0	467	n.a.
Mexican bean dip:							
(Hain), 4 tbsp.	60	4.0	9.0	1.0	5	260	n.a.
Mexican dinner, frozen (see also specific listings):							
(Patio Fiesta), 121/4 oz.	470	16.0	55.0	20.0	30	2040	m.q.
(Swanson Hungry Man), 201/4 oz. . .	820	25.0	88.0	41.0	m.q.	2080	m.q.
style:							
(Banquet), 12 oz.	490	18.0	62.0	18.0	m.q.	2000	m.q.
(Morton), 10 oz. . .	300	9.0	44.0	10.0	20	1390	m.q.
(Patio), 131/4 oz.	540	15.0	64.0	25.0	45	1940	m.q.
style, combination:							
(Banquet), 12 oz.	520	20.0	72.0	17.0	m.q.	1980	m.q.
(Swanson), 141/4 oz.	520	17.0	60.0	24.0	m.q.	1580	m.q.
Mexican entree, frozen:							
(Van de Kamp's), 1/2 pkg.	220	7.0	25.0	10.0	m.q.	640	m.q.

Food and Measure	cal.	prot. (gms)	carbo. (gms)	fat (gms)	chol. (mgs)	sod. (mgs)	fiber (gms)
Mexican seasoning:							
(Tone's), 1 tsp. . . .	6	.3	1.3	.1	tr.	4185	.4 d
rice (Lawry's Season-							
ing Blends), 1 pkg.	94	3.9	17.0	2.0	n.a.	3246	2.1 c
Milk, fluid, 1 cup, ex-							
cept as noted:							
buttermilk, cultured:							
(Crowley)	110	9.0	12.0	4.0	15	390	0
lowfat, unsalted							
(Friendship) . . .	120	9.0	12.0	4.0	14	125	0
whole:							
(Borden)	150	8.0	11.0	8.0	m.q.	130	0
(Crowley)	150	8.0	11.0	8.0	30	125	0
(Darigold)	150	8.0	11.0	8.0	33	125	0
lowfat, 2% fat:							
(Crowley/Crowley							
Tone Acidophilus)	120	8.0	11.0	5.0	15	125	0
(Darigold/Darigold							
Acidophilus) . . .	120	8.0	11.0	5.0	18	130	0
(Knudsen/Knudsen							
Acidophilus) . . .	140	10.0	13.0	5.0	m.q.	150	0
lowfat, 1% fat:							
(Borden)	100	8.0	11.0	2.0	m.q.	130	0
(Crowley)	100	8.0	11.0	2.0	10	130	0
(Crowley Protein							
Fortified)	120	10.0	14.0	2.0	10	150	0
w/lactose enzyme							
(Crowley Lactaid)	100	8.0	11.0	2.0	10	125	0
skim:							
(Borden)	90	8.0	12.0	1.0	m.q.	130	0
(Borden Skim-Line)	100	10.0	13.0	1.0	m.q.	150	0
(Crowley)	90	9.0	12.0	<1.0	<1	130	0
(Darigold/Darigold							
Trim)	80	8.0	11.0	1.0	4	130	0
Milk, canned:							
condensed, sweet-							
ened:							
1 tbsp.	61	1.5	10.4	1.7	6	24	0

Food and Measure	cal.	prot. (gms)	carbo. (gms)	fat (gms)	chol. (mgs)	sod. (mgs)	fiber (gms)
Milk, canned, condensed, sweetened *(cont.)*							
(Borden), 1/3 cup	320	7.0	54.0	8.0	m.q.	115	0
(Eagle), 1/3 cup . .	320	7.0	52.0	9.0	m.q.	120	0
evaporated, 1/2 cup:							
(Pet)	170	8.0	12.0	10.0	36	140	0
imitation, filled							
(Diehl)	150	8.0	12.0	8.0	5	135	0
skim *(Pet 99)* . . .	100	9.0	14.0	0	1	150	0
Milk, chocolate, see "Chocolate milk"							
Milk, dry:							
buttermilk:							
sweet cream, 1 cup	464	41.2	58.8	6.9	83	621	0
sweet cream,							
1 tbsp.	25	2.2	3.2	.4	5	34	0
whole, 1 oz.	141	7.5	10.9	7.6	27	105	0
whole, 1 cup	635	33.7	49.2	34.2	124	475	0
instant *(Sanalac)*, .8 oz.	80	8.0	12.0	.1	5	85	0
nonfat:							
regular, 1 cup . . .	435	43.4	62.4	.9	24	642	0
instant, 3.2-oz. pkt.	244	23.9	35.5	.5	12	373	0
instant *(Carnation)*, 5 level tbsp. . .	80	8.0	12.0	.2	5	125	0
Milk, goat:							
whole, 1 cup	168	8.7	10.9	10.1	28	122	0
Milk, human:							
whole, 1 cup	171	2.5	17.0	10.8	34	42	0
"Milk," imitation:							
fluid[1], 1 cup	150	4.3	15.0	8.3	tr.	191	0
soy, see "Soy milk"							
Milk, sheep:							
whole, 1 cup	264	14.7	13.1	17.2	m.q.	108	0
Milk beverage, see specific flavors							
Milkfish, meat only:							
raw, 1 lb.	673	93.1	0	30.5	235	m.q.	0

[1] *Containing blend of hydrogenated vegetable oils.*

Food and Measure	cal.	prot. (gms)	carbo. (gms)	fat (gms)	chol. (mgs)	sod. (mgs)	fiber (gms)
raw, 1 oz.	42	5.8	0	1.9	15	m.q.	0
Milkshake, frozen, 11.5 oz.: chocolate							
(MicroMagic) . . .	340	5.0	55.0	8.0	40	120	(0)
strawberry							
(MicroMagic) . . .	340	5.0	54.0	9.0	40	120	(0)
vanilla (MicroMagic)	380	8.0	60.0	13.0	45	150	0
Millet:							
raw, 1 oz.	107	3.1	20.7	1.2	0	1	.3 c
cooked, 4 oz.	135	4.0	26.8	1.1	0	2	.4 c
Mincemeat, see "Pie filling"							
Miso:							
1 oz.	58	3.3	7.9	1.7	0	1034	1.5 d
1/2 cup	284	16.3	38.6	8.4	0	5032	7.6 d
Molasses, 1 tbsp.:							
dark (Brer Rabbit) . .	60	0	14.0	0	0	15	(0)
gold (Grandma's) . .	70	0	17.0	0	0	28	(0)
green (Grandma's)	70	0	16.0	0	0	57	(0)
light (Brer Rabbit) . .	60	0	14.0	0	0	10	(0)
Monkfish, meat only:							
raw, 1 lb.	343	65.7	0	6.9	115	84	0
raw, 1 oz.	22	4.1	0	.4	7	5	0
Monosodium glutamate:							
(Tone's), 1 tsp. . . .	0	0	0	0	0	638	0
Mortadella:							
beef and pork, 1 oz.	88	4.6	.9	7.2	16	353	0
Mostaccioli entree, frozen:							
(Banquet Family Entrees), 7 oz.	170	7.0	28.0	3.0	m.q.	m.q.	m.q.
Mothbean:							
boiled, 4 oz.	133	8.9	23.8	.6	0	11	1.5 c
Mother's loaf:							
pork, 1 oz.	80	3.4	2.1	6.3	13	320	(0)

Food and Measure	cal.	prot. (gms)	carbo. (gms)	fat (gms)	chol. (mgs)	sod. (mgs)	fiber (gms)
Mousse, see specific listings							
Muffin, 1 piece, except as noted:							
apple:							
(Awrey's)	220	3.0	30.0	10.0	35	350	1.0 d
cinnamon, mini							
(Hostess), 1 pkg.	160	2.0	17.0	9.0	0	100	m.q.
streusel (Awrey's)	340	6.0	50.0	13.0	35	540	1.0 d
banana nut							
(Awrey's)	370	4.0	55.0	15.0	30	400	1.0 d
banana walnut, mini							
(Hostess), 1 pkg.	160	2.0	17.0	9.0	0	90	m.q.
blueberry:							
(Awrey's)	210	3.0	31.0	8.0	20	280	1.0 d
mini (Hostess),							
1 pkg.	150	2.0	18.0	7.0	0	90	m.q.
cranberry (Awrey's)	120	2.0	20.0	4.0	10	210	0
corn (Awrey's)	220	4.0	33.0	8.0	25	430	1.0 d
English:							
(Pepperidge Farm, 12/pkg.)	140	4.0	28.0	2.0	0	180	m.q.
(Pepperidge Farm, 6/pkg.)	140	5.0	27.0	1.0	0	220	m.q.
(Pepperidge Farm Bonus Pack) . .	150	4.0	27.0	2.0	0	200	m.q.
(Roman Meal Original)	146	6.4	28.5	1.8	0	350	2.7 d
(Thomas')	130	4.3	25.4	1.3	0	206	m.q.
(Wonder)	130	4.0	26.0	1.0	0	280	1.2 d
(Hi Fiber)	110	5.0	21.0	1.0	0	280	5.0 d
cinnamon-apple (Pepperidge Farm)	140	4.0	27.0	1.0	0	210	m.q.
cinnamon chip (Pepperidge Farm)	160	4.0	28.0	3.0	0	180	m.q.

Food and Measure	cal.	prot. (gms)	carbo. (gms)	fat (gms)	chol. (mgs)	sod. (mgs)	fiber (gms)
cinnamon raisin (Hi Fiber)	110	4.0	21.0	1.0	0	275	5.0 d
cinnamon raisin or honey and oatmeal (Oatmeal Goodness) . . .	140	5.0	26.0	2.0	0	160	1.5 d
cinnamon raisin (Pepperidge Farm, 6/pkg.)	150	4.0	29.0	2.0	0	200	m.q.
cinnamon raisin (Pepperidge Farm Bonus Pack) . .	150	4.0	27.0	2.0	0	200	m.q.
honey wheat (Thomas')	129	5.0	24.0	1.1	0	200	.4 c
multi-grain (Hi Fiber)	120	4.0	23.0	1.0	0	240	4.0 d
oat bran (Thomas')	116	4.2	26.0	1.2	0	192	2.9 d
raisin (Thomas') . .	153	4.5	30.4	1.5	0	200	.2 c
rye (Thomas') . . .	120	5.0	27.0	1.0	0	210	3.0 d
sourdough (Pepperidge Farm) . . .	135	4.0	27.0	1.0	0	260	m.q.
oat bran:							
(Awrey's)	180	5.0	27.0	7.0	0	330	2.0 d
(Hostess)	170	2.0	22.0	8.0	0	140	2.0 d
pineapple raisin (Awrey's)	180	5.0	26.0	6.0	0	320	2.0 d
raisin (Wonder Raisin Rounds)	140	4.0	27.0	2.0	0	280	1.2 d
raisin-bran (Awrey's)	190	3.0	30.0	7.0	20	280	2.0 d
sourdough (Wonder)	130	4.0	27.0	1.0	0	250	1.2 d
Muffin, frozen, 1 piece:							
apple cinnamon spice (Sara Lee)	220	4.0	36.0	8.0	n.a.	280	m.q.
banana nut (Pepperidge Farm Old Fashioned)	170	3.0	28.0	6.0	30	220	1.0 d

Food and Measure	cal.	prot. (gms)	carbo. (gms)	fat (gms)	chol. (mgs)	sod. (mgs)	fiber (gms)
Muffin, frozen, *(cont.)*							
blueberry *(Pepperidge Farm Old Fashioned)*	170	2.0	27.0	7.0	25	250	1.0 d
blueberry *(Sara Lee)*	200	3.0	34.0	8.0	n.a.	290	m.q.
cinnamon swirl *(Pepperidge Farm Old Fashioned)*	190	2.0	30.0	6.0	35	170	1.0 d
corn *(Pepperidge Farm Old Fashioned)*	180	3.0	27.0	7.0	30	260	2.0 d
corn, golden *(Sara Lee)*	250	4.0	31.0	13.0	n.a.	330	m.q.
multigrain Muesli *(Pepperidge Farm Old Fashioned)*	200	4.0	30.0	8.0	0	230	2.0 d
oat bran *(Sara Lee)*	220	4.0	36.0	8.0	n.a.	380	m.q.
oat bran w/apple *(Pepperidge Farm Old Fashioned)* . .	190	3.0	29.0	7.0	0	200	2.0 d
raisin bran *(Pepperidge Farm Old Fashioned)*	170	4.0	30.0	6.0	0	280	3.0 d
raisin bran *(Sara Lee)*	220	4.0	37.0	7.0	n.a.	400	m.q.
Muffin, mix[1]**, 1 piece:**							
apple cinnamon or blackberry *(Martha White)*[2]	140	2.0	25.0	3.0	3	250	m.q.
applesauce *(Robin Hood/Gold Medal)*[2]	160	3.0	26.0	5.0	m.q.	240	m.q.
banana *(Robin Hood/ Gold Medal)*[2] . . .	150	3.0	24.0	5.0	m.q.	240	m.q.
blueberry:							
(Duncan Hines Bakery Style) . .	190	2.0	32.0	6.0	n.a.	250	m.q.
(Martha White) . .	140	2.0	25.0	3.0	3	260	m.q.

[1] *Prepared according to package directions.*
[2] *Prepared 6 per package.*

Food and Measure	cal.	prot. (gms)	carbo. (gms)	fat (gms)	chol. (mgs)	sod. (mgs)	fiber (gms)
(Robin Hood/Gold Medal)	170	3.0	26.0	6.0	m.q.	240	m.q.
wild (Duncan Hines)	110	2.0	17.0	3.0	n.a.	155	m.q.
bran (Martha White)	150	3.0	24.0	5.0	14	330	m.q.
bran and honey:							
(Duncan Hines) . .	120	2.0	18.0	4.0	n.a.	170	m.q.
(Duncan Hines Bakery Style) . .	200	2.0	32.0	7.0	n.a.	220	m.q.
caramel (Robin Hood/ Gold Medal)	150	3.0	23.0	5.0	m.q.	250	m.q.
cinnamon swirl (Duncan Hines Bakery Style) . . .	200	2.0	32.0	7.0	n.a.	245	m.q.
corn:							
(Dromedary)	120	3.0	20.0	4.0	n.a.	270	m.q.
(Flako)	116	1.8	19.8	3.3	n.a.	351	.7 d
(Robin Hood/Gold Medal)[1]	130	3.0	24.0	2.0	m.q.	250	m.q.
cranberry orange nut (Duncan Hines Bakery Style) . . .	200	2.0	30.0	8.0	n.a.	215	m.q.
honey bran (Robin Hood/Gold Medal)[1]	170	5.0	25.0	6.0	m.q.	240	m.q.
oat bran:							
apple cinnamon (Hain)	140	4.0	28.0	3.0	0	200	5.0 d
banana nut (Hain)	140	4.0	26.0	4.0	0	190	4.0 d
raspberry spice (Hain)	140	5.0	27.0	3.0	0	190	4.0 d
orangeberry (Martha White)	140	2.0	25.0	3.0	2	220	m.q.
pecan crunch (Duncan Hines Bakery Style)	220	3.0	27.0	11.0	n.a.	250	m.q.
raspberry (Martha White)	140	2.0	25.0	3.0	3	184	m.q.
strawberry (Martha White)[1]	140	2.0	25.0	3.0	3	270	m.q.

[1] Prepared 6 per package.

Food and Measure	cal.	prot. (gms)	carbo. (gms)	fat (gms)	chol. (mgs)	sod. (mgs)	fiber (gms)
Mulberry:							
10 berries, .5 oz. . . .	7	.2	1.5	.1	0	2	.1 c
1/2 cup	31	1.0	6.9	.3	0	7	.7 c
Mullet, striped, meat only:							
raw, 1 lb.	530	87.8	0	17.2	224	294	0
raw, 1 oz.	33	5.5	0	1.1	14	18	0
baked, broiled, or microwaved, 4 oz. . .	170	28.1	0	5.5	71	81	0
Mung bean:							
boiled, 1/2 cup	107	7.1	19.3	.4	0	2	2.5 d
Mung bean, sprouted:							
fresh:							
raw, 1 oz.	9	.9	1.7	.1	0	2	.3 d
boiled, drained, 1/2 cup	13	1.3	2.6	.1	0	6	.3 c
canned (La Choy), 2 oz.	8	.8	1.0	.1	0	20	.7 d
Mungo bean:							
boiled, 1/2 cup	95	6.8	16.5	.5	0	7	1.2 c
Mushroom:							
fresh:							
raw, untrimmed, 1 lb.	111	9.2	20.5	1.9	0	16	5.7 d
raw, pieces, 1/2 cup	9	.7	1.6	.2	0	1	.5 d
boiled, drained, pieces, 1/2 cup	21	1.7	4.0	.4	0	2	1.7 d
canned:							
(B in B), 1/4 cup . .	12	1.0	2.0	0	0	240	1.0 d
all cuts (Green Giant), 1/2 cup . . .	25	2.0	5.0	0	0	430	1.0 d
pieces and stems (Allens), 1/2 cup	20	2.0	3.0	<1.0	0	450	m.q.
pieces and stems (Empress), 2 oz.	14	1.0	2.0	n.a.	0	260	m.q.

Food and Measure	cal.	prot. (gms)	carbo. (gms)	fat (gms)	chol. (mgs)	sod. (mgs)	fiber (gms)
in butter sauce *(Green Giant)*, ½ cup	30	2.0	4.0	1.0	n.a.	330	.6 d
frozen, whole *(Birds Eye* Deluxe), 2.6 oz.	20	2.0	4.0	0	0	0	2.0 d
frozen, battered *(Stilwell Quick Krisp)*, 2 oz. . . .	140	2.0	15.0	8.0	5	280	m.q.
Mushroom, Japanese honey:							
trimmed, *(Frieda* of California), 1 oz.	9	.6	1.2	<.1	0	m.q.	m.q.
Mushroom, Oriental straw, canned:							
(Green Giant), 2 oz.	12	1.0	2.0	0	0	290	1.0 d
Mushroom, oyster:							
(Frieda of California), 1 oz.	7	.6	1.3	.1	0	1	.2 d
Mushroom, shiitake:							
fresh, cooked, 4 medium or ½ cup pieces	40	1.1	10.4	.2	0	3	1.4 c
dried, 4 medium, .5 oz.	44	1.4	11.3	.2	0	2	1.7 c
Mushroom gravy, canned:							
(Franco-American), 2 oz.	25	0	3.0	1.0	n.a.	290	n.a.
(Heinz), 2 oz. . . .	20	0	3.0	1.0	n.a.	200	n.a.
Mussel, blue, meat only:							
raw, 1 oz.	24	3.4	1.0	.7	8	81	0
raw, 1 cup	129	17.9	5.5	3.4	42	429	0
boiled or steamed, 4 oz.	195	27.0	8.4	5.1	64	418	0

Food and Measure	cal.	prot. (gms)	carbo. (gms)	fat (gms)	chol. (mgs)	sod. (mgs)	fiber (gms)
Mustard, prepared, 1 tbsp., except as noted:							
(Heinz Pourable), 1 tsp.	5	.3	.5	.2	0	70	0
(Kraft Pure)	10	0	1.0	1.0	0	170	0
brown:							
(Heinz), 1 tsp. . . .	8	.4	.5	.4	0	60	0
(Gulden's Spicy), 1/4 oz.	8	0	0	0	0	45	0
creamy mild *(Gulden's),* 1/4 oz.	6	0	0	0	0	60	0
Dijon:							
(French's), 1 tsp.	8	0	0	1.0	0	140	0
(Grey Poupon) . .	18	0	0	1.0	0	450	0
w/horseradish *(French's)*	16	1.0	1.0	1.0	0	265	n.a.
horseradish *(Kraft)*	14	1.0	1.0	1.0	0	135	0
hot *(Gulden's* Diablo), 1/4 oz.	8	0	0	0	0	55	0
jalapeño *(Great Impressions),* 2 tsp.	7	.4	.7	.3	0	173	n.a.
Medford *(French's)*	16	1.0	1.0	1.0	0	240	n.a.
mild *(Heinz),* 1 tsp.	5	.3	.5	.2	0	70	0
mild, creamy *(Gulden's),* 1/4 oz.	6	0	0	0	0	60	0
w/onion *(French's),* 1 tsp.	8	0	2.0	0	0	70	n.a.
spicy *(French's* Bold'n Spicy), 1 tsp. . . .	6	0	0	0	0	50	n.a.
stone ground *(Hain)*	14	1.0	1.0	1.0	0	185	n.a.
yellow *(French's)* . .	10	1.0	1.0	1.0	0	180	n.a.
Mustard greens:							
fresh, chopped:							
raw, 1 oz., 1/2 cup	7	.8	1.4	.1	0	7	.2 d
boiled, drained, 1/2 cup	11	1.6	1.5	.2	0	11	.5 c

Food and Measure	cal.	prot. (gms)	carbo. (gms)	fat (gms)	chol. (mgs)	sod. (mgs)	fiber (gms)
canned, chopped *(Allens)*, 1/2 cup . . .	20	1.0	2.0	<1.0	0	35	m.q.
frozen, chopped:							
(Frosty Acres),							
3.3 oz.	20	2.0	3.0	0	0	20	1.0 c
(Seabrook), 3.3 oz.	20	2.0	3.0	0	0	20	1.0 c
Mustard powder:							
(Spice Islands), 1 tsp.	9	.5	.3	.6	0	<1	<.1 c
Mustard sauce, hot:							
(Sauceworks), 1 tbsp.	35	0	3.0	2.0	5	85	n.a.
Mustard seed:							
yellow, 1 tsp.	15	.8	1.2	1.0	0	tr.	.2 c
Mustard spinach:							
raw, chopped, 1/2 cup	17	1.7	2.9	.2	0	m.q.	.8 c
boiled, drained,							
chopped, 1/2 cup	14	1.5	2.5	.2	0	m.q.	.7 c
Mustard tallow:							
1 tbsp.	115	0	0	12.8	13	0	0

N

Food and Measure	cal.	prot. (gms)	carbo. (gms)	fat (gms)	chol. (mgs)	sod. (mgs)	fiber (gms)
Nacho, mix:							
(Tio Sancho Micro-							
wave Snacks):							
chips, 4 oz.	567	8.5	74.4	26.1	n.a.	590	4.0 c
cheese sauce,							
3.5 oz.	247	14.5	2.3	20.0	m.q.	995	.4 c
Nacho seasoning:							
(Lawry's), 1 pkg. . . .	141	6.7	15.0	6.8	n.a.	2168	1.6 c
Natto:							
1/2 cup	187	15.6	12.6	9.7	0	6	1.4 c
Navy bean, 1/2 cup:							
boiled	129	7.9	24.0	.5	0	1	3.3 d
canned:							
w/liquid	148	9.9	26.8	.6	0	587	2.4 c
(Allens)	160	8.0	24.0	<1.0	0	440	m.q.
Navy bean,							
sprouted:							
raw, 1/2 cup	35	3.2	6.8	.4	0	m.q.	1.3 c
boiled, drained, 4 oz.	88	8.0	17.0	.9	0	m.q.	3.3 c
Nectarine:							
1 medium, 21/2″ diam.	67	1.3	16.0	.6	0	tr.	2.2 d
sliced, 1/2 cup	34	.7	8.1	.3	0	tr.	1.1 d
New England Brand							
Sausage:							
(Eckrich), 1-oz. slice	35	5.0	1.0	1.0	m.q.	370	(0)
(Oscar Mayer), .8-oz.							
slice	31	3.8	.4	1.6	14	293	(0)

Food and Measure	cal.	prot. (gms)	carbo. (gms)	fat (gms)	chol. (mgs)	sod. (mgs)	fiber (gms)
New Zealand spinach:							
raw, 1 oz. or 1/2 cup chopped	4	.4	.7	.1	0	37	.2 c
boiled, drained, chopped, 1/2 cup	11	1.2	2.0	.2	0	97	.6 c
Newberg sauce, canned:							
w/sherry *(Snow's),* 1/3 cup	120	3.0	10.0	8.0	n.a.	520	0
Noodle, Chinese:							
cellophane or long rice, dehydrated, 2 oz.	199	.1	48.8	<.1	0	6	<.1 c
chow mein, 1 cup . .	237	3.8	25.9	13.8	0	197	1.8 d
Noodle, egg:							
uncooked, 2 oz.:							
(Creamette)	221	8.0	40.0	2.5	70	3	.8 d
(Mueller's)	220	8.0	40.0	3.0	55	10	m.q.
(Prince)	210	8.0	40.0	2.0	65	35	m.q.
cooked:							
1 cup	212	7.6	39.7	2.4	53	11	3.5 d
spinach, 1 cup . .	211	8.1	38.8	2.5	52	20	m.q.
Noodle, Japanese:							
soba:							
dry, 2 oz.	192	8.2	42.5	.4	0	451	m.q.
cooked, 1 cup . . .	113	5.8	24.4	.1	0	40	m.q.
somen:							
dry, 2 oz.	203	6.5	42.2	.5	0	1049	2.4 d
cooked, 1 cup . . .	230	7.0	48.5	.3	0	284	.4 c
udon:							
dry, 2 oz.	159	3.9	32.3	.7	0	340	m.q.
cooked, 4 oz. . . .	115	2.8	23.0	.6	0	51	m.q.
Noodle and chicken dinner, frozen:							
(Banquet), 10 oz. . .	350	10.0	42.0	15.0	45	460	m.q.
(Swanson), 10 1/2 oz.	260	11.0	35.0	9.0	m.q.	860	m.q.

Food and Measure	cal.	prot. (gms)	carbo. (gms)	fat (gms)	chol. (mgs)	sod. (mgs)	fiber (gms)
Noodle and chicken dinner, *(cont.)*							
(Banquet Family Favorites), 10 oz. . .	340	11.0	42.0	15.0	45	455	m.q.
Noodle dishes, canned, 7.5 oz.:							
and beef, in sauce							
(Heinz)	170	8.0	17.0	8.0	m.q.	825	m.q.
and chicken:							
(Heinz)	160	6.0	19.0	7.0	m.q.	930	m.q.
(Hormel/Dinty Moore Micro-Cup)	180	7.0	18.0	8.0	20	1000	m.q.
and tuna *(Heinz)* . .	170	11.0	20.0	5.0	m.q.	950	m.q.
Noodle dishes, mix[1], 1/2 cup, except as noted:							
Alfredo:							
(Lipton Noodles and Sauce)[2]	220	7.0	24.0	10.0	m.q.	580	m.q.
(Minute Microwave Family Size)[3] . .	170	7.0	23.0	6.0	45	670	m.q.
(Minute Microwave Single Size)[3] . .	160	7.0	23.0	5.0	40	660	m.q.
(Mueller's Chef's Series)	190	5.0	23.0	9.0	m.q.	580	m.q.
beef *(Lipton* Noodles and Sauce)[4]	180	5.0	23.0	7.0	m.q.	700	m.q.
butter:							
(Lipton Noodles and Sauce)[4]	200	6.0	23.0	10.0	m.q.	510	m.q.
and herb *(Lipton* Noodles and Sauce)[4]	190	5.0	23.0	9.0	m.q.	520	m.q.

[1] *Prepared according to package directions, except as noted.*
[2] *Prepared with 1/2 cup whole milk and 2 tbsp. butter.*
[3] *Prepared with salted butter.*
[4] *Prepared with 2 tbsp. butter.*

Food and Measure	cal.	prot. (gms)	carbo. (gms)	fat (gms)	chol. (mgs)	sod. (mgs)	fiber (gms)
carbonara Alfredo (Lipton Noodles and Sauce)[2]	210	6.0	22.0	11.0	m.q.	530	m.q.
cheese:							
(Kraft Dinner), 3/4 cup[1]	340	10.0	37.0	17.0	50	630	m.q.
(Lipton Noodles and Sauce)[2]	190	5.0	25.0	8.0	m.q.	530	m.q.
chicken or chicken flavor:							
(Kraft Dinner), 3/4 cup[1]	240	8.0	31.0	9.0	35	880	m.q.
(Lipton Noodles and Sauce)[2]	180	5.0	23.0	8.0	m.q.	450	m.q.
(Minute Microwave Family Size)[3] . .	160	6.0	23.0	5.0	35	570	m.q.
(Minute Microwave Single Size)[3] . .	160	6.0	25.0	4.0	35	610	m.q.
(Mueller's Chef's Series)	160	3.0	21.0	8.0	m.q.	550	m.q.
broccoli (Lipton Noodles and Sauce)[4]	200	6.0	24.0	9.0	m.q.	500	m.q.
mushroom (Noodle Roni), 1 serving	160	6.0	25.0	4.0	m.q.	550	m.q.
fettuccini (Noodle Roni), 1 serving . .	300	7.0	29.0	18.0	m.q.	560	m.q.
garlic butter (Mueller's Chef's Series) . . .	170	3.0	21.0	7.0	m.q.	480	m.q.
garlic butter (Noodle Roni), 1 serving . .	300	7.0	29.0	17.0	m.q.	630	m.q.
herb butter (Noodle Roni), 1 serving . .	160	5.0	19.0	7.0	m.q.	290	m.q.

[1] Prepared without added salt.
[2] Prepared with 2 tbsp. butter.
[3] Prepared with salted butter.
[4] Prepared with 1/2 cup whole milk and 2 tbsp. butter.

Food and Measure	cal.	prot. (gms)	carbo. (gms)	fat (gms)	chol. (mgs)	sod. (mgs)	fiber (gms)
Noodle dishes, mix *(cont.)*							
Parmesan:							
(*Lipton* Noodles and Sauce)[1]	210	7.0	23.0	11.0	m.q.	480	m.q.
(*Minute* Microwave Family Size)[2] . .	170	6.0	23.0	6.0	45	470	m.q.
(*Minute* Microwave Single Size)[2] . .	160	6.0	23.0	5.0	40	460	m.q.
(*Noodle Roni*), 1 serving	240	7.0	23.0	13.0	m.q.	470	m.q.
pesto (*Noodle Roni*), 1 serving	220	6.0	23.0	12.0	m.q.	340	m.q.
Romanoff (*Noodle Roni*), 1 serving . .	240	8.0	28.0	11.0	m.q.	730	m.q.
sour cream and chives:							
(*Lipton* Noodles and Sauce)[3]	200	5.0	24.0	9.0	m.q.	500	m.q.
(*Mueller's Chef's Series*)	190	4.0	22.0	8.0	m.q.	470	m.q.
Stroganoff:							
(*Lipton* Noodles and Sauce)[1]	200	7.0	23.0	9.0	m.q.	410	m.q.
(*Mueller's Chef's Series*)	190	5.0	22.0	9.0	m.q.	620	m.q.
(*Noodle Roni*), 1 serving	350	11.0	37.0	17.0	m.q.	1190	m.q.
Noodle entree:							
canned, 7.5 oz.:							
and beef (*Heinz*)	170	8.0	17.0	8.0	m.q.	825	m.q.
and chicken (*Heinz*)	160	6.0	19.0	7.0	m.q.	930	m.q.
and chicken (*Hormel/Dinty Moore Micro-Cup*) . . .	180	7.0	18.0	8.0	20	1000	m.q.
and tuna (*Heinz*)	170	11.0	20.0	5.0	m.q.	950	m.q.

[1] *Prepared with 1/2 cup whole milk and 2 tbsp. butter.*
[2] *Prepared with salted butter.*
[3] *Prepared with 2 tbsp. butter.*

Food and Measure	cal.	prot. (gms)	carbo. (gms)	fat (gms)	chol. (mgs)	sod. (mgs)	fiber (gms)
freeze-dried, and chicken *(Mountain House)*, 1 cup . . .	270	10.0	34.0	10.0	m.q.	201	m.q.
frozen:							
and beef w/gravy *(Banquet Family Entrees)*, 8 oz.	200	13.0	22.0	7.0	m.q.	m.q.	m.q.
and julienne beef *(Banquet Family Entrees)*, 7 oz.	170	12.0	22.0	3.0	m.q.	m.q.	m.q.
Romanoff *(Stouffer's)*, 4 oz. . . .	170	7.0	15.0	9.0	m.q.	840	m.q.
Nut topping:							
(Planters), 1 oz. . . .	180	5.0	6.0	16.0	0	0	m.q.
Nutmeg, ground:							
1 tsp.	12	.1	1.1	.8	0	tr.	.1 c
Nuts, see specific listings							
Nuts, mixed, 1 oz.:							
w/peanuts *(Guy's)*	170	8.0	3.0	14.0	0	140	m.q.
dry-roasted:							
(Planters)	160	5.0	7.0	14.0	0	250	m.q.
(Planters Unsalted)	170	6.0	7.0	15.0	0	0	m.q.
w/peanuts	169	4.9	7.2	14.6	0	3	.3 c
w/peanuts, salted	169	4.9	7.2	14.6	0	190	.3 c
oil-roasted:							
(Flavor House) . .	180	5.0	6.0	18.0	0	125	m.q.
w/peanuts	175	4.8	6.1	16.0	0	3	2.6 d
w/peanuts, salted	175	4.8	6.1	16.0	0	185	2.6 d

O

Food and Measure	cal.	prot. (gms)	carbo. (gms)	fat (gms)	chol. (mgs)	sod. (mgs)	fiber (gms)
Oat (see also "Cereal"):							
whole-grain, 1 oz. . . .	110	4.8	18.8	2.0	0	1	m.q.
flakes (Arrowhead Mills), 2 oz.	220	10.0	39.0	4.0	0	1	8.1 d
rolled or oatmeal:							
dry, 1 oz.	109	4.5	19.0	1.8	0	1	2.9 d
cooked, 1 cup . . .	145	6.0	25.2	2.4	0	1	.4 c
cooked, salted, 1 cup	145	6.0	25.2	2.4	0	374	.4 c
Oat bran:							
raw, 1 oz.	70	4.9	18.8	2.0	0	1	4.5 d
cooked, 1 cup	87	7.0	25.1	1.9	0	2	.8 c
Oat flour:							
whole grain (Arrowhead Mills), 2 oz.	200	7.0	43.0	1.0	0	1	8.3 d
blend (Gold Medal), 4 oz. or 1 cup . . .	390	14.0	81.0	3.0	0	0	4.0 d
Ocean perch, Atlantic, meat only:							
raw, 1 lb.	427	84.5	0	7.4	191	339	0
raw, 1 oz.	27	5.3	0	.5	12	21	0
baked, broiled, or microwaved, 4 oz. . .	137	27.1	0	2.4	61	109	0
Ocean perch, frozen:							
(Booth), 4 oz.	100	20.0	0	1.0	m.q.	250	0
(Gorton's Fishmarket Fresh), 5 oz.	140	25.0	2.0	3.0	m.q.	100	0
(Van de Kamp's Natural), 4 oz.	110	21.0	2.0	2.0	65	60	0

Food and Measure	cal.	prot. (gms)	carbo. (gms)	fat (gms)	chol. (mgs)	sod. (mgs)	fiber (gms)
Ocean perch entree, frozen:							
breaded (Mrs. Paul's Crispy Crunchy), 2 pieces	310	14.0	19.0	20.0	40	460	m.q.
breaded (Van de Kamp's Light), 1 piece	260	17.0	19.0	13.0	40	400	m.q.
October bean, canned:							
w/pork (Luck's), 7¼ oz.	230	12.0	32.0	6.0	m.q.	550	10.0 d
Octopus, meat only:							
raw, 1 lb.	372	67.6	10.0	4.7	219	m.q.	0
raw, 1 oz.	23	4.2	.6	.3	14	m.q.	0
Oheloberry:							
10 berries, .4 oz. . .	3	<.1	.8	<.1	0	tr.	.2 c
½ cup	20	.3	4.8	.2	0	1	.9 c
Oil, 1 tbsp.:							
almond, cocoa butter, coconut, corn, cottonseed, hazelnut, nutmeg butter, palm, palm kernel, or poppyseed . . .	120	0	0	13.6	0	0	0
avocado or mustard	124	0	0	14.0	0	0	0
cod liver:							
regular/mint (Hain)	120	0	0	14.0	85	0	0
cherry (Hain) . . .	120	0	0	14.0	75	0	0
olive, peanut, safflower, sesame, soybean, sunflower, vegetable, or walnut	120	0	0	14.0	0	0	0
Okra:							
fresh:							
raw, trimmed, 1 oz.	11	.6	2.2	<.1	0	2	.3 c
raw, sliced, ½ cup	19	1.0	3.8	.1	0	4	.5 c

Food and Measure	cal.	prot. (gms)	carbo. (gms)	fat (gms)	chol. (mgs)	sod. (mgs)	fiber (gms)
Okra, fresh *(cont.)*							
boiled, drained, 8 pods, 3" × 5/8"	27	1.6	6.1	.1	0	5	.8 c
boiled drained, sliced, 1/2 cup	25	1.5	5.8	.1	0	4	.7 c
frozen:							
whole *(Seabrook)*, 3.3 oz.	30	2.0	7.0	0	0	2	1.0 c
whole *(Southern)*, 3.5 oz.	35	1.9	7.4	.2	0	20	m.q.
whole, baby *(Frosty Acres)*, 3.3 oz.	30	2.0	7.0	0	0	2	1.0 c
cut *(Seabrook)*, 3.3 oz.	25	1.0	6.0	0	0	3	1.0 c
cut *(Southern)*, 3.5 oz.	31	1.6	6.5	.2	0	20	m.q.
Old fashioned mix:							
bottled *(Holland House)*, 1 fl. oz. . .	33	0	8.0	0	0	6	0
Old fashioned loaf:							
(Oscar Mayer), 1 oz.	64	4.0	2.5	4.2	15	334	(0)
Olive, pickled:							
all varieties, all sizes *(S&W)*, 1 oz. . . .	46	0	0	5.1	0	215	m.q.
green, w/pits:							
10 small	33	.4	.4	3.6	0	686	.7 d
10 large	45	.5	.5	4.9	0	926	1.0 d
10 giant	76	.9	.9	8.3	0	1572	1.7 d
green, pitted, 1 oz.	33	.4	.4	3.6	0	680	.7 d
ripe, Manzanillo or mission, pitted:							
all sizes *(Lindsay)*, 1 oz.	32	.2	1.8	3.0	0	247	.9 d
(Lindsay), 10 small	37	.3	2.0	3.5	0	283	1.0 d
(Lindsay), 10 medium	44	.3	2.4	4.1	0	336	1.2 d
(Lindsay), 10 large	50	.4	2.8	4.8	0	388	1.4 d

Food and Measure	cal.	prot. (gms)	carbo. (gms)	fat (gms)	chol. (mgs)	sod. (mgs)	fiber (gms)
(Lindsay), 10 extra large	63	.5	3.5	5.9	0	484	1.8 d
ripe, mixed varieties:							
pitted *(Vlasic)*, 1 oz.	37	.3	.7	3.9	0	230	.4 c
sliced *(Lindsay)*, ½ cup	70	.6	4.1	6.5	0	598	2.0 d
ripe, salt-cured, Greek style:							
10 medium	65	.4	1.7	6.9	0	631	m.q.
10 extra large . . .	89	.6	2.3	9.5	0	868	m.q.
pitted, 1 oz.	96	.6	2.5	10.2	0	932	m.q.
ripe, Sevillano and Ascolano, pitted:							
all sizes *(Lindsay)*, 1 oz.	23	.3	1.6	1.9	0	255	.7 d
(Lindsay), 10 jumbo	66	.8	4.7	5.7	0	745	2.1 d
(Lindsay), 10 colossal	90	1.1	6.3	7.7	0	1010	2.8 d
(Lindsay), 10 super colossal	122	1.5	8.5	10.4	0	1365	3.8 d
Olive loaf:							
(Boar's Head), 1 oz.	60	3.0	1.0	4.5	10	360	(0)
(Eckrich), 1 oz. . . .	80	3.0	2.0	6.0	m.q.	320	(0)
(Hormel Perma-Fresh), 2 slices	110	7.0	5.0	7.0	m.q.	810	(0)
(Oscar Mayer), 1 oz.	62	3.2	2.9	4.2	13	402	(0)
Olive oil, see "Oil"							
Omelet, see "Egg breakfast"							
Onion, mature:							
fresh or stored:							
raw, 1 oz.	11	.3	2.4	<.1	0	1	.5 d
raw, chopped, ½ cup	30	.9	6.9	0.1	0	2	1.3 d
raw, chopped, 1 tbsp.	4	1	.9	<.1	0	tr.	.2 d
boiled, drained, chopped, ½ cup	47	1.4	10.7	.2	0	3	.7 c

Food and Measure	cal.	prot. (gms)	carbo. (gms)	fat (gms)	chol. (mgs)	sod. (mgs)	fiber (gms)
Onion *(cont.)*							
canned:							
cocktail, spiced							
(Vlasic), 1 oz. . . .	4	0	1.0	0	0	410	m.q.
sweet *(Heinz)*, 1 oz.	40	0	9.0	0	0	165	m.q.
whole, small *(S&W)*,							
1/2 cup	35	1.0	9.0	0	0	345	m.q.
frozen:							
whole, small *(Birds*							
Eye), 4 oz. . . .	40	1.0	10.0	0	0	10	2.0 d
whole, small *(Sea-*							
brook), 3.3 oz.	35	1.0	8.0	0	0	9	1.0 c
chopped, boiled,							
drained, 1 tbsp.	4	.1	1.0	<.1	0	2	.1 c
chopped *(Ore-Ida)*,							
2 oz.	20	0	4.0	<1.0	0	10	m.q.
chopped *(Sea-*							
brook), 1 oz. . .	8	0	2.0	0	0	2	0
w/cream sauce,							
small *(Birds Eye*							
Combinations),							
5 oz.	140	2.0	12.0	10.0	0	400	1.0 d
Onion, dried:							
flakes, 1 tbsp.	16	.5	4.2	<.1	0	1	.2 c
minced, w/green							
onion *(Lawry's)*,							
1 tsp.	7	.4	1.6	.2	0	1	.6 c
Onion, green (scal-							
lion):							
raw, trimmed, w/top:							
chopped, 1/2 cup	16	.9	3.7	.1	0	8	1.2 d
chopped, 1 tbsp.	2	.1	.4	<.1	0	1	.1 d
Onion, Welsh:							
trimmed, 1 oz.	10	.5	1.8	.1	0	n.a.	.3 c
Onion dip:							
bean *(Hain)*, 4 tbsp.	70	4.0	10.0	1.0	5	270	m.q.
creamy *(Kraft* Pre-							
mium), 2 tbsp. . . .	45	1.0	2.0	4.0	10	125	n.a.

Food and Measure	cal.	prot. (gms)	carbo. (gms)	fat (gms)	chol. (mgs)	sod. (mgs)	fiber (gms)
French:							
(Bison), 1 oz. . . .	60	1.0	2.0	5.0	20	180	n.a.
(Kraft), 2 tbsp. . .	60	1.0	3.0	4.0	0	240	n.a.
(Kraft Premium),							
2 tbsp.	45	1.0	2.0	4.0	10	150	n.a.
(Nasoya Vegi-Dip),							
1 oz.	50	2.0	4.0	3.0	0	100	n.a.
green (Kraft), 2 tbsp.	60	1.0	3.0	4.0	0	170	n.a.
Onion flavor snack:							
(Funyuns), 1 oz. . . .	140	2.0	18.0	6.0	0	275	n.a.
rings (Wise), 1 oz. . .	130	<1.0	21.0	5.0	0	360	n.a.
Onion gravy:							
canned (Heinz), 2 oz.	25	0	4.0	1.0	n.a.	150	n.a.
mix[1] (McCormick/							
Schilling), 1/4 cup	22	.6	3.6	.6	n.a.	337	n.a.
Onion powder:							
(Spice Islands), 1 tsp.	8	.2	1.7	<.1	0	1	.1 c
Onion rings, frozen:							
(Ore-Ida Onion Ring-							
ers), 2 oz.	140	2.0	18.0	7.0	0	190	m.q.
battered:							
(Stilwell), 3 oz. . .	250	2.0	22.0	16.0	<1.0	300	m.q.
(Farm Rich), 4 oz.	260	3.0	32.0	13.0	n.a.	580	m.q.
crispy:							
(Farm Rich Onion							
O's), 5 rings . .	190	3.0	26.0	9.0	0	480	m.q.
(Mrs. Paul's), 2.5 oz.	180	2.0	20.0	10.0	n.a.	270	m.q.
Onion salt:							
(Tone's), 1 tsp. . . .	1	.1	.4	tr.	0	1599	<.1 d
Opossum, meat only:							
roasted, 4 oz.	251	34.2	0	11.6	m.q.	m.q.	0
Orange:							
California navel:							
2 7/8"-diam. orange	65	1.4	16.3	.1	0	1	.6 c
sections w/out							
membrane,							
1/2 cup	38	.9	9.6	.1	0	1	.4 c

[1] Prepared according to package directions.

Food and Measure	cal.	prot. (gms)	carbo. (gms)	fat (gms)	chol. (mgs)	sod. (mgs)	fiber (gms)
Orange *(cont.)*							
California Valencia:							
2⅝"-diam. orange sections w/out membrane,	59	1.3	14.4	.4	0	0	.6 c
½ cup	44	.9	10.7	.3	0	0	.5 c
Florida:							
2¹¹⁄₁₆"-diam. orange sections w/out membrane,	69	1.1	17.4	.3	0	0	.5 c
½ cup	42	.7	10.7	.2	0	1	.3 c
Orange, canned, Mandarin, see "Tangerine"							
Orange drink, 6 fl. oz., except as noted:							
(Bama), 8.45 fl. oz.	120	0	29.0	0	0	60	(0)
(Crowley), 8 fl. oz. . .	130	0	32.0	0	0	15	(0)
(Hawaiian Punch) . .	100	0	24.0	0	0	20	(0)
(Hi-C)	95	.1	23.3	<.1	0	17	(0)
(Veryfine), 8 fl. oz. . .	130	<1.0	33.0	0	0	<70	(0)
frozen¹ or chilled, breakfast *(Bright & Early)*	90	.1	20.8	.2	0	18	(0)
mix²:							
(Kool-Aid), 8 fl. oz.	100	0	25.0	0	0	0	(0)
(Kool-Aid Presweetened), 8 fl. oz.	80	0	20.0	0	0	0	(0)
breakfast *(Tang)*	90	0	22.0	0	0	0	(0)
Orange extract:							
(Virginia Dare), 1 tsp.	22	0	0	0	0	0	0

¹ *Diluted according to package directions.*
² *Prepared according to package directions.*

Food and Measure	cal.	prot. (gms)	carbo. (gms)	fat (gms)	chol. (mgs)	sod. (mgs)	fiber (gms)
Orange juice, 6 fl. oz., except as noted:							
fresh	83	1.3	19.3	.4	0	2	.2 c
canned, bottled or boxed:							
(Campbell's Juice Bowl)	90	1.0	21.0	0	0	40	m.q.
(Del Monte Un-sweetened) . . .	80	1.0	19.0	0	0	< 10	m.q.
(Minute Maid), 8.45 fl. oz.	129	1.9	30.8	.2	0	20	m.q.
(Ocean Spray) . .	90	1.0	18.0	1.0	0	5	m.q.
(S&W)	83	2.0	18.0	0	0	2	m.q.
(Sippin' Pak), 8.45 fl. oz.	110	1.0	26.0	0	0	25	m.q.
(Stokely Un-sweetened) . . .	89	1.0	21.0	1.0	0	5	m.q.
(Tree Top)	90	1.0	22.0	0	0	5	m.q.
(TreeSweet)	78	1.0	18.0	0	0	15	m.q.
(Veryfine 100%), 8 fl. oz.	121	1.5	24.0	0	0	< 10	m.q.
blend (Minute Maid Juices to Go), 11.5 fl. oz. . . .	178	2.1	44.5	.7	0	37	m.q.
blend (Minute Maid On The Go), 10 fl. oz.	155	1.8	38.7	.6	0	32	m.q.
blend (Veryfine 100%), 8 fl. oz.	120	< 1.0	30.0	0	0	< 35	m.q.
or chilled (Sunkist)	84	1.3	20.0	.1	0	2	m.q.
chilled:							
(Citrus Hill Plus Calcium/Select) . .	90	< 1.0	20.0	< 1.0	0	10	m.q.
(Crowley), 8 fl. oz.	110	2.0	26.0	0	0	5	m.q.
(Kraft Pure 100% Unsweetened)	80	1.0	19.0	0	0	0	m.q.
(Sunkist)	84	1.3	20.1	.1	0	2	m.q.

Food and Measure	cal.	prot. (gms)	carbo. (gms)	fat (gms)	chol. (mgs)	sod. (mgs)	fiber (gms)
Orange juice, chilled *(cont.)*							
(Sunkist Fresh Squeezed) . . .	77	1.2	17.7	.3	0	2	m.q.
chilled or frozen[1]:							
(Minute Maid) . . .	91	1.4	21.9	.1	0	19	m.q.
calcium fortified *(Minute Maid)* . .	93	1.4	21.9	.1	0	19	m.q.
reduced acid *(Minute Maid)*	89	1.4	21.9	.1	0	19	m.q.
frozen[1]:							
(Sunkist), 8 fl. oz.	112	1.7	26.8	.1	0	3	m.q.
(TreeSweet)	84	1.0	20.0	0	0	15	m.q.
cocktail *(Welch's* Orchard), 10 fl. oz.	150	0	37.0	0	0	0	0
Orange juice drink:							
(Citrus Hill Lite Premium), 6 fl. oz. . .	60	<1.0	14.0	<1.0	0	10	(0)
(Kool-Aid Koolers), 8.45 fl. oz.	110	0	30.0	0	0	10	(0)
(Minute Maid Light'N Juicy), 6 fl. oz. . .	16	.3	3.8	<.1	0	17	(0)
(Tang Fruit Box), 8.45 fl. oz.	130	0	31.0	0	0	10	(0)
tropical *(Tang* Fruit Box), 8.45 fl. oz.	150	0	37.0	0	0	10	(0)
Orange sauce:							
Mandarin *(La Choy)*, 1 tbsp.	24	<.1	6.1	tr.	0	38	.1 d
Orange-banana juice:							
(Smucker's Naturally 100%), 8 fl. oz. . .	120	0	30.0	0	0	10	m.q.
Orange-grapefruit juice:							
canned, 6 fl. oz. . . .	80	1.1	19.1	.2	0	6	m.q.
chilled *(Kraft* Pure 100%), 6 fl. oz. . .	80	1.0	19.0	0	0	0	m.q.

[1] *Diluted according to package directions.*

Food and Measure	cal.	prot. (gms)	carbo. (gms)	fat (gms)	chol. (mgs)	sod. (mgs)	fiber (gms)
Orange-pineapple juice:							
chilled *(Kraft Pure 100%)*, 6 fl. oz. . . .	80	1.0	19.0	0	0	0	m.q.
Oregano, dried:							
(Spice Islands), 1 tsp.	6	.2	1.0	.1	0	<1	.2 c
Oriental 5-spice:							
(Tone), 1 tsp.	9	.3	1.9	.3	0	2	.5 d
Oyster, meat only:							
Eastern:							
raw, 1 lb.	311	32.0	17.7	11.2	248	507	0
raw, 6 medium, 3 oz.	58	5.9	3.3	2.1	46	94	0
steamed or poached, 4 oz.	155	16.0	8.9	5.6	124	254	0
Pacific:							
raw, 1 lb.	370	42.9	22.5	10.4	m.q.	481	0
raw, 1 oz.	23	2.7	1.4	.7	m.q.	30	0
raw, 1 medium . .	41	4.7	2.5	1.2	m.q.	53	0
Oyster, canned:							
Eastern, w/liquid, 4 oz.	78	8.0	4.4	2.8	62	127	0
(Bumble Bee), 1 cup	218	25.4	15.4	5.3	m.q.	185	0
whole *(S&W Fancy)*, 2 oz.	95	12.0	4.0	3.0	m.q.	m.q.	0
Oyster stew, see "Soup"							

P

Food and Measure	cal.	prot. (gms)	carbo. (gms)	fat (gms)	chol. (mgs)	sod. (mgs)	fiber (gms)
P&B loaf:							
(Kahn's), 1 slice . . .	40	5.0	1.0	2.0	m.q.	270	0
(JM), 1-oz. slice . . .	70	3.0	2.0	5.0	m.q.	330	0
Pancake, frozen:							
(Aunt Jemima Original							
Microwave), 3.5 oz.	211	6.2	40.3	3.6	n.a.	801	1.8 d
(Pillsbury Original Mi-							
crowave), 3 pieces	240	6.0	47.0	4.0	n.a.	550	m.q.
blueberry:							
(Aunt Jemima),							
3.5 oz.	220	6.2	42.3	3.7	21	826	1.7 d
(Downyflake),							
2 pieces	170	3.0	22.0	7.0	n.a.	500	m.q.
(Pillsbury Micro-							
wave), 3 pieces	250	5.0	49.0	4.0	n.a.	540	m.q.
buttermilk:							
(Aunt Jemima Mi-							
crowave), 3.5 oz.	210	6.4	41.3	3.0	20	860	1.8 d
(Aunt Jemima Lite							
Microwave),							
3.5 oz.	140	7.0	28.0	3.0	n.a.	660	m.q.
(Pillsbury Micro-							
wave), 3 pieces	260	6.0	51.0	4.0	n.a.	590	m.q.
wheat, harvest *(Pills-*							
bury Microwave),							
3 pieces	240	6.0	48.0	4.0	n.a.	420	m.q.
Pancake batter,							
frozen, 3.6 oz.:							
(Aunt Jemima Original)	183	5.7	36.5	2.4	19	763	1.8 d
blueberry *(Aunt Je-*							
mima)	204	5.0	38.7	4.0	27	688	1.8 d

Food and Measure	cal.	prot. (gms)	carbo. (gms)	fat (gms)	chol. (mgs)	sod. (mgs)	fiber (gms)
buttermilk *(Aunt Jemima)*	180	5.5	36.0	2.3	27	778	1.8 d
Pancake breakfast, frozen:							
and blueberries in sauce *(Swanson Great Starts)*, 7 oz.	410	8.0	72.0	10.0	n.a.	800	m.q.
and sausages *(Swanson Great Starts)*, 6 oz.	470	14.0	53.0	22.0	m.q.	900	m.q.
and strawberries in sauce *(Swanson Great Starts)*, 7 oz.	430	8.0	74.0	11.0	n.a.	860	m.q.
Pancake and waffle mix[1], 3 pieces, 4″ each:							
(Aunt Jemima Original)	116	3.4	25.4	.8	0	609	1.4 d
(Aunt Jemima Original Complete)	253	7.0	50.2	3.6	16	1024	2.1 d
(Bisquick Shake'N Pour)	260	6.0	48.0	5.0	0	850	m.q.
(Hungry Jack Extra Lights)	210	6.0	30.0	7.0	n.a.	490	m.q.
(Hungry Jack Extra Lights Complete)	190	4.0	37.0	2.0	n.a.	700	m.q.
(Hungry Jack Panshakes)	250	7.0	43.0	6.0	n.a.	880	m.q.
blueberry *(Hungry Jack)*	320	6.0	41.0	15.0	n.a.	820	m.q.
buckwheat *(Aunt Jemima)*	143	5.5	31.7	1.6	n.a.	773	5.0 d
buttermilk:							
(Aunt Jemima) . .	122	4.2	26.1	.7	1.0	698	1.3 d
(Aunt Jemima Complete)	231	7.2	46.4	2.8	8.7	950	2.0 d
(Aunt Jemima Lite Complete)	130	7.0	25.0	2.0	n.a.	570	m.q.

[1] *Prepared according to package directions.*

Food and Measure	cal.	prot. (gms)	carbo. (gms)	fat (gms)	chol. (mgs)	sod. (mgs)	fiber (gms)
Pancake and waffle mix, buttermilk *(cont.)*							
(Bisquick Shake'N Pour)	260	7.0	47.0	5.0	0	860	m.q.
(Hungry Jack) . . .	240	7.0	29.0	11.0	n.a.	570	m.q.
(Hungry Jack Complete)	180	4.0	39.0	1.0	n.a.	710	m.q.
(Hungry Jack Complete Packets)	180	4.0	35.0	3.0	n.a.	680	m.q.
oat bran *(Bisquick Shake'N Pour)* . .	240	7.0	45.0	4.0	0	580	1.0 d
whole wheat *(Aunt Jemima)*	161	7.0	34.5	1.0	0	892	3.6 d
Pancake syrup, 1 fl. oz., except as noted:							
table blends, 1 tbsp.:							
cane and maple . .	50	0	12.8	0	0	tr.	0
chiefly corn	59	0	15.4	0	0	n.a.	0
(Aunt Jemima Butter-Lite)*	50	0	13.0	0	0	65	(0)
(Aunt Jemima Lite)	54	.1	13.1	.1	0	92	.3 d
(Aunt Jemima Original)	109	0	27.1	0	0	32	(0)
(Log Cabin)	100	0	26.0	0	0	35	(0)
(Log Cabin Country Kitchen)*	100	0	26.0	0	0	20	(0)
(Log Cabin Lite) . . .	50	0	13.0	0	0	90	(0)
(Vermont Maid), 1 tbsp.	50	0	13.0	0	0	5	(0)
Pancreas, braised:							
beef, 4 oz.	307	30.7	0	19.5	m.q.	68	0
lamb, 4 oz.	265	25.9	0	17.1	454	59	0
pork, 4 oz.	248	32.3	0	12.2	357	48	0
veal (calf), 4 oz. . . .	290	33.0	0	16.6	m.q.	m.q.	0
Papaya:							
1-lb. papaya, 3½" × 5⅛" . . .	117	1.9	29.8	.4	0	8	2.8 d
peeled, seeded, cubed, ½ cup . . .	27	.4	6.9	.1	0	2	.6 d

Food and Measure	cal.	prot. (gms)	carbo. (gms)	fat (gms)	chol. (mgs)	sod. (mgs)	fiber (gms)
Papaya nectar:							
(Libby's), 6 fl. oz. . .	110	0	28.0	0	0	10	m.q.
Papaya punch:							
(Veryfine), 8 fl. oz. . .	120	<1.0	30.0	0	0	<10	m.q.
Paprika:							
1 tsp.	6	.3	1.2	.3	0	1	.4 c
Parsley:							
fresh:							
untrimmed, 1 lb. . .	140	9.5	29.8	1.3	0	169	19.0 d
10 sprigs	3	.2	.7	<.1	0	4	.4 d
chopped, 1/2 cup	10	.7	2.1	.1	0	12	1.3 d
dried, 1 tsp.	1	.1	.2	.1	0	1	tr.c
freeze-dried, 1 tbsp.	1	.1	.2	<.1	0	2	<.1 c
Parsley root:							
1 oz.	3	.8	.7	.2	0	28	.4 d
Parsley seasoning:							
all purpose (McCor-mick/Schilling Parsley Patch), 1 tsp.	6	.3	1.0	0	0	3	m.q.
Parsnip:							
raw, untrimmed, 1 lb.	289	4.6	69.4	1.2	0	39	7.7 c
raw, sliced, 1/2 cup	50	.8	12.1	.2	0	7	1.3 c
boiled, drained:							
1 medium, 9" × 2 1/4" diam.	130	2.1	31.3	.5	0	17	4.3 d
sliced, 1/2 cup . . .	63	1.0	15.2	.2	0	8	2.1 d
Passion fruit, purple:							
trimmed, 1 oz.	27	.6	6.6	.2	0	n.a.	3.1 c
1 medium	18	.4	4.2	.1	0	n.a.	2.0 c
Passion fruit juice:							
fresh:							
purple, 4 fl. oz. . .	63	.5	16.8	.1	0	n.a.	.1 c
yellow, 4 fl. oz. . .	75	.8	17.8	.2	0	n.a.	.2 c
cocktail, bottled or frozen[1] (Welch's Orchard Tropicals), 6 fl. oz.	100	0	25.0	0	0	20	0

[1] Diluted according to package directions.

Food and Measure	cal.	prot. (gms)	carbo. (gms)	fat (gms)	chol. (mgs)	sod. (mgs)	fiber (gms)
Passion fruit-orange tropical re-fresher:							
(Veryfine), 8 fl. oz. . . .	110	<1.0	26.0	0	0	<25	n.a.
Pasta, dry (see also "Macaroni"):							
uncooked, 2 oz.:							
plain	211	7.3	42.6	.9	0	4	1.4 d
(Ronzoni)	210	7.0	41.0	1.0	0	<5	m.q.
all varieties, except whole wheat *(Al Dente)*	220	8.0	40.0	2.0	m.q.	20	m.q.
corn, wheat-free *(De Boles)* . . .	210	4.0	44.0	2.0	0	30	m.q.
w/egg *(Creamette)*	221	8.0	40.0	2.5	70	3	.8 d
garlic and parsley, Jerusalem ar-tichoke or spin-ach *(De Boles)*	210	8.0	43.0	1.0	0	3	m.q.
rainbow *(Creamette)*	210	8.0	42.0	1.0	0	5	1.3 d
spinach, w/egg *(Creamette)* . . .	220	8.0	40.0	3.0	70	65	.8 d
tomato and basil or vegetable rainbow *(De Boles)* . . .	200	8.0	41.0	1.0	0	8	m.q.
whole-wheat *(Al Dente)*	210	8.0	42.0	1.0	0	10	m.q.
whole wheat *(De Boles* Natural Gourmet)	200	7.0	40.0	<1.0	0	0	6.0 d
cooked, 1 cup:							
plain	197	6.7	39.7	.9	0	1	3.1 d
corn	176	3.7	39.1	1.0	0	1	m.q.
spinach	183	6.4	36.6	.9	0	20	1.7 c
whole wheat . . .	174	7.5	37.2	.6	0	4	1.4 c
Pasta, fresh-refriger-ated, w/egg:							
uncooked:							
2 oz.	163	6.4	31.0	1.3	41	15	m.q.

Food and Measure	cal.	prot. (gms)	carbo. (gms)	fat (gms)	chol. (mgs)	sod. (mgs)	fiber (gms)
spinach, 2 oz. . . .	164	6.4	31.6	1.2	41	15	m.q.
cooked:							
4 oz.	149	5.8	28.3	1.2	37	7	m.q.
spinach, 4 oz. . . .	147	5.7	28.4	1.1	37	7	m.q.
Pasta dinner, frozen (see also specific pasta listings):							
shells, stuffed, 3-cheese *(Le Menu Light Style)*, 10 oz.	280	16.0	35.0	8.0	m.q.	720	m.q.
Pasta dishes, canned (see also specific pasta listings):							
garden medley *(Lipton Hearty Ones)*, 11 oz.	323	15.1	63.4	3.8	6	914	m.q.
Italiano *(Lipton Hearty Ones)*, 11 oz.	328	13.9	63.4	1.9	n.a.	1241	m.q.
w/meatballs, in sauce, rings or twists *(Buitoni)*, 7.5 oz.	210	8.0	28.0	7.0	20	850	m.q.
rings, in sauce *(Buitoni)*, 7.5 oz.	150	5.0	24.0	4.0	5	650	m.q.
twists, in pizza sauce *(Franco-American Hearty)*, 7.5 oz. . .	220	8.0	32.0	7.0	n.a.	850	m.q.
twists, in sauce *(Buitoni)*, 7.5 oz.	150	5.0	24.0	4.0	0	610	m.q.
Pasta dishes, frozen (see also "Pasta entree" and specific listings) 1/2 cup, except as noted:							
Alfredo, w/broccoli *(The Budget Gourmet Side Dish)*, 5.5 oz.	200	14.0	17.0	8.0	25	390	m.q.

Food and Measure	cal.	prot. (gms)	carbo. (gms)	fat (gms)	chol. (mgs)	sod. (mgs)	fiber (gms)
Pasta dishes, frozen *(cont.)*							
creamy cheddar *(Green Giant Pasta Accents)*	100	4.0	12.0	5.0	5	310	m.q.
Dijon *(Green Giant Garden Gourmet)*, 1 pkg.	260	7.0	21.0	17.0	55	630	4.0 d
garden herb *(Green Giant Pasta Accents)*	80	3.0	11.0	3.0	5	220	m.q.
garlic seasoning *(Green Giant Pasta Accents)*	110	3.0	13.0	5.0	5	280	m.q.
Florentine *(Green Giant Garden Gourmet)*, 1 pkg.	230	14.0	27.0	9.0	25	840	4.0 d
marinara *(Green Giant One Serving)*, 5.5 oz.	180	5.0	29.0	5.0	0	730	m.q.
Parmesan, w/sweet peas *(Green Giant One Serving)*, 5.5 oz.	170	9.0	24.0	5.0	10	510	m.q.
primavera *(Green Giant Pasta Accents)*	110	5.0	13.0	5.0	5	180	m.q.
and vegetables:							
in Stroganoff sauce *(Birds Eye Custom Cuisine)*, 4.6 oz.[1]	120	5.0	15.0	5.0	30	700	0
in white cheese sauce *(Birds Eye Custom Cuisine)*, 4.6 oz.[1]	150	7.0	19.0	6.0	15	440	1.0 d

---

[1] *Without added ingredients.*

Food and Measure	cal.	prot. (gms)	carbo. (gms)	fat (gms)	chol. (mgs)	sod. (mgs)	fiber (gms)
Pasta dishes, mix[1]							
(see also specific listings), 1/2 cup, except as noted:							
Alfredo (McCormick/ Schilling Pasta Prima)	253	7.0	27.0	13.0	n.a.	1178	m.q.
bacon vinaigrette (Country Recipe Pasta Salad) . . .	140	4.0	24.0	4.0	n.a.	210	m.q.
broccoli:							
cheddar w/fusilli (Lipton Pasta & Sauce)[2]	200	7.0	25.0	9.0	n.a.	520	m.q.
creamy (Lipton Pasta Salad)[3] . .	200	5.0	23.0	10.0	n.a.	190	m.q.
buttermilk, country (Mueller's Salad Bar)	250	5.0	22.0	16.0	n.a.	410	m.q.
carbonara Alfredo (Lipton Pasta and Sauce)	140	4.6	20.2	4.2	n.a.	459	0
cheese:							
cheddar (Minute Microwave Family Size)[4]	160	6.0	20.0	7.0	15	530	m.q.
cheddar (Minute Microwave Single Size)[4]	160	6.0	20.0	6.0	15	520	m.q.
cheddar, tangy (Hain Pasta & Sauce), 1/4 pkg.	180	6.0	24.0	6.0	n.a.	350	m.q.
supreme (Lipton Pasta and Sauce)	139	5.8	24.0	2.3	n.a.	406	.2 c

[1] Prepared according to package directions, except as noted.
[2] Prepared with 1/2 cup whole milk and 2 tbsp. butter.
[3] Prepared with 3 tbsp. milk and 3 tbsp. mayonnaise or salad dressing.
[4] Prepared with salted butter.

Food and Measure	cal.	prot. (gms)	carbo. (gms)	fat (gms)	chol. (mgs)	sod. (mgs)	fiber (gms)
Pasta dishes, mix, cheese *(cont.)*							
Parmesan, creamy *(Hain* Pasta & Sauce), 1/4 pkg.	150	8.0	22.0	3.0	10	400	m.q.
chicken broccoli *(Lipton* Pasta and Sauce)	129	5.4	22.4	2.0	n.a.	425	m.q.
cucumber, creamy *(Mueller's* Salad Bar)	250	4.0	22.0	16.0	n.a.	460	m.q.
Dijon, creamy *(Country Recipe* Pasta Salad)	190	4.0	24.0	10.0	n.a.	310	m.q.
garlic, creamy *(Lipton* Pasta & Sauce)[1]	210	6.0	27.0	10.0	m.q.	620	m.q.
herb and garlic *(McCormick/Schilling Pasta Prima)*, 1 cup	326	9.0	45.0	12.0	m.q.	869	m.q.
herb tomato *(Lipton* Pasta & Sauce)[2]	180	5.0	26.0	7.0	n.a.	420	m.q.
homestyle *(Mueller's* Salad Bar)	250	4.0	22.0	16.0	n.a.	390	m.q.
Italian:							
creamy *(Country Recipe* Pasta Salad)	160	4.0	22.0	7.0	n.a.	340	m.q.
creamy *(Mueller's* Salad Bar) . . .	290	3.0	20.0	22.0	n.a.	550	m.q.
herb *(Fantastic* Pasta Salad)[3] . .	167	4.0	19.0	9.0	n.a.	176	m.q.
herb *(Hain* Pasta & Sauce), 1/5 pkg.	110	4.0	17.0	2.0	n.a.	160	m.q.
robust *(Lipton* Pasta Salad)[4]	190	5.0	25.0	8.0	n.a.	300	m.q.

[1] *Prepared with 1/2 cup whole milk and 2 tbsp. butter.*
[2] *Prepared with 2 tbsp. butter.*
[3] *Prepared with oil, vinegar, and tomato.*
[4] *Prepared with 2 tbsp. oil.*

Food and Measure	cal.	prot. (gms)	carbo. (gms)	fat (gms)	chol. (mgs)	sod. (mgs)	fiber (gms)
zesty *(Mueller's Salad Bar)* . . .	140	3.0	21.0	5.0	n.a.	400	m.q.
marinara:							
(Hain Pasta & Sauce), 1/4 pkg.	120	5.0	23.0	1.0	<5	390	m.q.
(McCormick/Schilling Pasta Prima), 1 pkg. dry	74	1.0	16.0	0	0	690	m.q.
mushroom, creamy *(Lipton* Pasta & Sauce)[1]	210	6.0	26.0	9.0	m.q.	500	m.q.
mushroom and chicken flavors *(Lipton* Pasta and Sauce)	124	5.8	23.4	.8	n.a.	435	.2 c
Oriental:							
w/fusilli *(Lipton* Pasta and Sauce)	130	5.4	25.5	.7	n.a.	506	.3 c
spicy *(Fantastic* Pasta Salad)[2] . .	175	3.0	19.0	10.0	n.a.	168	m.q.
pasta salad *(McCormick/Schilling Pasta Prima),* 1 cup . . .	390	7.0	41.0	23.0	n.a.	822	m.q.
pesto *(McCormick/ Schilling Pasta Prima)*	193	6.0	29.0	6.0	n.a.	356	m.q.
primavera *(Hain* Pasta & Sauce), 1/4 pkg.	140	7.0	20.0	4.0	10	430	m.q.
ranch *(Country Recipe* Pasta Salad) . . .	140	4.0	19.0	5.0	n.a.	300	m.q.
Swiss, creamy *(Hain* Pasta & Sauce), 1/5 pkg.	170	6.0	26.0	4.0	n.a.	360	m.q.

---

[1] *Prepared with 1/2 cup whole milk and 2 tbsp. butter.*
[2] *Prepared with oil, vinegar, and green onions.*

Food and Measure	cal.	prot. (gms)	carbo. (gms)	fat (gms)	chol. (mgs)	sod. (mgs)	fiber (gms)
Pasta entree, frozen, see also specific listings:							
baked, and cheese *(Celentano)*, 6 oz.	290	12.0	29.0	13.0	m.q.	350	m.q.
carbonara *(Stouffer's)*, 9¾ oz.	620	19.0	34.0	45.0	m.q.	780	m.q.
casino *(Stouffer's)*, 9¼ oz.	300	9.0	44.0	10.0	m.q.	800	m.q.
Mexicali *(Stouffer's)*, 10 oz.	490	16.0	36.0	31.0	m.q.	1020	m.q.
Oriental *(Stouffer's)*, 9⅞ oz.	300	8.0	35.0	14.0	m.q.	760	m.q.
primavera: *(Stouffer's)*, 10⅝ oz.	540	14.0	26.0	42.0	m.q.	1160	m.q.
(Weight Watchers), 8.5 oz.	260	15.0	22.0	11.0	5	800	m.q.
shells: and beef *(The Budget Gourmet)*, 10 oz.	340	20.0	34.0	14.0	35	985	m.q.
cheese, w/tomato sauce *(Stouffer's)*, 9¼ oz.	330	17.0	32.0	15.0	m.q.	850	m.q.
shells, stuffed: *(Buitoni* Single Serving), 9 oz.	460	18.0	46.0	13.0	80	840	m.q.
(Celentano), 8 oz.	330	18.0	41.0	11.0	m.q.	680	m.q.
w/vegetables *(Legume* Provencale), 11 oz.	240	15.0	26.0	12.0	0	660	6.2 d
trio *(Tyson Gourmet Selection)*, 11 oz.	450	21.0	53.0	17.0	n.a.	890	m.q.
Pasta salad, see "Pasta dishes, mix"							

Food and Measure	cal.	prot. (gms)	carbo. (gms)	fat (gms)	chol. (mgs)	sod. (mgs)	fiber (gms)
Pasta sauce, 4 oz., except as noted:							
(Enrico's All Natural)	60	2.0	9.0	1.0	0	345	m.q.
(Enrico's All Natural No Salt)	60	2.0	9.0	1.0	0	30	m.q.
(Hunt's Traditional)	70	2.0	12.0	2.0	0	530	m.q.
(Pastorelli Italian Chef)	81	3.0	11.0	3.0	n.a.	430	1.1 c
(Prego)	140	1.0	20.0	6.0	n.a.	630	m.q.
(Prego No Salt) . . .	100	2.0	11.0	6.0	n.a.	25	m.q.
(Ragu)	80	2.0	9.0	4.0	0	740	m.q.
(Ragu Chunky Garden Style)	70	2.0	10.0	3.0	0	440	m.q.
(Ragu Fresh Italian)	90	2.0	13.0	3.0	0	490	m.q.
(Ragu Homestyle) . .	50	2.0	6.0	2.0	0	390	m.q.
(Ragu Thick & Hearty)	100	2.0	·15.0	3.0	0	460	m.q.
w/beef, ground (Chef Boyardee)	90	2.0	14.0	3.0	m.q.	605	m.q.
marinara (Prego) . .	100	1.0	11.0	5.0	0	500	m.q.
meat or meat flavor:							
(Chef Boyardee), 3.75 oz.	80	2.0	11.0	3.0	n.a.	650	m.q.
(Chef Boyardee Original), 3.75 oz.	120	3.0	13.0	6.0	n.a.	650	m.q.
(Hunt's)	70	2.0	12.0	2.0	n.a.	570	m.q.
(Prego)	150	2.0	21.0	6.0	n.a.	630	m.q.
(Weight Watchers), 1/3 cup	50	2.0	9.0	1.0	n.a.	440	m.q.
meatless (Chef Boyardee)	60	1.0	11.0	1.0	n.a.	790	m.q.
mushroom or mush-room flavor:							
(Chef Boyardee), 3.75 oz.	60	1.0	11.0	1.0	n.a.	790	m.q.
(Chef Boyardee Jars)	70	1.0	11.0	2.0	n.a.	655	m.q.
(Chef Boyardee Original), 3.75 oz.	80	1.0	13.0	3.0	n.a.	680	m.q.

Food and Measure	cal.	prot. (gms)	carbo. (gms)	fat (gms)	chol. (mgs)	sod. (mgs)	fiber (gms)
Pasta sauce, mushroom or mushroom flavor *(cont.)*							
(Enrico's)	60	2.0	9.0	1.0	0	m.q.	m.q.
(Hunt's)	70	2.0	12.0	2.0	0	560	m.q.
(Prego)	140	1.0	21.0	5.0	n.a.	630	m.q.
(Weight Watchers), 1/3 cup	40	1.0	9.0	0	0	430	m.q.
w/mushrooms *(Enrico's* Pasta Sauce)	60	2.0	9.0	1.0	0	336	m.q.
mushroom and green pepper:							
(Enrico's All Natural)	60	2.0	9.0	1.0	0	345	m.q.
(Enrico's All Natural No Salt)	60	2.0	9.0	1.0	0	30	m.q.
(Prego Extra Chunky)	110	1.0	13.0	6.0	n.a.	440	m.q.
mushroom and onion *(Prego* Extra Chunky)	110	2.0	14.0	5.0	n.a.	540	m.q.
mushroom and tomato *(Prego* Extra Chunky)	110	1.0	13.0	6.0	n.a.	500	m.q.
sausage and green pepper *(Prego* Extra Chunky)	170	3.0	19.0	9.0	m.q.	480	m.q.
tomato:							
garden, w/mushrooms *(Prego* Al Fresco)	100	1.0	12.0	5.0	n.a.	560	m.q.
garden, w/peppers *(Prego* Al Fresco)	100	1.0	11.0	6.0	n.a.	560	m.q.
and onion *(Prego* Extra Chunky)	110	1.0	14.0	6.0	n.a.	470	m.q.
Pasta sauce mix, dry, 1 pkg.:							
(Lawry's Rich & Thick)	147	3.5	28.1	2.2	n.a.	2172	.5 c
(McCormick/Schilling)	26	.8	5.0	n.a.	n.a.	492	m.q.

Food and Measure	cal.	prot. (gms)	carbo. (gms)	fat (gms)	chol. (mgs)	sod. (mgs)	fiber (gms)
w/imported mush-rooms *(Lawry's)* . .	143	5.2	26.0	1.5	n.a.	2015	2.1 c
Pasta snack chip:							
(Bachman Pastapazazz), 1 oz. . . .	150	2.0	15.0	9.0	n.a.	340	m.q.
Pastrami:							
(Hillshire Farm Deli Select), 1 oz.	31	6.0	<1.0	.4	m.q.	290	0
(Oscar Mayer), .6-oz. slice	16	3.2	.1	.3	7	219	0
(Boar's Head), 1 oz.	40	6.0	<1.0	1.5	16	270	0
(Healthy Deli), 1 oz.	34	5.3	.8	1.1	14	195	0
turkey, see "Turkey pastrami"							
Pastry dough (see also "Pie crust"):							
pocket *(Pillsbury)*, 1 piece	230	4.0	25.0	13.0	5	550	m.q.
sheet, puff pastry *(Pepperidge Farm)*, 1/4 piece	260	4.0	22.0	17.0	n.a.	290	m.q.
shell:							
patty *(Pepperidge Farm)*, 1 piece	210	3.0	16.0	15.0	n.a.	180	m.q.
puff pastry, mini *(Pepperidge Farm)*, 1 piece	50	1.0	4.0	4.0	n.a.	40	m.q.
Pâté, canned:							
1 oz.	90	4.0	.4	7.9	m.q.	198	0
1 tbsp.	41	1.9	.2	3.6	m.q.	91	0
chicken liver, 1 oz.	57	3.8	1.9	3.7	m.q.	m.q.	0
chicken liver, 1 tbsp.	26	1.8	.9	1.7	m.q.	m.q.	0
goose liver, smoked, 1 oz.	131	3.2	1.3	12.4	43	m.q.	0
goose liver, smoked, 1 tbsp.	60	1.5	.6	5.7	20	m.q.	0

Food and Measure	cal.	prot. (gms)	carbo. (gms)	fat (gms)	chol. (mgs)	sod. (mgs)	fiber (gms)
Pea pod, Chinese, see "Peas, edible-podded"							
Peach:							
fresh:							
2¹/₂"-diam. peach, 4 per lb.	37	.6	9.7	.1	0	tr.	1.4 d
pulp, sliced, ¹/₂ cup	37	.6	9.4	.1	0	1	1.4 d
canned:							
(Mott's Peach Fruit Pak), 3.75 oz. . . .	75	0	18.0	0	0	7	m.q.
spiced, in heavy syrup, whole, ¹/₂ cup	90	.5	24.3	.1	0	5	.3 c
canned, freestone, halves or slices, ¹/₂ cup:							
(Del Monte)	90	0	23.0	0	0	<10	m.q.
(Del Monte Lite) . .	60	0	13.0	0	0	<10	m.q.
in heavy syrup *(S&W)*	100	0	26.0	0	0	10	m.q.
in extra heavy syrup	126	.6	34.1	<.1	0	11	.4 c
or yellow cling, in heavy syrup . . .	95	.6	25.5	.1	0	8	.4 c
canned, yellow cling, ¹/₂ cup halves or slices, except as noted:							
in water	29	.5	7.5	.1	0	4	.4 c
in juice	55	.8	14.3	<.1	0	6	.6 d
in light syrup . . .	68	.6	18.3	<.1	0	7	.4 c
in heavy syrup *(S&W)*	100	0	25.0	0	0	10	m.q.
in heavy syrup *(Del Monte)*	80	0	22.0	0	0	<10	m.q.
in heavy syrup *(Del Monte Lite)* . . .	50	0	13.0	0	0	<10	m.q.

Food and Measure	cal.	prot. (gms)	carbo. (gms)	fat (gms)	chol. (mgs)	sod. (mgs)	fiber (gms)
diced (Del Monte Fruit Cup), 5 oz.	110	0	28.0	0	0	<10	m.q.
spiced, w/pits (Del Monte), 3 1/2 oz.	80	0	20.0	0	0	<10	m.q.
spiced, whole (S&W)	90	0	23.0	0	0	10	m.q.
dried:							
(Del Monte), 2 oz.	140	2.0	35.0	0	0	<10	m.q.
sulfured, halves, 1/2 cup	192	2.9	49.1	.6	0	6	6.6 d
sulfured, 10 halves, 4.6 oz.	311	4.7	79.7	1.0	0	9	10.7 d
freeze-dried (Mountain House), 1/4 cup . .	50	1.0	12.0	0	0	<1	m.q.
frozen, sliced, sweet- ened, 1/2 cup . . .	118	.8	30.0	.2	0	8	.5 c
Peach butter:							
(Smucker's), 1 tsp.	15	0	4.0	0	0	0	m.q.
Peach cobbler, see "Cobbler"							
Peach drink:							
(Hi-C), 6 fl. oz.	101	.1	24.8	<.1	0	18	(0)
Peach juice:							
(Smucker's Naturally 100%), 8 fl. oz. . .	120	1.0	30.0	0	0	10	m.q.
orchard blend (Dole Pure & Light), 6 fl. oz.	90	0	24.0	0	0	10	m.q.
Peach nectar:							
(Libby's), 6 fl. oz. . .	100	0	24.0	0	0	5	m.q.
Peanut[1], 1 oz., except as noted:							
(Beer Nuts)	180	7.0	7.0	14.0	n.a.	60	m.q.
all varieties:							
unroasted, in shell, 1 lb.	1877	85.4	53.4	163.0	0	60	19.5 d
unroasted	159	7.2	4.5	13.8	0	5	1.7 d

[1] Shelled, except as noted.

Food and Measure	cal.	prot. (gms)	carbo. (gms)	fat (gms)	chol. (mgs)	sod. (mgs)	fiber (gms)
Peanut *(cont.)*							
boiled, salted	90	3.8	6.0	6.2	0	213	.6 c
dry-roasted:							
1 oz.	164	6.6	6.0	13.9	0	2	2.3 d
1/2 cup	428	17.3	15.7	36.3	0	4	5.8 d
salted	164	6.6	6.0	13.9	0	228	2.3 d
oil-roasted:							
1 oz.	163	7.4	5.3	13.8	0	2	2.5 d
1/2 cup	419	19.0	13.6	35.5	0	4	6.3 d
salted	163	7.4	5.3	13.8	0	121	2.5 d
cocktail, oil-roasted:							
(Planters)	170	7.0	5.0	15.0	0	160	m.q.
(Planters Unsalted)	170	7.0	5.0	15.0	0	0	m.q.
dry-roasted:							
(Flavor House) . .	180	8.0	5.0	14.0	0	200	m.q.
(Flavor House Un-							
salted)	180	8.0	5.0	14.0	0	0	m.q.
(Frito-Lay's), 1 1/8 oz.	190	7.0	7.0	16.0	0	300	m.q.
(Guy's)	170	8.0	3.0	14.0	0	310	m.q.
(Planters)	160	7.0	6.0	14.0	0	250	m.q.
(Planters Unsalted)	170	7.0	5.0	15.0	0	0	m.q.
honey roasted:							
(Eagle Honey							
Roast).	170	7.0	7.0	13.0	0	140	m.q.
(Flavor House) . .	160	6.0	9.0	11.0	0	120	m.q.
(Planters)	170	6.0	8.0	13.0	0	180	m.q.
dry-roasted *(Plant-*							
ers)	160	7.0	7.0	13.0	0	90	m.q.
oil-roasted:							
(Flavor House) . .	170	7.0	5.0	15.0	0	125	m.q.
(Planters)	170	7.0	5.0	15.0	0	160	m.q.
redskin *(Planters)*	170	7.0	5.0	15.0	0	150	m.q.
Spanish:							
(Guy's)	170	8.0	3.0	14.0	0	170	m.q.
dry-roasted *(Plant-*							
ers)	160	7.0	6.0	14.0	0	200	m.q.
oil-roasted *(Flavor*							
House)	170	7.0	5.0	15.0	0	125	m.q.

Food and Measure	cal.	prot. (gms)	carbo. (gms)	fat (gms)	chol. (mgs)	sod. (mgs)	fiber (gms)
Peanut butter, 2 tbsp.:							
chunk style:							
(Bama)	200	7.0	6.0	17.0	0	115	m.q.
(Jif)	190	9.0	6.0	16.0	0	155	m.q.
(Peter Pan Extra Crunchy)	190	9.1	5.1	16.3	0	122	m.q.
(Skippy Super Chunk)	190	9.0	4.0	17.0	0	130	.6 c
(Smucker's Chunky Natural)	200	8.0	6.0	16.0	0	125	m.q.
unsalted	188	7.7	6.9	16.0	0	5	2.1 d
smooth style:							
(Bama)	200	7.0	6.0	17.0	0	140	m.q.
(Jif)	190	9.0	6.0	16.0	0	155	m.q.
(Peter Pan Creamy)	190	8.6	5.7	16.4	0	150	m.q.
(Skippy Creamy)	190	9.0	4.0	17.0	0	150	.6 c
(Smucker's Natural)	200	8.0	6.0	16.0	0	125	m.q.
unsalted	188	7.9	6.6	16.0	0	5	1.9 d
jelly and, see "Jelly and peanut butter"							
Peanut butter flavor baking chips:							
(Reese's), 1/4 cup . .	230	7.0	19.0	13.0	5	90	m.q.
Peanut butter-cara-mel topping:							
(Smucker's), 2 tbsp.	150	3.0	29.0	2.0	0	105	m.q.
Peanut flour, 1 cup:							
defatted	196	31.3	20.8	.3	0	9	2.4 c
defatted, salted . . .	196	31.3	20.8	.3	0	108	2.4 c
lowfat	257	20.3	18.8	13.1	0	0	m.q.
Peanut oil, see "Oil"							
Pear:							
fresh:							
Bartlett, 1 medium, 2 1/2 per lb. . . .	98	.7	25.1	.7	0	1	4.3 d
w/peel, sliced, 1/2 cup	49	.3	12.5	.3	0	1	2.1 d

Food and Measure	cal.	prot. (gms)	carbo. (gms)	fat (gms)	chol. (mgs)	sod. (mgs)	fiber (gms)
Pear *(cont.)*							
canned, 1/2 cup							
halves or slices, except as noted:							
Bartlett *(Del Monte)*	80	0	22.0	0	0	<10	m.q.
Bartlett *(Del Monte Lite)*	50	0	14.0	0	0	<10	m.q.
in water, halves . .	36	.2	9.5	<.1	0	3	.7 c
in juice, halves . .	62	.4	16.0	.1	0	5	1.1 d
in juice *(Libby Lite)*	60	0	19.0	0	0	10	m.q.
in juice, slices *(S&W Natural Style)* . .	80	0	20.0	0	0	10	m.q.
in light syrup, halves	72	.2	19.0	<.1	0	7	.7 c
in heavy syrup, halves	94	.3	24.4	.2	0	7	.7 c
in heavy syrup, halves *(S&W)* . .	100	0	25.0	0	0	<10	m.q.
dried, sulfured:							
4 oz.	297	2.1	79.0	.7	0	7	6.5 c
halves, 1/2 cup . .	236	1.7	62.7	.6	0	5	5.1 c
Pear nectar, canned:							
6 fl. oz.	112	.2	29.6	<.1	0	7	1.2 d
Peas, see specific listings							
Peas, cream, canned:							
(Allens), 1/2 cup . . .	90	7.0	14.0	<1.0	0	440	m.q.
Peas, crowder:							
canned, fresh *(Allens),* 1/2 cup	80	5.0	15.0	<1.0	0	370	m.q.
frozen *(Seabrook),* 3 oz.	130	8.0	23.0	1.0	0	m.q.	1.0 c
Peas, edible-podded:							
fresh:							
raw, untrimmed, 1 lb.	180	11.9	32.2	.9	0	18	11.1 d
raw, 1/2 cup	30	2.0	5.4	.1	0	3	1.9 d
boiled, drained, 1/2 cup	34	2.6	5.6	.2	0	3	2.2 d

Food and Measure	cal.	prot. (gms)	carbo. (gms)	fat (gms)	chol. (mgs)	sod. (mgs)	fiber (gms)
frozen:							
boiled, drained, 1/2 cup	42	2.8	7.2	.3	0	4	2.4 c
Chinese (Chun King), 1.5 oz. . . .	20	1.0	3.0	0	0	<10	m.q.
Chinese (Seabrook), 2 oz.	20	2.0	4.0	0	0	n.a.	m.q.
snow (Birds Eye Deluxe), 3 oz. . . .	35	2.0	6.0	0	0	0	3.0 d
sugar snap (Birds Eye Deluxe), 2.6 oz.	45	2.0	9.0	0	0	5	4.0 d
sugar snap, carrots, water chestnuts (Birds Eye Farm Fresh), 3.2 oz.	50	2.0	11.0	0	0	20	4.0 d
Peas, field, canned, 1/2 cup:							
(Allens)	100	7.0	18.0	<1.0	0	370	m.q.
w/snaps (Allens) . .	100	5.0	20.0	<1.0	0	370	m.q.
tiny, w/snaps (Allens)	70	6.0	13.0	<1.0	0	340	m.q.
Peas, green or sweet:							
fresh:							
raw, in pod, 1 lb.	140	9.3	24.9	.7	0	8	5.9 d
raw, shelled, 1/2 cup	58	3.9	10.4	.3	0	3	2.4 d
boiled, drained, 1/2 cup	67	4.3	12.5	.2	0	2	3.0 d
canned, 1/2 cup:							
(Del Monte)	60	3.0	10.0	0	0	355	m.q.
(Del Monte No Salt)	60	3.0	11.0	0	0	<10	m.q.
(Stokely No Salt/ Sugar)	50	4.0	9.0	0	0	5	m.q.
dry early June (Allens)	80	5.0	15.0	<1.0	0	320	m.q.
early (Stokely) . . .	60	4.0	12.0	0	0	320	m.q.
early June (Green Giant)	50	3.0	12.0	0	0	330	3.4 d

Food and Measure	cal.	prot. (gms)	carbo. (gms)	fat (gms)	chol. (mgs)	sod. (mgs)	fiber (gms)
Peas, green or sweet canned, 1/2 cup *(cont.)*							
early June *(S&W Petit Pois)*	70	4.0	12.0	0	0	330	m.q.
seasoned *(Del Monte)*	60	3.0	11.0	0	0	355	m.q.
small *(Del Monte)*	50	3.0	9.0	0	0	355	m.q.
sweet *(Green Giant)*	50	4.0	11.0	0	0	320	4.8 d
sweet *(S&W Perfection)*	70	4.0	12.0	0	0	330	m.q.
sweet *(Stokely)* . .	60	4.0	10.0	0	0	320	m.q.
sweet, mini *(Green Giant)*	50	4.0	12.0	0	0	340	3.4 d
sweet, w/onions *(Green Giant)* . .	50	4.0	11.0	0	0	510	4.0 d
sweet, w/pearl onions *(S&W)* . . .	60	3.0	10.0	1.0	0	490	m.q.
freeze-dried *(Mountain House)*, 1/2 cup . .	70	4.0	12.0	1.0	0	21	m.q.
frozen, 3.3 oz., except as noted:							
(Birds Eye)	80	5.0	13.0	0	0	130	4.0 d
(Birds Eye Portion Pack), 3 oz. . . .	70	5.0	12.0	0	0	120	4.0 d
(Frosty Acres) . . .	80	5.0	13.0	0	0	91	2.0 c
(Seabrook)	80	5.0	13.0	0	0	91	2.0 c
(Stokely Singles), 3 oz.	65	4.0	12.0	1.0	0	95	m.q.
early June *(Green Giant)*, 1/2 cup	50	4.0	11.0	0	0	120	3.0 d
early June *(Green Giant Harvest Fresh)*, 1/2 cup	60	4.0	13.0	1.0	0	170	3.3 d
sweet *(Green Giant)*, 1/2 cup . . .	50	4.0	11.0	0	0	95	4.0 d
sweet *(Green Giant Harvest Fresh)*, 1/2 cup	50	4.0	12.0	0	0	200	3.4 d

Food and Measure	cal.	prot. (gms)	carbo. (gms)	fat (gms)	chol. (mgs)	sod. (mgs)	fiber (gms)
tender tiny (Birds Eye Deluxe) . . .	60	4.0	11.0	0	0	120	4.0 d
tiny (Frosty Acres)	60	4.0	11.0	0	0	127	2.0 c
frozen in butter sauce:							
early (Green Giant One Serving), 4.5 oz.	90	6.0	16.0	2.0	5	500	m.q.
early (LeSueur), 1/2 cup	80	5.0	14.0	2.0	5	440	2.8 d
sweet (Green Giant), 1/2 cup . . .	80	5.0	14.0	2.0	5	410	4.0 d
sweet (Stokely Singles), 4 oz. . . .	90	5.0	16.0	1.0	5	335	m.q.
frozen, w/cream sauce (Birds Eye Combinations), 5 oz.	180	5.0	16.0	11.0	0	480	3.0 d
Peas, green, combinations, frozen:							
and carrots, see "Peas and carrots"							
and cauliflower in cream sauce (The Budget Gourmet Side Dish), 5.75 oz.	170	6.0	16.0	7.0	20	280	m.q.
Le Sueur style (Green Giant Valley Combination), 1/2 cup . .	70	4.0	12.0	2.0	0	400	2.1 d
mini, w/pea pods and water chestnuts, in butter sauce (Le Sueur), 1/2 cup . .	80	4.0	10.0	2.0	n.a.	410	3.0 d
w/onions and carrots, in butter sauce (Le Sueur), 1/2 cup . .	80	4.0	11.0	3.0	n.a.	470	3.0 d
w/pearl onions:							
(Birds Eye Combinations), 3.3 oz. . .	70	5.0	13.0	0	0	440	3.0 d

Food and Measure	cal.	prot. (gms)	carbo. (gms)	fat (gms)	chol. (mgs)	sod. (mgs)	fiber (gms)
Peas, green, combinations w/pearl onions *(cont.)*							
in cheese sauce *(Birds Eye Cheese Sauce Combinations),* 5 oz.	140	6.0	17.0	5.0	5	470	3.0 d
and potatoes, w/ cream sauce *(Birds Eye Combinations),* 5 oz.	190	4.0	17.0	12.0	0	490	2.0 d
and water chestnuts Oriental *(The Budget Gourmet),* 5 oz.	120	5.0	15.0	3.0	5	240	m.q.
Peas, purple hull:							
canned, fresh *(Allens),* 1/2 cup	100	6.0	16.0	<1.0	0	370	m.q.
frozen *(Frosty Acres),* 3.3 oz.	130	9.0	23.0	0	0	6	m.q.
Peas, sprouted, mature seeds:							
raw, 1/2 cup	77	5.3	17.0	.4	0	12	1.7 c
boiled, drained, 4 oz.	134	8.0	24.8	.6	0	3	3.7 d
Peas, white acre, canned:							
fresh *(Allens),* 1/2 cup	90	7.0	14.0	<1.0	0	440	m.q.
Peas and carrots:							
canned, 1/2 cup:							
(Del Monte)	50	2.0	10.0	0	0	355	m.q.
(S&W)	50	3.0	9.0	0	0	310	m.q.
(Stokely)	50	3.0	9.0	0	0	320	m.q.
diced carrots *(Stokely* No Salt/ Sugar)	45	3.0	8.0	0	0	20	m.q.
w/pearl onions *(Green Giant)*	50	3.0	11.0	0	0	510	m.q.
frozen, 3.3 oz.:							
(Frosty Acres)	60	3.0	11.0	0	0	75	1.0 c
(Seabrook)	60	3.0	11.0	0	0	75	1.0 c

Food and Measure	cal.	prot. (gms)	carbo. (gms)	fat (gms)	chol. (mgs)	sod. (mgs)	fiber (gms)
Pecan, shelled:							
(Planters), 1 oz.	190	2.0	5.0	20.0	0	0	m.q.
dried:							
1 oz.	190	2.2	5.2	19.2	0	tr.	1.8 d
halves, 1 cup . . .	721	8.4	19.7	73.1	0	1	7.0 d
chopped, 1 cup . .	794	9.2	21.7	80.5	0	1	7.7 d
dry-roasted:							
1 oz.	187	2.3	6.3	18.4	0	tr.	.5 c
salted, 1 oz.	187	2.3	6.3	18.4	0	221	.5 c
oil-roasted:							
1 oz.	195	2.0	4.6	20.2	0	tr.	.5 c
salted, 1 oz.	195	2.0	4.6	20.2	0	214	.5 c
Pecan flour:							
1 oz.	93	9.1	14.4	.4	0	tr.	.4 c
Pecan topping:							
in syrup *(Smucker's)*,							
2 tbsp.	130	2.0	28.0	1.0	0	0	m.q.
Pepper, ground,							
1 tsp.:							
black	5	.2	1.4	.1	0	1	.3 c
chili *(Spice Islands)*	9	.3	1.2	.3	0	<1	.3 c
red or cayenne . . .	6	.2	1.0	.3	0	1	.5 c
white	7	.3	1.7	.1	0	tr.	.1 c
seasoned *(Lawry's)*	9	.3	1.8	.1	0	5	.2 c
Pepper, bell, see							
"Pepper, sweet"							
Pepper, cherry, 1 oz.:							
mild *(Vlasic)*	8	0	2.0	0	0	480	m.q.
Pepper, chili:							
raw, green and red,							
w/out seeds:							
1 medium, 1.6 oz.	18	.9	4.3	.1	0	3	.8 c
chopped, 1/2 cup	30	1.5	7.1	.2	0	5	1.4 c
canned, green:							
all styles *(Del*							
Monte), 1/2 cup	20	0	5.0	0	0	690	m.q.
all styles *(Ortega)*,							
1 oz.	10	0	3.0	0	0	20	m.q.

Food and Measure	cal.	prot. (gms)	carbo. (gms)	fat (gms)	chol. (mgs)	sod. (mgs)	fiber (gms)
Pepper, chili canned, green *(cont.)*							
whole *(Old El Paso)*,							
1 chili	8	0	1.0	0	0	105	m.q.
chopped *(Old El*							
Paso), 2 tbsp. . . .	8	0	2.0	0	0	70	m.q.
Pepper, jalapeño:							
all styles:							
(Ortega), 1 oz. . .	10	0	3.0	0	0	20	m.q.
(Del Monte), 1/2 cup	30	1.0	6.0	1.0	0	1690	m.q.
whole *(Old El Paso)*,							
2 peppers	14	0	1.0	1.0	0	480	m.q.
hot *(Vlasic)*, 1 oz. . .	10	0	2.0	0	0	470	m.q.
marinated *(La Victo-*							
ria), 1 tbsp.	4	<1.0	1.0	<1.0	0	251	m.q.
nacho *(La Victoria)*,							
1 tbsp.	2	<1.0	1.0	<1.0	0	335	m.q.
Pepper, pepper-							
oncini:							
salad *(Vlasic)*, 1 oz.	4	0	1.0	0	0	440	m.q.
Pepper, sweet:							
fresh, green and red:							
raw, 1 medium,							
3³/₄" × 3" diam.	20	.7	4.8	.1	0	1	1.2 d
raw, chopped,							
1/2 cup	13	.4	3.2	.1	0	1	.8 d
boiled, drained,							
1 medium	20	.7	4.9	.1	0	1	.3 c
boiled, drained,							
chopped, 1/2 cup	19	.6	4.6	.1	0	1	.3 c
canned, see "Pi-							
mento"							
freeze-dried, 1 tbsp.	1	.1	.3	<.1	0	1	<.1 c
frozen, 1 oz:							
green *(Seabrook)*	6	0	1.0	0	0	1	m.q.
red *(Seabrook)* . .	8	0	1.0	0	0	n.a.	m.q.

Food and Measure	cal.	prot. (gms)	carbo. (gms)	fat (gms)	chol. (mgs)	sod. (mgs)	fiber (gms)
Pepper, stuffed, entree, frozen:							
green, w/beef in tomato sauce *(Stouffer's)*, 7¾ oz. . . .	200	11.0	19.0	9.0	m.q.	940	m.q.
sweet red *(Celentano)*, 13 oz.	350	28.0	28.0	20.0	m.q.	710	m.q.
Pepper rings, 1 oz.:							
hot *(Vlasic)*	4	0	1.0	0	0	480	m.q.
Pepper sauce, hot:							
(Gebhardt Lousiana Style)*, ½ tsp. . . .	0	0	n.a.	0	0	45	(0)
(Tabasco), ¼ tsp. . .	<1	tr.	<1.0	tr.	0	9	(0)
Peppered loaf:							
(Eckrich), 1-oz. slice	35	5.0	2.0	1.0	m.q.	340	(0)
(Kahn's), 1 slice . . .	40	5.0	1.0	2.0	m.q.	340	(0)
(Oscar Mayer), 1 oz.	43	4.8	1.3	2.1	13	361	(0)
Pepperoni, 1 oz., except as noted:							
(Hickory Farms) . . .	140	6.0	1.0	13.0	23	578	0
(Hormel)	140	6.0	0	13.0	m.q.	462	0
(Hormel Chunk) . . .	140	6.0	0	12.0	m.q.	423	0
(Hormel Leoni Brand)	130	6.0	0	12.0	m.q.	508	0
(Hormel Perma-Fresh), 2 slices	80	3.0	0	7.0	m.q.	281	0
(Hormel Rosa)	140	6.0	0	13.0	m.q.	626	0
(Hormel Rosa Grande)	140	6.0	0	13.0	m.q.	512	0
(JM), ½ oz.	70	3.0	1.0	6.0	m.q.	290	0
Pepperoni bits:							
(Hormel), 1 tbsp. . .	35	2.0	0	3.0	m.q.	m.q.	0
Perch, meat only:							
raw, 1 lb.	413	87.9	0	4.2	407	280	0
raw, 1 oz.	26	5.5	0	.3	26	18	0
baked, broiled, or microwaved, 4 oz. . .	133	28.2	0	1.3	130	90	0
ocean, see "Ocean perch"							

Food and Measure	cal.	prot. (gms)	carbo. (gms)	fat (gms)	chol. (mgs)	sod. (mgs)	fiber (gms)
Perch, frozen:							
(Booth), 4 oz.	100	20.0	0	1.0	m.q.	90	0
(SeaPak), 4 oz.	100	19.0	0	2.0	m.q.	80	0
Perch entree, frozen:							
battered *(Van de Kamp's)*, 2 pieces	260	13.0	20.0	14.0	50	520	m.q.
breaded *(Mrs. Paul's Light)*, 4 1/4 oz.	270	18.0	19.0	13.0	m.q.	391	m.q.
Persimmon:							
Japanese:							
fresh, 1 medium, 2 1/2″ × 3 1/2″	118	1.0	31.2	.3	0	3	2.5 c
dried, 1 oz.	78	.4	20.8	.2	0	1	1.0 c
native, fresh, 1 medium, 1.1 oz.	32	.2	8.4	.1	0	tr.	.4 c
Pesto sauce:							
refrigerated *(Contadina Fresh)*, 2 1/3 oz.	350	6.0	6.0	34.0	10	420	m.q.
Pheasant, raw:							
meat w/skin, 1 oz.	51	6.4	0	2.6	m.q.	11	0
meat only:							
1 oz.	38	6.7	0	1.0	m.q.	10	0
1/2 breast, 6.4 oz.	243	44.4	0	5.9	m.q.	60	0
1 leg, 3.8 oz.	143	23.8	0	4.6	m.q.	48	0
Picante sauce (see also "Salsa"):							
(Gebhardt), 1 tbsp.	4	0	1.0	0	0	120	m.q.
(Old El Paso), 2 tbsp.	8	1.0	2.0	0	0	310	m.q.
(Pace), 2 tsp.	3	.1	.6	.1	0	111	m.q.
(Wise), 2 tbsp.	12	0	3.0	0	0	130	m.q.
mild *(Azteca)*, 1 tbsp.	4	0	1.0	0	0	85	m.q.
Pickle, 1 oz., except as noted:							
bread and butter:							
slices *(Claussen)*	20	.2	4.7	.1	0	172	m.q.
slices *(Heinz)*	25	0	6.0	0	0	170	m.q.

Food and Measure	cal.	prot. (gms)	carbo. (gms)	fat (gms)	chol. (mgs)	sod. (mgs)	fiber (gms)
slices (Mrs. Fanning's), 2/3 oz.	16	0	3.0	0	0	140	m.q.
chunks (Vlasic Old Fashion)	25	0	6.0	0	0	135	m.q.
sweet (Vlasic Sweet Butter Chips) . .	25	0	6.0	0	0	170	m.q.
sweet (Vlasic Sweet Butter Stix) . . .	18	0	5.0	0	0	170	m.q.
dill:							
(Vlasic Original) . .	4	0	1.0	0	0	390	m.q.
whole, 3¾″ long, 2.3 oz.	12	.4	2.7	.1	0	833	.8 d
whole (Heinz Genuine)	2	0	0	0	0	420	m.q.
whole, processed (Heinz)	2	0	0	0	0	435	m.q.
halves (Heinz Deli Style)	4	0	1.0	0	0	280	m.q.
spears (Claussen)	4	.1	.5	.1	0	330	m.q.
hamburger slices (Heinz)	2	0	0	0	0	405	m.q.
hamburger chips, half salt (Vlasic)	2	0	0	0	0	180	m.q.
no garlic (Claussen)	6	.2	1.0	.1	0	313	m.q.
no garlic, crunchy (Vlasic)	4	0	1.0	0	0	220	m.q.
Polish style, whole or spears (Heinz)	4	0	1.0	0	0	285	m.q.
zesty, spears or crunch (Vlasic)	4	0	1.0	0	0	280	m.q.
kosher:							
all styles (Vlasic)	4	0	1.0	0	0	220	m.q.
whole (Claussen)	3	.2	.5	.1	0	332	m.q.
whole (Heinz Old Fashioned) . . .	4	0	1.0	0	0	280	m.q.
halves (Claussen)	4	.1	.5	.1	0	330	m.q.
halves (Heinz Old Fashioned Deli)	4	0	1.0	0	0	275	m.q.

Food and Measure	cal.	prot. (gms)	carbo. (gms)	fat (gms)	chol. (mgs)	sod. (mgs)	fiber (gms)
Pickle, kosher (cont.)							
slices (Claussen)	3	.1	.5	.1	0	319	m.q.
dill, whole or spears							
(Heinz)	4	0	1,0	0	0	295	m.q.
dill, baby (Heinz)	4	0	1.0	0	0	285	m.q.
dill, chips (Heinz)	4	0	1.0	0	0	275	m.q.
dill, spears (Vlasic							
Half Salt)	4	0	1.0	0	0	110	m.q.
chips (Heinz Old							
Fashioned) . . .	4	0	1.0	0	0	270	m.q.
mixed, garden, hot							
and spicy (Vlasic)	4	0	1.0	0	0	480	m.q.
salad cubes, sweet							
(Heinz)	30	0	7.0	0	0	270	m.q.
sour	3	.1	.6	.1	0	342	.2 c
sweet:							
(Heinz)	35	0	8.0	0	0	210	m.q.
(Heinz Cucumber							
Stix)	25	0	6.0	0	0	145	m.q.
(Vlasic Sweet Butter							
Chips Half Salt)	30	0	7.0	0	0	85	m.q.
gherkins (Heinz) . .	35	0	8.0	0	0	210	m.q.
gherkins, midget							
(Heinz)	35	0	8.0	0	0	205	m.q.
mixed (Heinz) . . .	40	0	9.0	0	0	200	m.q.
sliced (Heinz) . . .	35	0	8.0	0	0	205	m.q.
sliced (Heinz Cu-							
cumber Slices)	20	0	5.0	0	0	195	m.q.
Pickle loaf:							
(Eckrich), 1-oz. slice	80	3.0	2.0	6.0	m.q.	270	(0)
(Eckrich Smorgas							
Pac), 1-oz. slice . .	80	3.0	2.0	6.0	m.q.	270	(0)
(Hormel Perma-Fresh),							
2 slices	102	8.0	3.0	7.0	m.q.	752	(0)
(Kahn's), 1 slice . . .	80	3.0	2.0	7.0	m.q.	280	(0)
(Kahn's Family Pack),							
1 slice	70	3.0	2.0	6.0	m.q.	220	(0)

Food and Measure	cal.	prot. (gms)	carbo. (gms)	fat (gms)	chol. (mgs)	sod. (mgs)	fiber (gms)
beef *(Kahn's* Family Pack), 1 slice . . .	60	2.0	1.0	5.0	m.q.	210	(0)
Pickle and pimento loaf:							
(Oscar Mayer), 1 oz.	63	3.4	3.4	3.9	13	394	m.q.
Pickling spice:							
(Tone's), 1 tsp. . . .	10	.3	1.2	.6	n.a.	1	.3 d
Picnic loaf:							
(Oscar Mayer), 1 oz.	62	4.2	1.4	4.4	15	334	0
Pie, frozen:							
apple:							
(Banquet Family Size), 1/6 pie . .	250	2.0	37.0	11.0	n.a.	290	m.q.
(Mrs. Smith's Pie In Minutes), 1/8 pie	210	2.0	29.0	9.0	0	250	m.q.
(Weight Watchers), 1/2 pkg.	200	2.0	39.0	5.0	5	280	m.q.
banana cream:							
(Banquet), 1/6 pie	180	2.0	21.0	10.0	n.a.	150	m.q.
(Pet-Ritz), 1/6 pie	170	2.0	22.0	9.0	n.a.	155	m.q.
blackberry *(Banquet* Family Size), 1/6 pie	270	3.0	40.0	11.0	n.a.	350	m.q.
blueberry:							
(Banquet Family Size), 1/6 pie . .	270	3.0	40.0	11.0	n.a.	350	m.q.
(Mrs. Smith's Pie In Minutes), 1/8 pie	220	2.0	32.0	9.0	0	240	m.q.
Boston cream, see "Cake, frozen"							
cherry:							
(Banquet Family Size), 1/6 pie . .	250	3.0	36.0	11.0	n.a.	260	m.q.
(Mrs. Smith's Pie In Minutes), 1/8 pie	220	2.0	32.0	9.0	0	200	m.q.
chocolate cream:							
(Banquet), 1/6 pie	190	2.0	24.0	10.0	n.a.	110	m.q.
(Pet-Ritz), 1/6 pie	190	1.0	27.0	8.0	n.a.	145	m.q.

Food and Measure	cal.	prot. (gms)	carbo. (gms)	fat (gms)	chol. (mgs)	sod. (mgs)	fiber (gms)
Pie, frozen (cont.)							
coconut cream:							
(Banquet), 1/6 pie	190	2.0	22.0	11.0	n.a.	120	m.q.
(Pet-Ritz), 1/6 pie	190	2.0	27.0	8.0	n.a.	145	m.q.
lemon cream:							
(Banquet), 1/6 pie	170	2.0	23.0	9.0	n.a.	120	m.q.
(Pet-Ritz), 1/6 pie	190	2.0	26.0	9.0	n.a.	150	m.q.
lemon meringue (Mrs. Smith's), 1/8 pie . .	210	2.0	38.0	5.0	n.a.	130	m.q.
mincemeat (Banquet Family Size), 1/6 pie	260	3.0	38.0	11.0	n.a.	370	m.q.
neapolitan cream (Pet-Ritz), 1/6 pie	180	1.0	17.0	10.0	n.a.	185	m.q.
peach:							
(Banquet Family Size), 1/6 pie . .	245	3.0	35.0	11.0	n.a.	280	m.q.
(Mrs. Smith's Pie In Minutes), 1/8 pie	210	2.0	29.0	9.0	0	190	m.q.
pecan (Mrs. Smith's Pie In Minutes), 1/8 pie	330	3.0	51.0	13.0	35	200	m.q.
pumpkin:							
(Banquet Family Size), 1/6 pie . .	200	3.0	29.0	8.0	n.a.	350	m.q.
(Mrs. Smith's Pie In Minutes), 1/8 pie	190	3.0	30.0	6.0	35	230	m.q.
strawberry cream:							
(Banquet), 1/6 pie	170	2.0	22.0	9.0	n.a.	120	m.q.
(Pet-Ritz), 1/6 pie	170	2.0	20.0	9.0	n.a.	145	m.q.
Pie, snack, 1 piece:							
apple:							
(Drake's)	210	2.0	29.0	10.0	0	135	m.q.
(Hostess)	390	4.0	56.0	19.0	13	490	m.q.
(Tastykake)	345	3.5	55.4	12.2	n.a.	385	m.q.
Dutch (Little Debbie)	270	2.0	48.0	8.0	<1	170	m.q.
French (Tastykake)	399	3.8	67.9	12.5	n.a.	340	m.q.
blackberry (Hostess)	380	4.0	55.0	15.0	15	360	m.q.

Food and Measure	cal.	prot. (gms)	carbo. (gms)	fat (gms)	chol. (mgs)	sod. (mgs)	fiber (gms)
blueberry:							
(Hostess)	410	5.0	60.0	17.0	1	450	m.q.
(Tastykake)	359	3.5	60.0	11.7	n.a.	340	m.q.
apple (Drake's) . .	210	2.0	30.0	10.0	0	135	m.q.
cherry:							
(Hostess)	410	5.0	59.0	17.0	2	420	m.q.
(Tastykake)	368	3.7	59.7	12.7	n.a.	325	m.q.
apple (Drake's) . .	220	2.0	30.0	10.0	0	135	m.q.
chocolate pudding:							
(Hostess)	490	5.0	76.0	19.0	21	439	m.q.
(Tastykake)	443	6.0	68.3	16.2	n.a.	m.q.	m.q.
coconut creme (Tastykake)	432	5.8	52.0	22.3	n.a.	285	m.q.
lemon:							
(Drake's)	210	2.0	27.0	11.0	0	115	m.q.
(Hostess)	400	4.0	58.0	20.0	19	430	m.q.
(Tastykake)	361	4.2	56.2	13.2	n.a.	369	m.q.
oatmeal creme (Little Debbie), 2.75 oz.	350	4.0	51.0	14.0	<1	260	m.q.
peach:							
(Hostess)	380	4.0	53.0	15.0	13	380	m.q.
(Tastykake)	343	3.6	54.4	12.4	n.a.	322	m.q.
pecan (Little Debbie)	280	3.0	60.0	3.0	<1	340	m.q.
pineapple (Tastykake)	362	3.9	59.7	12.0	n.a.	372	m.q.
pumpkin (Tastykake)	356	5.1	51.9	14.2	n.a.	339	m.q.
raisin creme (Little Debbie)	290	2.0	47.0	10.0	<1	190	m.q.
strawberry:							
(Hostess)	340	5.0	56.0	16.0	10	400	m.q.
(Tastykake)	373	3.4	63.1	11.9	n.a.	308	m.q.
(Tastykake Tasty Klair)	436	6.3	59.3	19.4	n.a.	240	m.q.
vanilla pudding:							
(Hostess)	470	4.0	75.0	17.0	18	400	m.q.
(Tastykake)	437	5.8	61.8	18.5	n.a.	m.q.	m.q.

Food and Measure	cal.	prot. (gms)	carbo. (gms)	fat (gms)	chol. (mgs)	sod. (mgs)	fiber (gms)
Pie, snack, frozen, 1 serving:							
apple, country (Sara Lee)	230	2.0	39.0	7.0	n.a.	170	m.q.
Boston cream, see "Cake, snack, frozen"							
fudge brownie (Sara Lee)	280	4.0	35.0	14.0	n.a.	170	m.q.
Mississippi mud (Pepperidge Farm) . . .	310	3.0	23.0	23.0	60	45	m.q.
pecan, southern (Sara Lee)	260	4.0	31.0	13.0	n.a.	200	m.q.
Pie crust shell, (see also "Pastry dough"):							
frozen or refrigerated:							
(Mrs. Smith's, 8"), 1/8 shell :	80	1.0	8.0	5.0	0	105	m.q.
(Mrs. Smith's 9"), 1/8 shell	90	1.0	10.0	5.0	0	125	m.q.
(Mrs. Smith's 95/8"), 1/8 shell	120	2.0	12.0	7.0	0	160	m.q.
(Pet-Ritz), 1/6 shell	110	1.0	11.0	7.0	n.a.	110	m.q.
(Pet-Ritz, 95/8"), 1/6 shell	170	2.0	15.0	11.0	n.a.	180	m.q.
(Pillsbury All Ready), 1/8 of 2-crust pie . . .	240	2.0	24.0	15.0	15	210	m.q.
deep dish (Pet-Ritz), 1/6 shell	130	1.0	12.0	8.0	n.a.	120	m.q.
deep dish, whole grain (Pet-Ritz), 1/6 shell	130	1.0	14.0	8.0	n.a.	125	m.q.
graham cracker (Pet-Ritz), 1/6 shell	110	1.0	8.0	6.0	n.a.	80	m.q.

Food and Measure	cal.	prot. (gms)	carbo. (gms)	fat (gms)	chol. (mgs)	sod. (mgs)	fiber (gms)
mix[1] *(Flako)*, 1 serving	247	3.7	24.4	15.0	9	393	1.2 d
Pie filling, canned, 3.5 oz., except as noted:							
apple:							
(Comstock)	120	0	30.0	0	0	15	.4 d
(Comstock Lite) . .	80	0	20.0	0	0	10	.4 d
(Musselman's), 4 oz.	120	0	30.0	0	0	60	m.q.
(White House) . . .	121	0	29.0	1.0	0	44	m.q.
turnover, diced *(Musselman's),* 4 oz.	120	0	30.0	0	0	60	m.q.
apricot:							
(Comstock)	110	0	29.0	0	0	100	.4 d
(Musselman's), 4 oz.	150	0	39.0	0	0	90	m.q.
banana *(Comstock)*	110	1.0	22.0	2.0	0	300	.5 d
blackberry *(Musselman's)*, 4 oz. . .	120	1.0	31.0	0	0	140	m.q.
blueberry:							
(Comstock)	110	0	28.0	0	0	15	.6 d
(Comstock Lite) . .	75	0	17.0	0	0	15	.6 d
(White House) . . .	118	0	28.0	1.0	0	48	m.q.
boysenberry *(Musselman's)*, 4 oz. . .	120	1.0	31.0	0	0	140	m.q.
cherry:							
(Comstock)	110	0	28.0	0	0	15	.3 d
(Comstock Lite) . .	75	0	19.0	0	0	15	.3 d
(Musselman's), 4 oz.	120	1.0	29.0	0	0	50	m.q.
(White House) . . .	141	0	33.0	1.0	0	54	m.q.
chocolate *(Comstock)*	130	1.0	26.0	3.0	0	240	.2 d
coconut *(Comstock)*	120	1.0	22.0	3.0	0	290	.2 d
gooseberry *(Musselman's)*, 4 oz. . .	180	0	45.0	0	0	30	m.q.

[1] *Prepared according to package directions.*

Food and Measure	cal.	prot. (gms)	carbo. (gms)	fat (gms)	chol. (mgs)	sod. (mgs)	fiber (gms)
Pie filling *(cont.)*							
lemon:							
(Comstock)	140	0	34.0	1.0	0	110	.1 d
(Musselman's),							
4 oz.	200	0	48.0	2.0	0	235	m.q.
French *(Mus-*							
selman's), 4 oz.	180	0	42.0	1.0	0	140	m.q.
mincemeat:							
(Borden None							
Such), 1/3 cup	200	1.0	48.0	1.0	n.a.	280	m.q.
(Comstock)	150	0	39.0	1.0	0	180	.7 d
(Musselman's),							
4 oz.	190	0	48.0	1.0	n.a.	145	m.q.
w/brandy *(S&W* Old							
Fashioned) . . .	234	1.1	55.6	2.3	n.a.	234	m.q.
w/brandy and rum							
(Borden None							
Such), 1/3 cup	220	1.0	48.0	2.0	n.a.	260	m.q.
condensed *(Borden*							
None Such),							
1/4 pkg.	220	1.0	50.0	2.0	n.a.	310	m.q.
peach:							
(Comstock)	110	0	26.0	0	0	20	.2 d
(Musselman's),							
4 oz.	150	0	37.0	0	0	65	m.q.
(White House) . . .	117	0	28.0	1.0	0	30	m.q.
pineapple:							
(Comstock)	100	0	28.0	0	0	65	.4 d
(Musselman's),							
4 oz.	110	0	30.0	0	0	65	m.q.
pumpkin:							
(Comstock)	100	0	24.0	0	0	180	m.q.
(Musselman's),							
4 oz.	170	1.0	33.0	4.0	n.a.	200	m.q.
(Stokely), 1/2 cup	170	1.0	44.0	0	0	420	m.q.
raisin:							
(Comstock)	120	0	32.0	0	0	80	m.q.

Food and Measure	cal.	prot. (gms)	carbo. (gms)	fat (gms)	chol. (mgs)	sod. (mgs)	fiber (gms)
(Musselman's), 4 oz.	130	1.0	34.0	1.0	0	120	m.q.
raspberry:							
black (Musselman's), 4 oz.	190	0	43.0	0	0	50	m.q.
red (Musselman's), 4 oz.	190	0	46.0	0	0	80	m.q.
strawberry:							
(Comstock)	100	0	25.0	0	0	20	.6 d
(Musselman's), 4 oz.	120	0	30.0	0	0	75	m.q.
strawberry-rhubarb (Musselman's), 4 oz.	120	0	31.0	0	0	95	m.q.
vanilla creme (Musselman's), 4 oz. . .	150	0	32.0	3.0	n.a.	145	n.a.
Pie filling mix, see "Pudding mix"							
Pie mix[1], 1/8 pie:							
banana cream (Jell-O No Bake)	240	3.0	27.0	14.0	30	300	m.q.
chocolate:							
mint (Royal No-Bake)	260	5.0	25.0	15.0	n.a.	280	m.q.
mousse (Jell-O No Bake)	260	4.0	25.0	17.0	30	430	m.q.
mousse (Royal No-Bake)	230	4.0	27.0	12.0	n.a.	260	m.q.
coconut cream (Jell-O No Bake)	260	3.0	27.0	16.0	30	300	m.q.
lemon meringue (Royal No-Bake)	310	3.0	50.0	11.0	n.a.	250	m.q.
pumpkin (Jell-O No Bake)	250	4.0	31.0	13.0	30	450	m.q.
Pigeon, see "Squab"							

Prepared according to package directions.

Food and Measure	cal.	prot. (gms)	carbo. (gms)	fat (gms)	chol. (mgs)	sod. (mgs)	fiber (gms)
Pigeon peas:							
fresh:							
raw, in pod, 1 lb.	296	15.7	52.0	3.6	0	11	5.8 c
raw, 1/2 cup	105	5.5	18.4	1.3	0	4	2.1 c
boiled, drained,							
1/2 cup	86	4.6	15.0	1.1	0	3	2.2 c
mature, boiled, 1/2 cup	102	5.7	19.5	.3	0	5	3.9 d
Pig's feet:							
simmered, 4 oz. . . .	220	21.8	0	14.1	113	m.q.	0
pickled:							
cured, 1 oz.	58	3.8	<.1	4.6	26	m.q.	0
(Penrose), 1 piece	220	19.0	2.0	15.0	m.q.	2890	0
Pig's knuckles, pick-							
led:							
(Penrose), 1 piece . .	290	23.0	1.0	21.0	m.q.	2380	0
Pike:							
northern, meat only:							
raw, 1 lb.	401	87.3	0	3.1	177	177	0
raw, 1 oz.	25	5.5	0	.2	11	11	0
baked, broiled, or							
microwaved, 4 oz.	128	28.0	0	1.0	57	56	0
walleye, meat only:							
raw, 1 lb.	420	86.6	0	5.5	390	230	0
raw, 1 oz.	26	5.4	0	.3	24	14	0
Pili nut, dried:							
in shell, 1 lb.	619	9.3	3.4	68.5	0	3	2.4 c
shelled, 1 oz.	204	3.1	1.1	22.6	0	4	.8 c
Pimento, 1 oz.:							
all varieties, drained							
(Dromedary)	10	0	2.0	0	0	5	m.q.
Pimento spread:							
(Price's), 1 oz.	80	3.0	2.0	6.0	n.a.	m.q.	n.a.
Pina colada mix:							
bottled *(Holland*							
House), 1 fl. oz. . .	33	0	8.0	0	0	4	m.q.
instant *(Holland*							
House), .56 oz. . . .	82	0	12.0	3.0	0	<1	m.q.

Food and Measure	cal.	prot. (gms)	carbo. (gms)	fat (gms)	chol. (mgs)	sod. (mgs)	fiber (gms)
Pine nut, dried:							
pignolia:							
1 oz.	146	6.8	4.0	14.4	0	1	.2 c
1 tbsp.	51	2.4	1.4	5.1	0	tr.	.1 c
pinyon:		—					
1 oz.	161	3.3	5.5	17.3	0	20	1.3 c
10 kernels	6	.1	.2	.6	0	1	.1 c
Pineapple:							
fresh:							
untrimmed, 1 lb. . .	117	.9	29.2	1.0	0	2	2.8 d
diced, 1/2 cup . . .	39	.3	9.6	.3	0	<1	.9 d
(Del Monte), 2 slices, 31/2″ × 3/4″ . . .	90	1.0	24.0	0	0	<5	m.q.
canned, in juice:							
4 oz.	68	.5	17.8	.1	0	1	.9 d
all cuts (Dole), 1/2 cup	70	.5	17.5	.5	0	1	m.q.
spears (Del Monte), 2 spears	50	0	14.0	0	0	10	m.q.
slices (S&W 100% Hawaiian), 1/2 cup	70	0	17.0	0	0	10	m.q.
slices, chunks, tidbits or crushed (Del Monte), 1/2 cup	70	0	18.0	0	0	<10	m.q.
crushed (Empress), 1/2 cup	70	0	18.0	0	0	<10	m.q.
canned, in heavy syrup:							
4 oz.	88	.4	22.9	.1	0	1	.5 c
(Mott's Fruit Pak), 3.75 oz.	86	0	21.0	0	0	2	m.q.
all cuts (Del Monte), 1/2 cup	90	0	23.0	0	0	<10	m.q.
all cuts (Dole), 1/2 cup	95	.4	24.8	.2	0	2	m.q.

Food and Measure	cal.	prot. (gms)	carbo. (gms)	fat (gms)	chol. (mgs)	sod. (mgs)	fiber (gms)
Pineapple, canned, in heavy syrup *(cont.)*							
slices *(S&W 100% Hawaiian),*							
2 slices	90	0	23.0	0	0	0	m.q.
chunks, tidbits or							
crushed, 1/2 cup	100	.5	25.8	.1	0	2	.6 c
frozen, sweetened,							
chunks, 1/2 cup . .	104	.5	27.1	.1	0	2	.4 c
Pineapple juice:							
canned, bottled or							
boxed, 6 fl. oz., ex-							
cept as noted:							
(Del Monte)	100	0	25.0	0	0	<10	m.q.
(Dole)	103	.8	25.4	.2	0	2	m.q.
(Minute Maid),							
8.45 fl. oz. . . .	139	1.1	34.1	.8	0	27	m.q.
(Minute Maid On							
The Go), 10 fl. oz.	165	.3	40.4	.1	0	32	m.q.
(Mott's), 9.5 fl. oz.	169	0	42.0	0	0	0	m.q.
(S&W)	100	0	25.0	0	0	0	m.q.
(Veryfine 100%),							
8 fl. oz.	125	.7	31.0	0	0	<10	m.q.
nectar *(Libby's)* . .	110	0	27.0	0	0	30	m.q.
chilled or frozen[1]:							
(Dole)	100	0	25.0	n.a.	0	7	m.q.
(Minute Maid) . . .	99	.8	24.2	.1	0	19	m.q.
Pineapple topping:							
(Kraft), 1 tbsp.	50	0	13.0	0	0	0	m.q.
(Smucker's), 2 tbsp.	130	0	32.0	0	0	0	m.q.
Pineapple-banana							
juice cocktail:							
bottled or frozen[1]							
(Welch's Orchard							
Tropicals), 6 fl. oz.	100	0	24.0	0	0	20	0
Pineapple-grapefruit							
juice, 6 fl. oz.:							
(Dole)	90	1.0	23.0	n.a.	0	8	m.q.

[1] *Diluted according to package directions.*

Food and Measure	cal.	prot. (gms)	carbo. (gms)	fat (gms)	chol. (mgs)	sod. (mgs)	fiber (gms)
w/pink grapefruit							
(Dole)	101	.4	25.4	.1	0	tr.	m.q.
cocktail (Ocean Spray)	110	0	26.0	0	0	5	m.q.
Pineapple-grapefruit juice drink:							
regular or pink (Del Monte), 6 fl. oz. . . .	90	0	24.0	0	0	50	m.q.
Pineapple-orange drink:							
(Veryfine), 8 fl. oz. . . .	130	0	32.0	0	0	<10	m.q.
Pineapple-orange juice, 6 fl. oz.:							
(Dole)	100	1.0	23.0	n.a.	0	8	m.q.
chilled or frozen[1] (Minute Maid)	98	.8	23.9	.1	0	19	m.q.
Pineapple-orange juice drink:							
(Del Monte), 6 fl. oz.	90	0	24.0	0	0	20	m.q.
Pineapple-orange-banana juice:							
(Dole), 6 fl. oz.	90	.8	23.0	.1	0	5	m.q.
Pink bean:							
boiled, 1/2 cup	125	7.6	23.5	.4	0	2	3.7 d
Pinto bean:							
boiled, 1/2 cup	117	7.0	21.8	.4	0	1	3.4 d
canned:							
(Allens), 1/2 cup . .	105	5.0	18.0	<1.0	0	480	m.q.
(Gebhardt), 4 oz.	197	12.8	35.7	.5	0	608	m.q.
(Green Giant/Joan of Arc), 1/2 cup	90	6.0	20.0	1.0	0	280	5.2 d
(Old El Paso), 1/2 cup	100	6.0	19.0	0	0	320	8.0 d
baked, w/pork, (Luck's), 7.5 oz.	220	12.0	30.0	6.0	m.q.	787	7.0 d

[1] Diluted according to package directions.

Food and Measure	cal.	prot. (gms)	carbo. (gms)	fat (gms)	chol. (mgs)	sod. (mgs)	fiber (gms)
Pinto bean, canned *(cont.)*							
baked, and great northern beans, w/pork *(Luck's)*, 7.25 oz.	200	12.0	29.0	5.0	m.q.	822	m.q.
dried, 1/2 cup . . .	93	5.5	17.5	.4	0	499	1.5 c
Picante style *(Green Giant/Joan of Arc)*, 1/2 cup . .	100	7.0	21.0	1.0	0	580	6.6 d
frozen *(Seabrook)*, 3.2 oz.	160	9.0	29.0	0	0	m.q.	m.q.
Pinto bean, sprouted:							
boiled, drained, 4 oz.	25	2.1	4.6	.4	0	58	1.1 c
Pistachio nut[1]**:**							
dried:							
in shell, 1 lb. . . .	1309	46.7	56.3	109.7	0	13	24.5 d
1 oz.	164	5.8	7.1	13.7	0	2	3.1 d
dry-roasted:							
in shell, 1 lb. . . .	1429	35.2	64.9	124.5	0	14	4.3 c
in shell, salted, 1 lb.	1429	35.2	64.9	124.5	0	1840	4.3 c
1 oz.	172	4.2	7.8	15.0	0	2	.5 c
1 cup	776	19.1	35.2	67.6	0	8	2.3 c
salted, 1 oz.	172	4.2	7.8	15.0	0	221	.5 c
(Planters), 1 oz. . .	170	5.0	6.0	15.0	0	250	m.q.
roasted *(Dole)*, 1 oz.	163	6.0	7.0	14.0	0	2	m.q.
Pitanga:							
1 medium, .3 oz. . .	2	.1	.5	<.1	0	tr.	<.1 c
1/2 cup	29	.7	6.5	.3	0	3	.5 c
Pizza, frozen:							
bacon *(Totino's* Party Pizza), 1/2 pie . . .	370	11.0	35.0	20.0	m.q.	1030	m.q.
bacon *(Totino's* Temptin' Toppings), 1/4 pie	220	7.0	21.0	11.0	m.q.	640	m.q.

[1] *Shelled, except as noted.*

Food and Measure	cal.	prot. (gms)	carbo. (gms)	fat (gms)	chol. (mgs)	sod. (mgs)	fiber (gms)
Canadian-style bacon:							
(Totino's Party							
Pizza), 1/2 pie . .	310	13.0	35.0	14.0	m.q.	1150	m.q.
(Jeno's Crisp'n							
Tasty), 1/2 pie . .	250	11.0	27.0	11.0	m.q.	880	m.q.
(Tombstone), 1/4 pie	340	22.0	34.0	13.0	40	910	m.q.
(Totino's Temptin'							
Toppings), 1/4 pie	190	9.0	21.0	8.0	m.q.	650	m.q.
cheese:							
(Celentano 9-Slice),							
2.7 oz.	150	6.0	22.0	4.0	m.q.	390	m.q.
(Celentano Thick							
Crust), 4.3 oz.	290	13.0	35.0	11.0	m.q.	700	m.q.
(Celeste), 1/4 pie	317	14.2	27.8	16.6	20	770	2.2 d
(Celeste Pizza For							
One), 1 pie . . .	497	21.2	48.0	24.5	40	1070	3.6 d
(Celeste Suprema),							
1/4 pie	381	16.8	29.2	24.1	15	1090	3.0 d
(Celeste Suprema							
Pizza For One),							
1 pie	678	26.5	54.0	39.3	20	1610	4.5 d
(Jeno's Crisp'n							
Tasty), 1/2 pie . .	270	10.0	28.0	14.0	m.q.	770	m.q.
(Jeno's Snacks),							
4 pies	130	5.0	12.0	7.0	m.q.	440	m.q.
(Jeno's 4-Pack),							
1 pie	160	6.0	17.0	8.0	m.q.	460	m.q.
(John's 3-Pack),							
1 pie	300	14.0	33.0	12.0	m.q.	1040	m.q.
(Pillsbury Micro-							
wave), 1/2 pie . .	240	10.0	28.0	10.0	m.q.	540	m.q.
(Stouffer's), 1/2 pkg.	320	14.0	32.0	15.0	m.q.	640	m.q.
(Stouffer's Extra							
Cheese), 1/2 pkg.	370	17.0	33.0	19.0	m.q.	720	m.q.
(Tombstone), 1/4 pie	330	20.0	34.0	13.0	30	700	m.q.
(Totino's My Classic							
Deluxe), 1/6 pie	210	10.0	23.0	9.0	m.q.	420	m.q.

Food and Measure	cal.	prot. (gms)	carbo. (gms)	fat (gms)	chol. (mgs)	sod. (mgs)	fiber (gms)
Pizza, frozen, cheese (cont.)							
(Totino's Party), 1/2 pizza	340	13.0	34.0	17.0	m.q.	1000	m.q.
(Totino's Slices), 1 slice	170	7.0	20.0	7.0	m.q.	350	m.q.
(Totino's Small Microwave), 3.9 oz.	250	10.0	34.0	8.0	m.q.	760	m.q.
(Totino's Temptin' Toppings), 1/4 pie	210	8.0	21.0	10.0	m.q.	630	m.q.
(Weight Watchers), 5.75 oz.	310	21.0	39.0	8.0	40	910	m.q.
cheese, double:							
and hamburger (Tombstone Double Top), 1/4 pie	530	37.0	35.0	27.0	75	1480	m.q.
and sausage (Tombstone Double Top), 1/4 pie . . .	510	38.0	35.0	25.0	80	1360	m.q.
and sausage (Tombstone Double Top Deluxe), 1/4 pie	520	38.0	36.0	25.0	80	1360	m.q.
cheese, three:							
(Tombstone Double Top), 1/4 pie . . .	490	30.0	36.0	25.0	65	1110	m.q.
(Tombstone Microwave), 7.7-oz. . .	520	29.0	41.0	27.0	60	1130	m.q.
(Totino's Pan Pizza), 1/6 pie	290	15.0	33.0	10.0	m.q.	510	m.q.
cheese, two (Tombstone Thin Crust), 1/4 pie	330	20.0	25.0	16.0	35	670	m.q.
cheese and hamburger:							
(Tombstone), 1/4 pie	360	21.0	34.0	16.0	40	910	m.q.
(Tombstone Thin Crust), 1/4 pie . .	320	19.0	23.0	17.0	40	810	m.q.

Food and Measure	cal.	prot. (gms)	carbo. (gms)	fat (gms)	chol. (mgs)	sod. (mgs)	fiber (gms)
cheese and pepper-oni:							
(Tombstone), 1/4 pie	380	20.0	34.0	18.0	30	950	m.q.
(Tombstone Micro-wave), 7.5-oz. . .	530	30.0	39.0	29.0	50	1300	m.q.
(Tombstone Thin Crust), 1/4 pie . .	330	18.0	23.0	19.0	30	820	m.q.
cheese and sausage:							
(Tombstone), 1/4 pie	350	22.0	34.0	14.0	40	850	m.q.
(Tombstone Thin Crust), 1/4 pie . .	330	19.0	23.0	18.0	40	710	m.q.
cheese, sausage and mushroom *(Tomb-stone)*, 1/4 pie . . .	360	23.0	35.0	15.0	40	860	m.q.
combination:							
(Jeno's 4-Pack), 1 pie	180	7.0	17.0	9.0	m.q.	470	m.q.
(Pappalo's Pan Pizza), 1/6 pie . .	340	17.0	34.0	15.0	m.q.	700	m.q.
(Pappalo's Thin Crust), 1/6 pie . .	260	13.0	29.0	10.0	m.q.	590	m.q.
(Pillsbury Micro-wave), 1/2 pie . .	310	14.0	29.0	15.0	m.q.	780	m.q.
(Totino's My Classic Deluxe), 1/6 pie	270	13.0	23.0	14.0	m.q.	630	m.q.
(Totino's Party), 1/2 pie	380	13.0	35.0	21.0	m.q.	1230	m.q.
(Totino's Slices), 1 slice	200	7.0	20.0	10.0	m.q.	630	m.q.
(Weight Watchers Deluxe), 6.75 oz.	300	20.0	37.0	8.0	35	700	m.q.
deluxe:							
(Celeste), 1/4 pie	378	15.5	29.3	22.1	20	910	3.1 d
(Celeste Pizza For One)*, 1 pie . . .	582	22.7	51.2	31.8	20	1370	4.4 d
(Stouffer's), 1/2 pkg.	370	16.0	33.0	19.0	m.q.	590	m.q.
golden topping:							
(Fox Deluxe), 1/2 pie	240	9.0	25.0	11.0	m.q.	600	m.q.

Food and Measure	cal.	prot. (gms)	carbo. (gms)	fat (gms)	chol. (mgs)	sod. (mgs)	fiber (gms)
Pizza, frozen, golden topping *(cont.)*							
(John's), 1/2 pie . .	240	9.0	25.0	11.0	m.q.	600	m.q.
hamburger:							
(Fox Deluxe), 1/2 pie	260	11.0	26.0	12.0	m.q.	700	m.q.
(Jeno's Crisp'n Tasty)*, 1/2 pie . .	290	12.0	28.0	15.0	m.q.	810	m.q.
(Jeno's 4-Pack)*, 1 pie	180	8.0	17.0	9.0	m.q.	500	m.q.
(Pappalo's Pan Pizza)*, 1/6 pie . .	310	17.0	34.0	12.0	m.q.	580	m.q.
(Pappalo's Thin Crust)*, 1/6 pie . .	240	14.0	28.0	8.0	m.q.	470	m.q.
(Totino's Party Pizza)*, 1/2 pie . .	370	15.0	35.0	19.0	m.q.	1060	m.q.
(Totino's Temptin' Toppings)*, 1/4 pie	210	9.0	21.0	10.0	m.q.	660	m.q.
Mexican style:							
(Totino's Party Pizza)*, 1/2 pie . .	380	13.0	35.0	21.0	m.q.	970	m.q.
(Totino's Temptin' Toppings)*, 1/4 pie	220	8.0	21.0	12.0	m.q.	530	m.q.
pepperoni:							
(Celeste), 1/4 pie	368	15.0	29.2	21.3	15	1000	m.q.
(Celeste Pizza For One)*, 1 pie	546	20.2	49.7	29.6	20	1360	3.9 d
(Fox Deluxe), 1/2 pie	250	8.0	26.0	13.0	m.q.	640	m.q.
(Jeno's Crisp'n Tasty)*, 1/2 pie . .	280	10.0	27.0	15.0	m.q.	760	m.q.
(Jeno's 4-Pack)*, 1 pie	170	6.0	17.0	9.0	m.q.	460	m.q.
(Jeno's Snacks)*, 4 pies	140	5.0	12.0	8.0	m.q.	470	m.q.
(Pappalo's Pan Pizza)*, 1/6 pie . .	330	16.0	34.0	14.0	m.q.	710	m.q.
(Pappalo's Thin Crust)*, 1/6 pie . .	270	13.0	28.0	11.0	m.q.	600	m.q.
(Pillsbury Micro-wave)*, 1/2 pie . .	300	13.0	29.0	15.0	m.q.	790	m.q.

Food and Measure	cal.	prot. (gms)	carbo. (gms)	fat (gms)	chol. (mgs)	sod. (mgs)	fiber (gms)
(Stouffer's), 1/2 pkg.	350	15.0	34.0	18.0	m.q.	820	m.q.
(Tombstone Real Deluxe), 1/4 pie	380	20.0	34.0	18.0	30	940	m.q.
(Totino's My Classic Deluxe), 1/6 pie	260	12.0	23.0	13.0	m.q.	630	m.q.
(Totino's Pan Pizza), 1/6 pie	330	16.0	34.0	14.0	m.q.	730	m.q.
(Totino's Party), 1/2 pie	370	13.0	35.0	20.0	m.q.	1310	m.q.
(Totino's Slices), 1 slice	190	7.0	20.0	9.0	m.q.	530	m.q.
(Totino's Small Microwave), 4 oz.	280	10.0	34.0	12.0	m.q.	880	m.q.
(Totino's Temptin' Toppings), 1/4 pie	220	8.0	22.0	11.0	m.q.	700	m.q.
(Weight Watchers), 5.87 oz.	320	22.0	38.0	9.0	45	870	m.q.
double cheese *(Tombstone Double Top)*, 1/4 pie	560	35.0	35.0	31.0	60	1490	m.q.
double cheese *(Tombstone Double Top Deluxe)*, 1/4 pie	550	33.0	36.0	30.0	55	1430	m.q.
sausage:							
(Celeste), 1/4 pie	376	15.6	29.7	21.7	15	910	3.3 d
(Celeste Pizza For One), 1 pie . . .	571	22.6	48.8	31.7	20	1370	4.2 d
(Fox Deluxe), 1/2 pie	260	10.0	26.0	13.0	m.q.	630	m.q.
(Jeno's Crisp'n Tasty), 1/2 pie . .	300	11.0	28.0	16.0	m.q.	850	m.q.
(Jeno's 4-Pack), 1 pie	180	7.0	17.0	9.0	m.q.	460	m.q.
(Jeno's Snacks), 4 pies	140	5.0	13.0	8.0	m.q.	430	m.q.
(John's), 1/2 pie . .	260	10.0	26.0	13.0	m.q.	630	m.q.

Food and Measure	cal.	prot. (gms)	carbo. (gms)	fat (gms)	chol. (mgs)	sod. (mgs)	fiber (gms)
Pizza, frozen, sausage (cont.)							
(John's Deluxe), 1/2 pie	260	10.0	26.0	13.0	m.q.	630	m.q.
(John's 3-Pack), 1 pie	300	15.0	34.0	11.0	m.q.	910	m.q.
(Pappalo's Pan Pizza), 1/6 pie . .	360	14.0	34.0	18.0	m.q.	550	m.q.
(Pappalo's Thin Crust), 1/6 pie . .	250	12.0	28.0	9.0	m.q.	490	m.q.
(Pillsbury Microwave), 1/2 pie . .	280	13.0	29.0	13.0	m.q.	680	m.q.
(Stouffers), 1/2 pkg.	360	16.0	32.0	18.0	m.q.	830	m.q.
(Tombstone Deluxe), 1/4 pie	350	22.0	34.0	14.0	40	840	m.q.
(Tombstone Deluxe Microwave), 1 pkg.	520	34.0	40.0	25.0	65	1280	m.q.
(Totino's Pan Pizza), 1/6 pie	320	16.0	34.0	13.0	m.q.	630	m.q.
(Totino's Party), 1/2 pie	390	14.0	35.0	21.0	m.q.	1180	m.q.
(Totino's Slices), 1 slice	200	7.0	20.0	10.0	m.q.	540	m.q.
(Totino's Small Microwave), 4.2 oz.	320	11.0	33.0	16.0	m.q.	870	m.q.
(Totino's Temptin' Toppings), 1/4 pie	210	8.0	20.0	11.0	m.q.	590	m.q.
(Weight Watchers), 6.25 oz.	310	22.0	37.0	8.0	· 45	810	m.q.
Italian (Tombstone Microwave), 8 oz.	550	32.0	39.0	29.0	65	1220	m.q.
smoked, w/pepperoni seasoning (Tombstone), 1/4 pie	350	21.0	34.0	14.0	40	900	m.q.
sausage combination: (Tombstone), 1/4 pie	370	23.0	33.0	16.0	45	980	m.q.

Food and Measure	cal.	prot. (gms)	carbo. (gms)	fat (gms)	chol. (mgs)	sod. (mgs)	fiber (gms)
sausage and mushroom *(Celeste* Pizza For One), 1 pie . .	592	23.9	51.3	32.3	20	1180	4.5 d
sausage and pepperoni:							
(Fox Deluxe), 1/2 pie	260	10.0	26.0	13.0	m.q.	640	m.q.
(Jeno's Crisp'n Tasty)*, 1/2 pie . .	300	10.0	27.0	16.0	m.q.	840	m.q.
(Stouffer's), 1/2 pkg.	380	16.0	33.0	21.0	m.q.	860	m.q.
(Tombstone Double Top), 1/4 pie . . .	540	36.0	35.0	29.0	70	1460	m.q.
(Tombstone Microwave), 8-oz. pkg.	560	34.0	39.0	29.0	65	1430	m.q.
(Totino's Small Microwave), 4.2 oz.	310	12.0	31.0	15.0	m.q.	970	m.q.
(Totino's Pan Pizza), 1/6 pie	340	16.0	34.0	15.0	m.q.	720	m.q.
(Totino's Temptin' Toppings), 1/4 pie	230	9.0	21.0	12.0	m.q.	670	m.q.
vegetable:							
(Celeste), 1/4 pie	310	13.0	28.0	16.0	m.q.	840	m.q.
(Celeste Pizza For One), 1 pie . . .	490	20.0	44.0	26.0	m.q.	1260	m.q.
(Totino's Party Pizza), 1/2 pie . .	300	11.0	36.0	13.0	m.q.	910	m.q.
(Totino's Temptin' Toppings), 1/4 pie	180	7.0	22.0	7.0	m.q.	560	m.q.
Pizza, croissant pastry, frozen, 1 pie:							
cheese *(Pepperidge Farm)*	430	15.0	41.0	23.0	m.q.	640	m.q.
deluxe *(Pepperidge Farm)*	440	16.0	43.0	23.0	m.q.	790	m.q.
pepperoni *(Pepperidge Farm)*	420	14.0	43.0	22.0	m.q.	690	m.q.

Food and Measure	cal.	prot. (gms)	carbo. (gms)	fat (gms)	chol. (mgs)	sod. (mgs)	fiber (gms)
Pizza, French bread, frozen:							
Canadian style bacon							
(Stouffer's), 1/2 pkg.	360	18.0	41.0	14.0	m.q.	960	m.q.
cheese:							
(Banquet Zap),							
4.5 oz.	310	14.0	41.0	10.0	35	800	m.q.
(Pappalo's), 1 piece	360	16.0	40.0	15.0	m.q.	830	m.q.
(Pillsbury Micro-							
wave), 1 piece	370	18.0	41.0	15.0	m.q.	680	m.q.
(Stouffer's), 1/2 pkg.	340	15.0	41.0	13.0	m.q.	840	m.q.
(Stouffer's Double							
Cheese), 1/2 pkg.	410	19.0	43.0	18.0	m.q.	950	m.q.
(Weight Watchers),							
5.12 oz.	310	18.0	31.0	12.0	15	680	m.q.
combination (Pap-							
palo's), 1 piece . .	430	19.0	41.0	21.0	m.q.	1120	m.q.
deluxe:							
(Banquet Zap),							
4.8 oz.	330	13.0	39.0	13.0	25	890	m.q.
(Stouffer's), 1/2 pkg.	430	18.0	41.0	21.0	m.q.	1130	m.q.
(Weight Watchers),							
6.12 oz.	310	19.0	31.0	13.0	10	780	m.q.
hamburger (Stouf-							
fer's), 1/2 pkg. . . .	410	19.0	40.0	19.0	m.q.	1010	m.q.
pepperoni:							
(Banquet Zap),							
4.5 oz.	350	15.0	36.0	16.0	40	1040	m.q.
(Pappalo's), 1 piece	410	16.0	41.0	20.0	m.q.	1130	m.q.
(Pillsbury Micro-							
wave), 1 piece	430	19.0	46.0	19.0	m.q.	940	m.q.
(Stouffer's), 1/2 pkg.	410	17.0	41.0	20.0	m.q.	1120	m.q.
(Weight Watchers),							
5.25 oz.	310	19.0	28.0	13.0	20	850	m.q.
pepperoni and mush-							
room (Stouffer's),							
1/2 pkg.	430	18.0	40.0	22.0	m.q.	1340	m.q.

Food and Measure	cal.	prot. (gms)	carbo. (gms)	fat (gms)	chol. (mgs)	sod. (mgs)	fiber (gms)
sausage:							
(Pappalo's), 1 piece	410	18.0	41.0	18.0	m.q.	1000	m.q.
(Pillsbury Micro-							
wave), 1 piece	410	18.0	48.0	16.0	m.q.	860	m.q.
(Stouffer's), 1/2 pkg.	420	18.0	41.0	20.0	m.q.	1110	m.q.
sausage and mush-							
room *(Stouffer's)*,							
1/2 pkg.	410	17.0	42.0	19.0	m.q.	1050	m.q.
sausage and pepper-							
oni:							
(Pillsbury Micro-							
wave), 1 piece	450	19.0	47.0	21.0	m.q.	950	m.q.
(Stouffer's), 1/2 pkg.	450	20.0	40.0	23.0	m.q.	1350	m.q.
vegetable deluxe							
(Stouffer's), 1/2 pkg.	420	18.0	41.0	20.0	m.q.	830	m.q.
Pizza crust:							
(Pillsbury All Ready),							
1/8 crust	90	3.0	16.0	1.0	0	170	m.q.
Pizza dinner, frozen:							
(Kid Cuisine), 6.5 oz.	240	10.0	41.0	4.0	20	390	m.q.
Pizza Hut:							
hand-tossed, medium							
pie, 2 slices:							
cheese	518	34.0	55.0	20.0	55	1276	7.0 d
pepperoni	500	28.0	50.0	23.0	50	1267	6.0 d
supreme	540	32.0	50.0	26.0	55	1470	7.0 d
super supreme . .	463	29.0	44.0	21.0	56	1336	5.0 d
pan pizza, medium							
pie, 2 slices:							
cheese	492	30.0	57.0	18.0	34	940	5.0 d
pepperoni	540	29.0	62.0	22.0	42	1127	5.0 d
supreme	589	32.0	53.0	30.0	48	1363	7.0 d
super supreme . .	563	33.0	53.0	26.0	55	1447	6.0 d
Personal Pan Pizza:							
pepperoni, 1 pie	675	37.0	76.0	29.0	53	1335	8.0 d
supreme, 1 pie . .	647	33.0	76.0	28.0	49	1313	9.0 d

Food and Measure	cal.	prot. (gms)	carbo. (gms)	fat (gms)	chol. (mgs)	sod. (mgs)	fiber (gms)
Pizza Hut *(cont.)*							
Thin 'n Crispy, medium pie, 2 slices:							
cheese	398	28.0	37.0	17.0	33	867	4.0 d
pepperoni	413	26.0	36.0	20.0	46	986	4.0 d
supreme	459	28.0	41.0	22.0	42	1328	5.0 d
super supreme . .	463	29.0	44.0	21.0	56	1336	5.0 d
Pizza pocket sandwich, frozen:							
(Lean Pockets Deluxe), 1 pkg. . .	280	14.0	34.0	9.0	n.a.	500	m.q.
pepperoni *(Hot Pockets),* 5 oz.	380	17.0	40.0	17.0	45	1240	m.q.
sausage *(Hot Pockets),* 5 oz.	360	15.0	40.0	16.0	65	590	m.q.
Pizza roll, frozen, 3 oz. or 6 rolls:							
cheese *(Jeno's)* . . .	240	8.0	23.0	12.0	m.q.	350	m.q.
hamburger *(Jeno's)*	240	9.0	21.0	13.0	m.q.	280	m.q.
pepperoni and cheese *(Jeno's)*	230	7.0	22.0	13.0	m.q.	390	m.q.
pepperoni and cheese *(Jeno's Microwave)*	240	7.0	23.0	13.0	m.q.	440	m.q.
sausage and cheese *(Jeno's Microwave)*	250	8.0	24.0	13.0	m.q.	440	m.q.
sausage and pepperoni *(Jeno's)*	230	7.0	22.0	13.0	m.q.	380	m.q.
Pizza sauce:							
(Contadina Quick & Easy), 1/4 cup . . .	30	1.0	5.0	1.0	n.a.	330	m.q.
(Enrico's Homemade Style), 4 oz.	60	2.0	9.0	1.0	0	m.q.	m.q.
(Enrico's Homemade Style No Salt), 4 oz.	60	2.0	9.0	1.0	0	30	m.q.
(Pastorelli Italian-Chef), 4 oz.	90	3.0	12.0	3.0	n.a.	430	m.q.
(Ragu Pizza Quick), 3 tbsp.	35	1.0	3.0	2.0	0	330	m.q.

Food and Measure	cal.	prot. (gms)	carbo. (gms)	fat (gms)	chol. (mgs)	sod. (mgs)	fiber (gms)
w/Italian cheese							
(Contadina), 1/4 cup	30	1.0	5.0	1.0	m.q.	380	m.q.
w/pepperoni (Contadina), 1/4 cup . .	40	1.0	5.0	2.0	m.q.	390	m.q.
Plantain:							
raw, 1 medium,							
9.7 oz.	218	2.3	57.1	.7	0	7	.9 c
raw, sliced, 1/2 cup	91	1.0	23.6	.3	0	3	.4 c
cooked, sliced, 1/2 cup	89	.6	24.0	.1	0	4	m.q.
Plum:							
fresh:							
w/pits, 1 lb. . . .	235	3.4	55.5	2.6	0	2	2.6 c
pitted, sliced,							
1/2 cup	46	.7	10.7	.5	0	1	.5 c
Japanese or hybrid,							
1 medium, 2 1/8″							
diam.	36	.5	8.6	.4	0	tr.	.4 c
canned, in juice:							
1/2 cup	73	.7	19.1	<.1	0	2	.5 d
3 plums and 2 tbsp.							
liquid	55	.5	14.4	<.1	0	1	.4 d
canned, in light syrup:							
1/2 cup	79	.5	20.5	.1	0	25	.4 c
3 plums and 2 3/4							
tbsp. liquid . . .	83	.5	21.7	.1	0	26	.5 c
(Stokely), 1/2 cup	100	0	16.0	0	0	20	m.q.
canned, in heavy							
syrup:							
1/2 cup	115	.5	30.0	.1	0	25	.4 c
3 plums and 2 3/4							
tbsp. liquid . . .	119	.5	30.9	.1	0	26	.4 c
(Stokely), 1/2 cup	130	0	30.0	0	0	25	m.q.
canned, in extra heavy							
syrup:							
1/2 cup	133	.5	34.3	.1	0	25	.4 c
3 plums and 2 3/4							
tbsp. liquid . . .	135	.5	35.0	.1	0	25	.4 c

Food and Measure	cal.	prot. (gms)	carbo. (gms)	fat (gms)	chol. (mgs)	sod. (mgs)	fiber (gms)
Plum canned, in extra heavy *(cont.)*							
halves or whole, un-peeled *(S&W Fancy),* 1/2 cup	135	0	35.0	0	0	25	m.q.
Plum sauce:							
tangy *(La Choy),* 1 oz.	45	.1	10.8	.1	0	17	m.q.
Poi:							
1/2 cup	134	.5	32.7	.2	0	14	.7 c
Pokeberry shoots:							
raw, 1/2 cup	18	2.1	3.0	.3	0	n.a.	m.q.
boiled, drained, 1/2 cup	16	1.9	2.5	.3	0	n.a.	m.q.
Polenta mix[1]:							
(Fantastic Polenta), 1/2 cup	106	3.0	18.0	2.0	n.a.	246	m.q.
Polish sausage (see also "Kielbasa"):							
(Hillshire Farm), 2 oz.	190	7.0	2.0	17.0	m.q.	520	0
(Hormel), 2 links . . .	170	9.0	0	14.0	m.q.	574	0
(OHSE), 1 oz.	80	4.0	1.0	7.0	m.q.	290	0
(Oscar Mayer International Sausages), 2.7-oz. link	229	9.7	2.1	20.2	31	740	0
(Pilgrim's Pride), 3 oz.	131	13.2	2.3	7.7	72	780	0
hot *(OHSE),* 1 oz. . . .	70	4.0	3.0	5.0	m.q.	270	0
Pollock, meat only:							
Atlantic, raw, 1 lb. . . .	416	88.2	0	4.4	320	391	0
Atlantic, raw, 1 oz. .	26	5.5	0	.3	20	24	0
walleye:							
raw, 1 lb.	365	77.9	0	3.6	323	449	0
raw, 1 oz.	23	4.9	0	.2	20	28	0
baked, broiled, or microwaved, 4 oz.	128	26.7	0	1.3	109	132	0
Pollock entree, frozen:							
breaded *(Mrs. Paul's Light),* 4 1/4 oz. . .	240	17.0	18.0	11.0	m.q.	530	m.q.

[1] *Prepared according to package directions.*

Food and Measure	cal.	prot. (gms)	carbo. (gms)	fat (gms)	chol. (mgs)	sod. (mgs)	fiber (gms)
Pomegranate:							
1 medium, 3³/₈″ ×							
3³/₄″, 9.7 oz.	104	1.5	26.4	.5	0	5	.3 c
Pompano, Florida,							
meat only:							
raw, 1 lb.	745	83.8	0	42.9	227	294	0
raw, 1 oz.	46	5.2	0	2.7	14	18	0
baked, broiled, or mi-							
crowaved, 4 oz. . .	239	26.4	0	13.8	73	86	0
Ponderosa, 1 serving:							
chicken, breast . . .	98	19.9	.9	2.1	54	400	0
chicken wings	213	10.7	10.7	9.0	75	610	m.q.
fish:							
bake 'r broil	230	19.0	10.0	13.0	50	330	m.q.
fried	190	9.0	17.0	9.0	15	170	m.q.
nuggets, 1 piece	31	1.7	1.9	1.7	8	52	m.q.
halibut, broiled . .	170	35.0	0	2.4	m.q.	68	0
roughy, broiled . .	138	20.6	n.a.	4.8	28	88	0
salmon, broiled . .	192	37.0	3.0	2.7	60	72	0
scrod, baked . . .	120	27.0	0	1.0	65	80	0
shrimp, fried,							
7 pieces	231	21.5	31.3	.5	105	612	m.q.
shrimp, mini,							
6 pieces	47	4.4	.9	1.7	11	8	0
swordfish, broiled	271	43.7	0	9.4	85	0	m.q.
trout, broiled . . .	228	29.4	1.0	3.9	110	51	0
hot dog	144	5.0	1.0	13.0	27	460	n.a.
steak:							
Kansas City Strip,							
5 oz.	138	21.0	.9	5.7	76	850	0
New York Strip,							
choice, 8 oz. . .	314	44.5	1.4	10.5	50	570	0
New York Strip,							
choice, 10 oz.	384	33.5	1.8	14.5	62	1420	0
porterhouse, choice,							
16 oz.	640	56.7	2.8	30.9	82	1130	0
ribeye, 5 oz.	219	25.2	.9	12.8	75	1130	0
ribeye, choice, 6 oz.	282	28.6	.1	14.2	60	570	0

Food and Measure	cal.	prot. (gms)	carbo. (gms)	fat (gms)	chol. (mgs)	sod. (mgs)	fiber (gms)
***Ponderosa,* steak** *(cont.)*							
sirloin, 7 oz.	241	34.6	1.4	10.8	63	570	0
sirloin tips, 5 oz. .	473	29.2	1.5	8.2	72	280	0
steak, chopped,							
4 oz.	225	18.5	.7	16.2	80	150	0
steak kabobs, meat							
only, 3 oz. . . .	153	25.8	1.7	4.8	67	280	0
steak sandwich,							
4 oz.	408	19.6	1.6	11.1	62	850	m.q.
steak teriyaki, 5 oz.	174	31.5	5.1	3.1	64	1420	0
T-bone, 8 oz. . . .	178	24.7	.6	8.5	71	850	0
T-bone, choice,							
10 oz.	444	33.7	1.7	18.4	80	850	0
side dishes:							
beans, baked, 4 oz.	170	6.0	21.0	6.0	0	330	m.q.
beans, green,							
3.5 oz.	20	.9	3.1	0	0	391	m.q.
cauliflower, breaded,							
4 oz.	115	4.1	23.0	.7	1	446	m.q.
carrots, 3.5 oz. . .	31	.9	7.0	.2	0	33	m.q.
corn, 3.5 oz.	90	3.0	21.0	.4	0	5	m.q.
macaroni and							
cheese, 1 oz. . .	17	.7	4.4	.5	1	80	m.q.
okra, breaded, 4 oz.	124	2.9	22.5	1.0	1	483	m.q.
onion rings,							
breaded, 4 oz.	213	3.2	30.3	8.8	2	620	m.q.
peas, 3.5 oz. . . .	67	5.1	11.7	.3	0	121	m.q.
potato, baked,							
7.2 oz.	145	4.0	32.8	.2	0	6	m.q.
potato, french fried,							
3 oz.	120	1.7	16.7	4.3	3	39	m.q.
potato, mashed,							
4 oz.	62	1.8	13.4	.2	20	191	m.q.
potato wedges,							
3.5 oz.	130	3.0	16.0	6.0	n.a.	171	m.q.
rice pilaf, 4 oz. . .	160	4.0	26.0	4.0	22	450	m.q.
shells, pasta, 2 oz.	78	2.4	16.1	.3	0	1	m.q.
stuffing, 4 oz. . . .	230	6.0	27.0	11.0	22	800	m.q.

Food and Measure	cal.	prot. (gms)	carbo. (gms)	fat (gms)	chol. (mgs)	sod. (mgs)	fiber (gms)
winter mix, 3.5 oz.	25	2.0	4.0	0	0	371	m.q.
zucchini, breaded, 4 oz.	102	3.1	17.8	.7	1	584	m.q.
salad bar:							
chicken salad, 3.5 oz.	213	11.2	7.6	15.4	42	335	n.a.
macaroni salad, 3.5 oz.	335	7.6	49.2	11.7	9	431	m.q.
pasta salad, 3.5 oz.	269	6.4	34.3	11.7	tr.	441	m.q.
potato salad, 3.5 oz.	126	1.4	16.1	5.9	7	300	m.q.
roll, dinner, 1 piece	184	5.0	33.0	3.4	0	311	m.q.
roll, sourdough, 1 piece	110	4.0	22.0	1.0	0	230	m.q.
turkey ham salad, 3.5 oz.	186	7.5	10.1	12.8	12	655	n.a.
sauces and gravy:							
BBQ sauce, 1 tbsp.	25	0	5.0	0	0	260	n.a.
brown gravy, 2 oz.	25	.6	3.9	1.0	0	167	n.a.
sweet/sour sauce, 1 oz.	37	.2	7.7	.5	0	80	n.a.
turkey gravy, 2 oz.	25	.7	5.1	.2	0	228	n.a.
desserts:							
banana pudding, 1 oz.	52	.4	6.4	2.4	0	29	(0)
ice milk, chocolate, 3.5 oz.	152	3.8	29.6	2.9	22	70	(0)
ice milk, vanilla, 3.5 oz.	150	4.0	29.7	2.6	20	58	0
mousse, chocolate, 1 oz.	78	0	6.9	4.4	0	18	n.a.
mousse, strawberry, 1 oz.	74	0	6.3	4.6	0	17	n.a.
wafer, vanilla, 2 cookies	35	0	6.0	1.0	5	25	n.a.
Popcorn, popped:							
(*Bachman*), 1/2 oz. . .	80	1.0	7.0	6.0	0	160	m.q.
(*Bachman* Lite), 1/2 oz.	50	1.0	10.0	1.0	0	35	2.0 d

Food and Measure	cal.	prot. (gms)	carbo. (gms)	fat (gms)	chol. (mgs)	sod. (mgs)	fiber (gms)
Popcorn *(cont.)*							
(Bearitos Organic Lite), 1 oz.	132	2.8	14.7	6.9	0	39	2.7 d
(Bearitos Organic No Salt), 1 oz.	108	3.6	21.7	.8	0	1	.7 d
(Bearitos Organic Traditional), 1 oz.	140	2.4	12.0	9.2	0	85	3.0 d
(Frito-Lay's), 1/2 oz.	70	1.0	9.0	3.0	0	200	m.q.
(Jiffy Pop Pan Popcorn), 4 cups . . .	130	3.0	16.0	6.0	0	270	2.0 d
(Laura Scudder's Tender Baby White), 1/2 oz.	80	1.0	6.0	6.0	0	140	m.q.
(Orville Redenbacher Natural), 3 cups . .	80	2.0	8.0	5.0	0	190	3.1 d
butter flavor:							
(Jiffy Pop Pan Popcorn), 4 cups . .	130	3.0	16.0	6.0	0	270	2.0 d
(Orville Redenbacher), 3 cups	80	2.0	8.0	5.0	0	150	3.1 d
caramel coated, see "Candy"							
cheese flavor:							
(Bachman), 1/2 oz.	90	1.0	7.0	6.0	n.a.	165	m.q.
(Bearitos Organic), 1 oz.	137	3.1	13.2	8.0	n.a.	122	2.0 d
(Frito-Lay's), 1/2 oz.	80	1.0	7.0	5.0	0	180	m.q.
cheddar *(Orville Redenbacher)*, 3 cups	160	3.0	12.0	12.0	2	310	3.1 d
cheddar, white:							
(Bachman), 1/2 oz.	70	1.0	7.0	4.0	n.a.	150	m.q.
(Cape Cod), 1/2 oz.	80	2.0	6.0	5.0	n.a.	150	m.q.
(Clover Club), 1/2 oz.	70	1.0	6.0	5.0	n.a.	140	m.q.
(Keebler Deluxe), 1 oz.	140	1.0	13.0	10.0	5	270	m.q.

Food and Measure	cal.	prot. (gms)	carbo. (gms)	fat (gms)	chol. (mgs)	sod. (mgs)	fiber (gms)
(Laura Scudder's),							
1/2 oz.	70	1.0	6.0	5.0	n.a.	140	m.q.
honey caramel *(Keebler Pop Deluxe)*,							
1 oz.	120	<1.0	22.0	3.0	0	180	m.q.
microwave:							
(Jiffy Pop), 4 cups	140	3.0	17.0	7.0	0	270	3.0 d
(Jolly Time Natural),							
3 cups	150	2.0	15.0	10.0	0	180	m.q.
(Orville Redenbacher Light Natural),							
3 cups	50	2.0	9.0	1.0	0	85	3.1 d
(Pillsbury Original),							
3 cups	210	3.0	20.0	13.0	0	410	m.q.
(Planters Natural),							
3 cups	140	2.0	14.0	9.0	0	560	m.q.
(Pop Weaver's Natural/Butter),							
4 cups	140	3.0	20.0	8.0	0	230	4.0 d
microwave, butter flavor:							
(Jiffy Pop), 4 cups	140	3.0	17.0	7.0	0	270	3.0 d
(Jolly Time), 3 cups	150	3.0	18.0	7.0	0	130	m.q.
(Orville Redenbacher Lite), 3 cups . .	50	2.0	9.0	2.0	0	70	3.1 d
(Planters), 3 cups	140	2.0	13.0	10.0	0	560	m.q.
microwave, cheddar							
(Jolly Time), 3 cups	180	3.0	17.0	11.0	0	200	m.q.
microwave, frozen, 3 cups:							
(Pillsbury Original)	210	3.0	20.0	13.0	0	420	m.q.
(Pillsbury Salt Free)	170	3.0	23.0	7.0	0	0	m.q.
butter flavor *(Pillsbury)*	210	3.0	20.0	13.0	n.a.	480	m.q.
white *(Jolly Time)*,							
4 cups	75	3.0	16.0	1.0	0	tr.	3.5 d

Food and Measure	cal.	prot. (gms)	carbo. (gms)	fat (gms)	chol. (mgs)	sod. (mgs)	fiber (gms)
Popcorn *(cont.)*							
yellow *(Jolly Time)*,							
4 cups	88	3.0	19.0	1.0	0	tr.	3.0 d
Popcorn seasoning:							
(Tone's), 1 tsp. . . .	0	0	0	0	0	2455	0
(McCormick/Schilling							
Parsley Patch),							
1 tsp.	10	.6	3.0	.1	0	4	n.a.
Poppyseed:							
1 tsp.	15	.5	.7	1.3	0	1	.2 c
Porgy, see "Scup"							
Pork, fresh, meat only							
(see also "Pork,							
boneless"):							
back rib, raw *(JM*							
Gourmet), 5½ oz.	220	15.0	0	18.0	m.q.	50	0
leg, see "Ham"							
loin, whole, lean w/							
fat:							
braised, 4 oz. . . .	417	30.8	0	31.6	116	74	0
broiled, 4 oz. . . .	392	26.7	0	30.9	107	75	0
broiled, 2.9 oz. (3.7							
oz. raw chop w/							
bone)	284	19.3	0	22.3	77	54	0
roasted, 4 oz. . . .	362	26.6	0	27.5	102	71	0
roasted, diced,							
1 cup	447	32.8	0	34.0	126	88	0
loin, whole, lean only:							
braised, 4 oz. . . .	310	37.4	0	16.6	119	85	0
broiled, 4 oz. . . .	291	31.6	0	17.3	108	85	0
broiled, 2.3 oz. (3.7							
oz. raw chop w/							
bone and fat) . .	169	18.4	0	10.1	63	49	0
roasted, 4 oz. . . .	272	30.5	0	15.8	102	78	0
roasted, diced,							
1 cup	336	37.7	0	19.5	126	97	0
loin, blade, lean w/fat:							
braised, 4 oz. . . .	465	27.2	0	38.7	122	78	0

Food and Measure	cal.	prot. (gms)	carbo. (gms)	fat (gms)	chol. (mgs)	sod. (mgs)	fiber (gms)
broiled, 4 oz. . . .	446	23.4	0	38.4	111	76	0
roasted, 4 oz. . . .	413	23.9	0	34.5	102	69	0
loin blade, lean only:							
braised, 4 oz. . . .	355	33.7	0	23.3	128	92	0
broiled, 4 oz. . . .	340	28.2	0	24.3	113	87	0
roasted, 4 oz. . . .	316	28.0	0	21.9	101	77	0
loin, center, lean w/ fat:							
braised, 4 oz. . . .	401	33.3	0	28.7	121	58	0
broiled, 4 oz. . . .	358	31.1	0	25.1	110	79	0
broiled, 3.1 oz. (3.7 oz. raw chop w/ bone)	275	23.9	0	19.2	84	61	0
fried in vegetable oil, 3.1 oz. (4 oz. raw chop w/ bone)	333	20.7	0	27.2	92	64	0
roasted, 4 oz. . . .	346	28.8	0	24.7	103	73	0
loin, center, lean only:							
braised, 4 oz. . . .	308	39.4	0	15.5	126	62	0
broiled, 4 oz. . . .	262	36.3	0	11.9	111	88	0
broiled, 2.5 oz. (3.7 oz. raw chop w/ bone and fat) . .	166	23.0	0	7.5	71	56	0
fried in vegetable oil, 2.4 oz. (4 oz. raw chop w/bone and fat)	178	19.3	0	10.7	71	57	0
roasted, 4 oz. . . .	272	32.3	0	14.8	103	78	0
loin, center rib, lean w/fat:							
braised, 4 oz. . . .	416	32.4	0	30.8	108	54	0
broiled, 4 oz. . . .	389	27.9	0	29.9	106	69	0
broiled, 2.7 oz. (3.7 oz. raw chop w/ bone)	264	18.9	0	20.3	72	47	0
roasted, 4 oz. . . .	361	28.1	0	26.8	92	50	0

Food and Measure	cal.	prot. (gms)	carbo. (gms)	fat (gms)	chol. (mgs)	sod. (mgs)	fiber (gms)
Pork *(cont.)*							
loin, center rib, lean only:							
braised, 4 oz. . . .	314	39.1	0	16.4	110	59	0
broiled, 4 oz. . . .	293	32.7	0	16.9	107	76	0
broiled, 2.2 oz. (3.7 oz. raw chop w/ bone and fat) . .	162	18.2	0	9.4	59	42	0
roasted, 4 oz. . . .	278	32.0	0	15.6	86	52	0
loin, top, lean w/fat:							
braised, 4 oz. . . .	432	31.4	0	33.1	108	53	0
broiled, 4 oz. . . .	408	26.9	0	32.5	105	67	0
broiled, 3 oz. (3.7 oz. raw chop w/ bone)	295	19.5	0	23.5	76	49	0
loin, top, lean only:							
braised, 4 oz. . . .	314	39.1	0	16.4	110	59	0
broiled, 4 oz. . . .	293	32.7	0	16.9	107	76	0
broiled, 2.3 oz. (3.7 oz. raw chop w/ bone and fat) . .	165	18.4	0	9.6	60	43	0
roasted, 4 oz. . . .	278	32.0	0	15.6	90	52	0
shoulder, whole, roasted:							
lean w/fat, 4 oz.	370	25.0	0	29.1	109	77	0
lean only, 4 oz. . .	277	28.8	0	17.0	110	86	0
shoulder, arm (picnic), roasted:							
lean w/fat, 4 oz.	375	25.3	0	29.6	107	79	0
lean w/fat, diced, 1 cup	463	31.3	0	36.5	132	97	0
lean only, 4 oz. . .	259	30.3	0	14.3	108	91	0
lean only, diced, 1 cup	319	37.4	0	17.7	133	112	0
shoulder, Boston blade, 4 oz.:							
braised, lean w/fat	421	29.9	0	32.5	126	76	0
braised, lean only	333	35.3	0	19.9	132	85	0

Food and Measure	cal.	prot. (gms)	carbo. (gms)	fat (gms)	chol. (mgs)	sod. (mgs)	fiber (gms)
broiled, lean w/fat	397	24.8	0	32.3	117	85	0
broiled, lean only	311	28.5	0	20.9	119	95	0
roasted, lean only	290	27.6	0	19.1	111	83	0
sirloin, lean w/fat:							
braised, 4 oz.	399	31.7	0	29.2	120	61	0
broiled, 4 oz.	375	27.4	0	28.6	110	62	0
broiled, 3 oz. (3.7 oz. raw chop w/ bone)	278	20.3	0	21.2	81	46	0
roasted, 4 oz.	330	28.4	0	23.1	103	67	0
sirloin, lean only:							
braised, 4 oz.	296	38.0	0	14.8	125	67	0
broiled, 4 oz.	276	32.1	0	15.4	111	68	0
broiled, 2.4 oz. (3.7 oz. raw chop w/ bone and fat) . .	165	19.2	0	9.2	67	41	0
roasted, 4 oz.	268	31.2	0	14.9	102	70	0
spareribs, lean w/fat:							
raw (JM Gourmet), 4 1/2 oz.	250	14.0	0	22.0	m.q.	70	0
braised, 6.3 oz. (1 lb. raw w/bone)	703	51.4	0	53.6	214	165	0
tenderloin, roasted:							
lean only, 4 oz. . .	188	32.6	0	5.5	105	76	0
lean only, diced, 1 cup	232	40.3	0	6.7	130	94	0
Pork, boneless, 3 oz., except as noted:							
chop (JM America's Cut), 6-oz. chop . .	330	38.0	0	20.0	m.q.	90	0
loin, center cut (JM)	190	16.0	0	13.0	m.q.	50	0
shoulder butt (JM) . .	210	13.0	0	18.0	m.q.	60	0
tenderloin (JM) . . .	120	17.0	0	5.0	m.q.	40	0
Pork, canned, 3 oz.:							
(Hormel)	240	11.0	2.0	21.0	m.q.	1056	0
chopped (Hormel) . .	200	12.0	2.0	16.0	m.q.	1073	0

Food and Measure	cal.	prot. (gms)	carbo. (gms)	fat (gms)	chol. (mgs)	sod. (mgs)	fiber (gms)
Pork, cured (see also "Ham"):							
arm (picnic), roasted:							
lean w/fat, 4 oz.	318	23.2	0	24.2	66	1216	0
lean only, 4 oz. . . .	193	28.3	0	8.0	54	1396	0
blade roll, lean w/fat, roasted, 4 oz.	325	19.6	.4	26.6	76	1103	0
Pork, ground:							
(JM), 3 oz.	190	15.0	0	14.0	m.q.	40	0
Pork belly:							
raw, 1 oz.	147	2.7	0	15.1	20	9	0
Pork dinner, frozen:							
loin (Swanson), 10³/₄ oz.	310	22.0	28.0	12.0	m.q.	770	m.q.
Pork entree, canned:							
chow mein (La Choy Bi-Pack), ³/₄ cup	80	6.0	7.0	3.0	14	970	2.0 d
Pork entree, frozen or refrigerated:							
barbecued:							
back ribs (John Morrell Pork Classics), 4³/₄ oz. . . .	240	12.0	8.0	17.0	62	480	0
chops (John Morrell Pork Classics), 4¹/₂ oz.	230	29.0	7.0	9.0	90	410	0
loin (John Morrell Pork Classics), 3 oz.	150	17.0	5.0	6.0	52	440	0
spare ribs (John Morrell Pork Classics), 4¹/₂ oz. . . .	250	12.0	7.0	18.0	51	470	0
tenderloin (John Morrell Pork Classics), 3 oz.	130	18.0	3.0	5.0	53	220	0
steak, breaded (Hormel), 3 oz.	220	12.0	11.0	15.0	m.q.	m.q.	m.q.

Food and Measure	cal.	prot. (gms)	carbo. (gms)	fat (gms)	chol. (mgs)	sod. (mgs)	fiber (gms)
sweet and sour (Chun King), 13 oz. . . .	400	11.0	78.0	5.0	m.q.	1460	n.a.
Pork entree mix[1]:							
Cajun (Hunt's Minute Gourmet), 7.9 oz.	500	19.0	46.0	28.0	m.q.	1290	m.q.
Pork fat:							
roasted, 1 oz.	167	2.2	0	17.5	24	177	0
Pork gravy, canned:							
(Franco-American), 2 oz.	40	0	3.0	3.0	n.a.	350	n.a.
(Heinz), 2 oz.	30	2.0	2.0	2.0	n.a.	130	n.a.
w/chunky pork (Hormel Great Beginnings), 5 oz.	140	14.0	5.0	8.0	m.q.	567	n.a.
Pork luncheon meat:							
(Eckrich Slender Sliced), 1 oz. . . .	45	5.0	1.0	2.0	m.q.	320	0
Pork rind snack:							
(Baken-ets), 1 oz. . .	160	12.0	2.0	10.0	25	850	n.a.
Pork seasoning and coating mix:							
(Shake'n Bake), 1/8 pouch	40	1.0	8.0	1.0	0	300	m.q.
barbecue (Shake'n Bake), 1/8 pouch	40	0	7.0	1.0	0	350	m.q.
extra crispy (Shake'n Bake Oven Fry), 1/4 pouch	120	3.0	21.0	3.0	0	690	m.q.
chop (McCormick/ Schilling Bag'n Season), 1 pkg.	103	1.1	23.6	.4	0	3126	m.q.
Pork and beans, see "Baked beans" and specific listings							

[1] Prepared according to package directions.

Food and Measure	cal.	prot. (gms)	carbo. (gms)	fat (gms)	chol. (mgs)	sod. (mgs)	fiber (gms)
Pot roast, see "Beef dinner" and "Beef entree"							
Pot roast seasoning mix, 1 pkg.:							
(*Lawry's* Seasoning Blends)	122	3.7	25.0	.7	0	4008	.5 c
(*McCormick/Schilling* Bag'n Season) . .	55	3.9	8.5	.6	0	3030	n.a.
Potato:							
raw:							
unpeeled, 1 lb. . . .	269	7.1	61.2	.3	0	21	5.4 d
peeled, 2½"-diam. potato	88	2.3	20.1	.1	0	7	1.8 d
peeled, diced, ½ cup	59	1.6	13.5	.1	0	5	1.2 d
baked in skin, 1 medium, 4¾" × 2⅓" diam.	220	4.7	51.0	.2	0	16	1.3 c
baked w/out skin:							
4 oz.	105	2.2	24.4	.1	0	6	1.7 d
½ cup	57	1.2	13.2	.1	0	3	.9 d
boiled in skin, peeled:							
2½"-diam. potato	119	2.5	27.4	.1	0	6	2.0 d
4 oz.	99	2.1	22.8	.1	0	5	1.7 d
½ cup	68	1.5	15.7	.1	0	3	1.2 d
boiled in skin, skin only, 2 oz.	44	1.6	9.8	.1	0	8	2.1 c
boiled w/out skin:							
2½"-diam. potato	116	2.3	27.0	.1	0	7	.5 c
4 oz.	98	1.9	22.7	.1	0	6	.4 c
½ cup	67	1.3	15.6	.1	0	4	.3 c
microwaved in skin:							
1 medium, 4¾" × 2⅓" diam.	212	4.9	48.7	.2	0	16	1.6 c
4 oz.	119	2.8	27.4	.1	0	9	.9 c
peeled, ½ cup . .	78	1.6	18.2	.1	0	5	.3 c

Food and Measure	cal.	prot. (gms)	carbo. (gms)	fat (gms)	chol. (mgs)	sod. (mgs)	fiber (gms)
skin only, 2 oz. . . .	75	2.5	16.8	.1	0	9	1.8 c
mashed, w/whole milk:							
1/2 cup	81	2.0	18.4	.6	2	318	.3 c
w/butter, 1/2 cup	111	2.0	17.5	4.4	13	309	.3 c
w/margarine, 1/2 cup	111	2.0	17.5	4.4	2	309	.3 c
Potato, canned, 1/2 cup, except as noted:							
w/liquid, 4 oz.	45	1.5	9.8	.2	0	341	.3 c
drained, 1 potato, 1.2 oz.	21	.5	4.8	.1	0	m.q.	.1 c
(Stokely)	50	2.0	11.0	0	0	360	m.q.
whole, new, extra small (S&W)	45	2.0	9.0	0	0	310	m.q.
whole or sliced (Del Monte)	45	1.0	10.0	0	0	355	m.q.
sliced or diced, white (Allens)	45	2.0	10.0	<1.0	0	360	m.q.
double diced, white (Allens)	45	2.0	10.0	<1.0	0	540	m.q.
Potato, freeze-dried:							
hash brown (Mountain House), 1 cup . . .	150	2.0	36.0	0	n.a.	m.q.	m.q.
Potato, frozen, (see also "Potato dishes, frozen"):							
whole:							
small (Ore-Ida), 3 oz.	70	2.0	16.0	<1.0	0	45	m.q.
white (Southern), 3.5 oz.	69	2.0	15.0	.1	0	20	m.q.
white, boiled (Seabrook), 3.2 oz.	60	2.0	13.0	0	0	5	m.q.
diced and hash shred (Seabrook), 4 oz.	80	2.0	19.0	0	0	41	m.q.

Food and Measure	cal.	prot. (gms)	carbo. (gms)	fat (gms)	chol. (mgs)	sod. (mgs)	fiber (gms)
Potato, frozen *(cont.)*							
fried, or french-fried, 3 oz., except as noted:							
(Heinz Deep Fries)	160	2.0	23.0	6.0	0	20	m.q.
(MicroMagic) . . .	290	3.0	40.0	13.0	n.a.	30	m.q.
(Ore-Ida Country Style Dinner Fries)	110	2.0	19.0	3.0	0	30	m.q.
(Ore-Ida Crispers!)	230	2.0	25.0	15.0	0	545	m.q.
(Ore-Ida Crispy Crowns)	160	2.0	20.0	9.0	0	525	m.q.
(Ore-Ida Golden Fries)	120	2.0	19.0	4.0	0	35	m.q.
(Ore-Ida Lites) . . .	90	2.0	16.0	2.0	0	30	m.q.
cottage cut *(Ore-Ida)*	120	2.0	19.0	5.0	0	25	m.q.
crinkle cut *(Heinz Deep Fries)* . . .	150	2.0	22.0	6.0	0	30	m.q.
crinkle cut *(Ore-Ida Golden Crinkles)*	120	2.0	19.0	4.0	0	35	m.q.
crinkle cut *(Ore-Ida Lites)*	90	1.0	16.0	2.0	0	35	m.q.
crinkle cut *(Ore-Ida Microwave),* 3.5 oz.	180	2.0	26.0	8.0	0	35	m.q.
crinkle cut *(Ore-Ida Pixie Crinkles)*	140	2.0	21.0	6.0	0	40	m.q.
crinkle cut *(Quick'n Crispy)*, 4 oz. . .	370	3.0	44.0	19.0	n.a.	50	m.q.
w/onions *(Ore-Ida Crispy Crowns)*	170	1.0	20.0	9.0	0	570	m.q.
shoestring *(Heinz Deep Fries)* . . .	200	2.0	25.0	10.0	0	20	m.q.
shoestring *(Ore-Ida)*	140	2.0	21.0	6.0	0	30	m.q.
shoestring *(Ore-Ida Lites)*	90	1.0	15.0	4.0	0	25	m.q.

Food and Measure	cal.	prot. (gms)	carbo. (gms)	fat (gms)	chol. (mgs)	sod. (mgs)	fiber (gms)
shoestring *(Quick'n Crispy)*, 4 oz. . .	390	3.0	48.0	20.0	n.a.	50	m.q.
skinny *(MicroMagic)*	350	4.0	49.0	15.0	n.a.	40	m.q.
sticks *(MicroMagic Tater Sticks)*, 4 oz.	390	2.0	43.0	22.0	n.a.	620	m.q.
thin cuts *(Quick'n Crispy)*, 4 oz. . .	370	3.0	44.0	19.0	n.a.	50	m.q.
wedges *(Quick'n Crispy)*, 4 oz. . .	280	3.0	36.0	13.0	n.a.	40	m.q.
wedges *(Ore-Ida Home Style Potato Wedges)* . .	100	2.0	17.0	3.0	0	45	m.q.
hash brown:							
(Ore-Ida Golden Patties), 2.5 oz.	140	1.0	15.0	8.0	0	295	m.q.
(Ore-Ida Microwave), 2 oz.	130	1.0	12.0	8.0	0	170	m.q.
(Ore-Ida Southern Style), 3 oz.	70	1.0	16.0	<1.0	0	35	m.q.
w/butter and onions *(Heinz Deep Fries)*, 3 oz.	110	1.0	14.0	7.0	5	80	m.q.
w/cheddar *(Ore-Ida Cheddar Browns)*, 3 oz.	90	2.0	13.0	2.0	10	415	m.q.
shredded *(Ore-Ida)*, 3 oz.	70	1.0	15.0	<1.0	0	40	m.q.
O'Brien *(Ore-Ida)*, 3 oz.	60	1.0	14.0	<1.0	0	25	m.q.
puffs, 3 oz., except as noted:							
(Ore-Ida Tater Tots)	140	1.0	19.0	7.0	0	550	m.q.
w/bacon flavor *(Ore-Ida Tater Tots)*	140	2.0	19.0	6.0	0	625	m.q.
(Ore-Ida Tater Tots Microwave), 4 oz.	200	2.0	29.0	9.0	0	670	m.q.

Food and Measure	cal.	prot. (gms)	carbo. (gms)	fat (gms)	chol. (mgs)	sod. (mgs)	fiber (gms)
Potato, frozen, puffs *(cont.)*							
w/onion *(Ore-Ida Tater Tots)* . . .	140	2.0	19.0	6.0	0	715	m.q.
shredded, w/vegetables in cheese sauce *(Stokely Singles)*, 4.5 oz. . . .	130	5.0	15.0	6.0	15	480	m.q.
sliced, w/bacon in cheddar cheese sauce *(Stokely Singles)*, 4.5 oz.	150	3.0	24.0	5.0	10	460	m.q.
Potato mix[1], 1/2 cup, except as noted:							
au gratin:							
(Betty Crocker) . .	150	4.0	21.0	5.0	m.q.	600	m.q.
(Fantastic Foods)[2]	196	6.0	25.0	8.0	m.q.	495	m.q.
(Idahoan)	130	3.0	18.0	5.0	m.q.	475	m.q.
tangy *(French's)* . .	130	4.0	20.0	5.0	n.a.	460	m.q.
bacon and cheddar *(Betty Crocker Twice Baked)* . .	210	6.0	21.0	11.0	m.q.	600	m.q.
cheddar:							
spicy *(Idahoan)* . .	140	3.0	21.0	5.0	m.q.	500	m.q.
and bacon casserole *(French's)*	130	4.0	18.0	5.0	n.a.	390	m.q.
country style:							
(Fantastic Foods)[3]	118	3.0	19.0	4.0	m.q.	362	m.q.
hash brown *(Idahoan Quick One-Pan)* . .	140	2.0	18.0	7.0	m.q.	400	m.q.
herb and butter *(Idahoan)*	150	2.0	21.0	6.0	m.q.	475	m.q.
herbed butter *(Betty Crocker Twice Baked)*	220	5.0	20.0	13.0	m.q.	540	m.q.

[1] *Prepared according to package directions, except as noted.*

[2] *Prepared with whole milk and 2 tbsp. salted butter.*

[3] *Prepared with 2 tbsp. salted butter.*

Food and Measure	cal.	prot. (gms)	carbo. (gms)	fat (gms)	chol. (mgs)	sod. (mgs)	fiber (gms)
mashed:							
(Country Store),							
⅓ cup flakes . .	70	1.0	16.0	0	0	10	m.q.
(French's Idaho)	130	2.0	16.0	6.0	n.a.	320	m.q.
(French's Idaho							
Spuds)	140	3.0	17.0	7.0	n.a.	380	m.q.
(Hungry Jack							
Flakes)	140	3.0	17.0	7.0	n.a.	380	m.q.
(Idahoan)	140	3.0	16.0	7.0	m.q.	320	m.q.
(Idahoan Instamash)	80	1.0	17.0	1.0	n.a.	175	m.q.
scalloped:							
(Betty Crocker) . .	140	3.0	20.0	5.0	n.a.	580	m.q.
(Idahoan)	140	3.0	20.0	5.0	m.q.	425	m.q.
cheese, real							
(French's)	140	4.0	19.0	5.0	n.a.	380	m.q.
cheesy *(Betty*							
Crocker)	140	3.0	20.0	5.0	m.q.	560	m.q.
Italian, creamy							
(French's)	120	4.0	19.0	3.0	n.a.	430	m.q.
crispy top w/savory							
onion *(French's)*	140	3.0	20.0	5.0	n.a.	430	m.q.
sour cream and							
chives:							
(Betty Crocker) . .	140	3.0	21.0	5.0	m.q.	520	m.q.
(Betty Crocker							
Twice Baked)* . .	200	5.0	19.0	11.0	m.q.	570	m.q.
(French's)	150	3.0	19.0	7.0	n.a.	550	m.q.
(Idahoan)	130	2.0	18.0	5.0	m.q.	400	m.q.
Stroganoff, creamy							
(French's)	130	3.0	20.0	4.0	n.a.	520	m.q.
western *(Idahoan)* . .	120	2.0	18.0	4.0	m.q.	400	m.q.
Potato, scalloped:							
and ham *(Hormel*							
Micro-Cup), 7.5 oz.	260	8.0	21.0	16.0	25	810	m.q.
Potato, stuffed, see							
"Potato dishes,							
frozen"							

Food and Measure	cal.	prot. (gms)	carbo. (gms)	fat (gms)	chol. (mgs)	sod. (mgs)	fiber (gms)
Potato, sweet, see "Sweet potato"							
Potato chips and crisps, 1 oz., except as noted:							
(Bachman)	160	2.0	14.0	10.0	0	270	m.q.
(Bachman Kettle Cooked)	140	2.0	16.0	8.0	0	115	m.q.
(Bachman Ridge/Ruffled)	160	2.0	14.0	10.0	0	260	m.q.
(Bachman Unsalted)	160	2.0	14.0	10.0	0	5	m.q.
(Barrel O'Fun)	150	2.0	14.0	10.0	0	160	.4 d
(Cape Cod/Cape Cod Waves)	150	2.0	16.0	8.0	0	120	m.q.
(Cape Cod No Salt)	150	2.0	16.0	8.0	0	0	m.q.
(Eagle Extra Crunchy/ Idaho Russet) . . .	150	2.0	16.0	8.0	0	180	m.q.
(Eagle Ridged/Thins)	150	2.0	15.0	10.0	0	220	m.q.
(Lay's)	150	1.0	15.0	10.0	0	200	m.q.
(Lay's Unsalted) . . .	150	2.0	15.0	10.0	0	10	m.q.
(Munchos)	150	1.0	16.0	9.0	0	290	m.q.
(O'Boisies)	150	1.0	16.0	9.0	0	180	m.q.
(Pringle's)	170	2.0	12.0	13.0	n.a.	170	m.q.
(Pringle's Idaho Rippled)	170	2.0	13.0	12.0	n.a.	150	m.q.
(Pringle's Light) . . .	150	2.0	17.0	8.0	n.a.	120	m.q.
(Ruffles)	150	1.0	15.0	10.0	0	190	m.q.
(Ruffles Light)	130	1.0	19.0	6.0	0	190	m.q.
(Snacktime Krunchers!)	150	2.0	16.0	9.0	0	170	m.q.
(Wise Plain/Rippled)	150	2.0	14.0	10.0	0	190	m.q.
(Wise New York Deli)	160	2.0	14.0	11.0	0	120	m.q.
(Zapp's Lite/Original Kettle)	150	2.0	16.0	8.0	0	45	m.q.
(Zapp's Lite/Original Kettle No Salt) . .	150	2.0	16.0	8.0	0	<1	m.q.
au gratin *(King Kold)*	150	2.0	15.0	8.0	n.a.	220	m.q.

Food and Measure	cal.	prot. (gms)	carbo. (gms)	fat (gms)	chol. (mgs)	sod. (mgs)	fiber (gms)
barbecue flavor:							
(Bachman)	150	2.0	14.0	9.0	0	280	m.q.
(Eagle Extra Crunchy)	150	2.0	16.0	8.0	0	220	m.q.
(Eagle Extra Crunchy Louisi-ana)	150	2.0	16.0	8.0	0	140	m.q.
(Eagle Thins) . . .	150	2.0	15.0	10.0	0	220	m.q.
(Lay's Bar-B-Q) . .	150	2.0	15.0	9.0	0	310	m.q.
(Pringle's Light) . .	150	2.0	17.0	8.0	n.a.	125	m.q.
(Ruffles)	150	1.0	16.0	9.0	0	320	m.q.
(Wise/Wise Ridgies)	150	2.0	14.0	10.0	0	240	m.q.
Cajun:							
(Ruffles Cajun Spice)	150	1.0	15.0	10.0	0	240	m.q.
(Zapp's Lite/Original Kettle)	150	2.0	16.0	8.0	0	94	m.q.
cheddar and sour cream (Ruffles) . .	150	2.0	16.0	9.0	0	260	m.q.
cheese (Pringle's Cheez-ums)	170	2.0	12.0	13.0	n.a.	200	m.q.
dill (King Kold)	150	2.0	16.0	8.0	n.a.	340	m.q.
dill and sour cream (Cape Cod)	150	2.0	16.0	8.0	0	160	m.q.
hot:							
(Bachman)	150	2.0	14.0	9.0	0	200	m.q.
(Wise)	160	2.0	14.0	11.0	0	290	m.q.
jalapeño flavor:							
(Snacktime Krunchers!) . . .	150	2.0	16.0	9.0	0	270	m.q.
(Zapp's Original Kettle)	150	2.0	16.0	8.0	n.a.	85	m.q.
mesquite barbecue:							
(Ruffles Mesquite Grille)	160	2.0	14.0	10.0	0	260	m.q.
(Snacktime Krunchers!) . . .	150	2.0	16.0	9.0	0	200	m.q.

Food and Measure	cal.	prot. (gms)	carbo. (gms)	fat (gms)	chol. (mgs)	sod. (mgs)	fiber (gms)
Potato chips and crisps, mesquite barbecue *(cont.)*							
(Zapp's Lite/Original Kettle)	150	2.0	16.0	8.0	0	87	m.q.
onion, French *(Pringle's Idaho Rippled)*	170	2.0	13.0	12.0	n.a.	175	m.q.
onion-garlic *(Wise)*	150	2.0	14.0	10.0	0	250	m.q.
ranch:							
(Pringle's Light) . .	150	2.0	17.0	8.0	n.a.	135	m.q.
(Ruffles)	160	2.0	15.0	10.0	0	240	m.q.
salt and vinegar *(Lay's)*	150	1.0	15.0	9.0	0	460	m.q.
Saratoga style *(Bachman Kettle Cooked)*	140	2.0	16.0	8.0	0	115	m.q.
skins:							
baked *(Tato Skins)*	150	1.0	17.0	8.0	0	160	m.q.
cheese n'bacon or sour cream n'chive *(Tato Skins)*	150	1.0	17.0	8.0	0	180	m.q.
sour cream and onion:							
(Bachman) . . .	150	2.0	14.0	9.0	0	200	m.q.
(Eagle Ridged) . .	150	2.0	15.0	10.0	0	280	m.q.
(Lay's)	160	2.0	15.0	10.0	0	250	m.q.
(O'Boisies)	150	2.0	15.0	9.0	0	190	m.q.
(Pringle's)	170	2.0	13.0	12.0	n.a.	135	m.q
(Ruffles)	150	2.0	15.0	9.0	0	240	m.q.
(Wise Ridgies) . .	160	2.0	14.0	11.0	n.a.	240	m.q.
(Zapp's Lite) . . .	150	2.0	16.0	8.0	n.a.	79	m.q.
taco and cheddar *(Pringle's Idaho Rippled)*	170	2.0	13.0	12.0	n.a.	160	m.q.
vinegar *(Bachman)*	150	2.0	15.0	9.0	0	610	m.q.
Potato dishes, frozen:							
au gratin:							
(Birds Eye For One), 5.5 oz.	240	8.0	24.0	13.0	30	590	1.0 d

Food and Measure	cal.	prot. (gms)	carbo. (gms)	fat (gms)	chol. (mgs)	sod. (mgs)	fiber (gms)
(Freezer Queen Family Side Dish), 4 oz.	100	2.0	19.0	2.0	n.a.	440	m.q.
(Green Giant One Serving), 5.5 oz.	200	7.0	20.0	10.0	20	560	m.q.
(Stouffer's), 1/3 pkg.	110	4.0	10.0	6.0	n.a.	510	m.q.
and broccoli, w/ cheese sauce:							
(Green Giant One Serving), 5.5 oz.	130	4.0	19.0	5.0	5	720	m.q.
(Freezer Queen Family Side Dish), 5.5 oz.	140	3.0	25.0	3.0	n.a.	790	m.q.
cheddared *(The Budget Gourmet),* 5.5 oz.	230	7.0	22.0	13.0	35	450	m.q.
cheddared, and broccoli *(The Budget Gourmet),* 5 oz. . . .	130	6.0	18.0	4.0	25	340	m.q.
nacho *(The Budget Gourmet),* 5 oz. . . .	180	10.0	14.0	10.0	30	360	m.q.
new, in sour cream sauce *(The Budget Gourmet),* 5 oz. . . .	120	3.0	15.0	6.0	20	300	m.q.
scalloped *(Stouffer's),* 1/3 pkg.	90	3.0	11.0	4.0	m.q.	420	m.q.
stuffed, 6 oz.:							
w/cheddar *(Oh Boy!)*	142	4.0	23.0	4.0	6	612	m.q.
w/bacon *(Oh Boy!)*	116	4.0	18.0	3.0	5	641	m.q.
w/sour cream & chives *(Oh Boy!)*	129	3.0	18.0	5.0	2	418	m.q.
stuffed, baked: w/broccoli and cheese *(Weight Watchers),* 10.5 oz.	250	13.0	33.0	7.0	40	770	m.q.

Food and Measure	cal.	prot. (gms)	carbo. (gms)	fat (gms)	chol. (mgs)	sod. (mgs)	fiber (gms)
Potato dishes, frozen, stuffed, baked *(cont.)*							
w/cheese flavored topping *(Green Giant)*, 5 oz. . .	200	4.0	33.0	6.0	n.a.	520	m.q.
w/chicken divan *(Weight Watchers)*, 11 oz.	270	19.0	38.0	4.0	65	820	m.q.
w/sour cream and chives *(Green Giant)*, 5 oz.	230	5.0	31.0	10.0	n.a.	580	m.q.
three cheese *(The Budget Gourmet Side Dish)*, 5.75 oz.	230	8.0	25.0	11.0	30	410	m.q.
Potato flour:							
1 cup	628	14.3	143.0	1.4	0	61	2.9 c
Potato pancake mix[1]:							
(French's Idaho), 3 cakes, 3″ each	90	3.0	16.0	2.0	n.a.	420	m.q.
Potato salad, canned:							
German *(Joan of Arc/ Read)*, 1/2 cup . . .	120	2.0	23.0	3.0	n.a.	550	1.6 d
homestyle *(Joan of Arc/Read)*, 1/2 cup	340	4.0	32.0	22.0	n.a.	1070	3.0 d
Potato salad seasoning:							
(Tone's), 1 tsp. . . .	5	.2	.3	.2	0	1498	.1 d
Potato starch:							
(Featherweight), 1 cup	620	0	154.0	1.0	0	51	n.a.
Potato sticks, shoe-string, canned:							
(Allens), 1 oz.	140	2.0	16.0	8.0	n.a.	190	m.q.
(Allens No Salt), 1 oz.	140	1.0	16.0	8.0	n.a.	10	m.q.
Poultry, see specific listings							
Poultry seasoning:							
1 tsp.	5	.1	1.0	.1	0	tr.	.2 c

[1] *Prepared according to package directions.*

Food and Measure	cal.	prot. (gms)	carbo. (gms)	fat (gms)	chol. (mgs)	sod. (mgs)	fiber (gms)
Pout, ocean, meat only:							
raw, 1 lb.	360	75.5	0	4.1	236	277	0
raw, 1 oz.	22	4.7	0	.3	15	17	0
Preserves, see "Jam and preserves"							
Pretzel, 1 oz., except as noted:							
(A & Eagle)	110	3.0	22.0	2.0	0	570	m.q.
(Bachman Nutzels)	110	3.0	21.0	2.0	0	470	m.q.
(Bachman Petite) . .	110	3.0	21.0	2.0	0	410	m.q.
(Bachman Petite Sodium Free)	110	3.0	21.0	2.0	0	2	m.q.
(Mr. Salty Juniors) . .	110	2.0	22.0	2.0	n.a.	500	m.q.
(Mr. Salty Mini) . . .	110	3.0	21.0	1.0	n.a.	450	m.q.
(Rold Gold Tiny Tim)	110	2.0	23.0	1.0	0	610	m.q.
beer (Quinlan)	110	2.6	21.6	1.4	0	446	.1 d
braids (Keebler Butter)	110	3.0	21.0	1.0	0	620	m.q.
cheddar flavor (Combos), 1.8 oz.	240	5.0	34.0	9.0	n.a.	580	m.q.
Dutch (Mr. Salty), 2 pieces	110	3.0	22.0	1.0	n.a.	440	m.q.
hard (Bachman) . . .	110	3.0	23.0	<1.0	0	290	m.q.
hard (Bachman Unsalted)	110	3.0	23.0	<1.0	0	50	m.q.
knots (Keebler Butter)	110	3.0	21.0	1.0	0	530	m.q.
logs (Bachman) . . .	110	3.0	21.0	2.0	0	470	m.q.
logs (Quinlan)	103	2.7	21.5	.8	0	388	.3 d
mixed (Mr. Salty Mini)	110	3.0	23.0	1.0	n.a.	480	m.q.
oat bran (Quinlan) . .	115	3.5	21.8	1.5	0	156	.3 d
rice bran (Quinlan No-Salt)	101	2.6	19.5	2.3	0	52	2.0 d
rings:							
(Bachman)	110	3.0	21.0	2.0	0	410	m.q.
(Mr. Salty)	110	3.0	21.0	2.0	n.a.	510	m.q.
butter flavor (Mr. Salty)	110	3.0	21.0	2.0	n.a.	570	m.q.

Food and Measure	cal.	prot. (gms)	carbo. (gms)	fat (gms)	chol. (mgs)	sod. (mgs)	fiber (gms)
Pretzel *(cont.)*							
rods:							
(Bachman)	110	3.0	21.0	2.0	0	240	m.q.
(Rold Gold)	110	3.0	22.0	2.0	0	550	m.q.
butter *(Seyfert's)*	110	3.0	21.0	1.0	n.a.	530	m.q.
sticks:							
(Mr. Salty)	110	3.0	22.0	1.0	n.a.	620	m.q.
(Quinlan)	105	2.7	22.3	.6	0	538	.3 d
(Rold Gold)	110	2.0	23.0	1.0	0	760	m.q.
butter flavor *(Mr. Salty)*	110	3.0	22.0	1.0	n.a.	620	m.q.
thins:							
(Bachman Thin'n Light)	110	3.0	21.0	2.0	0	410	m.q.
(Mr. Salty Veri-Thin)	110	3.0	22.0	1.0	n.a.	770	m.q.
(Quinlan)	104	2.8	22.0	.6	0	765	.1 d
(Quinlan Ultra Thins)	106	2.7	22.5	.6	0	618	.1 d
tiny *(Quinlan)* . . .	109	2.6	21.2	1.5	0	601	.2 d
tiny *(Quinlan No-Salt)*	115	2.7	22.4	1.6	0	10	.2 d
thins, treats or twists							
(Bachman)	110	3.0	21.0	2.0	0	410	m.q.
twists:							
(Mr. Salty), 5 pieces	110	3.0	21.0	2.0	n.a.	590	m.q.
(Rold Gold)	110	2.0	23.0	1.0	0	470	m.q.
Prickly pear:							
1 medium, 4.8 oz. . . .	42	.8	9.9	.5	0	6	1.9 c
Prosciutto:							
(Hormel), 1 oz. . . .	90	7.0	0	7.0	m.q.	502	0
Prune:							
canned, in heavy syrup:							
pitted, 4 oz.	119	1.0	31.5	.2	0	3	.8 c
1/2 cup	123	1.0	32.5	.2	0	3	.8 c
5 medium and 2 tbsp. liquid . .	90	.8	23.9	.2	0	2	.6 c

Food and Measure	cal.	prot. (gms)	carbo. (gms)	fat (gms)	chol. (mgs)	sod. (mgs)	fiber (gms)
dehydrated:							
uncooked, 1/2 cup	224	2.4	58.8	.5	0	4	1.9 c
cooked, 1/2 cup . .	158	1.7	41.6	.3	0	3	1.4 c
dried, 2 oz., except as noted:							
(Del Monte Moist Pak)	120	1.0	30.0	0	0	<10	m.q.
(Sunsweet)	120	1.0	32.0	0	0	<10	m.q.
w/pits, 1/2 cup . .	193	2.1	50.5	.4	0	3	5.8 d
w/pits *(Del Monte)*	120	1.0	31.0	0	0	<10	m.q.
pitted, 10 prunes	201	2.2	52.7	.4	0	3	6.0 d
pitted *(Del Monte)*	140	1.0	35.0	0	0	<10	m.q.
pitted *(Sunsweet)*	140	1.0	36.0	0	0	<10	m.q.
dried, stewed, w/pits, unsweetened,							
1/2 cup	113	1.2	29.8	.2	0	2	7.0 d
Prune juice 6 fl. oz.:							
(Del Monte)	120	1.0	33.0	0	0	<10	m.q.
(Mott's)	130	1.0	32.0	0	0	8	m.q.
(Mott's Country Style)	130	1.0	32.0	0	0	7	m.q.
(S&W)	120	1.0	31.0	0	0	20	m.q.
(Sunsweet)	130	1.0	33.0	0	0	<20	m.q.
Pudding, ready-to-serve:							
banana *(Del Monte* Pudding Cup), 5 oz.	180	3.0	30.0	5.0	n.a.	285	n.a.
butterscotch:							
(Crowley), 4.5 oz.	150	3.0	27.0	3.0	10	210	n.a.
(Del Monte Pudding Cup), 5 oz. . . .	180	3.0	31.0	5.0	n.a.	285	n.a.
(White House), 3.5 oz.	113	1.0	20.0	3.0	n.a.	195	n.a.
butterscotch-chocolate-vanilla swirl *(Jell-O* Pudding Snacks), 4 oz. . . .	180	3.0	28.0	6.0	0	140	n.a.
chocolate:							
(Crowley), 4.5 oz.	190	4.0	29.0	3.0	10	100	n.a.

Food and Measure	cal.	prot. (gms)	carbo. (gms)	fat (gms)	chol. (mgs)	sod. (mgs)	fiber (gms)
Pudding, chocolate *(cont.)*							
(Del Monte Pudding Cup), 5 oz. . . .	190	4.0	31.0	6.0	n.a.	280	n.a.
(Hunt's Snack Pack), 4.25 oz.	160	2.0	28.0	5.0	0	125	n.a.
(Hunt's Snack Pack Lite), 4 oz. . . .	100	3.0	20.1	2.0	0	120	n.a.
(Jell-O Light Pudding Snacks), 4 oz.	100	3.0	21.0	2.0	5	125	n.a.
(Swiss Miss), 4 oz.	180	3.0	27.0	6.0	1	200	n.a.
(Swiss Miss Lite), 4 oz.	100	3.0	20.1	n.a.	0	120	n.a.
(White House), 3.5 oz.	120	2.0	22.0	4.0	n.a.	130	n.a.
fudge *(Del Monte* Pudding Cup), 5 oz.	190	4.0	31.0	6.0	n.a.	260	n.a.
fudge *(Jell-O* Light Pudding Snacks), 4 oz.	100	3.0	22.0	1.0	5	125	n.a.
milk *(Jell-O* Pudding Snacks), 4 oz.	170	4.0	29.0	6.0	0	135	n.a.
regular or fudge *(Jell-O* Pudding Snacks), 4 oz.	170	3.0	28.0	6.0	0	130	n.a.
chocolate-caramel swirl *(Jell-O* Pudding Snacks), 4 oz. . . .	170	3.0	28.0	6.0	0	130	n.a.
chocolate fudge-milk chocolate swirl *(Jell-O* Pudding Snacks), 4 oz.	170	3.0	28.0	6.0	0	135	n.a.
chocolate-vanilla combo *(Jell-O* Light Pudding Snacks), 4 oz.	100	3.0	21.0	2.0	5	125	n.a.

Food and Measure	cal.	prot. (gms)	carbo. (gms)	fat (gms)	chol. (mgs)	sod. (mgs)	fiber (gms)
chocolate-vanilla swirl (Jell-O Pudding Snacks), 4 oz.	170	3.0	28.0	6.0	0	135	n.a.
lemon (White House), 3.5 oz.	152	0	37.0	1.0	n.a.	65	n.a.
rice:							
(Crowley), 4.5 oz.	125	4.0	22.0	2.0	10	80	n.a.
(White House), 3.5 oz.	111	1.0	20.0	3.0	n.a.	135	n.a.
tapioca:							
(Crowley), 4.5 oz.	135	4.0	27.0	1.0	5	70	n.a.
(Del Monte Pudding Cup), 5 oz. . . .	180	3.0	30.0	4.0	n.a.	250	n.a.
(Hunt's Snack Pack), 4.25 oz.	160	2.0	28.0	4.0	0	200	n.a.
(Hunt's Snack Pack Lite), 4 oz. . . .	100	2.0	18.1	2.0	0	105	n.a.
(Jell-O Pudding Snacks), 4 oz.	170	3.0	27.0	4.0	0	140	n.a.
(Swiss Miss), 4 oz.	150	2.0	26.0	4.0	1	190	n.a.
(Swiss Miss Lite), 4 oz.	100	2.0	18.1	2.0	0	105	n.a.
(White House), 3.5 oz.	131	1.0	19.0	6.0	n.a.	105	n.a.
vanilla:							
(Crowley), 4.5 oz.	140	3.0	26.0	3.0	10	130	n.a.
(Del Monte Pudding Cup), 5 oz. . . .	180	3.0	32.0	5.0	n.a.	285	n.a.
(Hunt's Snack Pack), 4.25 oz.	170	1.0	28.0	6.0	0	180	n.a.
(Hunt's Snack Pack Lite), 4 oz. . . .	100	2.0	18.1	2.0	0	110	n.a.
(Jell-O Light Pudding Snacks), 4 oz.	100	3.0	20.0	2.0	5	130	n.a.
(Jell-O Pudding Snacks), 4 oz.	180	3.0	28.0	7.0	0	140	n.a.
(Swiss Miss), 4 oz.	160	2.0	26.0	6.0	n.a.	200	n.a.

Food and Measure	cal.	prot. (gms)	carbo. (gms)	fat (gms)	chol. (mgs)	sod. (mgs)	fiber (gms)
Pudding, vanilla *(cont.)*							
(Swiss Miss Lite),							
4 oz.	100	2.0	18.1	2.0	0	110	n.a.
(White House),							
3.5 oz.	111	1.0	20.0	3.0	n.a.	135	n.a.
vanilla-chocolate swirl							
(Jell-O Pudding							
Snacks), 4 oz. . . .	180	3.0	28.0	6.0	0	140	n.a.
Pudding, frozen,							
3 oz.:							
butterscotch *(Rich's)*	130	2.0	18.0	6.0	0	130	n.a.
chocolate *(Rich's)* . .	140	2.0	18.0	7.0	0	135	n.a.
vanilla *(Rich's)*	130	2.0	18.0	6.0	0	160	n.a.
Pudding bar, frozen,							
1 bar:							
chocolate *(Jell-O* Pud-							
ding Pops)	80	2.0	13.0	2.0	0	85	n.a.
chocolate, fudge, milk							
or double swirl							
(Jell-O Pudding							
Pops)	80	2.0	13.0	2.0	0	90	n.a.
chocolate-vanilla swirl							
(Jell-O Pudding							
Pops)	80	2.0	13.0	2.0	0	70	n.a.
vanilla *(Jell-O* Pudding							
Pops)	80	2.0	13.0	2.0	0	55	n.a.
Pudding mix¹,							
1/2 cup, except							
as noted:							
banana *(Jell-O* Instant							
Sugar Free)² . . .	80	4.0	11.0	2.0	10	390	n.a.
banana cream:							
(Jell-O Instant) . .	160	4.0	28.0	4.0	15	410	n.a.
(Jell-O Microwave)	150	4.0	25.0	4.0	15	220	n.a.
(Royal)	160	4.0	27.0	4.0	m.q.	210	n.a.
(Royal Instant) . .	180	4.0	29.0	5.0	m.q.	390	n.a.

¹ *Prepared according to package directions with whole milk, except as noted.*
² *Prepared with 2% lowfat milk.*

Food and Measure	cal.	prot. (gms)	carbo. (gms)	fat (gms)	chol. (mgs)	sod. (mgs)	fiber (gms)
butter almond, toasted							
(*Royal* Instant) ..	170	4.0	30.0	4.0	m.q.	350	n.a.
butter pecan (*Jell-O*							
Instant)	170	4.0	28.0	5.0	15	410	n.a.
butterscotch:							
(*D-Zerta*)[1]	70	4.0	12.0	0	0	65	n.a.
(*Jell-O*)	170	4.0	30.0	4.0	15	190	n.a.
(*Jell-O* Instant) ..	160	4.0	28.0	4.0	15	450	n.a.
(*Jell-O* Instant							
Sugar Free)[2] ..	90	4.0	12.0	2.0	10	390	n.a.
(*Jell-O* Microwave)	170	4.0	28.0	4.0	15	180	n.a.
(*Royal*)	160	4.0	27.0	4.0	m.q.	210	n.a.
(*Royal* Instant) ..	180	4.0	29.0	5.0	m.q.	390	n.a.
(*Royal* Instant Sugar							
Free)[2]	100	4.0	16.0	2.0	m.q.	470	n.a.
chocolate:							
(*D-Zerta*)[1]	60	5.0	11.0	0	0	70	n.a.
(*Jell-O*)	160	5.0	28.0	4.0	15	170	n.a.
(*Jell-O* Instant) ..	180	4.0	31.0	4.0	15	480	n.a.
(*Jell-O* Instant							
Sugar Free)[2] ..	90	4.0	13.0	3.0	10	380	n.a.
(*Jell-O* Microwave)	170	5.0	28.0	5.0	15	190	n.a.
(*Jell-O* Sugar Free)[2]	90	5.0	13.0	3.0	10	160	n.a.
(*Royal*)	180	5.0	33.0	4.0	m.q.	150	n.a.
(*Royal* Instant) ..	190	5.0	35.0	4.0	m.q.	390	n.a.
(*Royal* Instant Sugar							
Free)[2]	110	5.0	17.0	3.0	m.q.	480	n.a.
chocolate chip							
(*Royal* Instant)	190	4.0	35.0	4.0	m.q.	390	n.a.
dark'n sweet (*Royal*)	180	5.0	33.0	4.0	m.q.	150	n.a.
dark'n sweet (*Royal*							
Instant)	190	4.0	35.0	4.0	m.q.	390	n.a.
milk (*Jell-O*)	160	4.0	28.0	4.0	15	170	n.a.
milk (*Jell-O* Instant)	180	5.0	31.0	5.0	15	470	n.a.
milk (*Jell-O* Micro-							
wave)	160	4.0	27.0	5.0	15	190	n.a.

[1] *Prepared with skim milk.*
[2] *Prepared with 2% lowfat milk.*

Food and Measure	cal.	prot. (gms)	carbo. (gms)	fat (gms)	chol. (mgs)	sod. (mgs)	fiber (gms)
Pudding mix *(cont.)*							
chocolate fudge:							
(Jell-O)	160	5.0	28.0	4.0	15	170	n.a.
(Jell-O Instant) . .	180	5.0	31.0	5.0	15	440	n.a.
(Jell-O Instant							
Sugar Free)[1] . .	100	5.0	14.0	3.0	10	330	n.a.
chocolate mint *(Royal*							
Instant)	190	4.0	35.0	4.0	m.q.	390	n.a.
coconut, toasted							
(Royal Instant) . .	170	4.0	30.0	4.0	m.q.	350	n.a.
coconut cream *(Jell-O*							
Instant)	180	4.0	27.0	6.0	15	320	n.a.
custard *(Royal)* . . .	150	4.0	22.0	5.0	m.q.	115	n.a.
custard, egg, golden							
(Jell-O Americana)	160	5.0	23.0	5.0	80	200	n.a.
flan *(Jell-O)*	150	4.0	26.0	4.0	15	65	n.a.
flan, w/caramel sauce							
(Royal)	150	4.0	22.0	5.0	m.q.	115	n.a.
lemon:							
(Jell-O Instant) . .	170	4.0	29.0	4.0	15	360	n.a.
(Royal)	160	1.0	30.0	3.0	m.q.	120	n.a.
(Royal Instant) . .	180	1.0	29.0	5.0	m.q.	350	n.a.
lime, key *(Royal)* . .	160	1.0	30.0	3.0	m.q.	120	n.a.
pistachio:							
(Jell-O Instant) . .	170	4.0	28.0	5.0	15	410	n.a.
(Jell-O Instant							
Sugar Free)[1] . .	90	4.0	12.0	3.0	10	390	n.a.
nut *(Royal* Instant)	170	4.0	30.0	4.0	m.q.	350	n.a.
raspberry *(Salada*							
Danish Dessert) . .	130	0	32.0	0	0	5	n.a.
rennet, custard:							
chocolate *(Junket)*	120	5.0	15.0	4.0	n.a.	65	n.a.
chocolate *(Junket)*[2]	90	5.0	15.0	0	(0)	70	n.a.
raspberry or straw-							
berry *(Junket)* . .	120	4.0	16.0	4.0	n.a.	60	n.a.

[1] *Prepared with 2% lowfat milk.*

[2] *Prepared with skim milk.*

Food and Measure	cal.	prot. (gms)	carbo. (gms)	fat (gms)	chol. (mgs)	sod. (mgs)	fiber (gms)
raspberry or straw-							
berry *(Junket)*[1]	90	4.0	16.0	0	(0)	65	n.a.
vanilla *(Junket)* . .	120	4.0	16.0	4.0	n.a.	65	n.a.
vanilla *(Junket)*[1] . .	90	4.0	16.0	0	(0)	70	n.a.
rice *(Jell-O Ameri-*							
cana)	170	5.0	30.0	4.0	15	160	n.a.
strawberry *(Salada*							
Danish Dessert) . .	130	0	32.0	0	0	5	n.a.
tapioca:							
vanilla *(Jell-O Amer-*							
icana)	160	4.0	27.0	4.0	15	170	n.a.
vanilla *(Royal)* . . .	160	4.0	27.0	4.0	m.q.	150	n.a.
vanilla:							
(D-Zerta)[1]	70	4.0	12.0	0	0	65	n.a.
(Jell-O)	160	4.0	26.0	4.0	15	200	n.a.
(Jell-O Instant) . .	170	4.0	29.0	4.0	15	410	n.a.
(Jell-O Instant							
Sugar Free)[2] . .	90	4.0	12.0	2.0	10	390	n.a.
(Jell-O Microwave)	160	4.0	26.0	4.0	15	180	n.a.
(Jell-O Sugar Free)[2]	80	4.0	11.0	2.0	10	200	n.a.
(Royal)	160	4.0	27.0	4.0	m.q.	210	n.a.
(Royal Instant) . .	180	4.0	29.0	5.0	m.q.	390	n.a.
(Royal Instant Sugar							
Free)[2]	100	4.0	16.0	2.0	m.q.	470	n.a.
French *(Jell-O)* . .	170	4.0	30.0	4.0	15	190	n.a.
French *(Jell-O* In-							
stant)	160	4.0	28.0	4.0	15	400	n.a.
Puff pastry, see							
"Pastry dough"							
Pummelo:							
1 medium, 5½"diam.	228	4.6	58.6	.2	0	7	1.1 c
sections, ½ cup . . .	36	.7	9.1	<.1	0	1	.2 c
Pumpkin:							
fresh:							
raw, pulp only, 1"							
cubes, ½ cup	15	.6	3.8	.1	0	1	.6 c

[1] *Prepared with skim milk.*
[2] *Prepared with 2% lowfat milk.*

Food and Measure	cal.	prot. (gms)	carbo. (gms)	fat (gms)	chol. (mgs)	sod. (mgs)	fiber (gms)
Pumpkin, fresh *(cont.)*							
boiled, drained,							
mashed, 1/2 cup	24	.9	6.0	.1	0	2	1.0 c
canned, 1/2 cup:							
w/ or w/out winter							
squash	41	1.3	9.9	.3	0	6	2.0 c
(Del Monte)	35	1.0	9.0	0	0	<10	m.q.
(Stokely)	40	2.0	10.0	0	0	15	m.q.
Pumpkin flower:							
raw, 1/2 cup	3	.2	.5	<.1	0	1	.1 c
boiled, drained,							
1/2 cup	10	.7	2.2	.1	0	4	.6 c
Pumpkin leaf:							
raw, 1/2 cup	4	.6	.5	.1	0	2	.2 c
boiled, drained,							
1/2 cup	7	1.0	1.2	.1	0	3	.4 c
Pumpkin pie spice:							
1 tsp.	6	.1	1.2	.2	0	1	.3 c
Pumpkin seed:							
roasted, whole, in							
shell:							
1 oz. or 85 seeds	127	5.3	15.3	5.5	0	5	10.2 c
1 cup	285	11.9	34.4	12.4	0	12	23.0 c
salted, 1 oz.	127	5.3	15.3	5.5	0	163	10.2 c
roasted, shelled:							
1 oz.	148	9.4	3.8	12.0	0	5	.5 c
salted, 1 oz.	148	9.4	3.8	12.0	0	163	.5 c
dried, shelled:							
1 oz. or 142 kernels	154	7.0	5.1	13.0	0	5	.6 c
Punch, see "Fruit							
punch"							
Purslane:							
raw, untrimmed, 1 lb.	56	4.5	11.8	.3	0	156	2.8 c
raw, 1/2 cup	4	.3	.7	<.1	0	10	.2 c
boiled, drained,							
1/2 cup	10	.9	2.1	.1	0	26	.5 c

Q

Food and Measure	cal.	prot. (gms)	carbo. (gms)	fat (gms)	chol. (mgs)	sod. (mgs)	fiber (gms)
Quail, raw:							
meat w/skin:							
1 quail, 3.8 oz.							
(4.3 oz. w/bone)	210	21.4	0	13.1	m.q.	58	0
1 oz.	54	5.6	0	3.4	m.q.	15	0
meat only:							
1 quail, 3.2 oz.							
(4.3 oz. w/bone							
and skin)	123	20.0	0	4.2	m.q.	47	0
1 oz.	38	6.2	0	1.3	m.q.	14	0
breast, meat only:							
1 breast, 2 oz. . .	69	12.7	0	1.8	m.q.	31	0
1 oz.	35	6.4	0	.8	m.q.	16	0
Quince:							
1 medium, 5.3 oz. . .	53	.4	14.1	.1	0	4	1.6 c
peeled and seeded,							
1 oz.	16	.1	4.3	<.1	0	1	.5 c
Quincy's:							
main dishes, 1 aver-age serving:							
catfish filets,							
2 pieces	309	26.0	19.0	12.0	m.q.	101	m.q.
chicken breast,							
grilled	145	35.0	0	.4	72	140	0
chicken strips,							
4 pieces	318	39.0	4.0	15.0	m.q.	m.q.	m.q.
hamburger, 1/4 lb.	403	25.0	32.0	19.0	m.q.	284	m.q.
hamburger, 1/4 lb.,							
w/cheese	451	28.0	32.0	23.0	m.q.	432	m.q.
shrimp, 7 pieces	248	22.0	11.0	12.0	m.q.	205	m.q.

Food and Measure	cal.	prot. (gms)	carbo. (gms)	fat (gms)	chol. (mgs)	sod. (mgs)	fiber (gms)
***Quincy's* main dishes** *(cont.)*							
sirloin tips, 4 oz.	236	37.0	0	9.0	m.q.	113	0
steak, chopped . .	466	40.0	0	34.0	m.q.	96	0
steak, chopped, lun- cheon	350	30.0	0	25.0	m.q.	72	0
steak, country style, w/mushroom sauce	288	18.0	17.0	19.0	m.q.	315	m.q.
steak, filet	331	51.0	0	12.0	m.q.	159	0
steak, ribeye . . .	665	31.0	0	60.0	m.q.	205	0
steak, sirloin	649	38.0	0	54.0	m.q.	206	0
steak, sirloin, large	852	50.0	0	70.0	m.q.	241	0
steak, sirloin, petite	446	26.0	0	37.0	m.q.	118	0
steak, sirloin club	283	44.0	0	10.0	m.q.	160	0
steak, T-Bone . . .	1045	43.0	0	95.0	m.q.	222	0
side dishes:							
baked potato, w/out butter	181	5.0	41.0	<1.0	0	8	m.q.
coleslaw, 2.1 oz.	60	<1.0	4.0	5.0	n.a.	75	m.q.
corn bread, 1.9 oz.	178	4.0	28.0	6.0	n.a.	263	m.q.
green beans, 4.3 oz.	40	2.0	7.0	1.0	0	500	m.q.
mushroom sauce, 3 oz.	27	1.0	5.0	<1.0	n.a.	366	m.q.
peppers and onions, 4 oz.	80	1.0	8.0	5.0	n.a.	11	m.q.
steak fries, 5.5 oz.	426	7.0	56.0	21.0	n.a.	90	m.q.
soups, 1 serving:							
cream of broccoli	193	3.0	13.0	14.0	n.a.	1045	m.q.
chili w/beans . . .	346	20.0	32.0	16.0	m.q.	1380	m.q.
clam chowder . . .	198	6.0	15.0	14.0	m.q.	1185	m.q.
vegetable beef . .	78	5.0	10.0	2.0	m.q.	1046	m.q.
Quinoa:							
1 oz.	106	3.7	19.5	1.6	0	n.a.	m.q.

R

Food and Measure	cal.	prot. (gms)	carbo. (gms)	fat (gms)	chol. (mgs)	sod. (mgs)	fiber (gms)
Rabbit, meat only:							
domesticated:							
roasted, 4 oz.	175	25.8	0	7.2	73	42	0
stewed, 4 oz.	234	34.5	0	9.5	98	42	0
stewed, diced,							
1 cup	288	42.5	0	11.8	120	52	0
wild, stewed:							
4 oz.	196	37.4	0	4.0	139	51	0
diced, 1 cup	242	46.2	0	4.9	172	63	0
Radish:							
10 medium, 3/4″–							
1″diam.	7	.3	1.6	.2	0	11	.2 c
sliced, 1/2 cup	10	.4	2.1	.3	0	14	.3 c
Radish, black:							
1 oz.	5	.3	1.0	<.1	0	5	m.q.
Radish, Oriental:							
raw, 1 medium,							
7″ × 21/4″ diam.	62	2.0	13.9	.3	0	71	2.2 c
raw, sliced, 1/2 cup	8	.3	1.8	<.1	0	9	.3 c
boiled, drained, sliced,							
1/2 cup	13	.5	2.5	.2	0	10	.4 c
dried, 1 oz.	77	2.2	18.0	.2	0	79	2.4 c
Radish, white-icicle:							
1 medium, .6 oz. . .	2	.2	.5	<.1	0	3	.1 c
sliced, 1/2 cup	7	.6	1.3	.1	0	8	.4 c
Raisin, 1/2 cup, except							
as noted:							
golden seedless:							
not packed	219	2.5	57.7	.3	0	9	1.0 c
(Del Monte), 3 oz.	260	3.0	68.0	0	0	<10	m.q.

Food and Measure	cal.	prot. (gms)	carbo. (gms)	fat (gms)	chol. (mgs)	sod. (mgs)	fiber (gms)
Raisin, golden seedless *(cont.)*							
(Dole)	260	3.0	63.0	0	0	25	m.q.
natural *(Del Monte)*, 3 oz.	250	3.0	68.0	0	0	15	m.q.
seeded, not packed	214	1.8	56.9	.4	0	21	.5 c
seedless:							
not packed	217	2.3	57.4	.3	0	9	3.8 d
(Cinderella Thompson)	250	3.0	66.0	0	0	15	5.8 d
(Dole)	260	3.0	63.0	0	0	25	m.q.
(Sun-Maid)	290	3.0	69.0	0	0	<15	m.q.
Raspberry, red:							
1 pint	154	2.8	36.1	1.7	0	tr.	15.3 d
1/2 cup	31	.6	7.1	.3	0	tr.	2.9 d
frozen, in light syrup *(Birds Eye* Quick Thaw), 5 oz.	100	1.0	25.0	1.0	0	0	4.0 d
Raspberry drink mix[1], 8 fl. oz.:							
(Kool-Aid)	100	0	25.0	0	0	25	0
(Kool-Aid) Presweetened) . .	80	0	20.0	0	0	25	0
Raspberry juice:							
blend *(Dole Pure & Light* Country Raspberry), 6 fl. oz. . .	87	.3	24.0	.2	0	15	(0)
red *(Smucker's* Naturally 100%), 8 fl. oz.	120	0	30.0	0	0	10	(0)
cocktail *(Welch's* Orchard), 10 fl. oz.	160	0	40.0	0	0	10	0
Ravioli, canned, 7 1/2 oz.:							
beef:							
in meat sauce *(Franco-American* Hearty Pasta) . .	280	9.0	35.0	11.0	m.q.	810	m.q.

[1] *Prepared according to package directions.*

Food and Measure	cal.	prot. (gms)	carbo. (gms)	fat (gms)	chol. (mgs)	sod. (mgs)	fiber (gms)
in meat sauce (Franco-American RavioliO's) . . .	250	9.0	35.0	8.0	m.q.	920	m.q.
mini (Chef Boyardee)	210	7.0	31.0	5.0	m.q.	1140	m.q.
in tomato sauce (Hormel Micro-Cup)	247	8.0	28.0	11.0	21	951	m.q.
in tomato meat sauce (Chef Boyardee)	220	8.0	35.0	5.0	m.q.	1120	m.q.
cheese:							
in beef tomato sauce (Chef Boyardee)	200	7.0	34.0	3.0	m.q.	1205	m.q.
in sauce (Buitoni)	190	7.0	27.0	6.0	5	790	m.q.
in tomato sauce (Chef Boyardee)	200	7.0	33.0	5.0	m.q.	990	m.q.
chicken (Chef Boyardee)	180	7.0	29.0	4.0	m.q.	1100	m.q.
chicken, mini (Chef Boyardee)	220	7.0	29.0	8.0	m.q.	1090	m.q.
meat, in sauce (Buitoni)	180	7.0	28.0	4.0	5	890	m.q.
Ravioli, frozen:							
(Celentano), 6.5 oz.	380	21.0	50.0	11.0	m.q.	510	m.q.
cheese (Buitoni), 4 oz.	360	12.0	31.0	8.0	65	220	m.q.
mini (Celentano), 4 oz.	250	13.0	39.0	5.0	m.q.	210	m.q.
Ravioli entree, fro-zen:							
cheese (The Budget Gourmet Slim Selects), 10 oz. . .	260	12.0	36.0	7.0	45	960	m.q.
cheese, baked (Weight Watchers), 9 oz.	290	19.0	30.0	12.0	85	550	m.q.

Food and Measure	cal.	prot. (gms)	carbo. (gms)	fat (gms)	chol. (mgs)	sod. (mgs)	fiber (gms)
Rax, 1 serving:							
sandwiches:							
BBC	720	30.0	40.0	49.0	137	1873	m.q.
BBQ	420	21.0	53.0	14.0	24	1343	m.q.
fish	460	14.0	58.0	17.0	<1	935	m.q.
ham and Swiss . .	430	23.0	42.0	23.0	37	1737	m.q.
Philly beef w/							
cheese	480	25.0	44.0	22.0	49	1346	m.q.
roast beef	320	20.0	33.0	11.0	36	969	m.q.
roast beef, large	570	22.0	41.0	35.0	36	1169	m.q.
roast beef, small							
(Uncle Al)	260	12.0	21.0	14.0	19	562	m.q.
turkey bacon club	670	29.0	41.0	43.0	87	1878	m.q.
french fries:							
large, salted	390	3.0	50.0	20.0	16	104	m.q.
regular, salted . . .	260	2.0	33.0	13.0	10	69	m.q.
potatoes:							
plain, w/margarine	370	8.0	60.0	11.0	0	170	m.q.
BBQ, w/cheese . .	730	24.0	104.0	24.0	18	1071	m.q.
cheese and bacon	780	22.0	110.0	28.0	23	910	m.q.
cheese and broccoli	760	19.0	112.0	26.0	11	489	m.q.
chili and cheese	700	22.0	101.0	23.0	25	599	m.q.
Mexican bar:							
cheese sauce,							
3.5 oz.	420	10.0	58.0	17.0	11	365	n.a.
cheese sauce,							
nacho, 3.5 oz.	470	10.0	57.0	22.0	11	190	n.a.
refried beans, 3 oz.	120	6.0	16.0	4.0	2	375	m.q.
sour topping, 3.5 oz.	130	3.0	5.0	11.0	<1	79	n.a.
Spanish rice, 3.5 oz.	90	3.0	20.0	<1.0	0	442	m.q.
spicy meat sauce,							
3.5 oz.	80	5.0	6.0	4.0	12	751	n.a.
taco sauce, 3.5 oz.	30	1.0	6.0	<1.0	0	806	n.a.
taco shells, 1 piece	40	<1.0	6.0	2.0	0	53	m.q.
tortillas, 1 piece . .	110	3.0	19.0	2.0	0	284	m.q.
tortilla chips, 1 oz.	140	2.0	17.0	7.0	0	100	m.q.
pasta bar, 3.5 oz.:							
Alfredo sauce . . .	80	2.0	12.0	3.0	10	70	n.a.

Food and Measure	cal.	prot. (gms)	carbo. (gms)	fat (gms)	chol. (mgs)	sod. (mgs)	fiber (gms)
pasta shells	170	7.0	27.0	4.0	0	2	m.q.
pasta/vegetable							
blend	100	4.0	12.0	4.0	0	11	m.q.
rainbow rotini . . .	180	6.0	30.0	4.0	2	9	m.q.
spaghetti	140	3.0	23.0	4.0	0	1	m.q.
spaghetti sauce . .	80	1.0	19.0	<1.0	<1	635	m.q.
spaghetti sauce w/							
meat	150	7.0	12.0	8.0	<1	419	m.q.
chocolate chip cookie,							
1 piece	130	1.0	17.0	6.0	<1	65	m.q.
milkshake, w/out							
whipped topping:							
chocolate	560	13.0	97.0	13.0	63	239	(0)
strawberry	560	13.0	97.0	13.0	62	226	(0)
vanilla	500	13.0	81.0	14.0	58	286	0
whipped topping,							
1 dollop	50	<1.0	4.0	4.0	2	6	0
Red bean, canned:							
(*Allens*), 1/2 cup . . .	115	7.0	20.0	<1.0	0	350	m.q.
(*Green Giant/Joan of*							
Arc), 1/2 cup	90	6.0	19.0	1.0	0	340	5.0 d
(*Van Camp's*), 1 cup	194	11.5	35.6	.6	0	928	2.4 c
small (*Hunt's*), 4 oz.	91	5.7	18.1	0	0	578	m.q.
Red snapper, see							
"Snapper"							
Redfish, see "Ocean							
perch"							
Refried beans,							
canned:							
(*Gebhardt*), 4 oz. . .	130	7.0	20.0	2.0	n.a.	490	m.q.
(*Little Pancho*), 1/2 cup	80	6.0	15.0	0	n.a.	330	m.q.
(*Old El Paso*), 1/4 cup	50	5.0	8.0	1.0	0	200	2.5 d
(*Rosarita*), 4 oz. . .	130	7.0	20.0	2.0	n.a.	460	m.q.
w/green chilies (*Old*							
El Paso), 1/4 cup	50	5.0	16.0	1.0	n.a.	400	m.q.
jalapeño (*Gebhardt*),							
4 oz.	110	7.0	18.0	2.0	n.a.	320	m.q.

Food and Measure	cal.	prot. (gms)	carbo. (gms)	fat (gms)	chol. (mgs)	sod. (mgs)	fiber (gms)
Refried beans *(cont.)*							
w/sausage *(Old El Paso)*, 1/4 cup . . .	180	6.0	8.0	8.0	m.q.	300	m.q.
spicy *(Del Monte)*, 1/2 cup	130	6.0	20.0	2.0	n.a.	480	m.q.
vegetarian *(Old El Paso)*, 1/4 cup . . .	45	3.0	8.0	4.0	0	360	m.q.
Relish, 1 oz.:							
dill *(Vlasic)*	2	0	0	0	0	450	m.q.
hamburger *(Heinz)*	30	0	7.0	0	0	325	m.q.
hot dog *(Heinz)* . . .	35	0	8.0	0	0	200	m.q.
hot dog *(Vlasic)* . . .	40	0	8.0	1.0	n.a.	260	m.q.
India *(Heinz)*	35	0	9.0	0	0	215	m.q.
pickle *(Claussen)* . .	26	.3	5.6	.3	0	170	m.q.
picalilli *(Heinz)*	30	0	7.0	0	0	145	m.q.
sweet *(Heinz)*	35	0	9.0	0	0	205	m.q.
sweet *(Vlasic)*	30	0	8.0	0	0	260	m.q.
Rhubarb:							
fresh:							
untrimmed, 1 lb. . .	71	3.0	15.4	.7	0	14	2.4 c
diced, 1/2 cup . . .	13	.6	2.8	.1	0	2	.4 c
frozen, cooked, sweetened, 1/2 cup . . .	139	.5	37.4	.1	0	2	1.0 c
Rib sauce, 1 oz.:							
(Dip n'Joy Saucey Rib)	60	0	14.0	0	0	250	n.a.
Rice, cooked[1]:							
basmati, white *(Texmati)*, 1/2 cup	82	3.0	31.0	0	0	0	m.q.
brown, long grain:							
(Carolina), 1/2 cup	110	2.0	23.0	0	0	0	m.q.
(Mahatma), 1/2 cup	110	2.0	23.0	0	0	<10	m.q.
(River), 1/2 cup . .	110	2.0	23.0	0	0	n.a.	m.q.
(S&W), 3.5 oz. . .	119	3.0	26.0	0	0	0	m.q.
(S&W Quick), 3.5 oz.	110	2.0	25.0	0	0	0	m.q.

[1] *Prepared according to package directions, without salt and butter.*

Food and Measure	cal.	prot. (gms)	carbo. (gms)	fat (gms)	chol. (mgs)	sod. (mgs)	fiber (gms)
(*Uncle Ben's* Whole Grain), 2/3 cup	130	3.0	27.0	0	0	0	m.q.
brown, medium grain, 1 cup	218	4.5	45.8	1.6	0	2	.6 c
glutinous or sweet, 1 cup	234	4.9	50.8	.5	0	13	.2 c
precooked (*Uncle Ben's*), 1/2 cup . .	90	2.0	21.0	1.0	0	11	1.0 d
white, long grain:							
(*Carolina/Mahatma/ River*), 1/2 cup	100	2.0	22.0	0	0	<10	m.q.
(*Uncle Ben's* Natural Whole Grain), 2/3 cup	130	3.0	28.0	1.0	0	0	m.q.
(*Water Maid*), 1/2 cup	100	2.0	22.0	0	0	<10	m.q.
parboiled (*Uncle Ben's Converted*), 2/3 cup	120	2.0	28.0	<1.0	0	0	m.q.
white, long grain, instant:							
(*Carolina/Mahatma* Enriched), 1/2 cup	110	2.0	23.0	0	0	n.a.	m.q.
(*Minute Rice/Minute* Premium), 2/3 cup	120	3.0	27.0	0	0	0	m.q.
(*Minute Rice* Boil-in-Bag), 1/2 cup . .	90	2.0	20.0	0	0	0	m.q.
(*S&W*), 3.5 oz. . .	106	2.0	23.0	0	0	0	m.q.
(*Success* Boil-in-Bag Enriched), 1/2 cup	100	2.0	21.0	0	0	0	m.q.
(*Uncle Ben's* Boil-in-Bag), 1/2 cup . .	90	2.0	20.0	<1.0	0	10	m.q.
(*Uncle Ben's* Rice In An Instant), 2/3 cup	120	3.0	27.0	<1.0	0	10	m.q.
white, medium grain, 1 cup	266	4.9	58.6	.4	0	1	.2 c

Food and Measure	cal.	prot. (gms)	carbo. (gms)	fat (gms)	chol. (mgs)	sod. (mgs)	fiber (gms)
Rice, wild, see "Wild rice"							
Rice bran, crude:							
1 cup	262	11.1	41.2	17.3	0	4	18.0 d
Rice cake, 1 piece, except as noted:							
plain:							
(*Hain*)	40	<1.0	8.0	<1.0	0	10	m.q.
(*Quaker*)	35	.8	7.1	.3	0	36	.3 d
mini (*Hain*), 1/2 oz.	50	1.0	12.0	<1.0	0	75	0
apple cinnamon, mini (*Hain*), 1/2 oz. . . .	50	1.0	12.0	<1.0	0	5	0
barbecue, mini (*Hain*), 1/2 oz.	70	1.0	10.0	3.0	0	70	0
barley and oats (*Mother's*)	34	.9	6.9	.3	0	41	.3 d
buckwheat (*Mother's* Unsalted)	35	.8	7.1	.3	0	0	.3 d
cheese, mini (*Hain*), 1/2 oz.	60	1.0	10.0	2.0	0	80	0
corn (*Quaker/Mother's*)	35	.8	7.2	.3	0	31	.3 d
five grain (*Hain*) . . .	40	<1.0	8.0	<1.0	0	10	m.q.
honey nut, mini (*Hain*), 1/2 oz.	60	1.0	12.0	1.0	0	15	0
multigrain (*Quaker/ Mother's*)	34	.9	6.9	.4	0	29	.4 d
rye (*Quaker*)	34	.8	6.9	.4	0	12	.4 d
sesame:							
(*Hain*)	40	<1.0	8.0	<1.0	0	10	m.q.
(*Quaker/Mother's*)	35	.8	7.1	.3	0	36	.3 d
teriyaki, mini (*Hain*), 1/2 oz.	50	1.0	11.0	<1.0	0	80	0
Rice dishes, canned:							
fried (*La Choy*), 3/4 cup	180	4.0	40.0	1.0	0	930	1.4 d
Spanish:							
(*Heinz*), 71/4 oz. . .	150	3.0	26.0	5.0	n.a.	1045	m.q.

Food and Measure	cal.	prot. (gms)	carbo. (gms)	fat (gms)	chol. (mgs)	sod. (mgs)	fiber (gms)
(Old El Paso),							
1/2 cup	70	1.0	15.0	1.0	0	400	1.0 d
(Van Camp's), 1 cup	150	3.1	28.2	2.7	n.a.	1358	.6 c
Rice dishes, freeze-dried:							
and chicken (Mountain House), 1 cup . . .	400	13.0	41.0	13.0	m.q.	241	m.q.
Rice dishes, frozen, (see also specific listings):							
(Green Giant Rice Originals Medley), 1/2 cup	100	3.0	19.0	1.0	5	310	m.q.
and broccoli, au gratin (Birds Eye For One), 5.75 oz.	180	6.0	27.0	6.0	5	430	1.0 d
and broccoli, in cheese sauce:							
(Green Giant One Serving), 4.5 oz.	180	5.0	25.0	6.0	5	550	m.q.
(Green Giant Rice Originals), 1/2 cup	120	3.0	18.0	4.0	n.a.	510	.2 c
French style (Birds Eye), 3.3 oz. . . .	110	3.0	23.0	0	0	610	m.q.
fried:							
w/chicken (Chun King), 8 oz.	260	14.0	41.0	4.0	m.q.	1460	m.q.
w/pork (Chun King), 8 oz.	270	10.0	44.0	6.0	m.q.	1210	m.q.
Italian, w/spinach in cheese sauce (Green Giant Rice Originals), 1/2 cup	140	4.0	22.0	4.0	10	400	m.q.
peas and mushrooms, w/sauce (Green Giant One Serving), 5.5 oz.	130	4.0	27.0	2.0	5	410	m.q.

Food and Measure	cal.	prot. (gms)	carbo. (gms)	fat (gms)	chol. (mgs)	sod. (mgs)	fiber (gms)
Rice dishes, frozen *(cont.)*							
pilaf:							
(Green Giant Rice Originals), 1/2 cup	110	2.0	21.0	1.0	2	530	m.q.
w/green beans *(The Budget Gourmet Side Dish)*, 5.5 oz.	240	4.0	35.0	9.0	10	350	m.q.
Oriental, and vegetables *(The Budget Gourmet Side Dish)*, 5.75 oz.	210	4.0	27.0	10.0	20	310	m.q.
Spanish style *(Birds Eye)*, 3.3 oz. . . .	110	3.0	24.0	0	0	540	m.q.
white and wild *(Green Giant Rice Originals)*, 1/2 cup . . .	130	3.0	24.0	2.0	0	540	m.q.
wild, sherry *(Green Giant Microwave Garden Gourmet)*, 1 pkg.	210	6.0	40.0	4.0	10	580	3.0 d
Rice dishes, mix[1], 1/2 cup, except as noted:							
almondine *(Hain 3-Grain Side Dish)*	130	3.0	17.0	5.0	0	260	m.q.
Alfredo *(Country Inn)*[2]	140	4.0	23.0	4.0	n.a.	570	m.q.
asparagus:							
au gratin *(Country Inn)*[2]	130	4.0	22.0	3.0	n.a.	310	m.q.
w/hollandaise *(Lipton Rice and Sauce)*[3]	170	4.0	25.0	7.0	m.q.	530	m.q.

---

[1] *Prepared according to package directions, except as noted.*
[2] *Prepared without butter.*
[3] *Prepared with 2 tbsp. butter.*

Food and Measure	cal.	prot. (gms)	carbo. (gms)	fat (gms)	chol. (mgs)	sod. (mgs)	fiber (gms)
w/hollandaise (Lipton Rice and Sauce)[1]	150	4.0	25.0	4.0	n.a.	500	m.q.
au gratin, herb:							
(Success)[2]	100	2.0	20.0	0	0	260	m.q.
(Country Inn)[2] . . .	140	4.0	25.0	3.0	n.a.	450	m.q.
beef flavor:							
(Golden Grain/Rice-A-Roni)	170	4.0	27.0	5.0	m.q.	930	m.q.
(Lipton Rice and Sauce)[3]	150	3.0	26.0	3.0	m.q.	600	m.q.
(Minute Microwave Family Size)[4] . .	160	4.0	28.0	3.0	10	560	m.q.
(Minute Microwave Single Size)[4] . .	150	4.0	28.0	2.0	5	550	m.q.
broccoli:							
almondine (Country Inn)[2]	130	4.0	23.0	2.0	n.a.	600	m.q.
au gratin (Country Inn)[2]	130	4.0	22.0	3.0	n.a.	300	m.q.
au gratin (Golden Grain/Rice-A-Roni Savory Classics)	180	4.0	21.0	9.0	m.q.	440	m.q.
brown and wild:							
(Uncle Ben's)[5] . .	150	4.0	27.0	4.0	m.q.	520	m.q.
mushroom recipe (Uncle Ben's) . .	130	4.0	27.0	1.0	n.a.	500	m.q.
Cajun (Lipton Rice and Sauce)[3]	150	4.0	26.0	3.0	m.q.	630	m.q.
cauliflower au gratin:							
(Country Inn)[2] . . .	130	4.0	23.0	3.0	n.a.	570	m.q.

[1] Prepared with 1 tbsp. margarine.
[2] Prepared without butter.
[3] Prepared with 1 tbsp. butter.
[4] Prepared with salted butter.
[5] Prepared with salt and butter.

Food and Measure	cal.	prot. (gms)	carbo. (gms)	fat (gms)	chol. (mgs)	sod. (mgs)	fiber (gms)
Rice dishes, mix, cauliflower au gratin *(cont.)*							
(Golden Grain/Rice-A-Roni Savory Classics)	170	4.0	23.0	7.0	m.q.	410	m.q.
cheddar, zesty							
(Golden Grain/Rice-A-Roni Savory Classics)	180	5.0	25.0	7.0	m.q.	580	m.q.
cheddar and broccoli							
(Minute Microwave Family Size)[1] . . .	160	4.0	26.0	5.0	10	530	m.q.
cheddar and broccoli							
(Minute Microwave Single Size)[1] . . .	160	4.0	26.0	4.0	10	520	m.q.
chicken flavor:							
(Golden Grain/Rice-A-Roni)	170	4.0	28.0	5.0	m.q.	780	m.q.
(Lipton Rice and Sauce)[2]	150	3.0	25.0	4.0	m.q.	470	m.q.
(Minute Microwave Family Size)[1] . .	160	3.0	27.0	4.0	10	670	m.q.
(Minute Microwave Single Size)[1] . .	150	3.0	27.0	3.0	5	660	m.q.
and broccoli *(Suzi Wan)*[3]	120	4.0	23.0	1.0	n.a.	500	m.q.
creamy, and mushroom *(Country Inn)*[3]	140	3.0	25.0	3.0	n.a.	510	m.q.
drumstick *(Minute)* [1]	150	3.0	25.0	4.0	10	690	m.q.
and mushroom *(Golden Grain/Rice-A-Roni)* . .	180	4.0	26.0	7.0	m.q.	860	m.q.
royale *(Country Inn)*[3]	120	4.0	25.0	1.0	n.a.	560	m.q.
stock *(Country Inn)*[3]	130	4.0	25.0	1.0	n.a.	560	m.q.

[1] *Prepared with salted butter.*
[2] *Prepared with 1 tbsp. butter.*
[3] *Prepared without butter.*

Food and Measure	cal.	prot. (gms)	carbo. (gms)	fat (gms)	chol. (mgs)	sod. (mgs)	fiber (gms)
and vegetables *(Country Inn Homestyle)*[1] . . .	140	4.0	25.0	3.0	n.a.	490	m.q.
w/vegetables *(Golden Grain/ Rice-A-Roni)* . .	150	4.0	25.0	4.0	m.q.	800	m.q.
w/vegetables *(Suzi Wan)*[1]	120	3.0	24.0	1.0	n.a.	550	m.q.
Florentine:							
(Country Inn)[1]	140	4.0	24.0	3.0	n.a.	380	m.q.
chicken *(Golden Grain/Rice-A-Roni Savory Classics)*	130	4.0	22.0	4.0	m.q.	910	m.q.
fried:							
(Minute)	160	3.0	25.0	5.0	0	550	m.q.
w/almonds *(Golden Grain/Rice-A-Roni)*	140	3.0	22.0	5.0	m.q.	710	m.q.
green bean almondine:							
(Golden Grain/Rice-A-Roni Savory Classics)	210	5.0	22.0	11.0	m.q.	490	m.q.
casserole *(Country Inn)*[1]	120	3.0	23.0	2.0	n.a.	370	m.q.
herb and butter:							
(Golden Grain/Rice-A-Roni)	140	3.0	22.0	4.0	m.q.	800	m.q.
(Lipton Rice and Sauce)[2]	150	3.0	24.0	5.0	m.q.	470	m.q.
long grain and wild:							
(Lipton Rice and Sauce Original)[2]	150	4.0	26.0	3.0	m.q.	560	m.q.
(Minute)[3]	150	3.0	25.0	4.0	10	570	m.q.
(Near East)	130	3.0	21.0	4.0	n.a.	430	m.q.

[1] *Prepared without butter.*
[2] *Prepared with 1 tbsp. butter.*
[3] *Prepared with salted butter.*

Food and Measure	cal.	prot. (gms)	carbo. (gms)	fat (gms)	chol. (mgs)	sod. (mgs)	fiber (gms)
Rice dishes, mix, long grain and wild *(cont.)*							
(Uncle Ben's Original)[1]	120	3.0	22.0	2.0	m.q.	520	m.q.
(Uncle Ben's Fast Cooking)[1]	130	3.0	21.0	4.0	m.q.	450	m.q.
chicken stock sauce (Uncle Ben's)[1]	160	4.0	27.0	5.0	m.q.	680	m.q.
mushrooms and herbs (Lipton Rice and Sauce)[2]	150	4.0	26.0	3.0	m.q.	360	m.q.
Mexican (Old El Paso)	140	2.0	28.0	2.0	n.a.	370	m.q.
mushroom: (Lipton Rice and Sauce)[2]	150	3.0	26.0	3.0	m.q.	580	m.q.
creamy, and wild rice (Country Inn)[3]	140	3.0	24.0	3.0	n.a.	310	m.q.
Oriental (Hain 3-Grain Goodness)	120	4.0	15.0	5.0	n.a.	300	m.q.
Parmesan, creamy, and herbs (Golden Grain/Rice-A-Roni Savory Classics)	170	5.0	22.0	7.0	m.q.	470	m.q.
pilaf: (Golden Grain/Rice-A-Roni)	190	5.0	30.0	6.0	n.a.	1220	m.q.
(Lipton Rice and Sauce)[4]	170	3.0	25.0	6.0	m.q.	470	m.q.
(Lipton Rice and Sauce)[5]	140	3.0	25.0	3.0	n.a.	440	m.q.
(Near East)	140	3.0	21.0	5.0	n.a.	450	m.q.
beef flavor (Near East)	140	3.0	21.0	5.0	n.a.	470	m.q.

[1] Prepared with salt and butter.

[2] Prepared with 1 tbsp. butter.

[3] Prepared without butter.

[4] Prepared with 2 tbsp. butter.

[5] Prepared with 1 tbsp. margarine.

Food and Measure	cal.	prot. (gms)	carbo. (gms)	fat (gms)	chol. (mgs)	sod. (mgs)	fiber (gms)
brown, w/miso (Quick Pilaf)[1] . .	145	3.0	21.0	5.5	m.q.	295	m.q.
chicken flavor (Near East)	140	3.0	21.0	5.0	n.a.	420	m.q.
garden (Golden Grain/Rice-A-Roni Savory Classics)	140	4.0	23.0	4.0	m.q.	1000	m.q.
lentil (Near East)	170	6.0	21.0	7.0	n.a.	430	m.q.
French (Minute Microwave Family Size)	130	2.0	24.0	3.0	10	420	m.q.
French (Minute Microwave Single Size)	120	2.0	24.0	2.0	5	410	m.q.
Spanish, brown (Quick Pilaf)[2] . .	136	2.0	21.0	5.0	m.q.	369	m.q.
vegetable (Country Inn)[3]	120	3.0	25.0	1.0	n.a.	280	m.q.
wheat (Near East)	150	3.0	21.0	6.0	n.a.	380	m.q.
rib roast (Minute)[4] . .	150	3.0	25.0	4.0	10	720	m.q.
risotto:							
(Golden Grain/Rice-A-Roni)	200	4.0	32.0	6.0	m.q.	1130	m.q.
chicken and cheese (Country Inn)[2] . .	120	3.0	23.0	2.0	n.a.	410	m.q.
Spanish:							
(Golden Grain/Rice-A-Roni)	150	4.0	25.0	4.0	m.q.	1090	m.q.
(Lipton Rice and Sauce)[5]	140	3.0	26.0	3.0	m.q.	570	m.q.
Stroganoff (Golden Grain/Rice-A-Roni)	190	4.0	27.0	8.0	m.q.	830	m.q.

[1] Prepared with 2 tbsp. butter.
[2] Prepared with 2 tbsp. salted butter.
[3] Prepared without butter.
[4] Prepared with salted butter.
[5] Prepared with 1 tbsp. butter.

Food and Measure	cal.	prot. (gms)	carbo. (gms)	fat (gms)	chol. (mgs)	sod. (mgs)	fiber (gms)
Rice dishes, mix *(cont.)*							
sweet and sour *(Suzi Wan)*[1]	130	3.0	28.0	1.0	n.a.	460	m.q.
teriyaki *(Suzi Wan)*[1]	120	3.0	25.0	1.0	n.a.	690	m.q.
three-flavor *(Suzi Wan)*[1]	120	4.0	24.0	1.0	n.a.	570	m.q.
vegetable medley *(Country Inn)*[1] . . .	140	4.0	28.0	1.0	n.a.	390	m.q.
w/vegetables, broccoli and cheddar *(Lipton Rice and Sauce)*[2]	180	3.0	26.0	7.0	m.q.	490	m.q.
w/vegetables, broccoli and cheddar *(Lipton Rice and Sauce)*[3]	160	3.0	26.0	5.0	n.a.	450	m.q.
vegetables, spring, and cheese *(Golden Grain/Rice-A-Roni Savory Classics)*	170	4.0	23.0	7.0	n.a.	420	m.q.
yellow:							
(Golden Grain/Rice-A-Roni)	250	5.0	43.0	7.0	n.a.	1180	m.q.
Rice flour:							
brown, 1 cup	574	11.4	120.8	4.4	0	12	7.3 d
white, 1 cup	578	9.4	126.6	2.2	0	1	3.9 d
Rigatoni entree, frozen:							
baked w/meat sauce and cheese *(Lean Cuisine)*, 9¾ oz.	260	18.0	25.0	10.0	40	870	m.q.
Risotto, see "Rice dishes, mix"							
"Roast," vegetarian, frozen:							
(Worthington Dinner Roast), 2 oz. . . .	120	7.0	5.0	8.0	0	440	m.q.

[1] *Prepared without butter.*

[2] *Prepared with 2 tbsp. butter.*

[3] *Prepared with 1 tbsp. margarine.*

Food and Measure	cal.	prot. (gms)	carbo. (gms)	fat (gms)	chol. (mgs)	sod. (mgs)	fiber (gms)
Robert sauce, 1 tbsp.:							
(Escoffier)	20	0	5.0	0	0	70	m.q.
Rockfish, meat only:							
raw, 1 lb.	427	85.1	0	7.1	156	272	0
raw, 1 oz.	27	5.3	0	.4	10	17	0
baked, broiled, or microwaved, 4 oz. . . .	137	27.3	0	2.3	50	87	0
Roe (see also "Caviar"):							
1 oz.	40	6.3	.4	1.8	106	m.q.	0
1 tbsp.	22	3.6	.2	1.0	60	m.q.	0
Roll, 1 piece, except as noted:							
assorted (Brownberry Hearth)	124	4.4	23.7	2.3	7	247	1.5 d
brown and serve: (Pepperidge Farm Hearth)	50	2.0	10.0	1.0	0	100	tr.
club (Pepperidge Farm)	100	3.0	19.0	1.0	0	190	.5 d
French (Pepperidge Farm 2/pkg.), 1/2 piece	180	6.0	36.0	2.0	0	380	.5 d
French, petite (du Jour)	230	9.0	45.0	2.0	0	490	1.8 d
gem style (Wonder)	80	2.0	13.0	2.0	n.a.	140	.6 d
Italian, crusty (du Jour)	80	3.0	16.0	1.0	0	200	.6 d
w/buttermilk (Wonder)	80	2.0	13.0	2.0	n.a.	140	.6 d
crescent, butter (Pepperidge Farm) . . .	110	2.0	13.0	6.0	15	150	tr.
croissant, see "Croissant"							
Dijon (Pepperidge Farm)	230	8.0	39.0	5.0	n.a.	380	m.q.

Food and Measure	cal.	prot. (gms)	carbo. (gms)	fat (gms)	chol. (mgs)	sod. (mgs)	fiber (gms)
Roll *(cont.)*							
dinner:							
(Arnold 24 Dinner							
Party)	51	1.9	9.4	1.2	1	81	.8 d
(Awrey's)	60	2.0	11.0	1.0	0	115	0
(Pepperidge Farm)	60	2.0	8.0	2.0	<5	95	tr.
(Pepperidge Farm							
Country Style)	50	2.0	9.0	1.0	0	90	0
(Pepperidge Farm							
Old Fashioned)	50	2.0	7.0	2.0	5	85	tr.
(Pepperidge Farm							
Party)	30	1.0	5.0	1.0	0	50	tr.
(Pepperidge Farm							
Soft)	100	4.0	18.0	2.0	0	190	.5 d
(Roman Meal Origi-							
nal)	50	1.9	8.4	.8	0	91	.8 d
(Wonder)	80	2.0	14.0	1.0	n.a.	140	.6 d
black forest							
(Awrey's)	50	2.0	10.0	1.0	0	110	0
cracked wheat							
(Awrey's)	50	2.0	10.0	1.0	0	120	0
crusty *(Awrey's)* . .	70	2.0	12.0	1.0	0	150	0
Parker House *(Pep-*							
peridge Farm) . .	60	2.0	9.0	1.0	5	80	tr.
poppy seed							
(Awrey's)	59	2.0	11.0	1.0	0	115	0
poppy seed, finger							
(Pepperidge							
Farm)	50	2.0	8.0	2.0	<5	80	tr.
sesame seed							
(Awrey's)	60	2.0	11.0	1.0	0	115	0
sesame seed, finger							
(Pepperidge							
Farm)	60	2.0	9.0	2.0	<5	85	tr.
wheat *(Home Pride)*	70	3.0	12.0	1.0	0	140	.6 d
white *(Home Pride)*	80	2.0	14.0	2.0	0	170	.6 d

Food and Measure	cal.	prot. (gms)	carbo. (gms)	fat (gms)	chol. (mgs)	sod. (mgs)	fiber (gms)
egg:							
(Levy's Old Country Deli), 1 oz. . . .	146	5.3	28.1	2.8	11	431	2.0 d
sandwich *(Arnold* Dutch)	123	4.5	21.6	3.3	1	203	1.9 d
French style:							
(Francisco International)	108	4.2	21.3	1.5	0	285	1.2 d
(Pepperidge Farm, 9/pkg)	100	4.0	20.0	1.0	0	230	.5 d
sourdough style *(Pepperidge Farm,* 9/pkg.)	100	4.0	19.0	1.0	0	240	.5 d
hamburger:							
(Arnold)	115	4.3	22.0	2.2	0	223	1.8 d
(Pepperidge Farm)	130	5.0	22.0	2.0	0	240	.5 d
(Roman Meal Original)	113	4.7	21.1	1.9	0	228	2.0 d
(Wonder)	120	4.0	21.0	2.0	n.a.	230	.9 d
(Wonder Light) . .	80	5.0	13.0	1.0	n.a.	210	4.0 d
hoagie:							
(Pepperidge Farm Soft)	210	8.0	34.0	5.0	0	320	1.0 d
(Wonder)	400	13.0	73.0	7.0	n.a.	800	3.0 d
hot dog or frankfurter:							
(Arnold)	100	3.2	19.6	1.8	0	162	1.2 d
(Arnold New England)	108	3.7	20.9	2.0	0	178	1.4 d
(Country Grain) . .	100	4.0	18.0	1.0	n.a.	230	.9 d
(Pepperidge Farm Side or Top Sliced)	140	5.0	24.0	3.0	0	270	.5 d
(Roman Meal Original)	104	4.3	19.5	1.9	0	210	1.8 d
(Wonder)	80	2.0	14.0	1.0	n.a.	150	.6 d
(Wonder Light) . .	80	5.0	13.0	1.0	n.a.	210	4.0 d
Dijon *(Pepperidge Farm)*	160	5.0	23.0	5.0	0	230	2.0 d

Food and Measure	cal.	prot. (gms)	carbo. (gms)	fat (gms)	chol. (mgs)	sod. (mgs)	fiber (gms)
Roll, hot dog or frankfurter *(cont.)*							
oat bran *(Awrey's)*	110	4.0	20.0	2.0	0	210	1.0 d
poppy seed *(Pepperidge Farm)* . .	130	6.0	23.0	2.0	0	280	1.0 d
kaiser:							
(Arnold Francisco)	184	7.0	35.4	2.9	5	338	2.0 d
(Brownberry Hearth)	152	5.4	29.3	2.8	9	318	1.9 d
Luigi *(Colombo Brand)*	146	7.6	25.4	1.6	n.a.	334	m.q.
onion *(Levy's* Old Country Deli), 1 oz.	153	6.1	30.8	1.9	11	380	1.8 d
pan *(Wonder)*	80	2.0	14.0	1.0	n.a.	140	.6 d
sandwich:							
oat bran *(Awrey's)*	120	4.0	22.0	2.0	0	250	1.0 d
onion w/poppy seeds *(Pepperidge Farm)* . . .	150	5.0	26.0	3.0	0	260	.5 d
potato *(Pepperidge Farm)*	160	4.0	28.0	4.0	0	260	1.0 d
salad *(Pepperidge Farm)*	110	4.0	16.0	4.0	10	150	m.q.
w/sesame seeds *(Pepperidge Farm)*	140	5.0	23.0	3.0	0	230	.5 d
seeded *(Pepperidge Farm)*	200	7.0	34.0	4.0	n.a.	270	m.q.
sourdough *(Pepperidge Farm)*	260	9.0	44.0	5.0	n.a.	370	m.q.
steak:							
sour *(Colombo Brand)*	200	10.1	35.1	2.2	n.a.	413	m.q.
sweet *(Colombo Brand)*	206	10.0	34.2	3.3	0	439	m.q.
twist, golden *(Pepperidge Farm)*	110	2.0	14.0	5.0	5	150	tr.
Roll, frozen, 1 piece:							
cinnamon:							
all butter *(Sara Lee)*	230	3.0	33.0	10.0	m.q.	200	m.q.

Food and Measure	cal.	prot. (gms)	carbo. (gms)	fat (gms)	chol. (mgs)	sod. (mgs)	fiber (gms)
all butter icing *(Sara Lee)*, 1 pkt. . . .	60	0	14.0	0	n.a.	0	n.a.
bun *(Rich's Ever Fresh)*	293	4.0	38.0	14.6	n.a.	n.a.	m.q.
honey bun, mini *(Rich's Ever Fresh)*	133	1.8	17.5	6.6	n.a.	n.a.	m.q.
Parkerhouse *(Bridgford)*	85	2.5	15.8	1.3	n.a.	172	m.q.
Roll, refrigerated, 1 piece, except as noted:							
butterflake *(Pillsbury)*	140	3.0	20.0	5.0	5	520	m.q.
cinnamon:							
(Pillsbury's Best Quick)	210	2.0	29.0	9.0	10	260	m.q.
iced *(Hungry Jack)*, 2 pieces	290	3.0	37.0	14.0	n.a.	570	m.q.
iced *(Pillsbury)* . .	110	1.0	17.0	5.0	0	260	m.q.
crescent *(Pillsbury)*	100	2.0	11.0	6.0	5	230	m.q.
Roll, sweet (see also "Roll, frozen" and "Roll, refrigerated"), 1 piece:							
cinnamon:							
homestyle *(Awrey's)*	240	4.0	40.0	7.0	5	200	1.0 d
swirl *(Awrey's Grande)*	340	4.0	46.0	16.0	10	370	1.0 d
honeybun, glazed *(Tastykake)*	330	6.1	48.1	12.9	n.a.	360	m.q.
honeybun, iced *(Tastykake)*	342	5.7	52.6	12.4	n.a.	333	m.q.
Roman bean, canned:							
(Progresso), 8 oz. . .	210	14.0	36.0	1.0	0	m.q.	m.q.
Roseapple:							
untrimmed, 1 lb. . . .	76	1.8	17.3	.9	0	1	3.3 c
1 oz.	7	.2	1.6	.1	0	tr.	.3 c
Roselle:							
1 oz. or ½ cup . . .	14	.3	3.2	.2	0	2	.3 c

Food and Measure	cal.	prot. (gms)	carbo. (gms)	fat (gms)	chol. (mgs)	sod. (mgs)	fiber (gms)
Rosemary, dried:							
1 tsp.	4	.1	.8	.2	0	1	.2 c
Rotini, frozen:							
cheddar *(Green Giant* Microwave Garden Gourmet), 1 pkg.	230	9.0	32.0	10.0	20	570	4.5 d
seafood *(Mrs. Paul's* Light), 9 oz.	240	12.0	34.0	6.0	25	570	m.q.
Roughy, orange, meat only, raw:							
1 lb.	571	66.7	0	31.8	91	286	0
1 oz.	36	4.2	0	2.0	6	18	0
Roy Rogers, 1 serving:							
danish or roll:							
apple swirl	328	5.0	62.0	7.0	n.a.	279	m.q.
cheese swirl	383	8.0	54.0	15.0	n.a.	369	m.q.
cinnamon roll . . .	376	5.0	55.0	15.0	n.a.	339	m.q.
crescent roll	287	5.0	27.0	18.0	<5	547	m.q.
crescent sandwich:							
regular	408	13.0	28.0	27.0	207	820	m.q.
w/bacon.	446	15.0	28.0	30.0	212	982	m.q.
w/ham	456	20.0	29.0	29.0	227	1243	m.q.
w/sausage	564	19.0	28.0	42.0	248	1145	m.q.
egg and biscuit platter:							
regular	557	18.0	44.0	34.0	417	1020	m.q.
w/bacon.	607	21.0	44.0	39.0	424	1236	m.q.
w/ham	605	25.0	44.0	36.0	437	1442	m.q.
w/sausage	713	25.0	44.0	49.0	458	1345	m.q.
pancake platter w/ syrup and butter:							
regular	386	5.0	63.0	13.0	51	547	m.q.
w/bacon.	436	8.0	63.0	17.0	58	763	m.q.
w/ham	434	11.0	64.0	15.0	71	969	m.q.
w/sausage	542	11.0	63.0	28.0	92	872	m.q.
chicken, fried:							
breast	412	33.0	17.0	24.0	118	609	m.q.

Food and Measure	cal.	prot. (gms)	carbo. (gms)	fat (gms)	chol. (mgs)	sod. (mgs)	fiber (gms)
breast and wing . .	604	44.0	25.0	37.0	165	894	m.q.
drumstick	140	12.0	6.0	8.0	40	190	m.q.
drumstick and thigh	436	30.0	17.0	28.0	125	596	m.q.
nuggets, 6 pieces	288	10.0	21.0	18.0	63	548	m.q.
thigh	296	18.0	12.0	20.0	85	406	m.q.
wing	192	11.0	9.0	13.0	47	285	m.q.
sandwiches:							
bacon cheeseburger	552	32.0	31.0	33.0	83	1025	m.q.
bar burger	573	36.0	38.0	31.0	96	1252	m.q.
cheeseburger . . .	525	29.0	37.0	29.0	76	830	m.q.
cheeseburger, small	275	15.0	24.0	13.0	36	558	m.q.
hamburger	472	26.0	37.0	25.0	64	607	m.q.
hamburger, small	222	12.0	23.0	9.0	26	336	m.q.
Expressburger . . .	561	27.0	42.0	32.0	70	899	m.q.
Express bacon cheeseburger . .	641	33.0	36.0	41.0	89	1317	m.q.
Express cheese-burger	613	30.0	42.0	37.0	82	1122	m.q.
fish	514	18.0	58.0	24.0	62	857	m.q.
roast beef	350	26.0	37.0	11.0	58	732	m.q.
roast beef, w/ cheese	403	29.0	37.0	15.0	70	954	m.q.
roast beef, large	373	35.0	31.0	12.0	82	840	m.q.
roast beef, large, w/ cheese	427	38.0	31.0	17.0	94	1062	m.q.
side dishes:							
biscuit	231	4.0	26.0	12.0	<5	575	m.q.
coleslaw	110	1.0	11.0	7.0	<5	261	m.q.
french fries	320	4.0	39.0	16.0	13	164	m.q.
french fries, small	238	3.0	29.0	12.0	10	122	m.q.
french fries, large	440	6.0	54.0	22.0	19	225	m.q.
shakes:							
chocolate	358	8.0	61.0	10.0	37	290	(0)
strawberry	315	8.0	49.0	10.0	37	261	(0)
vanilla	306	8.0	45.0	11.0	40	282	0
sundaes:							
caramel	293	7.0	52.0	9.0	23	193	(0)
hot fudge	337	7.0	53.0	13.0	23	186	(0)

Food and Measure	cal.	prot. (gms)	carbo. (gms)	fat (gms)	chol. (mgs)	sod. (mgs)	fiber (gms)
Roy Rogers sundaes *(cont.)*							
strawberry	216	6.0	33.0	7.0	23	99	(0)
Vitari, 1 oz.	30	n.a.	7.0	n.a.	9	n.a.	(0)
Rutabaga:							
fresh:							
raw, untrimmed,							
1 lb.	140	4.6	31.4	.8	0	77	4.2 c
raw, cubed, 1/2 cup	25	.8	5.7	.1	0	14	.8 c
boiled, drained,							
cubed, 1/2 cup	29	.9	6.6	.2	0	15	.9 c
boiled, drained,							
mashed, 1/2 cup	41	1.3	9.3	.2	0	22	1.3 c
canned, diced *(Al-*							
lens), 1/2 cup . . .	20	1.0	4.0	<1.0	0	260	m.q.
Rye, whole-grain:							
1 cup	567	25.0	117.9	4.2	0	10	2.5 c
Rye cake, 1 piece:							
(Quaker Grain Cakes)	35	1.4	6.5	.3	0	52	.8 d
Rye flour, 1 cup:							
dark	415	18.0	88.0	3.4	0	2	m.q.
light	374	8.6	81.8	1.4	0	2	14.9 d
medium:							
1 cup	361	9.9	79.0	1.8	0	3	14.9 d
(Pillsbury's Best)	400	12.0	83.0	2.0	0	0	m.q.
and wheat *(Pillsbury's*							
Best Bohemian							
Style)	400	11.0	86.0	1.0	0	0	m.q.

S

Food and Measure	cal.	prot. (gms)	carbo. (gms)	fat (gms)	chol. (mgs)	sod. (mgs)	fiber (gms)
Sablefish, meat only:							
raw, 1 lb.	886	60.8	0	69.4	222	254	0
raw, 1 oz.	55	3.8	0	4.3	14	16	0
smoked, 4 oz.	291	20.0	0	22.8	73	836	0
Safflower seed ker- **nel:**							
dried, 1 oz.	147	4.6	9.7	10.9	0	(0)	.7 c
Safflower seed meal:							
partially defatted,							
1 oz.	97	10.1	13.8	.7	0	n.a.	2.2 c
Saffron:							
1 tsp.	2	.1	.5	<.1	0	1	tr.c
Sage, ground:							
1 tsp.	2	.1	.4	.1	0	tr.	.1 c
Salad dip, 1 oz.:							
(Nasoya Vegi-Dip) . .	45	2.0	3.0	3.0	0	110	n.a.
Salad dress- **ing,** 1 tbsp., ex- cept as noted:							
bacon, creamy *(Kraft* Reduced Calorie)	30	0	2.0	2.0	0	150	n.a.
bacon and buttermilk *(Kraft)*	80	0	1.0	8.0	0	125	n.a.
bacon and tomato:							
(Kraft)	70	0	1.0	7.0	0	130	n.a.
(Kraft Reduced Cal- orie)	30	0	2.0	2.0	0	150	n.a.
balsamic vinegar and oil *(Great Impres- sions)*	67	<1.0	2.3	6.5	0	367	n.a.

Food and Measure	cal.	prot. (gms)	carbo. (gms)	fat (gms)	chol. (mgs)	sod. (mgs)	fiber (gms)
Salad dressing (cont.)							
blue cheese:							
(Roka Brand) . . .	60	1.0	1.0	6.0	10	170	n.a.
(Roka Brand Reduced Calorie)	16	1.0	1.0	1.0	<5	280	n.a.
chunky (Kraft) . . .	60	1.0	2.0	6.0	<5	230	n.a.
chunky (Kraft Reduced Calorie)	30	0	2.0	2.0	<5	240	n.a.
chunky (Wish-Bone)	75	.4	.7	7.9	1	149	n.a.
chunky (Wish-Bone Lite)	40	.3	1.5	3.7	1	197	n.a.
buttermilk:							
(Hain Old Fashioned)	70	0	0	7.0	0	100	n.a.
creamy (Kraft) . . .	80	0	1.0	8.0	<5	120	0
creamy (Kraft Reduced Calorie)	30	0	1.0	3.0	<5	125	n.a.
Caesar:							
(Lawry's Classic), 1 oz.	130	.8	1.0	13.5	n.a.	337	.1 c
(Wish-Bone)	77	.4	.9	8.0	1	248	n.a.
creamy (Hain) . . .	60	0	1.0	6.0	<5	220	n.a.
creamy (Hain Low Salt)	60	0	1.0	6.0	<5	15	n.a.
golden (Kraft) . . .	70	0	1.0	7.0	0	180	n.a.
(Catalina Reduced Calorie)	16	0	3.0	0	0	120	n.a.
Chinese vinegar w/ sesame and ginger (Lawry's Classic), 1 oz.	145	.2	2.4	15.0	0	325	0
coleslaw (Kraft) . . .	70	0	4.0	6.0	10	200	n.a.
creamy:							
(Rancher's Choice)	90	0	1.0	10.0	<5	140	n.a.
(Rancher's Choice Reduced Calorie)	30	0	1.0	3.0	<5	160	n.a.
cucumber:							
creamy (Kraft) . . .	70	0	1.0	8.0	0	190	n.a.

Food and Measure	cal.	prot. (gms)	carbo. (gms)	fat (gms)	chol. (mgs)	sod. (mgs)	fiber (gms)
creamy (Kraft Reduced Calorie)	25	0	1.0	2.0	0	220	n.a.
dill (Hain)	80	0	0	8.0	5	210	n.a.
Dijon mustard (Great Impressions) . . .	57	.4	.3	6.1	18	103	n.a.
Dijon vinaigrette:							
(Hain)	50	0	0	5.0	<5	180	n.a.
(Wish-Bone Lite Classic)	30	.1	1.1	2.8	0	176	n.a.
(Wish-Bone Classic)	60	.2	1.0	6.1	<1	171	n.a.
dill, creamy (Nasoya Vegi-Dressing) . . .	40	1.0	1.0	3.0	0	50	n.a.
French:							
(Catalina)	70	0	4.0	6.0	0	180	n.a.
(Kraft)	60	0	2.0	6.0	0	125	n.a.
(Kraft Miracle) . . .	70	0	3.0	6.0	0	240	n.a.
(Kraft Reduced Calorie)	25	0	3.0	2.0	0	150	n.a.
(Wish-Bone Deluxe)	60	.1	2.3	5.4	0	83	n.a.
(Wish-Bone Lite)	31	0	2.1	2.5	0	70	0
(Wish-Bone Lite Sweet'n Spicy)	18	0	3.2	.5	0	110	n.a.
(Wish-Bone Sweet'n Spicy)	63	.1	2.9	5.7	0	156	n.a.
creamy (Hain) . . .	60	0	1.0	6.0	0	80	n.a.
garlic (Wish-Bone)	55	.1	1.8	5.3	0	158	.1 c
red (Wish-Bone Lite)	17	.2	3.2	.4	0	155	n.a.
style (Wish-Bone Lite)	30	.1	1.9	2.5	0	67	n.a.
w/green pepper (Great Impressions)	64	.2	4.1	5.2	0	188	n.a.
garlic:							
creamy (Kraft) . . .	50	0	1.0	5.0	0	170	n.a.
creamy (Wish-Bone)	74	.1	.5	8.0	0	158	.6 c
French (Wish-Bone)	55	.1	1.8	5.3	0	158	.1 c

Food and Measure	cal.	prot. (gms)	carbo. (gms)	fat (gms)	chol. (mgs)	sod. (mgs)	fiber (gms)
Salad dressing, garlic *(cont.)*							
herb *(Nasoya Vegi-Dressing)*	40	1.0	1.0	3.0	0	50	n.a.
and sour cream *(Hain)*	70	0	0	7.0	0	100	n.a.
herb, savory *(Hain No Salt)*	90	0	0	10.0	0	25	n.a.
honey and sesame *(Hain)*	60	0	2.0	5.0	0	210	n.a.
Italian:							
(Hain Traditional)	80	0	0	8.0	0	330	n.a.
(Hain Traditional No Salt)	60	0	1.0	6.0	0	20	n.a.
(Kraft Presto) . . .	70	0	1.0	7.0	0	150	n.a.
(Nasoya Vegi-Dressing)	40	1.0	1.0	3.0	0	50	n.a.
(Ott's)	80	<.1	.2	9.1	<1	87	tr.d
(Wish-Bone)	46	0	1.5	4.5	0	280	n.a.
(Wish-Bone Lite)	7	.2	.9	.3	0	212	n.a.
(Wish-Bone Robusto)	47	.1	1.8	4.5	0	288	n.a.
blended *(Wish-Bone)*	37	0	1.2	3.6	0	199	n.a.
w/bleu cheese *(Lawry's* Classic), 1 oz.	186	.1	1.9	2.0	n.a.	385	.1 c
cheese vinaigrette *(Hain)*	55	0	0	6.0	<5	130	n.a.
w/cheese *(Wish-Bone)*	89	.2	1.0	9.2	<1	170	n.a.
creamy *(Hain)* . . .	80	0	0	8.0	0	100	n.a.
creamy *(Hain No Salt)*	80	0	1.0	8.0	0	25	n.a.
creamy *(Kraft* Reduced Calorie)	25	0	1.0	2.0	0	120	n.a.
creamy *(Wish-Bone)*	56	.1	1.5	5.5	<1	149	n.a.
creamy *(Wish-Bone Lite)*	26	.1	2.0	2.0	<1	148	n.a.

Food and Measure	cal.	prot. (gms)	carbo. (gms)	fat (gms)	chol. (mgs)	sod. (mgs)	fiber (gms)
w/real sour cream							
(Kraft)	50	0	1.0	5.0	0	120	n.a.
herbal (Wish-Bone							
Classics)	70	0	1.2	7.3	0	228	n.a.
no oil (Kraft)	4	0	1.0	0	0	220	n.a.
w/Parmesan							
(Lawry's Classic),							
1 oz.	156	0	4.5	15.1	n.a.	178	.1 c
zesty (Kraft)	70	0	1.0	8.0	0	270	n.a.
zesty (Kraft Re-							
duced Calorie)	20	0	1.0	2.0	0	230	n.a.
mayonnaise, see							
"Mayonnaise"							
mayonnaise type:							
(Bama)	50	0	3.0	4.0	n.a.	105	n.a.
(Miracle Whip) . .	70	0	2.0	7.0	5	85	n.a.
(Miracle Whip Light)	45	0	2.0	4.0	5	95	n.a.
(Spin Blend)	60	0	3.0	5.0	10	110	0
cholesterol free							
(Spin Blend) . .	40	0	2.0	4.0	0	110	0
oil and vinegar (Kraft)	70	0	1.0	8.0	0	210	0
olive oil:							
Italian (Wish-Bone							
Classic)	34	0	1.7	3.0	0	190	0
vinaigrette (Wish-							
Bone)	28	0	1.8	2.3	0	111	0
vinaigrette (Wish-							
Bone Lite) . . .	16	.1	1.9	.9	0	111	0
onion and chive:							
(Wish-Bone Lite)	37	.2	1.6	3.3	0	164	n.a.
creamy (Kraft) . . .	70	0	1.0	7.0	0	150	n.a.
(Ott's Famous) . . .	40	.1	4.1	2.7	<1	195	<.1 d
poppyseed (Hain							
Rancher's)	60	0	0	7.0	<5	105	n.a.
Ranch:							
(Wish-Bone)	78	.1	1.1	8.3	4	156	n.a.
(Wish-Bone Lite)	42	.2	2.5	3.5	5	148	n.a.

Food and Measure	cal.	prot. (gms)	carbo. (gms)	fat (gms)	chol. (mgs)	sod. (mgs)	fiber (gms)
Salad dressing, Ranch *(cont.)*							
creamy *(Weight Watchers)*	25	0	6.0	0	0	100	n.a.
red wine vinaigrette *(Wish-Bone)*	51	0	4.2	3.8	0	216	(0)
red wine vinegar:							
w/cabernet *(Lawry's Classic)*, 1 oz.	138	0	4.9	13.7	n.a.	178	0
and oil *(Great Impressions)*	64	<1.0	2.5	6.1	0	277	0
and oil *(Kraft)* . . .	60	0	4.0	4.0	0	200	0
Russian:							
(Kraft)	60	0	4.0	5.0	0	130	m.q.
(Kraft Reduced Calorie*)*	30	0	4.0	1.0	0	130	m.q.
(Wish-Bone)	46	.1	6.0	2.5	0	147	m.q.
(Wish-Bone Lite*)*	22	.1	3.9	.6	0	126	m.q.
creamy *(Kraft)* . . .	60	0	2.0	5.0	5	150	m.q.
San Francisco, w/Romano *(Lawry's Classic)*, 1 oz.	136	.6	2.0	14.0	n.a.	547	.1 c
sesame garlic *(Nasoya Vegi-Dressing)*	40	1.0	1.0	3.0	0	50	m.q.
sesame seed	68	.5	1.3	6.9	0	153	.1 c
sour *(Friendship Sour Treat)*, 1 oz.	36	1.0	2.0	3.0	0	15	n.a.
Swiss cheese vinaigrette *(Hain)*	60	0	0	7.0	<5	160	n.a.
Thousand Island:							
(Hain)	50	0	0	5.0	0	85	m.q.
(Kraft)	60	0	3.0	5.0	5	150	m.q.
(Kraft Reduced Calorie*)*	30	0	2.0	2.0	5	150	m.q.
(Wish-Bone)	63	.1	3.1	5.6	7	158	m.q.
(Wish-Bone Lite*)*	36	.2	1.9	3.0	9	99	m.q.
and bacon *(Kraft)*	60	0	2.0	6.0	0	100	m.q.

Food and Measure	cal.	prot. (gms)	carbo. (gms)	fat (gms)	chol. (mgs)	sod. (mgs)	fiber (gms)
vintage, w/sherry wine (Lawry's Classic), 1 oz.	110	4.3	2.5	10.5	n.a.	415	.1 c
white wine, w/chardonnay (Lawry's Classic), 1 oz. . . .	153	0	2.7	15.7	n.a.	178	.1 c
white wine vinegar and oil (Great Impressions)	63	<1.0	.8	6.6	0	242	n.a.
Salad dressing mix[1], 1 tbsp.:							
bleu cheese: and herbs (Good Seasons)	70	0	1.0	8.0	0	150	n.a.
buttermilk (Good Seasons Farm Style)	60	1.0	1.0	6.0	5	135	n.a.
cheese:							
garlic (Good Seasons)	70	0	1.0	8.0	0	170	n.a.
Italian (Good Seasons)	70	0	1.0	8.0	0	130	n.a.
Italian (Good Seasons Lite)	25	0	1.0	3.0	0	135	n.a.
garlic and herbs (Good Seasons)	70	0	1.0	8.0	0	190	n.a.
herb (Good Seasons Classic)	70	0	1.0	8.0	0	150	n.a.
Italian:							
(Good Seasons)	70	0	1.0	8.0	0	170	n.a.
(Good Seasons Lite)	25	0	1.0	3.0	0	180	n.a.
mild (Good Seasons)	70	0	1.0	8.0	0	190	n.a.
zesty (Good Seasons)	70	0	1.0	8.0	0	120	n.a.
zesty (Good Seasons Lite)	25	0	1.0	3.0	0	135	n.a.

[1] Prepared according to package directions.

Food and Measure	cal.	prot. (gms)	carbo. (gms)	fat (gms)	chol. (mgs)	sod. (mgs)	fiber (gms)
Salad dressing mix *(cont.)*							
lemon and herbs							
(Good Seasons)	70	0	1.0	8.0	0	140	n.a.
ranch *(Good Seasons)*	60	0	1.0	6.0	5	110	n.a.
ranch *(Good Seasons Lite)*	30	1.0	2.0	2.0	5	95	n.a.
Salad nuggets, 1/4 cup:							
garlic'n cheese *(Flavor Tree)*	167	3.2	11.0	12.4	n.a.	336	.1 c
onion *(Flavor Tree)*	163	3.6	11.5	11.0	n.a.	299	.1 c
sesame *(Flavor Tree)*	160	3.4	12.9	10.9	n.a.	435	.1 c
Salad seasoning:							
(McCormick/Shilling Salad Supreme), 1 tsp.	11	.7	.5	.7	0	2807	m.q.
Salami, 1 oz., except as noted:							
beef:							
(Boar's Head) . . .	60	5.0	<1.0	4.0	20	288	0
(Hebrew National)	80	7.0	<1.0	7.0	15	230	0
(Hormel Perma-Fresh), 2 slices	50	3.0	0	5.0	0	219	0
(Kahn's), 1 slice . .	70	3.0	1.0	6.0	m.q.	250	0
(Kahn's Family Pack), 1 slice . .	60	2.0	1.0	5.0	m.q.	190	0
(Oscar Mayer Machiaeh Brand), .8-oz. slice . . .	60	3.0	0	5.0	15	265	0
beer:							
(Eckrich)	70	4.0	1.0	6.0	m.q.	330	0
(Oscar Mayer Salami for Beer), .8-oz. slice . . .	55	3.2	.3	4.5	16	283	0
beef *(Oscar Mayer Salami for Beer),* .8-oz. slice . . .	66	3.0	.3	5.9	17	279	0

Food and Measure	cal.	prot. (gms)	carbo. (gms)	fat (gms)	chol. (mgs)	sod. (mgs)	fiber (gms)
cooked:							
(Kahn's), 1 slice . .	60	4.0	1.0	4.0	m.q.	300	0
(OHSE)	65	4.0	1.0	5.0	m.q.	330	0
cotto:							
(Eckrich)	70	4.0	1.0	6.0	m.q.	380	0
(Hormel Club) . . .	100	5.0	0	5.0	m.q.	385	0
(Hormel Perma-							
Fresh), 2 slices	105	9.0	1.0	7.0	m.q.	750	0
(JM)	80	4.0	2.0	6.0	m.q.	270	0
(Kahn's Family							
Pack), 1 slice . .	45	3.0	1.0	3.0	m.q.	230	0
(Oscar Mayer),							
.8-oz. slice . . .	54	3.0	.5	4.4	18	291	0
beef *(Eckrich)*,							
1.3 oz.	100	5.0	2.0	8.0	m.q.	460	0
beef *(Oscar Mayer)*,							
.8-oz. slice . . .	46	3.2	.4	3.4	18	298	0
dry or hard:							
(Hickory Farms) . .	120	6.0	0	10.0	30	535	0
(Hormel)	110	7.0	0	10.0	m.q.	468	0
(Hormel National)	120	6.0	0	11.0	m.q.	463	0
(Hormel Perma-							
Fresh), 2 slices	80	4.0	0	7.0	m.q.	339	0
(Hormel Sliced) . .	110	6.0	0	10.0	m.q.	483	0
(JM)	110	6.0	1.0	9.0	m.q.	580	0
(Oscar Mayer Hard),							
.3-oz. slice . . .	34	1.9	.2	2.8	8	169	0
Genoa:							
(Hickory Farms) . .	110	6.0	0	10.0	20	540	0
(Hormel)	110	6.0	0	10.0	m.q.	456	0
(Hormel DiLusso)	100	6.0	0	8.0	m.q.	443	0
(Hormel Gran							
Valore)	110	6.0	0	10.0	m.q.	453	0
(Hormel San Remo)	118	7.0	0	10.0	m.q.	541	0
(JM)	100	6.0	1.0	8.0	m.q.	540	0
(Oscar Mayer),							
.3-oz. slice . . .	34	1.9	.1	2.9	9	164	0
(Hormel Party)	90	5.0	0	8.0	m.q.	399	0

Food and Measure	cal.	prot. (gms)	carbo. (gms)	fat (gms)	chol. (mgs)	sod. (mgs)	fiber (gms)
Salami (cont.)							
piccolo (Hormel Stick)	120	6.0	0	11.0	m.q.	512	0
"Salami," vegetarian,							
frozen:							
roll (Worthington),							
1.5 oz.	90	8.0	3.0	5.0	0	760	m.q.
slices (Worthington),							
2 slices	80	7.0	3.0	4.0	0	675	m.q.
Salisbury steak, see							
"Beef dinner" and							
"Beef entree"							
Salmon, fresh, meat							
only:							
Atlantic:							
raw, 1 lb.	644	90.0	0	28.8	249	198	0
raw, 1 oz.	40	5.6	0	1.8	16	113	0
Chinook:							
raw, 1 lb.	816	91.0	0	47.4	299	213	0
raw, 1 oz.	51	5.7	0	3.0	19	13	0
smoked, 4 oz. . . .	133	20.7	0	4.9	26	889	0
lox, 4 oz.	133	20.7	0	4.9	26	2268	0
chum:							
raw, 1 lb.	544	91.3	0	17.1	336	449	0
raw, 1 oz.	34	5.7	0	1.1	21	14	0
Coho:							
raw, 1 lb.	662	98.1	0	27.0	177	211	0
raw, 1 oz.	41	7.6	0	1.7	11	13	0
boiled, poached, or							
steamed, 4 oz.	210	31.0	0	8.6	56	67	0
pink:							
raw, 1 lb.	527	90.4	0	15.6	236	302	0
raw, 1 oz.	33	5.7	0	1.0	15	19	0
sockeye:							
raw, 1 lb.	763	96.6	0	38.8	283	211	0
raw, 1 oz.	48	6.0	0	2.4	18	13	0
baked, broiled, or							
microwaved, 4 oz.	245	31.0	0	12.4	99	75	0

Food and Measure	cal.	prot. (gms)	carbo. (gms)	fat (gms)	chol. (mgs)	sod. (mgs)	fiber (gms)
Salmon, canned:							
chum:							
drained, 4 oz. . . .	160	24.3	0	6.2	44	552	0
keta *(Bumble Bee)*,							
1 cup	306	47.3	0	11.4	m.q.	m.q.	0
coho, Alaska *(Deming's)*, ½ cup . . .	140	22.0	0	5.0	m.q.	450	0
pink:							
(Bumble Bee),							
1 cup	310	45.1	0	13.0	m.q.	851	0
w/liquid *(Del Monte)*, ½ cup	160	22.0	0	7.0	m.q.	660	0
Alaska *(Deming's)*, ½ cup	140	20.0	0	6.0	65	450	0
chunk, in water *(Deming's)*, 3.25 oz.	120	17.0	0	5.0	m.q.	420	0
red:							
w/liquid *(Del Monte)*, ½ cup	180	23.0	0	9.0	m.q.	660	0
blueback *(Rubinstein's)*, ½ cup	170	20.0	0	9.0	m.q.	450	0
red, sockeye:							
(Bumble Bee), 1 cup	376	44.7	0	20.5	m.q.	1148	0
Alaska *(Deming's)*, ½ cup	170	20.0	0	9.0	65	450	0
Alaska, medium *(Deming's)*, ½ cup . . .	150	21.0	0	7.0	65	450	0
blueback *(S&W Fancy)*, ½ cup . .	190	25.0	0	10.0	m.q.	590	0
Salmon, frozen:							
steaks, w/out seasoning *(SeaPak)*, 8-oz. pkg.	270	46.0	0	9.0	170	115	0
Salsa:							
brava *(La Victoria)*, 1 tbsp.	6	<1.0	1.0	<1.0	0	100	m.q.

Food and Measure	cal.	prot. (gms)	carbo. (gms)	fat (gms)	chol. (mgs)	sod. (mgs)	fiber (gms)
Salsa *(cont.)*							
burrito *(Del Monte)*,							
¼ cup	20	0	4.0	0	0	355	m.q.
casera *(La Victoria)*,							
1 tbsp.	4	<1.0	1.0	<1.0	0	80	m.q.
green chili:							
(La Victoria), 1 tbsp.	3	<1.0	1.0	<1.0	0	44	m.q.
hot *(Ortega)*, 1 oz.	10	0	2.0	0	0	180	m.q.
mild *(Del Monte)*,							
¼ cup	20	0	3.0	0	0	590	m.q.
mild or medium							
(Ortega), 1 oz.	8	0	2.0	0	0	180	m.q.
green jalapeña *(La*							
Victoria), 1 tbsp.	4	<1.0	1.0	<1.0	0	105	m.q.
hot *(Hain)*, ¼ cup . .	22	1.0	4.0	0	0	480	m.q.
mild *(Hain)*, ¼ cup	20	1.0	4.0	0	0	410	m.q.
mild, medium or hot							
(Old El Paso							
Thick'n Chunky),							
2 tbsp.	6	0	1.0	0	0	170	m.q.
mild or hot, 2 tbsp.:							
(Enrico's Chunky)	8	1.0	2.0	0	0	34	m.q.
(Enrico's Chunky No							
Salt)	8	1.0	2.0	0	0	10	m.q.
omelette *(La Victoria)*,							
1 tbsp.	6	<1.0	1.0	<1.0	0	95	m.q.
picante *(see also* "Pi-							
cante sauce"):							
(La Victoria), 1 tbsp.	4	<1.0	1.0	<1.0	0	80	m.q.
(Old El Paso),							
2 tbsp.	10	0	2.0	0	0	160	m.q.
(Ortega), 1 oz. . .	10	0	2.0	0	0	300	m.q.
hot *(Del Monte)*,							
¼ cup	20	0	4.0	0	0	385	m.q.
hot and chunky *(Del*							
Monte), ¼ cup	15	0	3.0	0	0	405	m.q.
ranchera:							
(La Victoria), 1 tbsp.	6	<1.0	1.0	<1.0	0	85	m.q.

Food and Measure	cal.	prot. (gms)	carbo. (gms)	fat (gms)	chol. (mgs)	sod. (mgs)	fiber (gms)
(Ortega), 1 oz. . . .	12	0	3.0	0	0	250	m.q.
red jalapeña (La Victoria), 1 tbsp.	6	<1.0	1.0	<1.0	0	95	m.q.
roja, mild (Del Monte), 1/4 cup	20	0	4.0	0	0	510	m.q.
suprema (La Victoria), 1 tbsp.	4	<1.0	1.0	<1.0	0	95	m.q.
taco (see also "Taco sauce"):							
hot (Ortega), 1 oz.	10	0	2.0	0	0	300	m.q.
mild (Ortega), 1 oz.	10	0	2.0	0	0	290	m.q.
mild (Rosarita), 2 oz.	27	1.0	6.1	.1	<1	304	.1 d
Texas (Hot Cha Cha), 1 oz.	6	.3	2.5	0	0	2	.4 d
thick'n chunky (Old El Paso), 2 tbsp. . . .	6	0	1.0	0	0	170	m.q.
Victoria (La Victoria), 1 tbsp.	4	<1.0	1.0	<1.0	0	80	m.q.
Salsify:							
raw, untrimmed, 1 lb.	325	13.0	73.4	.8	0	79	7.1 c
raw, sliced, 1/2 cup	55	2.2	12.5	.1	0	13	1.2 c
boiled, drained, sliced, 1/2 cup	46	1.9	10.5	.1	0	11	1.0 c
Salsify, black:							
31/2 oz.	82	3.3	18.6	<.1	0	20	m.q.
Salt, 1 tsp., except as noted:							
1 tbsp.	0	0	0	0	0	6589	0
(Morton Lite Salt) . .	<1	0	tr.	0	0	1100	0
kosher (Morton) . . .	0	0	0	0	0	1880	0
non-iodized (Morton)	0	0	0	0	0	2300	0
sea (Hain)	0	0	0	0	0	2255	0
seasoned (see also specific listings):							
(Lawry's)	4	.1	.6	.1	0	1367	.1 c
(Lawry's Lite) . . .	8	.3	1.7	<.1	0	357	.1 c

Food and Measure	cal.	prot. (gms)	carbo. (gms)	fat (gms)	chol. (mgs)	sod. (mgs)	fiber (gms)
Salt, seasoned *(cont.)*							
(McCormick/Schilling)	4	.2	.6	n.a.	0	980	n.a.
(McCormick/Schilling Salt'n Spice)	3	.2	.5	n.a.	0	939	n.a.
(Morton)	4	<1.0	<1.0	<.1	0	1300	n.a.
(Morton Nature's Seasons)	3	<.1	<1.0	<.1	0	1400	n.a.
"Salt," substitute, 1 tsp.:							
(Lawry's Salt-Free 17)	10	.3	1.8	.2	0	2	.4 c
(Morton)	<1	0	.1	0	0	<1	n.a.
seasoned *(Lawry's Salt-Free)*	3	.1	.6	<.1	0	7	<.1 c
Salt pork:							
raw, 1 oz.	212	1.4	0	22.8	25	404	0
Sandwich, see specific listings							
Sandwich and soup, see "Soup combinations"							
Sandwich spread:							
meat *(Oscar Mayer Chub)*, 1 oz.	67	2.0	3.7	4.9	10	268	n.a.
meatless:							
(Hellman's/Best Foods), 1 tbsp.	50	0	2.0	5.0	5	170	m.q.
(Kraft), 1 tbsp. . .	50	0	3.0	5.0	5	95	m.q.
Sapodilla:							
1 medium, 3" × 2½"	140	.7	33.9	1.9	0	20	9.0 d
½ cup	100	.5	24.1	1.3	0	15	6.4 d
Sapote:							
1 medium, 11.2 oz.	301	4.8	76.0	1.4	0	21	4.3 c
trimmed, 1 oz.	38	.6	9.6	.2	0	3	.5 c
Sardine, fresh, see "Herring"							

Food and Measure	cal.	prot. (gms)	carbo. (gms)	fat (gms)	chol. (mgs)	sod. (mgs)	fiber (gms)
Sardine, canned:							
Atlantic, in oil, drained:							
2 oz.	118	14.8	0	6.5	81	286	0
2 medium,							
3″ × 1″ × 1/2″	50	5.9	0	2.8	34	121	0
Norwegian:							
in oil, drained *(Empress)*, 3.75 oz.	260	19.0	1.0	20.0	m.q.	m.q.	0
brisling *(S&W)*, 1.5 oz.	130	10.0	0	10.0	m.q.	220	0
Pacific, in tomato sauce, drained:							
2 oz.	658	60.5	n.a.	44.3	225	1532	.1 c
1 medium, 43/4″ × 11/8″ × 5/8″ . . .	68	6.2	n.a.	4.6	23	157	<.1 c
in tomato sauce *(Del Monte)*, 1/2 cup . .	360	19.0	45.0	12.0	m.q.	540	m.q.
kippered *(Brunswick Kippered Snacks)*, 31/2-oz. can	185	16.0	1.0	14.0	m.q.	610	0
Sauce, see specific listings							
Sauerkraut, canned, 1/2 cup:							
(Claussen)	17	.6	3.2	.2	0	517	m.q.
(Del Monte)	25	1.0	6.0	0	0	775	m.q.
(Snow Floss)	28	1.0	4.0	0	0	780	1.0 d
(Stokely Bavarian) . .	30	1.0	7.0	0	0	780	m.q.
shredded *(Allens)* . .	21	1.0	5.0	<1.0	0	880	m.q.
Sauerkraut juice:							
(S&W), 5 fl. oz. . . .	14	1.0	3.0	0	0	1120	m.q.

Food and Measure	cal.	prot. (gms)	carbo. (gms)	fat (gms)	chol. (mgs)	sod. (mgs)	fiber (gms)
Sausage, (see also "Sausage stick" and specific listings):							
beef:							
(Jones Dairy Farm Golden Brown), 1 link	75	3.8	tr.	6.1	18	159	0
and cheddar (Hillshire Farm Flavorseal), 2 oz. . . .	190	8.0	1.0	15.0	m.q.	500	0
brown and serve:							
(Eckrich Lean Supreme), 2 links	120	7.0	1.0	10.0	m.q.	440	0
(Hormel), 2 links	140	6.0	0	13.0	m.q.	430	0
(Jones Dairy Farm Light), 1 link . .	60	3.5	1.0	4.1	16	150	0
(Swift Premium Country Recipe), 1 link or pattie	130	4.0	1.0	12.0	m.q.	240	0
(Swift Premium Original), 1 link	130	3.0	1.0	12.0	m.q.	260	0
(Swift Premium Original), 1 pattie	120	4.0	1.0	12.0	m.q.	270	0
(Swift Premium Microwave), 1 link	120	4.0	1.0	12.0	m.q.	270	0
w/bacon (Swift Premium), 1 link . .	120	4.0	1.0	11.0	m.q.	270	0
beef (Swift Premium), 1 link . .	120	4.0	1.0	12.0	m.q.	250	0
w/ham (Swift Premium), 1 link . .	130	3.0	1.0	13.0	m.q.	260	0
maple flavor (Swift Premium), 1 link	120	3.0	1.0	12.0	m.q.	260	0
smoked flavor (Swift Premium), 1 link	120	4.0	1.0	11.0	m.q.	280	0
(Hickory Farms Safari), 1 oz.	98	5.0	1.0	9.0	14	343	0

Food and Measure	cal.	prot. (gms)	carbo. (gms)	fat (gms)	chol. (mgs)	sod. (mgs)	fiber (gms)
(Hillshire Farm Country Recipe), 2 oz.	180	7.0	2.0	16.0	m.q.	490	0
hot *(OHSE* Hot Links), 1 oz.	80	4.0	4.0	3.0	m.q.	310	0
Italian, see "Italian sausage"							
minced roll *(Eckrich)*, 1-oz. slice	80	4.0	1.0	7.0	m.q.	300	0
pickled:							
(Penrose Firecracker), 1 link	120	6.0	1.0	10.0	m.q.	620	0
(Penrose Firecracker), 1 giant link	170	9.0	1.0	14.0	m.q.	870	0
hot, red hot, Polish, beer or firecracker *(Penrose)*, .5-oz. link	40	2.0	1.0	3.0	m.q.	220	0
pork:							
fresh, cooked, .5 oz. (1 oz. raw link)	48	2.6	.1	4.1	11	168	0
(Hormel Little Sizzlers), 2 links . .	103	6.0	0	9.0	m.q.	172	0
(Hormel Midget), 2 links	143	7.0	0	13.0	m.q.	327	0
(JM Tasty Link), 2 cooked links	190	6.0	1.0	18.0	m.q.	290	0
(Jones Dairy Farm), 1 link	140	2.9	tr.	13.7	24	176	0
(Jones Dairy Farm Golden Brown Light), 1 link . .	55	3.3	.5	4.2	16	132	0
(Jones Dairy Farm Light), 1 link . .	70	4.2	1.0	5.0	21	232	0
(Oscar Mayer Little Friers), 1 cooked link	82	3.4	.2	7.5	17	219	0

Food and Measure	cal.	prot. (gms)	carbo. (gms)	fat (gms)	chol. (mgs)	sod. (mgs)	fiber (gms)
Sausage, pork *(cont.)*							
mild *(Jones Dairy Farm* Golden Brown), 1 link . .	100	2.6	tr.	9.8	18	150	0
spicy *(Jones Dairy Farm* Golden Brown), 1 link . .	100	2.8	tr.	9.5	18	159	0
pork, patty:							
fresh, cooked, 1 oz. (2 oz. raw patty)	100	5.3	.3	8.4	22	349	0
(JM), 1 cooked patty	70	2.0	1.0	6.0	m.q.	170	0
(Jones Dairy Farm), 1 patty	155	5.5	tr.	14.4	36	281	0
(Jones Dairy Farm Golden Brown), 1 patty	155	4.6	tr.	14.7	29	250	0
hot *(JM),* 1 cooked patty	70	2.0	1.0	6.0	m.q.	170	0
pork roll *(Jones Dairy Farm* Cello Roll), 1 slice	105	3.7	tr.	9.6	24	200	0
pork and bacon *(JM* Tasty Link), 2 cooked links . .	100	6.0	1.0	9.0	m.q.	240	0
smoked:							
(Eckrich Lean Supreme), 1 oz. . .	70	4.0	1.0	6.0	m.q.	230	0
(Eckrich Skinless), 1 link	180	7.0	2.0	16.0	m.q.	420	0
(Eckrich Smok-Y-Links), 2 links . .	160	6.0	2.0	14.0	m.q.	340	0
(Hillshire Farm Bun Size), 2 oz. . . .	180	8.0	2.0	16.0	m.q.	570	0
(Hillshire Farm Flavorseal), 2 oz. .	190	7.0	1.0	17.0	m.q.	500	0
(Hillshire Farm Links), 2 oz. . .	190	8.0	1.0	18.0	m.q.	520	0

Food and Measure	cal.	prot. (gms)	carbo. (gms)	fat (gms)	chol. (mgs)	sod. (mgs)	fiber (gms)
(Hillshire Farm Lite), 2 oz.	160	8.0	2.0	13.0	m.q.	m.q.	0
(Hormel Smokies), 2 links	160	9.0	2.0	14.0	m.q.	597	0
(OHSE), 1 oz. . . .	80	4.0	1.0	7.0	m.q.	320	0
(Oscar Mayer Little Smokies), 1 link	28	1.2	.1	2.5	6	91	0
(Oscar Mayer Smokie Links), 1 link	124	5.4	.6	11.1	28	435	0
(Oscar Mayer International Sausages), 1 oz. . . .	83	3.6	.5	7.4	15	263	0
(Pilgrim's Pride), 3 oz.	144	13.1	2.5	9.1	64	890	0
smoked, beef:							
(Eckrich), 1 oz. . .	100	3.0	<1.0	9.0	m.q.	270	0
(Eckrich Lean Supreme), 1 oz. . . .	80	4.0	1.0	7.0	m.q.	230	0
(Eckrich Smok-Y-Links), 2 links . .	160	6.0	2.0	14.0	m.q.	350	0
(Hillshire Farm Bun Size), 2 oz. . . .	180	8.0	2.0	16.0	m.q.	570	0
(Hillshire Farm Flavorseal), 2 oz.	180	7.0	2.0	16.0	m.q.	490	0
(Oscar Mayer Smokies), 1 link . . .	123	5.4	.6	11.0	27	430	0
smoked, cheese:							
(Eckrich Smok-Y-Links), 2 links . .	160	6.0	2.0	14.0	m.q.	360	0
(Hormel Smokie Cheezers), 2 links	168	9.0	1.0	15.0	m.q.	623	0
(Oscar Mayer Smokies), 1 link . . .	127	5.8	.8	11.2	29	453	0
smoked, ham (Eckrich Smok-Y-Links), 2 links	160	6.0	2.0	15.0	m.q.	500	0

Food and Measure	cal.	prot. (gms)	carbo. (gms)	fat (gms)	chol. (mgs)	sod. (mgs)	fiber (gms)
Sausage *(cont.)*							
smoked, hot:							
(Eckrich Smok-Y-Links), 2 links . .	150	6.0	1.0	14.0	m.q.	360	0
(Hillshire Farm Flavorseal), 2 oz.	180	7.0	2.0	16.0	m.q.	510	0
smoked, maple flavor							
(Eckrich Smok-Y-Links), 2 links . . .	160	6.0	2.0	14.0	m.q.	390	0
smoked, pork *(Hormel)*, 3 oz.	290	12.0	1.0	27.0	m.q.	m.q.	0
canned, 1 patty:							
hot *(Hormel)* . . .	150	7.0	0	13.0	m.q.	549	0
mild *(Hormel)* . . .	150	7.0	0	13.0	m.q.	541	0
"Sausage," vegetarian:							
canned *(Worthington Saucettes)*, 2 links	140	10.0	5.0	9.0	0	350	m.q.
frozen:							
(Morningstar Farms Breakfast Links), 3 links	190	12.0	3.0	14.0	0	500	m.q.
(Morningstar Farms Breakfast Patties), 2 patties	190	15.0	7.0	12.0	0	710	m.q.
(Worthington Prosage), 3 links	190	13.0	4.0	14.0	0	570	m.q.
(Worthington Prosage), 2 patties	210	18.0	4.0	14.0	0	780	m.q.
roll *(Worthington Prosage)*, 2.5 oz.	180	13.0	4.0	12.0	0	570	m.q.
Sausage breakfast biscuit:							
refrigerated:							
(Owens Border Breakfasts), 2 oz.	210	6.0	14.0	14.0	m.q.	400	m.q.

Food and Measure	cal.	prot. (gms)	carbo. (gms)	fat (gms)	chol. (mgs)	sod. (mgs)	fiber (gms)
egg and cheese *(Owens Border Breakfasts)*, 2.5 oz.	250	8.0	15.0	15.0	m.q.	500	m.q.
smoked *(Owens Border Breakfasts)*, 2 oz. . . .	200	4.0	15.0	6.0	m.q.	785	m.q.
frozen *(Swanson Great Starts)*, 4¾ oz.	410	14.0	36.0	22.0	m.q.	1180	m.q.
Sausage breakfast taco:							
(Owens Border Breakfasts), 2.17 oz. . .	190	7.0	11.0	12.0	65	345	m.q.
Sausage seasoning:							
pork *(Tone's)*, 1 tsp.	12	.4	2.7	.3	0	1	.7 d
Sausage stick, (see also "Beef jerky"), 1 piece, except as noted:							
(Hickory Farms Sportsman Stick), 1 oz.	138	9.0	4.0	10.0	40	1075	0
beef, 1.1 oz.:							
pepperoni *(Pemmican)*	170	8.0	2.0	14.0	m.q.	500	0
Tabasco *(Pemmican)*	120	5.0	2.0	10.0	m.q.	410	0
teriyaki *(Pemmican)*	150	8.0	5.0	11.0	m.q.	410	0
smoked:							
(Slim Jim Big Slim)	80	3.0	1.0	7.0	m.q.	220	0
(Slim Jim Giant Slim), 1.1 oz. . .	180	7.0	2.0	16.0	m.q.	470	0
(Slim Jim Jumbo Jim)	150	8.0	2.0	12.0	m.q.	430	0
(Slim Jim Super Slim Regular/Tabasco)	110	4.0	1.0	10.0	m.q.	300	0

Food and Measure	cal.	prot. (gms)	carbo. (gms)	fat (gms)	chol. (mgs)	sod. (mgs)	fiber (gms)
Sausage stick, smoked *(cont.)*							
mild, pepperoni, spicy or *Tabasco* (*Slim Jim* Handi- Paks)	50	2.0	1.0	4.0	m.q.	130	0
nacho (*Slim Jim Super Slim*) . . .	100	6.0	1.0	7.0	m.q.	350	0
summer sausage:							
beef (*Hickory Farms*), 1 oz. . . .	100	5.0	1.0	8.0	20	345	0
regular or teriyaki (*Pemmican*) . . .	110	5.0	1.0	10.0	m.q.	410	0
smoked (*Slim Jim*)	80	3.0	1.0	7.0	m.q.	200	0
Savory, ground:							
1 tsp.	4	.1	1.0	.1	0	tr.	.2 c
summer (*Tone's*), 1 tsp.	4	.1	1.0	.1	0	1	.2 c
Scallion, see "Onion, green"							
Scallop, meat only:							
raw, 1 lb.	400	76.1	10.7	3.4	152	730	0
raw, 2 large or 5 small	26	5.0	.7	.2	10	48	0
Scallop, frozen:							
fried (*Mrs. Paul's*), 3 oz.	200	9.0	22.0	8.0	m.q.	410	m.q.
"Scallop," imitation[1]:							
1 lb.	447	57.9	48.2	1.9	98	3606	0
1 oz.	28	3.6	3.0	.1	6	225	0
"Scallop," vegetar- ian, canned, 1/2 cup:							
(*Worthington Vegeta- ble Skallops*) . . .	90	15.0	4.0	2.0	0	430	m.q.
(*Worthington Vegeta- ble Skallops* No Salt*)	80	13.0	4.0	1.0	0	80	m.q.

[1] *Made from surimi.*

Food and Measure	cal.	prot. (gms)	carbo. (gms)	fat (gms)	chol. (mgs)	sod. (mgs)	fiber (gms)
Scallop and shrimp dinner, frozen:							
Mariner *(The Budget Gourmet),* 11.5 oz.	320	16.0	43.0	9.0	70	690	m.q.
Scallop squash:							
raw, untrimmed, 1 lb.	81	5.3	17.1	.9	0	5	2.5 c
raw, sliced, 1/2 cup	12	.8	2.5	.1	0	1	.4 c
boiled, drained:							
sliced, 1/2 cup . . .	14	.9	3.0	.2	0	1	.4 c
mashed, 1/2 cup . .	19	1.2	4.0	.2	0	1	.6 c
Scrapple:							
(Jones Dairy Farm), 1 slice	65	2.7	4.2	3.7	24	165	0
Scrod: fresh, see "Cod, Atlantic"							
Scrod entree, frozen:							
baked *(Gorton's Microwave Entrees),* 1 pkg.	320	22.0	17.0	18.0	80	420	m.q.
Scup, meat only, raw:							
1 lb.	477	85.6	0	12.4	m.q.	191	0
1 oz.	30	5.4	0	.8	m.q.	12	0
Sea bass, meat only:							
raw, 1 lb.	439	83.6	0	9.1	186	308	0
raw, 1 oz.	27	5.2	0	.6	12	19	0
baked, broiled, or microwaved, 4 oz. . .	141	26.8	0	2.9	60	99	0
Seafood, see specific listings							
Seafood cocktail sauce, see "Cocktail sauce"							
Seafood dinner, frozen:							
w/herbs *(Armour Classics Lite),* 10 oz.	190	13.0	29.0	2.0	35	1020	m.q.

Food and Measure	cal.	prot. (gms)	carbo. (gms)	fat (gms)	chol. (mgs)	sod. (mgs)	fiber (gms)
Seafood entree, frozen:							
casserole *(Pillsbury Microwave Classic)*, 1 pkg.	420	15.0	37.0	24.0	m.q.	950	m.q.
combination platter, breaded *(Mrs. Paul's)*, 9 oz. . . .	600	19.0	55.0	33.0	85	408	m.q.
creole, w/rice *(Swanson* Homestyle Recipe), 9 oz.	240	7.0	40.0	6.0	m.q.	810	m.q.
Newberg:							
(The Budget Gourmet), 10 oz. . . .	350	17.0	43.0	12.0	70	660	m.q.
(Healthy Choice), 8 oz.	200	13.0	30.0	3.0	55	440	m.q.
Seafood seasoning, see "Fish seasoning and coating mix"							
Seafood and crabmeat salad, 1 oz.:							
(Longacre Saladfest)	45	1.0	3.0	3.0	5	130	n.a.
Seasoned coating mix (see also specific listings), 1 oz.:							
breading *(Golden Dipt)*	90	3.0	20.0	0	0	630	m.q.
Sea trout, meat only:							
raw, 1 lb.	472	76.0	0	16.4	376	263	0
raw, 1 oz.	29	4.7	0	1.0	24	16	0
Seaweed, 1 oz.:							
agar:							
raw	7	.2	1.9	tr.	0	3	.1 c
dried	87	1.8	22.9	.1	0	29	.2 c
Irish moss, raw . . .	14	.4	3.5	<.1	0	19	m.q.
kelp, raw	12	.5	2.7	.2	0	66	.4 c

Food and Measure	cal.	prot. (gms)	carbo. (gms)	fat (gms)	chol. (mgs)	sod. (mgs)	fiber (gms)
laver, raw	10	1.6	1.4	.1	0	14	.1 c
spirulina:							
raw	8	1.7	.7	.1	0	28	.1 c
dried	82	16.3	6.8	2.2	0	297	1.0 c
wakame, raw	13	.9	2.6	.2	0	247	.2 c
Semolina, whole-grain:							
1 cup	602	21.2	121.6	1.8	0	2	6.5 d
Sesame butter, see "Sesame paste"							
Sesame chips:							
(Flavor Tree), 1/4 cup	163	3.2	10.6	9.2	0	380	.1 c
Sesame flour, 1 oz.:							
high fat	149	8.7	7.6	10.5	0	12	1.8 c
partially defatted . . .	109	11.5	10.0	3.4	0	12	1.7 c
lowfat	95	14.2	10.1	.5	0	11	1.4 c
Sesame meal, 1 oz.:							
partially defatted . . .	161	4.8	7.4	13.6	0	11	1.1 c
Sesame nut mix, 1 oz.:							
dry roasted *(Planters)*	160	5.0	8.0	12.0	0	330	m.q.
Sesame paste (see also "Tahini"):							
from whole sesame seeds, 1 tbsp.	95	2.9	4.1	8.1	0	2	.9 c
Sesame seasoning:							
all-purpose *(McCormick/Schilling Parsley Patch),* 1 tsp.	15	.6	1.0	1.0	0	2	n.a.
Sesame seeds:							
(Spice Islands), 1 tsp.	9	.5	.9	.4	0	1	.7 c
whole, roasted and toasted, 1 oz.	161	4.8	7.3	13.6	0	3	2.4 c
kernels, decorticated:							
dried, 1 tsp.	16	.7	.3	1.5	0	1	.1 c
toasted, 1 oz.	161	4.8	7.4	13.6	0	11	1.4 c

Food and Measure	cal.	prot. (gms)	carbo. (gms)	fat (gms)	chol. (mgs)	sod. (mgs)	fiber (gms)
Sesame sticks,							
¼ cup:							
(Flavor Tree)	133	3.1	10.6	9.1	0	358	.1 c
(Flavor Tree No Salt)	131	3.2	13.4	8.1	0	7	.1 c
Sesbania flower:							
raw, 1 cup	5	.3	1.4	<.1	0	3	.3 c
steamed, ½ cup . .	11	.6	2.7	<.1	0	6	.8 c
7-Eleven, 1 serving:							
Big Bite	287	10.2	20.3	18.1	27	781	1.1 d
Big Bite Super	460	17.0	20.6	34.1	54	1322	1.1 d
burrito:							
bean and cheese	616	23.3	84.3	23.1	46	1118	6.2 d
beef, bean, and							
cheese	395	14.9	41.5	20.5	40	738	2.8 d
beef and potato . .	394	13.2	48.0	18.4	32	607	2.4 d
chicken and rice	244	9.6	42.2	5.6	13	474	2.3 d
burrito, beef and							
bean:							
5 oz.	308	11.6	42.1	11.5	23	559	3.1 d
green chili	617	23.3	84.3	23.1	46	1118	6.1 d
red chili	308	11.6	42.1	11.5	23	559	3.1 d
red hot, 5 oz. . . .	310	11.7	42.6	11.6	23	561	3.2 d
red hot, 10 oz. . .	620	23.5	85.1	23.2	47	1122	6.3 d
red hot, premium	359	13.3	41.9	17.1	31	603	3.3 d
chicken breast, 4.8 oz.	405	17.6	48.6	15.7	29	441	m.q.
chimichanga, beef . .	363	15.0	42.3	14.9	m.q.	674	.4 d
enchilada, beef and							
cheese	369	18.6	27.6	21.7	55	524	3.5 d
fajitas	311	13.8	40.4	11.4	32	795	1.8 d
sandito:							
ham and cheese	347	17.7	35.9	16.0	40	1118	1.9 d
pizza	345	12.8	38.0	17.0	23	711	2.0 d
tacos, soft, twin . . .	399	17.3	40.7	19.7	50	862	2.5 d
Deli-Shoppe micro-							
wave products:							
bacon cheeseburger	558	24.1	42.7	28.7	11	1217	0 d
bagel and cream							
cheese	338	10.5	37.3	16.1	47	440	.9 d

Food and Measure	cal.	prot. (gms)	carbo. (gms)	fat (gms)	chol. (mgs)	sod. (mgs)	fiber (gms)
char sandwich, large	713	32.1	46.2	47.2	11	1478	.1 d
fish sandwich w/ cheese	433	20.4	54.1	14.5	11	955	0 d
sausage, red hot, large	845	31.0	43.3	59.2	128	2204	2.2 d
turkey wedge, 3.4 oz.	193	13.9	20.3	5.6	24	482	.7 d
Shad, meat only:							
raw, 1 lb.	891	76.8	0	62.5	m.q.	233	0
raw, 1 oz.	56	4.8	0	3.9	m.q.	14	0
Shakey's:							
chicken, fried:							
3 pieces w/potatoes	947	57.0	51.0	56.0	m.q.	2293	m.q.
5 pieces w/potatoes	1700	97.0	130.0	90.0	m.q.	5327	m.q.
Hot Ham and Cheese	550	36.0	56.0	21.0	m.q.	2135	m.q.
pizza, *Homestyle Pan Crust,* 1/10 of 12″ pie:							
cheese	303	14.1	31.0	13.7	21	591	m.q.
onion, green peppers, olives, mushrooms . . .	320	14.7	32.1	14.7	21	652	m.q.
pepperoni	343	15.8	31.1	15.4	27	740	m.q.
sausage, mushroom	343	16.4	31.4	16.9	24	677	m.q.
sausage, pepperoni	374	17.4	31.2	19.9	24	676	m.q.
Shakey's Special	384	17.9	31.6	20.7	29	878	m.q.
pizza, thick crust, 1/10 of 12″ pie:							
cheese	170	9.0	21.6	4.8	13	421	m.q.
green pepper, olives, mushrooms	162	9.1	22.2	4.1	13	418	m.q.
pepperoni	185	10.1	21.8	6.4	17	422	m.q.
sausage, mushrooms . . .	179	10.2	21.8	5.6	15	420	m.q.
sausage, pepperoni	177	11.1	21.7	8.0	19	424	m.q.

Food and Measure	cal.	prot. (gms)	carbo. (gms)	fat (gms)	chol. (mgs)	sod. (mgs)	fiber (gms)
Shakey's pizza, thick crust *(cont.)*							
Shakey's Special	208	13.1	22.3	8.3	18	423	m.q.
pizza, thin crust, 1/10 of 12" pie:							
cheese	133	8.4	13.2	5.2	14	323	m.q.
onion, green pepper, olives, mushrooms	125	7.2	13.8	4.5	11	313	m.q.
pepperoni	148	8.4	13.2	6.9	14	403	m.q.
sausage, mushroom	141	8.5	13.3	6.0	13	336	m.q.
sausage, pepperoni	166	9.4	13.2	8.4	17	397	m.q.
Shakey's Special	171	13.3	13.5	8.7	16	475	m.q.
potatoes, 15 pieces	950	17.0	120.0	36.0	n.a.	3703	m.q.
Shakey's Super Hot Hero	810	36.0	67.0	44.0	m.q.	2688	m.q.
spaghetti w/meat sauce and garlic bread	940	26.0	134.0	33.0	m.q.	1904	m.q.
Shallot:							
fresh or stored:							
peeled, 1 oz. . . .	20	.7	4.8	<.1	0	3	.2 c
chopped, 1 tbsp.	7	.3	1.7	<.1	0	1	.1 c
freeze-dried, 1 tbsp.	3	.1	.7	tr.	0	1	<.1 c
Shark, meat only:							
raw, 1 lb.	591	95.2	0	20.5	232	360	0
raw, 1 oz.	37	5.9	0	1.3	14	22	0
batter-dipped, 4 oz.	259	21.1	7.2	15.7	67	138	.2 c
Sheepshead, meat only:							
raw, 1 lb.	490	91.7	0	10.9	m.q.	324	0
raw, 1 oz.	31	5.7	0	.7	m.q.	20	0
baked, broiled, or microwaved, 4 oz. . . .	143	29.5	0	1.8	m.q.	83	0
Shellie bean, canned:							
w/liquid, 1/2 cup . . .	37	2.1	7.6	.2	0	408	.7 c
(Stokely), 1/2 cup . .	35	2.0	7.0	0	0	470	m.q.

Food and Measure	cal.	prot. (gms)	carbo. (gms)	fat (gms)	chol. (mgs)	sod. (mgs)	fiber (gms)
Shells, stuffed, see "Pasta Dishes" or "Pasta Dinner"							
Sherbet (see also "Sorbet"):							
orange:							
(Bordon), 1/2 cup	110	1.0	25.0	1.0	m.q.	40	n.a.
(Darigold), 1/2 cup	120	1.0	26.0	1.0	m.q.	25	n.a.
rainbow *(Baskin-Robbins)*, 1 regular scoop	160	1.0	34.0	2.0	6	85	n.a.
Shortening, 1 tbsp.:							
lard and vegetable oil	115	0	0	12.8	m.q.	(0)	0
hydrogenated soybean and cottonseed or palm	113	0	0	12.8	0	(0)	0
vegetable, regular or butter flavor *(Crisco)*	110	0	0	12.0	0	0	0
Shrimp, meat only:							
raw:							
1 lb.	481	92.1	4.1	7.8	692	673	0
1 oz. or 4 large . .	30	5.7	.3	.5	43	42	0
boiled or steamed:							
4 oz.	112	23.7	m.q.	1.2	221	254	0
4 large	22	4.6	m.q.	.2	43	49	0
Shrimp, canned, drained:							
1 cup	154	29.6	1.3	2.5	222	216	0
(Louisiana Brand), 2 oz.	58	12.0	0	1.0	m.q.	m.q.	0
Shrimp dinner, frozen:							
baby bay *(Armour Classics Lite)*, 9.75 oz.	220	12.0	31.0	6.0	105	890	m.q.
Creole, 11.25 oz.:							
(Armour Classics Lite)	260	6.0	53.0	2.0	45	900	m.q.

Food and Measure	cal.	prot. (gms)	carbo. (gms)	fat (gms)	chol. (mgs)	sod. (mgs)	fiber (gms)
Shrimp dinner, Creole *(cont.)*							
(Healthy Choice)	210	8.0	42.0	1.0	65	560	m.q.
marinara *(Healthy*							
Choice), 10.5 oz.	220	9.0	42.0	1.0	50	320	m.q.
Shrimp entree, canned:							
chow mein *(La Choy*							
Bi-Pack)*, 3/4 cup	50	3.0	7.0	1.0	19	860	2.0 d
Shrimp entree, frozen:							
battered:							
(SeaPak), 4 oz. . . .	260	11.0	20.0	15.0	20	470	m.q.
w/crabmeat stuffing							
(SeaPak), 4 oz.	260	8.0	27.0	13.0	m.q.	780	m.q.
breaded:							
butterfly *(SeaPak*							
Mikado)*, 4 oz.	160	12.0	26.0	1.0	110	710	m.q.
butterfly *(Gorton's)*,							
4 oz.	160	19.0	16.0	<1.0	m.q.	540	m.q.
butterfly, round							
(SeaPak), 4 oz.	150	14.0	20.0	1.0	m.q.	m.q.	m.q.
fried *(Mrs. Paul's)*,							
3 oz.	200	9.0	16.0	11.0	m.q.	430	m.q.
crisps *(Gorton's)*,							
4 oz.	280	9.0	26.0	15.0	m.q.	740	m.q.
crunchy *(Gorton's*							
Microwave)*, 5 oz.	380	14.0	35.0	20.0	65	870	m.q.
Cajun *(Mrs. Paul's*							
Light)*, 9 oz.	230	9.0	37.0	5.0	60	740	m.q.
and chicken Cantonese, w/noodles *(Lean Cuisine)*,							
10 1/8 oz.	270	22.0	25.0	9.0	100	920	m.q.
and clams w/linguini *(Mrs. Paul's Light)*,							
10 oz.	240	12.0	36.0	5.0	40	750	m.q.

Food and Measure	cal.	prot. (gms)	carbo. (gms)	fat (gms)	chol. (mgs)	sod. (mgs)	fiber (gms)
and fettuccine (The Budget Gourmet), 9.5 oz.	375	10.0	38.0	20.0	145	660	m.q.
fettuccine Alfredo (Booth), 10 oz. . .	260	19.0	28.0	8.0	m.q.	620	m.q.
w/garlic butter sauce and vegetable rice, (Booth), 10 oz. . .	400	13.0	40.0	25.0	m.q.	750	m.q.
w/lobster sauce (La Choy Fresh & Lite), 10 oz.	240	12.0	36.4	6.2	118	946	2.8 d
New Orleans, w/wild rice (Booth), 10 oz.	230	13.0	35.0	5.0	m.q.	950	m.q.
Oriental, w/pineapple rice (Booth), 10 oz.	190	11.0	30.0	3.0	m.q.	950	m.q.
primavera: (Mrs. Paul's Light), 9 1/2 oz.	180	11.0	28.0	3.0	125	840	m.q.
(Right Course), 9 5/8 oz.	240	12.0	32.0	7.0	50	590	m.q.
w/fettuccine (Booth), 10 oz.	200	16.0	28.0	3.0	m.q.	760	m.q.
scampi (Gorton's Microwave Entrees), 1 pkg.	470	12.0	33.0	32.0	130	720	m.q.
"Shrimp," imitation[1]:							
1 lb.	458	56.2	41.4	6.7	163	3198	0
1 oz.	29	3.5	2.6	.4	10	200	0
Shrimp salad, 1 oz.:							
(Longacre Saladfest)	45	2.0	2.0	3.0	25	150	n.a.
w/seafood (Longacre Saladfest)	42	2.0	2.0	3.0	15	160	n.a.
Shrimp spice, 1 tsp.:							
(Tone's Craboil) . . .	10	.3	1.2	.6	1	1	.3 d
Skipper's, 1 serving:							
thick-cut cod:							
3 piece, fries . . .	665	27.0	68.0	32.0	38	1054	m.q.

[1] Made from surimi (See "Surimi").

Food and Measure	cal.	prot. (gms)	carbo. (gms)	fat (gms)	chol. (mgs)	sod. (mgs)	fiber (gms)
Skipper's, **thick-cut cod** *(cont.)*							
4 piece, fries . . .	759	34.0	74.0	36.0	50	1388	m.q.
5 piece, fries . . .	853	42.0	80.0	41.0	62	1723	m.q.
famous fish fillets:							
1 fish, fries	558	17.0	51.0	28.0	55	408	m.q.
2 fish, fries	733	28.0	71.0	38.0	108	765	m.q.
3 fish, fries	908	39.0	82.0	48.0	160	1122	m.q.
seafood combo w/ fries:							
shrimp, 1 fish . . .	728	24.0	77.0	37.0	105	943	m.q.
jumbo shrimp, 1 fish	720	24.0	75.0	36.0	91	1268	m.q.
clam strips, 1 fish	868	25.0	81.0	54.0	61	667	m.q.
oysters, 1 fish . . .	885	25.0	95.0	44.0	80	809	m.q.
seafood basket w/ fries:							
shrimp . . . . \ . . .	723	20.0	82.0	36.0	102	1121	m.q.
jumbo shrimp . . .	707	20.0	79.0	35.0	73	911	m.q.
clam strips	1003	22.0	90.0	70.0	14	569	m.q.
oysters	1038	28.0	118.0	51.0	52	853	m.q.
Skipper's Platter	1038	32.0	97.0	63.0	111	1202	m.q.
chicken tenderloin strips w/fries:							
5 piece	793	44.0	69.0	38.0	77	798	m.q.
3 piece, 1 fish . . .	805	80.0	72.0	40.0	100	858	m.q.
3 piece, shrimp . .	800	36.0	77.0	39.0	97	1036	m.q.
salads & lite catch:							
2 fish, small salad	409	25.0	27.0	23.0	119	937	m.q.
3 chicken, small salad	305	26.0	17.0	15.0	58	673	m.q.
1 fish, 2 chicken, small salad . . .	399	29.0	24.0	21.0	96	880	m.q.
small salad	59	3.0	6.0	3.0	13	223	m.q.
shrimp and seafood salad	167	23.0	15.0	3.0	80	657	m.q.
Create A Catch:							
chicken sandwich	606	31.0	44.0	32.0	82	976	m.q.
chicken strip . . .	82	8.0	4.0	4.0	15	150	m.q.
fish sandwich . . .	524	19.0	43.0	33.0	86	1191	m.q.

Food and Measure	cal.	prot. (gms)	carbo. (gms)	fat (gms)	chol. (mgs)	sod. (mgs)	fiber (gms)
fish sandwich,							
double	698	30.0	54.0	73.0	139	1548	m.q.
fish fillet	175	11.0	11.0	10.0	53	357	m.q.
fries	383	6.0	50.0	18.0	<2	51	m.q.
clam chowder cup	100	3.0	14.0	3.5	12	525	m.q.
clam chowder pint	200	5.0	19.0	7.0	24	1050	m.q.
coleslaw, 5 oz. . .	289	2.0	10.0	27.0	50	329	m.q.
condiments, 1 tbsp.:							
barbecue sauce . .	25	0	5.0	1.0	0	226	n.a.
cocktail sauce . . .	20	0	5.0	0	0	216	n.a.
tartar sauce	65	0	0	7.0	4	102	n.a.
salad dressing, 1 pkt.:							
blue cheese, pre-							
mium	222	1.0	4.0	23.0	8	240	n.a.
Italian, gourmet . .	140	0	2.0	15.0	0	200	n.a.
Italian, lo-cal . . .	17	0	2.0	1.0	0	680	n.a.
ranch house	188	1.0	2.0	20.0	0	302	n.a.
thousand island . .	160	0	8.0	14.0	6	415	n.a.
Sloppy joe season-							
ing:							
(Lawry's Seasoning							
Blends), 1 pkg. . .	126	2.8	27.7	.4	0	3442	.8 c
(Tone's), 1 tsp. . . .	14	.3	3.1	.1	0	347	m.q.
mix *(French's),*							
1/8 pkg.	16	0	4.0	0	0	390	m.q.
mix *(McCormick/Schil-*							
ling), 1 serving . .	18	.3	3.9	0	0	500	m.q.
Smelt, rainbow, meat							
only:							
raw, 1 lb.	440	80.0	0	11.0	318	272	0
raw, 1 oz.	27	5.0	0	.7	20	17	0
baked, broiled, or mi-							
crowaved, 4 oz. . .	141	25.6	0	3.5	102	87	0
Snack mix, 1 oz., ex-							
cept as noted:							
(Eagle)	140	4.0	18.0	6.0	0	370	m.q.
(Flavor Tree Party							
Mix), 1/4 cup	163	3.4	12.3	11.0	0	407	.1 c

Food and Measure	cal.	prot. (gms)	carbo. (gms)	fat (gms)	chol. (mgs)	sod. (mgs)	fiber (gms)
Snack mix *(cont.)*							
(Flavor Tree Party Mix No Salt)*, ¼ cup	163	3.9	13.2	10.8	0	8	.1 c
(Pepperidge Farm Classic)	140	4.0	14.0	8.0	0	360	1.0 d
(Ralston Chex Traditional)	120	3.0	19.0	5.0	0	320	m.q.
(Super Snax)	137	3.4	17.0	6.5	0	207	m.q.
cheddar, golden *(Ralston Chex)*	130	3.0	19.0	5.0	n.a.	300	m.q.
cheese, nacho *(Ralston Chex)*	130	3.0	19.0	5.0	n.a.	430	m.q.
smoked, lightly *(Pepperidge Farm)* . . .	150	4.0	13.0	9.0	0	350	1.0 d
sour cream and onion *(Ralston Chex)* . .	130	3.0	19.0	5.0	n.a.	300	m.q.
spicy *(Pepperidge Farm)*	140	4.0	14.0	8.0	<5	340	1.0 d
Snail, sea, see "Whelk"							
Snapper, meat only:							
raw, 1 lb.	452	93.0	0	6.1	168	291	0
raw, 1 oz.	28	5.8	0	.4	10	18	0
baked, broiled, or microwaved, 4 oz. . .	145	3.0	0	2.0	53	65	0
Snow peas, see "Peas, ediblepodded"							
Soft drinks and mixers, 12 fl. oz., except as noted:							
all flavors *(Schweppes Royal)*, 6 fl. oz. . .	35	0	8.0	0	0	<5	0
berry, red *(Shasta)*	158	0	43.0	0	0	20	0
cherry, black *(Shasta)*	162	0	44.0	0	0	29	0
cherry cola:							
(Coca-Cola), 6 fl. oz.	76	0	20.0	0	0	4	0
(Pepsi Wild Cherry)	163	0	43.2	0	0	2	0

Food and Measure	cal.	prot. (gms)	carbo. (gms)	fat (gms)	chol. (mgs)	sod. (mgs)	fiber (gms)
(Shasta)	140	0	38.0	0	0	22	0
cherry-lime *(Spree)*	158	0	43.0	0	0	2	0
chocolate *(Yoo-Hoo)*, 9 fl. oz.	140	3.0	27.0	1.0	n.a.	130	0
citrus mist *(Shasta)*	170	0	46.0	0	0	19	0
club soda:							
(Schweppes), 6 fl. oz.	0	0	0	0	0	25	0
(Shasta)	0	0	0	0	0	46	0
cola:							
(Coca-Cola Regular/Free), 6 fl. oz.	77	0	20.0	0	0	4	0
(Coca-Cola Classic), 6 fl. oz.	72	0	19.0	0	0	7	0
(Jolt), 6 fl. oz. . . .	85	0	20.7	0	0	10	0
(Pepsi Regular/Free)	160	0	39.6	0	0	2	0
(Shasta)	147	0	40.0	0	0	3	0
(Shasta Free) . . .	151	0	41.0	0	0	2	0
(Spree)	147	0	40.0	0	0	1	0
collins mixer:							
(Canada Dry), 8 fl. oz.	80	0	20.0	0	0	17	0
(Schweppes), 6 fl. oz.	75	0	18.0	0	0	51	0
(Shasta)	118	0	32.0	0	0	23	0
cream:							
(A&W), 1 fl. oz. . .	14	.1	3.6	tr.	0	2	0
(Shasta Creme) . .	154	0	42.0	0	0	23	0
(Dr. Diablo)	140	0	38.0	0	0	14	0
(Dr. Pepper Regular/Free)	150	0	38.4	0	0	18	0
fruit punch *(Shasta)*	173	0	47.0	0	0	32	0
ginger ale:							
(Canada Dry), 8 fl. oz.	90	0	21.0	0	0	7	0
(Canada Dry Golden)*, 8 fl. oz.	100	0	24.0	0	0	24	0

Food and Measure	cal.	prot. (gms)	carbo. (gms)	fat (gms)	chol. (mgs)	sod. (mgs)	fiber (gms)
Soft drinks and mixers, ginger ale *(cont.)*							
(Fanta), 6 fl. oz. . . .	63	0	16.0	0	0	14	0
(Schweppes),							
6 fl. oz.	65	0	16.0	0	0	10	0
(Shasta)	120	0	33.0	0	0	23	0
(Spree)	120	0	33.0	0	0	1	0
raspberry							
(Schweppes),							
6 fl. oz.	65	0	16.0	0	0	10	0
ginger beer							
(Schweppes),							
6 fl. oz.	70	0	17.0	0	0	30	0
grape:							
(Canada Dry Con-							
cord), 8 fl. oz. . .	130	0	32.0	0	0	21	0
(Fanta), 6 fl. oz. . .	86	0	22.0	0	0	7	0
(Schweppes),							
6 fl. oz.	95	0	23.0	0	0	15	0
(Shasta)	177	0	48.0	0	0	34	0
grapefruit:							
(Schweppes),							
6 fl. oz.	80	0	20.0	0	0	28	0
(Spree)	154	0	42.0	0	0	1	0
(Wink), 8 fl. oz. . .	120	0	30.0	0	0	19	0
half & half *(Canada*							
Dry), 8 fl. oz. . . .	110	0	26.0	0	0	17	0
kiwi-passion fruit							
(Schweppes Royal),							
6 fl. oz.	35	0	8.0	0	0	<5	0
lemon, bitter							
(Schweppes),							
6 fl. oz.	82	0	20.0	0	0	13	0
lemon sour							
(Schweppes),							
6 fl. oz.	79	0	19.0	0	0	12	0
lemon-lime:							
(Schweppes),							
6 fl. oz.	72	0	18.0	0	0	30	0

Food and Measure	cal.	prot. (gms)	carbo. (gms)	fat (gms)	chol. (mgs)	sod. (mgs)	fiber (gms)
(Shasta)	146	0	39.0	0	0	19	0
(Slice)	150	0	38.4	0	0	<69	0
(Spree)	154	0	42.0	0	0	1	0
lemon tangerine							
(Spree)	165	0	45.0	0	0	1	0
lime, Mandarin *(Spree)*	154	0	42.0	0	0	1	0
(Mello Yello), 6 fl. oz.	87	0	22.0	0	0	14	0
(Mountain Dew) . . .	179	0	44.4	0	0	31	0
(Mr. Pibb), 6 fl. oz. . .	71	0	19.0	0	0	10	0
orange:							
(Fanta), 6 fl. oz. . .	88	0	23.0	0	0	7	0
(Minute Maid),							
6 fl. oz.	87	0	22.0	0	0	tr.	0
(Shasta)	177	0	48.0	0	0	28	0
Mandarin *(Slice)*	193	0	50.4	0	0	<1	0
sparkling							
(Schweppes),							
6 fl. oz.	88	0	22.0	0	0	17	0
pop, red *(Shasta)* . .	158	0	43.0	0	0	20	0
root beer:							
(A&W), 1 fl. oz. . . .	15	<.1	3.5	<.1	0	5	0
(Fanta), 6 fl. oz. . . .	78	0	20.0	0	0	10	0
(Mug)	168	0	42.0	0	0	39	0
(Ramblin'), 6 fl. oz. .	88	0	23.0	0	0	17	0
(Schweppes),							
6 fl. oz.	76	0	19.0	0	0	17	0
(Shasta)	154	0	42.0	0	0	31	0
(Spree)	154	0	42.0	0	0	2	0
seltzer, 6 fl. oz.:							
(Schweppes Low							
Sodium)	0	0	0	0	0	7	0
flavored, all flavors							
(Schweppes) . .	0	0	0	0	0	<5	0
(7Up)	144	0	36.2	0	0	32	0
(7Up Cherry)	148	0	38.7	0	0	32	0
(Sprite), 6 fl. oz. . . .	71	0	18.0	0	0	23	0
strawberry *(Shasta)*	147	0	40.0	0	0	36	0

Food and Measure	cal.	prot. (gms)	carbo. (gms)	fat (gms)	chol. (mgs)	sod. (mgs)	fiber (gms)
Soft drinks and mixers (cont.)							
tonic:							
(Canada Dry),							
8 fl. oz.	90	0	22.0	0	0	7	0
(Schweppes),							
6 fl. oz.	64	0	16.0	0	0	8	0
(Shasta)	121	0	33.0	0	0	17	0
tropical blend (Spree)	146	0	41.0	0	0	2	0
vichy water							
(Schweppes),							
6 fl. oz.	0	0	0	0	0	76	0
Sole, fresh, see "Flat-fish"							
Sole, frozen:							
(Gorton's Fishmarket Fresh), 5 oz.	110	24.0	1.0	1.0	m.q.	140	0
(SeaPak), 4 oz. . . .	90	20.0	0	1.0	m.q.	135	0
(Van de Kamp's Natural), 4 oz.	80	17.0	0	1.0	70	70	0
Atlantic (Booth), 4 oz.	90	19.0	0	1.0	m.q.	180	0
Sole dinner, frozen:							
au gratin (Healthy Choice), 11 oz. . .	270	16.0	40.0	5.0	55	470	m.q.
fillet of (Le Menu), 10 oz.	360	18.0	40.0	14.0	m.q.	940	m.q.
Sole entree, frozen:							
breaded:							
(Mrs. Paul's Light), 4¼ oz.	260	14.0	28.0	11.0	m.q.	536	m.q.
(Van de Kamp's Light), 1 fillet . .	240	15.0	19.0	12.0	45	460	m.q.
in lemon butter (Gorton's Micro-wave Entrees), 1 pkg.	380	25.0	17.0	24.0	120	560	m.q.
w/lemon butter sauce (Healthy Choice), 8.25 oz.	230	16.0	33.0	4.0	45	390	m.q.

Food and Measure	cal.	prot. (gms)	carbo. (gms)	fat (gms)	chol. (mgs)	sod. (mgs)	fiber (gms)
stuffed, w/newburg sauce *(Weight Watchers)*, 10.5 oz.	310	19.0	38.0	9.0	5	940	m.q.
in wine sauce *(Gorton's Micro-wave Entrees)*, 1 pkg.	180	25.0	3.0	8.0	90	770	m.q.
Sorbet (see also "Sherbet" and "Ice"):							
key lime, and vanilla ice cream *(Häagen-Dazs)*, 1/2 cup . . .	200	2.0	34.0	6.0	m.q.	35	n.a.
orange, mandarin *(Dole)*, 4 oz.	110	.5	28.0	.1	0	9	n.a.
orange, and vanilla ice cream *(Häagen-Dazs)*, 1/2 cup . . .	200	3.0	30.0	8.0	m.q.	30	n.a.
peach *(Dole)*, 4 oz.	120	.6	28.0	.6	0	11	n.a.
pineapple *(Dole)*, 4 oz.	120	.5	28.0	.1	0	11	n.a.
raspberry:							
(Dole), 4 oz.	110	.4	28.0	<.1	0	12	n.a.
red *(Baskin-Rob-bins)*, 1 regular scoop	140	0	34.0	0	0	25	n.a.
and vanilla ice cream *(Häagen-Dazs)*, 1/2 cup . .	180	3.0	26.0	7.0	m.q.	30	n.a.
strawberry *(Dole)*, 4 oz.	110	.5	28.0	.1	0	11	n.a.
Sorghum, whole-grain:							
1 cup	650	21.7	143.3	6.3	0	n.a.	4.6 c
Sorghum syrup:							
1/2 cup	424	0	112.2	0	0	n.a.	0
1 tbsp.	53	0	14.0	0	0	n.a.	0
Sorrel, see "Dock"							

Food and Measure	cal.	prot. (gms)	carbo. (gms)	fat (gms)	chol. (mgs)	sod. (mgs)	fiber (gms)
Soup, canned, ready-to-serve, 9.5 oz., except as noted:							
bean:							
(Grandma Brown's), 1 cup	190	9.0	30.9	3.4	<1	700	9.8 d
w/ham, chowder (Hormel Micro-Cup Hearty), 1 cont.	191	10.0	31.0	3.0	30	664	m.q.
w/ham (Campbell's Chunky Old Fashioned), 9⅝ oz.	250	12.0	33.0	8.0	m.q.	960	m.q.
beef:							
(Campbell's Chunky)	170	12.0	21.0	4.0	m.q.	960	m.q.
(Progresso)	160	14.0	12.0	6.0	m.q.	1440	m.q.
hearty (Campbell's Home Cookin')	130	10.0	16.0	3.0	m.q.	910	m.q.
beef barley:							
(Progresso)	150	13.0	16.0	4.0	m.q.	1180	m.q.
beef broth:							
(College Inn), 1 cup	18	2.0	1.0	0	m.q.	1280	0
(Swanson), 7¼ oz.	18	2.0	0	1.0	m.q.	750	0
beef minestrone (Progresso)	170	17.0	15.0	5.0	m.q.	1030	m.q.
beef noodle (Progresso)	160	14.0	17.0	4.0	m.q.	1230	m.q.
beef Stroganoff style (Campbell's Chunky), 10¾-oz. can	320	15.0	28.0	16.0	m.q.	1230	m.q.
beef vegetable:							
(Hormel Micro-Cup Hearty), 1 cont.	71	5.0	12.0	1.0	9	811	m.q.
(Lipton Hearty Ones), 11-oz. cont.	229	10.4	40.0	3.0	29	921	m.q.

Food and Measure	cal.	prot. (gms)	carbo. (gms)	fat (gms)	chol. (mgs)	sod. (mgs)	fiber (gms)
(Progresso)	150	12.0	18.0	3.0	m.q.	1140	m.q.
borscht, 1 cup:							
(Gold's)	100	4.0	21.0	0	0	1280	m.q.
(Rokeach)	96	.8	23.0	.3	0	985	.3 c
(Rokeach Unsalted)	103	.8	23.0	.3	0	50	.5 c
w/beets *(Manis-chewitz)*	80	1.0	20.0	0	0	660	m.q.
low calorie *(Gold's)*	20	1.0	5.0	<1.0	0	1160	m.q.
low calorie *(Manis-chewitz)*	20	1.0	4.0	0	0	725	m.q.
chickarina *(Progresso)*	110	9.0	7.0	5.0	m.q.	1110	m.q.
chicken:							
(Campbell's Chunky Old Fashioned)	150	10.0	18.0	4.0	m.q.	1050	m.q.
(Progresso Home-style)	90	8.0	8.0	3.0	m.q.	1130	m.q.
hearty *(Progresso)*	140	12.0	12.0	4.0	m.q.	960	m.q.
chicken barley *(Progresso)*, 9¼ oz.	120	11.0	16.0	2.0	m.q.	940	m.q.
chicken broth:							
(Campbell's Low Sodium), 10½ oz.	40	3.0	2.0	2.0	m.q.	70	n.a.
(College Inn), 1 cup	35	1.0	0	3.0	m.q.	1320	0
(Hain), 8¾ oz. . .	70	2.0	0	6.0	5	870	0
(Hain No Salt), 8¾ oz.	60	3.0	0	5.0	5	75	0
(Swanson), 7¼ oz.	30	2.0	2.0	2.0	m.q.	910	n.a.
chicken, cream of, w/mushrooms *(Progresso)*	180	8.0	13.0	11.0	m.q.	760	m.q.
chicken minestrone *(Progresso)*	160	12.0	13.0	6.0	m.q.	1210	m.q.
chicken mushroom, creamy *(Campbell's* Chunky), 9⅜ oz.	290	10.0	10.0	23.0	m.q.	1200	m.q.
chicken w/noodles:							
(Campbell's Home Cookin')*	120	12.0	10.0	3.0	m.q.	1000	m.q.

Food and Measure	cal.	prot. (gms)	carbo. (gms)	fat (gms)	chol. (mgs)	sod. (mgs)	fiber (gms)
Soup, canned, ready-to-serve, chicken w/noodles *(cont.)*							
(Campbell's Low Sodium), 10¾ oz.	160	13.0	15.0	5.0	m.q.	85	m.q.
chicken noodle:							
(Campbell's Chunky)	180	12.0	18.0	6.0	m.q.	1010	m.q.
(Hain)	120	10.0	12.0	4.0	40	930	m.q.
(Hain No Salt) . . .	110	9.0	10.0	4.0	50	90	m.q.
(Hormel Micro-Cup Hearty), 1 cont.	108	7.0	14.0	3.0	22	686	m.q.
(Lipton Hearty Ones Homestyle), 11-oz. cont. . . .	227	10.1	37.4	4.0	37	989	m.q.
(Progresso)	130	11.0	10.0	4.0	m.q.	990	m.q.
chicken nuggets w/ vegetables and noo-dles *(Campbell's Chunky)*	190	9.0	20.0	8.0	m.q.	930	m.q.
chicken w/rice *(Campbell's Chunky)*	140	10.0	15.0	4.0	m.q.	1050	m.q.
chicken rice *(Progresso)*	120	8.0	14.0	3.0	m.q.	870	m.q.
chicken vegetable:							
(Campbell's Chunky)	170	10.0	19.0	6.0	m.q.	1080	m.q.
(Progresso)	140	11.0	9.0	3.0	m.q.	900	m.q.
country *(Campbell's Home Cookin')*	110	3.0	18.0	2.0	m.q.	900	m.q.
and rice *(Hormel Micro-Cup Hearty),* 1 cont.	114	5.0	16.0	3.0	7	1025	m.q.
chili beef *(Campbell's Chunky),* 9¾ oz.	260	18.0	33.0	6.0	m.q.	990	m.q.
clam chowder, Man-hattan:							
(Campbell's Chunky)	150	6.0	22.0	4.0	m.q.	980	m.q.

Food and Measure	cal.	prot. (gms)	carbo. (gms)	fat (gms)	chol. (mgs)	sod. (mgs)	fiber (gms)
(Progresso)	120	8.0	17.0	2.0	m.q.	1050	m.q.
clam chowder, New England:							
(Campbell's Chunky)	250	7.0	22.0	15.0	m.q.	1040	m.q.
(Hain), 9¼ oz. . .	180	8.0	26.0	4.0	25	780	m.q.
(Hormel Micro-Cup Hearty), 1 cont.	118	5.0	15.0	5.0	30	882	m.q.
(Progresso), 9¼ oz.	220	8.0	20.0	12.0	m.q.	950	m.q.
corn chowder							
(Progresso), 9¼ oz.	270	5.0	40.0	10.0	n.a.	980	m.q.
escarole in chicken broth *(Progresso)*, 9¼ oz.	30	1.0	4.0	1.0	m.q.	880	m.q.
fisherman's chowder *(Campbell's Chunky)*	230	9.0	22.0	13.0	m.q.	1140	m.q.
gazpacho, 1 cup . . .	57	8.7	.8	2.2	0	1183	.8 c
ham and bean *(Progresso)*	180	12.0	30.0	2.0	m.q.	1130	m.q.
ham and butter bean *(Campbell's Chunky)*, 10¾-oz. can	280	12.0	34.0	10.0	m.q.	1180	m.q.
lentil:							
(Progresso)	170	10.0	24.0	4.0	n.a.	780	m.q.
hearty *(Campbell's Home Cookin')*	150	9.0	26.0	1.0	n.a.	830	m.q.
vegetarian *(Hain)*	160	9.0	25.0	3.0	0	690	m.q.
w/sausage *(Progresso)* . . .	180	9.0	20.0	7.0	m.q.	940	m.q.
macaroni and bean *(Progresso)*	170	8.0	25.0	4.0	n.a.	1090	m.q.
minestrone:							
(Campbell's Chunky)	170	6.0	25.0	5.0	n.a.	890	m.q.

Food and Measure	cal.	prot. (gms)	carbo. (gms)	fat (gms)	chol. (mgs)	sod. (mgs)	fiber (gms)
Soup, canned, ready-to-serve, minestrone *(cont.)*							
(Campbell's Home Cookin' Old World)	130	4.0	20.0	3.0	n.a.	1070	m.q.
(Hain)	170	8.0	28.0	2.0	0	1060	m.q.
(Hain No Salt) . . .	160	7.0	27.0	4.0	0	35	m.q.
(Health Valley), 7½ oz.	120	4.0	18.0	3.0	0	80	5.8 d
(Hormel Micro-Cup Hearty), 1 cont.	104	7.0	15.0	2.0	10	903	m.q.
(Lipton Hearty Ones), 11-oz. cont.	189	8.0	36.1	3.2	6	821	m.q.
(Progresso)	160	8.0	24.0	3.0	n.a.	730	m.q.
extra zesty *(Progresso)* . . .	180	7.0	20.0	8.0	n.a.	1140	m.q.
mushroom:							
cream of *(Campbell's* Low Sodium), 10½ oz.	190	3.0	16.0	13.0	n.a.	60	m.q.
cream of *(Progresso),* 9¼ oz.	140	4.0	11.0	8.0	n.a.	920	m.q.
creamy *(Campbell's* Chunky), 9⅜ oz.	240	4.0	12.0	19.0	n.a.	1130	m.q.
creamy *(Hain),* 9¼ oz.	110	4.0	16.0	4.0	15	740	m.q.
mushroom barley *(Hain)*	100	4.0	17.0	2.0	10	600	m.q.
pea, split:							
(Campbell's Low Sodium), 10½ oz.	240	11.0	38.0	5.0	n.a.	25	m.q.
(Grandma Brown's), 1 cup	208	11.7	31.0	4.1	<1	522	5.8 d
(Hain)	170	11.0	28.0	1.0	0	970	m.q.
(Hain No Salt) . . .	170	11.0	29.0	1.0	0	40	m.q.
green *(Progresso)*	180	11.0	28.0	3.0	n.a.	830	m.q.

Food and Measure	cal.	prot. (gms)	carbo. (gms)	fat (gms)	chol. (mgs)	sod. (mgs)	fiber (gms)
w/ham (Campbell's Chunky)	210	11.0	30.0	5.0	m.q.	950	m.q.
w/ham (Campbell's Home Cookin')	190	12.0	26.0	4.0	m.q.	1090	m.q.
w/ham (Progresso)	170	11.0	24.0	4.0	m.q.	970	m.q.
pepper steak (Campbell's Chunky)	160	12.0	21.0	3.0	m.q.	920	m.q.
schav (Gold's), 8 oz.	25	2.0	4.0	0	15	1380	m.q.
sirloin burger (Campbell's Chunky)	200	10.0	21.0	8.0	m.q.	1100	m.q.
steak and potato (Campbell's Chunky)	170	12.0	21.0	4.0	m.q.	990	m.q.
tomato:							
garden (Campbell's Home Cookin')	130	1.0	25.0	3.0	n.a.	820	m.q.
w/tomato pieces (Campbell's Low Sodium), 10½ oz.	180	3.0	29.0	5.0	n.a.	40	m.q.
tomato beef w/rotini (Progresso)	170	11.0	19.0	6.0	m.q.	1250	m.q.
tomato w/tortellini (Progresso), 9¼ oz.	140	6.0	17.0	5.0	n.a.	1080	m.q.
tomato w/vegetables (Progresso)	110	4.0	20.0	2.0	n.a.	950	m.q.
tortellini (Progresso)	80	5.0	8.0	3.0	n.a.	1070	m.q.
turkey rice (Hain) . .	100	8.0	9.0	3.0	40	1020	m.q.
turkey vegetable (Campbell's Chunky), 9⅜ oz.	150	9.0	16.0	6.0	m.q.	1060	m.q.
vegetable:							
(Campbell's Chunky)	140	3.0	22.0	4.0	n.a.	970	m.q.
(Progresso)	100	4.0	13.0	3.0	n.a.	1130	m.q.

Food and Measure	cal.	prot. (gms)	carbo. (gms)	fat (gms)	chol. (mgs)	sod. (mgs)	fiber (gms)
Soup, canned, ready-to-serve, vegetable (cont.)							
country (Hormel Micro-Cup Hearty), 1 cont.	89	5.0	13.0	2.0	1	865	m.q.
Mediterranean (Campbell's Chunky)	160	4.0	24.0	5.0	n.a.	1020	m.q.
vegetarian (Hain)	140	4.0	22.0	4.0	0	920	m.q.
vegetarian (Hain No Salt)	150	5.0	23.0	5.0	0	45	m.q.
vegetable beef:							
(Campbell's Chunky Old Fashioned)	160	11.0	18.0	5.0	m.q.	980	m.q.
(Campbell's Home Cookin' Old Fashioned)	140	12.0	15.0	3.0	m.q.	1010	m.q.
vegetable chicken:							
(Hain)	120	8.0	14.0	4.0	15	930	m.q.
(Hain No Salt) . . .	120	9.0	14.0	3.0	30	140	m.q.
vegetable pasta, Italian:							
(Hain)	160	4.0	25.0	5.0	20	910	m.q.
(Hain Low Sodium)	140	4.0	22.0	6.0	20	90	m.q.
Soup, canned, condensed[1], 8 oz., except as noted:							
asparagus, cream of:							
(Campbell's)	90	2.0	11.0	4.0	n.a.	840	m.q.
(Campbell's Creamy Natural)	100	1.0	13.0	5.0	n.a.	640	m.q.
(Campbell's Creamy Natural)[2]	170	5.0	18.0	9.0	m.q.	690	m.q.
barley and mushroom (Rokeach), 1 cup	85	3.4	17.3	.2	n.a.	904	m.q.
bean w/bacon:							
(Campbell's)	120	6.0	22.0	4.0	m.q.	850	m.q.

[1] Prepared according to package directions with water, except as noted.
[2] Prepared with whole milk.

Food and Measure	cal.	prot. (gms)	carbo. (gms)	fat (gms)	chol. (mgs)	sod. (mgs)	fiber (gms)
(Campbell's Special Request)	140	6.0	21.0	4.0	5	470	m.q.
bean, black *(Campbell's)*	110	5.0	17.0	2.0	n.a.	950	m.q.
beef:							
(Campbell's)	80	5.0	10.0	2.0	m.q.	840	m.q.
broth or bouillon *(Campbell's)* . .	16	3.0	1.0	0	n.a.	820	n.a.
consomme w/gelatin *(Campbell's)*	25	4.0	2.0	0	n.a.	760	n.a.
beef noodle:							
(Campbell's)	70	4.0	7.0	3.0	m.q.	830	m.q.
(Campbell's Home-style)	80	6.0	8.0	3.0	m.q.	810	m.q.
beef, sirloin *(Campbell's Golden Classic)*	70	5.0	6.0	3.0	m.q.	870	n.a.
broccoli:							
(Campbell's Creamy Natural)	70	1.0	10.0	3.0	n.a.	670	m.q.
(Campbell's Creamy Natural)[1]	140	5.0	15.0	7.0	m.q.	720	m.q.
cauliflower:							
(Campbell's Creamy Natural)	130	1.0	13.0	9.0	n.a.	800	m.q.
(Campbell's Creamy Natural)[1]	200	5.0	18.0	13.0	m.q.	850	m.q.
celery, cream of *(Campbell's)*	100	1.0	8.0	7.0	n.a.	830	m.q.
cheese:							
cheddar *(Campbell's)* . .	130	3.0	10.0	8.0	n.a.	750	n.a.
nacho *(Campbell's)*	110	3.0	9.0	8.0	n.a.	750	n.a.
nacho *(Campbell's)*[1]	180	7.0	14.0	12.0	m.q.	810	n.a.
chicken alphabet *(Campbell's)*	70	3.0	10.0	2.0	m.q.	810	m.q.

[1] *Prepared with whole milk.*

Food and Measure	cal.	prot. (gms)	carbo. (gms)	fat (gms)	chol. (mgs)	sod. (mgs)	fiber (gms)
Soup, canned, condensed *(cont.)*							
chicken barley							
(Campbell's)	70	3.0	10.0	2.0	m.q.	850	m.q.
chicken broth:							
(Campbell's)	35	1.0	3.0	2.0	m.q.	750	n.a.
and noodles							
(Campbell's) . .	60	2.0	8.0	2.0	m.q.	870	m.q.
and rice							
(Campbell's) . .	50	1.0	8.0	1.0	m.q.	850	m.q.
chicken, cream of:							
(Campbell's)	110	3.0	9.0	7.0	n.a.	810	n.a.
(Campbell's Special							
Request)	110	3.0	9.0	7.0	10	490	n.a.
chicken and dump-							
lings *(Campbell's*							
Chicken 'n Dump-							
lings)	80	4.0	9.0	3.0	m.q.	980	m.q.
chicken gumbo							
(Campbell's)	60	2.0	8.0	2.0	m.q.	900	m.q.
chicken mushroom,							
creamy *(Campbell's)*	120	3.0	9.0	8.0	m.q.	940	m.q.
chicken noodle:							
(Campbell's)	70	3.0	8.0	2.0	m.q.	910	m.q.
(Campbell's Noodle-							
O's)	70	3.0	9.0	2.0	m.q.	820	m.q.
(Campbell's Special							
Request)*	60	3.0	8.0	2.0	15	440	m.q.
chicken w/rice:							
(Campbell's)	60	2.0	7.0	2.0	m.q.	800	m.q.
(Campbell's Special							
Request)*	60	2.0	7.0	3.0	10	480	m.q.
chicken and stars							
(Campbell's)	60	3.0	7.0	2.0	m.q.	870	m.q.
chicken vegetable:							
(Campbell's)	70	3.0	8.0	3.0	m.q.	850	m.q.
w/wild rice							
(Campbell's							
Golden Classic)*	80	3.0	11.0	3.0	m.q.	740	m.q.

Food and Measure	cal.	prot. (gms)	carbo. (gms)	fat (gms)	chol. (mgs)	sod. (mgs)	fiber (gms)
chili beef *(Campbell's)*	140	5.0	19.0	5.0	m.q.	740	m.q.
clam chowder, Manhattan:							
(Campbell's)	70	2.0	11.0	2.0	m.q.	830	m.q.
(Doxsee), 7.5 oz.	70	3.0	11.0	2.0	m.q.	780	m.q.
(Snow's), 7.5 oz.	70	3.0	11.0	2.0	m.q.	780	m.q.
clam chowder, New England:							
(Campbell's)	80	3.0	12.0	3.0	m.q.	870	m.q.
(Campbell's)[1] . . .	150	7.0	17.0	7.0	m.q.	930	m.q.
(Gorton's), 1/4 can[1]	140	7.0	17.0	5.0	15	740	m.q.
(Snow's), 7.5 oz.[1]	140	8.0	13.0	6.0	m.q.	670	m.q.
corn chowder *(Snow's)*, 7.5 oz.[1]	150	5.0	18.0	6.0	n.a.	640	m.q.
fish chowder *(Snow's)*, 7.5 oz.[1]	130	9.0	11.0	6.0	m.q.	620	m.q.
meatball alphabet *(Campbell's)*	100	4.0	11.0	4.0	m.q.	910	m.q.
minestrone *(Campbell's)*	80	3.0	14.0	2.0	n.a.	910	m.q.
mushroom, beefy *(Campbell's)*	60	4.0	5.0	3.0	m.q.	960	m.q.
mushroom, cream of:							
(Campbell's)	100	1.0	9.0	7.0	n.a.	820	m.q.
(Campbell's Special Request)	100	1.0	8.0	7.0	<5	480	m.q.
mushroom, golden *(Campbell's)*	80	2.0	10.0	3.0	n.a.	870	m.q.
noodle:							
and ground beef *(Campbell's)* . .	90	4.0	10.0	4.0	m.q.	830	m.q.
curly, w/chicken *(Campbell's)* . .	80	3.0	9.0	3.0	m.q.	960	m.q.
onion:							
cream of *(Campbell's)* . .	100	2.0	12.0	5.0	n.a.	830	m.q.

[1] *Prepared with whole milk.*

Food and Measure	cal.	prot. (gms)	carbo. (gms)	fat (gms)	chol. (mgs)	sod. (mgs)	fiber (gms)
Soup, canned, condensed, onion *(cont.)*							
cream of							
(Campbell's)[1]	140	4.0	15.0	7.0	m.q.	860	m.q.
French (Campbell's)	60	2.0	9.0	2.0	n.a.	900	m.q.
oyster stew:							
(Campbell's)	80	3.0	5.0	5.0	m.q.	830	m.q.
(Campbell's)[2] . . .	150	6.0	10.0	9.0	m.q.	880	m.q.
pea, green							
(Campbell's)	160	8.0	25.0	3.0	n.a.	830	m.q.
pea, split:							
w/egg barley							
(Rokeach), 1 cup	132	8.2	23.6	.5	n.a.	757	m.q.
w/ham and bacon							
(Campbell's) . .	150	8.0	24.0	4.0	m.q.	800	m.q.
pepper pot							
(Campbell's)	90	5.0	9.0	4.0	n.a.	960	m.q.
potato:							
(Campbell's Creamy							
Natural)	120	1.0	12.0	7.0	n.a.	640	m.q.
(Campbell's Creamy							
Natural)[1]	190	5.0	17.0	11.0	m.q.	690	m.q.
cream of							
(Campbell's) . .	70	1.0	11.0	3.0	n.a.	880	m.q.
cream of							
(Campbell's)[1]	110	3.0	14.0	4.0	m.q.	910	m.q.
Scotch broth							
(Campbell's)	80	4.0	9.0	3.0	n.a.	870	m.q.
seafood chowder							
(Snow's), 7.5 oz.[2]	140	8.0	14.0	6.0	m.q.	670	m.q.
shrimp, cream of:							
(Campbell's)	90	2.0	8.0	6.0	m.q.	800	m.q.
(Campbell's)[2] . . .	160	5.0	13.0	10.0	m.q.	850	m.q.
spinach:							
(Campbell's Creamy							
Natural)	90	1.0	9.0	6.0	n.a.	680	m.q.

[1] *Prepared with 4 oz. soup, 2 oz. water, and 2 oz. whole milk.*
[2] *Prepared with whole milk.*

Food and Measure	cal.	prot. (gms)	carbo. (gms)	fat (gms)	chol. (mgs)	sod. (mgs)	fiber (gms)
(Campbell's Creamy Natural)[1]	160	5.0	14.0	10.0	m.q.	730	m.q.
tomato:							
(Campbell's)	90	1.0	17.0	2.0	n.a.	670	m.q.
(Campbell's)[2] . . .	160	5.0	22.0	6.0	m.q.	730	m.q.
(Campbell's Special Request)	90	1.0	17.0	2.0	0	430	m.q.
bisque (Campbell's)	120	1.0	23.0	3.0	n.a.	790	m.q.
zesty (Campbell's)	90	2.0	19.0	1.0	n.a.	770	m.q.
tomato, cream of:							
(Campbell's Home-style)	110	1.0	20.0	3.0	n.a.	730	m.q.
(Campbell's Home-style)[2]	180	5.0	25.0	7.0	m.q.	780	m.q.
tomato rice (Campbell's Old Fashioned)	110	1.0	22.0	2.0	n.a.	730	m.q.
tortellini and vegetable (Campbell's Golden Classic)	80	2.0	12.0	3.0	n.a.	870	m.q.
turkey noodle (Campbell's)	70	3.0	8.0	3.0	m.q.	870	m.q.
turkey vegetable (Campbell's)	70	2.0	8.0	3.0	m.q.	710	m.q.
vegetable:							
(Campbell's)	80	3.0	14.0	2.0	n.a.	800	m.q.
(Campbell's Home-style)	60	2.0	10.0	2.0	n.a.	880	m.q.
(Campbell's Old Fashioned) . . .	60	2.0	9.0	2.0	n.a.	890	m.q.
w/beef stock (Campbell's Special Request) . .	90	3.0	14.0	2.0	<5	500	m.q.
vegetable beef:							
(Campbell's)	70	4.0	10.0	2.0	m.q.	750	m.q.

[1] Prepared with 4 oz. soup, 2 oz. water, and 2 oz. whole milk.
[2] Prepared with whole milk.

Food and Measure	cal.	prot. (gms)	carbo. (gms)	fat (gms)	chol. (mgs)	sod. (mgs)	fiber (gms)
Soup, canned, condensed, vegetable beef (cont.)							
(Campbell's Special Request)	70	4.0	10.0	2.0	10	470	m.q.
vegetable, vegetarian (Campbell's)	80	2.0	14.0	2.0	0	780	m.q.
won ton (Campbell's)	45	3.0	5.0	1.0	n.a.	870	m.q.
Soup, canned, semicondensed[1], 11 oz.:							
bean w/ham (Campbell's Old Fashioned Soup-For-One)	220	8.0	30.0	7.0	m.q.	1340	m.q.
clam chowder, New England (Campbell's Soup-For-One)[2]	190	9.0	23.0	7.0	m.q.	1410	m.q.
chicken, golden, and noodles (Campbell's Soup-For-One) . .	120	6.0	14.0	4.0	m.q.	1450	m.q.
mushroom, savory cream of (Campbell's Soup-For-One)	180	3.0	14.0	13.0	n.a.	1500	m.q.
tomato royale (Campbell's Soup-For-One)	180	3.0	35.0	3.0	n.a.	1290	m.q.
vegetable (Campbell's Old World Soup-For-One)	130	4.0	18.0	4.0	n.a.	1470	m.q.
Soup, frozen, 6 fl. oz., except as noted:							
asparagus, cream of:							
(Kettle Ready) . . .	62	.8	5.1	4.3	n.a.	406	m.q.
(Myers), 9.75 oz.	152	11.0	10.0	8.0	n.a.	992	m.q.

[1] Prepared according to package directions, with water, except as noted.
[2] Prepared with whole milk.

Food and Measure	cal.	prot. (gms)	carbo. (gms)	fat (gms)	chol. (mgs)	sod. (mgs)	fiber (gms)
bean, savory, w/ham *(Kettle Ready)* . . .	113	6.8	20.2	3.6	m.q.	459	m.q.
beef, hearty, vegetable *(Kettle Ready)*	85	4.2	10.7	3.0	m.q.	448	m.q.
black bean, w/ham *(Kettle Ready)* . . .	154	8.1	23.0	6.2	m.q.	613	m.q.
broccoli, cream of:							
(Kettle Ready) . . .	94	.9	6.4	7.2	n.a.	417	m.q.
(Myers), 9.75 oz.	174	8.0	11.0	11.0	n.a.	905	m.q.
cauliflower, cream of							
(Kettle Ready) . . .	93	2.3	5.5	7.0	n.a.	445	m.q.
cheddar cheese:							
cream of *(Kettle Ready)*	158	4.1	7.3	12.5	n.a.	616	.1 c
and broccoli, cream of *(Kettle Ready)*	137	4.0	4.7	11.3	n.a.	533	m.q.
cheese and broccoli *(Myers)*, 9.75 oz.	325	12.0	19.0	23.0	n.a.	1257	m.q.
chicken:							
cream of *(Kettle Ready)*	98	5.7	5.0	6.2	m.q.	668	m.q.
gumbo *(Kettle Ready)*	94	3.5	12.1	3.5	m.q.	473	m.q.
noodle *(Kettle Ready)*	94	5.0	12.0	3.0	m.q.	569	m.q.
noodle *(Myers)*, 9.75 oz.	87	8.0	5.0	5.0	m.q.	1046	m.q.
chili:							
traditional *(Kettle Ready)*	161	11.7	14.0	6.5	n.a.	454	m.q.
jalapeño *(Kettle Ready)*	173	11.0	14.7	8.0	n.a.	531	m.q.
clam chowder:							
Boston *(Kettle Ready)*	131	3.5	13.0	7.3	m.q.	417	m.q.
Manhattan *(Kettle Ready)*	69	3.6	8.0	2.6	m.q.	549	m.q.

Food and Measure	cal.	prot. (gms)	carbo. (gms)	fat (gms)	chol. (mgs)	sod. (mgs)	fiber (gms)
Soup, frozen, clam chowder *(cont.)*							
New England *(Kettle Ready)*	116	3.0	11.4	6.5	m.q.	373	m.q.
New England *(Myers)*, 9.75 oz. . .	152	7.0	21.0	5.0	m.q.	910	m.q.
New England *(Stouffer's)*, 8 oz.	180	8.0	16.0	9.0	m.q.	790	m.q.
corn and broccoli chowder *(Kettle Ready)*	102	1.4	13.0	5.0	n.a.	323	m.q.
minestrone, hearty *(Kettle Ready)* . . .	104	3.3	15.2	4.4	n.a.	577	m.q.
mushroom, cream of *(Kettle Ready)* . . .	85	.6	6.2	6.4	n.a.	371	m.q.
onion, French *(Kettle Ready)*	42	.7	5.0	2.2	n.a.	562	m.q.
pea:							
split, w/ham *(Kettle Ready)*	155	11.1	25.3	4.4	m.q.	483	m.q.
tortellini, in tomato *(Kettle Ready)*	122	3.5	15.0	5.4	n.a.	447	m.q.
seafood bisque *(Myers)*, 9.75 oz. . . .	163	9.0	13.0	8.0	m.q.	1393	m.q.
spinach, cream of:							
(Myers), 9.75 oz.	174	9.0	10.0	11.0	n.a.	905	m.q.
(Stouffer's), 8 oz.	210	7.0	12.0	15.0	n.a.	1020	m.q.
vegetable, garden *(Kettle Ready)* . . .	85	2.6	12.3	3.0	n.a.	296	m.q.
vegetable beef *(Myers)*, 9.75 oz. . . .	120	9.0	8.0	6.0	m.q.	1030	m.q.
Soup base:							
beef *(Tone's)*, 1 tsp.	11	.2	1.2	.6	n.a.	1	n.a.

Food and Measure	cal.	prot. (gms)	carbo. (gms)	fat (gms)	chol. (mgs)	sod. (mgs)	fiber (gms)
Soup combinations, 1 pkg.:							
broccoli, cream of, and ham and cheese croissant sandwich *(Campbell's Souper-Combo)*	450	14.0	40.0	26.0	m.q.	1420	m.q.
clam chowder, New England, and fish sandwich *(Campbell's Souper-Combo)*	460	19.0	53.0	19.0	m.q.	1260	m.q.
chicken noodleO's and hot dog on bun *(Campbell's Souper-Combo)*	310	15.0	29.0	15.0	m.q.	1360	m.q.
chicken noodle soup and grilled ham and cheese sandwich *(Campbell's Souper-Combo)*	470	20.0	50.0	21.0	m.q.	1950	m.q.
chicken rice soup and vegetable egg rolls *(Campbell's Souper-Combo)*	320	9.0	42.0	12.0	m.q.	1580	m.q.
chicken and stars soup and chicken nuggets *(Campbell's Souper-Combo)* . .	320	21.0	25.0	15.0	m.q.	1220	m.q.
tomato soup and grilled cheese sandwich *(Campbell's Souper-Combo)* . .	400	9.0	42.0	22.0	m.q.	1590	m.q.
vegetable soup and cheeseburger *(Campbell's Souper-Combo)*	410	18.0	34.0	22.0	m.q.	1420	m.q.

Food and Measure	cal.	prot. (gms)	carbo. (gms)	fat (gms)	chol. (mgs)	sod. (mgs)	fiber (gms)
Soup mix[1], 6 fl. oz., except as noted:							
beef or beef flavor:							
(Lipton Cup-A-Soup)	44	1.7	7.6	.7	n.a.	746	n.a.
hearty, and noodles (Lipton), 7 fl. oz.	107	3.5	20.2	1.4	n.a.	698	.2 c
broccoli:							
creamy (Lipton Cup-A-Soup)	62	1.1	9.1	2.4	n.a.	610	.3 c
creamy, and cheese (Lipton Cup-A-Soup)	70	1.7	9.8	3.4	n.a.	595	m.q.
golden (Lipton Cup-A-Soup Lite) . .	42	1.3	6.3	1.2	1	427	m.q.
cheddar, creamy, w/ noodles (Fantastic Noodles), 7 oz. . .	178	7.0	21.0	8.0	n.a.	578	m.q.
cheese:							
(Hain Savory Soup & Sauce Mix) . .	250	6.0	20.0	16.0	n.a.	890	n.a.
and broccoli (Hain Soup & Recipe Mix)	310	7.0	19.0	22.0	n.a.	980	m.q.
chicken or chicken flavor:							
broth (Lipton Cup-A-Soup)	20	.4	3.3	.6	1	605	n.a.
cream of (Lipton Cup-A-Soup) . .	84	1.4	9.7	4.4	n.a.	757	n.a.
creamy, w/vegetables (Lipton Cup-A-Soup)	93	1.7	14.4	3.1	n.a.	708	m.q.
creamy, w/white meat (Campbell's Cup 2 Minute Soup)	120	4.0	15.0	5.0	m.q.	850	n.a.

[1] Prepared according to package directions.

Food and Measure	cal.	prot. (gms)	carbo. (gms)	fat (gms)	chol. (mgs)	sod. (mgs)	fiber (gms)
with sweet corn *(Lipton Cup-A-Soup Country Style)*	133	3.3	17.5	5.5	n.a.	704	.2 c
Florentine *(Lipton Cup-A-Soup Lite)*	42	10.0	7.6	.5	6	481	n.a.
hearty *(Lipton Cup-A-Soup Country Style)*	69	3.8	11.1	1.1	n.a.	688	n.a.
hearty, supreme *(Lipton Cup-A-Soup)*	107	2.0	11.4	5.9	n.a.	848	n.a.
lemon *(Lipton Cup-A-Soup Lite)* . .	48	2.0	9.1	.4	4	419	n.a.
supreme *(Lipton Cup-A-Soup Country Style)*	107	1.7	11.8	5.9	n.a.	757	m.q.
chicken noodle:							
(Campbell's Quality Soup & Recipe), 1 cup	100	5.0	16.0	2.0	n.a.	810	m.q.
(Lipton), 1 cup . .	81	4.3	12.0	1.8	n.a.	792	m.q.
(Lipton Cup-A-Soup)	48	3.0	6.6	1.1	n.a.	635	m.q.
(Mrs. Grass Chickeny Rich), 1/4 pkg.	70	2.0	10.0	2.0	n.a.	900	m.q.
hearty *(Lipton)*, 1 cup	83	4.4	13.3	1.3	n.a.	753	m.q.
hearty *(Lipton Lots-A-Noodles Cup-A-Soup)*, 7 fl. oz.	110	4.0	20.0	1.6	n.a.	587	m.q.
hearty, creamy *(Lipton Lots-A-Noodles Cup-A-Soup)*, 7 fl. oz.	179	5.1	21.4	8.2	n.a.	639	m.q.
w/meat *(Lipton Cup-A-Soup)* . .	46	2.6	6.6	1.0	m.q.	660	m.q.

Food and Measure	cal.	prot. (gms)	carbo. (gms)	fat (gms)	chol. (mgs)	sod. (mgs)	fiber (gms)
Soup mix, chicken noodle *(cont.)*							
w/white meat (Campbell's Cup 2 Minute Soup)	90	6.0	11.0	2.0	m.q.	720	m.q.
w/white meat, diced (Lipton), 1 cup	81	4.3	12.1	1.8	m.q.	795	m.q.
w/vegetables, hearty (Lipton), 1 cup	75	3.0	12.3	1.6	n.a.	687	m.q.
chicken rice:							
(Lipton Cup-A-Soup)	47	2.2	7.7	.8	n.a.	667	m.q.
w/white meat (Campbell's Quality Soup & Recipe), 1 cup . . .	90	3.0	16.0	2.0	m.q.	800	m.q.
chicken vegetable (Campbell's Cup 2 Minute Soup)	90	3.0	14.0	2.0	n.a.	770	m.q.
(Lipton Cup-A-Soup)	47	2.5	7.8	.6	8	566	.2 c
lentil (Hain Savory Soup Mix)	130	4.0	20.0	2.0	n.a.	810	m.q.
minestrone:							
(Hain Savory Soup Mix)	110	4.0	20.0	1.0	n.a.	870	m.q.
(Manischewitz) . .	50	3.0	9.0	<1.0	n.a.	160	m.q
mushroom:							
(Hain Savory Soup & Recipe Mix)	210	4.0	11.0	15.0	n.a.	710	m.q.
beef flavor (Lipton), 1 cup	38	1.7	6.7	.5	n.a.	763	m.q.
cream of (Lipton Cup-A-Soup) . .	71	1.3	9.1	3.2	n.a.	756	m.q.
noodle:							
(Campbell's Quality Soup & Recipe), 1 cup	110	4.0	20.0	2.0	n.a.	760	m.q.
(Lipton Cup-A-Soup Ring Noodle) . .	47	2.7	7.6	.7	n.a.	650	m.q.

Food and Measure	cal.	prot. (gms)	carbo. (gms)	fat (gms)	chol. (mgs)	sod. (mgs)	fiber (gms)
beef (Cup O'Noodles), 1 cup . . .	290	8.0	33.0	14.0	n.a.	1490	m.q.
beef flavor (Oodles of Noodles/Top Ramen), 1 cup	390	9.0	49.0	18.0	n.a.	1810	m.q.
beefy, hearty, w/ vegetables (Lipton), 1 cup . . .	85	2.5	16.7	.9	n.a.	810	m.q.
chicken (Cup O'Noodles), 1 cup	300	9.0	32.0	16.0	n.a.	1790	m.q.
chicken flavor (Oodles of Noodles/ Top Ramen), 1 cup	400	10.0	48.0	18.0	n.a.	1910	m.q.
chicken, country (Cup O'Noodles Hearty), 1 cup	300	8.0	35.0	14.0	n.a.	1210	m.q.
w/chicken broth (Campbell's Cup 2 Minute Soup)	100	4.0	17.0	2.0	n.a.	700	m.q.
w/chicken broth (Lipton Giggle Noodle), 1 cup	77	2.9	11.4	2.1	n.a.	784	m.q.
w/chicken broth (Lipton Ring-O-Noodle), 1 cup	71	2.7	10.4	2.0	n.a.	784	m.q.
hearty, w/vegetables (Lipton), 1 cup	75	3.0	12.3	1.6	n.a.	687	m.q.
Oriental (Oodles of Noodles/Top Ramen), 1 cup	390	10.0	49.0	18.0	n.a.	1660	m.q.
pork (Oodles of Noodles/Top Ramen), 1 cup	390	10.0	51.0	20.0	n.a.	2060	m.q.
seafood, savory (Cup O'Noodles Hearty), 1 cup	300	7.0	34.0	15.0	n.a.	1170	m.q.

Food and Measure	cal.	prot. (gms)	carbo. (gms)	fat (gms)	chol. (mgs)	sod. (mgs)	fiber (gms)
Soup mix, noodle *(cont.)*							
shrimp *(Cup O'Noodles)*, 1 cup	300	10.0	32.0	14.0	n.a.	1480	m.q.
vegetable, hearty, old fashioned *(Cup O'Noodles)*, 1 cup	290	6.0	34.0	15.0	n.a.	1250	m.q.
vegetable beef *(Cup O'Noodles Hearty)*, 1 cup	290	8.0	36.0	15.0	n.a.	1150	m.q.
onion:							
(Campbell's Quality Soup & Recipe)*, 1 cup	50	1.0	10.0	0	n.a.	730	m.q.
(Hain Savory Soup, Dip & Recipe Mix)	50	2.0	6.0	2.0	n.a.	900	m.q.
(Lipton), 1 cup . .	20	.7	4.3	.2	n.a.	632	m.q.
(Lipton Cup-A-Soup)	27	.9	4.7	.5	n.a.	665	.1 c
(Mrs. Grass Soup & Dip Mix)*, 1/4 pkg.	35	1.0	6.0	<1.0	0	1070	m.q.
beefy *(Lipton)*, 1 cup	29	.8	4.2	1.0	n.a.	803	m.q.
creamy *(Lipton Cup-A-Soup)*	70	1.2	9.5	3.2	n.a.	678	.2 c
golden, w/chicken broth *(Lipton)*, 1 cup	62	1.1	11.0	1.5	n.a.	716	m.q.
mushroom *(Campbell's* Quality Soup & Recipe)*, 1 cup . . .	50	1.0	9.0	1.0	n.a.	740	m.q.
mushroom *(Lipton)*, 1 cup	41	1.4	6.8	.9	n.a.	684	m.q.
Oriental *(Lipton Cup-A-Soup Lite)*	45	1.5	5.8	1.7	3	457	m.q.
oxtail, 1 cup	71	2.8	9.0	2.6	3	1210	.1 c
pea, green *(Lipton Cup-A-Soup)* . . .	113	4.2	14.4	4.2	n.a.	553	.2 c

Food and Measure	cal.	prot. (gms)	carbo. (gms)	fat (gms)	chol. (mgs)	sod. (mgs)	fiber (gms)
pea, split:							
(Hain Savory Soup Mix)	310	4.0	16.0	10.0	n.a.	940	m.q.
(Manischewitz) . .	45	3.0	9.0	<1.0	0	320	m.q.
pea, Virginia *(Lipton Cup-A-Soup* Country Style)*	148	5.3	17.3	6.4	n.a.	828	.8 c
potato leek *(Hain Savory Soup Mix)* . .	260	4.0	20.0	18.0	n.a.	690	m.q.
seafood chowder *(Golden Dipt),* 1/4 pkg. dry	70	2.0	12.0	2.0	2	730	m.q.
shrimp bisque *(Golden Dipt),* 1/4 pkg. dry	30	1.0	5.0	1.0	2	570	m.q.
tomato:							
(Hain Savory Soup & Recipe Mix)	220	3.0	19.0	14.0	n.a.	770	m.q.
(Lipton Cup-A-Soup)	103	2.5	21.2	.9	n.a.	524	m.q.
creamy, and herb *(Lipton Cup-A-Soup* Lite)*	66	1.6	14.1	.3	2	305	m.q.
vegetable:							
(Hain Savory Soup Mix)	80	2.0	13.0	1.0	n.a.	730	m.q.
(Lipton), 1 cup . .	39	1.6	6.9	.5	n.a.	640	.4 c
(Manischewitz) . .	50	3.0	9.0	<1.0	0	65	m.q.
country *(Lipton),* 1 cup	80	2.6	15.7	.7	n.a.	803	m.q.
curry, w/noodles *(Fantastic Noo- dles),* 7 oz.	150	5.0	18.0	7.0	n.a.	472	m.q.
garden *(Lipton Lots- A-Noodles Cup-A- Soup),* 7 fl. oz.	123	4.3	23.1	1.5	n.a.	720	m.q.
harvest *(Lipton Cup- A-Soup* Country Style)*	91	1.7	18.8	1.2	n.a.	459	.5 c

Food and Measure	cal.	prot. (gms)	carbo. (gms)	fat (gms)	chol. (mgs)	sod. (mgs)	fiber (gms)
Soup mix, vegetable *(cont.)*							
miso, w/noodles *(Fantastic Noodles)*, 7 oz.	152	5.0	19.0	7.0	n.a.	434	m.q.
noodle w/meatballs *(Lipton Cup-A-Soup Country Style)*	95	4.9	15.4	1.6	n.a.	764	.5 c
spring *(Lipton Cup-A-Soup)*	33	1.1	5.9	.8	6	746	.3 c
tomato, w/noodles *(Fantastic Noodles)*, 7 oz.	158	5.0	20.0	7.0	n.a.	434	m.q.
vegetable beef, w/sirloin *(Campbell's Cup 2 Minute Soup)*	110	3.0	19.0	2.0	n.a.	900	m.q.
Sour cream, see "Cream, sour"							
Sour cream sauce mix:							
(McCormick/Schilling), 1 pkg.	176	4.8	14.9	6.1	n.a.	1088	n.a.
Sour cream and onion snack sticks:							
(Flavor Tree), ¼ cup	127	3.0	12.5	8.3	n.a.	360	.1 c
Soursop:							
1 medium, 2.1 lb. . .	416	6.3	105.3	1.9	0	87	6.9 c
½ cup	75	1.1	18.9	.3	0	16	1.2 c
Souse loaf:							
(Kahn's), 1 slice . . .	90	4.0	1.0	7.0	m.q.	190	0
Soy flour, stirred:							
full-fat:							
raw, 1 cup	371	29.4	29.9	17.6	0	11	4.0 c
roasted, 1 cup . .	375	29.6	28.6	18.6	0	11	1.9 c
defatted, 1 cup . . .	329	47.0	38.4	1.2	0	20	4.3 c
lowfat, 1 cup	287	40.9	33.4	2.4	0	16	3.7 c

Food and Measure	cal.	prot. (gms)	carbo. (gms)	fat (gms)	chol. (mgs)	sod. (mgs)	fiber (gms)
Soy meal, defatted:							
raw, 1 cup	414	54.8	49.0	2.9	0	3	14.0 d
Soy milk, 8 fl. oz.:							
fluid	79	6.6	4.3	4.6	0	30	2.6 d
powder[1] *(Soyamel)*	130	7.0	10.0	7.0	0	210	n.a.
Soy protein, concentrate, 1 oz.:							
w/alcohol	94	16.5	8.8	.1	0	1	1.1 c
acid/water wash . . .	94	16.5	8.8	.1	0	255	1.1 c
Soy sauce:							
(Kikkoman), 1 tbsp.	10	n.a.	.9	tr.	tr.	892	0
(Kikkoman Lite), 1 tbsp.	11	n.a.	1.3	tr.	tr.	600	0
(La Choy), 1 tsp. . .	<1	.2	.3	0	0	429	0
(La Choy Lite), 1 tsp.	<1	.2	.3	0	0	220	0
tamari, 1 tbsp.	11	1.9	1.0	<.1	0	1005	0
shoyu, 1 tbsp.	9	.9	1.5	tr.	0	1029	0
Soybean, 1/2 cup:							
green:							
raw, shelled	188	16.6	14.1	8.7	0	n.a.	2.6 c
boiled, drained . .	127	11.1	10.0	5.8	0	n.a.	1.7 c
dried:							
raw	387	33.9	28.1	18.5	0	2	11.6 d
boiled	149	14.3	8.5	7.7	0	1	1.8 c
dry-roasted	387	34.0	28.1	18.6	0	2	4.6 c
roasted	405	30.3	28.9	21.8	0	140	4.0 c
Soybean, fermented, see "Miso" and "Natto"							
Soybean, sprouted:							
raw, 1 lb.	580	59.4	50.7	30.4	0	62	10.4 c
raw, 1/2 cup	45	4.6	3.9	2.3	0	5	.8 c
steamed, 1/2 cup . .	38	4.0	3.1	2.1	0	5	.9 c
Soybean cake or curd, see "Tofu"							

[1] *Prepared according to package directions.*

Food and Measure	cal.	prot. (gms)	carbo. (gms)	fat (gms)	chol. (mgs)	sod. (mgs)	fiber (gms)
Soybean kernels, roasted and toasted:							
1 oz. or 95 kernels	129	10.5	8.7	6.8	0	1	1.0 c
whole, 1 cup	490	40.0	33.0	25.9	0	4	3.8 c
salted, whole, 1 cup	490	40.0	33.0	25.9	0	176	3.8 c
Spaghetti, see "Pasta"							
Spaghetti dinner, frozen:							
w/meat sauce (Kid Cuisine), 9.25 oz.	310	9.0	43.0	12.0	35	690	m.q.
and meatballs:							
(Banquet), 10 oz.	290	11.0	44.0	10.0	30	580	m.q.
(Morton), 10 oz. . . .	200	6.0	39.0	3.0	10	1090	m.q.
(Swanson), 12 1/2 oz.	370	12.0	45.0	16.0	m.q.	1010	m.q.
Spaghetti dishes, mix[1]:							
(Kraft American Style Dinner), 1 cup . . .	300	10.0	50.0	7.0	0	630	m.q.
w/meat sauce (Kraft Dinner), 1 cup . . .	360	12.0	47.0	14.0	15	880	m.q.
tangy (Kraft Italian Style Dinner), 1 cup	310	11.0	49.0	8.0	5	670	m.q.
Spaghetti entree, canned, 7.5 oz., except as noted:							
and beef:							
(Chef Boyardee)	240	7.0	30.0	9.0	m.q.	1120	m.q.
(Chef Boyardee Beef-O-Getti) . .	220	7.0	27.0	9.0	m.q.	1240	m.q.
in tomato sauce w/ cheese (Franco-American), 7 3/8 oz.	190	5.0	36.0	2.0	n.a.	810	m.q.

[1] Prepared according to package directions, without added salt.

Food and Measure	cal.	prot. (gms)	carbo. (gms)	fat (gms)	chol. (mgs)	sod. (mgs)	fiber (gms)
in tomato and cheese sauce (*Franco-American* Spaghetti-O's)	170	4.0	34.0	2.0	n.a.	920	m.q.
w/franks:							
(*Franco-American* SpaghettiO's), 7³/₈ oz.	220	7.0	26.0	9.0	m.q.	980	m.q.
(*Van Camp's Skettee Weenee*), 1 cup	243	9.4	34.7	7.4	m.q.	1128	.5 c
and meatballs:							
(*Chef Boyardee*), 8.5 oz.	250	8.0	30.0	11.0	m.q.	1210	m.q.
in sauce (*Buitoni*)	190	9.0	21.0	8.0	20	940	m.q.
w/meatballs:							
(*Chef Boyardee*)	230	8.0	30.0	9.0	m.q.	970	m.q.
(*Franco-American*), 7³/₈ oz.	220	9.0	28.0	8.0	m.q.	850	m.q.
(*Franco-American* SpaghettiO's), 7³/₈ oz.	210	9.0	25.0	8.0	m.q.	950	m.q.
Spaghetti entree, freeze-dried:							
w/meat and sauce (*Mountain House*), 1 cup	260	12.0	41.0	5.0	m.q.	m.q.	m.q.
Spaghetti entree, frozen:							
w/beef:							
(*Dining Lite*), 9 oz.	220	12.0	25.0	8.0	20	440	m.q.
and mushroom sauce (*Lean Cuisine*), 11¹/₂ oz.	280	16.0	38.0	7.0	25	940	m.q.
w/Italian sausage (*The Budget Gourmet*), 10 oz.	400	17.0	3.0	19.0	48	770	m.q.

Food and Measure	cal.	prot. (gms)	carbo. (gms)	fat (gms)	chol. (mgs)	sod. (mgs)	fiber (gms)
Spaghetti entree, frozen *(cont.)*							
w/meat sauce:							
(Banquet Casserole), 8 oz. . . .	270	14.0	35.0	8.0	m.q.	1250	m.q.
(Freezer Queen Single Serve), 10 oz.	350	14.0	47.0	12.0	m.q.	610	m.q.
(Healthy Choice), 10 oz.	310	16.0	48.0	6.0	15	440	m.q.
(Stouffer's), 12⁷/8 oz.	370	18.0	49.0	11.0	m.q.	1510	m.q.
(Weight Watchers), 10.5 oz.	280	19.0	34.0	7.0	35	910	m.q.
w/meatballs:							
(Stouffer's), 12⁵/8 oz.	380	20.0	42.0	15.0	m.q.	1510	m.q.
Italian style *(Swanson* Homestyle Recipe), 13 oz.	460	16.0	56.0	19.0	m.q.	1010	m.q.
Spaghetti sauce, see "Pasta sauce"							
Spaghetti squash:							
baked or boiled, drained, 1/2 cup . .	23	.5	5.0	.2	0	14	1.1 c
Spaghettini entree:							
(Hormel Top Shelf), 1 serving	240	13.0	35.0	5.0	5	1020	m.q.
Spare ribs, see "Pork"							
Spice loaf, 1 slice:							
(Kahn's Family Pack)	70	3.0	1.0	6.0	m.q.	180	0
beef *(Kahn's* Family Pack)	60	2.0	1.0	5.0	m.q.	200	0
Spinach:							
fresh, 1/2 cup:							
raw, chopped . . .	6	.8	1.0	.1	0	22	.7 d
boiled, drained . .	21	2.7	3.4	.2	0	63	2.0 d

Food and Measure	cal.	prot. (gms)	carbo. (gms)	fat (gms)	chol. (mgs)	sod. (mgs)	fiber (gms)
canned, 1/2 cup:							
(Allens Low Sodium)	28	2.0	3.0	<1.0	0	35	m.q.
(S&W Premium Northwest) . . .	25	2.0	3.0	0	0	395	m.q.
(Stokley)	30	2.0	3.0	0	0	420	m.q.
whole (Del Monte No Salt)	25	2.0	4.0	0	0	35	m.q.
whole or chopped (Del Monte) . . .	25	2.0	4.0	0	0	355	m.q.
sliced or chopped, curly (Allens) . .	28	2.0	3.0	<1.0	0	330	m.q.
frozen, 3.3 oz., except as noted:							
(Birds Eye Portion Pack), 3.2 oz. . .	20	3.0	3.0	0	0	70	2.0 d
(Green Giant Polybag), 1/2 cup	25	3.0	6.0	0	0	100	4.6 d
(Green Giant Harvest Fresh), 1/2 cup	25	3.0	4.0	0	0	250	2.8 d
whole (Birds Eye)	20	3.0	4.0	0	0	90	3.0 d
whole (Frosty Acres)	20	3.0	4.0	0	0	75	1.0 c
chopped (Birds Eye)	20	3.0	3.0	0	0	90	3.0 d
creamed (Birds Eye Combinations), 3 oz.	60	2.0	5.0	4.0	0	310	1.0 d
creamed (Green Giant), 1/2 cup . . .	60	4.0	9.0	2.0	2	510	2.5 d
creamed (Stouffer's), 4.5 oz. . .	170	4.0	7.0	14.0	n.a.	380	m.q.
au gratin (The Budget Gourmet), 6 oz.	120	5.0	14.0	5.0	40	410	m.q.
in butter sauce (Green Giant), 1/2 cup	40	3.0	6.0	2.0	5	380	3.5 d

Food and Measure	cal.	prot. (gms)	carbo. (gms)	fat (gms)	chol. (mgs)	sod. (mgs)	fiber (gms)
Spinach, New Zealand, see "New Zealand spinach"							
Spinach souffle, frozen:							
(Stouffer's), 4 oz. . .	140	6.0	8.0	9.0	n.a.	500	m.q.
Spiny lobster, meat only, raw:							
1 lb.	506	93.4	11.0	6.9	318	803	0
1 oz.	32	5.8	.7	.4	20	50	0
Split peas:							
boiled, 1/2 cup	116	8.2	20.7	.4	0	2	2.3 d
Spot, meat only:							
raw, 1 lb.	559	84.0	0	22.2	m.q.	130	0
raw, 1 oz.	35	5.2	0	1.4	m.q.	8	0
Spring onion, see "Onion, green"							
Sprouts, see specific bean listings							
Squab, fresh, raw:							
meat w/skin, 1 oz. . .	83	5.2	0	6.7	m.q.	m.q.	0
meat only, breast, 1 oz.	38	6.2	0	1.3	26	m.q.	0
Squash:							
fresh, see specific listings							
frozen (see also specific listings):							
(Frosty Acres), 3.3 oz.	18	1.0	4.0	0		1	1.0 c
winter (Birds Eye), 4 oz.	45	1.0	11.0	0	0	0	2.0 d
Squid, meat only:							
raw, 1 lb.	416	70.7	14.0	6.3	1059	199	0
raw, 1 oz.	26	4.4	.9	.4	66	12	0
Star fruit, see "Carambola"							
Steak sauce:							

Food and Measure	cal.	prot. (gms)	carbo. (gms)	fat (gms)	chol. (mgs)	sod. (mgs)	fiber (gms)
(A.1.), 1 tbsp.	12	0	3.0	0	0	280	n.a.
(French's), 1 tbsp. . .	25	0	6.0	0	0	150	n.a.
(Heinz 57), 1 tbsp.	15	0	3.0	0	0	270	n.a.
(Lea & Perrins), 1 oz.	40	<1.0	10.0	<1.0	0	220	n.a.
(Steak Supreme), 1 tbsp.	20	0	5.0	0	0	25	n.a.
Steak seasoning:							
blackened *(Tone's)*, 1 tsp.	9	.4	1.6	.3	0	486	n.a.
broiled *(McCormick/ Schilling* Spice Blends)*, 1/4 tsp. . . .	1	.1	.1	n.a.	0	273	n.a.
Stir-fry sauce:							
(Kikkoman), 1 tsp. . . .	6	.3	2.3	tr.	0	120	tr.d
(Lawry's), 1/4 cup . .	120	1.9	19.6	3.8	n.a.	1128	.2 c
Stomach, pork:							
raw, 1 oz.	44	4.7	0	2.7	55	15	0
Strawberry:							
fresh:							
1 pint	97	2.0	22.5	1.2	0	4	8.3 d
1/2 cup	23	.5	5.2	.3	0	1	1.9 d
canned, in heavy syrup, 1/2 cup . . .	117	.7	29.9	.3	0	5	m.q.
freeze-dried *(Mountain House)*, 1/4 cup . .	45	1.0	12.0	0	0	<1	m.q.
frozen in syrup:							
whole *(Birds Eye Lite)*, 4 oz. . . .	80	1.0	20.0	0	0	0	2.0 d
halves *(Birds Eye Quick Thaw)*, 5 oz.	120	1.0	30.0	0	0	0	2.0 d
halves *(Birds Eye Lite Quick Thaw)*, 5 oz.	90	1.0	22.0	0	0	5	2.0 d

Food and Measure	cal.	prot. (gms)	carbo. (gms)	fat (gms)	chol. (mgs)	sod. (mgs)	fiber (gms)
Strawberry flavor drink mix[1], 8 fl. oz.:							
(Kool-Aid)	100	0	25.0	0	0	25	(0)
(Kool-Aid Presweetened) . .	80	0	20.0	0	0	25	(0)
wild (Wyler's Crystals)	85	0	20.7	.3	0	43	(0)
Strawberry flavor milk drink:							
canned:							
(Frostee), 1 cup . .	180	2.0	27.0	7.0	n.a.	150	(0)
(Sego Very Strawberry), 10 fl. oz.	225	11.0	34.0	5.0	n.a.	360	(0)
mix, powder:							
1 oz.	110	<.1	28.1	.1	0	11	<.1 c
(Carnation Instant Breakfast), 1 pkt.	130	6.0	25.0	.2	3	210	.1 d
(Nestlé Quik), 3/4 oz. or 2 1/2 heaping tsp.	80	0	21.0	0	0	n.a.	m.q.
(Pillsbury Instant Breakfast), 1 pkt.	130	5.0	27.0	0	0	180	m.q.
Strawberry fruit roll, see "Fruit snack"							
Strawberry juice drink:							
(Tang Fruit Box), 8.45 fl. oz.	120	0	32.0	0	0	10	(0)
Strawberry nectar:							
(Libby's), 6 fl. oz. . .	110	0	27.0	0	0	0	m.q.
Strawberry syrup:							
(S&W), 1 tsp.[2]	4	0	1.0	0	0	25	n.a.
Strawberry topping:							
(Kraft), 1 tbsp.	50	0	13.0	0	0	0	n.a.
(Smucker's), 2 tbsp.	120	0	30.0	0	0	0	n.a.

[1] Prepared according to package directions.

[2] Saccharin sweetened.

Food and Measure	cal.	prot. (gms)	carbo. (gms)	fat (gms)	chol. (mgs)	sod. (mgs)	fiber (gms)
String bean, see "Green bean"							
Stroganoff entree, vegetarian, mix:							
creamy *(Tofu Classics),* 1/2 cup[1] . . .	127	7.0	11.0	7.0	m.q.	310	m.q.
Stroganoff sauce mix:							
(Lawry's), 1 pkg. . . .	123	4.5	25.5	.3	n.a.	2814	.8 c
(Natural Touch), 4 oz.[2]	90	4.0	10.0	3.0	n.a.	n.a.	n.a.
Stuffing, 1 oz.:							
apple and raisin *(Pepperidge Farm Distinctive)*	110	3.0	21.0	1.0	0	410	m.q.
chicken, classic *(Pepperidge Farm Distinctive)*	110	4.0	20.0	1.0	0	410	m.q.
corn *(Brownberry)* . .	103	3.7	20.6	1.6	0	350	1.5 d
cornbread *(Pepperidge Farm)*	110	3.0	22.0	1.0	0	320	m.q.
cube *(Pepperidge Farm)*	110	3.0	22.0	1.0	0	400	m.q.
herb:							
(Brownberry) . . .	100	3.6	20.7	1.3	0	297	1.6 d
country garden *(Pepperidge Farm Distinctive)* . . .	120	4.0	18.0	4.0	0	300	m.q.
seasoned *(Pepperidge Farm)* . . .	110	3.0	22.0	1.0	0	380	m.q.
vegetable, harvest, and almond *(Pepperidge Farm Distinctive)*	110	4.0	19.0	3.0	n.a.	250	m.q.
wild rice and mushroom *(Pepperidge Farm Distinctive)*	130	4.0	17.0	5.0	n.a.	310	m.q.

[1] *Prepared according to package directions, with tofu and 2 tbsp. salted butter.*
[2] *Prepared according to package directions.*

Food and Measure	cal.	prot. (gms)	carbo. (gms)	fat (gms)	chol. (mgs)	sod. (mgs)	fiber (gms)
Stuffing, frozen,							
1/2 cup:							
chicken (Green Giant Stuffing Originals)	170	4.0	21.0	7.0	n.a.	670	m.q.
cornbread (Green Giant Stuffing Originals)	170	3.0	25.0	6.0	n.a.	660	m.q.
mushroom (Green Giant Stuffing Originals)	150	4.0	19.0	7.0	n.a.	780	m.q.
wild rice (Green Giant Stuffing Originals)	160	3.0	21.0	7.0	n.a.	540	m.q.
Stuffing mix:							
dry:							
(Croutettes), .7 oz.	70	3.0	14.0	0	0	260	0
Cajun style (Golden Dipt), 1/4 cup	40	1.0	9.0	0	0	590	n.a.
cheddar and French (Golden Dipt), 1/4 cup	80	4.0	9.0	3.0	14	580	n.a.
garden herb (Golden Dipt), 1/4 cup	40	1.0	9.0	0	0	330	n.a.
prepared[1], 1/2 cup:							
(Stove Top Americana San Francisco)	170	4.0	20.0	9.0	20	650	m.q.
beef (Stove Top)	180	4.0	21.0	9.0	20	590	m.q.
broccoli and cheese (Stove Top Microwave)	170	4.0	20.0	8.0	15	580	m.q.
chicken (Stove Top)	180	4.0	20.0	9.0	20	570	m.q.
chicken (Stove Top Flexible Serving)	170	4.0	20.0	9.0	15	580	m.q.
chicken (Stove Top Microwave)	160	4.0	20.0	7.0	10	480	m.q.

[1] Prepared according to package directions, with salted butter.

Food and Measure	cal.	prot. (gms)	carbo. (gms)	fat (gms)	chol. (mgs)	sod. (mgs)	fiber (gms)
cornbread *(Stove Top)*	170	3.0	21.0	9.0	20	570	m.q.
cornbread *(Stove Top* Flexible Serving)	180	4.0	22.0	9.0	15	600	m.q.
cornbread, home-style *(Stove Top* Microwave) . . .	160	3.0	20.0	7.0	10	450	m.q.
herb, homestyle *(Stove Top* Flexible Serving) . . .	170	4.0	20.0	9.0	15	520	m.q.
herb, savory *(Stove Top)*	170	4.0	20.0	9.0	20	590	m.q.
long grain and wild rice *(Stove Top)*	180	4.0	22.0	9.0	20	560	m.q.
mushroom and on-ion *(Stove Top)*	180	4.0	20.0	9.0	20	490	m.q.
mushroom and on-ion *(Stove Top* Microwave) . . .	170	4.0	21.0	7.0	10	510	m.q.
pork *(Stove Top)*	170	4.0	20.0	9.0	20	570	m.q.
pork *(Stove Top* Flexible Serving)	170	4.0	20.0	9.0	15	630	m.q.
w/rice *(Stove Top)*	180	4.0	22.0	9.0	20	570	m.q.
turkey *(Stove Top)*	170	4.0	20.0	9.0	20	640	m.q.
Sturgeon, meat only:							
raw, 1 lb.	478	73.2	0	18.3	m.q.	m.q.	0
raw, 1 oz.	30	4.6	0	1.1	m.q.	m.q.	0
baked, broiled, or mi-crowaved, 4 oz. . .	153	23.5	0	5.9	m.q.	m.q.	0
smoked, 4 oz.	196	35.4	0	5.0	m.q.	m.q.	0
Succotash:							
fresh, boiled, drained, 1/2 cup	111	4.9	23.4	.8	0	16	1.3 c
canned, 1/2 cup:							
w/cream-style corn	102	3.5	23.4	.7	0	325	1.7 c
w/whole kernel corn	81	3.3	17.9	.6	0	283	.8 c

Food and Measure	cal.	prot. (gms)	carbo. (gms)	fat (gms)	chol. (mgs)	sod. (mgs)	fiber (gms)
Succotash canned *(cont.)*							
(S&W Country							
Style)	80	4.0	16.0	1.0	0	250	m.q.
(Stokely)	90	3.0	20.0	0	0	300	m.q.
frozen *(Frosty Acres),*							
3.3 oz.	100	4.0	19.0	0	0	47	1.0 c
Sucker, white, meat							
only, raw:							
1 lb.	419	76.0	0	10.5	187	181	0
1 oz.	26	4.8	0	.7	12	11	0
Sugar, beet or cane:							
brown:							
1 oz.	106	0	27.3	0	0	1	0
1 cup, not packed	541	0	139.8	0	0	44	0
1 cup, packed . . .	821	0	212.1	0	0	66	0
cane baton *(Frieda of*							
California), 1 oz.	21	<.1	49.9	.1	0	n.a.	(0)
granulated:							
1 oz.	109	0	28.2	0	0	<1	0
1 cup	770	0	199.0	0	0	<1	0
1 tbsp.	46	0	11.9	0	0	tr.	0
1 tsp.	15	0	4.0	0	0	tr.	0
2 cubes, 1/2" . . .	19	0	5.0	0	0	tr.	0
powdered or confec-							
tioner's:							
1 oz.	109	0	28.2	0	0	<1	0
1 cup, sifted	385	0	99.5	0	0	1	0
1 tbsp., unsifted . .	31	0	8.0	0	0	tr.	0
Sugar, maple:							
1-oz. piece	99	n.a.	25.5	0	0	4	0
"Sugar," substitute:							
(Sprinkle Sweet),							
1 tsp.	2	0	.5	0	0	1	0
(Sweet 'n Low), 1 pkt.	4	0	1.0	0	0	0	0
(Sweet* 10), 1/8 tsp.	0	0	0	0	0	2	0
Sugar, turbinado:							
(Hain), 1 tbsp.	50	0	12.0	0	0	0	(0)

Food and Measure	cal.	prot. (gms)	carbo. (gms)	fat (gms)	chol. (mgs)	sod. (mgs)	fiber (gms)
Sugar apple:							
1 medium, 2⁷/₈″ × 3¹/₄″, 9.9 oz. . . .	146	3.2	36.6	.5	0	15	2.3 c
¹/₂ cup	118	2.6	29.6	.4	0	12	1.8 c
Sugar snap peas, see "Peas, edible-podded"							
Summer sausage (see also "Thuringer cervelat"):							
(Eckrich), 1-oz. slice	80	4.0	1.0	7.0	m.q.	320	0
(Hillshire Farm), 2 oz.	180	9.0	1.0	16.0	m.q.	670	0
(Hormel Perma-Fresh), 2 slices	140	10.0	0	11.0	m.q.	706	0
(Hormel Tangy, Chub), 1 oz.	90	5.0	0	7.0	m.q.	317	0
(Hormel Thuringer), 1 oz.	90	4.0	0	9.0	m.q.	332	0
(Oscar Mayer), .8-oz. slice	73	3.5	.2	6.5	19	332	0
beef:							
(Hillshire Farm), 2 oz.	190	9.0	1.0	17.0	m.q.	m.q.	0
(Hormel Beefy), 1 oz.	100	5.0	0	9.0	m.q.	313	0
(Oscar Mayer), .8-oz. slice . . .	72	3.4	.6	6.2	18	327	0
w/cheese *(Hillshire Farm)*, 2 oz.	200	9.0	1.0	18.0	m.q.	m.q.	0
Sunfish, pumpkin-seed, meat only, raw:							
1 lb.	404	88.0	0	3.2	304	363	0
1 oz.	25	5.5	0	.2	19	23	0
Sunflower seed:							
dried, kernels:							
1 oz.	162	6.5	5.3	14.1	0	1	1.2 c
1 cup	821	32.8	27.0	71.4	0	4	6.0 c

Food and Measure	cal.	prot. (gms)	carbo. (gms)	fat (gms)	chol. (mgs)	sod. (mgs)	fiber (gms)
Sunflower seed (cont.)							
dry-roasted, kernels:							
1 oz.	165	5.5	6.8	14.1	0	1	.5 c
1 cup	745	24.8	30.8	63.7	0	4	2.3 c
salted, 1 oz.	165	5.5	6.8	14.1	0	221	.5 c
(Flavor House),							
1 oz.	180	8.0	4.0	15.0	0	200	m.q.
oil-roasted, kernels:							
1 oz.	175	6.1	4.2	16.3	0	1	1.9 d
1 cup	830	28.8	19.9	77.6	0	4	9.2 d
salted, 1 oz.	175	6.1	4.2	16.3	0	171	1.9 d
toasted, kernels:							
1 oz.	176	4.9	5.9	16.1	0	1	.5 c
1 cup	829	23.1	27.6	76.1	0	4	2.4 c
salted, 1 oz.	176	4.9	5.9	16.1	0	174	.5 c
Sunflower seed but-							
ter:							
1 oz.	165	5.6	7.8	13.6	0	1	1.4 d
1 tbsp.	93	3.2	4.4	7.6	0	1	.8 d
salted, 1 oz.	165	5.6	7.8	13.6	0	147	1.4 d
Sunflower seed							
flour:							
partially defatted,							
1 cup	261	38.5	28.7	1.3	0	2	4.2 c
Surimi[1]**:**							
1 lb.	449	68.9	31.1	4.1	135	649	0
1 oz.	28	4.3	1.9	.3	9	41	0
Swamp cabbage:							
raw, untrimmed, 1 lb.	67	9.1	11.0	.7	0	395	3.8 c
raw, .6-oz. shoot . .	2	.3	.4	<.1	0	15	.1 c
boiled, drained,							
chopped, 1/2 cup	10	1.0	1.8	.1	0	60	.4 c
Swedish sausage:							
(Hickory Farms), 1 oz.	100	5.0	0	9.0	20	380	0
Sweet potato:							
raw, 1 medium,							
5″ × 2″ diam. . . .	136	2.1	31.6	.4	0	17	3.9 d

[1] Processed from walleye (Alaska) pollock.

Food and Measure	cal.	prot. (gms)	carbo. (gms)	fat (gms)	chol. (mgs)	sod. (mgs)	fiber (gms)
baked in skin:							
1 medium, 5″ diam.	118	2.0	27.7	.1	0	12	3.4 d
mashed, 1/2 cup . .	103	1.7	24.3	.1	0	10	3.0 d
boiled w/out skin:							
4 oz.	119	1.9	27.5	.3	0	15	1.0 c
mashed, 1/2 cup . .	172	2.7	39.8	.5	0	21	1.4 c
Sweet potato,							
canned, 1/2 cup:							
in water, cut (Allens)	70	1.0	16.0	<1.0	0	20	m.q.
in light syrup (Joan of							
Arc/Princella/Royal							
Prince)	110	1.0	28.0	0	0	25	m.q.
in syrup:							
w/liquid	101	1.1	23.9	.2	0	50	.5 c
drained	106	1.3	24.9	.3	0	38	1.8 d
whole (Allens) . . .	90	2.0	20.0	<1.0	0	40	m.q.
cut (Allens)	90	2.0	20.0	<1.0	0	20	m.q.
in heavy syrup (Joan							
of Arc/Princella/							
Royal Prince) . . .	130	1.0	34.0	0	0	35	m.q.
in extra heavy syrup							
(S&W Southern)	139	1.0	31.0	1.0	0	27	m.q.
in pineapple orange							
sauce (Joan of Arc/							
Princella/Royal							
Prince)	210	1.0	54.0	0	0	35	m.q.
candied (Joan of Arc/							
Princella/Royal							
Prince)	240	1.0	60.0	0	0	15	m.q.
candied (S&W) . . .	180	1.0	44.0	0	0	355	m.q.
mashed (Joan of Arc/							
Princella/Royal							
Prince)	90	1.0	24.0	0	0	45	m.q.
vacuum pack:							
pieces	92	1.7	21.1	.2	0	54	.7 c
mashed	117	2.1	26.9	.3	0	68	.9 c

Food and Measure	cal.	prot. (gms)	carbo. (gms)	fat (gms)	chol. (mgs)	sod. (mgs)	fiber (gms)
Sweet potato, frozen:							
baked, cubed, 1/2 cup	88	1.5	20.6	.1	0	7	1.3 d
candied:							
(Mrs. Paul's), 4 oz.	190	1.0	47.0	0	0	60	m.q.
w/apples (Mrs. Paul's Sweets 'N Apples), 4 oz. . . .	160	0	38.0	0	0	70	m.q.
Sweet potato leaf:							
raw, chopped, 1/2 cup	6	.7	1.1	.1	0	2	.2 c
steamed, 1/2 cup . .	11	.7	2.3	.1	0	4	.4 c
Sweet and sour drink mix:							
liquid (Holland House), 1 fl. oz.	34	0	8.0	0	0	107	n.a.
Sweet and sour sauce:							
(Hickory Farms), 2 tbsp.	102	0	25.5	0	0	<1	n.a.
(Kikkoman), 1 tbsp.	18	n.a.	4.0	0	0	63	n.a.
(La Choy), 1 tbsp. . .	30	n.a.	7.0	n.a.	0	320	n.a.
(Sauceworks), 1 tbsp.	25	0	5.0	0	0	50	n.a.
duck sauce (La Choy), 1 tbsp.	26	<.1	6.9	tr.	0	59	0
Hawaiian (Hickory Farms), 2 tbsp. . .	102	0	25.5	0	0	2	n.a.
mix[1], 1/2 cup	147	.4	36.3	<.1	0	390	n.a.
Sweetbreads, see "Pancreas" and "Thymus"							
Swiss chard:							
raw, untrimmed, 1 lb.	81	7.5	15.6	.8	0	888	3.3 c
raw, chopped, 1/2 cup	3	.3	.7	<.1	0	38	.1 c
boiled, drained, chopped, 1/2 cup	18	1.7	3.6	1	0	158	.8 c
Swiss steak, see "Beef dinner"							

[1] Prepared with water and vinegar.

Food and Measure	cal.	prot. (gms)	carbo. (gms)	fat (gms)	chol. (mgs)	sod. (mgs)	fiber (gms)
Swordfish, fresh, meat only:							
raw, 1 lb.	548	89.8	0	18.2	178	408	0
raw, 1 oz.	34	5.6	0	1.1	11	26	0
baked, broiled, or microwaved, 4 oz. . . .	176	28.8	0	5.8	57	130	0
Swordfish, frozen:							
steaks, w/out seasoning mix *(Sea-Pak)*, 6-oz. pkg.	210	34.0	0	7.0	70	155	0
Syrup, see specific listings							
Szechwan sauce:							
hot and spicy *(La Choy)*, 1 oz.	48	.1	12.0	.2	0	141	0

T

Food and Measure	cal.	prot. (gms)	carbo. (gms)	fat (gms)	chol. (mgs)	sod. (mgs)	fiber (gms)
Tabbouleh mix:							
(Fantastic Foods),							
1/2 cup[1]	161	2.0	17.0	10.0	0	250	m.q.
(Near East), 1/2 cup[2]	170	3.0	20.0	9.0	0	290	m.q.
salad *(Casbah),* 1 oz.							
dry	126	4.0	28.0	1.0	0	m.q.	m.q.
Taco Bell, 1 serving:							
burrito:							
bean, green sauce	351	12.9	52.9	10.2	9	888	m.q.
bean, red sauce	357	13.1	54.4	10.2	9	763	m.q.
beef, green sauce	398	22.4	37.7	17.3	57	926	m.q.
beef, red sauce .	403	22.5	39.1	17.3	57	1051	m.q.
burrito supreme:							
double beef, green							
sauce	451	23.4	40.3	21.8	57	928	m.q.
double beef, red							
sauce	457	23.6	41.7	21.8	57	1053	m.q.
green sauce .	407	17.8	45.2	17.5	33	769	m.q.
red sauce . .	413	17.9	46.6	17.6	33	921	m.q.
cinnamon crispas . .	259	2.7	27.5	15.3	1	127	m.q.
Enchirito, green sauce	371	19.5	28.1	19.7	54	993	m.q.
Enchirito, red sauce	382	19.8	30.9	19.7	54	1243	m.q.
fajita, chicken .	226	13.6	19.8	10.2	44	619	m.q.
fajita, steak . . .	234	14.6	19.5	10.9	14	485	m.q.
guacamole, 3/4 oz.	34	.4	2.9	2.3	0	113	m.q.
jalapeños, 3.3 oz. . .	20	1.0	4.0	.2	0	1370	m.q.
Meximelt	266	12.9	18.7	15.4	38	689	n.a.

[1] *Prepared according to package directions with oil and tomatoes.*
[2] *Prepared according to package directions.*

Food and Measure	cal.	prot. (gms)	carbo. (gms)	fat (gms)	chol. (mgs)	sod. (mgs)	fiber (gms)
nachos	346	7.5	37.5	18.5	9	399	m.q.
nachos *Bellgrande*	649	21.6	60.0	35.3	36	997	m.q.
Pico de Gallo, 1 oz.	8	.3	1.1	.2	tr.	88	n.a.
pintos and cheese:							
green sauce	184	8.8	17.5	8.7	16	·518	m.q.
red sauce	190	8.9	18.9	8.7	16	642	m.q.
pizza, Mexican	575	21.3	39.7	36.8	52	1031	m.q.
taco:							
regular	183	10.3	10.6	10.8	32	276	m.q.
Bellgrande	355	18.3	17.7	23.1	56	472	m.q.
combo, super . . .	286	14.1	20.9	15.9	40	462	m.q.
light	410	18.9	18.1	28.8	56	594	m.q.
soft	228	11.8	17.9	11.8	32	515	m.q.
soft, supreme . . .	275	12.6	19.1	16.3	32	516	m.q.
taco salad:							
w/salsa	941	35.9	63.1	61.3	80	1662	m.q.
w/salsa, w/out shell	520	30.6	29.9	31.4	80	1431	m.q.
w/out shell	502	29.5	26.3	31.3	80	1056	m.q.
tostada, green sauce	237	9.3	25.2	11.1	16	471	m.q.
tostada, red sauce	243	9.5	26.6	11.1	16	596	m.q.
sour cream, 3/4 oz.	46	.6	.9	4.4	m.q.	n.a.	0
Taco dip:							
(Wise), 2 tbsp.	12	0	3.0	0	0	115	n.a.
and sauce *(Hain),*							
4 tbsp.	25	1.0	5.0	1.0	5	350	n.a.
Taco John's, 1 serv-ing:							
apple grande	257	5.0	44.0	8.0	n.a.	231	m.q.
beans, refried	331	19.0	79.0	6.0	n.a.	1195	m.q.
burrito:							
bean	249	10.0	36.0	6.0	n.a.	636	m.q.
beef	355	16.0	25.0	18.0	m.q.	666	m.q.
combo	302	11.0	30.0	12.0	m.q.	651	m.q.
super	434	17.0	66.0	11.0	m.q.	1022	m.q.
w/green chili	405	18.0	38.0	24.0	n.a.	995	m.q.
w/Texas chili . . .	518	23.0	48.0	24.0	n.a.	746	m.q.
chili, Texas	430	23.0	35.0	22.0	m.q.	1580	m.q.
chimi	487	16.0	54.0	19.0	m.q.	1226	m.q.

Food and Measure	cal.	prot. (gms)	carbo. (gms)	fat (gms)	chol. (mgs)	sod. (mgs)	fiber (gms)
Taco John's (cont.)							
churro	122	1.7	12.0	7.0	n.a.	153	m.q.
enchilada	379	19.0	33.0	18.0	m.q.	431	m.q.
nachos	407	11.0	42.0	19.0	m.q.	307	m.q.
nachos, super	657	23.0	57.0	34.0	m.q.	857	m.q.
Potato Ole Large . .	414	6.0	96.0	6.0	n.a.	1595	m.q.
taco:							
burger	332	14.0	31.0	14.0	m.q.	660	m.q.
Bravo, super . . .	485	18.0	51.0	20.0	m.q.	1006	m.q.
regular	228	11.0	15.0	13.0	m.q.	347	m.q.
soft shell	276	13.0	23.0	13.0	m.q.	505	m.q.
taco salad, super . .	450	16.0	48.0	18.0	n.a.	880	m.q.
tostada	228	11.0	15.0	13.0	n.a.	347	m.q.
Taco mix[1]:							
(Old El Paso), 1 taco	67	2.0	8.0	3.0	n.a.	423	n.a.
(Tio Sancho Dinner Kit):							
sauce, 2 oz.	62	1.6	13.4	.2	n.a.	750	.5 c
seasoning, 1.25 oz.	104	2.1	20.9	1.4	n.a.	2500	1.7 c
shell	64	1.1	8.1	3.1	n.a.	1	.5 c
vegetarian *(Natural Touch)*, 2 tbsp. . .	90	10.0	6.0	2.0	0	m.q.	m.q.
Taco sauce:							
(Lawry's Sauce'n Seasoner)*, ¼ cup . .	40	.7	7.6	.6	0	636	0
all styles *(Old El Paso)*, 2 tbsp.	10	0	2.0	0	0	130	m.q.
chunky *(Lawry's)*, ¼ cup	22	.9	4.0	.4	0	549	.4 c
green *(La Victoria)*, 1 tbsp.	4	<1.0	1.0	<1.0	0	85	m.q.
hot *(Del Monte)*, ¼ cup	15	0	4.0	0	0	440	m.q.
hot *(Ortega)*, 1 oz. . .	12	0	3.0	0	0	210	m.q.
mild:							
(Del Monte), ¼ cup	15	0	4.0	0	0	480	m.q.

[1] *Prepared according to package directions.*

Food and Measure	cal.	prot. (gms)	carbo. (gms)	fat (gms)	chol. (mgs)	sod. (mgs)	fiber (gms)
(Enrico's No Salt Added), 2 tbsp.	14	1.0	3.0	0	0	25	m.q.
(Ortega), 1 oz. . .	12	0	3.0	0	0	220	m.q.
or medium *(Heinz),* 1 tbsp.	6	0	1.0	0	0	m.q.	m.q.
red *(La Victoria),* 1 tbsp.	6	<1.0	1.0	<1.0	0	85	m.q.
red, mild *(El Molino),* 2 tbsp.	10	0	2.0	0	0	170	m.q.
western style *(Ortega),* 1 oz.	8	0	2.0	0	0	180	m.q.
Taco seasoning mix, 1 pkg., except as noted:							
(Lawry's Seasoning Blends)	118	3.4	23.6	1.1	0	1441	1.0 c
(McCormick/Schilling)	103	5.0	18.0	n.a.	0	2656	m.q.
(Old El Paso)	100	1.0	21.0	1.0	0	3570	m.q.
(Tio Sancho)	132	2.9	26.0	1.7	0	2623	2.0 c
meat *(Ortega),* 1 oz.[1]	60	4.0	1.0	4.0	20	105	m.q.
salad *(Lawry's* Seasoning Blends) . .	124	4.0	24.7	.9	0	1451	1.6 c
Taco shell, 1 piece, except as noted:							
(Gebhardt)	30	0	4.0	2.0	0	0	m.q.
(Lawry's)	50	.8	8.0	2.1	0	123	.2 c
(Lawry's Super) . . .	86	1.4	13.0	3.6	0	210	.4 c
(Old El Paso)	55	0	6.0	3.0	0	50	.5 d
(Old El Paso Super)	100	1.0	11.0	6.0	0	95	1.5 d
(Ortega)	50	0	8.0	2.0	0	5	m.q.
(Tio Sancho)	64	1.1	8.1	3.1	0	1	.5 c
(Tio Sancho Super)	94	1.6	11.3	4.7	0	2	.7 c
corn *(Azteca)*	60	1.0	7.0	3.0	0	65	m.q.
miniature *(Old El Paso),* 3 pieces . .	70	1.0	7.0	4.0	0	60	1.0 d
salad, flour *(Azteca)*	200	3.0	18.0	12.0	n.a.	130	m.q.

[1] *Prepared according to package directions, with 1 lb. ground beef and 1 1/2 cups water.*

Food and Measure	cal.	prot. (gms)	carbo. (gms)	fat (gms)	chol. (mgs)	sod. (mgs)	fiber (gms)
Taco starter:							
(Del Monte), 8 oz. . . .	140	3.0	28.0	1.0	n.a.	2180	n.a.
Tahini, 1 tbsp., except as noted:							
from unroasted kernels	85	2.5	2.5	7.9	0	tr.	1.3 d
from roasted and toasted kernels . .	89	2.6	3.2	8.1	0	17	1.4 d
mix *(Casbah)*, 1 oz. dry	25	2.0	2.0	5.0	0	m.q.	m.q.
Tamale:							
canned:							
(Old El Paso), 2 pieces	190	5.0	16.0	12.0	m.q.	380	m.q.
(Wolf Brand), 7.5 oz.	328	8.3	24.9	24.5	m.q.	1181	1.5 c
beef *(Hormel)*, 2 pieces	140	4.0	8.0	10.0	m.q.	550	m.q.
beef *(Hormel* Hot'N Spicy), 2 pieces	140	4.0	9.0	10.0	m.q.	612	m.q.
w/sauce *(Van Camp's)*, 1 cup	293	8.3	28.6	16.2	m.q.	1132	2.2 c
frozen, beef *(Hormel)*, 1 piece	140	6.0	13.0	7.0	m.q.	555	m.q.
Tamale dinner, frozen:							
(Patio), 13 oz.	470	12.0	58.0	21.0	35	1850	m.q.
Tamalito, canned:							
in chili gravy *(Dennison's)*, 7.5 oz. . . .	310	6.0	37.0	16.0	m.q.	1395	m.q.
Tamari, see "Soy sauce"							
Tamarind:							
1 fruit, 3" × 1"	5	.1	1.3	<.1	0	1	.1 c
pulp, 1/2 cup	144	1.7	37.5	.4	0	17	3.1 c
(Frieda of California Tamarindos), 31/2 oz.	239	2.8	62.5	.6	0	51	m.q.
Tangerine:							

Food and Measure	cal.	prot. (gms)	carbo. (gms)	fat (gms)	chol. (mgs)	sod. (mgs)	fiber (gms)
fresh:							
1 medium, 2³/₈" diam.	37	.5	9.4	.2	0	1	.3 c
sections w/out membrane,							
½ cup	43	.6	10.9	.2	0	2	.3 c
canned:							
(Del Monte Mandarin), 5½ oz. . . .	100	0	25.0	0	0	<10	m.q.
in juice, ½ cup . .	46	.8	11.9	<.1	0	7	.1 c
in light syrup:							
½ cup	76	.6	20.4	.1	0	8	.2 c
(Dole), ½ cup . .	76	.6	20.0	.1	0	8	m.q.
(Empress),							
5½ oz.	100	0	25.0	0	0	<10	m.q.
in heavy syrup							
(S&W), ½ cup	76	0	20.0	0	0	10	m.q.
natural style (S&W),							
½ cup	60	0	15.0	0	0	10	m.q.
Tangerine juice:							
fresh, 6 fl. oz.	80	.9	18.7	.4	0	2	.2 c
chilled:							
(Dole Pure & Light Mandarin Tangerine), 6 fl. oz. . .	97	.6	25.0	.1	0	20	m.q.
or frozen¹ (Minute Maid), 6 fl. oz.	91	.9	21.9	.2	0	19	m.q.
Tapioca, pearl, dry:							
1 oz.	97	<.1	25.1	tr.	0	tr.	.3 d
Taro:							
raw, sliced, ½ cup	56	.8	13.8	.1	0	6	.4 c
cooked, sliced, ½ cup	94	.3	22.8	.1	0	10	.6 c
Taro chips:							
1 oz.	135	.6	19.1	7.2	0	105	.3 c
½ cup	57	.3	8.1	3.1	0	44	.1 c

¹ Diluted according to package directions.

Food and Measure	cal.	prot. (gms)	carbo. (gms)	fat (gms)	chol. (mgs)	sod. (mgs)	fiber (gms)
Taro leaf:							
raw:							
untrimmed, 1 lb. . .	115	13.5	18.3	2.0	0	8	5.5 c
1 leaf, 11″ × 6½″	4	.5	.7	.1	0	tr.	.2 c
½ cup	6	.7	.9	.1	0	1	.3 c
steamed, ½ cup . .	18	2.0	3.0	.3	0	2	.4 c
Taro shoots:							
raw:							
1 shoot, 15½″ ×							
1⅛″ diam.	9	.8	1.9	.1	0	1	.5 c
sliced, ½ cup . . .	5	.4	1.0	<.1	0	<1	.3 c
cooked, sliced, ½ cup	10	.5	2.2	.1	0	1	.4 c
Taro, Tahitian:							
raw, sliced, ½ cup	25	1.7	4.3	.6	0	31	1.1 c
cooked, sliced, ½ cup	30	2.8	4.7	.5	0	37	1.6 c
Tarragon, ground:							
1 tsp.	5	.4	.8	.1	0	1	.1 c
Tartar sauce, 1 tbsp.:							
(Golden Dipt)	70	0	2.0	7.0	10	100	n.a.
(Golden Dipt Lite) . .	50	0	4.0	4.0	5	40	n.a.
(Great Impressions)	86	.2	1.2	9.0	10	76	n.a.
(Hellmann's/Best							
Foods)	70	0	0	8.0	5	220	n.a.
(Sauceworks)	70	0	1.0	8.0	5	160	n.a.
natural lemon and							
herb flavor							
(Sauceworks) . . .	70	0	1.0	8.0	5	85	n.a.
Tea, brewed:							
(Nestea), 6 fl. oz. . . .	0	0	0	0	0	0	0
caffeine-free (Celestial							
Seasonings),							
8 fl. oz.	4	tr.	.8	tr.	0	5	tr.d
instant, regular or de-							
caffeinated (Lipton),							
6 fl. oz.	0	0	0	0	0	0	0
instant, lemon flavor							
(Lipton), 6 fl. oz. . .	3	.1	.6	0	0	1	0

Food and Measure	cal.	prot. (gms)	carbo. (gms)	fat (gms)	chol. (mgs)	sod. (mgs)	fiber (gms)
Tea, flavored or special blend:							
all varieties *(Bigelow)*, 5¼ fl. oz.	1	<.1	<.2	tr.	0	<1	0
all varieties except chocolate orange *(Celestial Seasonings)*, 8 fl. oz. . . .	<4	<.1	<.7	tr.	0	<3	tr.d
chocolate orange *(Celestial Seasonings Bavarian Chocolate Orange)*, 8 fl. oz.	7	tr.	1.6	tr.	0	5	tr.d
Tea, herbal, brewed:							
all varieties except *Roastaroma (Celestial Seasonings)*, 8 fl. oz.	<6	<.1	<2.0	tr.	0	<9	tr.d
all varieties except spice *(Lipton)*, 8 fl. oz.	<5	0	<2.0	0	0	0	0
all varieties except apple and roasted grain *(Bigelow)*, 5 fl. oz.	<2	<.1	<.4	tr.	0	<4	0
(Celestial Seasonings Roastaroma), 8 fl. oz.	11	<.1	2.0	<.1	0	4	<.1 d
grains, roasted, w/ carob *(Bigelow)*, 5 fl. oz.	3	<.1	.6	tr.	0	1	0
spice *(Lipton Toasty Spice)*, 8 fl. oz. . .	6	0	1.0	0	0	0	0

Food and Measure	cal.	prot. (gms)	carbo. (gms)	fat (gms)	chol. (mgs)	sod. (mgs)	fiber (gms)
Tea, iced, lemon flavor:							
canned or chilled, 8 fl. oz., except as noted:							
(Lipton Presweetened)	83	0	20.2	0	0	11	0
(Nestea Sugar Sweetened) . . .	70	0	17.0	0	0	0	0
(Veryfine)	80	<1.0	16.0	0	0	<10	0
natural *(Lipton),* 8.45 oz.	96	1.6	24.0	.3	0	20	0
(Wylers Fruit Tea Punch), 12 fl. oz.	118	0	29.6	0	0	1	0
mix[1], 8 fl. oz., except as noted:							
(Nestea 100%) . .	2	0	0	0	0	0	0
all flavors *(Nestea Ice Teasers)* . .	6	0	1.0	0	0	0	0
lemon *(Lipton),* 6 fl. oz.	55	0	14.3	0	0	1	0
lemon *(Lipton Decaf),* 6 fl. oz. . .	55	0	14.2	0	0	<1	0
lemon *(Nestea Presweetened)*	70	0	19.0	0	0	0	0
Tempeh:							
1 oz.	56	5.4	4.8	2.2	0	2	.8 c
1/2 cup	165	15.7	14.1	6.4	0	5	2.5 c
Tempura batter mix:							
(Golden Dipt), 1 oz.	100	3.0	22.0	0	0	130	m.q.
Teriyaki sauce:							
(Kikkoman), 1 tbsp.	15	n.a.	2.7	tr.	tr.	630	n.a.
(Kikkoman Baste & Glaze), 1 tbsp. . .	27	n.a.	6.0	tr.	0	420	n.a.
(La Choy Sauce and Marinade), 1 oz. . .	30	1.0	5.0	0	n.a.	1640	n.a.

[1] *Prepared according to package directions.*

Food and Measure	cal.	prot. (gms)	carbo. (gms)	fat (gms)	chol. (mgs)	sod. (mgs)	fiber (gms)
(La Choy Thick & Rich), 1 oz.	41	.7	9.4	.1	<1	509	<.1 d
ginger marinade *(Golden Dipt),* 1 fl. oz.	120	1.0	12.0	7.0	0	920	n.a.
Thirst quencher drink:							
8 fl. oz.	60	tr.	15.2	tr.	0	96	0
Thuringer cervelat (see also "Summer sausage"), 1 oz.:							
(Hormel Old Smokehouse)	90	4.0	1.0	8.0	m.q.	328	0
(Hormel Old Smokehouse Chub) . . .	100	5.0	0	9.0	m.q.	332	0
(Hormel Viking Club Cervelat)	90	5.0	0	8.0	m.q.	325	0
(JM Cervalot)	70	4.0	1.0	6.0	m.q.	260	0
beef *(JM* Thuringer)	80	5.0	1.0	7.0	m.q.	340	0
Thyme, ground:							
1 tsp.	4	.1	.9	.1	0	1	.3 c
Thymus:							
beef, braised, 4 oz.	362	24.8	0	28.3	333	132	0
veal, braised, 4 oz.	197	35.8	0	4.9	532	75	0
Tilefish, meat only:							
raw, 1 lb.	433	79.4	0	10.5	m.q.	239	0
raw, 1 oz.	27	5.0	0	.7	m.q.	15	0
baked, broiled, or microwaved, 4 oz. . .	167	27.8	0	5.3	m.q.	67	0
Toaster muffins and pastries, 1 piece:							
apple:							
cinnamon *(Pepperidge Farm* Croissant Toaster Tarts)	170	3.0	25.0	7.0	0	120	m.q.

Food and Measure	cal.	prot. (gms)	carbo. (gms)	fat (gms)	chol. (mgs)	sod. (mgs)	fiber (gms)
Toaster muffins and pastries, apple *(cont.)*							
spice *(Toaster Muffins)*	130	2.0	21.0	5.0	n.a.	100	m.q.
banana nut:							
(Thomas' Toast-r-Cakes)	111	1.7	16.7	4.4	10	192	.6 d
(Toaster Muffins)	130	2.0	19.0	6.0	n.a.	85	m.q.
(Toaster Strudel Breakfast Pastries)	190	2.0	28.0	8.0	n.a.	190	m.q.
blueberry:							
(Thomas' Toast-r-Cakes)	108	1.6	18.0	3.3	n.a.	158	m.q.
(Toaster Strudel Breakfast Pastries)	190	2.0	28.0	8.0	n.a.	200	m.q.
wild Maine *(Toaster Muffins)*	120	2.0	23.0	3.0	n.a.	135	m.q.
bran *(Thomas' Toast-r-Cakes)*	103	1.7	17.6	2.9	n.a.	163	m.q.
cheese *(Pepperidge Farm Croissant Toaster Tarts)* . . .	190	5.0	22.0	10.0	10	180	m.q.
cherry *(Toaster Strudel Breakfast Pastries)*	190	2.0	26.0	9.0	n.a.	200	m.q.
cinnamon *(Toaster Strudel Breakfast Pastries)*	190	2.0	26.0	8.0	n.a.	200	m.q.
corn:							
(Thomas' Toast-r-Cakes)	120	1.8	19.2	4.0	n.a.	142	m.q.
old fashioned *(Toaster Muffins)*	120	2.0	17.0	5.0	n.a.	200	m.q.
oat bran w/raisins *(Awrey's Toastums)*	130	3.0	17.0	5.0	0	310	1.0 d
raisin bran *(Toaster Muffins)*	120	3.0	16.0	5.0	n.a.	220	m.q.

Food and Measure	cal.	prot. (gms)	carbo. (gms)	fat (gms)	chol. (mgs)	sod. (mgs)	fiber (gms)
raspberry or strawberry *(Toaster Strudel* Breakfast Pastries)	190	2.0	27.0	8.0	n.a.	200	m.q.
strawberry *(Pepperidge Farm* Croissant Toaster Tarts) . . .	190	3.0	28.0	7.0	0	120	m.q.
Tofu:							
raw:							
1 oz.	22	2.3	.5	1.4	0	2	.3 d
1/2 cup	94	10.0	2.3	5.9	0	9	1.5 d
firm, 1 oz.	41	4.5	1.2	2.5	0	4	<.1 c
firm, 1/2 cup	183	19.9	5.4	11.0	0	17	.2 c
pasteurized *(Frieda of California),* 4.2 oz.	86	9.6	2.9	m.q.	0	8	m.q.
dried-frozen (koya-dofu), 1 oz.	136	13.6	4.1	8.6	0	2	<.1 c
flavored, Chinese 5-spice or French country herb *(Nasoya),* 5 oz. . .	150	15.0	2.0	8.0	0	15	m.q.
fried, 1 oz.	77	4.9	3.0	5.7	0	5	<.1 c
okara, 1 oz.	22	.9	3.6	.5	0	3	1.2 c
okara, 1/2 cup	47	2.0	7.7	1.1	0	6	2.5 c
salted and fermented (fuyu), 1 oz.	33	2.3	1.5	2.3	0	814	.1 c
Tofu dishes, see specific listings							
Tofu patty, frozen, 1 patty:							
(Natural Touch Okara)	160	11.0	7.0	10.0	0	420	m.q.
garden *(Natural Touch)*	90	10.0	3.0	4.0	0	260	m.q.

Food and Measure	cal.	prot. (gms)	carbo. (gms)	fat (gms)	chol. (mgs)	sod. (mgs)	fiber (gms)
Tofu spread,							
canned:							
green chili or herb and spice *(Natural Touch Tofu Topper)*, 2 tbsp.	50	2.0	2.0	4.0	0	m.q.	m.q.
Mexican *(Natural Touch Tofu Topper)*, 2 tbsp.	60	2.0	2.0	5.0	0	m.q.	m.q.
Tomatillo:							
(Frieda of California), 3 1/2 oz.	25	1.4	4.2	.5	0	n.a.	m.q.
Tomatillo entero:							
(La Victoria), 1 tbsp.	4	<1.0	1.0	<1.0	n.a.	102	n.a.
Tomato:							
raw:							
2 3/5"-diam. tomato	26	1.0	5.7	.4	0	11	1.6 d
chopped, 1/2 cup	19	.8	4.2	.3	0	8	1.2 d
boiled, 1/2 cup	32	1.3	7.0	.5	0	13	1.0 c
Tomato, canned, 1/2 cup, except as noted:							
whole:							
(Contadina)	25	1.0	5.0	<1.0	0	260	m.q.
(Del Monte)	25	1.0	5.0	0	0	220	m.q.
(Hunt's), 4 oz. . . .	20	1.0	5.0	0	0	415	m.q.
(S&W)	25	1.0	6.0	0	0	220	m.q.
(Stokely)	25	1.0	5.0	0	0	190	m.q.
Italian-style, pear *(Contadina)* . . .	25	1.0	5.0	<1.0	0	220	m.q.
Italian style pear, w/ basil *(S&W)* . . .	25	1.0	5.0	0	0	200	m.q.
cut, peeled *(S&W Ready-Cut)*	25	1.0	6.0	0	0	220	m.q.
wedges:							
in tomato juice . .	34	1.0	8.3	.2	0	285	.6 c
w/liquid *(Del Monte)*	30	1.0	8.0	0	0	355	m.q.

Food and Measure	cal.	prot. (gms)	carbo. (gms)	fat (gms)	chol. (mgs)	sod. (mgs)	fiber (gms)
Aspic, supreme							
(S&W)	60	1.0	16.0	0	0	860	m.q.
diced, in rich puree							
(S&W)	35	1.0	8.0	0	0	290	m.q.
crushed:							
(Hunt's), 4 oz. . . .	25	1.1	5.2	.2	0	297	m.q.
in puree (Contadina)	30	1.0	6.0	<1.0	0	350	m.q.
w/green chilies (Old							
El Paso), 1/4 cup	14	0	3.0	0	0	480	m.q.
w/jalapeños (Ortega),							
1 oz.	8	0	1.0	0	0	120	m.q.
paste, see "Tomato							
paste"							
puree:							
1/2 cup	51	2.1	12.5	.1	0	499	2.9 d
(Contadina)	40	2.0	8.0	<1.0	0	35	m.q.
(Hunt's), 4 oz. . . .	45	2.0	10.0	.2	0	170	m.q.
(S&W)	60	2.0	14.0	0	0	35	m.q.
stewed:							
1/2 cup	34	1.2	8.3	.2	0	325	.5 c
(Contadina)	35	1.0	8.0	<1.0	0	350	m.q.
(Del Monte)	35	1.0	8.0	0	0	355	m.q.
(Del Monte No Salt)	35	1.0	8.0	0	0	45	m.q.
(Hunt's), 4 oz. . . .	35	1.0	8.0	0	0	460	m.q.
(Hunt's No Salt),							
4 oz.	35	1.0	8.0	0	0	20	m.q.
(S&W 50% Salt Re-							
duced)	35	1.0	9.0	0	0	180	m.q.
(Stokely)	35	1.0	8.0	0	0	220	m.q.
sliced or Italian							
(S&W)	35	1.0	9.0	0	0	355	m.q.
Italian style (Con-							
tadina)	35	1.0	8.0	<1.0	0	250	m.q.
w/jalapeños (Con-							
tadina)	35	1.0	8.0	<1.0	0	250	m.q.
Mexican style							
(S&W)	40	1.0	8.0	0	0	360	m.q.

Food and Measure	cal.	prot. (gms)	carbo. (gms)	fat (gms)	chol. (mgs)	sod. (mgs)	fiber (gms)
Tomato, green:							
2³/₅″-diam. tomato	30	1.5	6.3	.3	0	16	.6 c
Tomato, pickled:							
(Claussen), 1 oz. . .	5	.2	1.0	<1.0	0	330	m.q.
Tomato juice,							
6 fl. oz., except							
as noted:							
6 fl. oz.	32	1.4	7.7	.1	0	658	.7 c
low-sodium	32	1.4	7.7	.1	0	18	.7 c
(Campbell's)	35	1.0	8.0	0	0	570	m.q.
(Hunt's)	30	1.0	7.0	0	0	640	m.q.
(S&W California) . . .	35	1.0	8.0	0	0	600	m.q.
(Stokely), 4 fl. oz. . .	20	1.0	4.0	0	0	330	m.q.
(Welch's)	35	1.0	7.0	0	0	550	0
Tomato paste,							
canned:							
1 oz.	24	1.1	5.3	.3	0	224	1.2 d
(Contadina), 2 oz. . .	50	2.0	11.0	<1.0	0	40	m.q.
(Del Monte), ³/₄ cup	150	6.0	34.0	1.0	0	110	m.q.
(Hunt's), 2 oz.	45	2.0	11.0	0	0	140	m.q.
(Hunt's No Salt), 2 oz.	45	2.0	11.0	0	0	30	m.q.
(S&W), 6 oz.	150	6.0	35.0	0	0	100	m.q.
Italian (Contadina),							
2 oz.	65	2.0	12.0	1.0	0	520	m.q.
Tomato sauce,							
canned (see also							
"Pasta sauce"):							
¹/₂ cup	37	1.6	8.8	.2	0	738	1.8 d
(Contadina), ¹/₂ cup	30	1.0	7.0	<1.0	0	580	m.q.
(Contadina Thick and							
Zesty), ¹/₂ cup . .	40	2.0	8.0	<1.0	0	650	m.q.
(Del Monte), 1 cup	70	3.0	16.0	1.0	0	1330	m.q.
(Hunt's), 4 oz.	30	1.0	7.0	0	0	730	m.q.
(Hunt's No Salt), 4 oz.	35	1.0	8.0	0	0	20	m.q.
(Hunt's Special), 4 oz.	35	1.0	8.0	0	0	320	m.q.
(S&W), ¹/₂ cup	40	2.0	9.0	0	0	620	m.q.
(Stokely), ¹/₂ cup . .	30	2.0	7.0	0	0	810	m.q.

Food and Measure	cal.	prot. (gms)	carbo. (gms)	fat (gms)	chol. (mgs)	sod. (mgs)	fiber (gms)
Italian style:							
(Contadina), 1/2 cup	30	1.0	7.0	< 1.0	0	670	m.q.
(Rokeach), 3 oz.	60	1.0	8.0	2.0	0	243	m.q.
marinara:							
1/2 cup	86	2.0	12.7	4.2	0	786	.8 c
(Buitoni), 1/2 cup	70	1.0	11.0	3.0	0	570	m.q.
(Rokeach), 3 oz.	60	1.0	9.0	2.0	0	257	m.q.
w/mushrooms, 1/2 cup	42	1.8	10.3	.2	0	552	1.0 c
w/onions:							
1/2 cup	52	1.9	12.1	.2	0	672	1.0 c
(Del Monte), 1 cup	100	3.0	23.0	1.0	0	1150	m.q.
w/tomato tidbits, low-sodium, 1/2 cup . .	39	1.6	8.7	.5	0	18	1.3 c
Tomato sauce, re-frigerated:							
marinara *(Contadina Fresh)*, 7.5 oz. . . .	100	4.0	12.0	4.0	0	700	m.q.
plum, w/basil *(Contadina Fresh)*, 7.5 oz.	100	3.0	14.0	4.0	5	700	m.q.
Tom collins mix:							
bottled *(Holland House)*, 1 fl. oz. . .	47	0	11.0	0	0	96	n.a.
instant *(Holland House)*, .56 oz. . .	65	0	16.0	0	0	14	n.a.
Tomato-beef cock-tail:							
(Beefamato), 6 fl. oz.	80	1.0	19.0	0	n.a.	240	m.q.
Tomato-chile cock-tail:							
(Snap-E-Tom), 6 fl. oz.	40	2.0	7.0	0	0	980	m.q.
Tomato-clam juice cocktail:							
(Clamato), 6 fl. oz. . .	96	1.0	23.0	0	n.a.	815	m.q.
Tongue:							
fresh, braised:							
beef, 4 oz.	321	25.1	.4	23.5	121	68	0
lamb, 4 oz.	312	24.5	0	23.0	214	76	0

Food and Measure	cal.	prot. (gms)	carbo. (gms)	fat (gms)	chol. (mgs)	sod. (mgs)	fiber (gms)
Tongue fresh, braised (cont.)							
pork, 4 oz.	307	27.3	0	21.1	166	124	0
veal (calf), 4 oz.	229	29.3	0	11.5	m.q.	73	0
canned, cured (Hormel, 8 lb.), 3 oz.	190	17.0	0	13.0	m.q.	966	0
Tortellini, frozen:							
beef w/marinara sauce (Stouffer's), 10 oz.	360	18.0	45.0	12.0	m.q.	780	m.q.
cheese:							
(The Budget Gourmet Side Dish), 5.5 oz.	180	7.0	25.0	9.0	15	400	m.q.
in Alfredo sauce (Stouffer's), 87/8 oz.	600	28.0	32.0	40.0	m.q.	930	m.q.
marinara (Green Giant), 5.5 oz. . . .	260	8.0	37.0	9.0	m.q.	m.q.	m.q.
in tomato sauce (Birds Eye For One), 5.5 oz. . .	210	11.0	31.0	5.0	30	500	0
w/tomato sauce (Stouffer's), 95/8 oz.	360	18.0	37.0	16.0	m.q.	860	m.q.
w/vinaigrette (Stouffer's), 67/8 oz. . .	400	15.0	24.0	27.0	m.q.	540	m.q.
meatless (Tofutti), 2 oz.	220	12.0	38.0	2.0	0	110	m.q.
nondairy, regular/spinach (Tofutti), 2 oz.	210	12.0	32.0	4.0	0	158	m.q.
Provencale (Green Giant Microwave Garden Gourmet), 1 pkg.	210	7.0	36.0	5.0	15	720	4.0 d
veal, in Alfredo sauce (Stouffer's), 85/8 oz.	500	25.0	32.0	30.0	m.q.	860	m.q.

Food and Measure	cal.	prot. (gms)	carbo. (gms)	fat (gms)	chol. (mgs)	sod. (mgs)	fiber (gms)
Tortellini, packaged:							
w/shrimp and seafood (Hormel Top Shelf), 10 oz.	278	16.0	36.0	8.0	89	1341	m.q.
in marinara sauce (Hormel Top Shelf), 10 oz.	211	10.0	37.0	3.0	35	663	m.q.
Tortellini, refriger- ated, 4.5 oz.:							
egg:							
w/cheese (Con- tadina Fresh) . .	380	21.0	60.0	6.0	70	570	m.q.
w/chicken and pro- sciutto (Contadina Fresh)	370	24.0	53.0	7.0	75	560	m.q.
w/meat (Contadina Fresh)	380	22.0	60.0	6.0	75	580	m.q.
spinach:							
w/cheese (Con- tadina Fresh) . .	380	21.0	60.0	6.0	70	590	m.q.
w/chicken and pro- sciutto (Contadina Fresh)	340	24.0	53.0	7.0	75	580	m.q.
w/meat (Contadina Fresh)	380	22.0	60.0	6.0	75	610	m.q.
Tortilla, 1 piece:							
corn (Azteca)	45	1.0	9.0	0	0	10	0
corn (Old El Paso) .	60	1.0	10.0	1.0	0	170	n.a.
flour:							
(Azteca), 9″ diam.	130	3.0	23.0	3.0	0	180	0
(Azteca), 7″ diam.	80	2.0	14.0	2.0	0	110	0
(Old El Paso) . . .	150	4.0	27.0	3.0	0	360	n.a.
Tortilla entree, fro- zen:							
grande (Stouffer's), 9⅝ oz.	530	24.0	34.0	33.0	n.a.	910	m.q.

Food and Measure	cal.	prot. (gms)	carbo. (gms)	fat (gms)	chol. (mgs)	sod. (mgs)	fiber (gms)
Tortilla chips, see "Corn chips and similar snacks"							
Tostaco shell:							
(Old El Paso), 1 piece	100	1.0	11.0	5.0	0	10	1.0 d
Tostada shell:							
(Lawry's), 1 piece . .	73	1.2	9.5	3.5	0	147	.4 c
(Old El Paso), 2 pieces	110	1.0	12.0	6.0	0	130	1.5 d
(Ortega), 1 piece . .	50	0	8.0	2.0	0	5	m.q.
(Tio Sancho), 1 piece	67	1.2	8.4	3.2	0	1	.5 c
Tree fern, cooked:							
chopped, 1/2 cup . .	28	.2	7.8	.1	0	3	.4 c
Triticale, whole-grain:							
1 cup	646	25.1	138.5	4.0	0	10	34.8 d
Triticale flour:							
whole-grain, 1 cup . .	440	17.1	95.1	2.4	0	3	19.0 d
Trout, meat only:							
raw, 1 lb.	673	94.2	0	30.0	264	236	0
raw, 1 oz.	42	5.9	0	1.9	16	15	0
rainbow:							
raw, 1 lb.	535	93.2	0	15.2	257	122	0
raw, 1 oz.	33	5.8	0	1.0	16	8	0
baked, broiled, or microwaved, 4 oz.	171	29.9	0	4.9	83	39	0
sea, see "Sea trout"							
Tumeric, ground:							
1 tsp.	8	.2	1.4	.2	0	1	.2 c
Tuna, fresh, meat only:							
bluefin:							
raw, 1 lb.	652	105.8	0	22.2	173	177	0
raw, 1 oz.	41	6.6	0	1.4	11	11	0
baked, broiled, or microwaved, 4 oz.	209	33.9	0	7.1	56	57	0
skipjack:							
raw, 1 lb.	468	99.8	0	4.6	213	167	0
raw, 1 oz.	29	6.2	0	.3	13	10	0

Food and Measure	cal.	prot. (gms)	carbo. (gms)	fat (gms)	chol. (mgs)	sod. (mgs)	fiber (gms)
yellowfin:							
raw, 1 lb.	492	106.0	0	4.3	203	168	0
raw, 1 oz.	31	6.6	0	.3	13	10	0
Tuna, canned,							
drained, 2 oz.:							
solid light, in oil:							
(Star-Kist Prime							
Catch)	150	13.0	<1.0	13.0	25	310	0
solid light, in water:							
(Empress)	60	12.0	0	1.0	m.q.	310	0
(Star-Kist/Star-Kist							
Prime Catch) . .	60	14.0	<1.0	<1.0	25	310	0
chunk light, in oil:							
(Bumble Bee) . . .	110	12.0	0	12.0	30	310	0
(S&W Fancy) . . .	140	13.0	0	10.0	m.q.	450	0
(Star-Kist)	150	13.0	<1.0	13.0	25	310	0
chunk light, in water:							
(Bumble Bee) . . .	50	12.0	0	1.0	30	310	0
(S&W Fancy) . . .	60	13.0	0	1.0	m.q.	500	0
(Star-Kist)	60	13.0	<1.0	<1.0	25	310	0
(Star-Kist Select-							
60% Less Salt)	65	14.0	<1.0	1.0	25	120	0
distilled water *(Star-*							
Kist Diet)	65	14.0	<1.0	<1.0	25	35	0
solid white, albacore,							
·in oil:							
(Bumble Bee) . . .	100	14.0	0	8.0	30	310	0
(Star-Kist)	140	14.0	<1.0	10.0	25	310	0
(S&W Fancy) . . .	160	13.0	0	12.0	m.q.	450	0
solid white, albacore,							
in water:							
(Bumble Bee) . . .	60	14.0	0	2.0	30	310	0
(Star-Kist)	70	15.0	<1.0	1.0	25	310	0
chunk white, in oil:							
(Bumble Bee) . . .	110	12.0	0	12.0 ·	30	310	0
(Star-Kist)	140	14.0	<1.0	10.0	25	310	0
chunk white, in water:							
(Bumble Bee) . . .	60	12.0	0	2.0	30	310	0

Food and Measure	cal.	prot. (gms)	carbo. (gms)	fat (gms)	chol. (mgs)	sod. (mgs)	fiber (gms)
Tuna, canned, chunk white, in water *(cont.)*							
(Star-Kist Select-60% Less Salt)	70	15.0	<1.0	<1.0	25	120	0
distilled water *(Star-Kist Diet)*	70	15.0	<1.0	1.0	25	30	0
Tuna, frozen:							
steak, w/out seasoning mix *(SeaPak)*, 6 oz.	180	40.0	0	2.0	75	65	0
"Tuna," vegetarian, frozen:							
(Worthington Tuno), 2 oz.	100	5.0	3.0	7.0	0	310	m.q.
Tuna entree, frozen:							
noodle casserole *(Stouffer's)*, 10 oz.	310	17.0	31.0	13.0	m.q.	1340	m.q.
pie *(Banquet)*, 7 oz.	540	17.0	44.0	33.0	30	810	m.q.
Tuna entree mix[1]:							
au gratin *(Tuna Helper)*, 6 oz. . . .	280	16.0	30.0	11.0	m.q.	980	m.q.
fettucini Alfredo *(Tuna Helper)*, 7 oz. . . .	300	16.0	30.0	13.0	m.q.	1000	m.q.
mushroom, creamy *(Tuna Helper)*, 7 oz.	220	14.0	28.0	6.0	m.q.	740	m.q.
noodle:							
cheesy *(Tuna Helper)*, 7.75 oz.	250	15.0	28.0	9.0	m.q.	980	m.q.
creamy *(Tuna Helper)*, 8 oz. . .	300	14.0	30.0	14.0	m.q.	960	m.q.
pot pie *(Tuna Helper)*, 5.1 oz.	420	13.0	31.0	27.0	m.q.	890	m.q.
rice, buttery *(Tuna Helper)*, 6 oz. . . .	280	13.0	32.0	11.0	m.q.	1040	m.q.
salad *(Tuna Helper)*, 5.5 oz.	420	14.0	29.0	27.0	m.q.	870	m.q.
tetrazzini *(Tuna Helper)*, 6 oz. . . .	240	15.0	27.0	8.0	m.q.	780	m.q.

[1] *Prepared according to package directions, with water-packed tuna.*

Food and Measure	cal.	prot. (gms)	carbo. (gms)	fat (gms)	chol. (mgs)	sod. (mgs)	fiber (gms)
Tuna salad, 1 oz.:							
(Longacre)	58	2.0	3.0	4.0	10	130	n.a.
(Longacre Saladfest)	52	3.0	2.0	4.0	10	180	n.a.
Tuna sandwich, frozen:							
(Mrs. Paul's Microwave), 1 sandwich	200	10.0	23.0	6.0	m.q.	590	m.q.
Turbot, European, meat only:							
raw, 1 lb.	432	72.8	0	13.4	m.q.	678	0
raw, 1 oz.	27	4.6	0	.8	m.q.	43	0
Turkey, fresh, all classes, roasted:							
meat w/skin, 4 oz.	236	31.9	0	11.0	93	77	0
meat only:							
4 oz.	193	33.2	0	5.6	86	79	0
diced, 1 cup	238	41.0	0	7.0	107	99	0
skin only, 1 oz. . . .	125	5.6	0	11.2	32	15	0
light meat:							
w/skin, 4 oz. . . .	223	32.4	0	9.4	86	71	0
meat only, 4 oz. . .	178	33.9	0	3.7	78	73	0
meat only, diced, 1 cup	219	41.9	0	4.5	97	89	0
dark meat:							
w/skin, 4 oz. . . .	251	31.2	0	13.1	101	86	0
meat only, 4 oz. . .	212	32.4	0	8.2	96	90	0
meat only, diced, 1 cup	262	40.0	0	10.1	119	110	0
back, meat w/skin, 4 oz.	276	30.2	0	16.3	103	83	0
breast, meat w/skin:							
1/2 breast, 1.9 lb., (4.2 lbs. raw w/ bone)	1637	248.1	0	64.1	643	541	0
4 oz.	214	32.6	0	8.4	84	71	0
leg, meat w/skin:							
1 leg, 1.2 lb. (1.5 lbs. raw w/bone)	1133	152.2	0	53.6	466	420	0

Food and Measure	cal.	prot. (gms)	carbo. (gms)	fat (gms)	chol. (mgs)	sod. (mgs)	fiber (gms)
Turkey leg, meat w/skin *(cont.)*							
4 oz.	236	31.6	0	11.1	96	87	0
wing, meat w/skin:							
1 wing, 6.6 oz. (9.9 oz. raw w/bone)	426	50.9	0	23.1	150	114	0
4 oz.	260	31.0	0	14.1	92	69	0
Turkey, frozen or refrigerated:							
breast, raw:							
(Longacre Cook-N-Bag), 1 oz. . . .	27	6.0	<1.0	<1.0	10	120	0
(Longacre Ready-to-Cook), 1 oz. . .	39	8.0	0	<1.0	m.q.	150	0
w/gravy *(Norbest),* 4 oz.	115	20.7	1.1	2.4	m.q.	492	0
steaks, cubed *(Norbest),* 4-oz. steak	135	27.8	<.1	<2.0	m.q.	81	0
strips and tips *(Norbest Tasti-Lean),* 4 oz. . . .	135	27.8	<.1	<2.0	m.q.	81	0
tenderloin *(Norbest Tasti-Lean* Tenders), 4 oz. . . .	135	27.8	<.1	<2.0	m.q.	81	0
breast, cooked:							
(Land O'Lakes), 3 oz.	100	20.0	0	1.0	50	55	0
(Longacre Cook-N-Bag), 1 oz. . . .	38	8.0	<1.0	<1.0	15	85	0
barbecued *(Louis Rich),* 1 oz. . . .	35	5.0	1.0	1.0	10	315	0
barbecue, quarter *(Mr. Turkey* Chub), 1 oz. . . .	34	5.4	1.0	1.0	11	251	0
hickory smoked *(Louis Rich),* 1 oz.	35	5.0	1.0	1.0	10	350	0
honey roasted *(Louis Rich),* 1 oz.	35	5.0	1.0	1.0	10	360	0

Food and Measure	cal.	prot. (gms)	carbo. (gms)	fat (gms)	chol. (mgs)	sod. (mgs)	fiber (gms)
oven prepared, quarter *(Mr. Turkey Chub)*, 1 oz.	34	5.8	.4	1.0	12	266	0
oven roasted *(Louis Rich)*, 1 oz.	30	5.0	<1.0	1.0	10	300	0
smoked, quarter *(Mr. Turkey Chub)*, 1 oz. . .	35	6.1	.3	1.0	10	263	0
and dark, roasted *(Louis Rich)*, 1 oz.	30	5.0	1.0	<1.0	15	290	0
cutlets, raw *(Norbest Tasti-Lean)*, 4 oz.	135	27.8	<.1	<2.0	m.q.	81	0
dark meat:							
hickory smoked, roasted *(Louis Rich)*, 1 oz. . . .	35	5.0	1.0	<1.0	20	305	0
skinless, roasted *(Swift Butterball)*, 3.5 oz.	195	26.0	n.a.	10.0	130	90	0
drumsticks:							
(Land O'Lakes), 3 oz.	120	17.0	0	5.0	m.q.	85	0
(Louis Rich), 1 oz. cooked	55	8.0	<1.0	3.0	30	20	0
w/gravy, raw *(Norbest)*, 4 oz. . .	115	20.3	1.1	2.7	m.q.	600	0
ground, see "Turkey, ground"							
hindquarter roast *(Land O'Lakes)*, 3 oz.	140	17.0	0	8.0	m.q.	80	0
thigh:							
(Land O'Lakes), 3 oz.	150	17.0	0	10.0	m.q.	75	0
(Louis Rich), 1 oz. cooked	65	7.0	<1.0	4.0	30	20	0

Food and Measure	cal.	prot. (gms)	carbo. (gms)	fat (gms)	chol. (mgs)	sod. (mgs)	fiber (gms)
Turkey, frozen or refrigerated *(cont.)*							
white meat, skinless, roasted *(Swift Butterball)*, 3.5 oz. . .	160	30.0	n.a.	4.0	80	130	0
white and dark meat w/skin roasted *(Swift Butterball)*, 3.5 oz.	195	27.0	n.a.	10.0	100	115	0
whole, cooked, 1 oz.:							
boneless *(Norbest)*	42	6.2	.3	1.5	m.q.	105	0
boneless, smoked *(Norbest)*	42	6.4	.3	1.6	m.q.	218	0
w/out giblets *(Louis Rich)*	55	8.0	<1.0	3.0	20	20	0
wings:							
(Land O'Lakes), 3 oz.	120	18.0	0	5.0	m.q.	65	0
(Louis Rich), 1 oz. cooked	55	7.0	<1.0	3.0	25	15	0
(Louis Rich Drumettes)*, 1 oz. cooked	50	8.0	<1.0	2.0	25	20	0
portions *(Louis Rich)*, 1 oz. cooked	55	7.0	<1.0	3.0	25	15	0
young, 3 oz.:							
(Land O'Lakes) . .	130	17.0	<1.0	7.0	65	55	0
butter basted *(Land O'Lakes)*	140	17.0	<1.0	8.0	85	135	0
self-basting, broth *(Land O'Lakes)*	120	18.0	<1.0	5.0	77	145	0
Turkey, luncheon meat and boneless, cooked, 1 oz., except as noted:							
bologna, see "Turkey bologna"							

Food and Measure	cal.	prot. (gms)	carbo. (gms)	fat (gms)	chol. (mgs)	sod. (mgs)	fiber (gms)
breast:							
(*Butterball* Cold Cuts)	30	5.0	1.0	1.0	m.q.	230	0
(*Butterball Deli* No Salt Added) . . .	45	7.0	0	2.0	m.q.	15	0
(*Butterball Slice 'n Serve*)	35	5.0	<1.0	1.0	m.q.	230	0
(*Healthy Deli* Gourmet)	28	4.9	.5	.6	9	170	0
(*Healthy Deli* Lessalt)	25	4.5	.4	.5	9	140	0
(*Hormel* Perma-Fresh), 2 slices	60	9.0	0	2.0	m.q.	484	0
(*Longacre* Premium)	30	4.0	1.0	1.0	10	250	0
(*Longacre* Salt Watchers)	32	7.0	0	<1.0	15	10	0
(*Louis Rich*)	45	8.0	<1.0	2.0	15	20	0
(*Louis Rich* Sliced)	40	8.0	<1.0	1.0	15	25	0
(*Mr. Turkey*)	31	5.8	.3	.7	10	233	0
barbecue (*Butterball Slice 'n Serve*)	40	5.0	1.0	2.0	m.q.	210	0
browned, glazed (*Longacre* Premium)	30	4.0	1.0	1.0	10	300	0
browned, roasted (*Longacre* Premium)	30	4.0	1.0	1.0	10	300	0
honey (*Healthy Deli*)	28	4.9	.5	.5	9	170	0
honey-roasted (*Louis Rich*) . . .	30	5.0	1.0	1.0	15	310	0
golden (*Boar's Head*)	35	6.0	<1.0	1.0	20	200	0
golden, skinless (*Boar's Head*) . .	30	6.0	<1.0	<1.0	10	m.q.	0
lean lite, skinless or smoked (*Longacre Deli*)	35	6.0	0	1.0	15	160	0

Food and Measure	cal.	prot. (gms)	carbo. (gms)	fat (gms)	chol. (mgs)	sod. (mgs)	fiber (gms)
Turkey, luncheon meat and boneless, breast *(cont.)*							
oven cooked							
(Healthy Deli) . .	26	4.7	.4	.2	8	180	0
oven roasted *(Louis*							
Rich)	30	5.0	1.0	1.0	10	325	0
oven roasted *(Oscar*							
Mayer), 3/4 oz.	22	3.9	.5	.5	9	289	0
roast *(Louis Rich)*	40	8.0	<1.0	1.0	20	20	0
breast, w/skin:							
(Norbest Orange							
Label)	28	5.7	.1	.3	m.q.	232	0
prebrowned							
(Norbest Orange							
Label)	29	5.1	.2	.8	m.q.	259	0
smoked *(Norbest*							
Orange Label)	30	5.3	.9	.5	m.q.	284	0
breast, skinless:							
(Longacre Premium)	30	4.0	1.0	<1.0	10	250	0
(Norbest Orange							
Label)	26	5.1	.5	.2	m.q.	239	0
(Norbest Norfresh)	27	5.2	.5	.3	m.q.	269	0
breast, smoked:							
(Butterball Cold							
Cuts)	35	5.0	0	1.0	m.q.	190	0
(Healthy Deli) . . .	29	4.8	.5	.5	8	180	0
(Healthy Deli Gour-							
met)	31	5.8	.4	.5	11	170	0
(Hormel Perma-							
Fresh), 2 slices	60	10.0	0	2.0	m.q.	540	0
(Longacre)	35	6.0	0	1.0	15	240	0
(Louis Rich), .7-oz.							
slice	20	4.0	<1.0	<1.0	10	210	0
(Mr. Turkey)	31	5.9	.3	.7	10	332	0
(Norbest Gold La-							
bel)	29	6.4	.1	<.6	m.q.	270	0
(OHSE)	30	5.0	1.0	1.0	m.q.	340	0
(Oscar Mayer),							
3/4 oz.	20	4.2	.2	.3	9	317	0

Food and Measure	cal.	prot. (gms)	carbo. (gms)	fat (gms)	chol. (mgs)	sod. (mgs)	fiber (gms)
hickory (Butterball Slice 'n Serve)	35	5.0	1.0	1.0	m.q.	250	0
sliced (Longacre)	26	5.0	1.0	<1.0	10	260	0
breast steaks (Louis Rich)	40	8.0	<1.0	1.0	20	25	0
breast tenderloin (Louis Rich)	40	8.0	<1.0	<1.0	10	20	0
breast and white: (Longacre Deli Chef)	35	5.0	1.0	1.0	15	240	0
breast, browned: roasted (Longacre Deli Chef)	40	5.0	1.0	2.0	15	240	0
skinless (Longacre Deli Chef)	40	4.0	1.0	2.0	15	240	0
breast, diced, white meat (Norbest) . .	31	4.4	1.0	.9	m.q.	318	0
ham, see "Turkey ham"							
ham flavor, hickory smoked, dark meat (Norbest Gourmet)	39	4.6	.1	2.2	m.q.	335	0
loaf (Louis Rich) . . .	45	5.0	<1.0	3.0	15	265	0
luncheon loaf, spiced (Mr. Turkey)	51	4.2	.5	3.6	11	292	0
oven cooked (OHSE)	30	5.0	1.0	1.0	m.q.	190	0
pastrami, see "Turkey pastrami"							
roll: white meat (Norbest Orange Label)	29	4.1	.5	.9	m.q.	299	0
white and dark meat (Norbest Orange Label)	36	4.0	.3	2.0	m.q.	314	0
salami, see "Turkey salami"							
sausage, see "Turkey sausage"							

Food and Measure	cal.	prot. (gms)	carbo. (gms)	fat (gms)	chol. (mgs)	sod. (mgs)	fiber (gms)
Turkey, luncheon meat and boneless *(cont.)*							
smoked:							
(Butterball Cold Cuts)	35	5.0	1.0	1.0	m.q.	220	0
(Butterball Turkey Variety Pak), ³/₄ oz.	25	4.0	1.0	1.0	m.q.	160	0
(Louis Rich)	30	5.0	<1.0	1.0	15	290	0
Turkey, canned:							
chunk *(Hormel),* 6³/₄ oz.	230	37.0	0	10.0	m.q.	1278	0
white *(Swanson),* 2¹/₂ oz.	90	16.0	0	2.0	m.q.	260	0
white and dark *(Swanson),* 2¹/₂ oz. . . .	90	15.0	1.0	3.0	m.q.	280	0
Turkey, ground (see also "Turkey sausage"), 1 oz.:							
(Longacre)	60	5.0	0	4.0	30	20	0
(Mr. Turkey)	54	4.5	0	4.0	20	27	0
(Hudson's)	55	5.0	0	3.7	m.q.	35	0
cooked:							
(Louis Rich 85% Lean)	60	7.0	<1.0	4.0	25	25	0
(Louis Rich 90% Lean)	50	6.0	<1.0	3.0	25	30	0
"Turkey," vegetarian:							
canned, 2 slices:							
(Worthington Turkee Slices)	130	9.0	3.0	9.0	0	430	m.q.
(Worthington 209)	120	8.0	3.0	8.0	0	m.q.	m.q.
frozen, smoked, roll or slices *(Worthington),* 2.7 oz.	180	13.0	5.0	12.0	0	820	m.q.

Food and Measure	cal.	prot. (gms)	carbo. (gms)	fat (gms)	chol. (mgs)	sod. (mgs)	fiber (gms)
Turkey bologna, 1 oz., except as noted:							
*(Butterball Deli/Slice 'n Serve/*Cold Cuts)	70	4.0	2.0	6.0	m.q.	370	0
(Butterball Turkey Variety Pak), ¾ oz. . .	50	3.0	1.0	4.0	m.q.	280	0
(Longacre Sliced) . .	61	4.0	0	5.0	25	270	0
(Louis Rich)	60	3.0	<1.0	5.0	20	235	0
(Norbest Blue Label, 2/2.5 lb.)	68	3.5	.5	5.6	m.q.	331	0
(OHSE)	70	3.0	2.0	6.0	m.q.	300	0
mild *(Louis Rich)* . .	60	4.0	<1.0	5.0	15	300	0
Turkey and corned beef:							
(Healthy Deli Double-decker), 1 oz. . . .	30	5.1	.6	.7	12	195	0
Turkey dinner, frozen:							
(Banquet), 10.5 oz.	390	18.0	35.0	20.0	40	1110	m.q.
(Banquet Extra Helping), 19 oz.	750	29.0	68.0	42.0	65	1980	m.q.
(Morton), 10 oz. . . .	230	15.0	28.0	6.0	45	1300	m.q.
(Swanson), 11½ oz.	350	20.0	42.0	11.0	m.q.	1110	m.q.
(Swanson Hungry Man), 17 oz. . . .	550	36.0	61.0	18.0	m.q.	1810	m.q.
breast: *(Healthy Choice),* 10.5 oz.	290	21.0	39.0	5.0	45	420	m.q.
Dijon *(The Budget Gourmet),* 11.2 oz.	340	20.0	37.0	12.0	65	860	m.q.
roast *(Stouffer's Dinner Supreme),* 10¾ oz.	330	27.0	32.0	10.0	m.q.	1290	m.q.
breast, sliced: *(The Budget Gourmet),* 11.1 oz. . .	290	16.0	36.0	9.0	45	1200	m.q.

Food and Measure	cal.	prot. (gms)	carbo. (gms)	fat (gms)	chol. (mgs)	sod. (mgs)	fiber (gms)
Turkey dinner, breast, sliced *(cont.)*							
in mushroom sauce *(Lean Cuisine)*, 8 oz.	240	23.0	20.0	7.0	50	790	m.q.
w/mushroom gravy *(Le Menu)*, 10½ oz.	270	17.0	37.0	6.0	m.q.	1020	m.q.
Divan *(Le Menu* Light Style), 10 oz. . . .	280	22.0	26.0	9.0	m.q.	840	m.q.
w/dressing and gravy *(Armour Classics)*, 11.5 oz.	320	19.0	34.0	12.0	50	1280	m.q.
sliced *(Freezer Queen)*, 10 oz. . .	280	16.0	36.0	8.0	m.q.	1210	m.q.
Turkey entree, freeze-dried:							
tetrazzini *(Mountain House)*, 1 cup . . .	200	13.0	20.0	8.0	m.q.	m.q.	m.q.
Turkey entree, fro-zen:							
(Tyson Gourmet Se-lection), 11.5 oz.	380	19.0	51.0	11.0	m.q.	1350	m.q.
à la king, w/rice *(The Budget Gourmet)* 10 oz.	390	20.0	36.0	18.0	75	740	m.q.
breast, stuffed *(Weight Watchers)*, 8.5 oz.	260	20.0	24.0	10.0	80	910	m.q.
casserole: *(Pillsbury Microwave Classic)*, 1 pkg.	430	20.0	31.0	25.0	m.q.	880	0
w/gravy and dress-ing *(Stouffer's)*, 9¾ oz.	360	23.0	29.0	17.0	m.q.	1090	m.q.
croquettes, gravy and *(Freezer Queen Family Suppers)*, 7 oz.	250	13.0	19.0	13.0	m.q.	940	m.q.

Food and Measure	cal.	prot. (gms)	carbo. (gms)	fat (gms)	chol. (mgs)	sod. (mgs)	fiber (gms)
Dijon (Lean Cuisine), 9½ oz.	270	24.0	22.0	10.0	60	900	m.q.
w/dressing and potatoes (Swanson Homestyle Recipe), 9 oz.	290	17.0	30.0	13.0	m.q.	1020	m.q.
glazed (The Budget Gourmet Slim Selects), 9 oz. . . .	270	17.0	39.0	5.0	50	760	m.q.
and gravy, w/dressing (Freezer Queen Deluxe Family Suppers), 7 oz.	160	12.0	18.0	5.0	m.q.	1130	m.q.
pie:							
(Banquet), 7 oz. . . .	510	16.0	39.0	31.0	40	860	m.q.
(Banquet Supreme Microwave), 7 oz.	430	15.0	30.0	27.0	35	740	m.q.
(Morton), 7 oz. . . .	420	14.0	27.0	28.0	40	740	m.q.
(Stouffer's), 10 oz.	540	20.0	35.0	36.0	m.q.	1300	m.q.
(Swanson), 7 oz.	390	10.0	38.0	22.0	m.q.	720	m.q.
(Swanson Hungry Man), 16 oz. . .	750	27.0	65.0	42.0	m.q.	1670	m.q.
sliced, breast, in mushroom sauce (Lean Cuisine), 8 oz.	240	23.0	20.0	7.0	50	750	m.q.
sliced, gravy and:							
(Banquet Cookin' Bags), 5 oz.	100	7.0	5.0	6.0	m.q.	m.q.	m.q.
(Banquet Family Entrees), 8 oz.	150	12.0	8.0	8.0	m.q.	m.q.	m.q.
(Freezer Queen Cook-In-Pouch), 5 oz.	70	7.0	6.0	2.0	m.q.	880	m.q.
(Freezer Queen Family Suppers), 7 oz.	110	9.0	8.0	5.0	m.q.	1160	m.q.

Food and Measure	cal.	prot. (gms)	carbo. (gms)	fat (gms)	chol. (mgs)	sod. (mgs)	fiber (gms)
Turkey entree, frozen *(cont.)*							
sliced, and gravy, w/ dressing *(Freezer Queen* Single Serve), 9 oz. . . .	230	17.0	32.0	5.0	m.q.	1130	m.q.
sliced, in curry sauce w/rice pilaf *(Right Course)*, 8¾ oz.	320	23.0	40.0	8.0	50	570	m.q.
tetrazzini *(Stouffer's)*, 10 oz.	380	22.0	28.0	20.0	m.q.	1170	m.q.
Turkey fat:							
1 tbsp	115	0	0	12.8	13	0	0
Turkey frankfurter:							
(Butterball), 1 link . .	140	7.0	2.0	11.0	m.q.	610	0
(Longacre), 1 oz. . . .	66	4.0	0	6.0	30	260	0
(Mr. Turkey), 1.6 oz.	106	5.5	.9	8.9	31	440	0
cheese *(Mr. Turkey)*, 1.6 oz.	109	5.9	.9	9.1	29	526	0
Turkey giblets, simmered:							
4 oz.	189	30.1	2.4	5.8	474	67	0
chopped or diced, 1 cup	243	38.5	3.0	7.4	606	85	0
Turkey gravy:							
canned:							
(Franco-American), 2 oz.	30	0	3.0	2.0	n.a.	290	n.a.
(Heinz), 2 oz. . . .	30	1.0	2.0	2.0	n.a.	140	n.a.
w/chunky turkey *(Hormel Great Beginnings)*, 5 oz.	138	11.0	7.0	8.0	m.q.	585	n.a.
mix[1]:							
(Lawry's), 1 cup . .	102	2.6	13.4	4.1	n.a.	1400	.1 c
(McCormick/Schilling), ¼ cup . .	22	.5	4.0	.5	n.a.	353	n.a.

[1] *Prepared according to package directions.*

Food and Measure	cal.	prot. (gms)	carbo. (gms)	fat (gms)	chol. (mgs)	sod. (mgs)	fiber (gms)
Turkey ham, 1 oz., except as noted:							
(*Butterball* Cold Cuts)	35	5.0	1.0	1.0	m.q.	390	0
(*Butterball* Slice 'n Serve)	35	5.0	1.0	2.0	m.q.	340	0
(*Longacre* Deli Lean Lite)	37	6.0	0	2.0	25	150	0
(*Louis Rich* Round/un-sliced)	35	5.0	<1.0	1.0	20	300	0
(*Louis Rich* Square), 3/4-oz. slice	25	4.0	<1.0	<1.0	15	215	0
breakfast, smoked (*Mr. Turkey*)	33	5.0	.4	1.3	16	306	0
buffet style, smoked (*Mr. Turkey*)	32	4.7	.4	1.3	17	340	0
chopped (*Louis Rich*)	40	5.0	<1.0	2.0	15	260	0
chopped (*Mr. Turkey*)	37	5.4	.3	1.6	17	301	0
chunk (*Longacre*) . .	37	5.0	0	2.0	25	360	0
cured thigh meat: (*Norbest* Tavern, 2–2.5 lb. half) . . .	29	4.7	.6	.8	m.q.	312	0
Canadian style (*Norbest*)	35	5.1	.3	1.4	m.q.	331	0
honey cured: (*Butterball* Cold Cuts)	35	5.0	1.0	1.0	m.q.	380	0
(*Butterball* Slice 'n Serve)	40	5.0	1.0	2.0	m.q.	370	0
(*Louis Rich*), 3/4 oz.	25	4.0	<1.0	<1.0	15	220	0
chopped (*Butterball* Coldcuts)	35	5.0	2.0	1.0	m.q.	290	0
roll (*Norbest*)	31	4.6	.5	1.1	m.q.	346	0
sliced (*Butterball* Deli Thin)	35	5.0	1.0	1.0	m.q.	390	0
sliced (*Longacre*) . .	33	6.0	0	1.0	20	310	0
smoked: (*Mr. Turkey*)	32	5.4	.3	1.0	18	286	0
(*Mr. Turkey* Chub)	32	4.7	.4	1.3	17	340	0

Food and Measure	cal.	prot. (gms)	carbo. (gms)	fat (gms)	chol. (mgs)	sod. (mgs)	fiber (gms)
Turkey and ham:							
(Healthy Deli Double-decker), 1 oz. . . .	30	4.8	.8	.9	11	185	0
Turkey ham salad:							
(Longacre), 1 oz. . .	53	2.0	3.0	4.0	10	190	n.a.
(Longacre Saladfest), 1 oz.	58	2.0	2.0	4.0	10	270	n.a.
Turkey luncheon meat, see "Turkey, luncheon meat and boneless"							
Turkey nuggets:							
cooked[1] *(Louis Rich),* .7-oz. piece	65	3.0	4.0	4.0	8	160	n.a.
Turkey pastrami, 1 oz., except as noted:							
(Butterball Cold Cuts)	30	5.0	0	1.0	m.q.	290	0
(Butterball Slice 'n Serve)	35	5.0	1.0	1.0	m.q.	320	0
(Louis Rich Round)	35	5.0	<1.0	1.0	20	300	0
(Louis Rich Square), .8-oz. slice	25	4.0	<1.0	<1.0	15	265	0
(Mr. Turkey)	28	4.8	.1	.9	17	383	0
(Norbest, 3 lb.) . . .	29	4.8	.3	.9	m.q.	302	0
sliced *(Longacre)* . .	32	5.0	0	1.0	20	260	0
Turkey patty:							
cooked[1] *(Louis Rich),* 2.9-oz. patty	220	12.0	13.0	13.0	10	555	m.q.
Turkey pie, see "Turkey entree"							
Turkey salad, 1 oz.:							
(Longacre)	70	3.0	3.0	5.0	10	200	n.a.
(Longacre Saladfest)	68	3.0	2.0	5.0	15	180	n.a.

[1] *Prepared according to package directions.*

Food and Measure	cal.	prot. (gms)	carbo. (gms)	fat (gms)	chol. (mgs)	sod. (mgs)	fiber (gms)
Turkey salami, 1 oz., except as noted:							
*(Butterball Deli/Slice 'n Serve/*Cold Cuts)	50	4.0	1.0	4.0	m.q.	350	0
(Butterball Turkey Variety Pak), 3/4 oz. . .	40	3.0	1.0	3.0	m.q.	260	0
(Longacre Sliced) . .	52	4.0	1.0	4.0	20	290	0
(Louis Rich)	55	4.0	<1.0	4.0	20	260	0
(Norbest Blue Label, 2–2.5 lb.)	45	4.2	.9	2.6	m.q.	314	0
(OHSE)	50	4.0	1.0	3.0	m.q.	260	0
cooked	56	4.6	.2	3.9	23	285	0
cotto:							
(Louis Rich)	50	4.0	<1.0	4.0	20	270	0
(Mr. Turkey)	45	4.3	.4	2.9	16	369	0
Turkey sausage, 1 oz:							
(Butterball)	50	4.0	<1.0	4.0	m.q.	250	0
(Norbest Tasti-Lean)	53	4.6	.3	2.8	m.q.	179	0
breakfast:							
(Mr. Turkey)	58	4.6	.4	4.3	16	181	0
ground *(Hudson's)*	65	4.3	0	5.3	m.q.	180	0
ground, cooked *(Louis Rich)* . . .	55	6.0	<1.0	4.0	25	210	0
Polish:							
(Louis Rich Polska)	50	5.0	<1.0	3.0	20	260	0
(Mr. Turkey Polska)	59	4.4	.5	4.4	15	264	0
smoked:							
(Louis Rich)	50	5.0	<1.0	3.0	20	255	0
(Mr. Turkey)	47	4.5	.5	3.4	19	230	0
w/cheese *(Louis Rich)*	55	5.0	<1.0	4.0	20	275	0
Turkey sticks:							
(Louis Rich), 1 stick[1]	80	4.0	5.0	5.0	10	200	m.q.
Turkey summer sausage:							
(Louis Rich), 1 oz. . .	55	5.0	<1.0	4.0	25	325	0

[1] *Prepared according to package directions.*

Food and Measure	cal.	prot. (gms)	carbo. (gms)	fat (gms)	chol. (mgs)	sod. (mgs)	fiber (gms)
Turmeric:							
(Spice Islands), 1 tsp.	7	.2	1.3	.2	0	<1	.1 c
Turnip:							
fresh or stored:							
raw, untrimmed,							
1 lb.	100	3.3	22.9	.4	0	248	6.6 d
raw, cubed, 1/2 cup	18	.6	4.1	.1	0	44	1.2 d
boiled, drained,							
cubed, 1/2 cup	14	.6	3.8	.1	0	39	1.6 d
boiled, drained,							
mashed, 1/2 cup	21	.8	5.6	.1	0	58	2.3 d
canned, 1/2 cup:							
(Stokely)	20	2.0	3.0	0	0	350	m.q.
diced *(Allens)* . . .	16	2.0	2.0	<1.0	0	25	m.q.
frozen:							
boiled, drained,							
4 oz.	26	1.7	4.9	.3	0	41	.8 c
diced *(Southern)*,							
3.5 oz.	17	1.0	2.9	.2	0	50	m.q.
Turnip greens:							
fresh:							
raw, untrimmed,							
1 lb.	85	4.8	18.2	1.0	0	126	7.6 d
raw, chopped,							
1/2 cup	7	.4	1.6	.1	0	11	.7 d
boiled, drained,							
chopped, 1/2 cup	15	.8	3.1	.2	0	21	2.2 d
canned, 1/2 cup:							
w/liquid	17	1.6	2.8	.4	0	325	.7 c
chopped *(Allens)*	21	2.0	3.0	<1.0	0	15	m.q.
chopped, w/diced							
turnips *(Allens)*	19	2.0	1.0	<1.0	0	15	m.q.
w/diced turnips							
(Stokely)	20	2.0	0	0	0	340	m.q.
frozen, chopped:							
(Frosty Acres),							
3.3 oz.	20	2.0	4.0	0	0	10	1.0 c
(Seabrook), 3.3 oz.	20	2.0	4.0	0	0	11	1.0 c

Food and Measure	cal.	prot. (gms)	carbo. (gms)	fat (gms)	chol. (mgs)	sod. (mgs)	fiber (gms)
(Southern), 3.5 oz. w/diced turnips	25	2.5	3.6	.3	0	70	m.q.
(Seabrook), 3.3 oz.	20	3.0	3.0	0	0	n.a.	m.q.
Turnover, frozen or refrigerated, 1 piece:							
apple *(Pepperidge Farm)*	300	3.0	34.0	17.0	n.a.	210	m.q.
apple *(Pillsbury)* . . .	170	2.0	23.0	8.0	5	320	m.q.
blueberry *(Pepperidge Farm)*	310	3.0	32.0	19.0	n.a.	230	m.q.
cherry *(Pepperidge Farm)*	310	3.0	32.0	19.0	n.a.	280	m.q.
cherry *(Pillsbury)* . . .	170	2.0	24.0	8.0	5	310	m.q.
peach *(Pepperidge Farm)*	310	3.0	34.0	18.0	n.a.	260	m.q.
raspberry *(Pepperidge Farm)*	310	3.0	36.0	17.0	n.a.	260	m.q.

V

Food and Measure	cal.	prot. (gms)	carbo. (gms)	fat (gms)	chol. (mgs)	sod. (mgs)	fiber (gms)
Vanilla extract:							
(Virginia Dare), 1 tsp.	10	0	.3	0	0	0	0
Vanilla flavor drink:							
canned *(Sego* Very							
Vanilla), 10 fl. oz.	225	11.0	34.0	5.0	n.a.	360	n.a.
mix *(Pillsbury* Instant							
Breakfast), 1 pouch	140	6.0	29.0	0	n.a.	210	n.a.
Veal, meat only, 4 oz.:							
cubed, lean only,							
braised or stewed	213	39.6	0	4.9	164	105	0
ground, broiled . . .	195	27.6	0	8.6	117	94	0
leg:							
braised, lean w/fat	239	41.0	0	7.2	152	76	0
braised, lean only	230	41.6	0	5.8	159	76	0
fried, lean w/fat . .	239	36.0	0	9.5	119	86	0
fried, lean only . .	208	37.6	0	5.2	121	87	0
roasted, lean w/fat	181	31.4	0	5.3	117	77	0
roasted, lean only	170	31.8	0	3.8	117	77	0
loin:							
braised, lean w/fat	322	34.2	0	19.5	134	91	0
braised, lean only	256	38.1	0	10.4	142	95	0
roasted, lean w/fat	246	28.1	0	14.0	117	105	0
roasted, lean only	198	29.8	0	7.9	120	109	0
rib:							
braised, lean w/fat	285	36.8	0	14.2	158	108	0
braised, lean only	247	39.1	0	8.9	163	112	0
roasted, lean w/fat	259	27.2	0	15.8	125	104	0
roasted, lean only	201	29.2	0	8.4	130	110	0
shoulder, whole:							
braised, lean w/fat	259	36.4	0	11.5	143	108	0

Food and Measure	cal.	prot. (gms)	carbo. (gms)	fat (gms)	chol. (mgs)	sod. (mgs)	fiber (gms)
braised, lean only	226	38.2	0	6.9	147	110	0
roasted, lean w/fat	209	28.7	0	9.5	128	109	0
roasted, lean only	193	29.3	0	7.5	129	110	0
shoulder, arm:							
braised, lean w/fat	268	38.1	0	11.6	168	99	0
braised, lean only	228	40.5	0	6.0	176	102	0
roasted, lean w/fat	208	28.9	0	9.4	122	102	0
roasted, lean only	186	29.6	0	6.6	124	103	0
shoulder, blade:							
braised, lean w/fat	255	35.4	0	11.4	174	111	0
braised, lean only	224	37.0	0	7.3	179	115	0
roasted, lean w/fat	211	28.5	0	9.8	133	113	0
roasted, lean only	194	29.1	0	7.8	135	116	0
sirloin:							
braised, lean w/fat	286	35.4	0	14.9	122	90	0
braised, lean only	231	38.5	0	7.4	128	92	0
roasted, lean w/fat	229	28.5	0	11.9	116	94	0
roasted, lean only	191	29.8	0	7.1	118	96	0
Veal dinner, frozen:							
marsala *(Le Menu Light Style)*, 10 oz.	260	20.0	31.0	6.0	m.q.	800	m.q.
parmigiana:							
(Armour Classics), 11.25 oz.	400	18.0	34.0	22.0	55	1320	m.q.
(Morton), 10 oz. . . .	260	10.0	35.0	8.0	35	1510	m.q.
(Swanson), 12¼ oz.	450	22.0	40.0	22.0	m.q.	1100	m.q.
(Swanson Hungry Man), 18¼ oz.	560	30.0	64.0	23.0	m.q.	2080	m.q.
(Stouffer's Dinner Supreme), 11¼ oz.	350	27.0	30.0	13.0	m.q.	1090	m.q.
breaded *(Freezer Queen)*, 5 oz. . . .	220	11.0	17.0	12.0	m.q.	560	m.q.
platter *(Freezer Queen)*, 10 oz.	400	22.0	32.0	20.0	m.q.	870	m.q.

Food and Measure	cal.	prot. (gms)	carbo. (gms)	fat (gms)	chol. (mgs)	sod. (mgs)	fiber (gms)
Veal entree, frozen:							
parmigiana:							
(Swanson Home-style Recipe), 10 oz.	330	19.0	35.0	13.0	m.q.	960	m.q.
(Banquet Cookin' Bags), 4 oz. . . .	230	10.0	20.0	11.0	m.q.	m.q.	m.q.
(Freezer Queen Cook-In-Pouch), 5 oz.	220	11.0	17.0	12.0	m.q.	560	m.q.
(Freezer Queen Deluxe Family Suppers), 7 oz.	300	17.0	22.0	15.0	m.q.	820	m.q.
patty *(Banquet Family Entrees),* 8 oz.	370	18.0	33.0	18.0	m.q.	m.q.	m.q.
patty *(Weight Watchers),* 8.44 oz.	220	23.0	8.0	10.0	65	760	m.q.
primavera *(Lean Cuisine),* 9 1/8 oz. . . .	250	23.0	19.0	9.0	80	790	m.q.
steak, 4 oz.:							
(Hormel)	130	22.0	2.0	4.0	m.q.	m.q.	n.a.
breaded *(Hormel)*	240	17.0	13.0	13.0	m.q.	m.q.	m.q.
Vegetable entree:							
canned:							
chow mein, meat-less *(La Choy),* 3/4 cup	35	2.0	6.0	.4	0	820	2.2 d
stew *(Dinty Moore),* 8 oz.	170	5.0	20.0	8.0	n.a.	1047	m.q.
freeze-dried, stew, w/ beef *(Mountain House),* 1 cup . . .	230	11.0	27.0	7.0	m.q.	77	m.q.
frozen, and pasta mornay, w/ham *(Lean Cuisine),* 9 3/8 oz.	280	15.0	29.0	11.0	35	970	m.q.

Food and Measure	cal.	prot. (gms)	carbo. (gms)	fat (gms)	chol. (mgs)	sod. (mgs)	fiber (gms)
Vegetable juice, 6 fl. oz., except as noted:							
("V-8")	35	1.0	8.0	0	0	600	m.q.
("V-8" No Salt) . . .	40	1.0	9.0	0	0	45	m.q.
(Veryfine 100%) . . .	32	1.6	6.0	0	0	<600	m.q.
hearty (Smucker's), 8 fl. oz.	58	.6	13.0	<.1	0	714	m.q.
hot and spicy (Smucker's), 8 fl. oz. . . .	58	.6	13.0	<.1	0	650	m.q.
spicy hot ("V-8") . .	35	1.0	8.0	0	0	600	m.q.
cocktail	34	1.1	8.3	.2	0	664	.4 c
Vegetable oyster, see "Salsify"							
Vegetable sticks, frozen:							
(Farm Rich), 4 oz. . .	240	4.0	34.0	10.0	n.a.	980	m.q.
(Stilwell Quickkrisp), 3 oz.	240	3.0	40.0	8.0	<1	670	m.q.
Vegetables, see specific listings							
Vegetables, mixed, canned, 1/2 cup:							
drained	39	2.1	7.6	.2	0	122	2.0 d
(Del Monte)	40	2.0	7.0	0	0	355	m.q.
(Green Giant Garden Medley)	45	1.0	9.0	0	0	360	m.q.
(S&W Old Fashioned Harvest)	35	1.0	6.0	0	0	380	m.q.
(Stokely)	40	2.0	8.0	0	0	300	m.q.
(Stokely No Salt/ Sugar)	40	2.0	8.0	0	0	25	m.q.
Chinese (La Choy)	12	1.0	2.0	.1	0	30	1.1 d
chop suey (La Choy)	9	.7	2.0	.1	0	330	1.0 d
Vegetables, mixed, frozen, 3.3 oz., except as noted:							
(Birds Eye)	60	3.0	13.0	0	0	40	2.0 d

Food and Measure	cal.	prot. (gms)	carbo. (gms)	fat (gms)	chol. (mgs)	sod. (mgs)	fiber (gms)
Vegetables, mixed, frozen *(cont.)*							
(Birds Eye Portion							
Pack), 3 oz.	50	2.0	12.0	0	0	35	2.0 d
(Frosty Acres)	65	3.0	13.0	0	0	50	1.0 c
(Green Giant), 1/2 cup	40	2.0	9.0	0	0	40	2.3 d
(Green Giant Harvest							
Fresh), 1/2 cup . .	40	2.0	10.0	0	0	210	2.5 d
(Seabrook)	65	3.0	13.0	0	0	50	1.0 c
(Southern), 3.5 oz.	69	3.2	13.9	0	0	60	m.q.
(Stokely Singles),							
3 oz.	60	3.0	12.0	1.0	0	40	m.q.
in butter sauce *(Green*							
Giant), 1/2 cup . . .	60	2.0	11.0	2.0	5	300	2.0 d
Chinese style *(Birds*							
Eye Stir-Fry)	35	2.0	8.0	0	0	540	2.0 d
chow mein style:							
(Birds Eye Interna-							
tional)	90	2.0	12.0	4.0	0	370	1.0 d
in Oriental sauce							
(Birds Eye Cus-							
tom Cuisine),							
4.6 oz.[1]	80	3.0	14.0	2.0	0	570	1.0 d
Dutch style *(Frosty*							
Acres), 3.2 oz. . .	30	2.0	5.0	0	0	30	m.q.
w/herb sauce for							
chicken or shrimp							
(Birds Eye Custom							
Cuisine), 4.6 oz.[1]	90	3.0	8.0	5.0	0	460	2.0 d
Italian style *(Birds Eye*							
International) . . .	100	2.0	11.0	5.0	0	490	2.0 d
Japanese style:							
(Birds Eye Stir-Fry)	30	2.0	7.0	0	0	510	2.0 d
(Birds Eye Interna-							
tional)	90	2.0	10.0	5.0	0	420	2.0 d

---

[1] *Without added ingredients.*

Food and Measure	cal.	prot. (gms)	carbo. (gms)	fat (gms)	chol. (mgs)	sod. (mgs)	fiber (gms)
w/mushroom sauce for beef (Birds Eye Custom Cuisine), 4.6 oz.[1]	60	3.0	9.0	2.0	5	450	2.0 d
w/mustard sauce, Dijon, for chicken or fish (Birds Eye Custom Cuisine), 4.6 oz.[1]	70	4.0	9.0	3.0	5	310	1.0 d
New England style (Birds Eye International)	130	3.0	14.0	7.0	0	430	2.0 d
w/onion sauce (Birds Eye Combinations), 2.6 oz.	100	2.0	12.0	5.0	0	340	1.3 d
w/Oriental sauce for beef (Birds Eye Custom Cuisine), 4.6 oz.[1]	90	6.0	11.0	4.0	0	350	2.0 d
Oriental style (Birds Eye International)	70	2.0	8.0	4.0	0	300	1.0 d
pasta primavera style (Birds Eye International)	120	5.0	14.0	5.0	5	340	2.0 d
w/rice in teriyaki sauce (Stokely Singles), 4 oz.	100	3.0	24.0	0	0	580	m.q.
w/rotini in cheddar sauce (Stokely Singles), 4 oz.	100	4.0	15.0	3.0	10	380	m.q.
San Francisco style (Birds Eye International)	100	2.0	11.0	5.0	0	400	1.0 d
w/shells in Italian style sauce (Stokely Singles), 4 oz.	170	3.0	5.0	15.0	5	270	m.q.

[1] Without added ingredients.

Food and Measure	cal.	prot. (gms)	carbo. (gms)	fat (gms)	chol. (mgs)	sod. (mgs)	fiber (gms)
Vegetables, mixed, frozen (cont.)							
soup mix (Frosty Acres), 3 oz. . . .	45	4.0	11.0	0	0	35	m.q.
stew:							
(Frosty Acres), 3 oz.	42	3.0	10.0	0	0	21	m.q.
(Kohl's)	50	1.0	10.0	<1.0	0	30	m.q.
(Ore-Ida), 3 oz. . .	60	1.0	12.0	<1.0	0	40	m.q.
w/tomato basil sauce for chicken (Birds Eye Custom Cuisine), 4.6 oz.[1] . . .	110	5.0	17.0	3.0	0	360	1.0 d
w/white and wild rice pilaf (Stokely Singles), 4 oz.	80	3.0	17.0	0	5	290	m.q.
w/wild rice in wine sauce for chicken (Birds Eye Custom Cuisine), 4.6 oz.[1]	100	3.0	19.0	0	0	510	1.0 d
Vegetarian entree, frozen (see also specific listings):							
(Natural Touch Dinner Entree), 3-oz. patty	230	20.0	6.0	14.0	0	300	m.q.
Vegetarian foods, see specific listings							
Venison, meat only:							
roasted, 4 oz.	179	34.3	0	3.6	127	61	0
Vienna sausage, canned:							
(Hormel), 4 links . . .	200	7.0	1.0	18.0	n.a.	479	n.a.
in barbecue sauce (Libby's), 2½ oz.	180	8.0	2.0	15.0	m.q.	420	0
in beef broth (Libby's, 5 oz.), 2 oz. or 3½ links	160	6.0	1.0	15.0	m.q.	330	0

[1] Without added ingredients.

Food and Measure	cal.	prot. (gms)	carbo. (gms)	fat (gms)	chol. (mgs)	sod. (mgs)	fiber (gms)
beef and pork, 2″ link, .6 oz.	45	1.7	.3	4.0	8	152	0
Vine spinach:							
raw, 1 lb.	86	8.2	15.4	1.4	0	m.q.	3.2 c
Vinegar:							
cider:							
(Heinz), 1 tbsp. . . .	2	0	1.0	0	0	1	0
(White House), 1 fl. oz.	4	0	2.0	0	0	5	0
white, distilled (Heinz), 1 tbsp.	2	0	0	0	0	1	0
wine:							
all varieties (Regina), 1 fl. oz. . .	4	0	0	0	0	0	0
basil or garlic (Great Impressions), 1 tbsp.	7	0	.6	0	0	<1	0
raspberry (Great Impressions), 1 tbsp.	7	0	1.0	0	0	<1	0
red (Great Impressions), 1 tbsp.	6	0	.6	0	0	<1	0

W

Food and Measure	cal.	prot. (gms)	carbo. (gms)	fat (gms)	chol. (mgs)	sod. (mgs)	fiber (gms)
Waffle, frozen,							
1 piece, except							
as noted:							
(*Aunt Jemima* Original)	173	4.3	27.8	5.6	6	591	1.5 d
(*Downyflake*), 2 pieces	120	3.0	20.0	3.0	n.a.	420	m.q.
(*Downyflake* Jumbo),							
2 pieces	170	4.0	30.0	4.0	n.a.	500	m.q.
(*Eggo* Homestyle) . .	120	3.0	16.0	5.0	10	250	m.q.
(*Eggo* Nutri-Grain) . .	130	3.0	18.0	5.0	0	250	2.0 d
(*Roman Meal*),							
2 pieces	280	5.0	33.0	14.0	n.a.	680	3.0 d
apple cinnamon:							
(*Aunt Jemima*) . .	176	4.5	28.8	5.6	6	616	2.0 d
(*Eggo*)	130	3.0	18.0	5.0	n.a.	250	m.q.
blueberry:							
(*Aunt Jemima*) . .	175	4.2	29.2	5.2	5	684	1.3 d
(*Downyflake*),							
2 pieces	180	4.0	32.0	4.0	n.a.	570	m.q.
(*Eggo*)	130	3.0	18.0	5.0	n.a.	250	m.q.
buttermilk:							
(*Aunt Jemima*) . .	179	4.4	28.7	5.8	7	615	1.3 d
(*Downyflake*							
Jumbo), 2 pieces	170	4.0	30.0	4.0	n.a.	630	m.q.
(*Eggo*)	120	3.0	16.0	5.0	10	250	m.q.
oat bran:							
(*Eggo Common*							
Sense)	110	3.0	16.0	4.0	0	220	2.0 d
w/fruit and nut							
(*Eggo Common*							
Sense)	120	3.0	17.0	5.0	0	220	2.0 d

Food and Measure	cal.	prot. (gms)	carbo. (gms)	fat (gms)	chol. (mgs)	sod. (mgs)	fiber (gms)
raisin and bran (Eggo Nutri-Grain)	130	3.0	18.0	5.0	0	250	2.0 d
strawberry (Eggo) . .	130	3.0	18.0	5.0	n.a.	250	m.q.
whole grain wheat (Aunt Jemima) . .	154	5.9	29.4	2.8	n.a.	676	3.0 d
Waffle mix, see "Pancake and waffle mix"							
Walnut, dried:							
black:							
in shell, 1 lb.	661	26.5	13.2	61.6	0	2	5.4 d
shelled, 1 oz.	172	6.9	3.4	16.1	0	tr.	1.4 d
chopped, 1 cup . .	759	30.4	15.1	70.7	0	2	6.3 d
(Planters), 1 oz. . .	180	7.0	3.0	17.0	0	0	m.q.
English or Persian, dried:							
in shell, 1 lb.	1310	29.2	37.4	126.3	0	21	9.8 d
shelled, 1 oz.	182	4.1	5.2	17.6	0	3	1.4 d
pieces, 1 cup . . .	770	17.2	22.0	74.2	0	12	5.8 d
halves, 1 cup . . .	642	14.3	18.3	61.9	0	10	4.8 d
(Diamond), 1 oz. . .	192	5.0	4.0	19.0	0	n.a.	m.q.
all varieties (Planters), 1 oz.	190	4.0	3.0	20.0	0	0	m.q.
Walnut topping:							
in syrup (Smucker's), 2 tbsp.	130	2.0	27.0	1.0	0	0	m.q.
Waterchestnut, Chinese:							
fresh:							
untrimmed, 1 lb. . . .	369	4.9	83.6	.4	0	50	2.8 c
4 medium, 1¼"–2" diam.	38	.5	8.6	<.1	0	5	.3 c
sliced, ½ cup . . .	66	.9	14.8	.1	0	9	.5 c
canned:							
4 medium or 1 oz. w/liquid, sliced,	14	.3	3.5	<.1	0	2	.2 c
½ cup	35	.6	8.7	<.1	0	6	.4 c
(La Choy), 1.28 oz.	18	.3	4.5	<.1	0	3	m.q.

Food and Measure	cal.	prot. (gms)	carbo. (gms)	fat (gms)	chol. (mgs)	sod. (mgs)	fiber (gms)
Watercress:							
untrimmed, 1 lb. . . .	46	9.6	5.4	.4	0	170	9.6 d
10 sprigs, 11¼″ long	3	.6	.3	<.1	0	10	.6 d
chopped, ½ cup . .	2	.4	.2	<.1	0	7	.4 d
Watermelon:							
untrimmed, 1 lb. . . .	74	1.5	16.9	1.0	0	5	.9 d
1 slice, 10″							
diam. × 1″ thick	152	3.0	34.6	2.0	0	10	1.9 d
diced, ½ cup	25	.5	5.7	.3	0	2	.3 d
Watermelon seed:							
dried, kernels, 1 oz.	158	8.1	4.4	13.5	0	28	.9 c
Wax bean:							
fresh, see "Green bean"							
canned, ½ cup:							
(Allens)	15	1.0	3.0	<1.0	0	260	m.q.
(Stokely)	20	1.0	4.0	0	0	360	m.q.
all cuts (Del Monte)	20	0	4.0	0	0	355	m.q.
frozen, 3 oz.:							
(Frosty Acres) . . .	25	2.0	5.0	0	0	1	1.0 c
cut (Seabrook) . .	25	2.0	5.0	0	0	1	1.0 c
Wax gourd:							
boiled, drained, cubed,							
½ cup	11	.4	2.6	.2	0	93	.4 c
Welsh rarebit (see also "Cheese sauce"):							
canned (Snow's),							
½ cup	170	9.0	10.0	11.0	n.a.	460	n.a.
frozen (Stouffer's),							
10 oz.	350	13.0	8.0	30.0	n.a.	680	n.a.
Wendy's, 1 serving:							
breakfast:							
apple danish . . .	360	6.0	53.0	14.0	n.a.	380	m.q.
apple topping, 1 pkt.	130	<1.0	32.0	<1.0	0	120	n.a.
blueberry topping,							
1 pkt.	60	<1.0	15.0	<1.0	0	65	n.a.
breakfast sandwich	370	17.0	33.0	19.0	200	770	m.q.

Food and Measure	cal.	prot. (gms)	carbo. (gms)	fat (gms)	chol. (mgs)	sod. (mgs)	fiber (gms)
cheese danish ..	430	8.0	52.0	21.0	n.a.	500	m.q.
cinnamon raisin danish	410	7.0	55.0	18.0	n.a.	430	m.q.
French toast, 2 slices	400	11.0	45.0	19.0	115	850	m.q.
omelet, ham and cheese	290	18.0	7.0	21.0	355	570	m.q.
omelet, ham, cheese, mush- room	250	18.0	6.0	17.0	450	405	m.q.
omelet, ham, cheese, onion, peppers	280	19.0	7.0	19.0	525	485	m.q.
omelet, mushrooms, peppers, onion	210	14.0	7.0	15.0	460	200	m.q.
potatoes, breakfast	360	4.0	37.0	22.0	20	745	m.q.
sausage, 1 patty	200	8.0	<1.0	18.0	45	405	0
sandwiches:							
bacon Swiss burger	710	37.0	58.0	44.0	90	1390	m.q.
Big Classic	580	24.0	47.0	34.0	80	1015	m.q.
Big Classic, w/ cheese	640	28.0	47.0	40.0	100	1310	m.q.
cheeseburger, sin- gle	410	25.0	29.0	22.0	80	710	m.q.
cheeseburger, sin- gle, w/everything	490	26.0	36.0	28.0	85	1100	m.q.
cheeseburger, small	320	17.0	31.0	15.0	50	805	m.q.
chicken sandwich	430	26.0	41.0	19.0	60	705	m.q.
hamburger, plain, single	350	21.0	29.0	16.0	65	420	m.q.
hamburger, small	260	13.0	31.0	9.0	20	510	m.q.
Kid's Meal	260	13.0	30.0	9.0	30	510	m.q.
Kid's Meal, w/ cheese	320	17.0	30.0	15.0	50	805	m.q.
Philly Swiss burger	510	30.0	46.0	24.0	65	975	m.q.
chicken nuggets:							
crispy[1], 6 pieces	310	15.0	14.0	21.0	50	660	m.q.

[1] *Cooked in vegetable oil.*

Food and Measure	cal.	prot. (gms)	carbo. (gms)	fat (gms)	chol. (mgs)	sod. (mgs)	fiber (gms)
Wendy's, chicken nuggets *(cont.)*							
crispy[1], 6 pieces	290	16.0	11.0	21.0	55	615	m.q.
chili, 8.3 oz.	240	19.0	24.0	8.0	25	990	m.q.
chili, new, 9 oz. . . .	230	40.0	46.0	37.0	35	1110	m.q.
baked stuffed potato:							
plain	250	6.0	52.0	2.0	tr.	60	m.q.
bacon and cheese	570	19.0	57.0	30.0	22	1180	m.q.
broccoli and cheese	500	13.0	54.0	25.0	22	430	m.q.
cheese	590	17.0	55.0	34.0	22	450	m.q.
chili and cheese	510	22.0	63.0	20.0	22	610	m.q.
sour cream and							
chives	460	6.0	53.0	24.0	15	230	m.q.
salads and side							
dishes:							
chef salad, take out	180	15.0	10.0	9.0	120	140	m.q.
fries, regular	300	5.0	35.0	15.0	0	135	m.q.
garden salad, take							
out	102	7.0	9.0	5.0	0	110	m.q.
taco salad	660	40.0	46.0	37.0	35	1110	m.q.
frosty, dairy, small . .	400	8.0	59.0	14.0	50	220	(0)
pudding, 1/4 cup:							
chocolate	90	n.a.	12.0	4.0	tr.	70	n.a.
butterscotch	90	1.0	11.0	4.0	tr.	85	n.a.
Western dinner, frozen:							
(Banquet), 11 oz. . .	630	28.0	40.0	41.0	90	720	m.q.
(Morton), 10 oz.	290	14.0	29.0	14.0	35	1450	m.q.
style *(Swanson),*							
11 1/2 oz.	450	22.0	43.0	21.0	m.q.	1010	m.q.
Wheat, whole-grain:							
durum, 1 cup	650	26.3	136.6	4.7	0	3	m.q.
hard red:							
spring, 1 cup . . .	631	29.6	130.6	3.7	0	4	4.4 c
winter, 1 cup . . .	628	24.2	136.7	3.0	0	4	4.4 c
soft red winter, 1 cup	556	17.4	124.7	2.6	0	4	2.9 c
hard white, 1 cup . .	656	21.7	145.7	3.3	0	n.a.	m.q.
soft white, 1 cup . .	571	18.0	126.6	3.3	0	n.a.	m.q.

[1] *Cooked in animal/vegetable oil.*

Food and Measure	cal.	prot. (gms)	carbo. (gms)	fat (gms)	chol. (mgs)	sod. (mgs)	fiber (gms)
Wheat, parboiled, see "Bulgur"							
Wheat, sprouted:							
1 cup	214	8.1	45.9	1.4	0	18	m.q.
Wheat bran (see also "Bran"):							
crude:							
1 oz.	61	4.4	18.3	1.2	0	<1	12.0 d
2 tbsp.	15	1.1	4.5	.3	0	tr.	3.0 d
toasted *(Kretschmer),* 1 oz. or 1/3 cup . .	57	5.7	14.8	2.3	0	2	11.4 d
Wheat cake:							
(Quaker Grain Cakes), 1 piece	34	1.4	6.7	.3	0	52	.8 d
Wheat flour, 1 cup, except as noted:							
whole-grain:							
1 cup	407	16.4	87.1	2.2	0	1	15.1 d
(Ceresota/Heckers)	400	15.0	80.0	2.0	0	0	m.q.
(Pillsbury's Best)	400	15.0	80.0	2.0	0	10	m.q.
white, all-purpose:							
1 cup	455	12.9	95.4	1.2	0	2	3.4 d
(Ballard/Pillsbury's Best)	400	11.0	87.0	1.0	0	0	m.q.
(Ceresota/Heckers), 4 oz.	390	12.5	82.5	1.0	0	0	m.q.
unbleached *(Pillsbury's Best)* . . .	400	12.0	86.0	1.0	0	0	m.q.
white, bread *(Pillsbury's Best)*	400	14.0	83.0	2.0	0	0	m.q.
white, cake	395	8.9	85.1	.9	0	2	m.q.
white, self-rising:							
1 cup	442	12.4	92.8	1.2	0	1587	.3 c
(Ballard/Pillsbury's Best)	380	9.0	84.0	1.0	0	1290	m.q.
enriched *(Aunt Jemima),* 1/4 cup	109	3.0	23.6	.3	0	368	.1 c
tortilla mix	449	10.7	74.5	11.8	0	751	.2 c

Food and Measure	cal.	prot. (gms)	carbo. (gms)	fat (gms)	chol. (mgs)	sod. (mgs)	fiber (gms)
Wheat germ, 1 oz.:							
(Kretschmer)	103	9.3	12.3	3.4	0	2	3.3 d
crude	102	6.6	14.7	2.8	0	3	4.3 d
honey crunch (Kretschmer)	105	7.6	15.2	2.8	0	2	3.0 d
toasted, 1 oz.	108	8.3	14.1	3.0	0	1	3.7 d
Wheat gluten, 1 oz.: vital (Arrowhead Mills)	100	15.0	9.0	1.0	0	1	.9 d
Wheat pilaf mix: (Casbah), 1 oz. dry or 1/2 cup	100	3.0	20.0	0	0	m.q.	m.q.
Whelk, meat only, raw:							
1 lb.	623	108.1	35.2	1.8	294	934	0
1 oz.	39	6.8	2.2	.1	18	54	0
Whey:							
acid, dry, 1 oz.	96	3.3	20.8	.2	(0)	274	0
acid, fluid, 1 cup . . .	59	1.9	12.6	.2	(0)	118	0
sweet, dry, 1 oz. . . .	100	3.7	21.1	.3	2	306	0
sweet, fluid, 1 cup . .	66	2.1	12.6	.9	5	132	0
Whiskey, see "Liquor"							
Whiskey sour mix:							
bottled (Holland House), 1 fl. oz. . .	37	0	9.0	0	0	105	n.a.
instant (Holland House), .56 oz. dry	64	0	16.0	0	0	16	n.a.
White bean, 1/2 cup:							
dried:							
boiled	125	8.6	22.6	.3	0	6	2.2 c
boiled, small	127	8.1	23.2	.6	0	2	3.7 d
canned, w/liquid . . .	153	9.5	28.7	.4	0	595	.9 c
White Castle, 1 serving:							
cheeseburger	200	7.8	15.5	11.2	m.q.	361	2.7 d
chicken sandwich . .	186	12.5	32.1	11.7	m.q.	497	1.7 d

Food and Measure	cal.	prot. (gms)	carbo. (gms)	fat (gms)	chol. (mgs)	sod. (mgs)	fiber (gms)
fish sandwich, w/out tartar sauce	155	5.8	20.9	5.0	m.q.	201	1.4 d
hamburger	161	5.9	15.4	7.9	m.q.	266	2.1 d
sausage sandwich . .	196	6.7	13.3	12.3	m.q.	488	2.0 d
sausage w/egg sandwich	322	12.6	16.1	22.0	m.q.	698	3.0 d
side dishes:							
french fries	301	2.5	37.7	14.7	n.a.	193	4.6 d
onion chips	329	3.7	38.8	16.6	n.a.	823	3.5 d
onion rings	245	2.9	26.6	13.4	n.a.	566	2.6 d
White sauce mix:							
1¾-oz. pkt.	230	5.4	25.1	13.2	tr.	1691	.1 c
Whitefish, meat only:							
raw, 1 lb.	610	86.6	0	26.6	272	232	0
raw, 1 oz.	38	5.4	0	1.7	17	14	0
smoked, 4 oz.	122	26.5	0	1.1	37	1156	0
Whiting, meat only:							
raw, 1 lb.	408	83.1	0	6.0	303	326	0
raw, 1 oz.	26	5.2	0	.4	19	20	0
baked, broiled, or microwaved, 4 oz. . .	130	26.6	0	1.9	95	150	0
Whiting, frozen:							
(Booth), 4 oz.	100	19.0	0	1.0	m.q.	90	0
individually wrapped (Booth), 4 oz.	80	19.0	0	1.0	m.q.	85	0
Wild rice:							
raw, 1 oz.	101	4.2	21.2	.3	0	2	1.5 d
cooked, 1 cup	166	6.5	35.0	.6	0	6	.5 c
Wild rice dishes, see "Rice dishes"							
Wine, 1 fl. oz.:							
dessert or aperitif[1] . .	41	tr.	2.3	0	0	1	0
dry or table[2]	25	tr.	1.2	0	0	1	0

[1] Includes wines containing more than 15% alcohol (sherries, port, Tokay, vermouths, etc.).

[2] Includes wines containing less than 15% alcohol (Burgundy, Chablis, Champagnes, Rhine wines, rosés, etc.).

Food and Measure	cal.	prot. (gms)	carbo. (gms)	fat (gms)	chol. (mgs)	sod. (mgs)	fiber (gms)
Wine, cooking:							
burgundy or sauterne							
(Regina), 1/4 cup	2	<1.0	<1.0	<1.0	0	365	0
marsala *(Holland*							
House), 1 fl. oz. . .	9	0	2.3	0	0	186	0
red *(Holland House)*,							
1 fl. oz.	6	0	1.5	0	0	186	0
sherry *(Holland*							
House), 1 fl. oz. . .	5	0	1.2	0	0	186	0
sherry *(Regina)*,							
1/4 cup	20	<1.0	5.0	<1.0	0	70	0
vermouth or white							
(Holland House),							
1 fl. oz.	2	0	<1.0	0	0	186	0
Winged bean:							
fresh:							
raw, untrimmed,							
1 lb.	218	30.9	19.2	3.9	0	17	11.4 c
raw, sliced, 1/2 cup	11	1.5	1.0	.2	0	1	.6 c
boiled, drained,							
1/2 cup	12	1.6	1.0	.2	0	1	.4 c
dried:							
raw, 1/2 cup	372	27.0	38.0	14.9	0	35	14.1 d
boiled, 1/2 cup . . .	126	9.1	12.8	5.0	0	11	2.1 c
Winged bean leaves:							
trimmed, 1 lb. . . .	336	26.5	64.0	5.0	0	n.a.	11.3 c
trimmed, 1 oz.	21	1.7	4.0	.3	0	n.a.	.7 c
Winged bean tuber:							
trimmed, 1 lb.	268	52.6	127.5	4.1	0	n.a.	33.6 c
trimmed, 1 oz.	45	3.3	8.0	.3	0	n.a.	2.1 c
Wolf fish, meat only,							
Atlantic, raw, 1 lb. . .	437	79.4	0	10.8	209	386	0
Atlantic, raw, 1 oz.	27	5.0	0	.7	13	24	0
Wonton skin:							
(Nasoya), 1 piece . .	23	1.0	4.5	0	0	19	m.q.

Food and Measure	cal.	prot. (gms)	carbo. (gms)	fat (gms)	chol. (mgs)	sod. (mgs)	fiber (gms)
Worcestershire sauce:							
(Lea & Perrins), 1 tsp.	5	<1.0	1.0	<1.0	0	55	(0)
regular or smoky *(French's)*, 1 tbsp.	10	0	2.0	0	0	160	(0)
white wine *(Lea & Perrins)*, 1 tsp. ..	3	<1.0	1.0	<1.0	0	42	(0)

Y

Food and Measure	cal.	prot. (gms)	carbo. (gms)	fat (gms)	chol. (mgs)	sod. (mgs)	fiber (gms)
Yam:							
baked or boiled, 1/2 cup	79	1.0	18.8	.1	0	6	m.q.
canned or frozen, see "Sweet potato"							
Yam, mountain, Hawaiian:							
raw, cubed, 1/2 cup	46	.9	11.1	.1	0	9	.3 c
steamed, cubed, 1/2 cup	59	1.2	14.4	.1	0	9	.4 c
Yam bean tuber:							
raw, sliced, 1/2 cup	25	.8	5.3	.1	0	4	.4 c
boiled, drained, 4 oz.	52	1.3	11.8	.1	0	7	1.3 c
Yardlong bean:							
fresh, sliced, 1/2 cup:							
raw	22	1.3	3.8	.2	0	2	m.q.
boiled, drained . .	25	1.3	4.8	.1	0	2	.8 c
dried, 1/2 cup:							
raw	292	20.4	52.0	1.1	0	14	4.0 c
boiled	102	7.1	18.1	.4	0	4	1.4 c
Yeast, baker's:							
(*Fleischmann's* Active Dry/RapidRise), 1/4 oz.	20	3.0	3.0	0	0	10	m.q.
(*Red Star* Active Dry), 1/4 oz.	20	3.0	2.7	.3	0	4	1.2 c
fresh or household (*Fleischmann's*), .6 oz.	15	2.0	2.0	0	0	5	m.q.

Food and Measure	cal.	prot. (gms)	carbo. (gms)	fat (gms)	chol. (mgs)	sod. (mgs)	fiber (gms)
Yellow bean, dried:							
boiled, 1/2 cup	126	8.1	22.2	1.0	0	4	1.0 c
Yellow eye bean:							
canned, baked style							
(B&M), 8 oz. . . .	362	15.0	50.0	7.0	n.a.	770	11.0 d
Yellow squash, see							
"Crookneck							
squash"							
Yellowtail, meat only:							
raw, 1 lb.	662	105.0	0	23.8	m.q.	177	0
raw, 1 oz.	41	6.6	0	1.5	m.q.	11	0
Yogurt:							
plain, 1 cup, except as							
noted:							
(Bison Lowfat) . .	150	12.0	17.0	4.0	10	180	0
(Bison Nonfat) . .	120	12.0	16.0	0	0	170	0
(Crowley)	160	10.0	14.0	8.0	30	150	0
(Crowley Lowfat)	140	12.0	17.0	2.0	10	180	0
(Crowley Nonfat)	120	13.0	17.0	<1.0	<1	180	0
(Dannon Lowfat),							
8 oz.	140	10.0	16.0	4.0	15	160	0
(Dannon Nonfat),							
8 oz.	110	11.0	16.0	0	5	160	0
(Friendship Lowfat)	150	12.0	17.0	3.0	14	190	0
(Meadow Gold							
Lowfat)	160	12.0	16.0	5.0	m.q.	160	0
(Mountain High) . .	200	12.0	16.0	9.0	m.q.	140	0
(Yoplait), 6 oz.	130	10.0	15.0	3.0	15	140	0
all fruit flavors:							
(Crowley Nonfat),							
1 cup	100	8.0	17.0	<1.0	<1	135	m.q.
(Crowley Sundae							
Style), 1 cup . .	250	9.0	47.0	2.0	10	170	m.q.
(Crowley Swiss							
Style), 1 cup . .	240	8.0	48.0	2.0	10	150	m.q.
(Dannon Fruit-on-							
the-Bottom), 8 oz.	240	9.0	43.0	3.0	10	120	m.q.

Food and Measure	cal.	prot. (gms)	carbo. (gms)	fat (gms)	chol. (mgs)	sod. (mgs)	fiber (gms)
Yogurt, all fruit flavors *(cont.)*							
(Dannon Extra							
Smooth), 4.4 oz.	130	5.0	24.0	2.0	10	80	m.q.
(Dannon Hearty							
Nuts & Raisins),							
8 oz.	260	11.0	48.0	3.0	10	120	m.q.
(Ripple 70), 6 oz.	70	5.0	13.0	0	5	85	m.q.
(Yoplait), 6 oz. . . .	190	8.0	32.0	3.0	10	110	m.q.
(Yoplait Fat Free),							
6 oz.	150	7.0	31.0	0	5	· 95	m.q.
(Yoplait Light), 6 oz.	90	7.0	14.0	0	<5	100	m.q.
except cherry and							
mixed berry							
(Yoplait Custard							
Style), 6 oz. . . .	190	7.0	32.0	4.0	20	95	m.q.
apple crisp *(New*							
Country), 6 oz. . .	150	5.0	30.0	2.0	m.q.	85	m.q.
berries, mixed:							
(New Country),							
6 oz.	150	5.0	31.0	2.0	m.q.	85	m.q.
(Yoplait Breakfast							
Yogurt), 6 oz. . . .	210	8.0	40.0	3.0	10	95	2.0 d
blueberry:							
(Dannon Fresh							
Flavors), 8 oz.	200	10.0	34.0	4.0	10	160	m.q.
(New Country Su-							
preme), 6 oz. . .	150	5.0	31.0	2.0	m.q.	90	m.q.
blend *(Mountain*							
High), 1 cup . .	220	10.0	31.0	6.0	m.q.	140	m.q.
cherry *(New Country*							
Supreme), 6 oz. . .	150	5.0	32.0	2.0	m.q.	90	m.q.
cherry and mixed							
berry *(Yoplait Cus-*							
tard Style), 6 oz.	180	7.0	30.0	4.0	20	95	m.q.
cherry w/almonds							
(Yoplait Breakfast							
Yogurt), 6 oz. . . .	200	8.0	38.0	3.0	10	90	2.0 d

Food and Measure	cal.	prot. (gms)	carbo. (gms)	fat (gms)	chol. (mgs)	sod. (mgs)	fiber (gms)
coffee:							
(Bison Lowfat), 1 cup	210	11.0	33.0	4.0	10	160	0
(Dannon Fresh Flavors), 8 oz.	200	10.0	34.0	3.0	10	140	0
(Friendship Lowfat), 1 cup	210	11.0	35.0	3.0	14	170	0
fruit:							
crunch *(New Country* Lowfat), 6 oz.	150	5.0	30.0	2.0	m.q.	90	m.q.
tropical *(Yoplait Breakfast Yogurt),* 6 oz.	210	7.0	39.0	4.0	10	90	2.0 d
Hawaiian salad *(New Country* Lowfat), 6 oz.	150	5.0	31.0	2.0	m.q.	90	m.q.
lemon:							
(Bison Lowfat), 1 cup	210	11.0	33.0	4.0	10	160	n.a.
(Dannon Fresh Flavors), 8 oz.	200	10.0	34.0	3.0	10	140	n.a.
(New Country Supreme), 6 oz. ...	150	5.0	31.0	2.0	m.q.	90	n.a.
orange *(New Country* Supreme), 6 oz. ...	150	5.0	31.0	2.0	m.q.	90	n.a.
peaches'n cream *(New Country* Lowfat), 6 oz. ...	150	5.0	31.0	2.0	m.q.	90	m.q.
piña colada *(Yoplait),* 6 oz.	190	8.0	32.0	3.0	10	110	m.q.
raspberry:							
(Dannon Fresh Flavors), 8 oz.	200	10.0	34.0	4.0	10	160	m.q.
(New Country Supreme), 6 oz. ...	150	5.0	31.0	2.0	m.q.	90	m.q.
strawberry:							
(Crowley Nonfat), 1 cup	190	12.0	35.0	<1.0	<1	190	m.q.

Food and Measure	cal.	prot. (gms)	carbo. (gms)	fat (gms)	chol. (mgs)	sod. (mgs)	fiber (gms)
Yogurt, strawberry (cont.)							
(Dannon Fresh Flavors), 8 oz.	200	10.0	34.0	4.0	10	160	m.q.
(New Country Supreme), 6 oz. . . .	150	5.0	30.0	2.0	m.q.	90	m.q.
fruit cup (New Country Lowfat), 6 oz.	150	5.0	30.0	2.0	m.q.	85	m.q.
strawberry-almond (Yoplait Breakfast Yogurt), 6 oz. . . .	200	8.0	38.0	3.0	10	90	2.0 d
strawberry-banana:							
(Dannon Fresh Flavors), 8 oz.	200	10.0	34.0	4.0	10	160	m.q.
(New Country Lowfat), 6 oz. . .	150	5.0	31.0	2.0	m.q.	85	m.q.
(Yoplait Breakfast Yogurt), 6 oz. . . .	220	8.0	42.0	3.0	10	90	2.0 d
vanilla:							
(Bison Lowfat), 1 cup	210	11.0	33.0	4.0	10	160	0
(Crowley Lowfat), 1 cup	200	12.0	33.0	2.0	10	170	0
(Dannon Fresh Flavors), 8 oz.	200	10.0	34.0	3.0	10	140	0
(Dannon Hearty Nuts & Raisins), 8 oz.	270	9.0	48.0	5.0	10	120	n.a.
(Friendship Lowfat), 1 cup	210	11.0	35.0	3.0	14	170	0
French (New Country Lowfat), 6 oz.	150	5.0	31.0	2.0	m.q.	90	0
(Yoplait), 6 oz. . . .	180	9.0	29.0	3.0	15	120	0
(Yoplait Custard Style), 6 oz. . . .	180	7.0	30.0	4.0	20	110	0
(Yoplait Fat Free), 6 oz.	150	8.0	28.0	0	<5	110	0

Food and Measure	cal.	prot. (gms)	carbo. (gms)	fat (gms)	chol. (mgs)	sod. (mgs)	fiber (gms)
Yogurt, frozen, 4 fl. oz., except as noted:							
all fruit flavors							
(Dreyer's Inspirations), 3 oz.	80	2.0	15.0	1.0	5	40	(0)
cherry:							
(Crowley), 3 fl. oz.	80	2.0	16.0	1.0	5	40	(0)
black *(Breyers)* . .	120	3.0	24.0	1.0	10	50	(0)
black *(Sealtest Free)*	110	2.0	24.0	0	0	50	(0)
chocolate:							
(Bison), 3¹/₂ fl. oz.	94	3.0	18.0	2.0	5	50	(0)
(Breyers)	120	3.0	24.0	1.0	10	65	(0)
(Crowley), 3 fl. oz.	80	2.0	15.0	2.0	10	40	(0)
(Dreyer's Inspirations), 3 oz.	80	2.0	15.0	1.0	5	40	(0)
(Sealtest Free) . .	110	3.0	24.0	0	0	55	(0)
peach:							
(Breyers)	110	3.0	22.0	1.0	10	50	(0)
(Crowley), 3 fl. oz.	80	2.0	16.0	1.0	5	40	(0)
(Sealtest Free) . .	100	2.0	23.0	0	0	35	(0)
raspberry:							
(Crowley), 3 fl. oz.	80	2.0	16.0	1.0	5	40	(0)
red *(Breyers)* . . .	120	3.0	23.0	1.0	10	50	(0)
red *(Sealtest Free)*	100	2.0	23.0	0	0	40	(0)
strawberry:							
(Breyers)	110	3.0	22.0	1.0	10	45	(0)
(Crowley), 3 fl. oz.	80	2.0	16.0	1.0	5	40	(0)
(Sealtest Free) . .	100	2.0	22.0	0	0	35	(0)
strawberry-banana							
(Breyers)	110	3.0	22.0	1.0	10	45	(0)
vanilla:							
(Breyers)	120	3.0	23.0	1.0	15	55	0
(Crowley), 3 fl. oz.	80	2.0	15.0	2.0	10	40	0
(Dreyer's Inspirations), 3 oz.	80	2.0	15.0	1.0	5	50	0
(Sealtest Free) . .	100	2.0	23.0	0	0	45	0

Food and Measure	cal.	prot. (gms)	carbo. (gms)	fat (gms)	chol. (mgs)	sod. (mgs)	fiber (gms)
Yogurt, frozen *(cont.)*							
vanilla-raspberry swirl *(Dreyer's Inspirations)*, 3 oz.	80	2.0	15.0	1.0	5	45	(0)
Yogurt, frozen, soft-serve:							
all flavors, 1 oz.:							
(Bresler's Gourmet)	29	.9	5.5	.5	2	15	(0)
(Bresler's Lite) . .	27	1.1	6.0	0	0	11	(0)
plain *(Crowley* Peaks of Perfection), 3.5 fl. oz.	90	2.0	20.0	1.0	5	40	0
banana *(Crowley* Peaks of Perfection), 3.5 fl. oz. . .	100	3.0	19.0	2.0	5	50	(0)
blueberry *(Dannon)*, 4 fl. oz.	100	3.0	18.0	2.0	5	50	(0)
butter pecan or cappuccino *(Dannon)*, 4 fl. oz.	100	3.0	18.0	2.0	5	55	(0)
cheesecake *(Dannon)*, 4 fl. oz.	100	4.0	18.0	2.0	5	55	(0)
chocolate:							
(Crowley Peaks of Perfection), 3.5 fl. oz.	100	4.0	19.0	2.0	5	60	(0)
(Dannon), 4 fl. oz.	120	5.0	23.0	2.0	5	65	(0)
lemon, raspberry or strawberry *(Crowley* Peaks of Perfection), 3.5 fl. oz. . .	100	3.0	19.0	2.0	5	50	(0)
lemon meringue, peach or piña colada *(Dannon)*, 4 fl. oz.	100	4.0	18.0	2.0	5	55	(0)
raspberry:							
(Dannon), 4 fl. oz.	100	3.0	18.0	2.0	5	50	(0)

Food and Measure	cal.	prot. (gms)	carbo. (gms)	fat (gms)	chol. (mgs)	sod. (mgs)	fiber (gms)
red (Dannon Nonfat), 4 fl. oz.	90	3.0	21.0	0	0	65	(0)
rum raisin (Dannon Nonfat), 4 fl. oz. . . .	90	3.0	22.0	0	0	65	(0)
strawberry or golden vanilla (Dannon Nonfat), 4 fl. oz. . . .	90	3.0	22.0	0	0	65	(0)
strawberry or strawberry-banana (Dannon), 4 fl. oz.	100	3.0	18.0	2.0	5	50	(0)
vanilla (Crowley Peaks of Perfection), 3.5 fl. oz.	100	3.0	19.0	2.0	5	50	0
Yogurt drink, 8 oz.:							
all flavors (Dan'up)	190	6.0	32.0	4.0	10	110	(0)
Yogurt and fruit bar, see "Fruit bar"							

Z

Food and Measure	cal.	prot. (gms)	carbo. (gms)	fat (gms)	chol. (mgs)	sod. (mgs)	fiber (gms)
Ziti, frozen:							
in marinara sauce							
(The Budget Gour-							
met Side Dish),							
6.25 oz.	220	9.0	25.0	9.0	15	380	m.q.
Zucchini:							
fresh:							
raw, w/ends, 1 lb.	62	5.0	12.5	.6	0	11	2.2 d
raw, sliced, 1/2 cup	9	.8	1.9	.1	0	2	.3 d
boiled, drained,							
sliced, 1/2 cup	14	.6	3.5	.1	0	2	.5 c
boiled, drained,							
mashed, 1/2 cup	19	.8	4.7	.1	0	3	.6 c
canned, in tomato							
juice:							
4 oz. or 1/2 cup . .	33	1.2	7.8	.1	0	424	.6 c
(Del Monte), 1/2 cup	30	1.0	8.0	0	0	485	m.q.
frozen:							
(Seabrook), 3.3 oz.	16	1.0	3.0	0	0	2	1.0 c
(Southern), 3.5 oz.	18	1.2	3.6	.1	0	20	m.q.
breaded *(Stilwell*							
Quickkrisp),							
3.3 oz.	200	4.0	24.0	10.0	15	410	m.q.
w/carrots, pearl on-							
ions, mushrooms							
(Birds Eye Farm							
Fresh), 4 oz. . .	30	1.0	7.0	0	0	15	1.0 d